HEALTH LAW

FRAMEWORKS AND CONTEXT

Drawing upon a range of disciplinary perspectives, *Health Law: Frameworks and Context* adopts a theoretically informed and principles-based approach to examining health law.

Appealing to students and academic scholars alike, the text moves beyond traditional medical law frameworks to provide a broader contextual understanding of the way in which law intersects with health.

A clear and accessible style of writing, combined with a sophisticated and nuanced approach, takes this rich and challenging field to a new level of analysis.

Written by respected academics within the field, *Health Law: Frameworks and Context* is essential reading for students and scholars looking to grasp the fundamental concepts of this rapidly expanding area of law, as well as those who wish to deepen their knowledge and understanding of health law in Australia and internationally.

Anne-Maree Farrell: Professor and Chair of Health Law and Society, ARC Future Fellow and Director, Centre for Health Law and Society, La Trobe University, Melbourne.

John Devereux: Professor of Law, TC Beirne School of Law, University of Queensland.

Isabel Karpin: Professor of Law, Faculty of Law, University of Technology Sydney.

Penelope Weller: Associate Professor, Graduate School of Business and Law, RMIT University, Melbourne.

HEALTH LAW

FRAMEWORKS AND CONTEXT

Anne-Maree Farrell, John Devereux,
Isabel Karpin & Penelope Weller

CAMBRIDGE
UNIVERSITY PRESS

CAMBRIDGE
UNIVERSITY PRESS

University Printing House, Cambridge CB2 8BS, United Kingdom

One Liberty Plaza, 20th Floor, New York, NY 10006, USA

477 Williamstown Road, Port Melbourne, VIC 3207, Australia

4843/24, 2nd Floor, Ansari Road, Daryaganj, Delhi – 110002, India

79 Anson Road, #06–04/06, Singapore 079906

Cambridge University Press is part of the University of Cambridge.

It furthers the University's mission by disseminating knowledge in the pursuit of education, learning and research at the highest international levels of excellence

www.cambridge.org
Information on this title: www.cambridge.org/9781107455474

© Cambridge University Press 2017

First published 2017

Cover designed by Tanya De Silva-McKay
Typeset by Integra Software Services Pvt. Ltd.
Printed in China by C & C Offset Printing Co. Ltd., February 2017

A catalogue record for this publication is available from the British Library

A Cataloguing-in-Publication entry is available from the catalogue of the National Library of Australia at www.nla.gov.au

ISBN 978-1-107-45547-4 Paperback

Please be aware that this publication may contain several variations of Aboriginal and Torres Strait Islander terms and spellings; no disrespect is intended. Please note that the terms 'Indigenous Australians' and 'Aboriginal and Torres Strait Islander peoples' may be used interchangeably in this publication.

For Josephine Upton Farrell

CONTENTS

B Institutions and Regulation

PART II CONTEXT

A Patients, Doctors and Healthcare

C Law and the Human Body

FIGURES AND TABLES

CONTRIBUTORS

Stephen Gray   Senior Lecturer in Law, Monash University (Chapter 21)

Kate Mulvany   Trial Division Researcher, Supreme Court of Victoria (Chapter 24)

Justin Oakley   Associate Professor, Centre for Human Bioethics, Monash University (Chapter 2)

Karen O'Connell   Senior Lecturer in Law, University of Technology Sydney (Chapters 4 and 20, co-authored with Isabel Karpin)

Gabrielle Wolf   Lecturer in Law, Deakin University (Chapter 7)

PREFACE

This book explores health in its socio-legal context in Australia and beyond. It critically examines key frameworks and contexts which underpin the relationship between law and health. This is done with a view to better conceptualising this relationship in what is a burgeoning area of national and international academic study and policy interest. As such, it offers a new way forward within legal scholarship in the field, which will be of interest to a range of audiences, including academics, policy-makers, health professionals and students. As we developed this approach, we have been greatly assisted by the insightful feedback we have received on each of the chapters from independent peer reviewers. We would like to thank them for their time and contribution. The policy and law described in this book is current as at 1 January 2017.

Anne-Maree Farrell would like to acknowledge the support of the Australian Research Council (ARC) in relation to Chapters 17, 18 and 19, which draw on research undertaken while in receipt of the ARC Future Fellowship, *Regulating Human Body Parts: Principles Institutions and Politics* (FT130101768). Isabel Karpin would like to acknowledge the support of the ARC in relation to Chapters 4 and 20 (together with Karen O'Connell) and 22, which draw in part on research undertaken for the ARC Discovery Grant, *The Legal Regulation of Behaviour as a Disability* (DP150102935). In relation to Chapter 13, Isabel Karpin would also like to acknowledge such support in relation to the ARC Discovery Grant, *Regulating Relations: Forming Families Inside and Outside Law's Reach* (DP150101057).

The authors would also like to acknowledge the ongoing support provided by Cambridge University Press throughout this project, in particular by Lucy Russell, Senior Academic Commissioning Editor. We very much appreciate the contribution of additional individual chapters by our academic colleagues Stephen Gray, Kate Mulvany, Justin Oakley, Karen O'Connell and Gabrielle Wolf. We are also very grateful for the research and editorial assistance provided by Naomi Burstyner, as well as by Valerie Gutenev-Hale, Sarah McHutchison, Kate Mulvany and Marnie Manning. Finally, we would also like to thank our families for their support and patience throughout the process of writing this book. As always, it is much appreciated.

TABLE OF CASES

Australia

Colombia

Europe

India

New Zealand

United Kingdom

United States of America

TABLE OF STATUTES

South Australia

Victoria

LIST OF ABBREVIATIONS

ABS – Australian Bureau of Statistics

ACL – Australian Consumer Law (creates a strict liability regime for products which are considered to have 'safety defects', and imposes statutory guarantees on manufacturers regarding their products)

ACSQHC – Australian Commission on Safety and Quality in Health Care (In the wake of the findings from the QAHCS study, this was a Commonwealth initiative which Australian governments embarked upon, to improve safety and quality in healthcare.)

ACT – Australian Capital Territory

Additional Protocol – Additional Protocol on the Transplantation of Organs and Tissue of Human Origin

ADT – New South Wales Administrative Decision Tribunal

AHPRA – Australian Health Practitioner Regulation Agency (Boards rely on this national agency for administrative support.)

AHWMC – Australian Health Workforce Ministerial Council (comprising government health ministers, appoints Board members, approves their registration standards and provides policy direction)

AIDS – Acquired Immune Deficiency Syndrome

AIHW – Australian Institute of Health and Welfare

AKX – Australian Paired Kidney Exchange (this program has been established to facilitate kidney transplants with KPD)

ALRC – Australian Law Reform Commission

AMA – American Medical Association

ANZICS – Australian and New Zealand Intensive Care Society (represents intensive care physicians involved with potential donor patients and their families, as well as in the care of donor recipients immediately following organ donation)

ANZICS Statement – Australian and New Zealand Intensive Care Society Statement on Death and Organ Donation

AODR – Australian Organ Donation Register

AOMS – Australian Organ Matching Service (The OTA has announced plans to develop the AOMS, which will employ best practice algorithms to allow for optimal matching of organ recipients on a national basis.)

APP – Australian Privacy Principle

APRA – Australian Prudential Regulation Authority

APSEF – Australian Patient Safety Education Framework (sets out the knowledge, skills and behaviours required by health professionals and other staff in the area of patient safety)

ARCBS – Australian Red Cross Blood Service

ARGB – Australian Regulatory Guidelines for Biologicals (regulate human cell and tissue-based products as distinct therapeutic goods, known as 'biologicals')

ART – Assisted Reproductive Technologies

ARTG – Australian Register of Therapeutic Goods (Only once 'biologicals' are on the ARTG can they be marketed and supplied in Australia.)

ATCA – Australasian Transplant Coordinators Association (represents organ and tissue donor and transplant coordinators and publishes guidance on protocols and procedures for health professionals in relation to organ and tissue donation, transplantation and allocation)

ATSI – Aboriginal and Torres Strait Islander

ATSICPP – Aboriginal and Torres Strait Islander Child Placement Principle (an overarching principle that establishes child removal as a last resort, and requires that a child's connection to family and culture be supported if removed)

BRCA1 – A human gene and its protein product (breast cancer gene)

CEDAW – Convention for the Elimination of all Forms of Discrimination Against Women

CHC – Council of Australian Governments' Health Council

COAG – Council of Australian Governments

Commission – Australia's Productivity Commission

CRC – Convention on the Rights of the Child

CRPD – Convention on the Rights of Persons with Disabilities

Cth – Commonwealth

CVS – Chorionic Villus Sampling

DALY – Daily Adjusted Life Years (a metric which serves as a basis for comparison of the impact of disabilities across nations, established by the World Health Organization together with the World Bank)

DBTV – Donor Tissue Bank of Victoria

DCD – Donation after circulatory death

DDA – *Disability Discrimination Act 1992* (Cth)

DNA – Deoxyribonucleic Acid (hereditary material which stores biological information)

DOHad – Developmental Origins of Health and Disease

DPMP – Donor per Million Population

DPP – Director of Public Prosecutions

DSM – (American Psychiatric Association) Diagnostic and Statistical Manual of Mental Disorders

ECHR – European Convention on Human Rights

ECT – Electroconvulsive Therapy

ECtHR – European Court of Human Rights

EDR – Electronic Donor Record

EPA – Enduring Powers of Attorney (given to individuals appointed by family members or carers as substitute decision-makers).

ESKD – End Stage Kidney Disease

EU – European Union

FCTC – Framework Convention on Tobacco Control

FLA – *Family Law Act 1975* (Cth)

GDP – Gross Domestic Product

GP – General Physician

HCCC – Health Care Complaints Commission

HCE – Health Complaints Entities (colloquially referred to as Commissions)

hES cell – Human Embryonic Stem cell

HFEA – Human Fertilisation and Embryology Authority

HFE Act – *Human Fertilisation and Embryology Act 2008* (Cth)

HGDP – Human Genome Diversity Project (a United States-backed initiative aimed to collect genetic information from indigenous populations around the world)

HGP – Human Genome Project

HIV – Human Immunodeficiency Virus

HREC – Human Research Ethics Committee

HSC – Health Services Commissioner

HT Acts – Human Tissue Acts (state/territory Acts)

HUGO – Human Genome Organisation

ICESCR – International Covenant on Economic, Social and Cultural Rights

ICF – International Classification of Functioning, Disability and Health (used in conjunction with other accepted measures such as, for mental and behavioural disorders, the DSM)

ICU – Intensive care unit

IHR – International Health Regulations (these replaced the ISR in 1969, and are the only global regulations for the control of infectious diseases)

IMR – Income management regime (a scheme under which a proportion of welfare recipients' payments would be quarantined, ostensibly so that it would not be spent on alcohol)

iPS cells – Induced Pluripotent Stem cells

IPV – Intimate partner violence

ISBER – International Society for Biological and Environmental Repositories

ISDS – Investor-state dispute settlement (a mechanism in the TPP which provides that investor companies may obtain compensation from signatory states for the implementation of health law and regulation that lead to investor losses)

ISO – International Standards Organisation

ISR – International Sanitary Conventions

IVD – In vitro diagnostic device

IVF – In vitro fertilisation

JSCOT – Joint Standing Committee on Treaties

KPD – Kidney paired donation

MAOA – Monoamine Oxidase A Gene (a gene which has been referred to as the 'crime gene')

MDG – Millennium Development Goals (eight goals which formed part of the Millennium Declaration adopted by the Millennium Development Summit convened by the UN in 2000)

MI Principles – UN Principles for the Care and Treatment of People with Mental Illness (1991)

MSH6 – MutS, E. COLI, HOMOLOG OF, 6 (a gene which has been associated with certain cancers or carcinomas)

MTA – Material Transfer Agreement (which aims to ensure that third parties comply with all relevant laws in relation to the use of data identifiability, linkage and storage, in addition to any conditions specified by human research ethics committees and the National Statement)

National Law – Health Practitioner Regulation National Law (legislation hosted by the Queensland jurisdiction, as the Schedule to the *Health Practitioner National Law Act 2009* (Qld). The Northern Territory, South Australia, Tasmania and Victoria adopted and applied the National Law as a law of their jurisdictions. Western Australia and the Australian Capital Territory passed corresponding legislation that adopted the National Law, but made some modifications to it.)

National Statement – National Statement on the Ethical Conduct in Human Research

NCD – Non-communicable diseases

NDIS – National Disability Insurance Scheme

NGO – Non-government organisation

NHMRC – National Health and Medical Research Council

NHMRC ART Guidelines – National Health and Medical Research Council Assisted Reproductive Technologies Guidelines

NIIS – National Injury Insurance Scheme

NIPT – Non-invasive prenatal testing

NOMS – National Organ Matching Service

NPSEF – National Patient Safety Education Framework

NRAS – National Registration and Accreditation Scheme

NT – Northern Territory

NTER – NT Intervention, or the NT Emergency Response (a result of the 2007 announcement by the Commonwealth government that it would make an 'immediate and urgent response' to the perceived problem of child sexual abuse in the NT)

NWHP – National Women's Health Policy

OD Standard – Australian Open Disclosure (OD) Standard (which was published in 2003 and which established a framework that could be used in health service organisations for managing adverse events, as well as open communication about such events with patients)

OECD – Organisation for Economic Co-operation and Development

OGTR – Office of the Gene Technology Regulator (oversees approval of gene therapy in Australia, in association with the TGA 1989)

OIC – Office of the Information Commissioner

OID Report – Overcoming Indigenous Disadvantage: Key Indicators 2014

OTA – Organ and Tissue Authority (longer name is Australian Organ and Tissue Donation and Transplantation Authority)

OTDAs – Organ and Tissue Donation Agencies

PBAC – Pharmaceutical Benefits Advisory Committee

PBS – Pharmaceutical Benefits Scheme

PCEHR Act – *Personally Controlled Electronic Health Records Act 2012* (Cth)

PEG – Percutaneous Endoscopic Gastronomy (a form of medical treatment for artificial feeding, which involves the placement of a tube through the abdominal wall and into the stomach)

PGD – Preimplantation Genetic Diagnosis (a procedure where cells are removed from an embryo created using IVF, prior to implantation in a woman, to check for the presence of a genetic anomaly)

PHCR Act – *Prohibition of Human Cloning for Reproduction Act 2002* (Cth)

PHIAC – Private Health Insurance Administration Council

PHEIC – Public Health Emergency of International Concern

QAHCS – Quality in Australian Health Care Study (a landmark study, published in 1995, which examined the rate of [preventable] adverse events in healthcare settings in Australia)

Qld – Queensland

RANZCOG – Royal Australian and New Zealand College of Obstetricians

RCMI – Responsible Children's Marketing Initiative (aims to provide a 'framework for food and beverage companies to help promote healthy dietary choices and lifestyles to Australian children')

RIHE Act – *Research Involving Human Embryos Act 2002* (Cth)

RTC – Reproductive Technology Council

RTAC – Reproductive Technology Accreditation Committee

SA – South Australia

SCNT – Somatic Cell Nuclear Transfer (which involves taking the nucleus of an adult cell and inserting it into a denucleated egg cell which is then triggered to develop into an embryo. Where undertaken with reference to iPS, SCNT requires the creation of an embryo from which stem cells are then harvested, destroying the embryo in the process.)

SDG – Sustainable Development Goal(s)

SLLODP – Supporting Leave for Living Organ Donors Programme (reimburses employers for payments or leave credits provided to their employees for time taken off to donate a kidney or partial liver and to recover from surgery)

SNAICC – Secretariat of National Aboriginal and Islander Child Care

Tas – Tasmania

TGA 1989 – *Therapeutic Goods Act 1989* (Cth)

TGA – Therapeutic Goods Administration

TPP – Trans Pacific Partnership

TSANZ – Transplantation Society of Australia and New Zealand

UDHR – Universal Declaration of Human Rights

UK – United Kingdom

UN – United Nations

UNESCO – United Nations Educational, Social and Cultural Organisation

UPIAS – Union of the Physically Impaired Against Segregation

US – United States of America

VCAT – Victorian Civil and Administrative Tribunal

Vic – Victoria

WA – Western Australia

WB – World Bank

WHA – World Health Assembly

WHO – World Health Organization

WHO Guiding Principles – WHO Guiding Principles on Organ Donation and Transplantation

WIT – Warm Ischaemic Time (the time an organ or tissue remains at body temperature after its blood supply has been reduced or cut off but before it is cooled or reconnected to a blood supply)

WU – Washington University

YLD – The years of life lost due to a disability, adjusted for the severity of the disability

YLL – The sum of years of life lost from premature mortality in the population, adjusted for the severity of the disability

INTRODUCTION

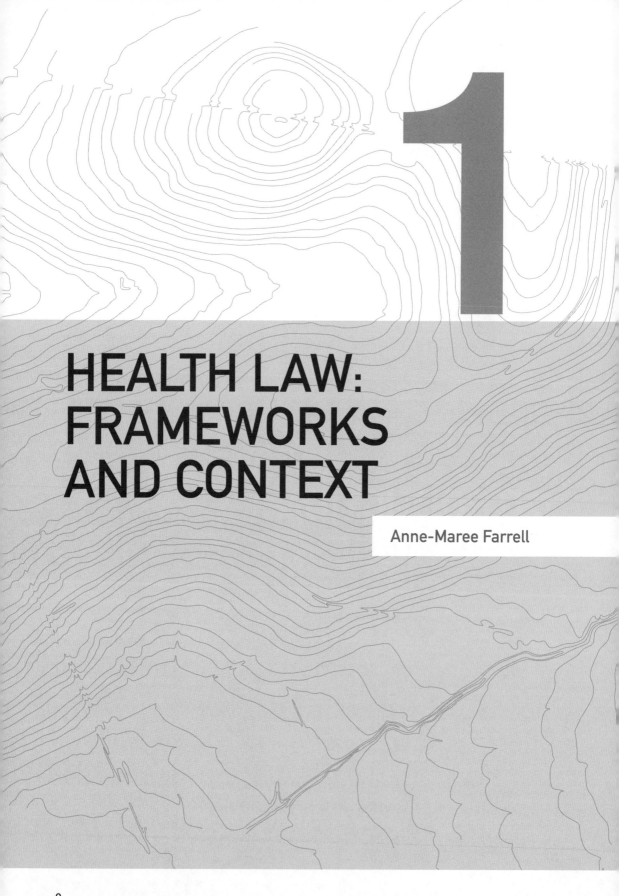

1

HEALTH LAW: FRAMEWORKS AND CONTEXT

Anne-Maree Farrell

In this book, we critically examine and reflect upon the relationship between law and health. Our approach is informed by a socio-legal perspective or 'law in context' approach. We start from the premise that health includes both good and ill-health at individual and population levels and should be viewed as a social and cultural construct that is influenced by science, medicine and technology, as well as by the law itself. We take a broad view of what constitutes law and we are particularly interested in how it is used as a method of social, political and behavioural control. We emphasise the importance of a contextual approach to understanding law's role in influencing the dynamics of patient-doctor relations and the provision of healthcare, the definition of health and ill-health, and the refashioning of human bodies, identity, normalcy and relationships through biomedical practices and technological innovation. In doing so, we explore how we should understand the ethical, social, institutional and equity issues that influence and constitute law's role at an individual, and population, level. In this introductory chapter, we briefly explore the evolution of health law. We then set out the particular approach we use in this book, before concluding with an outline of the organisation of the book.

Health law

From the late 1970s onwards, there was growing interest in the relationship between law and medicine in a range of common law jurisdictions, including Australia. The origins of such interest lay in the perceived growth in medical malpractice claims by patients who had been harmed during the course of medical treatment.[1] This was combined with a greater appreciation that law's coercive aspects could be used to facilitate an ethically principled approach in clinical practice.[2] This contributed to the development of a new legal sub-discipline, known as medical law. Drawing predominantly on the law of tort and contract, as well as the criminal law, it focused on a range of core areas covering the legal obligations involved in the doctor-patient relationship, including consent, confidentiality and privacy, and negligence. Indeed, law's role in such a relationship, underpinned by (philosophical) bioethical critique, remains a core aspect of study and scholarship in the field.[3]

More recently, the influence of human rights discourse and jurisprudence in the field has been the subject of considerable academic debate. Some commentators have argued that medical law should be seen as a 'subset of human rights law'.[4] While this was a claim that could be made in other common law jurisdictions, such as England and Canada,[5] the influence of human rights law in the Australian context has been limited by the fact that there is

---

1   Tamara Hervey and Jean McHale, *Health Law and the European Union* (Cambridge University Press [CUP], 2004) 11.

2   Jonathan Montgomery, 'Time for a Paradigm Shift: Medical Law in Transition' (2000) 53(1) *Current Legal Problems* 363.

3   Anne-Maree Farrell et al., 'Pioneering Healthcare Law' in Catherine Stanton et al. (eds), *Pioneering Healthcare Law: Essays in Honour of Margaret Brazier* (Routledge, 2016) 2. In the Australian context, see, for example, Loane Skene, *Law and Medical Practice: Rights, Duties, Claims and Defences*, 3rd edn (LexisNexis Butterworths, 2008); Bernadette Richards and Jennie Louise, *Medical Law and Ethics: A Problem-Based Approach* (LexisNexis Butterworths, 2013).

4   Ian Kennedy and Andrew Grubb, *Medical Law: Text With Materials*, 3rd edn (Butterworths, 2000) 3. For a more critical conceptualisation, see Thérèse Murphy, *Health and Human Rights* (Hart, 2013).

5   *Human Rights Act 1998* (UK) c. 42; Canadian Charter of Rights and Freedoms, Part 1, *Constitution Act 1982*.

no national legally binding human rights instrument, save for those of limited remit in the ACT and Victoria.[6] Having said that, human rights discourse is now much more influential, as a result of the incorporation of international human rights instruments into Australian law in health-related areas.[7]

Over time, the growth in health services, institutions and administration, combined with more emphasis being placed on a multi-disciplinary team-based approach to treating patients, has led some academic commentators to argue that the narrow focus on the doctor-patient relationship in medical law was no longer appropriate. Instead, it was suggested that the term 'healthcare law' better captured this change, as it encompassed a range of health professions, the administration of health services and the law's role in maintaining public health.[8] Incorporating insights from family law and public law, this shifted the focus to structural and systemic aspects of the health system, and recognised the importance of social care and welfare provision. Notwithstanding this more expansive approach, the provision of healthcare to patients remained a core aspect of analysis.[9]

The increased use of the term 'health law' marks a further conceptual shift. It recognises that the primary focus is on analysis of the relationship between law and health. *Health* is defined to include good and ill-health at both individual and population levels,[10] in circumstances where health is viewed as a socio-cultural construct which is influenced by science, medicine, technology and law. This has led to insights from a range of other disciplinary areas, including feminist studies, sociology, regulatory studies and the behavioural sciences, being incorporated into the field of health law[11]

In this book, *law* is broadly defined to include common law, legislation, courts/tribunals, norms, guidance, procedures and regulation.[12] It is understood as context driven and contingent on social understandings and political dynamics. The term 'regulation' is defined as a method of social control, incorporating both 'soft' and 'hard' legal mechanisms which are designed to promote standard-setting, information, and behaviour modification.[13] Adopting

---

6   See *Human Rights Act 2004* (ACT); *Charter of Human Rights and Responsibilities Act 2006* (Vic).

7   See Belinda Bennett, 'Human Rights and Health Law' in Ben White, Fiona McDonald and Lindy Willmott (eds), *Health Law in Australia*, 2nd edn (LawBook Co, 2014) 103–24; see also Chapter 5 in this book.

8   Jonathan Montgomery, *Health Care Law*, 2nd edn (Oxford University Press [OUP], 2002) 4.

9   See Margaret Brazier and Nicola Glover, 'Does Medical Law Have a Future?' in David Hayton (ed.), *Law's Futures* (Hart, 2000) 371–88.

10   John Coggon, *What Makes Health Public? A Critical Evaluation of Moral, Legal, and Political Claims in Public Health* (CUP, 2012); Lawrence Gostin, *Global Public Health Law* (Harvard University Press, 2014); Roger Magnusson and Paul Griffiths (eds), 'Mini-Symposium; Who's Afraid of the Nanny State? Freedom, Regulation and Public Health' (2015) 129(8) *Public Health* 1015–34; see also Chapters 24 and 25 in this book.

11   See, for example, Ruth Fletcher, Marie Fox and Julie McCandless, 'Legal Embodiment: Analysing the Body of Healthcare Law' (2008) 16 *Medical Law Review* 321; Muireann Quigley, 'Nudging for Health: On Public Policy and Designing Choice Architecture' (2013) 21 *Medical Law Review* 588. On the use of qualitative research methodologies in health law, see, for example, Isabel Karpin et al., 'Analysing IVF Participant Understanding of, Involvement in, and Control over Embryo Storage and Destruction in Australia' (2013) 20(4) *Journal of Law and Medicine* 811.

12   Norms may or may not be overt, particularly in case law in the field: see Jonathan Montgomery, Caroline Jones and Hazel Biggs, 'Hidden Law-Making in the Province of Medical Jurisprudence' (2014) 77(3) *Modern Law Review* 343.

13   Julia Black, 'What is Regulatory Innovation?' in Julia Black, Martin Lodge and Mark Thatcher (eds), *Regulatory Innovation: A Comparative Analysis* (Edward Elgar, 2005) 11.

this interpretation allows for a more flexible approach to understanding the diverse ways in which regulation intersects with health provision, systems, services and technologies in multi-level governance environments.[14]

Our approach

Health law: terminology and remit

It is for the reasons noted above that we use the term 'health law' in this book. We view the relationship between law and health as being one which is conceptually and analytically broader than that between law and medicine, although we recognise that the latter is an important aspect of study in the field. We note that there has been some academic debate over time about whether it should be recognised as a distinct field of legal study, and if so, what its remit should be.[15] However, the exponential growth in academic study in the field, its expansive engagement with a range of other disciplines, and its critical engagement in law reform, shows that such debate has now concluded in favour of its recognition as a thriving and exciting area of academic scholarship in the 21st century.

Frameworks and context

This book examines key frameworks which we argue influence law's relationship with health, both in terms of principles and in practice. Part I identifies and explores such frameworks. The first section is headed 'Theories, Perspectives and Ethics in Health' and contains chapters which explore the relationship between philosophical bioethics and health law; socio-legal perspectives on patient-doctor relations; the social determinants of health and the law; and human rights and health law. The second section is headed 'Institutions and Regulation' and covers overarching institutional and regulatory arrangements impacting the health system, including the regulation of health professionals and patient safety and redress.

Our choice of key frameworks underscores the importance we attach to examining health law in context. In adopting this approach, we draw inspiration from the socio-legal studies literature. There are differing opinions as to what is distinctive about this approach. One view is that socio-legal inquiry is about the study of law in its social context, in circumstances where law is viewed as one among a range of social phenomena. Another view is that it is concerned with the study of law and legal institutions from other disciplinary (social science) perspectives. As one commentator has observed, consensus on a definition is likely to prove elusive. In the circumstances, it is perhaps best to view socio-legal inquiry as a 'broad church', offering the opportunity and the space to engage in a critical examination of the role of law, legal institutions and practices from different disciplinary lenses, or in the context of other disciplines.[16]

---

14   Anne-Maree Farrell et al., 'Regulatory "Desirables" for New Health Technologies' (2013) 21(1) *Medical Law Review* 1–171 (journal special issue).

15   See, for example, Derek Morgan, *Issues in Medical Law and Ethics* (Cavendish, 2001) Ch 1; Kenneth Veitch, *The Jurisdiction of Medical Law* (Ashgate, 2007); Ben White, Fiona McDonald and Lindy Willmott, 'Health Law: Scope, Sources and Forces' in Ben White, Fiona McDonald and Lindy Willmott (eds), *Health Law in Australia*, 2nd edn (LawBook Co, 2014) 7–11.

16   Kerry Petersen, 'Socio-Legality and La Trobe University: Introducing and Celebrating a Broad Church of Ideas' (2013) 29(2) *Law in Context* 1.

While an in-depth examination of these debates is not possible here,[17] we argue that what is valuable about such an approach is the type of critique it offers regarding assumptions of law's neutrality and benign power in the field of health. In adopting a socio-legal analysis of health, we are able to explore the way in which law constitutes, and is constituted by, health discourses and practices. This may lead us to ask about the extent to which law is constitutive of the relationship between doctors and patients. Or conversely, the extent to which the particular area of health under examination determines law's role and response. While the starting point may be law, the end point of socio-legal inquiry may show that a range of non-legal factors – social, cultural, economic, institutional – influence the ways in which we answer such questions, and those ways are ones that may be omitted or not deemed relevant by those engaged in doctrinal study of the law.[18]

Socio-legal inquiry also highlights the importance of an interdisciplinary approach which seeks to understand and critique the way in which legal issues, practices and institutions are constituted by their social context and vice versa. While there is a long tradition of interdisciplinary engagement at the intersection between bioethics and the law,[19] we argue that socio-legal inquiry requires a more expansive approach in both theoretical and methodological terms, incorporating insights from a broader range of disciplinary perspectives, including sociology, economics, politics and anthropology.[20] Adopting such an approach offers a richer, more nuanced analysis of the health law topics covered in the book.

Organisation of the book

The book is organised into two Parts. As noted previously, Part I examines key ethical, social, equity and human rights frameworks that we argue must be taken into account in any examination or analysis of discrete topics in health law (Chapters 2–5). Thereafter, an examination is provided of overarching institutional and regulatory arrangements impacting the health system in Australia (Chapter 6), health professionals (Chapter 7) and patients (Chapter 8). Part II is divided into a number of areas which cover select issues in health law. The first section is entitled 'Patients, Doctors and Healthcare' and covers core legal topics relevant to the relationship between patients and doctors. The first topic is consent to medical treatment, which explores how the law deals with a failure to obtain consent through actions in

---

17   There is a voluminous literature examining the nature, scope of and rationale for socio-legal studies. For example, see Donald Harris, 'The Development of Socio-Legal Studies in the United Kingdom' (1983) 3 *Legal Studies* 315; Phillip Thomas (ed.), *Socio-Legal Studies* (Dartmouth, 1997); Brian Tamanaha, *A General Jurisprudence of Law and Society* (OUP, 2001); Paddy Hillyard, 'Invoking Indignation: Reflections on Future Directions of Socio-Legal Studies' (2002) 29(4) *Journal of Law and Society* 645; Austin Sarat (ed.), *The Blackwell Companion to Law and Society* (Blackwell Publishing, 2004); Roger Cotterell, *Law, Culture and Society: Legal Ideas in the Mirror of Social Theory* (Ashgate, 2006); David Nelken, *Beyond Law in Context: Developing a Sociological Understanding of Law* (Ashgate, 2009); Dermot Feenan (ed.), *Exploring the 'Socio' of Socio-Legal Studies* (Palgrave Macmillan, 2013); Kerry Petersen (ed.), 'Socio-Legality: An Odyssey of Ideas and Context' (2013) 29(2) *Law in Context* (special issue); David Cowan and Daniel Wincott (eds), *Exploring the 'Legal' in Socio-Legal Studies* (Palgrave Macmillan, 2015).

18   Sally Wheeler and Phillip Thomas, 'Socio-Legal Studies' in David Hayton (ed.), *Law's Future(s)* (Hart, 2000) 267–79, 273.

19   Ian Freckleton, 'The Emergence and Evolution of Health Law' (2013) 29(2) *Law in Context* 74.

20   See Annelise Riles, 'Representing In-Between: Law, Anthropology, and the Rhetoric of Interdisciplinarity' (1994) *University of Illinois Law Review* 597, 601.

contract and battery, and includes a section on consent and capacity in relation to children (Chapter 9). This is followed by a chapter on substituted decision-making which examines a range of legal and other processes and mechanisms for people who lack capacity and are unable to make decisions for themselves in respect of specific medical treatment or their healthcare more generally (Chapter 10). The next chapter examines how the law addresses harm caused to patients as a result of medical treatment (Chapter 11). The final chapter in this section examines ethical and legal issues that arise in the area of confidentiality and privacy in the patient-doctor relationship, as well as the circumstances in which patients are able to access their medical records (Chapter 12).

The second section is headed 'Law at the Beginning and the End of Life'. Topics covered include the regulation of reproduction, which covers assisted reproductive technologies (ART) and aspects of pregnancy, including prenatal screening, abortion and surrogacy (Chapter 13). This is followed by an examination of a number of emerging reproductive technologies and the socio-legal implications likely to accompany such innovations (Chapter 14). The next two chapters examine ethical, social and legal issues in relation to end-of-life decision-making and care. The first examines the withdrawal and withholding of medical treatment near the end of life, including the management of post-coma unresponsive or minimally responsive patients (Chapter 15). Case law and law reform debates concerning euthanasia and assisted suicide are examined in the following chapter, which includes an overview of recent prosecutions and other legal challenges in the area in a range of jurisdictions (Chapter 16).

The next section is headed 'Law and the Human Body'. The four chapters in this section deal with different aspects of the law relating to human tissue and genetic information and data. The first of these chapters deals with organ and tissue donation and transplantation, covering living and deceased donation, consent models, markets and trade, the diagnosis of death and transplantation allocation criteria (Chapter 17). The law covering ownership and control of human bodies, parts and tissue is explored in the next chapter, as well as the merits or otherwise of a property-based approach in the area (Chapter 18). This is followed by an examination of biobanks, which store human tissue and related genetic information, issues of consent, privacy and confidentiality, property rights, and commercialisation (Chapter 19). The final chapter in this section provides an overview of the law as it applies to genetic technologies and their therapeutic uses. It engages with disparate legal areas including therapeutic goods regulation, discrimination, privacy, Indigenous rights and ownership. Developments in the area of epigenetics are also identified and their relationships with understandings of the social determinants of health are discussed (Chapter 20).

The final section in Part II is entitled 'Law and Populations'. The first three chapters in this section engage with specific populations that have been constituted as vulnerable, marginal or otherwise stigmatised in terms of the relationship between law and health. The first of these chapters explores the deeply troubling relationship between Indigenous people, health and the law in Australia, showing how a complex interplay of historical, social, political and systemic factors have adversely impacted Indigenous health and compromised law's role in the provision of healthcare in this population (Chapter 21). The next chapter explores the way in which the idea of disability is constructed through medical, social and legal discourses, as well as interrogating whether, and if so how, we should conceptualise the relationship between health law and disability. It also considers how disability has been defined and interpreted, as well as reviewing contemporary scholarship on models of disability (Chapter 22). The following chapter draws on and develops some of the key issues raised in the previous chapter in order to explore the relationship between law and mental health. It identifies how mental illness has been defined and interpreted, before going on to examine how law deals with mental illness in the health system, with a specific focus on laws that permit detention and involuntary treatment (Chapter 23).

The final two chapters in this section deal with the relationship between law and health at the general population level. In the first of these chapters, the relationship between public health and the law is examined, by reference to definitions, sources, principles and institutional arrangements. By way of example, public health challenges in Australia are also identified (Chapter 24). The next and final chapter in the book explores the (potential) role of law in global health. It begins with an overview of the emergence of the global health agenda and the role of key institutions in developing such an agenda. The way in which the law intersects with global health is examined and its impact in Australia is considered, drawing on examples from health security, non-communicable diseases and trade agreements (Chapter 25).

There is potentially a wide range of topics that we could have included in Part II, given that health law is a rapidly expanding area of academic legal study. Choices had to be made as to what would be included. This was done on the basis of topical interest, as well as the fact that particular topics were within the authors' research expertise. A contextual approach was taken to the examination of these topics, with a view to linking them into one or more of the key frameworks identified in Part I. Although the chapters are primarily Australia-focused in terms of their examination of legal issues, comparative and international perspectives have been incorporated, where relevant and appropriate.

PART

FRAMEWORKS

THEORIES, PERSPECTIVES AND ETHICS IN HEALTH

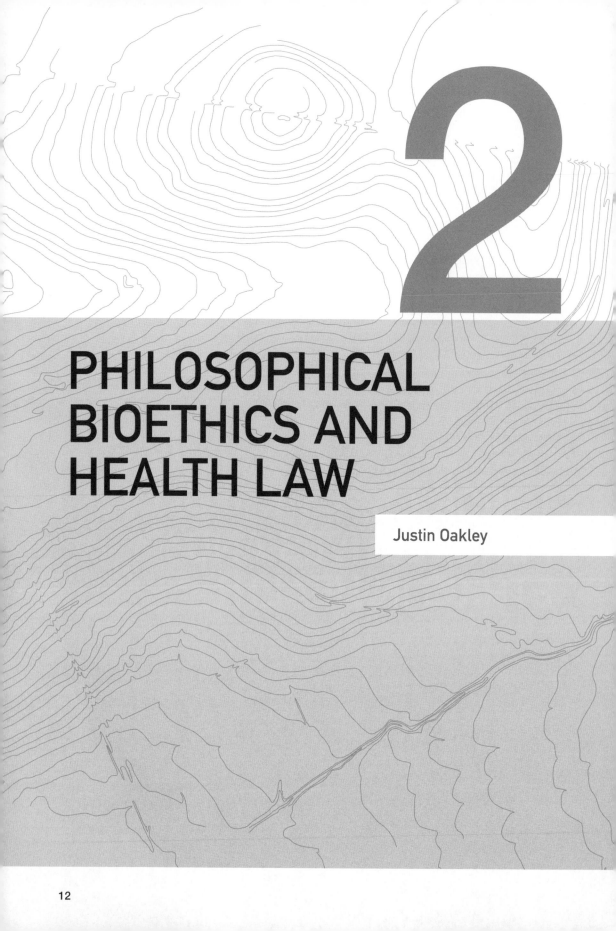

PHILOSOPHICAL BIOETHICS AND HEALTH LAW

Justin Oakley

Introduction

Discussions of ethical issues in healthcare and reproduction often move quickly from judgments about the morality of a certain practice to judgments about how that practice ought to be regulated. However, it is important to distinguish between these two levels of analysis. Someone might believe, for example, that abortion is morally wrong in certain circumstances. However, they might not believe that abortion should be prohibited by law in those circumstances. One may hold that there is a variety of reasonable views about the morality of abortion, but that the law should not be enforcing one such view. So, being justified in judging a certain practice as immoral or unethical might not provide sufficient reason to hold that such a practice should be deemed unlawful.

Ethical theories and concepts can therefore be used to evaluate individual health decisions and laws, and also to justify changes to healthcare practices and law reforms in this area. Two distinct levels of ethical frameworks are commonly appealed to in philosophical bioethics. They can serve as a basis for judgments about regulating a practice, as well as for judgments about the morality of the practice itself. There are broad-based ethical theories and approaches, such as Kantian ethics, Utilitarianism, Virtue ethics, and Feminist ethics, and there are also more practical ethical frameworks specifically addressing healthcare practice, such as the well-known 'principlist' framework developed by Beauchamp and Childress. The key elements of this framework are the concepts of autonomy, beneficence (including non-maleficence, or doing no harm), and justice.[1] This chapter outlines both these broader and more specific ethical frameworks, and briefly explains the constituent concepts involved in each of them.

Rights-based approaches

While a range of rights-based ethical theories have been applied to healthcare practices, the most influential contemporary rights-based theories have been developed from an approach devised by the 18th-century German philosopher, Immanuel Kant. Kant argued that it is through using reason to govern actions that human beings become truly self-determining and therefore free. On this approach, only reason can reveal to us how we ought to act, and any human being with a capacity for rationality can recognise what is right and wrong, and can perform morally right actions. As a key figure in the Enlightenment, Kant aimed to develop a morality in which any person, insofar as they are rational, has the opportunity to live a moral life, to act in ways which are morally good, and is owed a certain basic respect. Because Kant saw reason as a means through which anyone can seek ethical guidance, he sought to underwrite an ethic of respect for persons which was independent of the contingencies of fortuitous birth or social circumstances.

Kant's basic approach to the evaluation of actions revolves around what he calls the 'Categorical Imperative', which provides a criterion for assessing actions whereby the principles or 'maxims' upon which a person is acting are examined. Kant initially formulates

---

1   Tom Beauchamp and James Childress, *Principles of Biomedical Ethics*, 7th edn (Oxford University Press [OUP], 2012).

the Categorical Imperative in a rather abstract way (which his subsequent formulations flesh out):

> Act only according to that maxim by which you can at the same time will that it should become a universal law.[2]

One example Kant uses to illustrate this criterion involves a person asking to borrow money from another, and falsely promising to repay it. Kant argues that borrowing money on the basis of a false promise contravenes the Categorical Imperative, because acting on such a maxim could not feasibly exist as a universal practice. Under a universal practice of false promising, a promisee would 'only laugh at any such assertion [of a promise] as vain pretense'.[3] Thus, deception is morally impermissible because it cannot consistently be universally willed without self-contradiction. Kant uses this kind of approach to derive a range of duties, such as the general duty that we must not make false promises, and the duty to provide much-needed help to others when we can.

By using the reasoning employed in the Categorical Imperative, Kantians provide a theory of basic moral rights. These rights include a right not to be deceived, and a right not to be coerced or manipulated by others. Acts are then evaluated according to what would or would not infringe those basic rights. So, if we observe the duties which correlate with those rights, we will not act wrongly. This will be so even if we thereby fail to bring about the greatest welfare or happiness for the parties involved in the situation.

The key idea, which later Kantians have appealed to in applying Kant's theory to practical issues, is that we should act with a due regard for the autonomy of other moral agents. In doing so, subsequent theorists have been guided by Kant's second formulation of the Categorical Imperative:

> Act so that you treat humanity, whether in your own person or in that of another, always as an end and never as a means only.[4]

In other words, we should act so that we treat others as autonomous, self-legislating, moral agents. Thus, for Kantians, autonomy – the capacity for rational, universalisable self-legislation – is intrinsically valuable, because it is in deciding and acting autonomously that we express our true humanity as free, rational beings. This approach provides a clear ethical rationale for practices such as obtaining informed consent from patients for medical treatment, and maintaining patient confidentiality, as such practices serve as important ways of respecting the personal autonomy of the patients involved. When applied to health policy and regulation, Kantians typically argue that the state has a responsibility to uphold basic respect for persons, through, for example, enacting laws which discourage people from demeaning or degrading themselves or others. Some Kantians argue that commercial surrogacy arrangements and selling one's organs are necessarily demeaning or degrading to some or all of the parties involved.[5]

---

2   Immanuel Kant, *Foundations of the Metaphysics of Morals* (trans. LW Beck, Bobbs-Merrill, 1959) Ak 421.
3   Ibid Ak 423.
4   Ibid Ak 429.
5   For a detailed critical analysis of ethical and legal issues that arise in the context of (cross-border) commercial surrogacy and organ donation, see Chapters 13 and 17 respectively.

Kantian ethics illustrates well how rights-based approaches do not regard considerations of welfare as paramount in determining what we ought to do. While some rights-based theories see the impact of an action on the overall welfare of the affected parties as morally relevant, such theories do not regard such factors as settling the matter. Even if a certain action or practice would maximise the welfare of the parties involved – such as complying with relatives' requests to withhold a diagnosis of terminal illness from a patient with full decision-making capacity – it may still be thought wrong, for it may violate an individual's moral rights. The directive to respect others' rights is thus taken as a constraint on what can be justifiably done to benefit others.

Utilitarianism

Where Kantian ethics focuses on personal autonomy and respecting people's rights, Utilitarian approaches to ethics in health consider the impact of a decision or practice on the welfare of the parties involved. That is, Utilitarianism judges a particular decision, action, or policy according to the total effect it can reasonably be expected to have on people generally, and specifically, according to whether overall welfare is increased or decreased – where 'welfare' is understood as pleasure, happiness, or preference satisfaction.

Advocates of Utilitarianism present this theory as providing a more scientific and humane approach to dealing with questions about what we ought to do than appeals to human rights. For instance, one of the founding fathers of Utilitarianism, Jeremy Bentham, argued that the justifiability of various forms of punishment for convicted criminals is to be determined by looking at whether a certain system of punishment makes the relevant parties better off overall (by reforming the criminal and by deterring future crimes), rather than by whether any individual or communal rights to retribution have been fulfilled.[6] The early 19th century view of certain British settlements in Australia as social laboratories made them quite receptive to the reformist emphasis of Utilitarianism, which was being developed by Bentham at the same time that Australia was being colonised by Great Britain. Indeed, early examples of the influence of Utilitarianism in Australia are Bentham's panopticon-style prisons at the penal settlements of Port Arthur, Fremantle and Norfolk Island, in which guards at the hub could efficiently monitor prisoners in the cells which radiated out from the centre like spokes on a wheel.[7]

The general doctrine of Utilitarianism holds that:

> A practice is right if, and only if, it can reasonably be expected to produce the most utility, compared to its alternatives.

Earlier Utilitarians used the notion of utility to refer to pleasure or happiness, but many modern Utilitarians understand utility in terms of preference satisfaction, which they regard as more feasibly measured than pleasure or happiness. Utilitarianism can be applied to the evaluation of individual acts, or to the evaluation of general practices, rules, or policies; and maximisation of utility is the yardstick used to judge the rightness and wrongness of acts and

---

6   Jeremy Bentham, *An Introduction to the Principles of Morals and Legislation* (Hafner, 1961).
7   For discussion of Bentham's panopticon and its use in Port Arthur, see Julia Driver, *Ethics: The Fundamentals* (Blackwell, 2007) 42–3.

practices – thus, if an act fails to maximise utility, then it is wrong. This is meant to factor in the intensity with which those preferences are held, in that satisfying a strong preference counts for more than satisfying a weak preference. For example, RM Hare explains how Utilitarianism would decide which of two people ought to have access to a parking spot which they are both vying for:

> Suppose you are trying to park your car in a place where I have left my bicycle, and you have a *strong* preference to park your car in this spot, while I have a *mild* preference to leave my bicycle where it is. Suppose these are the only preferences which will be affected by your action. Then I ought to let you park your car in this spot. The fact that it is *my* bicycle, or that I got there first, is morally irrelevant. All that counts are our preferences and their strength.[8]

Thus, in the context of evaluating healthcare practices, such as upholding confidentiality in patient care, Utilitarians evaluate whether or not confidentiality can ever be justifiably breached by considering whether breaching confidentiality in certain circumstances – say, to protect a third party from a mentally ill patient who has confided in a clinician a threat to harm such party – would likely produce more benefit to the various parties involved than would maintaining absolute confidentiality.

When applied to public policy, Utilitarianism asks whether legalising a practice – such as commercial surrogacy – would maximise overall utility, even if the actions of the parties in a particular commercial surrogacy would not thereby maximise utility, considered on their own.[9]

Legal prohibitions of various activities often have all sorts of negative consequences. For example, a foreseeable consequence of a legal prohibition against abortion is that some women will be injured through turning to illegal 'backyard' abortionists in order to terminate a pregnancy. Whatever one's view of the morality of abortion, many think that the undesirable consequences of anti-abortion laws are sufficient to make such laws unjustifiable. Utilitarians argue that the justifiability of creating a law against a certain practice is entirely dependent on what we could expect the consequences of outlawing that activity to be. Thus, while there might be sound utilitarian reasons why a certain practice is wrong, there may nevertheless be sound utilitarian reasons against making such a practice unlawful, as legal prohibition may do more harm than good.

Of course, questions about whether to *prohibit* a certain practice by law are not the only legislative decisions faced by the state. Governments must also often decide whether or not to enact legislation which *decriminalises* certain practices in particular circumstances. For example, governments must decide whether or not to permit voluntary euthanasia and, if so, under what conditions. Utilitarian justifications of legislation decriminalising activities often point out how such legislation allows the state to exercise some kind of control over them, so that they are conducted properly. This is done to minimise harms which can result when the criminal law leads to such activities being practised covertly. However, critics of

---

8   Richard Mervyn Hare, *Moral Thinking: Its Levels, Methods and Point* (Clarendon Press, 1981) 111. See also John JC Smart, 'An Outline of a System of Utilitarian Ethics', in John JC Smart and Bernard Williams, *Utilitarianism: For and Against* (CUP, 1973).

9   See Richard Mervyn Hare, 'Public Policy in a Pluralist Society', in Peter Singer et al. (eds), *Embryo Experimentation* (CUP, 1990).

utilitarian approaches to law-making argue that while the consequences of enacting laws are important considerations, they do not settle the issue of what the law should be. For some critics, important moral rights and serious breaches of moral principles are the proper business of the law, whether or not creating laws protecting such rights and principles might have harmful consequences overall.

Virtue ethics

Instead of asking whether an action is in accordance with a particular duty or is likely to maximise the good, Virtue ethics asks a different sort of question: what sort of person would do a thing like that? For example, we can ask whether an action was generous or mean-spirited, courageous or cowardly, friendly or unfriendly. We can also ask whether this is the sort of thing which a kind person, a just person, or a self-respecting person, would do in the circumstances.

A Virtue ethics criterion of what makes an action right can thus be stated initially in broad terms as follows:[10]

> An action is right if, and only if, it is what an agent with a virtuous character would do in the circumstances.

On this approach, a right action is one that is in accordance with what a virtuous person would do in the circumstances, and what *makes* the action right is that it is what someone with a virtuous character would do. For example, it is right to help a stranger in distress because this is what someone with the virtue of benevolence would do. A person with the virtue of benevolence would do this because benevolence is directed at the good of others, and having this virtue involves being disposed to help others in circumstances where assistance is likely to be beneficial to them.[11]

Several forms of Virtue ethics have been developed recently, but the most influential is that based on Aristotle's ethics. Aristotle argued that there are certain sorts of things or activities which it is in our nature as humans to have and to do. For example, we are naturally social animals who have friendships and loving relationships. We naturally seek understanding of the world around us, we use reason to guide our lives, and we care about or are moved by what we value. These are the things which a good human being aims at having and achieving.[12]

Thus, two distinctive features of Virtue ethics are its emphasis on the connections between right action and the agent's motives, and its pluralist view of the good. Acting rightly, in many situations, requires acting from a particular sort of motivation, since this is an important aspect of doing what a virtuous person would do in the circumstances.[13] In

---

10   Rosalind Hursthouse, *On Virtue Ethics* (OUP, 1999) 28–31.

11   Philippa Foot, 'Euthanasia' (1977) *Philosophy and Public Affairs* 6(2).

12   See Aristotle, *The Nicomachean Ethics* (trans. WD Ross) (OUP, 1980).

13   An exception to this is the 'target-centred' pluralistic form of Virtue ethics developed by Christine Swanton, *Virtue Ethics, A Pluralistic View* (OUP, 2003) 294, 245–6, who argues that one can hit the target of a particular virtue from no relevant inner state at all. As such, Swanton appears to reject the idea that hitting the target of the contextually relevant virtue always requires acting from a particular virtuous motive or disposition.

contrast, most versions of Utilitarianism and Kantian ethics generally hold that one can act rightly whatever motivation one acts from. As long as one maximises expected utility, or acts in accordance with duty, one has done the right thing, whether or not one's motives were praiseworthy. Another important distinguishing feature between Virtue ethics and most versions of Utilitarianism is that contemporary Virtue ethicists commonly regard virtues as intrinsic goods whose value is not reducible to a single underlying value, such as utility. For instance, the value of personal integrity goes beyond its utility (eg. its pleasure) to oneself or others.[14]

In recent years, Virtue ethicists have applied the above criterion of right action in the context of various roles, such as medical practice, parenting, and personal relationships. Accounts have been developed of role virtues that demonstrably serve the proper goals of the profession or practice in question, mirroring Aristotle's goal-directed or 'teleological' account of how broad-based virtues enable us to live humanly flourishing lives. A key feature of these Virtue ethics evaluations of actions within roles is the central place given to the proper goals of the profession or practice in question, and to showing how a commitment to these goals should regulate or govern a practitioner's conduct in the context of that role. For example, in the healthcare context, Virtue ethics advises doctors to provide truthful diagnoses to their patients, not because patients have a right to know this information, or because truth-telling maximises utility, but because this is what is involved in a doctor having the virtue of truthfulness. A disposition to tell patients the truth serves the doctor's goal of achieving good health for the patient without breaching the patient's autonomy.

Other key virtues for doctors are medical beneficence, medical courage, and trustworthiness. Medical beneficence counts as a virtue because it focuses doctors on their patients' interests and blocks inclinations towards unnecessary interventions characterised by defensive medicine. Medical courage helps doctors work towards healing patients by helping doctors to face risks of serious infection when necessary, without rashly disregarding proper precautions against becoming infected themselves. Trustworthiness assists with effective diagnosis and treatment by helping patients feel comfortable about disclosing intimate information.[15]

One way of applying Virtue ethics to evaluating health regulation focuses on whether or not permitting a certain practice threatens to jeopardise doctors' medical virtues by undermining therapeutic relationships with patients. For example, the therapeutic orientation of doctor-patient relationships can be distorted by doctors' links with the pharmaceutical industry, and by direct-to-consumer advertising of pharmaceuticals. When the state supports (or fails to support) doctors developing and maintaining therapeutic relationships with their patients, it is supporting (or failing to support) doctors having and acting on the medical virtues they committed to having when they joined the profession. Therefore, the state needs to consider whether to allow practices which may threaten such professional relationships and virtues.

---

14   See Justin Oakley 'Varieties of Virtue Ethics' (1996) 9(2) *Ratio* 139–40.
15   Justin Oakley and Dean Cocking, *Virtue Ethics and Professional Roles* (CUP, 2001) 93.

Feminist approaches to bioethics

Feminist philosophers highlight the shortcomings of traditional bioethical theories, which, they argue, pay inadequate attention to gender inequities, as well as disparities in health, that result from differences in class, race, ethnicity and susceptibility to genetic disease. While there has been significant feminist analysis of key bioethical concepts such as autonomy (see below), separate consideration of the contribution of feminist bioethical critique as a distinct field is warranted. It is important to keep in mind, however, that there are a range of feminist approaches to bioethics, and that these resist encapsulation into a single criterion of right action.[16]

One prominent approach which originated from the work of feminist psychologist Carol Gilligan is an ethics of care. She claimed that there were female patterns of moral reasoning that emphasised relationships, as well as responsibilities within those relationships.[17] Unlike Virtue ethics, which focuses on the value of certain character traits and their role in a humanly flourishing life, care ethics focuses on the value of relationships, such as those between parents and children, spouses, partners, and friends. Care ethicists commonly emphasise how one's family typically plays a crucial role in the development of one's moral agency. They argue that the picture of moral agents in traditional ethical theories as self-sufficient and independent, rather than as relationally embedded and vulnerable, is misleading and unrealistic. Rather than viewing issues in terms of any rights individual agents may have, care ethics sees moral problems in terms of our responsibilities to others, and it encourages the development and maintenance of relationships which are both caring and equitable.[18]

As Shildrick notes, however, more recent feminist critique of the ethics of care challenges the central idea that biomedicine has, as its primary aim, either cure or care. Instead, she argues that 'health care is as much about control, containment and normalization as it is about treatment'.[19] Feminist scholars, such as Tong and Lanoix, have called for a reconsideration of the ethics of familial, as opposed to societal, responsibilities in the area of health.[20] Yet others, such as Fineman, have argued that the focus should instead be on inevitable dependency, rather than individual autonomy;[21] and Rogers has called for greater recognition of the importance of a feminist critique of public health.[22]

16   For a good summary, see Stanford Encyclopedia of Philosophy, *'Feminist Bioethics'* <http://plato .stanford.edu/entries/feminist-bioethics>.

17   Carol Gilligan, *In a Different Voice: Psychological Theory and Women's Development* (Harvard University Press, 1982).

18   Virginia Held, *The Ethics of Care: Personal, Political, and Global* (OUP, 2006).

19   Margrit Shildrick and Roxanne Mykitiuk (eds), *Ethics of the Body: Postconventional Challenges* (MIT Press, 2005) 17.

20   Rosemarie Tong, 'Long-term Care for the Elderly Worldwide: Whose Responsibility Is It?' (2009) 2(2) *International Journal of Feminist Approaches to Bioethics* 5; Monique Lanoix, 'Caring for Money: Communicative and Strategic Action in Ancillary Care' (2013) 6(2) *International Journal of Feminist Approaches to Bioethics* 94.

21   Martha A Fineman, 'Masking Dependency: The Political Role of Family Rhetoric' (1995) 81 *Virginia Law Review* 2181.

22   Wendy A Rogers, 'Feminism and Public Health Ethics' (2006) 32 *Journal of Medical Ethics* 351.

It is also worth noting one further area in which feminist bioethics has had a significant impact on bioethical critique, and that is the field known as feminism of the body.[23] Scholars working in this field argue that mainstream bioethics tends to use universalising ethical principles that work only for decontextualised and disembodied individuals, who bear little resemblance to material persons who exist in the world. These scholars argue that such approaches, where they do relate to the embodied and embedded person, tend to favour those whose bodies are most accommodated or normalised: that is, white, middle-class, able-bodied men. Instead, it is argued that mainstream bioethics should take account of non-normative, marginalised bodies – not in order to find ways to normalise them, but rather to embrace difference and to build theoretical models that recognise diversity.[24] One of the key contributions of feminist bioethicists in this regard has been to argue that biomedical discourse is an incredibly powerful force in the construction of normalcy, and this makes it incumbent on mainstream bioethics to take account of such critique in ethical analysis of healthcare practices.

Autonomy

In the 1980s, the value of personal autonomy was at the forefront of the critique of medical paternalism, which inaugurated the field of bioethics. It remains a central concept in the justification of various aspects of decision-making in healthcare practice. The ethical demand to respect the autonomous decisions and actions of patients is a crucial requirement upon health professionals. To be autonomous is to be self-determining in one's decisions and actions. To act or decide autonomously is to do so in accordance with one's values. We saw above that Kantian ethics places respect for autonomy at the centre of ethical decision-making; however, many philosophers who emphasise the importance of patient autonomy adopt conceptions of autonomy which are less demanding than Kantian accounts, and which allow a person's desires and emotions to play a greater role in constituting and expressing autonomous decisions.

Various philosophical theories have been put forward regarding what constitutes autonomy. Mainstream bioethics asserts that the capacity for autonomy involves two broad components: a *cognitive* component, which requires that one decides on the basis of one's understanding of relevant information about what one proposes to do; and a *volitional* component, which requires that one makes a voluntary decision, not prompted by inner compulsions, and without being coerced by others' threats or manipulated by others who deliberately target one's weaknesses.[25] Thus, when people talk about autonomy in clinical care, they often talk in terms of informed and voluntary decision-making by patients. For example, the recent emergence of advance care planning, where individuals are encouraged to develop and express better informed views about possible clinical interventions

---

23   This work must be read alongside the growing body of ethical critique in disability studies; for a detailed discussion of such work, see Chapter 22.

24   Shildrick and Mykitiuk, above n 19, 16.

25   For an overview of how the ethical position on autonomy maps onto the law of consent in the context of both capacity and incapacity, see Chapters 9 and 10.

towards the end of their lives, is based squarely on the idea that personal autonomy must be respected by health professionals.[26]

Feminist philosophers have also been critical of this mainstream approach to conceptualising autonomy, suggesting that it can operate only in circumstances that do not exist for most (if any) people. Instead, they have argued for recognition of the concept of 'relational autonomy', which views individual capacity to act as existing only or largely in the context of social relationships, and as being shaped by a complex interplay of social determinants, such as race, class, gender and ethnicity.[27] Yet other feminist scholars have rejected mainstream bioethical conceptions of autonomy altogether, arguing that our inevitable dependency on each other and our universal vulnerability ought to be the ordering principles for a system of ethical exchange.[28]

Beneficence

To act beneficently towards a patient is to act so as to benefit them, or at least to protect them from harm. Given that serving patient health is clearly a central goal of clinical practice, the ethical requirement to act beneficently towards patients is arguably of paramount value. Indeed, whatever else the idea of professional integrity in clinical practice might involve, it clearly includes a commitment to act in the best interests of one's patients. However, there are debates among health professionals about how the concept of 'best interests' is to be understood – consider here, for example, controversies about the meaning of 'medical futility' – and these debates often reflect philosophical disagreements about the nature of human wellbeing or welfare.[29]

A key issue here is how the quantity of life likely to be gained by a certain intervention is to be compared with the quality of life the patient is likely to subsequently experience. Some accounts of best interests hold that the quality of a patient's life is ultimately determined by their own subjective values or preferences; whereas other accounts understand quality of life in more objective terms. As an example of the latter, the 'capabilities approach' to wellbeing was devised as an alternative to preference-utilitarian approaches to measuring quality of life. As one of its originators, Martha Nussbaum, puts it: 'we want to know not only how people feel about what is happening to them … we also want to know what they are actually able to do and be'.[30] In any case, it is widely held that we can have a general duty of beneficence to help a stranger in considerable distress. In patient care, there are specific duties of beneficence deriving from institutional roles and the commitments to patients which such roles involve.

---

26   For an overview of advance care planning, end-of-life issues and the role of law, see Chapter 15.
27   Catriona Mackenzie and Natalie Stoljar (eds), *Relational Autonomy: Feminist Perspectives on Autonomy, Agency, and the Social Self* (OUP, 2000) 4. See Chapter 4 for a detailed discussion of how such social determinants impact health, as well as law's role in shaping such impact.
28   Fineman, above n 21; Catriona Mackenzie, Wendy Rogers and Susan Dodds (eds), *Vulnerability: New Essays in Ethics and Feminist Philosophy* (OUP, 2014).
29   See Lawrence J Schneiderman, Nancy S Jecker and Albert R Jonsen, 'Medical Futility: Its Meaning and Ethical Implications' (1990) 112 *Annals of Internal Medicine* 949; James Griffin, *Well-Being: Its Meaning, Measurement and Moral Importance* (OUP, 1986).
30   Martha Nussbaum, *Frontiers of Justice* (Harvard University Press, 2006) 73.

Justice

Beneficence and autonomy are not the only broad ethical principles needed for justifying decision-making in healthcare. For example, even if we have a duty of beneficence to put a particular patient on a kidney dialysis machine, it may not be right to do so because this might be unjust. This is because such devices may well be a scarce resource and another patient might have a stronger justice-based claim to the device. So healthcare decision-making and practice should also be governed by an overarching principle of justice. The values of autonomy and beneficence focus on how it is proper to treat individual patients, whereas the principle of justice looks at how a patient is to be properly treated within the broader context of whether a treatment they may have autonomously consented to ought to be provided to them, or to another patient who might have a stronger justice-based claim to it.

An important principle of justice in healthcare practice, stated abstractly, is that scarce health resources ought to be distributed according to morally relevant features of individuals, rather than according to morally irrelevant features (such as a patient's social status). A range of different specific allocative principles has been advocated by bioethicists. For instance, some argue that justice requires that such resources be distributed according to the urgency of a patient's needs; others argue that resources should be distributed according to the relative benefit that the patient stands to gain from the resource, compared with other potential recipients of this resource. Yet others argue that resources should be allocated in accordance with policies which promote consumers' freedom of choice among health programs.[31]

How might these three ethical principles work together?

One way of understanding how the values of autonomy, beneficence and justice might function effectively together in an overall ethics for healthcare is that respect for patient autonomy should be regarded as a side constraint rather than a goal of healthcare practice. Each profession has its own distinctive goal(s), which a health professional's role should be geared towards serving. For example, good health is a central goal of medicine, and effective caring is an important goal of nursing. Patient autonomy becomes morally significant in this context because whatever a health professional does to help restore or promote the health of a patient, it must be done in a way that does not violate their autonomy. Respect for the autonomy of patients is an important side constraint on the ethical pursuit of any proper professional goal, but this demand assumes particular importance for the health professions. This is because illness makes us especially vulnerable to various internal and external influences, which can undermine our capacity for autonomous decision-making. As a result, this places health professionals in a particularly powerful position when compared to other professionals.

It is also important to distinguish between justified and unjustified restrictions of a patient's autonomy. For example, assume that only one of two patients can be given an

---

31   See Norman Daniels, *Just Health: Meeting Health Needs Fairly* (CUP, 2008).

intensive care bed. Suppose a patient with advanced renal failure is denied admission to the intensive care unit in favour of a patient who stands to benefit far more from treatment in the unit. Here, the former patient's autonomy is certainly restricted by being refused admission to intensive care; but if justice requires that the bed be provided to the other patient instead, then the restriction of the first patient's autonomy in denying them an intensive care bed is ethically justifiable. A patient's autonomy counts as being violated when their autonomy is restricted unjustifiably. The requirement for health professionals to respect patients' autonomy demands that health professionals do not restrict their patients' autonomy unjustifiably. Such a requirement does not demand that health professionals meet whatever informed and voluntary requests patients make of them.[32]

Conclusion

Understanding key concepts in philosophical bioethics is important for clarifying the various contested issues that arise in health law and regulation. Lawyers and doctors need conceptual tools in order to critique such issues, and in order to find a principled way forward through these issues. In this chapter, we have seen how healthcare practice, law and regulation can be evaluated according to comprehensive, broad-based ethical theories and approaches, such as Kantian ethics, Utilitarianism, Virtue ethics, and feminist ethics. We can also draw on a more specific ethical framework in healthcare practice, whereby the concepts of autonomy, beneficence and justice (and the principles containing them) serve as crucial cornerstones. In outlining these ethical theories and concepts, this chapter has indicated their key differences, along with the motivations behind their development. This can help to clarify what is at stake in key ethical controversies which are relevant to healthcare practice, law and regulation. In addition, the need for such ethical frameworks as a basis for evaluating any proposed changes and law reform is likely to become increasingly important, given encroaching market and political pressures in the health sector more generally.

---

32   Oakley and Cocking, above n 15, 84–5.

SOCIO-LEGAL PERSPECTIVES ON PATIENT-DOCTOR RELATIONS

Anne-Maree Farrell

From the 1970s onwards, growing interest in the critical examination of the relationship between law and medicine led to the emergence of a new area of academic study known as medical law. While the initial catalyst for such interest was the exponential growth in medical negligence litigation in a number of common law jurisdictions, including Australia,[1] it was also influenced by an appreciation of law's potential role in promoting an ethically principled approach to the doctor-patient relationship.[2] Law's role in such a relationship, underpinned by (philosophical) bioethical critique, remains a core aspect of study and scholarship in the field of medical law, as well as within the expanding field of health law.[3]

While the relationship between bioethics and the law has become an established approach to understanding and critiquing the moral dilemmas and challenges that arise in the doctor-patient relationship,[4] what it lacks is a more nuanced and contextual account of other important social dynamics that influence such a relationship.[5] In turn, this may impact upon what law does and does not take into account in determining the acceptable parameters of such relationships. Law's role in this regard includes, for example, the regulation of the health system, the health professions and patient safety (Chapters 7–9); legislation which may either directly or indirectly impact upon such relations (Chapters 4 and 10), and redress mechanisms for harm caused to patients in healthcare settings (Chapters 8, 11 and 12).

Through a number of illustrative examples, the aim of this chapter is to highlight the importance of a contextual analysis of the patient in the study of health law, which is embedded in their day-to-day experiences with their treating doctors (as well as other health professionals). The objective in doing so is to facilitate a more critical reflection of the limits of the traditional twinning of ethical and legal analysis in seeking to understand how patients interact with their treating doctors, and to encourage a broader engagement in health law with both theoretical and empirical research in the social sciences.

The first part of the chapter presents a brief consideration of the social context in which patients access and receive healthcare, as well as law's role in that context. The social determinants impacting health are important in this context and they are considered in much more detail in Chapter 4. This part also includes a discussion of the primacy accorded to the principle of autonomy in mainstream bioethics and law and how it is (or should be) balanced against patient responsibilities. In the second part of the chapter, the power imbalance in patient-doctor relations is explored. This includes examining medicine's claim to expert knowledge; how such imbalance plays out in the framing of patients as good or difficult; and in the disclosure of risks in medical treatment. The final part of the chapter briefly considers law's role in shaping risk disclosure in this context.

1   Ian Freckleton, 'The Emergence and Evolution of Health Law' (2013) 29(2) *Law in Context* 74.

2   Jonathan Montgomery, 'Time for a Paradigm Shift: Medical Law in Transition' (2000) 53(1) *Current Legal Problems* 363.

3   See Chapter 1 for an overview of the development of medical and health law; see also chapters in Part II, A: Patients, Doctors and Healthcare.

4   Jose Miola, *Medical Ethics and Medical Law: A Symbiotic Relationship* (Hart, 2007); see, for example, J Kenyon Mason and Graeme T Laurie, *Law and Medical Ethics*, 9th edn (OUP, 2013); Ian Kerridge et al., *Ethics and Law for the Health Professions*, 4th edn (Federation Press, 2013).

5   See Ruth Fletcher, Marie Fox and Julie McCandless, 'Legal Embodiment: Analysing the Body of Healthcare Law' (2008) 16 *Med L Rev* 321, 322–3.

The patient in context

Within clinical settings, patients are individuals who are in ill-health or have a disease, and are receiving medical treatment. Patients may be young or old, poor or rich, have acute or chronic illness, and come from different racial, ethnic or identity backgrounds and geographical locations. Such diversity may be reflected in the extent to which they consider themselves to be sick or ill, whether or not they are considered to have (legal) capacity, and whether they feel marginalised, either as an individual or as part of a particular group. Depending on the type of treatment needed, patients may access the public or private healthcare sector or a mixture of both, which in turn may depend upon personal preferences, finances and location. Patients may present alone or be accompanied by family and friends. How they approach decision-making about their healthcare may also vary depending on their relations with family, friends and the broader community to which they belong.

Individuals who present as patients are in a relational, interconnected world, and are embedded in a range of social and cultural relations and practices. Within the social sciences literature, the concept of embodiment has been used to highlight the importance of taking account of the subjective experience of patients in dealing with ill-health and disease, as well as their experience in accessing and receiving healthcare. There is a recognition that patients (and their bodies) cannot be seen as solely biological objects, subject to control through medicine and technology.[6] Patients' 'being-in-the-world' – sensation, emotions and experience – comes with them, and affects the way in which they access and receive healthcare, as well as the way in which they navigate health professional and institutional practices.[7]

So where does bioethics position itself in conceptualisng the patient? As highlighted in Chapter 2, feminist approaches to bioethics, such as the ethics of care, recognise that patients are relationally embedded with family and friends and that moral problems need to be addressed in terms of our relations with others.[8] Others have argued that our vulnerability as human beings and the consequent dependency that brings to our relationships, should guide ethical decision-making and behaviour.[9] For those in favour of a relational autonomy approach, atomistic accounts of autonomous choice in healthcare decision-making by patients fail to take account of the context in which such decision-making takes place, which is informed by a range of social determinants, such as race, class, gender and ethnicity.[10]

Communitarianism acknowledges the importance of community and the social good. This requires that account be taken of meaning, implications and context in determining

---

6   See, for example, Nancy Scheper-Hughes and Margaret Lock, 'The Mindful Body: A Prolegomenon to Future Work in Medical Anthropology' (1987) 1 *Medical Anthropology Quarterly* 6; Mike Featherstone et al., *The Body: Social Process and Cultural Theory* (Sage, 1991); Thomas J Cordas, 'Introduction: The Body as Representation and Being-in-the-World' in Thomas J Csordas (ed.), *Embodiment and Experience: The Existential Ground of Culture and Self* (CUP, 1994) 3–6; Fletcher et al., above n 5, 321–2.

7   Csordas, above n 6, 8.

8   See Virginia Held, *The Ethics of Care: Personal, Political, and Global* (OUP, 2006).

9   See Catriona Mackenzie, Wendy Rogers and Susan Dodds (eds), *Vulnerability: New Essays in Ethics and Feminist Philosophy* (OUP, 2014).

10   See Catriona Mackenzie and Natalie Stoljar (eds), *Relational Autonomy: Feminist Perspectives on Autonomy, Agency, and the Social Self* (OUP, 2000); see also Chapter 4 for a detailed discussion of the social determinants of health.

what constitutes an ethically principled approach in healthcare, rather than relying solely on the autonomous choice of individuals.[11] In contrast, more mainstream bioethics, as exemplified in the principlist framework, is concerned primarily with the one-on-one relationship between patients and doctors.[12] The focus is on promoting the autonomous choices of individual patients and the use of ethical decision-making in clinical practice, rather than on the social and political issues impacting patients.[13]

Largely mirroring mainstream bioethics, the development of common law principles, and indeed legal precedent in general, has been predicated on the one-to-one relationship between patient and doctor. Law's role has been primarily to set out the scope of patients' rights and protections, as well as to determine what will be permitted (or not) in relation to patients' bodies. Mind/body dualism is largely perpetuated, with patients' bodies viewed as biological objects around which choice or rights have been infringed, and/or where harm has been done. More often than not, this is conceptualised in terms of the need to uphold or respect patient autonomy, which we consider in more detail in the next section.

Patient autonomy

Autonomy has become the pre-eminent ethical principle underpinning patient-doctor relations. Its importance has also been recognised by the courts,[14] with the most prominent affirmation to be found in the law of consent.[15] Although framed differently, it is also given effect in (international) human rights instruments and jurisprudence.[16] The importance of patient autonomy is also recognised in the patient-centred care approach in healthcare settings. The promotion of autonomous decision-making by patients is seen as important in enhancing patient satisfaction; in ensuring that treatment and medication regimes are adhered to; and in bringing about better health outcomes overall.[17]

What does it mean to uphold patient autonomy in clinical practice? First and foremost, respect for autonomy does not on its own mean that doctors must automatically respect and follow decisions by patients regarding their healthcare. Instead, to attract such respect patients must be considered to have made a decision (or choice) that is 'maximally

---

11   Daniel Callahan, 'Individual Good and Common Good: A Communitarian Approach to Bioethics' (2003) 46(4) *Perspectives in Biology and Medicine* 496–507.

12   Tom L Beauchamp and James F Childress, *Principles of Biomedical Ethics*, 7th edn (OUP, 2013).

13   Fletcher et al., above n 5, 322–3. As to whether the principlist framework actually informs day-to-day clinical practice, see Katie Page, 'The Four Principles: Can They Be Measured and Do They Predict Ethical Decision Making?' (2012) 13 *BMC Medical Ethics* 10.

14   See, for example, *Secretary, Department of Health and Community Services v JWB and SMB* (Marion's Case) (1992) 175 CLR 218; *Rogers v Whitaker* (1992) 175 CLR 479; *Re T (adult: refusal of medical treatment)* [1993] Fam 95, 102 (CA); *Chester v Afshar* [2005] 1 AC 134; *Montgomery v Lanarkshire Health Board* [2015] UKSC 11.

15   There is a voluminous academic literature in the area. For recent examples, see Alisdair MacLean, *Autonomy, Informed Consent and Medical Law: A Relational Challenge* (CUP, 2009); Sheila McLean, *Autonomy, Consent and the Law* (Routledge, 2010); Mary Donnelly, *Healthcare Decision-Making and the Law* (CUP, 2014); see also Chapter 9 for a detailed examination of the law of consent in the context of medical treatment in Australia.

16   For a critical overview, see Thérèse Murphy, *Health and Human Rights* (Hart, 2013); see also Chapter 5.

17   Nicola Mead and Peter Bower, 'Patient-Centredness: A Conceptual Framework and Review of the Empirical Literature' (2000) 51 *Social Science & Medicine* 1087.

autonomous – an informed and free decision made by someone with the capacity to make such a choice'.[18] In certain circumstances, the law has imposed limits on the autonomy of some individuals and their bodies, as exemplified in the English line of cases involving women being forced to undergo caesarean sections against their wishes.[19] Law's neutrality in such cases is subject to challenge, particularly given the long history of marginalisation of women's bodies in social and legal terms.[20] This is in addition to difficulties experienced by both the courts and legislatures in conceptualising the maternal-fetal relationship, notwithstanding the lack of legal recognition of the fetus.[21]

The pre-eminence of respect for autonomy as the dominant ethical principle in clinical practice raises the question as to whether, and if so what sort of, legal limits might be imposed on the expression of such a principle. Clearly, legal limits have been imposed due to incapacity,[22] but what of the competent patient? The law has upheld the right of an adult competent patient to refuse medical treatment, regardless of the outcome.[23] However, it has not followed that a competent patient will be entitled to demand medical treatment if their treating doctor is of the view that it is not clinically indicated or appropriate.[24] Treating doctors are not required to continue with treatment they consider to be futile[25]

Whether there should be ethical and legal limits imposed on the principle of autonomy has been the subject of academic debate, particularly with regard to where the balance should lie between patient autonomy and responsibility, particularly in the context of publicly funded health systems.[26] In ethical terms, it has been argued that patients have moral responsibilities in their relationship with doctors, as well as to the health system more generally. For commentators such as Sorell and Draper, the focus in ethical analysis on doctors' responsibilities in treating patients has been too one-sided. Traditionally, the ethical positon has been to place a 'big and largely unconditional responsibility on doctors to treat patients "no questions asked"'.[27] This has resulted in doctors becoming 'captive helpers', even in

---

18   Margaret Brazier and Emma Cave, *Medicine, Patients and the Law*, 5th edn (Penguin, 2011) para 3.3.

19   For an overview of the English line of cases, see Sara Fovargue and Jose Miola, 'Are We Still "Policing Pregnancy"?' in Catherine Stanton et al. (eds), *Pioneering Healthcare Law: Essays in Honour of Margaret Brazier* (Routledge, 2016) 243–54.

20   Margaret Brazier, 'The Body in Time' (2015) 7(2) *Law Innovation and Technology* 161, 179–84.

21   Fovargue and Miola, above n 19. See also public debate over fetal legal personhood which arose in the context of an ultimately unsuccessful legislative proposal in NSW which sought to criminalise harm caused to late-term fetuses due to injuries inflicted on their mother: see Hannah Robert, 'Why Losing My Daughter Means I Don't Support Zoe's Law', *The Conversation* (8 November 2013) <http://theconversation.com/why-losing-my-daughter-means-i-dont-support-zoes-law-19985>.

22   See Chapters 10, 15 and 24.

23   See, for example, *Brightwater Care Group v Rossiter* (2009) 40 WAR 84; *Medical Treatment Act 1988* (Vic).

24   *R (Burke) v General Medical Council* [2005] EWCA Civ 1003. Note that in the case of an incompetent adult patient, a best interests test would apply: see, for example, *Messiha v South East Health* [2004] NSWSC 1061.

25   See Chapter 15 for an overview of ethical and legal issues impacting the withholding and withdrawal of medical treatment.

26   See Margaret Brazier, 'Do No Harm – Do Patients Have Responsibilities Too?' (2006) 65(2) *Cambridge Law Journal* 397.

27   Heather Draper and Tom Sorell, 'Patients' Responsibilities and Medical Ethics' (2002) 16(4) *Bioethics* 335, 337.

circumstances where their patients are not acting in accordance with the medical advice provided.[28] While Sorell and Draper accept that patients may be vulnerable in seeking healthcare, this does not mean that patients can do no wrong.[29] They suggest that patients should be seen as moral agents with responsibilities for their own health: this requires them to follow the advice given to them by their treating doctors, and in doing so to limit their claims on the finite resources of publicly funded health systems.[30] Of course such reasoning assumes that doctors are best placed to mediate such claims.

Brazier also argues that patients have moral responsibilities, which exist in an environment in which the actions of patients, health professionals and institutions, as well as the community, are all engaged.[31] She acknowledges that one of the advantages of identifying patients' moral responsibilities may be to identify the limits of doctors' obligations to patients,[32] suggesting that it is this reciprocity which may determine the acceptability of moral (and perhaps even legal) responsibility.[33] While remaining wary of law's engagement in this area, she argues that there is a need for more critical reflection as to when and how such responsibilities should be balanced against the empowerment of patients brought about by the law's promotion of autonomy. She concludes that to do otherwise would be to potentially put at risk the advances which have been made as a result of the recognition of patients' rights.[34]

While there is a need to engage with academic debates about what should constitute the moral and legal boundaries of patient autonomy, there is also a need to recognise that such debates bring a range of other social and political factors into play. In making arguments about the importance of patients' moral responsibilities, there is a risk that this transforms into a political demand that individuals accept personal responsibility with respect to their own health,[35] without taking account of the broader social determinants of health which may adversely impact upon individuals' health, and over which they may have little control.[36] This may be used to create financial, institutional or indeed legal obstacles to accessing and receiving healthcare, often for those who need it the most. It may also result in a lack of political commitment to engaging in preventive health policy and regulation on a population basis.[37]

---

28   Ibid 346.

29   Ibid 339.

30   Ibid 347, 350–2.

31   Brazier, above n 26, 401.

32   Ibid 413. Note that Brazier excludes from her examination questions of self-responsibility (eg. where excess alcohol consumption may preclude eligibility for a liver transplant).

33   Ibid. Indeed, it may even raise the (albeit rare) prospect of contributory negligence being recognised as a defence in medical negligence claims. For example, see Jennifer Yule, 'Defences in Medical Negligence: To What Extent Has Tort Law Reform in Australia Limited the Liability of Health Professionals?' (2011) 4(1–2) *JALTA* 53, 54–6.

34   Brazier, above n 26, 422.

35   Gerald Dworkin, 'Voluntary Health Risks and Public Policy' (1981) 11(5) *Hastings Center Report* 26; Daniel Wikler, 'Who Should Be Blamed for Being Sick?' (1987) 14(1) *Health Education Quarterly* 11.

36   See Chapter 4 for a more detailed discussion of the social determinants of health and the role of law.

37   See Chapter 24, which examines how the political context has adversely affected preventive public health initiatives in Australia in recent years.

A question of power

The rise in patient autonomy is said to have been accompanied by patient empowerment, and represents a move away from the dark days of medical paternalism, where patients were passive and deferential towards their treating doctors, as well as uncritically accepting of the medical advice they received.[38] It is asserted that patients have been empowered through a more patient-centred approach to healthcare, which emphasises shared decision-making between patients and doctors.[39] Yet empirical evidence shows that such assertions may be aspirational at best in the face of the power imbalances which exist in patient-doctor interactions. From the perspective of patients, there are a number of factors contributing to such imbalance, which include knowledge about the illness or disease, treatment options and personal preferences; perceptions about what constitutes the 'good patient'; interpersonal characteristics and communication skills of treating doctors; and institutional practices which shape interactions between patients and doctors.[40]

In general terms, one of the ways in which power may be asserted is through claims to having expertise in a particular area. Those who make such claims often engage in boundary work to establish their expertise,[41] which includes distinguishing between expert and lay forms of knowledge.[42] Michel Foucault used the term the 'clinical gaze' to describe how claims to expert knowledge in the medical sphere were used to underpin doctors' social prestige, influence and power.[43] With this in mind, he conceptualised the relationship between knowledge and power in the following terms:

> We should admit … that power produces knowledge (and not simply by encouraging it because it serves power or by applying it because it is useful); that power and knowledge directly imply one another; that there is no power relation without the correlative constitution of a field of knowledge, nor any knowledge that does not presuppose and constitute at the same time power relations.[44]

In the face of what has been described by Lupton as the 'competence gap'[45] brought about by the knowledge/power nexus, patients may respond by presenting themselves in particular ways in their interactions with doctors, as a form of protection in the face of their vulnerability.

---

38   Brazier, above n 26, 401.

39   Cathy Charles, Amiram Gafni and Tim Whelan, 'Decision-making in the Physician-Patient Encounter: Revisiting the Shared Treatment Decision-Making Model' (1999) 49 *Social Science & Medicine* 651.

40   Natalie Joseph-Williams, Glyn Elwyn and Adrian Edwards, 'Knowledge is Not Power for Patients: A Systematic Review and Thematic Synthesis of Patient-Reported Barriers and Facilitators to Shared Decision Making' (2014) 94(3) *Patient Education and Counselling* 291.

41   Thomas F Gieryn, 'Boundary-Work and the Demarcation of Science from Non-science: Strains and Interests in Professional Ideologies of Scientists' (1983) 48 *American Sociological Review* 781.

42   Brian Wynne, 'May the Sheep Safely Graze? A Reflexive View of the Expert–Lay Knowledge Divide', in Scott Lash, Bronislaw Szerszynski and Brian Wynne (eds), *Risk, Environment and Modernity: Towards a New Ecology* (Sage, 1996) 44–83.

43   Michel Foucault, *The Birth of the Clinic: An Archaeology of Medical Perception* (Routledge, 1973); see also Bryan S Turner, *Medical Power and Social Knowledge*, 2nd edn (Sage, 1995).

44   Michel Foucault, *Discipline and Punish: The Birth of the Prison* (Vintage Books, 1977) 27.

45   Deborah Lupton, *Medicine as Culture: Illness, Disease and the Body in Western Society* (Sage, 2003) 113.

Good v difficult patients

In order to foster better relations with their treating doctors, research has shown that patients can internalise the need to be seen as a 'good patient', a position characterised by passivity and compliance.[46] Where an individual is receiving ongoing treatment for a chronic condition, how to be seen as a good patient becomes more complex. Although such an individual may acquire more knowledge about their condition over time, as well as becoming more confident about self-management, there is also a need to maintain good ongoing relationships with treating doctors and other health professionals. This may involve being suitably deferential and compliant in order to facilitate access to medication or health services they would like to receive, as well as ensuring the quality and safety of the treatment they receive.[47] This may be made more difficult by the fact that they need to navigate institutional practices in which power asymmetries and paternalistic behaviour towards patients may be entrenched, particularly in publicly funded health systems where resources are finite.[48]

What of the situation where patients encounter doctors with whom they experience difficulties in communicating about their health and medical treatment? Empirical research has shown that patients place a high value on being able to communicate in a meaningful way with their treating doctors. This allows them to express their fears and concerns, as well as to obtain information and feedback about their treatment and its likely outcomes.[49] A range of difficulties may arise if either doctors have poor communication skills or patients are unable (for a range of reasons) to communicate in a full and frank way with their treating doctors.[50]

In such circumstances, patients run the risk of being branded as 'difficult' by their treating doctors. Although it has been suggested that there is a tendency on the part of the medical profession to view this as a one-sided affair, with blame lying solely with patients,[51] the findings from empirical research have shown that it may in fact involve both 'difficult patients' and 'difficult doctors'. In the case of doctors, this may be attributable to particular personality characteristics, accompanied by poor communication skills. Where this combination occurs, it may result in worse short-term health outcomes for patients.[52] Such findings only reinforce the need for doctors to be more consciously aware of the power they hold and are able to exert in their relations with patients, as well as what ethical – and indeed legal – obligations may arise as a result of failures in communication with their patients.[53]

46   Joseph-Williams et al., above n 40.

47   Su-Yin Hor et al., 'Finding the Patient in Patient Safety' (2013) 17(6) *Health: An Interdisciplinary Journal for the Social Study of Health Illness and Medicine* 567–8.

48   Alison Pilnick and Robert Dingwall, 'On the Remarkable Persistence of Asymmetry in Doctor/Patient Interaction' (2011) 72 *Social Science & Medicine* 1374, 1381.

49   Hor et al., above n 47, 576; Anne-Maree Farrell and Sarah Devaney, 'When Things Go Wrong: Patient Harm, Responsibility and (Dis)empowerment' in Catherine Stanton et al. (eds), *Pioneering Healthcare Law: Essays in Honour of Margaret Brazier* (Routledge, 2016) 103–15.

50   Such reasons may include anxiety/depressive disorders, lack of trust and recent episodes of stress. See Sheri A Hinchey and Jeffrey L Jackson, 'A Cohort Study Assessing Difficult Patient Encounters in a Walk-In Primary Care Clinic, Predictors and Outcomes' (2011) 26(6) *Journal of General Internal Medicine* 588.

51   Jean Abbott, 'Difficult Patients, Difficult Doctors: Can Consultants Interrupt the "Blame Game"?' (2012) 12(5) *American Journal of Bioethics* 18.

52   Hinchey and Jackson, above n 50.

53   Michael Jefford and John R Zalcberg, 'Broken Doctor-Patient Relationships; Why Won't They Listen?' (2014) 201(6) *Medical Journal of Australia* 347; Loane Skene, 'Legal Issues When a Doctor's Relationship with a "Difficult" Patient Breaks Down' (2014) 201(6) *Medical Journal of Australia* 350.

Information disclosure and the role of law

As highlighted in the Introduction, there are a range of legal mechanisms in place to regulate interactions between patients and doctors in Australia, and any adverse consequences of those interactions. Clearly, the law has sought to promote the principle of autonomy in order to uphold patients' rights and protections in such relationships. The question is whether the law has been able to fully take account of the broader social and political contexts which may affect how patients access and receive healthcare and interact with their treating doctors.

In the seminal case of *Rogers v Whitaker*,[54] the High Court considered what sort of 'material risks' should be disclosed to patients by doctors in relation to their medical treatment. Acknowledging the need to take account of the particular circumstances in a given case, the Court stated that the types of risks that should be disclosed were those which 'a reasonable person in the patient's position, if warned of the risk, would be likely to attach significance to' or where the doctor 'is or should reasonably be aware that the particular patient, if warned of the risk, would be likely to attach significance to it'.[55] In this instance, the knowledge of the patient about the sorts of risks they might be prepared to undertake was given preference over what their treating doctors might consider to be clinically indicated or relevant.

Despite concerns on the part of the medical profession that the case would open the litigation floodgates, this has not eventuated. Indeed, empirical research has subsequently shown that many doctors remained ill-informed about their legal obligations regarding the disclosure of risks to patients, and 'routinely underestimate the importance of a small set of risks that vex patients'.[56] In addition, the High Court has since adopted a fairly strict interpretation of causation in subsequent information disclosure cases, which has operated as a control mechanism to mitigate any prospect of the floodgates opening.[57] This approach has been reinforced by the adoption of politically contentious restrictive tort law change in Australia in the early 2000s, at a time when there were increasing concerns about a personal injury litigation and insurance crisis.[58] These concerns led to the adoption of state/territory legislation in which patients' views on what they would have done if they had been warned of a material risk in relation to their medical treatment are not to be taken into account.[59]

Following yet another restrictive interpretation of causation by the High Court in a recent unsuccessful information disclosure case brought by a patient in *Wallace v Kam*,[60] one commentator felt compelled to observe that the Court was clearly showing 'undue deference to a

---

54   (1992) 175 CLR 479 [16] per Mason CJ, Brennan, Dawson, Toohey and McHugh JJ.
55   The test of material risk was held by the majority of the High Court to be subject to therapeutic privilege. For further details of this exception, see Chapter 11.
56   Marie Bismark et al., 'Legal Disputes Over Duties to Disclose Treatment Risks to Patients: A Review of Negligence Claims and Complaints in Australia' (2012) 9 *PLoS Medicine* e1001283.
57   See, for example, High Court judgments in *Chappel v Hart* (1998) 195 CLR 232; *Rosenberg v Percival* (2001) 205 CLR 434; *Wallace v Kam* (2013) 250 CLR 375.
58   See Review of the Law of Negligence: Final Report (the Ipp Report) (Commonwealth of Australia, 2002).
59   This is subject to the exception where statements given by patients would be against their own interests, see *Civil Liability Act 2002* (NSW) s 5D(3)(b); *Civil Liability Act 2003* (Qld) s 11(3(b); *Civil Liability Act 2002* (WA) s 5C(3)(b); *Civil Liability Act 2002* (Tas) s 13(3)(b). For a more detailed discussion, see Chapter 11.
60   (2013) 250 CLR 37.

fundamentally unjust stream of legislative change' which had been driven by powerful political and economic interests, rather than by any sound evidence of a litigation or insurance crisis.[61] Twenty-five years on from *Rogers v Whitaker*, Australian case law on information disclosure regarding the risks of medical treatment to patients provides an example of how the law has been influenced by the broader political context, shifting towards a restrictive judicial and legislative approach which limits rather than enhances patient autonomy. It also now stands in stark contrast to the more expansive approach taken in other jurisdictions, such as England. [62]

Conclusion

This chapter has offered a socio-legal perspective on patient-doctor relations. It has presented an analysis of how issues such as autonomy, responsibility, power and risk impact upon such relations, with an empirically grounded focus on the patient perspective. Using a contextual analysis of the patient into the study of health law should be encouraged, as it contributes to a more developed account of the dynamics of patient interactions with doctors and other health professionals. It also has the potential to offer insights into how law constitutes, and is constituted by, the broader social and political contexts which shape such interactions.

---

61   Thomas Faunce, 'Disclosure of Material Risk as Systems-Error Tragedy: *Wallace v Kam* (2013) 87 ALJR 648; [2013] HCA 19' (2013) 21 *Journal of Law and Medicine* 53, 64.

62   See Anne-Maree Farrell and Margaret Brazier, 'Not So New Directions in the Law of Consent? Examining *Montgomery v Lanarkshire Health Board*' (2016) 42(2) *Journal of Medical Ethics* 85.

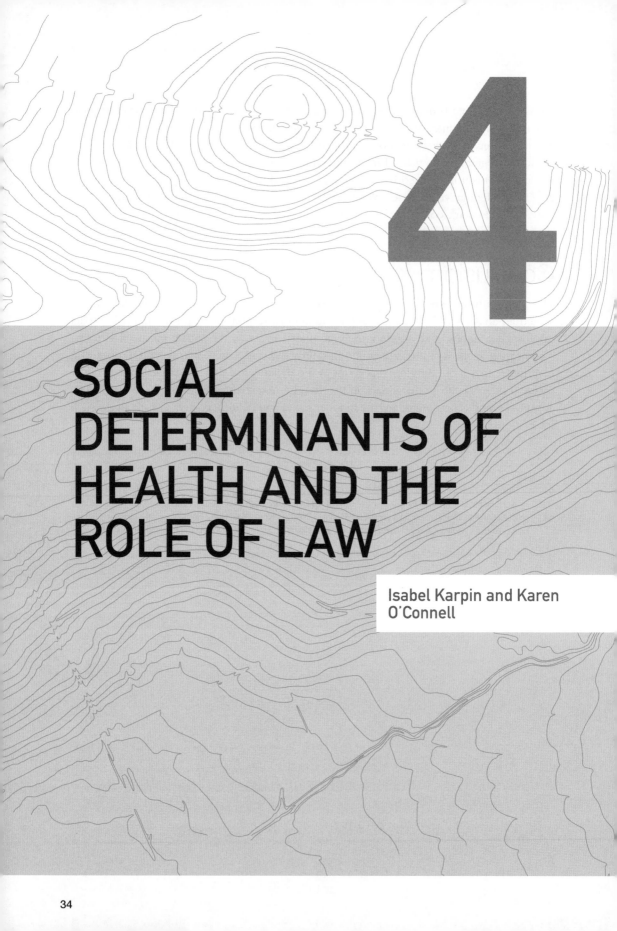

4

SOCIAL DETERMINANTS OF HEALTH AND THE ROLE OF LAW

Isabel Karpin and Karen O'Connell

Introduction

Social determinants of health are the contextual factors – environmental, relational, institutional, economic – that impact upon health status and outcomes, shaping access to services, and experiences of health. Law or legal structures, as socially constituted institutions, also form a crucial component of the social determinants of health. Law plays a direct and indirect role in shaping the conditions in which other social determinants of health might be created, amplified or mitigated.

Given the extraordinary complexity of the characteristics that make up the social determinants of health, and given the even more complex interaction between them, and how they might change over time and place, it is impossible to give a comprehensive overview in one short chapter. Rather, in this chapter we provide a snapshot of the way in which some social determinants of health within Australia lead to inequities that law might redress. In the first part, we examine the impact of select laws that either directly or indirectly determine health outcomes, with a focus on equality laws that are aimed at redressing social and health inequities. In the second part, we examine how social determinants of health differ for Indigenous Australians, women, and the embryo/fetus. While this last category is not viewed as a legal person with equality rights, we consider it here because significant regulatory and policy work is expended on the health and wellbeing of the embryo/fetus through the concept of the welfare of the future child. In the third part, we consider what constitutes both harm and health, as determined by social and biomedical markers. In the final part of the chapter, we consider some recent legislative measures that have been put in place to deal more effectively with social determinants of health.

Social determinants of health in a legal context: social inequities and equality law

Social determinants are the factors that influence health, such as education, socio-economic status, employment and access to (publicly funded) healthcare. The WHO defines social determinants of health as:

> the conditions in which people are born, grow, work, live, and age, and the wider set of forces and systems shaping the conditions of daily life. These forces and systems include economic policies and systems, development agendas, social norms, social policies and political systems.[1]

The WHO sees these issues as so important that it has a specific program focused on social determinants and has worked with the United Nations (UN) Member States to have the Rio Political Declaration at the World Conference on Social Determinants of Health[2] endorsed by the World Health Assembly (WHA). With a focus on five specific areas, the Declaration

---

1   WHO, *Social Determinants of Health* <www.who.int/social_determinants/en>.
2   WHO, *Rio Political Declaration on Social Determinants of Health* (October 2011) <www.who.int/sdhconference/declaration/en>.

broadly encompasses taking action on governance of health, reducing health inequities and monitoring progress.[3]

The list of social determinants of health is not closed, and apart from those mentioned above, includes social policy considerations such as economic stability, as well as public goods, such as access to greenery[4] and unpolluted air, transportation and adequate public services. Time is also a crucial factor in determining health. Adversity in the early years may impact on a person's health throughout their life, while a decline in financial security in older age, for example, can undermine earlier positive experiences.[5] Further, as scientific knowledge about the causes of poor health expands into new fields, understanding of the social determinants of health has correspondingly expanded. So, for example, the health impact of discrimination in the form of racism, sexism, cultural exclusion and stigmatisation has taken on a new significance in recent years. Though viewed as moral wrongs in most progressive societies, discrimination and prejudice were not generally included in lists identifying the social causes of ill-health.[6] Recent research in the area of epigenetics may, however, change this perception, with increasing evidence that:

> The health consequences of racism and discrimination can be persistent and passed from one generation to the next through the body's 'biological memory' of harmful experiences.[7]

The mechanism for transmission is not DNA mutations – for which we might screen – but rather occurs through the regulation of gene expression, that is, epigenetically. Waggoner and Uller describe epigenetics as 'the study of how environmental exposures (including those internal to the organism) alter gene activity without changing the genetic makeup of the individual'.[8] The most commonly discussed epigenetic mechanism is DNA methylation (methylation), which has as one of its functions, modification of gene expression.[9] Recent studies claim that exposure to environmental stress or trauma in one generation may cause a gene to turn on or off in the next generation, or even across several generations. These are heritable changes in gene expression, rather than changes to the gene or DNA itself. What is interesting about this new research is that it suggests that some social disparities in

---

3   The Rio Political Declaration, see above n 2, was endorsed by WHO Member States at the 65th WHA in May 2012. For details of the five specific areas, see WHO, *What Are Social Determinants of Health?* <www.who.int/social_determinants/sdh_definition/en>.

4   Nicholas Bakalar, 'Living Near Greenery May Help You Live Longer', *New York Times*, 14 April 2016.

5   Roxanne Mykitiuk and Jeff Nisker, 'Social Determinants of "Health" of Embryos' in Jeff Nisker et al. (eds), *The 'Healthy' Embryo* (CUP, 2010) 116.

6   Roxanne Mykitiuk et al., 'The Legal Construction and Regulation of the Gendered Body and of Disability in Health Law and Policy', *Commissioned Reports and Studies*, Paper 104, The National Network on Environments and Women's Health (2002); Mark Siegler and Richard Allen Epstein, 'Organizers' Introduction to the Conference on Social Determinants of Health and Disease' (2003) 46 Supp 3 *Perspectives in Biology and Medicine* S1; Dennis Raphael, 'Introduction to the Social Determinants of Health' in Dennis Raphael (ed.), *Social Determinants of Health: Canadian Perspectives* (Canadian Scholar's Press Inc, 2004).

7   Bridget J Goosby and Chelsea Heidbrink, 'The Transgenerational Consequences of Discrimination on African-American Health Outcomes' (2013) 7(8) *Sociology Compass* 630–43.

8   Miranda R Waggoner and Tobias Uller, 'Epigenetic Determinism in Science and Society' (2015) 34(2) *New Genetics and Society* 177.

9   Ibid 179.

health that appear across generations derive from systemic forms of discrimination. If this is the case, then anti-discrimination and human rights laws may not just serve the moral good of ensuring all people are equal, but may also be good for your health.[10]

Law forms a framework that intersects with social determinants of health, with the aim of protecting individuals from discriminatory harms, and preserving non-discriminatory access to health services.[11] At the same time, law may also permit differential provision of services where this is warranted as a result of past disadvantage.[12] While we suggest that law can do this, we also acknowledge that it currently does not. The equality framework in the Australian legal system (and in many other jurisdictions of which we might take note, such as the UK) is not consistent or reliable, since it is geared towards individuals bringing claims of harm with quite difficult hurdles of proof. It is difficult, for example, for an Aboriginal man to claim that his poor health is a result of racial discrimination, despite the fact that we know Aboriginal and Torres Strait Islander men have a life expectancy 11.5 years less than non-Aboriginal men in Australia.[13] A legal remedy directed at an individual is of limited use in addressing social determinants of health that may impact whole communities and are complex interactions of disparate elements over time.

Laws which are aimed more broadly at social inequities have also not fared well in guaranteeing positive health outcomes. For example, our positive obligations to provide universal health services are not entrenched in law in Australia. Recent cuts to Medicare bulk billing and a freeze on general practitioner (GP) rebates may also have a negative effect on communities with the least economic resources.[14] As outlined in Chapter 5, Australia lacks a stand-alone human rights legal framework that provides a right to health for all people. This is despite the fact that Australia is a signatory to many important international human rights treaties, including the Convention on the Rights of Persons with Disabilities (CRPD), the Universal Declaration of Human Rights (UDHR) and the International Covenant on Economic, Social and Cultural Rights (ICESCR), all of which work towards achieving the highest attainable standard of physical and mental health. In many respects, these international treaties remain aspirational, with significant components not having been enacted into enforceable legal rights.

Moreover, even where there are enforceable legal equality rights, other social factors may inhibit activation of those rights. For example, people may have a theoretical right to enforce their access to health services, through anti-discrimination law. However, people who are socially disadvantaged – whether through poor education, socio-economic status

---

10   See Chapter 5 for a detailed discussion of the relationship between health and human rights law.

11   See, for example, *McBain v Victoria* (2000) 99 FCR 116 (IVF Case) where the Court relied on section 22 of the *Sex Discrimination Act 1984* (Cth) to overcome then Victorian ART legislation restricting the provision of IVF services to unmarried women. It was upheld on appeal to the High Court, see *Re McBain* (2002) 209 CLR 372.

12   See, for example, *Proudfoot v Australian Capital Territory Board of Health* (1992) EOC 92–417, where the Commission also relied on the *Sex Discrimination Act 1984* (Cth) to find that women's health services were not discriminatory in part because they were a 'special measure' aimed at ameliorating women's disadvantage.

13   Australian Bureau of Statistics (ABS), *4704.0 – The Health and Welfare of Australia's Aboriginal and Torres Strait Islander Peoples* (October 2010) <www.abs.gov.au/AUSSTATS/abs@.nsf/lookup/4704.0 Chapter218Oct+2010>.

14   See Chapter 6 for an overview of the regulatory framework for health in Australia, which includes a discussion of Medicare and how it works.

or belonging to a health 'risk' group, such as Indigenous people – are less likely to access both appropriate health services and law. Indeed, as outlined in Chapter 21, in the case of Indigenous peoples, their compromised social and health status may bring them into contact with the punitive arm of the law rather than trigger access to remedial support. It is impossible to trace every way that law interacts with social determinants of health. However, it is clear that disadvantage – social, legal and identity-based – compounds the problem. At the same time, existing poor health can result in a feedback loop, where being sick means that a person cannot access the social and institutional support that may assist in overcoming illness.

Some of this disadvantage has been tackled through policy measures. The Commonwealth Department of Health has embraced the idea of social determinants of health in areas such as indigenous health,[15] women's health,[16] and men's health.[17] The creation of distinct policies based on sex and race is potentially problematic and yet may be necessary to address health inequalities. Such policies become problematic if the chosen categories are treated as biological categories, as this undermines the social component of their construction and thus their susceptibility to positive regulatory interventions. As Krieger and Fee have noted with respect to US health policy:

> Vital statistics present health information in terms of race and sex and age conceptualized only as biological variables – ignoring the social dimensions of gender and ethnicity.[18]

Once the social component of these variables is unpacked, we can see that cultural stereotypes, as well as discrimination based on sex and race, determine health behaviours and limit access to services. The effects of race and sex discrimination extend to lower socio-economic status, but lower socio-economic status is also in and of itself a social determinant of health.

Interaction of law and social determinants of health: some examples

Indigenous health[19]

A key consequence of identifying social determinants of health is that these necessarily expand the responsibility for health well beyond the institutions and relationships conventionally associated with health, such as hospitals, doctors and the health system. The

---

15 Department of Health, *Aboriginal and Torres Strait Islander Health Performance Framework* (9 June 2015) <www.health.gov.au/indigenous-hpf>.

16 Department of Health, *National Women's Health Policy* (10 June 2013) <www.health.gov.au/internet/main/publishing.nsf/Content/national%20womens%20health-1>.

17 Department of Health, *National Male Health Policy* (30 June 2014) <www.health.gov.au/internet/main/publishing.nsf/Content/national%20mens%20health-1>.

18 Nancy Krieger and Elizabeth Fee, 'Man-Made Medicine and Women's Health: The Biopolitics of Sex/Gender and Race/Ethnicity' in Nancy Krieger (ed.), *Embodying Inequality: Epidemiologic Perspectives* (Baywood Publishing Company, 2005) 239, 244.

19 See Chapter 21 for a detailed discussion of Indigenous health and the law.

National Aboriginal and Torres Strait Islander Health Plan 2013–2023 (Health Plan) takes on board the advice of the Close the Gap Steering Committee that it is:

> important to address the social and cultural determinants of health as there are many drivers of ill health that lie outside the direct responsibility of the health sector.[20]

The Health Plan notes that a large proportion of the life expectancy gap between Indigenous Australians and non-Indigenous Australians is due to social determinants of health.[21]

One startling example offered in the Health Plan shows the significant difference education and employment makes to the formation of life-shortening habits. It states that: 'Aboriginal and Torres Strait Islander adults are less likely to smoke if they have completed Year 12, are employed and if they have higher incomes'.[22] Clearly then, direct discrimination based on race is one factor that leads to poorer health, but indirect discrimination in the form of persistent intergenerational deprivation leading to poverty, lack of schooling and lack of access to health services, is also a key factor in determining whether or not an individual is healthy.

As part of the Health Plan, state and territory governments, as well as that of the Commonwealth, must develop implementation plans. Interestingly, the Commonwealth implementation plan does not include any specific legal strategies.[23] However, it does refer to the National Indigenous Law and Justice Framework 2009–2015 (Framework), which includes seven principles of recognition and six principles of action. The fourth principle of recognition states:

> 4. Aboriginal and Torres Strait Islander peoples have the right to live free from victimisation, racism and discrimination.

The second principle of action (the ninth in the combined list) requires governments to agree to:

> 9. Comprehensively respond to factors contributing to violent and criminal behaviour in Indigenous communities in particular mental health issues and the misuse and abuse of alcohol and other substances.[24]

---

20   Department of Health, *National Aboriginal and Torres Strait Islander Health Plan 2013–2023* (27 June 2013) <www.health.gov.au/internet/publications/publishing.nsf/Content/oatsih-healthplan-toc~determinants>, quoting Close the Gap Steering Committee 2012, *Submission to the Australian Government for the development of a National Aboriginal and Torres Strait Islander Health Plan*.

21   Department of Health, *National Aboriginal and Torres Strait Islander Health Plan 2013–2023* (27 June 2013) <www.health.gov.au/internet/publications/publishing.nsf/Content/oatsih-healthplan-toc~determinants>.

22   Department of Health, *National Aboriginal and Torres Strait Islander Health Plan 2013–2023* (27 June 2013) <www.health.gov.au/internet/publications/publishing.nsf/Content/oatsih-healthplan-toc~determinants> quoting Australian Health Ministers' Advisory Council 2012, *Aboriginal and Torres Strait Islander Health Performance Framework 2012*.

23   Department of Health, *National Indigenous and Torres Strait Islander Health Plan Implementation Plan 2013–2023* <www.health.gov.au/internet/main/publishing.nsf/Content/indigenous-implementation-plan>.

24   Standing Committee of Attorneys-General Working Group on Indigenous Justice, *National Indigenous Law and Justice Framework 2009–2015* <www.cabinet.qld.gov.au/documents/2009/sep/scag%20national%20indigenous%20law%20and%20justice%20framewoek/Attachments/NationalIndigenousLawandJusticeFramework.pdf>.

With respect to health, the Framework specifically notes that: 'health, substance misuse and wellbeing are issues closely linked to indigenous violence, offending and incarceration'.[25] Strategies to redress these concerns are included in the Framework,[26] but there has been limited success. In 2008, it was noted by the Australian Bureau of Statistics that:

> Nearly one-third (32 per cent) of the Aboriginal and Torres Strait Islander people aged 18 years and over had experienced high/very high levels of psychological distress, which was more than twice the rate for non-Indigenous people.[27]

As outlined in Chapter 21, evidence of the ongoing significantly higher levels of incarceration of Indigenous peoples compared to the general population suggest that standard mental health diversionary strategies and support systems are not effective. In 2015, Aboriginal and Torres Strait Islanders accounted for just over a quarter of the total Australian prison population, despite the fact that they make up only 2 per cent of the general Australian population.[28] The Australian Institute of Health and Welfare (AIHW) reports that:

> [N]on-Indigenous prison entrants were more likely than Indigenous prison entrants to have ever been told that they have a mental health disorder (51 per cent and 44 per cent, respectively), but the proportions taking mental health related medication was the same.[29]

It is clear that in the case of Aboriginal and Torres Strait Islander people, it is not sufficient to simply respond to mental health issues by intervening once an incident has occurred or a mental health issue has been recognised. Instead, there needs to be a fundamental strategy to address the long-term consequences of entrenched and systemic racism stemming from historic harms, such as dispossession and the unjust removal of children. This is in addition to more contemporary harms such as exclusion from social goods, poverty, and poor educational opportunities. By taking an approach that acknowledges that social context is a significant determinant of health, we can thus see that equality measures in law need to be developed in areas that are not immediately identified as health-related areas. These include the criminal law and employment law, as well as laws dealing with equality of opportunity and affirmative measures for redressing past harms and inequities.

Indigenous health issues in Australia also demonstrate that what are considered social determinants of health will vary by group and culture and over time. For example, past

---

25 Ibid 24.
26 Ibid 18. To this end the Framework includes implementation strategies such as: 2.3.3a Develop and implement specialised training to enable police to better identify Aboriginal and Torres Strait Islander people with mental health issues; 2.3.3b Develop and implement appropriate referral pathways to enable police to better respond to Aboriginal and Torres Strait Islander people with mental health issues; 2.3.3c Review court-based mental health initiatives to identify and promote culturally competent good practice; 2.3.3d Increase use of effective court-based mental health diversionary options; 2.3.3e Review current mental health care in corrective settings and develop and implement culturally competent mental health through care programs.
27 ABS, above n 13.
28 ABS, *4517.0 Prisoners in Australia* (2015) <www.abs.gov.au>.
29 Australian Institute for Health and Welfare (AIHW), 'Mental Health of Prison Entrants' <www.aihw.gov.au/prisoner-health/mental-health>.

government practice involved the removal of Aboriginal children from their families, based on the idea that it was better for the child (particularly if they had some non-Indigenous heritage) to be brought up away from Aboriginal culture and community. These very factors were identified in the *Bringing Them Home* Report as leading to terrible and ongoing health effects for Aboriginal people.[30] Citing the Report, the Closing the Gap Clearinghouse has recently observed that:

> The effects of colonisation and trauma surrounding forced removal from natural family has contributed to disadvantaged socio-economic conditions such as overcrowding, inadequate housing and unemployment in many Indigenous communities.[31]

Keeping Aboriginal children in their communities and connected to their culture wherever possible is now recognised as best for such children. The Aboriginal and Torres Strait Islander Child Placement Principle (ATSICPP) is an overarching principle that establishes child removal as a last resort, and requires that a child's connection to family and culture be supported if the child is removed.[32] This Principle has been enacted in various forms in every state and territory's child protection legislation.[33] What is accepted in government policy as social determinants of health for an Aboriginal child has thus changed drastically over time, and kinship and culture are now viewed as essential to an Aboriginal child's flourishing. However, it is important to note that this area remains contested, with concerns that the Principles are not upheld in practice. As the Secretariat of National Aboriginal and Islander Child Care (SNAICC) has observed: '[the] implementation of the ATSICPP remains grossly inadequate to promote and respect the rights of our children to family and cultural connection'.[34]

Women's health

The National Women's Health Policy (NWHP) provides a statement on the social factors affecting women's health and wellbeing.[35] These factors are to be taken into account when framing public policy on women's health and include such factors as intersecting social status (eg. Aboriginal and Torres Strait Islander women experience much worse health outcomes than non-Indigenous women, and this is exacerbated by living in remote locations)[36]

---

30   Human Rights and Equal Opportunity Commission, *Bringing them Home: Report of the National Inquiry into the Separation of Aboriginal and Torres Strait Islander Children from their Families* (HREOC, 1997).

31   Sarah Wise, *Improving the Early Life Outcomes of Indigenous Children: Implementing Early Childhood Development at the Local Level*, Issues Paper No. 6, produced for the Closing the Gap Clearinghouse (December 2013).

32   Clare Tilbury et al., *Aboriginal and Torres Strait Islander Child Placement Principle: Aims and core elements* (Secretariat of National Aboriginal and Islander Child Care [SNAICC], 2013).

33   Ibid Table 2, 17–18.

34   SNAICC, <www.snaicc.org.au/aboriginal-and-torres-strait-islander-child-placement-principle>.

35   Department of Health and Ageing, *National Women's Health Policy 2010* (27 April 2016) 85 <www .health.gov.au>.

36   AIHW, *Spatial Variation in Aboriginal and Torres Strait Islander Peoples' Access to Primary Health Care* (21 July 2015) <www.aihw.gov.au/publication-detail/?id=60129551602>.

and socially constructed gender roles which can inhibit access to appropriate healthcare. The NWHP states that:

> Gender roles and gender relations can affect women's capacity to access resources such as income, education and employment, which themselves promote health. These inequalities can create, maintain or exacerbate exposure to risk factors that endanger health. For example, gender can contribute to differences between and among women and men in financial security, paid and unpaid caring work and experiences of violence.[37]

This makes it clear that there is a wide range of laws that will impact the social determinants of women's health, including social security laws, labour laws (which allow for flexible work practices) and family violence laws. Each of these laws interacts with other practices, and institutions, to form a very complex picture of what is required to improve women's health outcomes.

To take one example, domestic and family violence directly impacts women's health through physical injury and has a cumulative impact on women's mental health. The risk factors for domestic and family violence, such as alcohol and drug abuse and childhood abuse, and the high at-risk groups (women with disabilities, Indigenous women, rural and remote women)[38] are already markers for poor health, which is then exacerbated by the long-term impact of such violence. Law reform in many areas of law has attempted to address domestic and family violence and to improve the protections offered to women (in particular) who experience such violence.

Examples include creating a statutory definition of 'consent' in NSW that requires a reasonable belief that a person is consenting to sex;[39] implementing quasi-criminal measures to prevent violence through apprehended family violence orders;[40] and putting in place a host of legal institutional measures (liaison officers, court support) to support women who seek and obtain such orders. More recently, workplace law and policy reforms, such as allowing workplace leave in situations of domestic and family violence,[41] as well as making being a 'victim of domestic violence' a protected attribute in discrimination law,[42] have extended again the range of laws that are aimed at tackling what is (also) a health issue. In order to address domestic and family violence, therefore, a whole host of laws in quite disparate areas, ranging from criminal laws to the laws of evidence, as well as workplace and discrimination laws, need to be engaged.

---

37   See Department of Health and Ageing, above n 35, 86.

38   Janet Phillips and Penny Vandenbroek, *Domestic, Family and Sexual Violence in Australia: An Overview of the Issues*, Research Paper Series 2014–15, Parliamentary Library, Parliament of Australia (2014) <www.aph.gov.au/About_Parliament/Parliamentary_Departments/Parliamentary_Library/pubs/rp/rp1415/ViolenceAust>.

39   *Crimes Amendment (Consent – Sexual Assault Offences) Act 2007* (NSW).

40   These were first introduced in NSW in 1982, and are now contained in the *Crimes (Domestic and Personal Violence) Act 2007*.

41   In collective bargaining agreements, for an assessment of the introduction of domestic violence clauses in workplace agreements, see Ludo McFerran, Natasha Cortis and Tahlia Trijbetz, *Gendered Violence & Work Domestic and Family Violence Clauses in your Workplace: Implementation and Good Practice*, Social Policy Research Centre & Centre for Gender Related Violence Studies University of New South Wales (2013) <www.arts.unsw.edu.au/media/FASSFile/Domestic_and_Family_Violence_Clauses_in_your_Workplace__Implementation_and_good_practice.pdf>.

42   For a discussion of how anti-discrimination laws are beginning to be used to provide support and protection for victims of family violence, see Belinda Smith and Tashina Orchiston, 'Family Violence Victims at Work: A Role for Anti-Discrimination Law?' (2012) 25(3) *Australian Journal of Labour Law* 209.

For women, sex-based inequality has clear, although complex, impacts on health outcomes. When we turn our attention to men, the strongest social determinants of health come from vulnerabilities other than sex. The Commonwealth government has developed a policy on men's health which lists some of the social determinants of health for men, such as socioeconomic status, which is exacerbated by unemployment, a lack of educational achievement and indigeneity. Where people are offered sex-specific services in health, such as women's health services, they are not discriminatory under Commonwealth anti-discrimination law, if they are 'special measures' designed to bring about equality.[43] Where a disadvantage has come about as a consequence of a privileged social status, as it arguably has in the case of some men's health issues, it is harder to argue that it is an issue of inequality that should be protected by law.[44]

Future children (embryos and fetuses)

Social determinants of health will change over the lifecycle and, in fact, begin before a person's birth. Moreover, some social determinants will have an intergenerational impact on people. For example, the conditions required to produce a healthy embryo or fetus often focus on policing women's bodies, both before and during pregnancy. Indeed, women may be held responsible for creating, out of the material of their own bodies, an optimally healthy environment for future and not-yet-conceived children. For example, the Royal Australasian College of Physicians and the Royal Australian and New Zealand College of Psychiatrists recently published an Alcohol Policy that recommended that there be 'routine screening and early interventions for women of reproductive age who misuse or have alcohol dependency'.[45] Significantly, the language applies to all women who are capable of pregnancy, not just women who are planning to have children. In such policy framing, women are characterised as both the conduit for potential harm to future children and the target for intervention.

As noted earlier in this chapter, current and emerging research on epigenetics suggests that intergenerational harm may be traced back to the way the body registers the impact of environmental stressors.[46] While these scientific findings represent an important

---

43   *Proudfoot v Australian Capital Territory Board of Health* (1992) EOC 92–417.

44   Will Courtenay, 'Theorising Masculinity and Men's Health' in Alex Broom and Philip Tovey (eds), *Men's Health; Body, Identity and Social Context* (Wiley-Blackwell, 2009) 9, 14.

45   The Royal Australasian College of Physicians and The Royal Australian and New Zealand College of Psychiatrists, 'Alcohol Policy' (15 March 2016) 37 <www.ranzcp.org/News-policy/News/RACP-and-RANZCP-release-updated-Alcohol-Policy.aspx>.

46   Megan Warin et al., 'Epigenetics and Obesity: The Reproduction of Habitus Through Intracellular and Social Environments' (2016) 22(4) *Body & Society* 53; Maurizio Meloni, 'Heredity 2.0: The Epigenetics Effect' (2015) 34(2) *New Genetics and Society* 117; Hannah Landecker and Aaron Panofsky, 'From Social Structure to Gene Regulation, and Back: A Critical Introduction to Environmental Epigenetics for Sociology' (2013) 39 *Annual Review of Sociology* 333; Shannon Sullivan, 'Inheriting Racist Disparities in Health: Epigenetics and the Transgenerational Effects of White Racism' (2013) 1(2) *Critical Philosophy of Race* 190; Arline Geronimus, 'Deep Integration: Letting Epigenome Out of the Bottle Without Losing Sight of the Structural Origins of Population Health' (2013) 103(S1) *American Journal of Public Health* S56; Michael Rutter, 'Gene-Environment Interdependence' (2012) 19(1) *European Journal of Developmental Psychology* 391; Mark A Rothstein, Yu Cai and Gary E Marchant, 'The Ghost in our Genes: Legal and Ethical Implications of Epigenetics' (2009) 19(1) *Health Matrix* 1.

development in knowledge about the determinants of health, there is a danger that the immediate regulatory effect will be a greater policing of women's bodies, since women are the node where the complex network of intergenerational harm transmission and intergenerational repair meet. Women then become even more responsible for health outcomes, particularly in relation to their offspring. This is despite the fact that men also transmit heritable epigenetic harms.

This is particularly noticeable in the new area of research that has come to be known as developmental origins of health and disease (DOHaD), which refers to the developmental environment of the embryo or fetus and that of its mother. While clearly DOHaD should also take into account paternal environmental development, in fact DOHaD research is overwhelmingly focused on the maternal side. According to Richardson, DOHaD theory is mobilised to 'model how the mother's social and environmental context during her own development – including social class – may be transmitted to the growing fetus, conditioning it for a life of inequality even before birth'.[47] Mykitiuk and Nisker argue that a social determinants approach to embryo health requires us to pay attention to the social environments in which women, men and embryos exist, rather than locating health and illness exclusively within a particular body – be it an embryonic body or that of a person.[48] At the same time, it must be remembered that any emphasis on particular social environments – such as those affecting the mother – when responding to such arguments may inadvertently reinforce gender inequality.[49]

Emerging biomedical approaches to social determinants of health

Social and biomedical determinants of health are increasingly intertwined. However, when considering what constitutes a social determinant of health, it is important to remember that there are two components to this question: first, what is a social determinant? (which has already been addressed in this chapter); and second, what is health? As health itself is a social construct, answering this second part of the question is not simple. In order to shed some light on the complexity of this construct, we now turn briefly to consider some interesting questions which are raised by a fascinating but problematic area of current health research: the identification of biomarkers for socially undesirable behaviours.

Research in this area is still in the early stages, but genetic markers for antisocial behaviour are already being enthusiastically sought. As Niv and Baker point out, 'several candidate genes related to antisocial and aggressive behaviour have emerged and have been

---

47   Sarah S Richardson, 'Maternal Bodies in the Postgenomic Order' in Sarah S Richardson and Hallan Stevens (eds), *Postgenomics Perspective on Biology after the Genome* (Duke University Press, 2015) 210, 222.

48   Mykitiuk and Nisker, above n 5, 121.

49   For a comprehensive discussion, see Isabel Karpin, 'Regulatory Responses to the Gendering of Transgenerational Harm' (2016) 31 *Australian Feminist Studies* 139.

supported in numerous studies'.[50] They go on to note that even the genes most implicated in anti-social behaviours are impacted by other factors, such as 'childhood adversity':

> MAOA's [monoamine oxidase A gene] influence on aggressive behaviour has been found to interact significantly with adverse environment; that is, gene expression depending heavily upon environmental conditions.[51]

By seeking biomarkers for social and behavioural conditions, health is correlated with good citizenship and biological 'flaws' with delinquency. At the same time, epigenetics and neuroscience are providing fascinating insights into the biological impact of social harm. For example, neuroscience is highlighting the impact on brain development of early childhood abuse, including exposure to violence. However, it does so in a way that biologises the harm of abuse within the individual child's body. Further, once disadvantage is understood as biological, the affected child is less likely to be construed as remediable than if the harm is viewed as having a more transitory social and circumstantial effect.[52]

While neuroscience examines the immediate impact of violence on children, epigenetics posits a transgenerational effect. For example, there have been studies exploring the transgenerational impact of intimate partner violence (IPV) on methylation (see earlier) that suggest that maternal stress due to IPV has an impact on epigenetic modifications that occur in utero. The epigenetic effect claimed is the production of socially aggressive children and grandchildren.[53] Socially undesirable behaviours are thus associated both with historical inequality and with an abiding state of poor neurological and genetic health that seemingly takes such behaviour outside the ambit of law. We await further research developments in this area, while at the same time recognising its significant limitations.

Health in all policies? Advancing social determinants of health policy in Australia

While this chapter has focused on the difficulties associated with legal attempts to bring about health equalities, there are some current attempts to take a broader legal and policy approach to improving social determinants of health. In 2013, the Senate Community Affairs References Committee published a report in response to the WHO's Commission on Social Determinants of Health, Closing the Gap in a Generation Report (WHO Report) (Senate Committee Report).[54] While the Senate Committee Report's list of recommendations

50   Sharon Niv and Laura A Baker, 'Genetic Markers for Antisocial Behaviour' in Christopher R Thomas and Kayla Pope (eds), *The Origins of Anti-Social Behaviour: A Developmental Perspective* (OUP, 2012) 3.

51   Ibid 13.

52   Karen O'Connell, 'Unequal Brains: Disability Discrimination Laws and Children with Challenging Behaviour' (2016) 24(1) *Medical Law Review* 76–98.

53   Maria Isabel Cordero et al., 'Evidence for Biological Roots in the Transgenerational Transmission of Intimate Partner Violence' (2012) 2 *Translational Psychiatry* e106.

54   Senate Community Affairs References Committee, Parliament of Australia, *Australia's Domestic Response to the World Health Organisation's (WHO) Commission on Social Determinants of Health report 'Closing the Gap Within a Generation'* (2013) <www.aph.gov.au/Parliamentary_Business/ Committees/Senate/Community_Affairs/Completed_inquiries/2010-13/socialdeterminantsofhealth/ report/index>.

is written in broad terms and is mostly aimed at administrative and policy changes, it also highlights some interesting legal measures adopted by Australian states to address the social determinants of health, a number of which we highlight here.

In SA, the concept of social determinants of health has been incorporated into government policy. So, for example, the Minister for Health and Ageing specifically referred to the WHO Report in his second reading speech for the *Public Health Act 2011* (SA), noting that:

> [The legislation] 'in part provides for South Australia's response to this challenge' and includes principles of sustainability, partnerships, equity and prevention, providing a mandate for working together and recognising that the social determinants of health are fundamental to improving population health outcomes.[55]

Specifically, the SA *Public Health Act* now includes an 'Equity Principle' which states:

> Decisions and actions should not, as far as is reasonably practicable, unduly or unfairly disadvantage individuals or communities and, as relevant, consideration should be given to health disparities between population groups and to strategies that can minimise or alleviate such disparities.[56]

In the Senate Committee Report, it was noted that arguments had been put forward that the approach taken in SA should not be adopted at the federal level, with the Commonwealth Department of Health noting in its supplementary submission to the Committee that:

> In the case of both the South Australian Government and Tasmanian Health in All Policies Collaboration, key drivers have been established through legislation; in particular Public Health Acts, as well as state based strategic plans and/or targets. Duplication of such approaches at a national level could add further complexity to an already complicated environment without a clear mandate for action.[57]

Nevertheless, the Senate Committee Report ultimately recommended that the Commonwealth government adopt a similar mechanism to the SA 'Health in All Policies' (HiAP) approach in relation to government action. Specifically it required the adoption of comprehensive measures 'that incorporate health as a shared goal across all parts of Government and addresses complex health challenges through an integrated policy response across portfolio boundaries'.[58] The Report also recommended that the Commonwealth government 'adopt the WHO Report and commit to addressing the social determinants of health relevant to the Australian context'.[59] Once such recommendations have been adopted there will need to be follow-up research to determine whether they are effective in achieving better health outcomes for people with unequal social resources.

---

55   Ibid 28.
56   *Public Health Act 2011* (SA) s 13.
57   Senate Community Affairs References Committee, Parliament of Australia, *Australia's domestic response to the World Health Organization's (WHO) Commission on Social Determinants of Health report 'Closing the gap within a generation'* (2013) <www.aph.gov.au/Parliamentary_Business/Committees/Senate/Community_Affairs/Completed_inquiries/2010-13/socialdeterminantsofhealth/report/index>.
58   Ibid 38.
59   Ibid.

Conclusion

It is clear that social determinants of health and disparities in the distribution of health resources play a very significant role in health outcomes. What we have shown in this chapter are a number of ways in which social determinants of health raise important issues for consideration in law. This has included consideration of the role of equality laws which aim to address social and health inequities; an exploration of the impact of social determinants on different communities; and a critical analysis of the way in which health is socially constructed, rather than being just a matter for biomedical determination. We have also presented a range of examples of the way in which the law has been used, with varying degrees of success, to create or amplify positive social determinants and to mitigate negative ones. Such examination offers a springboard for much-needed discussion about the important role law can play in redressing social inequities arising from disparities in the distribution of the social goods that lead to poor health.

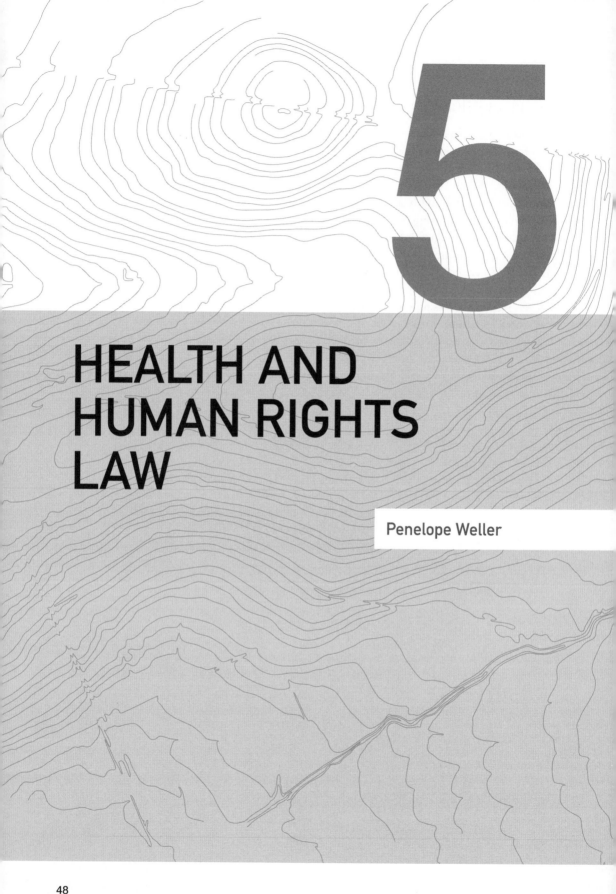

5

HEALTH AND HUMAN RIGHTS LAW

Penelope Weller

Introduction

Improving the health of human populations is one of the core objectives of modern societies. In recent decades, this objective has been pursued through human rights frameworks. In the Australian context, this has been facilitated by the growing influence of human rights norms in legal discourse in a range of health-related areas, underpinned by Australia's ratification of international human rights conventions. The influence of human rights in national law is interwoven with a range of topics examined in this book, including mental health, disability, end of life decision-making, organ and tissue donation, human genetics, indigenous health and public health. An informed and critical understanding of the role of human rights in advancing the national and global health agenda, in particular its role in addressing health inequities and its interface with health security, is therefore vital.

The scope of any examination of the relationship between health and human rights law is potentially very wide. Apart from the right to health, which is clearly of central concern, such an examination could also include civil and political rights, including the rights to life, to be free from torture, to respect for private life and to freedom of expression. Adopting such an approach has been described by academic commentators, such as Murphy, as the 'right-to-health plus'.[1] For reasons of space, however, a decision has been taken to focus in this chapter on the human right to health, given its status as one of the foundation principles in international human rights law. The right to health is now at the centre of international political debate and social policy, spurred by recognition of the interdependence of all human rights and the social determinants of health.[2]

In developed nations such as Australia, it is often assumed that good standards of living and public access to healthcare fulfil national and international obligations with respect to the right to health. This chapter argues that the right to health demands a more robust engagement with the social determinants of health and applicable human rights standards. National law and policy debates about health, healthcare and the social determinants of health are rarely posed in terms of the human right to health, despite the fact that Australia has ratified all the major international human rights conventions.[3] The chapter begins by discussing the status of human rights law and the 'soft' approach to international human rights standards in Australian law and policy. The second part outlines the established content of the right to health in international law. The third examines some of the debates and interests that have already influenced the expansion of the right and that will do so in the future. The fourth part provides an overview of human rights jurisprudence. The chapter concludes with a call for closer engagement with the right to health.

---

1   Thérèse Murphy, *Health and Human Rights* (Hart, 2013) 17.

2   John Harrington and Maria Stuttaford, 'Introduction' in John Harrington and Maria Stuttaford (eds), *Global Health & Human Rights* (Routledge, 2010) 1.

3   Mariette Brennan, 'The Good, the Bad and the Unhealthy: An Assessment of Australia's Compliance with the International Right to Health' (2015) 39(2) *University of Western Australia Law Review* 373, 374. The social determinants of health are discussed in more detail in Chapter 4.

Human rights law in Australia

The general principle in Australian law is that legislation must be passed in order to give legal protection to human rights. When the Australian government ratifies international human rights conventions, it attests to the conformity of Australian law with the requisite international standard. During the ratification process, the Joint Standing Committee on Treaties (JSCOT) conducts public consultations and makes recommendations to the Commonwealth government regarding the incorporation of treaties.[4] In areas of rapidly advancing human rights sensibility, such as the right to health, the decision to introduce legislation is largely dependent upon public appreciation of the scope of an emerging right. This approach downplays the significance of human rights norms. It lacks a process for 'updating' Australian law beyond the ratification process, and may not provide an obvious or suitable avenue for the enforcement of the treaty rights by individuals. Such limitations have underpinned an extended (but unsuccessful) campaign to adopt Commonwealth human rights legislation in Australia. Following the last formal debate about the issue,[5] the Commonwealth government opted for a 'soft' approach to human rights, proposing the development of a national human rights policy framework rather than national legislation.[6]

In contrast, Victoria and the ACT have adopted human rights legislation. Several other states are considering doing the same. The human rights statutes in the ACT and Victoria protect a relatively limited set of rights. Relevant to the right to health are the right to be free from inhuman or degrading treatment, which includes the right to be free from medical experimentation and the right to private life.[7] As is discussed in more detail below, the right to private life in the European Convention on Human Rights (ECHR) has provided a basis for recognition of the right to health by the European Court of Human Rights. In Victoria, the *Charter of Human Rights and Responsibilities Act 2006* has been successfully invoked to protect aspects of the right to access special healthcare in prison and the right to choose one's own accommodation.[8] These examples illustrate that a key contribution of human rights legislation is recognition of the justiciability of protected human rights.[9]

Content of the right to health

The 'right to the highest attainable standard of physical and mental health', or the right to health, is an embedded norm under international law and carries 'considerable legal weight'.[10] The right was first expresssed in article 25 of the Universal Declaration of Human Rights (UDHR):

---

4   JSCOT <http://www.aph.gov.au/house/committee/jsct/index.htm>.
5   Commonwealth Attorney-General's Department, *National Human Rights Consultation Report* (2009).
6   Commonwealth of Australia, *National Human Right Framework* (2010).
7   *Charter of Human Rights and Responsibilities Act 2006* (Vic) ss 9, 12; *Human Rights Act 2004* (ACT) ss 10, 13.
8   *Kracke v Mental Health Review Board* (2009) 29 VAR 1; *PJB v Melbourne Health* (Patrick's case) (2011) 39 VR 373; *Antunovic v Dawson* (2010) 30 VR 355; *Castles v Secretary of the Department of Justice* (2010) 28 VR 141; *Burgess v Director of Housing* [2014] VSC 648.
9   Penelope Weller, 'Human Rights and Social Justice: The Convention on the Rights of Persons with Disabilities and the Quiet Revolution in International Law' (2009) 4(1) *Public Space: The Journal of Law and Social Justice* 74, 81.
10   Brigit Toebes, 'Introduction' in Brigit Toebes, Rhonda Ferguson, Milan M Markovic and Obiajulu Nnamuchi (eds), *The Right to Health: A Multi-Country Study of Law, Policy and Practice* (Springer, 2014) xiii.

(1) Everyone has the right to a standard of living adequate for the health and well-being of himself and of his family, including food, clothing, housing and medical care and necessary social services, and the right to security in the event of unemployment, sickness, disability, widowhood, old age or other lack of livelihood in circumstances beyond his control.

(2) Motherhood and childhood are entitled to special care and assistance. All children, whether born in or out of wedlock, shall enjoy the same social protection.[11]

Some aspects of article 25 are expressed in article 12 of the International Covenant on Economic, Social and Cultural Rights (ICESCR), which is a binding human rights instrument giving effect to the UDHR:

1. The States Parties to the present Covenant recognize the right of everyone to the enjoyment of the highest attainable standard of physical and mental health.

2. The steps to be taken by the States Parties to the present Covenant to achieve the full realization of this right shall include those necessary for:

   (a) The provision for the reduction of the stillbirth-rate and of infant mortality and for the healthy development of the child;

   (b) The improvement of all aspects of environmental and industrial hygiene;

   (c) The prevention, treatment and control of epidemic, endemic, occupational and other diseases;

   (d) The creation of conditions that would assure to all medical service and medical attention in the event of sickness.[12]

Other elements of the right to health, as expressed in the UDHR, are contained in the right to work in article 6 of the ICESCR, to safety at work in article 7, to social security in article 9, to an adequate standard of living in article 11 and to special protection of the family in article 10.[13]

The right to health is a right to the physical and social conditions necessary to support health.[14] It protects the right to access the various conditions that enable human health. It is an expansive right, encompassing 'a wide range of socio-economic factors that promote

---

11   *Universal Declaration of Human Rights*, GA Res. 217A (III) at 71, UN GAOR, 3d Sess., 1st plen. mtg., UN Doc. A/810 (10 December 1948) (UNHR).

12   *International Covenant on Economic Social and Cultural Rights*, 19 December 1966 (entered into force 3 January 1976), 993 UNTS 3 (ICESCR).

13   Ibid.

14   John Eyles and Kevin J Woods, *The Social Geography of Medicine and Health* (Routledge, 2014); Jennifer Prah Ruger, 'Health Capability: Conceptualization and Operationalization' (2010) 100(1) *American Journal of Public Health* 41; Brigit Toebes, *The Right to Health as a Human Right in International Law* (Hart, 1999) 27–85; see also Judith Asher, *The Right to Health: A Resource Manual for NGOs* (Martinus Nijhoff Publishers, 2010); Padmini Murthy and Clyde Lanford Smith, *Women's Global Health and Human Rights* (Jones and Bartlett Learning, 2010); Eibe Riedel, Gilles Giacca and Christopher Golay, *Economic Social and Cultural Rights in International Law* (OUP, 2014); John Tobin, *The Right to Health in International Law* (OUP, 2012); Brigit Toebes, Rhonda Ferguson, Milan Markovic and Obiajulu Nnamuchi, *The Right to Health: A Multi-Country Study of the Law, Policy and Practice* (Springer, 2014); Jonathan Wolff, *The Human Right to Health* (WW Norton, 2013); Jose Zuniga, Stephen Marks and Lawrence Gostin (eds), *Advancing the Human Right to Health* (OUP, 2013).

conditions in which people can lead a healthy life'.[15] General Comment 14, on the 'right to the highest attainable standard of health', which was adopted by the United Nations in 2000, provides an authoritative articulation of the scope and meaning of article 24 in the ICESCR.[16] General Comment 14 affirms that the right to health contains freedoms, such as the right to control one's health and body, as well as entitlements, such as the right to a system of health protection.[17] It includes access to timely and appropriate healthcare, to the prevention, treatment and control of diseases, access to systems of health protection, and provision for the underlying and social determinants of health. The underlying and social determinants of health include 'access to safe and potable water and adequate sanitation, safe and healthy working conditions, and a healthy environment.'[18] General Comment 14 recognises the emergence of new social determinants of health, such as those related to resource distribution and gender difference, new diseases and the health burdens of rapidly growing world populations.[19]

The right to health requires state parties to respect, protect and fulfil (promote and provide for) the human right to health, recognising that the exact scope of the obligation depends on the prevailing conditions within the state.[20] Specifically, article 12 requires that healthcare and public health facilities and services should be available,[21] accessible,[22] acceptable[23] and of good quality.[24] State parties are required to: integrate gender perspectives in health-related policies; implement a national strategy for promoting women's health; abolish harmful traditional practices; provide a safe and supportive environment for adolescents; integrate health for older persons; address the health needs of people with disabilities, including people with mental health issues; and adopt measures with respect to the health of Indigenous peoples including the provision of resources for the design, delivery and control of such services.[25] The right to health also proscribes any discrimination in access to healthcare, including with respect to the underlying determinants of health, imposing a special obligation to provide services to those with insufficient means.[26] Importantly, the obligations with respect to non-discrimination are immediately realisable in international law.[27]

15   UN Committee on Economic, Social and Cultural Rights (CESCR), *General Comment No. 14: The Right to the Highest Attainable Standard of Health (Art 12 of the ICESCR)*, UN Doc E/C12/2000/4 (11 August 2000), para 4.

16   Ibid.

17   Ibid [8].

18   Ibid [4].

19   Ibid [10].

20   Ibid [12].

21   'Availability' refers to facilities, goods and services, including health systems, hospitals, clinics, trained medical professionals and medicines and to the underlying determinants of health such as safe and potable drinking water and adequate sanitation [12a].

22   'Accessibility' includes the overlapping dimensions of access without discrimination, and physical and economic access, including affordable and accessible health-related information [12b].

23   'Acceptability' refers to respect for medical ethics and cultural sensitivities [12c].

24   'Quality' refers to the availability of scientifically and medically appropriate skilled medical personnel, scientifically approved and unexpired drugs, hospital equipment, safe and potable water and adequate sanitation [12d].

25   Ibid [20]–[27].

26   Ibid [18], [19].

27   Michael Ashley Stein, Janet E Lord and Dorothy Weiss Tolchin, 'Equal Access to Health Care Under the UN Disability Rights Convention' in Rosamond Rhodes, Margaret P Battin and Anita Silvers (eds), *Medicine and Social Justice: Essays on the Distribution of Health Care* (OUP, 2012) 245.

General Comment 14 explains that article 12 permits limitations on the exercise of fundamental human rights relating to health, but only when it is strictly necessary to promote general welfare in a democratic society.[28] Such limitations must accord with the principle of least restriction and be subject to review.[29] In this respect, an influential but non-binding statement with respect to the right to mental health is provided by the Special Rapporteur on Health and the Special Rapporteur on Torture.[30] General Comment 14 also clarifies that the principle of 'progressive realisation' in article 2 of the ICESCR requires state parties to take deliberate, concrete and targeted steps towards the full realisation of the right to health.[31] 'Progressive realisation' means that state parties have a specific and continuing obligation to move as expeditiously and effectively as possible towards the full realisation of the right to health, understood in the context of available state resources.[32] It is also recognised that the right to health can be pursued through numerous complementary approaches and is closely related to, and dependent on, the realisation of other human rights that contribute to health, such as the right to food, housing, work, education, dignity, life, non-discrimination and equality, the prohibition against torture, the rights to privacy and to access to information, and the freedoms of association, assembly and movement. [33]

Specific aspects of the right to health are articulated in the thematic human rights conventions. Article 5(iv) of the International Convention on the Elimination of All Forms of Racial Discrimination[34] emphasises the non-discriminatory 'right to public health, medical care, social security and social services'; article 12 of the Convention on the Elimination of Discrimination Against Women (CEDAW)[35] emphasises the special needs of women in relation to reproduction. CEDAW prohibits discrimination on the grounds of maternity; requires the provision of safe working conditions during pregnancy; requires equal access to healthcare; and required appropriate services, care and nutrition for pregnancy, confinement and the postnatal period.[36] Article 24 of Convention on the Rights of the Child (CRC) includes the obligation to provide and ensure access to facilities for the treatment of illness and the rehabilitation of health; to reduce infant and child mortality; to provide medical assistance and primary healthcare; to combat disease and malnutrition; to ensure prenatal and postnatal care; to provide health education to parents; and to take measures to abolish harmful traditional practices.[37]

---

28 CESCR, above n 15, [28].

29 Ibid [29].

30 Paul Hunt, *Report of the Special Rapporteur on the Right of Everyone to the Enjoyment of the Highest Attainable Standard of Physical and Mental Health*, E/CN.4/2005/51 (11 February 2005); Center for Human Right and Humanitarian Law, *Torture in Healthcare Settings: Reflections on the Special Rapporteur on Torture's 2013 Thematic Report* (Washington College of Law, American University).

31 CESCR, above n 15, [30]; ICESCR Art 2.

32 Sigrun Skogly, 'The Requirement of Using the "Maximum of Available Resources" for Human Rights Realisation: A Question of Quality as Well as Quantity?' (2012) 12(3) *Human Rights Law Review* 393.

33 CESCR, above n 15, [3].

34 *International Convention on the Elimination of All Forms of Racial Discrimination* opened for signature 21 December 1965, 660 UNTS 195.

35 *Convention on the Elimination of Discrimination Against Women* (CEDAW) opened for signature 18 December 1979, 1249 UNTS 13 (entered into force 9 March 1981).

36 Ibid arts 11–12.

37 *Convention on the Rights of the Child* (CRC) opened for signature 20 November 1989, 1577 UNTS 3. See also the Committee on the Rights of the Child, *General Comment No. 15 (2013) on the Right of the Child to the Enjoyment of the Highest Attainable Standard of Health (Art 24)*, 62nd sess, UN Doc CRC/C/GC/15 (17 April 2013).

Article 25 of the Convention on the Rights of Persons with Disabilities (CRPD) requires states parties to provide healthcare services, including services related to the person's disability, on an equal basis with others.[38] Article 25 requires states parties to ensure that people with disabilities have access to gender-sensitive health services that are of the same range, quality and standard as those provided to other persons. This includes sexual and reproductive health and population-based public health programs, and services that provide the early identification and intervention designed to minimise and prevent further disabilities, including among children and older persons. The services must be as close as possible to people's own communities.

Article 25 also requires provision of services on the basis of free and informed consent. It requires states parties to raise awareness of the human rights, dignity, autonomy and needs of persons with disabilities through training and the promulgation of ethical standards for public and private healthcare. It prohibits discrimination against persons with disabilities in the provision of health insurance and life insurance, and requires states parties to prevent the discriminatory denial of healthcare or health services or food and fluids on the basis of disability.[39] Article 24 of the (non-binding) Declaration on the Rights of Indigenous Peoples recognises the right to traditional medicines and healthcare practice, as well as the right to access social and health services without discrimination.[40] Regional human rights instruments also incorporate the right to health: in article 10 of the Additional Protocol to the American Convention on Human Rights;[41] in articles 14 and 16 of the African Charter on Human and Peoples' Rights, which includes the dimension of spiritual health;[42] in article 29 of the Arab Charter on Human Rights;[43] and in article 11 of the European Social Charter.[44]

Minimum or core obligations

The expansive nature of the right to health means that its exact contours are difficult to define. Moreover, the principle of 'progressive realisation' means that the obligations of states parties differ significantly according to 'available resources'.[45] To deal with this issue, General Comment 14 sets out core minimum obligations.[46] These obligations are:

38   *Convention on the Rights of Persons with Disabilities* (CRPD), opened for signature 13 December 2006, GA Res 61/106 (entered into force 3 May 2008), UN Doc A/Res/61/106. For further discussion of the CRPD, see Chapter 10, which examines substituted and supported decision-making; Chapter 22, which examines models of disability and the CRPD; and Chapter 23, which examines how the CRPD is impacting mental health law and its reform in Australia.

39   Ibid Art 25 (Health).

40   UN General Assembly, *United Nations Declaration on the Rights of Indigenous Peoples*, adopted by General Assembly on 2 October 2007, A/RES/61/295; see Chapters 4 and 21 for further discussion of Indigenous health and the law.

41   *Additional Protocol to the American Convention on Human Rights in the areas of Economic, Social and Cultural Rights* (Protocol of San Salvador) adopted 17 November 1988 (entered in force 16 November 1999).

42   Organization of African Unity, *African Charter on Human and Peoples' Rights* (Banjul Charter) 27 June 1981, CAB/LEG/67/3 rev. 5, 21 I.L.M. 58 (1982).

43   League of Arab States, *Arab Charter on Human Rights*, 15 September 1994.

44   Council of Europe, *European Social Charter* (Revised) 3 May 1966, ETS 163 as amended by Protocols 11 and 14. Council of Europe, *Protocol 1 to the European Convention for the Protection of Human Rights and Fundamental Freedoms* (20 March 1952), ETS, 9.

45   ICESCR, above n 12, Art 2.

46   See Lisa Forman et al., 'Conceptualising Minimum Core Obligations Under the Right to Health: How Should We Define and Implement the "Morality of the Depths"' (2016) 20(4) *International Journal of Human Rights* 531.

(a) To ensure the right of access to health facilities, goods and services on a non-discriminatory basis, especially for vulnerable and marginalized groups; (b) To ensure access to the minimum essential food which is sufficient, nutritionally adequate and safe, and ensure freedom from hunger for everybody; (c) To ensure access to basic shelter, housing and sanitation and an adequate supply of safe and potable water; (d) To provide essential drugs; (e) To ensure equitable distribution of all health facilities, goods and services; and (f) To adopt and implement a national public health strategy and plan for action on the basis of evidence, addressing the health concerns of the whole population.[47]

The plan shall be devised and reviewed on the basis of a participatory and transparent process. It shall include health indicators and benchmarks by which progress can be monitored. Finally, it shall give particular attention to vulnerable and marginalised groups.[48]

Obligations of 'comparable priority' include (a) reproductive, maternal and child healthcare; (b) immunisation against major infectious diseases; (c) measures to prevent, treat and control epidemic and endemic diseases; (d) community education and access to information; and (e) appropriate training of health personnel, including about human rights.[49] All states are obliged to develop benchmarks and indicators that monitor the right to health.[50] The General Comment recognises that the right to health is endangered by unequal global development, noting that all governments have a responsibility to provide for the health of their peoples through the provision of adequate health and social measures.[51]

Integrating human rights and the social determinants of health

The content of the right to health has expanded in response to a series of debates about the concept of human health. In the postwar period, the international health community was deeply influenced by the principles of social medicine.[52] Social medicine, which became prominent in the UK in the 1940s, was principally concerned with the connections between poverty and ill-health, including interactions between the individual and his or her environment, family, workplace, community and social institutions.[53] Social medicine sought to incorporate into medicine emerging insights from sociology and psychology about the human social condition.[54] The social approach was endorsed by the World Health Organization (WHO) and is reflected in its Constitution, which defines 'health' as 'a state

---

47   The right to water has emerged as discrete human right. See ICESCR, *General Comment No. 15: The Right to Water* (Arts 11 and 12 of the Covenant) 20 January 2003, E/C12/2002/11. ICESCR, General Comment No. 14: The Right to the Highest Attainable Standard of Health (Art. 12) 11 August 2000, E/C12/2000/4, 43.

48   Ibid.

49   Ibid 44.

50   Ibid 46–52, 57–58.

51   Ibid. See Chapter 4 for a detailed discussion of contemporary approaches to the social determinants of health, including the WHO's program of action in the area.

52   Benjamin M Meier, 'Global Health Governance and the Contentious Politics of Human Rights: Mainstreaming the Right to Health for Public Health Advancement' (2010) 46 *Stanford Journal of International Law* 1–50.

53   Francis A Crew, 'Social Medicine' (1945) 1 *Medical Journal of Australia* 39–40.

54   Ibid 39.

of complete physical, mental and social wellbeing and not merely the absence of disease or infirmity'.[55] The WHO also recognised that the health of all peoples is 'fundamental to the attainment of peace and security'.[56] In the mid-20th century, however, a preference for biomedical perspectives in the WHO leadership severed the connections between WHO and the UN.[57]

Grassroots activism for health in 1970s spurred a renewed interest on the part of the WHO in preventive and social medicine, the environment, women's health and the social determinants of health.[58] The WHO Declaration of Alma-Ata on Primary Health Care in 1978 restated a commitment to the social determinants of health:

> The attainment of the highest possible level of health is a most important worldwide social goal whose realisation requires the action of many other social and economic sectors in addition to the health sector.[59]

The Declaration contained a pledge to develop primary healthcare systems and ensure effective and equitable distribution of resources for maintaining health.

In tandem with the recognition of the social determinants of health, the civil rights and women's movements began to conceptualise the connection between health and human rights in terms of access, disempowerment and discrimination.[60] Responding to the HIV/AIDS epidemic in the 1980s, human rights scholars and activists articulated a more precise and practical relationship between health and human rights.[61] Mann saw the analytical bridges between health and human rights in terms of the impact of health policies, programs and practices on human rights; the health impact of human rights violations; and the link between health and human rights demonstrated by public health responses to HIV/AIDS and maternal health.[62] This health and human rights scholarship provided a blueprint for human rights-based responses in public health, forming the intellectual foundations of a global movement for health. Meanwhile, the World Conference on Human Rights held in Vienna in 1993 affirmed that all human rights were integrated and interrelated,[63] opening the way for a reiteration of the scope and content of the right to health. In 2000, the UN appointed the first Special Rapporteur on Health, Paul Hunt, who actively raised the international profile of the human right to health.[64]

55   Adopted by the International Health Conference held in New York 19 June – 22 July 1946, signed by 61 states (Official Record, WHO 2, 100).
56   Ibid.
57   Meier, above n 52, 25.
58   Andrew Courtwright, 'Justice, Stigma and the New Epidemiology of Health Disparities' (2009) 23(2) *Bioethics* 90.
59   International Conference on Primary Health Care, Alma-Ata, USSR, 6–12 September 1978.
60   Jennifer Nelson, *More Than Medicine: A History of the Feminist Women's Health Movement* (NYU Press, 2015) 17.
61   Wolff, above n 14.
62   Jonathan Mann et al., 'Health and Human Rights' (1994) 1 *Health and Human Rights: An International Journal* 1; Jonathan Mann, 'Health and Human Rights' (1996) 3(12) *British Medical Journal* 924.
63   *Vienna Declaration and Programme of Action* adopted by the World Conference on Human Rights in Vienna on 25 June 1993, UN Doc A/CONF.157/23, Art 5.
64   Toebes, above n 14; see *Report of the Special Rapporteur on the Right To Health to the Commission on Human Rights*, UN Doc E/CN 4/2003/58 (13 February 2003) Annex 1.

When the Millennium Development Summit was convened by the UN in 2000, however, it declined to engage with the emerging discourse on health and human rights.[65] The Summit adopted the Millennium Declaration with its eight Millennium Development Goals (MDGs), including targets that were to be achieved by 2015.[66] Three of the eight MDGs are directly related to health: the reduction of child mortality; the improvement of maternal health; and undertaking measures to combat HIV/AIDS, malaria and other communicable diseases. The other five have an indirect relationship to health: the eradication of poverty; universal primary education; gender equality and empowerment of women; environmental sustainability; and a global partnership development.[67] Seventeen Sustainable Development Goals (SDGs), which replace the MDGs, have now been adopted by the UN.[68] Further examination of the SDGs and the promotion of global health (both directly and indirectly) is provided in Chapter 25.

Contemporary scholarship on the right to health has continued the expansive articulation of the right in the context of the social determinants of health. For example, Marks argues that analyses of the right to health should take into account all the health-related content in international human rights instruments.[69] He includes the right to health, freedom of speech and conscience, the protection of privacy, freedom from arbitrary detention or arrest, torture, cruel, inhuman or degrading treatment or punishment, freedom from medical experimentation and freedom of movement.[70] Marks also regards the right to participation in society, education, family, culture and political life, including the right to education, health education, cultural participation and freedom of association, as implicated in the right to health. This includes patient, gender and reproductive rights, environmental rights, the development of self-determination and the rights of minority peoples with respect to religion, culture and language.

The danger of such comprehensive interpretations is that the right to health may lose any real meaning. Chapman seeks to address this fragmentation in the right to health discourse by placing it within an overarching conceptualisation of human dignity.[71] Burci has argued for a renewed effort to create international normative standards, arguing that the key justification for pursuing the right to health is that 'improved global health can serve as a powerful tool for poverty reduction, equity, human rights, and security'.[72] On the other hand, Ferguson et al. conclude that achieving equitable access to health resources 'may require little more than the removal of discriminatory barriers'.[73]

65   Philip Alston, 'Ships Passing in the Night: The Current State of the Human Rights and Development Debate Seen Through the Lens of the Millennium Development Goals' (2005) 27 *Human Rights Quarterly* 755, 798–807.

66   UN Doc. A/55/49 (2000) ratified by 189 Member States.

67   UN Development Program, *Human Development Report 2003: Millennium Development Goals: A Compact Among Nations To End Human Poverty* (Geneva, 2003).

68   UN Sustainable Development Summit (September 2015) <www.un.org/sustainabedevelopment>.

69   Stephen P Marks, 'The Emergence and Scope of the Human Right to Health' in Jose Zuniga, Stephen Marks and Lawrence O Gostin (eds), *Advancing the Human Right to Health* (OUP, 2013) 22.

70   Ibid 11.

71   Audrey Chapman, 'The Foundations of a Human Right to Health: Human Rights and Bioethics in Dialogue' (2015) 17(1) *Health and Human Rights Journal* 6.

72   Gian Luca Barci, 'The Next One Hundred Years of Global Health' (2015) 39(1) *The Fletcher Forum of World Affairs* 87.

73   Rhonda Ferguson, Obiajulu Nnamuchi and Milan M Markovic, 'Conclusion' in Brigit Toebes et al. (eds), *The Right to Health: A Multi-Country Study of the Law, Policy and Practice* (Springer, 2014) 439, 444.

Litigation and the human right to health

The justiciability of the right to health is dependent on formal legal recognition of human rights. In nations that have provided such recognition, right to health litigation reflects the application of the right to health in practice.[74] Jurisdictions that have incorporated the right to health in their constitutions, such as South Africa, Colombia, Brazil and Argentina, have provided the 'first wave' of right to health litigation. For example, the Indian Supreme Court has expanded the justiciable right to life to include the right to live in dignity with adequate nutrition, clothing and shelter;[75] the right of mothers and children to receive medical care;[76] the right to appropriate conditions in mental hospitals;[77] and the provision of primary care in emergencies.[78] Another example is provided in Colombia. In 2008, the Constitutional Court of Columbia grouped together 22 individual appeals that had been brought in relation to the inadequacy of the health system. The Court required Colombian health authorities to undertake measures to resolve systemic issues, ultimately leading to the restructuring of Colombia's health system.[79] Between 1999 and 2005, 328,191 individual petitions about healthcare came before the Colombian courts, of which 80 per cent were granted.[80]

As noted above, systems of healthcare are integral to the realisation of the right to health. Most developed nations have systems involving free healthcare, at least for disadvantaged members of society, although the extent to which health and medical insurance systems provide 'free' healthcare varies considerably around the world. Whether a fully publicly funded healthcare system (UK),[81] a mixed public and private system (Australia), or a predominantly private system (US), is the most acceptable system continues to be debated. In 2010, the then US President Obama and his administration addressed the situation by introducing the *Patient Protection and Affordable Care Act*. The (federal) legislation was challenged in a series of legal actions heard in consolidation by the US Supreme Court in 2012. The Court ruled that all aspects of Act were valid.[82] In nations where there is public provision of health services, the limits of public provision have been tested. For example, the courts have considered whether or not public provision extends to foreign nationals,[83] or to novel medical

---

74   Oscar Cabrera and Ana Ayala, 'Advancing the Right to Health Through Litigation' in Jose Zuniga, Stephen Marks and Lawrence Gostin (eds), *Advancing the Human Right to Health* (OUP, 2013) 25, 27–29.

75   *Francis Coralie Mullin v Union Territory of Delhi* (1981) AIR 1981 SC 746.

76   *State of Punjab v Mohinder Singh Chawla* (1997) 2 SCC 83.

77   *Rakesh Chandra Narayan v Union of India* (1989) AIR 1989 SC 148.

78   *Pascim Banga Khet Mazdoor Samity v State of West Bengal* (1966) AIR SC 2426/(1996) 4 SCC 37.

79   Cabrera and Ayala, above n 74, 29; Constitutional Court of Colombia Judgment T-760/08, 31 July 2008: Part II, Sec 3.

80   Cabrera and Ayala, above n 74, 32.

81   See Matthew Weait, 'The United Kingdom: The Right to Health in the Context of a Nationalised Health Service' in Jose M Zuniga, Stephen P Marks and Lawrence O Gostin, *Advancing the Human Right to Health* (OUP, 2013) 209.

82   *National Federation of Independent Businesses v Sebelius, Secretary of Health and Human Services* 132 S Ct 2566 (2012). See Dabney P Evans, 'The Right to Health: The Next American Dream' in Brigit Toebes et al. (eds), *The Right to Health: A Multi-Country Study of the Law, Policy and Practice* (Springer, 2014).

83   For example, whether the UK should fund free abortions for women from Northern Ireland: *R (A) (a child) v Secretary of State for Health* [2015] EWCA Civ 771 (22 July 2015); whether asylum seekers in the UK are entitled to free healthcare: *R (YA) v Secretary of State for Health* [2009] EWCA Civ 225 (30 March 2009); whether EU citizens in the UK must have private health insurance: *Ahmad v Secretary of State for the Home Department* [2015] 1 All ER 953.

procedures.[84] In many countries, access to health insurance is essential, or at least facilitates access to health services.[85] Successful litigation has also been mounted challenging discrimination in insurance on the basis of disability.[86]

The European Court of Human Rights (ECtHR) has established itself as an international leader in the development of human rights norms generally, particularly with respect to the right to health.[87] ECtHR jurisprudence relating to the right to health has developed under article 3 (prohibition against torture), especially with respect to the right to access healthcare in prison; article 5 (right to liberty and security), especially with respect to mental health detention; and article 8 (right to respect for private and family life), especially with respect to the right to individual autonomy in health and other areas impacting private and family life. In the period 2007 to 2016, successful petitions concerned lack of access to healthcare or poor conditions in prisons;[88] the sterilisation of Romany women without their consent;[89] the deprivation of legal capacity on mental health grounds;[90] the right to access terminations of pregnancy;[91] the right to access appropriate antenatal care;[92] the right to be free from unjustified use of psychiatric examination;[93] and the right to be free from discrimination on the basis of homosexuality;[94] or HIV/AIDS.[95] Petitions to the court about the right to die, as discussed in Chapters 15 and 16, are also aspects of the right to health.

---

84   Whether gender dysphoria surgery is free in UK: *North West Lancashire Health Authority v A* [1999] EWCA Civ 2022 (29 July 1999).

85   Robert Boston and Brian Clifford, 'Laws Affecting Wellness Programs and Some Things They Make You Do' (2013) 39(1) *Employee Relations Law Journal* 30; Carrie Griffin Basas, 'What's Bad About Wellness? What the Disability Rights Perspective Offers About the Limitations of Wellness' (2014) 39(5) *Journal of Health Politics, Policy and Law* 1035; Stacey A Tovino, 'Will Neuroscience Redefine Mental Injury? Disability Benefit Law, Mental Health Parity Law, and Disability Discrimination Law' (2015) 12 *Indiana Health Law Review* 695.

86   *Ingram v QBE Insurance (Australia) Ltd* [2015] VCAT 1936. See also Kate Judd, 'Mental Health, Discrimination and Insurance in Australia' (2011) *New Paradigm* 24.

87   Council of Europe, *European Convention on Human Rights and Fundamental Freedoms*, as amended by Protocols 11 and 14, 4 November 1950, ETS, 5.

88   *Salakhov and Islyamova v Ukraine* (2013) App. No. 28005/08; *Elefteriadis v Romania* App. 38427/05; *Kharchenko v Ukraine* App. No. 40107/02; *Gladkiy v Russia* App. No. 3242/03; *Slawomir Muial v Poland* App. No. 28300/06; *Belashev v Russia; Branduse v Romania* App. No. 6586/03; *Mechenkov v Russia* App. No. 35421/05 (2008); *Khudobin v Russia* App No. 59696/00 (2006); *Testa v Croatia* App. No. 20877/04 (2008) *Jalloh v Germany* App No. 54810/00 (2007); *MSS v Belgium and Greece*. App. No. 30696/09; *Cf Hajol v Poland* App No. 1127/06; *Shelly v United Kingdom* App No. 23800/06 (2008); [2008] ECHR 108 where no violation was found.

89   *LH v Latvia* App. No. 52019/07 (2014); *NB v Slovakia* App. No. 29518/10 (2012); *VC v Slovkia* App. No. 18968/07 (2011); *KH v Slovakia* App. No. 32881/04 (2009).

90   *Sykora v Czech Republic* App. No. 23419/07; [2012] ECHR 1960; *Stanev v Bulgaria* App. No. 36760/06 (2012); *Shtukaturov v Russia* App. No. 44009/05 (2008); *cf Munjaz v United Kingdom* (2102) App. No. 2913/06 (2102); [2012] ECHR 1704.

91   *Tysiac v Poland* App. No. 5410/03 (2007); *L v Lithunia* App. No. 27527/03 (2008). *Sykora v Czech Republic* App. No. 23419/07; [2012] ECHR 1960; *Stanev v Bulgaria* App. No. 36760/06 (2012); *Shtukaturov v Russia* App. No. 44009/05 (2008); *cf Munjaz v United Kingdom* App. No. 2913/06 (2102); [2012] ECHR 1704.

92   *AK v Latvia* App. No. 33011/08 (2014); *RR v Poland* App. No. 27617/04 European Ct H. R. rep. 648 (2011).

93   *Fyodorov and Fyodorova v Ukraine* App. No. 39229/03.

94   *ABC v Ireland* App. No. 25579/05.

95   *Kiyutin v Russia* App. No. 2700/10.

Conclusion

The right to health is an expansive and developing human right based on recognition of the fundamental connection between health and human rights. Health and social interventions associated with the right to health include those that address the underlying determinants of health, remedy poverty, integrate human rights in health systems and empower individuals and civil society. This chapter has outlined the content of the right in international law, provided an overview of debates associated with the expansion of the right to health and briefly summarised recent right to health litigation. It was argued that the right to health in international law offers a powerful normative framework to advance justice in health. Debates about health in Australia have yet to fully engage with the right to health as it is understood in international law. Notwithstanding the absence of national human rights legislation, this would be welcome, offering the potential to invoke a new era of human rights debate.

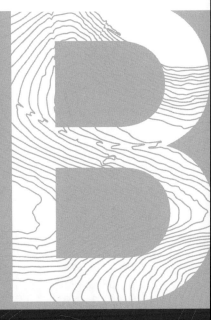

INSTITUTIONS AND REGULATION

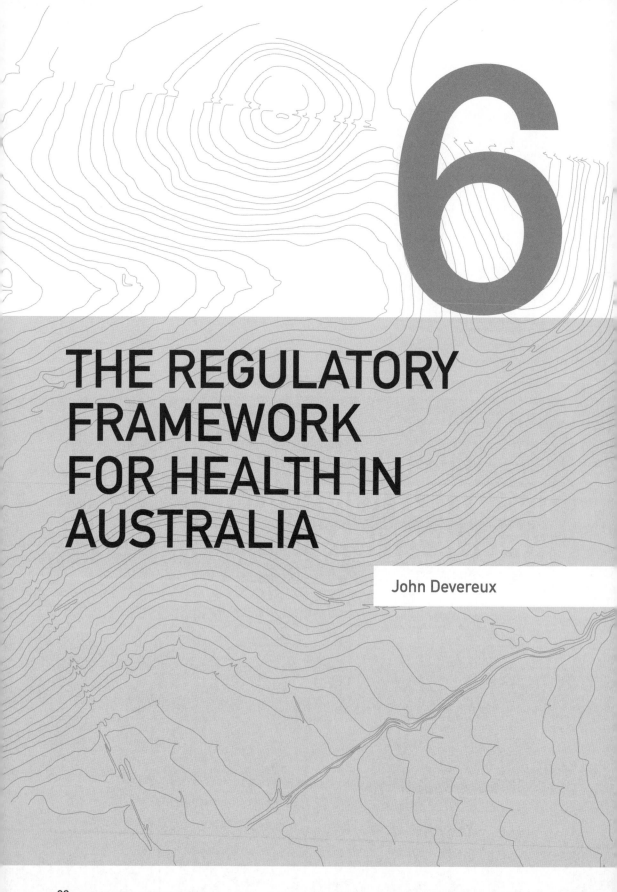

6

THE REGULATORY FRAMEWORK FOR HEALTH IN AUSTRALIA

John Devereux

Introduction

Delivery of health services in Australia is a complex and expensive undertaking. In its Report entitled *Australia's Health 2014*, the Australian Institute of Health and Welfare (AIHW) noted that 'in 2011–12, health spending in Australia was estimated to be $140.2 billion, or 9.5% of GDP. The amount was around 1.7 times as high as in 2001–02, with health expenditure growing faster than population growth'.[1] Perhaps unsurprisingly, there is a level of complexity surrounding allocation of health services and health expenditure in Australia. Ours is a system that has been described as a web of services, providers, recipients and organisational structures.[2]

This chapter explores the broad framework governing the allocation of health services. The aim of the chapter is to set out the macro-level regulation which seeks to direct the provision of health services. The first part briefly considers how the Australian political system impacts upon the provision of health services. The second examines the nature and scope of health powers under the Commonwealth Constitution. The final part of the chapter reviews key aspects of Australia's current health system. It is important to note that there is a broad range of legal controls which apply to health services, in the same way as they apply in respect of the conduct of any business. What is not covered in this chapter is how the law of contract, or tort, or anti-competition law may apply to the provision of health services. An examination of the regulatory regimes that apply to the registration and disciplining of health professionals, as well as patient safety and redress, are covered in detail in Chapters 7 and 8 respectively.

The Australian polity – a brief overview

A key reason for the complexity of health service regulation is the nature of Australian constitutional arrangements, which are discussed in more detail below. However, it should be acknowledged that there are also a range of historical and political factors at play. As Wheelwright notes:

> The Australian health system is the product of a diverse range of economic, social, technological, legal, constitutional and political factors, some of which are unique to Australia. The system is also a product of the historical evolution from the provision of care based on private philanthropy to a system which is largely government funded and controlled. The way health services are organised, funded and delivered is affected particularly by the existence of federalism as a major organising principle for the distribution of political power in Australia. This is complicated further by the philosophies of governments of different political persuasions about the role of the state in health service provision and funding and the appropriate balance between public and private service provision. Governments in turn are influenced to varying degrees by powerful interest groups in the health sector, including the organised medical profession, pharmaceutical manufacturers and the private health insurance

---

1   Australian Institute of Health and Welfare (AIHW), *Australia's Health 2014* (25 June 2014)
     <www.aihw.gov.au>.
2   Ibid.

industry. These political factors and influences cannot be overestimated because they have a profound influence on the preparedness of governments, in particular the Commonwealth government, to test their potential legal power.[3]

It is not possible to understand the provision of health services in Australia without first understanding the nature of the Australian political system. There are two dominant features of the Australian political system: first, Australia is a constitutional monarchy; and second, Australia is a federation. We now briefly consider each feature in turn, before briefly considering some constitutional limitations.

Constitutional monarchy

Australia is a constitutional monarchy. That is to say, though the head of state is a King or Queen, the monarch acts only on the advice of the Chief Minister. The monarch is represented in Australia by a Governor-General, and by a Governor in each constituent state of Australia. The Chief Minister is the person who holds the confidence of the Lower House of Parliament. This person is the person whose political party holds the majority of seats in that Lower House. Parliament at each level (state or federal) passes laws, according to the power to make laws granted to it under its respective governing Constitution.

Federation

Australia is a federation, a collection of former colonies which, on 1 January 1901, came together to form a nation, known as the Commonwealth of Australia. There are presently six constituent states, and two federal territories. By passing legislation, many states have created local governments, or councils, as they are routinely known. Unlike the Australian states, these councils are not constitutionally entrenched, so they may be created or disestablished at will by the states.

Each level of Australian government has involvement in the provision or regulation of health services. As examples, local governments regulate refuse, sewerage and water services; state governments run state hospitals; and the federal government funds health services through Medicare. In addition, there is a range of private providers, ranging from individual medical practitioners to private hospitals.

Constitutional limitations[4]

The allocation of powers between the Commonwealth (federal) government and the state governments is regulated by the Constitution of the Commonwealth of Australia (Constitution), which is an Act of the Parliament at Westminster in the UK.[5] Though it is

---

3   Karen Wheelwright 'Commonwealth and State Powers in Health – A Constitutional Diagnosis' (1995) 21(1) *Monash University Law Review* 53, 55.
4   The section of this chapter on constitutional limitations on the provision of health services and the case law discussing that issue draws heavily on John Devereux, *Australian Medical Law*, 3rd edn (Routledge, 2007) 118–31.
5   *Commonwealth of Australia Constitution Act 1900* (Imp).

theoretically possible for the UK Parliament to alter the balance of power between the federal and state governments, it has renounced its right to do so.[6]

Absent a successful referendum being carried out in accordance with section 128 of the Constitution, the allocation of power between the federal and state governments is fixed in the Constitution. This has posed challenges for Australia and its development, given that the Constitution was drafted over 100 years ago. The broad approach of the Constitution is that the federal government is given enumerated powers, with the balance of powers being left to the states. Given that health is a national issue, it might be assumed that there would be a grant of power over health matters to the federal government. This is not the case.

Health powers

There is no broad health power granted to the Commonwealth in the Constitution. There are some enumerated powers in the Constitution which permit the Commonwealth to regulate some health matters. So, for example, the following enumerated powers are to be found in section 51: quarantine (section 51(ix)); insurance (section 51(xiv)); and invalid and old age pensions (section 51(xxiii)). Attempts by the Commonwealth to broaden the base of its health powers have had a chequered history.

Pharmaceutical Benefits Act 1944 (Cth): An early attempt to legislate over health matters

The *Pharmaceutical Benefits Act 1944* (Cth) purported to provide free pharmaceuticals to Australians. Duties were imposed on medical practitioners and pharmacists who were to provide such medicines. The Act was challenged by the state of Victoria on the basis that the Commonwealth had no grant of legislative power which would support it. The Commonwealth purported to justify the Act on the basis of section 81 of the Constitution, which grants the Commonwealth the power to make laws for the purposes of the Commonwealth. It took the view that the purposes of the Commonwealth were those as set, from time to time, by the Commonwealth. As the Commonwealth Parliament had determined to enact a scheme to provide medicines, it followed that this was one of the purposes of the Commonwealth.

In *Attorney-General (Vic); Ex rel Dale v Commonwealth*[7] the High Court disagreed with the Commonwealth and struck down the scheme as being unconstitutional. The High Court decided that the phrase 'for the purposes of the Commonwealth' encompassed two matters. First, those express grants of power in section 51 of the Constitution, as well as matters ancillary to the existence of the Commonwealth as a federal government, such as payments for Members of Parliament. Second, there was no express grant of power to deal with public health, nor was there a broad grant of powers to the Commonwealth (unlike the plenary grant of power accorded to the federal government in the United States Constitution).

The position adopted by the High Court in *Attorney-General (Vic); Ex rel Dale v Commonwealth* has recently been affirmed. In *Pape v Federal Commissioner of Taxation*,[8] a

---

6   *Australia Act 1986* (Imp).
7   *Attorney-General (Vic); Ex rel Dale v Commonwealth* (1945) 71 CLR 237.
8   *Pape v Federal Commissioner of Taxation* (2009) 238 CLR 1.

decision concerning a tax bonus paid to Australians, the High Court held that section 81 of the Constitution does not, of itself, provide a head of power to authorise payments out of consolidated revenue. Rather, the source of such a power must be sought in an enumerated power in the Constitution.[9]

A second run at it – *Pharmaceutical Benefits Act 1947* (Cth)

The Commonwealth put a referendum to the Australian people in 1946. That referendum altered the Constitution by inserting a new section 51(xxiiiA). That section provided the Commonwealth had power to make laws in respect of:

> the provision of maternity allowances, widows' pensions, child endowment, unemployment, pharmaceutical, sickness and hospital benefits, medical and dental services (but not so as to authorize any form of civil conscription), benefits to students and family allowances.

Shortly thereafter, the *Pharmaceutical Benefits Act 1947* (Cth) was passed. Although similar in its terms to the *Pharmaceutical Benefits Act 1944* (Cth), there were two main differences. First, there was provision for the free supply of appliances in addition to the provision of medicines. Second, medical practitioners who supplied medicines or appliances under the scheme were obliged, on pain of imposition of penalty, to do so using a prescribed form. This latter requirement was to prove fatal.

In *Federal Council of the British Medical Association in Australia v Commonwealth*[10] the High Court considered a challenge to the *Pharmaceutical Benefits Act 1947* (Cth). Although the High Court decided that the scheme was supported by a head of power – that of section 51(xxiiiA) – the scheme was struck down because, by forcing doctors to use a form prescribed by the Commonwealth, it was considered that a form of civil conscription was involved. Though the High Court held the word 'conscription' had its ordinary meaning of compulsory enrolment of people in the armed forces, the idea of civil conscription was any compulsion on medical practitioners to provide medical services. The Commonwealth argued that the Act did not compel any medical practitioner to render any medical service, but only to use a form if they (in their absolute discretion) chose to provide access to the Commonwealth scheme. The High Court took a contrary view, holding that the writing of a prescription was a medical act. Since a doctor was obliged to use the Commonwealth's form, or risk losing a substantial amount of their practice, the Commonwealth was forcing a medical practitioner to render a medical service, which amounted to a form of civil

---

9   *Pape v Federal Commissioner of Taxation* (2009) 238 CLR 1. More recently, in *Williams v Commonwealth* (2012) 248 CLR 156, the High Court held that the Commonwealth could not seek to enlarge its powers by simply relying upon section 61 of the Constitution – the executive power of the Commonwealth – absent a grant of legislative power in the Constitution over the area it was seeking to regulate.

10 *Federal Council of the British Medical Association in Australia v Commonwealth* (1949) 79 CLR 201.

conscription. It imposed a duty to render a service to the Commonwealth (the filling out of a form) which was separate from, and formed no part of, the contract between doctor and patient.

Health Insurance Act 1973 (Cth) – the last hurrah

The matter was considered in the case of *General Practitioners Society in Australia v Commonwealth*.[11] That case concerned a provision of the *Health Insurance Act 1973* (Cth) which obliged a medical practitioner, if seeking the payment of benefits from the Commonwealth in respect of pathology services, to give certain undertakings and abide by a code of conduct. The General Practitioners Society alleged that such requirements were a form of civil conscription and thus prohibited by the Constitution. The High Court disagreed, and held that the meaning of conscription was the compulsory enlistment of people for military service. The Court drew a distinction between regulating the manner in which a service was to be provided – which was constitutionally permissible – and requiring the service to be performed, which was not. Justice Gibbs gave the example of a volunteer in the armed forces. Such a person would not, because he was forced to follow orders issued by his superiors, become a conscript. His Honour was of the view that the words 'any form of' did not extend the meaning of 'conscription'.[12]

More recently, this issue has been considered by the High Court in the case of *Wong v Commonwealth*.[13] In that case, the High Court held that provisions of the *Health Insurance Act 1973* (Cth) do not amount to a form of civil conscription, because doctors do not compulsorily provide services for the Commonwealth, or for other bodies on the Commonwealth's behalf. The Act does not force doctors to treat or not treat particular patients. Doctors are free to choose where and when they practise.

The impact of vertical fiscal imbalance

One further important constitutional development needs to be noted. In *South Australia v Commonwealth* (Uniform Tax Case),[14] the High Court upheld the Commonwealth's legislative competence to postpone the states' right to levy income taxes. The consequence has been that, although the Australian states have the majority of legislative powers, the Commonwealth has the majority of the revenue. The Commonwealth has successfully influenced the development of health policies and practices in Australia through its use of the grants power in the Constitution. Section 96 of the Constitution permits the Commonwealth to make grants to the states on such terms as it sees fit. This provision has, for example, permitted the Commonwealth to fund hospitals and medical treatments carried out at state level.

---

11 *General Practitioners Society in Australia v Commonwealth* (1980) 145 CLR 532.
12 Ibid.
13 *Wong v Commonwealth* (2009) 236 CLR 573.
14 *South Australia v Commonwealth* (1942) 65 CLR 373.

The Australian health system

The AIHW has produced an 'at a glance' diagram of the main services, funding responsibilities and providers of the Australian health system, together with accompanying commentary[15] (see Figure 6.1 below).

Figure 6.1   Health services funding and responsibility

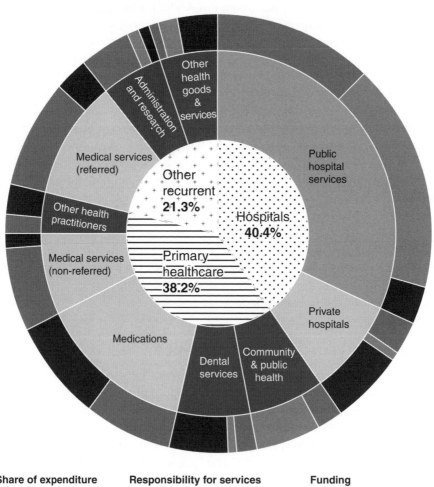

15   AIHW, above n 1, 34.

The inner segments show the relative size of the expenditure in each of the main sectors of the health system, being hospitals, primary healthcare and other areas of recurrent expenditure. In the case of the hospital sector, this includes all services provided by public and private hospitals. Primary healthcare includes a range of frontline health services delivered in the community, such as by a general practitioner (GP), physiotherapy and optometry services, dental services and all community and public health initiatives. It also includes the cost of medications not provided through hospital funding. The category 'other recurrent' includes areas of recurrent spending that were not paid for by hospitals but that which were not delivered through the primary healthcare sector either, such as medical services other than those provided by GPs, medical research, health aids and appliances, patient transport services and health administration. It is important to note that this list of examples is not exhaustive, and each group of services consists of many types of activities.

The middle ring indicates the relative expenditure on the specific service types within each sector, and who delivers the service. The outer ring shows the funding source for the services and the relative size of the funding. The colour coding in Figure 6.1 shows whether the service is provided by the private sector, public sector, or both. Private sector providers include private hospitals, medical practices and pharmacies. Public sector provision is the responsibility of state/territory governments, and includes public hospitals, for example. There is a mixture of federal, state/territory and local government provision for community and public health services.[16]

Key aspects of the current health system

Australia operates a healthcare system where GPs operate as gatekeepers. That is, a person with an illness will typically consult their GP first. If the GP is able to prescribe appropriate treatment, the GP does so. If not, the GP may offer a referral to a specialist. More complex procedures are carried out in hospitals. It is also possible for a person who feels ill to go straight to the emergency department of a hospital. In terms of regulation of healthcare, there are three main systems: Medicare; the Pharmaceutical Benefits Scheme (PBS); and private health insurance. We will now briefly consider each one in turn.

Medicare

The Medicare scheme was introduced in 1984, under amendments made to the *Health Insurance Act 1973* (Cth). Australian residents are issued with a Medicare card, on either a family or individual basis.[17] This card entitles them to claim rebates in respect of medical services provided by medical practitioners who have a Medicare provider number.[18] Medicare Australia is responsible for payments of benefits under the Act, as well as operational matters associated with Medicare. Rebates payable are summarised as follows:[19]

Services which attract a Medicare benefit can be located in tables in the schedules of the *Health Insurance Act 1973*. Each service is allocated an item number which must

---

16   Ibid.
17   *Health Insurance Act 1973* (Cth) s 10AA.
18   Ibid s 10.
19   See, generally, Phillip W Bates et al., *Australian Health and Medical Law Reporter* (CCH Australia Ltd, 2007–16) 60–130.

be identified when claiming a benefit. Services that are included in the schedules and amounts payable for each service are amended from time to time by regulation. The amount of rebate paid to service providers had its origins in the 'most common fee'. The 'most common fee' for individual services was a list drawn up by representatives of the Commonwealth, the Australian Medical Association and the benefit funds in 1968–1969 to be included in a schedule of medical benefits. The most common fee was not an average of fees charged but, as its name suggests, the most frequently charged fee for a particular service. The amount of benefit is now determined by a variety of means including an assessment of the cost of high technology investigations, an estimate of the time and complexity of a particular treatment and comparisons with similar treatments. The introduction of new techniques and equipment for pathology testing has resulted in a reduction in the benefit for some tests as they can now be performed more quickly and efficiently than previously.[20]

Pursuant to the scheme all Australians receive a rebate from the Commonwealth government, representing 100 per cent of the scheduled fee of services provided by a registered practitioner (which includes a GP, specialist, nurse practitioner or psychologist). However, no registered practitioner is obliged to charge only the scheduled fee.

Hospital care

There are public and private hospitals in Australia. Medicare provides free treatment and accommodation in public hospitals for public patients, through a mix of federal and state government funding. Private patients receive a rebate of 75 per cent of the scheduled fee for services in a public or private hospital. This does not include accommodation or theatre fees in private hospitals. Medicare does not fund cosmetic surgery or ambulances.

Prescription pharmaceuticals

The Pharmaceutical Benefits Scheme (PBS) allows Australians to access a range of prescription medication at a cost subsidised by the federal government.[21] Its operation is summarised as follows:

> For drugs to attract a benefit, the Minister must make a declaration in relation to individual preparations about which drugs are included in the scheme following recommendations of the Pharmaceutical Benefits Advisory Committee (PBAC). The Minister may determine how much of the drug by reference to dose and quantity should be dispensed with each prescription. The Minister may also declare that a particular drug shall cease to be part of the PBS. Before doing so he or she must obtain the advice of the PBAC in relation to ceasing benefits in relation to the drug.[22]

Provision is made for pensioners, low-income earners and people who have reached a pre-assigned 'safety net' threshold to obtain prescription medications at lower rates.

20   See also *Health Insurance Act 1973* (Cth) ss 11, 19A, 66, Sch 1, Sch 1A.
21   *National Health Act 1953* (Cth) Part VII.
22   See, generally, Bates et al., above n 19, 60–510.

Private health insurance

Private health insurance is regulated by the *Private Health Insurance Act 2007* (Cth). Whereas Medicare funds the provision of medical services as an inpatient in public hospitals and medical treatment provided by GPs, private health insurance in Australia typically covers the gap between the Medicare rebate and the fee charged by a medical practitioner; accommodation costs in private hospitals; and the funding of extras, such as dental, physiotherapy, and chiropractic treatments, for example. Any company wishing to offer private health insurance must first be registered to do so in accordance with Chapter 4 of the *Private Health Insurance Act 2007* (Cth).[23] Once registered, a number of obligations are imposed on a registered health insurance provider, including compliance with accounting and regulatory standards. Private health insurers are also obliged to produce a standard form product statement to facilitate easy comparison across policies. There is also a Private Health Insurance Administration Council (PHIAC) which administers and ensures compliance with respect to health benefit funds. On 1 July 2015, responsibility for the prudential supervision of private health insurers transferred from PHIAC to the Australian Prudential Regulation Authority (APRA).[24]

Most general insurance works on the basis of a premium being charged according to the assessed risk of an individual. However, this is not the case with private health insurance in Australia. Instead, premiums for such insurance are 'community rated'. That is to say, the same premium is charged to every person, irrespective or health or age.[25] Incentives are built into private health insurance by law. With limited exceptions, any person who does not take up such insurance prior to reaching their 31st birthday is charged higher premiums.[26] People on higher incomes are also charged a higher Medicare levy if they elect not to take out such insurance.[27] The Commonwealth provides a means-tested tax rebate for premiums paid by those who do have private health insurance.[28]

What health matters are governed by the states?

All of the matters referred to above are the subject of Commonwealth law. As noted by the AIHW, those health matters regulated by state governments include the power to license or register private hospitals. In addition, each state has legislation relevant to the operation of public hospitals. They are also largely responsible for health-relevant industry regulation, such as for the sale and supply of alcohol and tobacco-related products.[29]

In 2011, the Commonwealth government established Medicare Locals. These are bodies which are designed to plan and fund health needs for local communities. In 2014, Medicare Locals were replaced by Primary Health Networks (PHN) and they commenced operation on 1 July 2015. The aim of PHNs is to liaise with state health bodies to avoid duplication and waste. In conjunction with the above, state governments have established local hospital networks with the aim of improving access to health services.[30]

---

23   *Private Health Insurance Act 2007* (Cth) Part 4–4.
24   *Private Health Insurance (Prudential Supervision) Act 2015* (Cth).
25   *Private Health Insurance Act 2007* (Cth) Div 55.
26   Ibid Div 34.
27   *Medicare Levy Act 1986* (Cth).
28   *Private Health Insurance Act 2007* (Cth) Div 23.
29   AIHW, above n 1.
30   Ibid.

Conclusion

This chapter has examined the broad framework governing the allocation of health services in Australia, with a particular focus on macro-level regulation which seeks to direct the provision of such services. This included examining the constitutional position with respect to health powers, as well as identifying key aspects of Australia's health system and services. What is important to note is that there is no express grant of power to make laws with respect to health in the Constitution. Historically, this has meant that the development of a national approach to healthcare has been difficult. The Commonwealth currently utilises the grants power in the Constitution to fund the provision of health services and pharmaceutical benefits, as well as to regulate the provision of private health insurance, in Australia. Constitutional limitations, institutional arrangements and differing political ideologies all impact upon the way in which federal and state/territory governments seek to manage and fund the provision of health services in Australia.

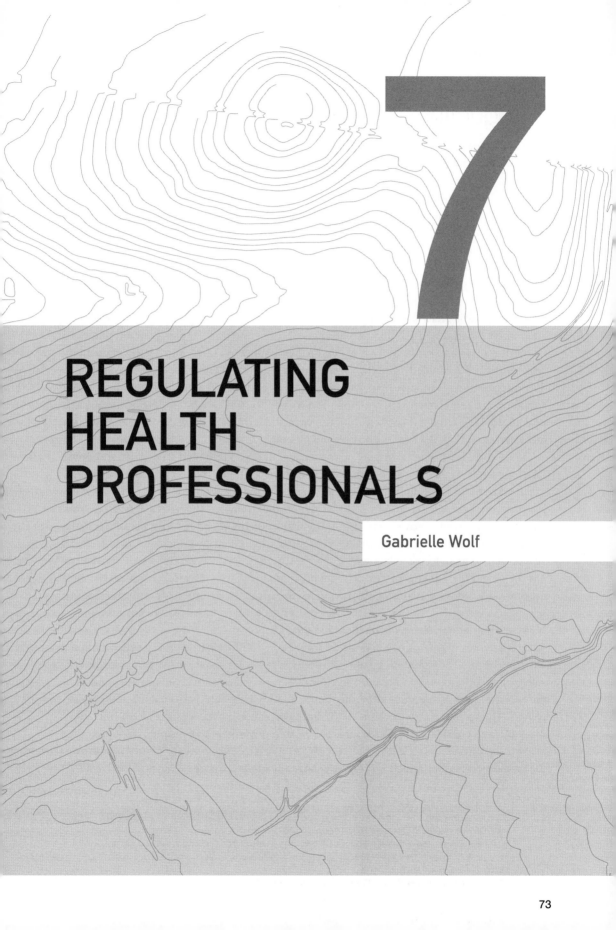

7

REGULATING HEALTH PROFESSIONALS

Gabrielle Wolf

Introduction

Until 2010, health professions in Australia were regulated separately from one another at a state and territory level, and according to the peer review model. Governments delegated power to the health professions to regulate themselves; each profession was governed independently and subject to the direction of representative members. Professionals within the same health profession were also regulated differently from one another according to the jurisdiction in which they practised. By 2010, there were eight health regulatory systems in Australia and at least 85 state and territory-based statutory boards, predominantly made up of health professionals and regulating various health professions. They set registration standards and codes of conduct, registered health professionals, and administered disciplinary procedures, but in different ways from one another.[1]

Health professionals who worked across jurisdictions and/or in more than one profession confronted varied regulation and administrative obstacles. For example, a doctor employed by the Royal Flying Doctor Service needed to apply under 'mutual recognition' legislation, which from 1992 enabled health professionals registered in one Australian jurisdiction to obtain registration in another by paying relevant fees and satisfying multiple registration and administrative requirements. In addition, doctors had to comply with professional standards promulgated by statutory boards in various states and territories, as well as by the Australian Medical Association, doctors' peak professional body.

From 2010, health professionals' representative bodies continued to protect and guide their constituents, but many health professions were united within a single regulatory scheme known as the National Registration and Accreditation Scheme (NRAS). Initially, ten professions fell within the NRAS's ambit, with a further four joining in 2012. It was intended that the NRAS would provide consistent regulation of health professions across Australia and reduce the autonomy of individual professions within the various jurisdictions. National Health Practitioner Boards (Boards), of which not more than two-thirds were 'practitioner members' and the remainder were 'community members', were created to govern the professions.[2] The NRAS was promoted as a panacea to perceived problems with the preceding regime. Nevertheless, this Scheme has proved to be a controversial initiative, not least because it has never been truly national in practice.

This chapter examines key aspects of the NRAS. The first part of the chapter explores why the NRAS – designed as a national, uniform regulatory system for 14 health professions – was introduced and how it operates. It then provides an overview of key aspects of the Scheme, such as registration requirements, as well as health, performance and conduct matters. The second part provides a critical appraisal of the advantages and disadvantages of the NRAS and considers its likely future. The matters covered in this chapter are relevant for all 14 health professions regulated by the NRAS, however, examples are mostly drawn from the medical profession, which is one of the larger health professions regulated by the NRAS.

---

1   Note that from 2007 the same legislative requirements governed 12 health professions within Victoria: see *Health Professions Registration Act 2005* (Vic). For a historical overview of the Victorian system, see Gabrielle Wolf, 'A Delayed Inheritance: The Medical Board of Victoria's 75-Year Wait to Find Doctors Guilty of "Infamous Conduct in a Professional Respect"' (2015) 22 *Journal of Law and Medicine* 568.

2   *Health Practitioner Regulation National Law Act 2009* (Qld) Sch s 33 (National Law).

In order to understand fully the regulatory context in which health professionals operate, it is important that account is taken of the overarching regulatory framework for health in Australia (Chapter 6), as well as the regulation of patient safety and redress (Chapter 8).

Impetus for reform

The NRAS was the brainchild of Australia's Productivity Commission (Commission). The Commission was requested by the Council of Australian Governments (COAG) to 'examine issues impacting on the health workforce ... and propose solutions'.[3] The Commission's report, delivered in 2006, revealed an inflexible, inefficient, inconsistent and costly regulatory system, with 'extraordinarily complex' health workforce arrangements.[4] It recommended that a national registration board with profession-specific panels be established to govern all regulated health professions and administer uniform registration standards based on qualifications formulated by a national accreditation board. COAG subsequently endorsed a national registration and accreditation scheme for health professionals to 'facilitate workforce mobility, improve safety and quality, and reduce red tape'.[5] Nevertheless, COAG agreed to create national, profession-specific boards, rather than approving a single registration board.[6]

Other unstated drivers for reform were public scandals involving doctors. Administrative failures of public hospitals and the Medical Boards of NSW and Queensland enabled Doctors Graeme Reeves, Jayant Patel and Abdalla Khalafalla to continue practising medicine, notwithstanding grave allegations having been made about their professional conduct and performance and, in Patel's case, when the relevant Board had failed to check his credentials.[7] Reeves was ultimately convicted of indecent assault and grievous bodily harm of patients.[8] Patel was eventually convicted of defrauding his registration body and he was initially convicted of the manslaughter of three patients and grievous bodily harm of another, although this was subsequently quashed by the High Court for evidentiary reasons.[9] In the case of Khalafalla, the Medical Board of Queensland eventually refused to renew his registration, with experts concluding that deficiencies in his training, qualifications and competence had seriously compromised his handling of surgical complications.[10]

---

3   Council of Australian Governments (COAG), *Communique* (14 July 2006) 4; *Intergovernmental Agreement for a National Registration and Accreditation Scheme for the Health Professions*, signed 26 March 2008, cl 2.1 (Intergovernmental Agreement).
4   Productivity Commission, Australia's Health Workforce: Productivity Commission Research Report (2005) iv, xiv, xix, xxxiv.
5   Intergovernmental Agreement, above n 3, cl 5.3.
6   Ibid cll 2.3, 2.5.
7   See Deirdre O'Connor, *Report of the Appointment, Management and Termination of Dr Graeme Reeves as a Visiting Medical Officer in the NSW Public Health System* (2008); Peter Garling, *Special Commission of Inquiry Acute Care Service in New South Wales Public Hospitals, Inquiry into the Circumstances of the Appointment of Graeme Reeves by the Former Southern Area Health Service, Final Report* (2008); Geoffrey Davies AO, *Queensland Public Hospitals Commission of Inquiry Report* (2005); Health Quality and Complaints Commission, *An Investigation into Concerns Raised by Mrs De-Anne Kelly about the Quality of Health Services at Mackay Base Hospital* (2008) (An Investigation into Concerns Raised by Mrs De-Anne Kelly).
8   *R v Reeves* [2011] Woods QC DCJ 1/7/2011; *Reeves v The Queen* (2013) 227 A Crim R 444.
9   *R v Patel* [2013] QDC Martin SC DCJ 21/11/2013; *R v Patel* [2010] QSC 199; *Patel v The Queen* (2012) 247 CLR 531.
10 An Investigation into Concerns Raised by Mrs De-Anne Kelly, above n 7, 19.

Implementation of the NRAS

There have been two regulatory approaches to the implementation of the NRAS: the 'applied laws' model and the 'co-regulatory' model. Pursuant to the *Intergovernmental Agreement for a National Registration and Accreditation Scheme for the Health Professions* (2008) (Intergovernmental Agreement), the Commonwealth, states and territories agreed to implement the NRAS through a national 'applied laws' model, whereby legislation is enacted in one jurisdiction and applied by other jurisdictions as a law of those jurisdictions.[11] Queensland hosted the substantive legislation, including the Health Practitioner Regulation National Law (National Law) as the Schedule to the *Health Practitioner Regulation National Law Act 2009* (Qld).[12] The NT, SA, Tasmania and Victoria adopted and applied the National Law as a law of their jurisdictions.[13] WA and the ACT passed corresponding legislation that adopted the National Law, but made some modifications to it.[14]

NSW and Queensland follow a co-regulatory model in which health professionals are regulated under both the National Law and other state legislation, and where health profession boards share regulatory responsibility with health complaints bodies.[15] Since the commencement of the NRAS, NSW (which wanted to retain its long-standing health complaints management system) has participated in the NRAS's registration and accreditation processes, but the Health Care Complaints Commission (HCCC) and state-based health profession Councils have handled matters relating to practitioners' health, performance and conduct. On 1 July 2014, Queensland became a co-regulatory jurisdiction too, due to perceived deficiencies in the NRAS's health complaints management system, especially delays in dealing with, and inadequate responses to, concerns raised about doctors.[16] The Health Ombudsman now manages serious complaints about health professionals practising in Queensland.

Initially, ten Boards were formed for professions that had already been regulated in most, or all, Australian jurisdictions: chiropractic; dental; medicine; nursing and midwifery; optometry; osteopathy; pharmacy; physiotherapy; podiatry; and psychology.[17] On 1 July 2012, Boards were created for Aboriginal and Torres Strait Islander health practice; Chinese

---

11   Intergovernmental Agreement, above n 3, cl 6; Parliamentary Counsel's Committee, Protocol on Drafting National Uniform Legislation (4th edn, 2014) 1.

12   National Law, above n 2.

13   *Health Practitioner Regulation (National Uniform Legislation) Act 2010* (NT); *Health Practitioner Regulation National Law (South Australia) Act 2010* (SA); *Health Practitioner Regulation National Law (Tasmania) Act 2010* (Tas); *Health Practitioner Regulation National Law (Victoria) Act 2009* (Vic).

14   See ACT: *Human Rights Commission Act 2005* (ACT); *Health Practitioner Regulation National Law (ACT) Act 2010* (ACT). See WA: *Health Practitioner Regulation National Law (WA) Act 2010* (WA).

15   NSW: *Health Practitioner Regulation Act 2009* (NSW); *Health Practitioner Regulation National Law (NSW)* Act No. 86a of 2009 (NSW) and *Health Care Complaints Act 1993* (NSW). Queensland: *Health Practitioner Regulation National Law Act 2009* (Qld) and *Health Ombudsman Act 2013* (Qld). See also David Thomas, 'The Co-Regulation of Medical Discipline: Challenging Medical Peer Review' (2004) 11 *Journal of Law and Medicine* 382, 383.

16   Explanatory Notes, Health Ombudsman Bill 2013 (Qld) 1; for relevant legislation, see above n 15.

17   Australian Health Practitioner Regulation Agency (AHPRA), *Annual Report 2010–11*, 7; Explanatory Notes, Health Practitioner Regulation National Law Bill 2009 (Qld) 3.

medicine; medical radiation practice; and occupational therapy, which previously had been unregulated, or regulated in only a few jurisdictions.

Some larger Boards have established state and territory Boards to which they delegate functions, including decision-making about individual health professionals. The Australian Health Workforce Ministerial Council (AHWMC), comprising government health ministers, appoints Board members, approves their registration standards and provides policy direction. The Boards rely for administrative support on the National Agency – the Australian Health Practitioner Regulation Agency (AHPRA) – which is governed by the AHPRA Agency Management Committee. AHPRA performs many functions, including managing processes for registering health professionals and investigating their health, performance and conduct.

The Boards refer matters to tribunals for adjudication if they believe a health professional has engaged in professional misconduct or their registration was obtained improperly; or if a health, performance and professional standards panel established by a Board requires them to do so.[18] Tribunals are empowered to adjudicate the most serious disciplinary matters and cancel health professionals' registration.[19] Allegations against health professionals must be proved on the balance of probabilities to the tribunal's reasonable satisfaction.[20] The tribunals may refer to expert evidence, regulatory policies and registration standards, and previous tribunal and judicial interpretations of professionals' conduct that warrants sanction. This jurisprudence highlights that determinations in disciplinary matters should protect the public, deter the individual and others from engaging in misconduct, maintain professional standards, and not punish health professionals.[21] Tribunals may consider demand for the health professional's services, given the NRAS's objective, 'to facilitate access to services provided by health practitioners in accordance with the public interest'.[22]

Some recent hearings concerning doctors demonstrate the range of matters involving health professionals on which tribunals adjudicate. The Victorian Civil and Administrative Tribunal (VCAT) reprimanded and placed conditions on two doctors for failing to provide adequate post-operative management of a patient who died due to complications from liposuction surgery.[23] The NT Health Professional Review Tribunal also ordered that a doctor who engaged in a sexual relationship with a patient, and wrote prescriptions for medication in his wife's name that were intended for his own use, be reprimanded and undergo mentoring.[24] The ACT Civil and Administrative Tribunal reprimanded a doctor and ordered that he undergo mentoring and not perform any supervisory role for failing both to refer a patient to another doctor for treatment when he had a conflict of interest and to notify the Medical Board of Australia of another doctor's sexual misconduct.[25]

---

18   National Law, above n 2, s 193.
19   Katie Elkin, 'Medical Practitioner Regulation: Is It All About Protecting the Public?' (2014) 21 *Journal of Law and Medicine* 682, 689; Australian Health Practitioner Regulation Agency, *Annual Report 2012–13*, 137; National Law, above n 2, s 196.
20   See *Briginshaw v Briginshaw* (1938) 60 CLR 336.
21   Ian Freckelton, 'Regulation of Health Practitioners: National Reform in Australia' (2010) 18 *Journal of Law and Medicine* 207, 217.
22   National Law, above n 2, s 3(2)(e); Elkin, above n 19, 697, 699.
23   *Medical Board of Australia v Dieu* [2014] VCAT 1597.
24   *Medical Board of Australia v Forrest* [2014] NTHPRT 1.
25   *Medical Board of Australia v Al-Naser* [2015] ACAT 15.

Registration of health professionals

The major uniformity in Australian regulation of health professionals is that they are all bound by the same requirements for registration, as outlined in Part 7 of the National Law. The Boards must register 'suitably qualified and competent' practitioners and, with AHPRA, maintain national registers of practitioners. Regardless of profession or jurisdiction, applicants for registration must fulfil the Boards' registration standards and assure them that they are 'suitable' to hold registration. Grounds for unsuitability include inability to practise competently and a criminal history that is relevant to practice of the health profession (this history is more likely to lead to refusal to grant registration if there is evidence that the health professional received a conviction and/or custodial sentence, the crime was committed when the professional was over 18 years of age, and/or the offence was part of a pattern of behaviour).[26]

Health professionals apply annually to renew their registration. Boards can endorse a health professional's registration, such as to supply scheduled medicines or to practise acupuncture, and impose conditions on registration to restrict the way in which a health professional practises the profession, or to ensure that the health professional practises the profession only if certain measures are undertaken or in particular circumstances.[27] For instance, the Medical Board of Australia may impose conditions on the practice of a doctor who has previously been found to have been drug-dependent, such as that s/he regularly provide samples for urinalysis and undertake counselling.

There are six categories of registration:

- **General:** This is the largest category and is open to applicants with relevant qualifications.
- **Specialist:** Applicants for this category must qualify for registration in a recognised specialty in their profession.
- **Provisional:** Health professionals apply for this category if they need to complete supervised practice to become eligible for general registration.
- **Limited:** Health professionals who are unqualified for general or specialist registration can apply for this category to undertake postgraduate training, supervised practice or assessment, to practise in an area of need or for a limited time or scope in the public interest, or to fill a teaching or research position.
- **Non-practising:** Health professionals who have held general or specialist registration are eligible for this category.
- **Student:** Boards grant this category of registration to those undertaking approved programs of study for a health profession.

Health, performance and conduct matters

A major inconsistency in Australian regulation of health professionals is how matters pertaining to their health, performance and conduct are addressed. Part 8 of the National Law as originally enacted in Queensland, which empowers the Boards to handle cases

---

26   National Law, above n 2, s 55; Medical Board of Australia, *Criminal History Registration Standard* (1 July 2010).
27   National Law, above n 2, ss 83, 94–8, 107.

where a health professional's or student's ill-health affects their capacity to practise or undertake training, or a health professional's conduct or practice of their profession is unsatisfactory, applies only in the NT, SA, Tasmania and Victoria and, with minor amendment, in WA.

In the ACT, the Health Services Commissioner (HSC) is integrally involved in the Boards' decision-making. The Boards' responsibilities are undertaken in NSW largely by the HCCC and health profession Councils. In Queensland, they are undertaken by the Health Ombudsman. The grounds on which concerns about registrants' health, performance and conduct can be made vary to some extent between jurisdictions. Such concerns are called 'notifications' if received by the Boards, or 'complaints' if they are directed to the HSC, the HCCC or the Health Ombudsman.

Anyone can make a 'voluntary' notification/complaint and there are several bases on which this can be done. They include where a health professional's professional conduct, knowledge, skill or care is below the expected standard, or where a health professional or student has an 'impairment' (defined as a physical or mental impairment, disability, condition or disorder that detrimentally affects a health professional's capacity to practise the profession or a student's capacity to undertake clinical training).[28] In all jurisdictions, registered health professionals and their employers are obliged to make notifications if they reasonably believe a health professional has practised while intoxicated; engaged in sexual misconduct; placed the public at risk due to their impairment; or significantly departed from professional standards.[29]

Health professionals and education providers (including tertiary education institutions and organisations that provide vocational training) must make notifications about students whom they believe to have an impairment that, in undertaking clinical training, could place the public at substantial risk.[30] In Queensland and WA, health professionals are exempted from these obligations if they form their belief while providing health services to the health professional/student. In Queensland, to be exempted, they must also believe their patient's conduct relates to an impairment that will not place the public at risk and is not professional misconduct.[31] As we have highlighted briefly here, there are some differences in the processes followed by state and territory regulatory bodies in dealing with health, performance and conduct matters. It is therefore important to check the applicable state/territory legislation with regard to such issues, which is likely to be updated from time to time.[32] Table 7.1 outlines differences in the processes followed by the state and territory regulatory bodies in dealing with health, performance and conduct matters.

---

28   Ibid ss 5, 144.
29   Ibid ss 140–2.
30   Ibid ss 5, 141(1)(b), 143.
31   National Law, above n 2, s 141, as amended by *Health Practitioner Regulation National Law Act 2009* (Qld) s 25(3); National Law s 141, as amended by *Health Practitioner Regulation National Law (WA) Act 2010* (WA) s 4(7).
32   See above n 3, 13–15.

Table 7.1: Regulation of Health Professionals in Australia

	PATHWAYS FOR HEALTH, PERFORMANCE AND CONDUCT MATTERS				
ISSUE	NT, SA, Tas, Vic	ACT	NSW	Qld	WA
Governing legislation	*Health Practitioner Regulation (National Uniform Legislation) Act 2010* (NT); *Health Practitioner Regulation National Law (South Australia) Act 2010* (SA); *Health Practitioner Regulation National Law (Tasmania) Act 2010* (Tas); *Health Practitioner Regulation National Law (Victoria) Act 2009* (Vic) (National Law)	*Human Rights Commission Act 2005* (ACT); *Health Practitioner Regulation National Law (ACT) Act 2010* (ACT)	*Health Practitioner Regulation (Adoption of National Law) Act 2009* (NSW); *Health Practitioner Regulation National Law (NSW) Act No. 86a of 2009* (NSW) (86a); *Health Care Complaints Act 1993* (NSW)	*Health Practitioner Regulation National Law Act 2009* (Qld); *Health Ombudsman Act 2013* (Qld) (HO Act)	*Health Practitioner Regulation National Law (WA) Act 2010* (WA)
Description of communication of concern about registered health professional/ student to regulatory authority	Notification	Notification	Complaint	Complaint	Notification
Grounds for making voluntary complaint/ notification about registered health professional	Professional conduct of lesser standard than expected by public or peers; knowledge, skill, judgment or care below standard expected; not suitable person to hold registration; impairment; contravened governing legislation; contravened condition of registration or undertaking to a National Health Practitioner Board (Board); registration improperly obtained (National Law s 144(1))	Same as NT, SA, Tas, Vic	Criminal conviction or finding; unsatisfactory professional conduct or professional misconduct; lack of competence; impairment; not suitable person (86a s 144)	Same as NT, SA, Tas, Vic	Same as NT, SA, Tas, Vic

Grounds for making voluntary complaint/notification about student	Charged with, convicted or found guilty of an offence punishable by 12 months imprisonment or more; impairment; contravention of condition of registration or undertaking to Board (National Law s 144(2))	Same as NT, SA, Tas, Vic	Charged with offence, convicted or made subject of criminal finding for offence punishable by at least 12 months imprisonment; impairment; contravention of condition of registration or undertaking given to Board (86a s 144A)	Same as NT, SA, Tas, Vic	Same as NT, SA, Tas, Vic
Who is obliged to make mandatory notification	Health practitioners, employers and education providers (National Law ss 141–3)	Same as NT, SA, Tas, Vic	Same as NT, SA, Tas, Vic	Same as NT, SA, Tas, Vic	Same as NT, SA, Tas, Vic
Grounds for making mandatory notification about registered health professional ('notifiable conduct')	Practised profession while intoxicated by alcohol or drugs; engaged in sexual misconduct; placed public at risk due to impairment; placed public at risk because practised in way that constitutes significant departure from accepted professional standards (National Law s 140)	Same as NT, SA, Tas, Vic	Same as NT, SA, Tas, Vic	Same as NT, SA, Tas, Vic	Same as NT, SA, Tas, Vic
Obligations of registered health professionals to make mandatory notifications	If in the course of practising their health profession they form a reasonable belief that another registered practitioner has behaved in way that constitutes notifiable conduct or a student has an impairment that in the course of undertaking clinical training may place the public at substantial risk of harm (National Law s 141(1))	Same as NT, SA, Tas, Vic	Same as NT, SA, Tas, Vic	Same as NT, SA, Tas, Vic	Same as NT, SA, Tas, Vic

Table 7.1: (cont.)

ISSUE	NT, SA, Tas, Vic	ACT	NSW	Qld	WA
Exemptions from obligations of registered health professionals to make mandatory notifications	Practitioner is employed/engaged by insurer that provides professional indemnity insurance relating to practitioner/student and they form reasonable belief as a result of disclosure made to them during legal proceeding or in providing legal advice arising from insurance policy; practitioner forms reasonable belief in the course of providing advice regarding notifiable conduct/ impairment for purposes of legal proceeding or preparation of legal advice; practitioner is legal practitioner and forms reasonable belief in course of providing legal services to practitioner/student regarding legal proceeding or preparation of legal advice in which notifiable conduct/impairment is issue; they form reasonable belief while exercising functions as member of quality assurance committee, council or other body approved or authorised under Act of participating jurisdiction and unable to disclose information that forms basis of the reasonable belief because provision of that Act prohibits disclosure of information; or practitioner knows/ reasonably believes AHPRA has been notified of conduct/impairment that forms basis of reasonable belief (National Law s 141(4))	Same as NT, SA, Tas, Vic	Same as NT, SA, Tas, Vic	Same as NT, SA, Tas, Vic, but also if forms reasonable belief as result of providing health service to practitioner and reasonably believes notifiable conduct relates to impairment that will not place public at substantial risk of harm and is not professional misconduct (National Law s 141(5)), as inserted by *HO Act 2009* (Qld) s 326)	Same as NT, SA, Tas, Vic, but also if forms reasonable belief while providing health service to practitioner/ student (National Law s 141(4)(da), as inserted by *Health Practitioner Regulation National Law (WA) Act 2010* item 4(7))

Obligations on employers of registered health professionals to make mandatory notifications	If reasonably believe practitioner has behaved in way that constitutes notifiable conduct (National Law s 142(1))	Same as NT, SA, Tas, Vic	Same as NT, SA, Tas, Vic	Same as NT, SA, Tas, Vic	Same as NT, SA, Tas, Vic
Obligations on education providers to make mandatory notifications	If reasonably believe student enrolled in program of study provided by them or for whom they have arranged clinical training has impairment that, in undertaking clinical training, may place public at substantial risk of harm (National Law s 143(1))	Same as NT, SA, Tas, Vic	Same as NT, SA, Tas, Vic	Same as NT, SA, Tas, Vic	Same as NT, SA, Tas, Vic
Who receives complaints/ notifications about registered health professional/ student	Australian Health Practitioner Regulation Agency (AHPRA)* or health complaints entity in jurisdiction	Same as NT, Tas, Vic	Health Care Complaints Commission (HCCC) or Councils for regulated health professions, or AHPRA if it is mandatory notification	Health ombudsman	Same as NT, SA, Tas, Vic
Who deals with complaint/ notification	Board that registered practitioner or health complaints entity if subject matter of notification would also provide ground for complaint to it or vice versa, and they must attempt to agree about who will deal with it (National Law s 150)	Board and HSC, who must attempt to agree on who will deal with it (National Law s 150(1), as amended by *Health Practitioner Regulation National Law (ACT) Act 2010* item 1.2)	Council or HCCC, as decided by both (86a ss 144G, 145A–C)	Health ombudsman; or ombudsman refers matter to AHPRA, unless it indicates practitioner may have behaved in way that constitutes professional misconduct or another ground may exist for suspension/cancellation of practitioner's registration; or director of proceedings who decides whether to refer it to tribunal or back to ombudsman (HO Act ss 38(3), 91, 102–3)	Same as NT, SA, Tas, Vic

Table 7.1: (cont.)

ISSUE	NT, SA, Tas, Vic	ACT	NSW	Qld	WA
Options for dealing with complaint/ notification	Take no further action; take 'immediate action'; investigate; require practitioner/student to undergo health assessment; require practitioner to undergo performance assessment; take 'relevant action' (caution, accept undertaking, impose condition on registration, refer matter to another entity); establish health panel (if Board believes practitioner/student has/may have impairment and it is necessary/appropriate to refer matter to panel) or performance and professional standards panel (if Board reasonably believes the way practitioner practises the health profession is/may be unsatisfactory, or practitioner's professional conduct is/may be unsatisfactory) (National Law ss 151, 155, 160, 169–70, 178, 181–2)	Same as NT, SA, Tas, Vic	Council can make inquiries about complaint; refer it to HCCC for investigation; refer it to Assessment Committee (for professions other than medical and nursing and midwifery) or Professional Standards Committee (PSC) (for medical and nursing and midwifery professions); deal with it by inquiry at Council meeting (for professions other than medical and nursing and midwifery); refer practitioner/student for health assessment; refer matter to Impaired Registrants Panel; refer practitioner's professional performance for performance assessment; direct practitioner/student to attend counselling; refer it to HCCC for conciliation; refer it to another entity, including Board; determine no further action should be taken; take immediate action. HCCC can refer complaint to Council, PSC or Board; refer complaint for conciliation; refer complaint to another entity; determine no further action should be taken; or take action it can take under the *Health Care Complaints Act 1993* (NSW) (86a ss 25B, 145B–C)	Same as NT, SA, Tas, Vic if Board is dealing with it, or ombudsman can take immediate action; investigate it; refer it to AHPRA; or refer it to director of proceedings for decision about whether to refer it to tribunal (HO Act, ss 38, 91)	Same as NT, SA, Tas, Vic

Grounds on which regulatory authority can decide to take no further action	If Board reasonably believes notification is frivolous, vexatious, misconceived or lacking in substance; given amount of time that elapsed since matter occurred, it is not practicable for Board to investigate or deal with it; person to whom notification relates has not been/is no longer registered and it is not in public interest for Board to investigate or deal with notification; subject matter of notification has already been dealt with adequately by Board; or subject of the notification is being dealt with/ has been dealt with adequately by another entity (National Law s 151)	Same as NT, SA, Tas, Vic, but subject to HSC agreeing with Board that no further action should be taken (National Law s 151(1), as amended by *Health Practitioner Regulation National Law (ACT) Act 2010* (ACT) item 1.6)	Unstated	Same as NT, SA, Tas, Vic for Board. Also if ombudsman reasonably considers complaint is frivolous, vexatious, trivial, not made in good faith, misconceived or lacking in substance, is being adequately dealt with by another entity, has been resolved or otherwise appropriately finalised by ombudsman or another entity, or despite reasonable efforts it cannot be resolved; complainant failed to cooperate with attempts to resolve complaint or comply with request for information; complaint is withdrawn or matter of complaint arose and the complainant was aware of matter at least two years before complaint was made (unless practitioner may have behaved in way that constitutes professional misconduct or another ground may exist for suspension/ cancellation of registration); complainant, health service provider or other relevant person dies and ombudsman reasonably considers it would be appropriate to take no further action (HO Act s 44)	Same as NT, SA, Tas, Vic

Table 7.1: (cont.)

ISSUE	NT, SA, Tas, Vic	ACT	NSW	Qld	WA
Grounds on which investigation may be conducted	Board decides it is necessary/appropriate because it received notification; Board believes practitioner/student has/may have impairment, or way practitioner practises the profession is or may be unsatisfactory, or practitioner's conduct is/may be unsatisfactory, or to ensure practitioner/student is complying with conditions on registration or undertaking given to Board (National Law s 160(1))	Same as NT, SA, Tas, Vic	Council refers complaint to HCCC for investigation; Council suspended/imposed conditions on practitioner's/student's registration; Council/Performance Review Panel considers matter raises significant issue of public health/safety that requires investigation and Council refers it to HCCC (86a ss 145B(2), 150D, 154A, 155C, 156B); Council/HCCC considers matter should be investigated; following assessment of complaint, HCCC considers complaint raises significant issue of public health/safety or significant question regarding appropriate care/treatment of client by health service provider, or if substantiated would provide grounds for disciplinary action against practitioner, involve gross negligence of practitioner, or result in being found guilty of offence under *Public Health Act 2010* (NSW) (advertising/promoting health services in a false/misleading manner or providing/promoting health services while deregistered) (*Health Care Complaints Act 1993* (NSW) ss 13, 23)	Matter is subject of health service complaint, systemic issue relating to provision of health service, or another matter where ombudsman considers investigation is relevant to achieving an objective of HO Act; or minister directs ombudsman to undertake investigation (HO Act ss 80–1)	Same as NT, SA, Tas, Vic

Power to suspend registration, impose conditions on registration, and accept undertaking or surrender of registration	Board reasonably believes because of practitioner's conduct, performance or health, they pose a serious risk to persons and its necessary to take immediate action to protect public health/safety; Board reasonably believes student poses serious risk to persons because they have been charged with, convicted or found guilty of an offence that is punishable by 12 months imprisonment or more, student has/may have impairment, or has/may have contravened condition on registration or undertaking to Board, and it is necessary to take immediate action to protect public health/safety; practitioner's registration was improperly obtained because practitioner/someone else gave Board false/misleading information; or practitioner's/student's registration has been cancelled or suspended in Australia or elsewhere (National Law s 156)	Same as NT, SA, Tas, Vic	Council satisfied it is appropriate to suspend/impose conditions on registration for protection of health/safety of a person/s, or satisfied this action is otherwise in the public interest (86a s 150)	Ombudsman reasonably believes because of practitioner's health, conduct or performance they pose a serious risk to persons and it is necessary to take action to protect public health/safety; ombudsman reasonably believes practitioner's registration was improperly obtained because practitioner/ someone else gave Board false/misleading information; or practitioner's registration has been cancelled/ suspended in Australia or elsewhere (HO Act s 58)	Same as NT, SA, Tas, Vic
Who can conduct investigation into performance, conduct or health matter	Investigator appointed by Board, who can be a member of AHPRA's staff or contractor engaged by AHPRA (National Law ss 160, 163)	Same as NT, SA, Tas, Vic	Officer of HCCC, authorised in writing by HCCC to do so (*Health Care Complaints Act 1993* (NSW) s 31)	Ombudsman (HO Act s 80)	Same as NT, SA, Tas, Vic

Table 7.1: (cont.)

ISSUE	NT, SA, Tas, Vic	ACT	NSW	Qld	WA
Definitions of conduct that warrants disciplinary action	'Unprofessional conduct': professional conduct of lesser standard than that which might reasonably be expected of practitioner by public/professional peers; 'unsatisfactory professional performance': knowledge, skill or judgment possessed, or care exercised by, practitioner in practice of profession is below standard reasonably expected of a practitioner of equivalent level of training/experience; 'professional misconduct': unprofessional conduct that amounts to conduct that is substantially below standard reasonably expected of practitioner of equivalent training or experience, more than one instance of unprofessional conduct that, when considered together, amounts to conduct that is substantially below standard reasonably expected of practitioner of equivalent training/ experience, and conduct, whether occurring in connection with practice of profession or not, that is inconsistent with practitioner being fit and proper person to hold registration in the profession (National Law s 5)	Same as NT, SA, Tas, Vic	'Unsatisfactory professional conduct': conduct significantly below standard reasonably expected of practitioner of equivalent training/experience; contravention of this law/requirement under *Health Care Complaints Act 1993* (NSW); contravention of condition of registration or undertaking given to Board; failure to comply with decision/order of PSC or tribunal; accepting benefit for referral/ recommendation to health service provider; accepting benefit for recommending health product; offering benefit for referral or recommendation; failure to disclose pecuniary interest in giving referral/ recommendation; overservicing; permitting employed, unregistered assistant to treat patients; other improper/unethical conduct relating to practice of profession plus additional matters for medical practitioners and pharmacists; 'professional misconduct': unsatisfactory professional conduct of sufficiently serious nature to justify suspension/cancellation of registration, more than one instance of unprofessional conduct that, when considered together, amount to conduct of sufficiently serious nature to justify suspension/cancellation of registration (86a ss 139B–E)	Same as NT, SA, Tas, Vic	Same as NT, SA, Tas, Vic

| **Possible decisions of panels/ committees** | Practitioner has no case to answer and no further action is to be taken; practitioner has behaved in way that constitutes unsatisfactory professional performance or unprofessional conduct; practitioner has impairment; matter must be referred to tribunal; matter must be referred to another entity for investigation/action; student has an impairment; matter regarding student must be referred to another entity; or student has no case to answer and no further action is to be taken (National Law s 191(1)) | Same as NT, SA, Tas, Vic | Performance Review Panel can find practitioner's professional performance is unsatisfactory and impose conditions on registration, order practitioner to complete educational course, report on practice and/ or seek and take advice regarding practice management, or recommend to Council that complaint be made against practitioner if matter raises significant issue of public health/safety that requires investigation by HCCC or raises prima facie case of professional misconduct or unsatisfactory professional conduct (86a s 156C). Impaired Registrants Panel may counsel practitioner/ student, recommend they undertake counselling, recommend they agree to conditions being placed on their registration or to suspension of their registration, recommend Council take action (86a s 152I) | Same as NT, SA, Tas, Vic | Same as NT, SA, Tas, Vic |

Table 7.1: (cont.)

ISSUE	NT, SA, Tas, Vic	ACT	NSW	Qld	WA
Disciplinary powers of panels/ committees	If panel decides practitioner/student has impairment or practitioner behaved in way that constitutes unsatisfactory professional performance or unprofessional conduct, panel may impose conditions on registration; health panel can suspend registration; performance and professional standards panel can caution or reprimand the practitioner (National Law s 191(2))	Same as NT, SA, Tas, Vic	If PSC finds subject matter of complaint proved or practitioner admits to it in writing to PSC, it can caution/reprimand practitioner, direct that conditions be imposed on practitioner's registration, order practitioner to undergo medical/psychiatric treatment/counselling, order practitioner to complete educational course, report on their practice, take advice regarding practice management, impose fine, recommend suspension/cancellation of registration if satisfied practitioner does not have sufficient physical and mental capacity to practise profession (86a ss 146A–E). If practitioner is subject of inquiry before Council, Council can caution/reprimand practitioner, withhold/refund payment of fees for services that are the subject of the complaint, direct that conditions be imposed on practitioner's registration, order practitioner to undergo medical/psychiatric treatment/counselling, complete educational course, report on practice or take practice management advice, caution/ reprimand student, direct that conditions be imposed on student's registration, order that student undergo medical/psychiatric treatment/counselling or complete educational course, impose fine on practitioner if guilty of unsatisfactory professional conduct and no other order is appropriate in the public interest, recommend registration be suspended/ cancelled if practitioner does not have sufficient physical/mental capacity to practise profession or student has impairment (86a ss 148E–G)		Same as NT, SA, Tas, Vic

	Health Professional Review Tribunal (NT), South Australian Health Practitioners Tribunal, Health Practitioners Tribunal (Tas), Victorian Civil and Administrative Tribunal	ACT Civil and Administrative Tribunal	NSW Civil and Administrative Tribunal	Queensland Civil and Administrative Tribunal	State Administrative Tribunal (WA)
Tribunal that hears matters regarding registered health professional/ student					
When matter must be referred to tribunal	Board reasonably believes practitioner has behaved in way that constitutes professional misconduct or registration was improperly obtained because practitioner/ someone else gave Board false/ misleading information/document; panel established by Board requires Board to refer matter to a tribunal (because practitioner/student asks panel for matter to be referred to tribunal, or panel reasonably believes practitioner may have behaved in way that constitutes professional misconduct or registration may have been improperly obtained) (National Law ss 190, 193)	Same as NT, SA, Tas, Vic	HCCC and Council form opinion that complaint may provide grounds for suspension/cancellation of registration (unless allegations relate solely/principally to practitioner's physical/mental capacity to practise profession or student's physical/ mental capacity to undertake clinical training); Council reasonably believes practitioner has contravened conditions imposed by PSC or failed to comply with tribunal order or conditions imposed by it (86a ss 145D, 146E, 149D); PSC forms opinion that complaint may provide grounds for suspension/cancellation of registration and allegations are not related solely/ principally to practitioner's physical/mental capacity to practise profession; Council/ HCCC has referred another complaint about practitioner to tribunal (86a s 171D)	Board refers matter to ombudsman when ombudsman requests it; because Board/panel reasonably believes practitioner has behaved in way that constitutes professional misconduct or there is another ground for suspension/cancellation of practitioner's registration; panel notifies Board that matter must be referred to tribunal; panel asks Board to refer matter to tribunal and it is not matter that must be referred to ombudsman (National Law ss 193, 193A–B, as inserted by *Health Practitioner Regulation National Law Act 2009* (Qld) item 50; HO Act s 103)	Same as NT, SA, Tas, Vic

Table 7.1: (cont.)

ISSUE	NT, SA, Tas, Vic	ACT	NSW	Qld	WA
Decisions and orders tribunal can make	Practitioner has no case to answer and no further action is to be taken; practitioner has behaved in way that constitutes unsatisfactory professional performance, unprofessional conduct or professional misconduct; practitioner has impairment; practitioner's registration was improperly obtained; student has impairment or has no case to answer and no further action is to be taken (National Law ss 196(1), 197(1)). Unless tribunal decides practitioner has no case to answer, it can caution/reprimand practitioner; impose condition on practitioner's registration; require practitioner to pay fine to Board; suspend or cancel practitioner's registration; or if tribunal decides the student has an impairment, impose condition on or suspend student's registration (National Law ss 196(2), 197(2))	Same as NT, SA, Tas, Vic	If tribunal finds complaint proved or practitioner/ student admits to it in writing to tribunal, tribunal can caution/reprimand practitioner; impose conditions on practitioner's registration; order practitioner to undergo medical/ psychiatric treatment/counselling; order practitioner to complete educational course, report on practice or take practice management advice; caution/reprimand student; impose conditions on student's registration; order student to undergo medical/psychiatric treatment/counselling, or complete educational course; impose fine on practitioner where tribunal finds practitioner guilty of unsatisfactory professional conduct or professional misconduct and is satisfied that no other order is appropriate in the public interest; suspend/ cancel practitioner's registration if practitioner is not competent to practise profession, is guilty of professional misconduct, has been convicted of/made the subject of a criminal finding for an offence, and circumstances of offence render practitioner unfit in the public interest to practise profession, or practitioner is not suitable person for registration; suspend/ cancel student's registration if student has been convicted/made the subject of criminal finding for offence and student is unfit in the public interest or not suitable to undertake clinical training; tribunal must cancel practitioner's/ student's registration if they contravene critical compliance order/condition (86a ss 149A–C)	Same as NT, SA, Tas, Vic, but where practitioner is ordered to pay fine, fine is ordered to be paid to ombudsman (HO Act s 107)	Same as NT, SA, Tas, Vic

*For information on making notifications to the Australian Health Practitioner Regulation Agency, see <www.ahpra.gov.au/Notifications/aspx>.

NRAS: Advantages

The NRAS's objectives, as outlined in the National Law, are unquestionably important and its innovations, typified by measures introduced to fulfil the principal aim – 'to provide for the protection of the public by ensuring that only health practitioners who are suitably trained and qualified to practise in a competent and ethical manner are registered'[33] – help to facilitate their achievement. To confirm that registrants are and remain fit to practise, Boards check applicants' criminal history, and may check existing registrants' identities and criminal history at any time; health professionals must meet nationally consistent registration standards (which include requirements for continuing professional development, English language skills and recency of practice), codes and guidelines; applicants seeking renewal of registration must declare that they have no impairment and have met registration standards, and they must also advise of changes to their criminal history, whether any complaints have been made about them, whether there are any restrictions on their right to practise, and if there has been any withdrawal of their billing privileges.[34] By prohibiting unregistered persons from holding themselves out to be registered, the National Law assures the public that practitioners who claim to be registered are appropriately qualified and regulated.[35]

Before the NRAS, if regulatory authorities did not publish their constraints on health professionals' registration, those professionals could surreptitiously obtain unrestricted registration and employment in other Australian jurisdictions. This risk is reduced by a publicly accessible national database of up-to-date information about the status of health professionals' registration, including restrictions on practice and reprimands, and registers of health professionals whose registration has been cancelled or surrendered.[36] Boards analyse notification trends in the register to refine public safety policies.[37] Tribunals can now prohibit health professionals whose registration they cancel from providing health services, so that, for example, a deregistered psychiatrist could be precluded from practising as a counsellor.[38] The national register and national registration also support the realisation of the NRAS's objectives to develop 'a flexible, responsive and sustainable Australian health workforce' and 'facilitate workforce mobility'.[39] The NRAS has overcome the need for 'mutual recognition'; now health professionals who work across borders or in different jurisdictions, and in locum and emergency roles, only need to register once annually.[40]

---

33   National Law, above n 2, s 3(2)(a).

34   Ibid ss 38, 78–9, 134–5, 109.

35   Ibid ss 113–20; AHPRA, above n 17, 10.

36   National Law, above n 2, s 225.

37   AHPRA, above n 17, 6–7.

38   National Law, above n 2, s 196(4)(b); *Health Practitioner Regulation National Law (NSW)* Act No. 86a of 2009 (NSW) s 149C(5). In NSW, the tribunal can also make a prohibition order regarding a person who is no longer registered: *Health Practitioner Regulation National Law (NSW)* Act No. 86a of 2009 s 149C(5A), as inserted by *Health Practitioner Regulation Legislation Amendment Act 2014* (NSW) Sch 1 item 3.

39   National Law, above n 2, s 3(2)(b), (f).

40   AHPRA, above n 19, 10.

NRAS: Disadvantages

Notwithstanding these advantages, the NRAS has been criticised in official reviews, and academic and public commentary, for various reasons. These include: inadequate and inappropriate administration of the Scheme; inconsistencies in the handling of health, conduct and performance matters; problems with mandatory reporting; persisting problems with peer review of conduct; and the adjudication of disciplinary matters without adherence to the fundamental requirements of court proceedings. We now consider each of those issues in turn.

Inadequate and inappropriate administration of the NRAS

While AHPRA lauds the NRAS's capacity to 'streamline' registration and notifications processes, minimise red tape and achieve 'economies of scale',[41] evaluations have highlighted administrative problems that have plagued the NRAS, partly due to inadequate planning for its commencement. Official reviews have criticised many aspects of how the NRAS has been administered. In 2011, the Commonwealth Parliament's Senate Finance and Public Administration References Committee inquiry concluded that the NRAS's implementation was not only 'far from well managed', but 'a dismal example of ... public administration', and that AHPRA had unduly delayed renewing health professionals' registration.[42] A year later, in 2012, the Commonwealth Parliament's House of Representative's Standing Committee on Health and Ageing published a report that observed that overseas-trained doctors experienced the NRAS as opaque, inefficient and discriminatory.[43]

In 2013, two reports published in Queensland criticised the workings of the NRAS. The first was the Forrester Report, which found that AHPRA and the Medical Board of Australia's Queensland Board had tardily and inappropriately managed notifications.[44] The second was the Hunter Report, which recommended that six doctors who had been the subject of complaints to the Medical Board of Australia's Queensland Board be referred to police to determine whether or not they had committed criminal offences.[45] This led to the resignation or removal of members of that board.[46] The *Health Ombudsman Act 2013* (Qld) was subsequently passed to create a co-regulatory jurisdiction.[47] Following Queensland's lead, the Victorian Parliament's Legislative Council Legal and Social Issues Legislation Committee published a report in 2014 which recommended that Victoria establish a co-regulatory

---

41   Ibid 11.

42   Senate Finance and Public Administration References Committee, Parliament of Australia, *Inquiry into the Administration of Health Practitioner Registration by the Australian Health Practitioner Regulation Agency* (2011) 111–12, 114, 116.

43   House of Representatives Standing Committee on Health and Ageing, Parliament of Australia, *Lost in the Labyrinth: Report on the Inquiry into Registration Processes and Support for Overseas Trained Doctors* (2012) x–xi.

44   Kim Forrester, Elizabeth Davies and Jim Houston, *Chesterman Report Recommendation 2 Review Panel, Final Report* (2013) xix, xxiii, 97.

45   The Hon Lawrence Springborg, Minister for Health, 'Police Asked to Investigate Six Queensland Doctors', Media Release (31 March 2013).

46   AHPRA, above n 19, 43.

47   Kim Forrester, 'A New Beginning for Health Complaints in Queensland: The Health Ombudsman Act 2013 (Qld)' (2013) 21 *Journal of Law and Medicine* 273, 273–4.

jurisdiction as well.[48] If this does happen in Victoria, it would further undermine the original rationale for establishing the NRAS: namely, the creation of a uniform, national approach to the regulation of health professionals. Yet this rationale barely justifies the existence of the Scheme now.

Inconsistencies in handling of health, conduct and performance matters

There are significant inconsistencies in how matters regarding health professionals' health, conduct and performance are managed in different jurisdictions, and especially between jurisdictions that follow the applied laws model and those that are co-regulatory. The different processes can cause confusion and result in inconsistent experiences of regulation and varying outcomes for complainants/notifiers and health professionals.

For example, in NSW, Queensland and the ACT, complainants are likely to be involved in the resolution of matters because health complaints entities are closely involved in decision-making about health professionals' regulation.[49] In other jurisdictions, unless the Boards refer a notification to a health complaints entity to deal with, a notifier may be involved in a matter merely as a witness, as the Boards manage risk, rather than resolve complaints.[50] In addition, regulatory authorities pursue varying pathways for dealing with a complaint/notification depending on the jurisdiction in which they operate, and are permitted to take disciplinary action on different grounds from one another.

Discrepancies can also arise in the management of notifications within jurisdictions governed by Part 8 of the National Law and in processing registration matters. This is because innumerable decisions (such as whether to grant or renew registration) are made daily and locally in the NRAS, without referring in each case to how similar applications have been managed in other jurisdictions. Despite the capacity for health professions to collaborate and learn from each other, differences in their cultures and expectations also account for inconsistencies, as do the varied nature of complaints/notifications.[51]

Problems arising from mandatory reporting

Another inconsistency within the NRAS – mandatory reporting obligations – has dominated commentary about the NRAS by academics, the media and representative bodies of health professionals. Such commentary has focused less on the differences between those obligations in various jurisdictions than on their alleged potential to diminish patient safety. The Scheme extended obligations that had already been imposed on doctors in some Australian jurisdictions, including in NSW (in 2008) and Queensland (in 2009), following the Reeves,

---

48   Legislative Council Legal and Social Issues Legislation Committee, Parliament of Victoria, *Inquiry into the Performance of the Australian Health Practitioner Regulation Agency, Final Report* (2014) 134; see also Gabrielle Wolf, 'Sticking Up for Victoria? Victoria Inquires into the Performance of the Australian Health Practitioner Regulation Agency' (2014) 40(3) *Monash University Law Review* 890.

49   See *Health Practitioner Regulation National Law (ACT) Act 2010* (ACT); *Health Practitioner Regulation National Law (NSW) Act* No. 86a of 2009; *Health Ombudsman Act 2013* (Qld).

50   National Law, above n 2, s 150; AHPRA, above n 19, 137.

51   Jayne Hewitt, 'Is Whistleblowing Now Mandatory? The Impact of Mandatory Reporting Law on Trust Relationships in Health Care' (2013) 21 *Journal of Law and Medicine* 82, 86.

Patel and Khalafalla scandals. This was mainly due to concerns that health professionals, in particular doctors, were reluctant to comply with ethical codes and report colleagues' misconduct.[52] Some argue that in responding to health professionals' failure to self-regulate adequately and protect the public, mandatory reporting has appropriately prioritised patient safety over health professionals' autonomy.[53]

Yet the expansion of mandatory reporting requirements has also fuelled concern that health professionals may now be more reluctant to report suspected misconduct for fear of professional reprisal and breaching patients' confidentiality, and that such obligations may impede practitioners' collaboration by eroding mutual trust and support.[54] Certain commentators dispute that mandatory reporting can cause such problems or is open to abuse. This is because the threshold for reporting is high and health professionals can be disciplined for vexatious reports, while those who make notifications in good faith are indemnified from liability.[55] Nevertheless, health professionals may still neglect to seek help from peers regarding their own ill-health, as well as performance or conduct problems, for fear of being reported.[56] Some argue that the WA exemption from mandatory reporting for health professionals in relation to other health professionals who are their patients should apply in all jurisdictions to ensure that those 'who need support receive it'.[57] In any case, it is still unclear whether mandatory reporting enhances or erodes public protection. [58]

Persistence of peer review

Other elements of the NRAS continue the erosion of the peer review model, which had traditionally underpinned Australian health professionals' regulation. Health profession boards' community membership has increased; lay health complaints authorities are more involved in disciplinary processes, especially in the ACT, NSW and Queensland; and tribunals, whose panels include health professionals, but are independent of the Boards, are empowered to adjudicate the most serious disciplinary matters.[59] Nevertheless, in many jurisdictions, the

---

52   *Medical Practice Act 1992* (NSW) s 71A; *Medical Practitioners Registration Act 2001* (Qld) s 166; Malcolm Parker, 'Full Steam Ahead on the SS "External Regulator"? Mandatory Reporting, Professional Independence, Self-Regulation and Patient Harm' (2009) 17 *Journal of Law and Medicine* 29, 33, 35.

53   Malcolm Parker, 'Embracing the New Professionalism: Self-Regulation, Mandatory Reporting and Their Discontents' (2011) 18 *Journal of Law and Medicine* 456, 457.

54   Hewitt, above n 51, 83, 86, 98; Freckelton, above n 21, 220.

55   Marie M Bismark, Jen M Morris and Christopher Clarke, 'Mandatory Reporting of Impaired Medical Practitioners: Protecting Patients, Supporting Practitioners' (2014) 44(12a) *Internal Medicine Journal* 1165, 1167; Kim Forrester, 'Notifications and Mandatory Reporting – Two Years On' (2012) 20 *Journal of Law and Medicine* 273, 279; National Law, above n 2, s 237.

56   Roy G Beran, 'Mandatory Notification of Impaired Doctors' (2014) 44(12a) *Internal Medicine Journal* 1162, 1164; Hon Nick Goiran MLC et al., 'Mandatory Reporting of Health Professionals: The Case for a Western Australian Style Exemption for All Australian Practitioners' (2014) 22 *Journal of Law and Medicine* 209, 219.

57   Mary Langcake, 'Support or Report', *Medical Journal of Australia Insight* (16 February 2015); David Nathan, 'Mandatory Consequences', *Medical Journal of Australia Insight* (31 October 2011); Goiran et al., above n 56, 219–20.

58   Goiran et al., above n 56, 215; Marie M Bismark et al., 'Mandatory Reports of Concerns about Health, Performance and Conduct of Health Practitioners' (2014) 201(7) *Medical Journal of Australia* 399.

59   See, for example, *Victorian Civil and Administrative Tribunal Act 1998* Sch 1 Part 5AAB cl 11AJ; Thomas, above n 15, 383; Elkin, above n 19, 689; AHPRA, above n 19, 137; National Law, above n 2, s 33(4), (6).

Boards still determine which matters warrant referral to a tribunal hearing and retain other powers that affect health professionals' registration, including authority to take immediate action before an independent decision-maker considers all relevant evidence.[60] Moreover, problems identified with the peer review model may still afflict the NRAS.

The justification for delegating power to health professions to self-regulate was that their expertise made them best placed to determine standards, evaluate health professionals' conduct and discipline them.[61] Yet statutory boards mainly comprising health professionals were criticised for failing to discipline appropriately, allegedly because they protected their own, respected professionals' autonomy and/or misunderstood applicable law.[62] Their processes have also arguably contravened the separation of powers doctrine that requires different authorities to exercise legislative, executive and judicial powers respectively and keep a check on one another. The Boards continue to make the law by formulating standards, implement the law by investigating allegations of their breach, and make judgments by imposing sanctions.[63]

Lack of judicial involvement in decision-making about health professionals

It has been suggested that courts would be more appropriate arbiters of disciplinary matters than tribunals, which are not compelled to follow rules of evidence, and that apply a civil standard of proof, including in cases involving criminal allegations. In addition, they are not bound by precedent, so are free to impose divergent sanctions which, despite their stated intent, can have a punitive impact by blighting a practitioner's reputation and livelihood.[64]

The future of the NRAS

The AHWMC commissioned Kim Snowball to conduct an Independent Review of the NRAS at its three-year anniversary, as required by the Intergovernmental Agreement.[65] The Review found that stakeholders had expressed 'overwhelming support' for its introduction,[66] and Snowball made 33 recommendations to improve aspects of the Scheme. The AHWMC has acknowledged 'the significant achievements' of the NRAS that the Review highlighted.[67]

---

60   Danuta Mendelson, 'Disciplinary Powers of Medical Practice Boards and the Rule of Law' (2000) 8 *Journal of Law and Medicine* 142, 147–9.

61   Anne-Louise Carlton, 'National Models for Regulation of the Health Professions' in Ian Freckelton (ed.), *Regulating Health Practitioners* (Federation Press, 2006) 21, 27.

62   Ibid 27–8; Thomas, above n 15, 386; Parker, above n 52, 34; cf Katie Elkin et al., 'Doctors Disciplined for Professional Misconduct in Australia and New Zealand, 2000–2009' (2011) 194(9) *Medical Journal of Australia* 452, 455. Note that the authors suggest that medical boards have been willing to take action against doctors who engaged in risky behaviour, even where they did not harm patients, solely for the purpose of addressing 'quality-of-care concerns'.

63   Anthony Ogus, 'Rethinking Self-Regulation' (1995) 15 *Oxford Journal of Legal Studies* 97, 99.

64   Mendelson, above n 60, 145–6, 148–9, 151.

65   Intergovernmental Agreement, above n 3, cl 14.1; Kim Snowball, *Independent Review of the National Registration and Accreditation Scheme for Health Professions*, Final Report (December 2014) 1.

66   Snowball, above n 65, 3.

67   COAG Health Council, meeting as the Australian Health Workforce Ministerial Council, *Communique* (7 August 2015) 1.

The AHWMC has also demonstrated its openness to reforming the Scheme, accepting nine recommendations, and a further 11 in principle.[68] In addition, it has decided to implement additional changes to the NRAS even though they were not raised by the Review.[69]

Some of the AHWMC's proposed reforms have the potential to mitigate disadvantages of the NRAS. In particular, it accepted the recommendations of the Review that focused on improving the efficiency and transparency of the NRAS's administrative processes, and its communications with consumers of health professionals' services.[70] The AHWMC has also encouraged AHPRA and the Boards 'to establish mechanisms to support the development of consistent and best practice approaches to regulation'.[71] It will be critical that all the AHWMC's reforms are pursued, especially since it has now decided to include paramedics in the Scheme and is also contemplating including social workers.[72] Already criticised for its remote and extensive bureaucracy,[73] further expansion of the NRAS risks it becoming even more unwieldy.

The AHWMC also accepted the recommendations of the Review that may in practice further erode the peer review model of regulation. These involve amending the National Law to enable the AHWMC to appoint either a practitioner or a community member of a Board as its Chairperson[74] and establishing processes for the sharing of investigations and reports between the Boards, AHPRA and health complaints entities and for the Boards to refer matters to those entities for alternative dispute resolution.[75]

Notwithstanding these changes, the AHWMC has not yet meaningfully addressed concerns that health professionals' disciplinary matters are not heard by bodies that are compelled to follow the requirements of courts of record. In addition, there remain significant inconsistencies in the handling of health, conduct and performance matters within the NRAS. It appears that inconsistency, in particular, will continue to be a thorn in the side of the NRAS, especially given that NSW and Queensland are unlikely to relinquish their co-regulatory arrangements.

Although the Review also recommended that the National Law be amended so that treating health professionals in all jurisdictions share the WA exemption from mandatory reporting,[76] this was not accepted by the AHWMC at that time, but the AHWMC indicated that it will reconsider the recommendation when further research has been conducted. In any case, it could be argued that the exemption could inhibit the Boards' ability to protect the public if treating health professionals do not report those of their patients who pose a risk to the community.

---

68   Snowball, above n 65, 5–9; COAG Health Council, above n 67, 3.

69   See COAG Health Council, meeting as the Australian Health Workforce Ministerial Council, *Communique* (8 April 2016).

70   Snowball, above n 65, 6, 8; COAG Health Council, above n 67, 4, 6, 11.

71   COAG Health Council, above n 69.

72   Ibid.

73   Kerry Breen, 'National Registration Scheme at 5 Years: Not What It Promised' (2016) *Australian Health Review* <www.publish.csiro.au/paper/AH15187.htm>.

74   Snowball, above n 65, 8; COAG Health Council, above n 67, 5.

75   Snowball, above n 65, 6; COAG Health Council, above n 67, 4.

76   Snowball, above n 65, 6.

Conclusion

This chapter has provided an overview of the regulation of health professionals in Australia under the NRAS. It analysed how the NRAS was implemented and how it operates at present, focusing in particular on the regulation of doctors. The chapter evaluated the NRAS by considering its advantages and criticisms of it. Problems identified with the administration of the NRAS are likely to be resolved in the medium term, but substantive elements of the NRAS will probably draw ongoing criticism. A major challenge for AHPRA, the Boards and the AHWMC will continue to be how best to instil greater confidence in the Scheme amongst key stakeholders.

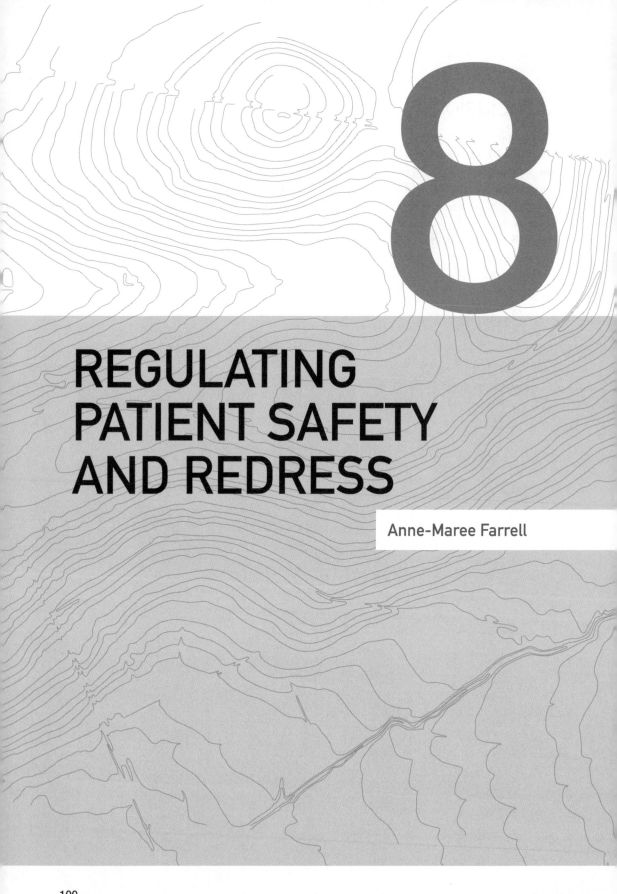

8

REGULATING PATIENT SAFETY AND REDRESS

Anne-Maree Farrell

Introduction

Over twenty years ago, a landmark study which examined the extent of (preventable) harm suffered by patients in the Australian health system was published.[1] The findings from the study led to a series of governance initiatives at both state and Commonwealth levels to address the issue as part of an emerging national agenda to enhance safety and quality in healthcare. The first part of this chapter provides an overview of that agenda, focusing on key terms, institutions and recent initiatives. The second part examines what patients want when things go wrong in healthcare provision, as well as what redress options may be open to them. The final part provides an overview of a range of redress options that are available, before briefly reviewing select reform in the area.[2]

The governance of safety and quality in healthcare in Australia

Key terms

By way of background, it is useful to define some of the key terms that are often used in this area. The term 'safety and quality in healthcare' refers to a wider health system agenda in which aspects of safety and quality may be measured in a number of ways. Broadly speaking, the term means the extent to which a health service organisation produces a desired outcome. More specifically, it can be used to assess whether a health system is performing at an appropriate level to improve individual and population health and wellbeing.[3]

In this chapter, we are particularly interested in 'patient safety', which has been defined as:

> The reduction of risk of unnecessary harm associated with health care to an acceptable minimum. An acceptable minimum refers to the collective notions of current knowledge, resources available and the context in which care was delivered, weighed against the risk of non-treatment or other treatment.[4]

Adverse events and outcomes occur when there is unsafe or poor quality healthcare. 'Adverse events' are defined as incidents in which harm resulted to a person receiving healthcare. They include healthcare-associated infections; problems with medication and medical devices; inappropriate use of blood products; falls resulting in injuries in healthcare settings; and problems with medication and medical devices. Some of these

---

1 Ross Wilson et al., 'The Quality in Australian Health Care Study' (1995) 163(9) *Medical Journal of Australia* 458.

2 When the term 'patient' is used in this chapter, it includes patients' families, patients' advocates, and substituted decision-makers.

3 Australian Institute of Health and Welfare (AIHW), *Definitions of Safety and Quality in Healthcare* <www.aihw.gov.au/sqhc-definitions>.

4 World Health Organization (WHO), *The International Classification for Patient Safety* (WHO, 2009) 15.

adverse events are preventable.[5] An 'adverse outcome' is an outcome of an illness or its treatment that has not met the expectations of either clinicians or patients for improvement or cure.[6]

A commitment to patient safety, as well as minimising or avoiding adverse events and outcomes, is important in promoting a 'patient-centred' approach in healthcare provision. It is an approach that is said to contribute to the embedding of practices – and changes – in professional culture that enhance safety and quality in healthcare.[7] It involves patients being treated with dignity and respect and ensuring that there is information sharing between patients and their treating health professionals. This is in addition to encouraging participation and collaboration in healthcare processes where patients are able, and wish, to do so. It is argued that there are important tangible benefits associated with promoting such an approach, which include greater patient satisfaction, increased adherence to treatment regimens and better health outcomes overall.[8]

The role of law

So where do we position the role of law in promoting patient safety? When we speak about law in this context, we use a broad definition which includes legislation, regulation, guidelines and standards, in addition to the civil and criminal law. Over the past decade there has been a growing appreciation that patient safety should not be left entirely to health systems, institutions or providers. Instead, law is seen as having a positive role to play in preventing and dealing with the consequences of (preventable) adverse events, as well as contributing more broadly to the safety and quality of healthcare.[9] This has led to the increased use of a range of regulatory frameworks to provide oversight, accountability and supervision.[10] It is important to note that there is no national patient safety legislation per se, given the Commonwealth's limited constitutional remit within the field of health.[11] Nevertheless, the law does interact in various ways with the promotion of patient safety and its role has grown in recent decades in the wake of a range of Commonwealth and state/territory initiatives in the area.

---

5   AIHW, *Hospital Performance: Adverse Events Treated in Hospitals* (2011–12) <www.aihw.gov.au/ haag11-12/adverse-events>.

6   Australian Commission on Safety and Quality in Health Care (ACSQHC), *Australian Open Disclosure Framework: Better Communication, A Better Way to Care*, 1 <www.safetyandquality.gov .au/wpcontent/uploads/2013/03/Australian-Open-Disclosure-FrameworkFeb-2014.pdf>.

7   Tessa Richards et al., 'Time to Deliver Patient Centred Care' (2015) 350 *British Medical Journal* h530.

8   Moira Stewart, 'Towards a Global Definition of Patient-Centred Care' (2001) 322 *British Medical Journal*, 444, 445.

9   Donella Piper et al., 'The Role of the Law in Communicating Patient Safety' in Rick Iedema et al. (eds), *Communicating Quality and Safety in Healthcare* (CUP, 2015) 317.

10   Jocelyn Downie et al., *Patient Safety Law: From Silos to Systems*, Final Report (Health Canada, 2006) iv; see, generally, Judith Healy, *Improving Health Care Safety and Quality: Reluctant Regulators* (Ashgate, 2011).

11   See Chapter 6 for a detailed discussion of the Commonwealth's limited constitutional powers in health.

Institutional arrangements

In 1995, a landmark study known as the Quality in Australian Health Care Study (QAHCS) was published. It examined the rate of (preventable) adverse events in healthcare settings in Australia.[12] The findings from the QAHCS study revealed that 16.6 per cent of people admitted to hospitals in the study sample experienced an adverse event associated with their healthcare.[13] Just over half these events (51 per cent) were considered to be preventable. Subsequent re-evaluation of the data showed that this estimate was too high and the figure was probably closer to 10 per cent, which was comparable with findings in other countries.[14]

In the wake of the QAHCS study, Australian governments embarked upon a series of initiatives to improve safety and quality in healthcare. At Commonwealth level, this included establishing the Australian Council for Safety and Quality in Health Care (2000–2005), which was later replaced by the Australian Commission on Safety and Quality in Health Care (ACSQHC).[15] Various government agencies and departmental units dealing with quality and safety in healthcare have also been established at state/territory level.[16]

As part of its remit, the ACSQHC has developed the Australian Safety and Quality Framework for Health Care, which was endorsed by Health Ministers in 2010. The Framework has three core principles: care is consumer-centred, driven by information, and organised for safety. It has 21 areas for action that all participants in the health system can use to improve safety and quality in healthcare settings.[17] In addition, the ACSQHC has published ten national quality and safety standards as part of national accreditation processes for health service organisations.[18] As part of the National Health Reform Agreement, which was adopted by the Council of Australian Governments (COAG) in 2011,[19] funding arrangements for the Australian health system are linked to improved quality outcomes in healthcare, with support from the Independent Hospital Pricing Authority, the National Health Funding Body and the National Health Performance Authority.[20] In addition to the creation of these framework agreements and key institutions, a number of important policies have been developed to promote safety and quality in healthcare at a systems level, a select number of which are considered below.

---

12   The QAHCS study was mirrored in a range of other countries, in lockstep with a growing interest, from the 1990s onwards, in dealing with adverse events in healthcare. For an overview, see Anne-Maree Farrell, Sarah Devaney and Amber Dar, *No-Fault Compensation Schemes for Medical Injury: A Review*, No Fault Compensation Review Group, Report and Recommendations, Volume II, February 2010, <www.scotland.gov.uk/Resource/0039/00394407.pdf>.

13   Wilson et al., above n 1.

14   See Ross Wilson et al., WHO Patient Safety EMRO/AFRO Working Group, 'Patient Safety in Developing Countries: Retrospective Estimation of Scale and Nature of Harm to Patients in Hospital' (2012) 344 *British Medical Journal* e832.

15   For an overview of ACSQHC, see *National Health Reform Act 2011* (Cth) ch 2.

16   For example, see Department of Health Patient Safety Unit (Qld), Commission for Hospital Improvement (Vic), Clinical Excellence Commission (NSW), Office of Quality and Safety in Healthcare (WA).

17   Australian Safety and Quality Framework for Health Care <www.safetyandquality.gov.au/wp-content/uploads/2012/01/32296-Australian-SandQ-Framework1.pdf>.

18   ACSQHC, *Information for Health Service Organisations*, <www.safetyandquality.gov.au/our-work/accreditation-and-the-nsqhs-standards/information-for-health-service-organisations/#Who-needs-to-implement-the-NSQHS-Standards>.

19   COAG, *National Health Reform Agreement*, <www.federalfinancialrelations.gov.au/content/npa/health_reform/national-agreement.pdf>.

20   John Hamilton et al., 'After the Quality in Australian Health Care Study, What Happened?' (2014) 201(1) *Medical Journal of Australia* 23; see also *National Health Reform Act 2011* (Cth).

Open disclosure

A key policy initiative has been to promote open disclosure of adverse events. The key elements of open disclosure are: (1) an expression of regret; (2) a factual explanation of what happened; (3) a description of the potential consequences; and (4) the steps that are being taken to manage the event and prevent recurrence.[21] The Australian Open Disclosure (OD) Standard was published in 2003. The aim of the Standard was to establish a framework that could be used by health service organisations to manage adverse events, as well as to ensure open communication about such events with patients. A pilot program which involved 40 facilities in seven jurisdictions, including the private sector, was undertaken. It examined the development of open disclosure policies, protocols and tools within those jurisdictions and participating facilities.[22]

Difficulties have been experienced in implementing the Standard effectively. They have included ongoing uncertainty about how open disclosure interacts with existing legal, medical indemnity insurance and quality assurance requirements, as well as with statutory protections for apologies which have been adopted as part of civil liability reform.[23] Health professionals, in particular doctors, have expressed concern about the threat of medical negligence litigation in the event that they act in accordance with the Standard.[24] This is so notwithstanding their ethical obligation to be open and honest with their patients.[25] Research conducted into patients' experiences with open disclosure revealed that many were unhappy with the way in which health professionals and institutions attempted to engage with the Standard. A range of areas were identified as being in need of improvement, including better communication and greater sensitivity to the needs of individual patients and their families.[26]

In 2012, the ACSQHC published its review of the OD Standard. The Review found that although the Standard remained relevant, it would benefit from 'further refinement'. This included encouraging better training of health professionals in relation to open disclosure; increasing patient involvement in open disclosure; and providing resources to assist in the successful and sustained implementation of the Standard.[27] Following the Review, the ACSQHC published an updated and revised version of the OD Standard in 2013, which is now known as the Australian Open Disclosure Framework.[28]

---

21   ACSQHC, *Open Disclosure Standard Review Report* (June 2012) <www.safetyandquality.gov.au/wp-content/uploads/2013/05/Open-Disclosure-Standard-Review-Report-Final-Jun2012.pdf>.

22   See Rick Iedema et al., 'The National Open Disclosure Pilot: Evaluation of a Policy Implementation Initiative' (2008) 188 *Medical Journal of Australia* 397.

23   David Studdert and Mark Richardson, 'Legal Aspects of Open Disclosure: A Review of Australian Law' (2010) 193(5) *Medical Journal of Australia* 273.

24   David Studdert et al., 'Legal Aspects of Open Disclosure II: Attitudes of Health Professionals – Findings from a National Survey' (2010) 193(6) *Medical Journal of Australia* 351.

25   Medical Board of Australia, *Good Medical Practice: A Code of Conduct for Doctors in Australia*, para 3.10.

26   Rick Iedema et al., 'Patients' and Family Members' Views on How Clinicians Enact and How They Should Enact Incident Disclosure: The "100 Patient Stories" Qualitative Study' (2011) 343 *British Medical Journal* d4423.

27   ACSQHC, above n 21, 4.

28   ACSQHC, *Australian Open Disclosure Framework: Better Communication, A Better Way to Care* (2013) <www.safetyandquality.gov.au/wp-content/uploads/2013/03/Australian-Open-Disclosure-FrameworkFeb-2014.pdf>.

Australian Charter of Healthcare Rights

The Australian Charter of Healthcare Rights sets out the rights of patients (and others) who use the Australian health system. Following stakeholder consultation, the Charter was endorsed by Australian Health Ministers in 2008. The overarching objective of the Charter is to embed patients' rights to safe and high quality healthcare in the Australian health system. Guiding principles set out in the Charter recognise the right of access to healthcare as essential for the Charter to be meaningful. This is in addition to affirming the Australian government's commitment to relevant international human rights obligations in the area,[29] as well as respect for cultural differences. Specific rights include access, safety, respect, communication, participation and privacy, as well as the right of patients to comment on their care and to have their concerns addressed.[30] Given that the Charter is not a legally binding instrument, however, it remains largely aspirational.

Patient safety education

In 2005, the Australian Health Ministers endorsed the Australian Patient Safety Education Framework (APSEF). This framework sets out the knowledge, skills and behaviours required by health professionals and other staff in the area of patient safety.[31] One of the underlying rationales for the development of the APSEF was the realisation that health professionals had not been properly educated to deal with the issue.[32] Traditionally, patient safety teaching and curricula were designed for particular groups of health professionals, covering adverse event reporting, minimising falls and medical errors. In contrast, the NPSEF places the patient at the centre of healthcare provision and identifies all the competencies a health worker requires, irrespective of their position or role in an organisation.[33] Although patient safety education and training now form part of health education programs and curricula, questions have been raised as to the extent to which this has been translated effectively into healthcare practice.[34]

Patient redress

Having examined key aspects of the national safety and quality in healthcare agenda, we now turn to examining the options that are available to patients when things go wrong in healthcare provision. This includes where patients suffer harm resulting from an adverse event which may have been preventable. It also includes patient concerns about a lack of respect or loss of dignity resulting from poor communication and/or misunderstandings about diagnosis, treatment and care between patients and health professionals and health service organisations.

29   See Chapter 5 for a discussion of the relationship between health and human rights law, which also includes an examination of Australia's human rights law.

30   ACSQHC, *Australian Charter of Healthcare Rights* <www.safetyandquality.gov.au/wp-content/uploads/2012/01/Charter-PDf.pdf>.

31   ACSQHC, *Australian Patient Safety Education Framework* <www.safetyandquality.gov.au/wp-content/uploads/2012/01/framework0705.pdf>.

32   Merrilyn Walton, 'Responding to Patient Harm: Patient Safety Initiatives in Australia' in John Tingle and Pippa Bark (eds), *Patient Safety, Law Policy and Practice* (Routledge, 2011) 225, 227.

33   Merrilyn Walton et al., 'Developing a National Patient Safety Education Framework for Australia' (2006) 15(6) *Quality and Safety in Health Care* 437.

34   Walton, above n 32, 228–9.

When patients suffer harm as a result of a (preventable) adverse event in healthcare provision, findings from empirical research have shown that patients' concerns or grievances are an 'often complex and overlapping mix of concerns about communication breakdown, poor staff attitudes, inadequate general care and generally feeling disempowered'.[35] What is also clear is that, in many cases, patients are reluctant to pursue available redress options, even where they have grounds to do so.[36] When they do decide to take action, such research has also revealed that what patients most often want is a 'redress package': appropriate explanations and apologies; adequate financial compensation; health professionals being held to account for what happened; and institutional lesson learning so that what happened to them does not happen to other patients.[37] In the sections that follow, we examine some key redress options available to patients.

Healthcare complaints process

A patient may lodge a formal complaint about the problems or harm they experienced in healthcare provision. Australian state and territory governments have established a range of health complaints entities (HCEs) (colloquially referred to as Commissions) to deal with healthcare complaints made about health professionals and health service providers/organisations.[38] In the first instance, it is suggested that patients seek to resolve their complaints informally and directly with the health professional or health service organisation concerned. In turn, the latter should ideally respond in an open and responsive manner in line with the OD Framework (see earlier).

If this does not resolve the matter to the patient's satisfaction, a formal complaint can be made to the relevant state/territory HCE. Although there are differences in approach among the HCEs, in general terms, after a complaint is received from a patient, HCEs must determine whether there are recognised legislative grounds for the complaint. If not, it will be rejected. If the complaint is within the HCE's legislative remit, then there are a range of options open to HCEs regarding the investigation, conciliation processes between parties, and requirements regarding reporting and outcomes resulting from the complaint.[39] Patients can also make what is called a voluntary 'notification' to the Australian Health Practitioner Regulation

35   Frank Stephen et al., *A Study of Medical Negligence Claiming in Scotland*, Research Findings No. 113/2012, Government Social Research, Scotland <www.scotland.gov.uk/Resource/0039/00394437 .pdf>.

36   See Alexy Buck et al., 'Do Citizens Know How to Deal with Legal Issues? Some Empirical Insights' (2008) 27(4) *Journal of Social Policy* 661, 671–3, 678.

37   See Charles Vincent et al., 'Why Do People Sue Doctors? A Study of Patients and Relatives Taking Legal Action' (1994) 343 *The Lancet* 1609; Rick Iedema and Donella Piper, 'Do Patients Want and Expect Compensation Following Harm?' (2013) 116 *Precedent* 48.

38   Health Services Commissioner (ACT); Commissioner for Health and Community Services Complaints (NT); Health and Community Services Complaints Commissioner (SA); Health Complaints Commissioner (Tas); Health Complaints Commissioner (Vic); Health and Disability Services Complaints Office (WA). In NSW, healthcare complaints are dealt with by the Health Care Complaints Commission (HCCC) and a range of Councils (see Health Professional Councils Authority (HPCA)). In Queensland, healthcare complaints are dealt with by the Health Ombudsman.

39   For an overview of HCEs' functions, powers and responsibilities, see their governing legislation: *Human Rights Commission Act 2005* (ACT); *Health Care Complaints Act 1993* (NSW) and *Health Practitioner Regulation National Law (NSW)* Act No. 86a of 2009; *Health Ombudsman Act 2013* (Qld); *Health and Community Services Complaints Act 1998* (NT); *Health and Community Services Complaints Act 2004* (SA); *Health Complaints Act 1995* (Tas); *Health Complaints Act 2016* (Vic); *Health Services (Conciliation and Review) Act 1995* (WA).

Agency (AHPRA) about a registered health professional under the National Registration and Accreditation Scheme (NRAS). AHPRA can only respond to such notifications if they fall within the grounds set out in its governing legislation (*National Law*).[40]

Where there is an unresolved complaint against a health professional, different approaches may be taken depending on whether they are registered or unregistered. As outlined in Chapter 7, further discussions may need to take place between HCEs and the AHPRA where the complaint involves a registered health professional who comes under the Agency's remit.[41] If the complaint is referred to the AHPRA, it may be considered further by the relevant National Board for the health professional in question.[42] In relation to unregistered health practitioners, the AHPRA can also investigate the behaviour of non-registered health professionals, if it has been reported that they are breaking the National Law.[43] There are also a number of Australian states that have adopted Codes of Conduct in relation to unregistered health practitioners. Where this is the case, HCEs may deal with and investigate complaints made by patients directly.[44]

Recent research has shown that it is generally not happenstance as to whether health professionals find themselves subject to complaints by patients. Instead, it is clear that certain specialties, as well as certain doctors, are over-represented in terms of complaints made against them. For example, in research published on complaints data from private practice in Victoria, approximately 1 per cent of health professionals in this sector accounted for nearly 20 per cent of all complaints made.[45] In a published review of nearly 19,000 formal healthcare complaints lodged against doctors in Australia between 2000 and 2011, it was found that 'approximately three per cent of practicing doctors accounted for half of all complaints. The number of prior complaints doctors had experienced was a particularly strong predictor of a short-term risk of further complaints' being made against them.[46] It has been suggested that this type of data could be used to drive prevention programs for health professionals, as well as to address patient dissatisfaction on a system-wide basis.[47]

40   *Health Practitioner Regulation National Law Act 2009* (Qld) (National Law) s 144. For further information about such grounds, see AHPRA, *Notifications and Outcomes* <www.ahpra.gov.au/Notifications.aspx>.

41   AHPRA has a Memorandum of Understanding (MOU) with HCEs (apart from NSW and now Qld) in relation to the handling of healthcare complaints pursuant to Division 5, Part 8 of the *Health Practitioner Regulation National Law Act 2009* (Qld)) (National Law), see <www.ahpra.gov.au/Notifications/About-notifications/Working-with-health-complaints-entities/Health-complaints-entities>. NSW and Queensland have their own arrangements for the handling of healthcare complaints: see <www.ahpra.gov.au/Notifications/What-is-a-notification.aspx#nsw-process>.

42   AHPRA, *National Boards* <www.ahpra.gov.au/National-Boards.aspx>. For further details of how the Boards operate, see Chapter 7.

43   AHPRA, *Notifications and Outcomes* <www.ahpra.gov.au/Notifications.aspx>.

44   *Public Health Regulation 2012* (NSW) Sch 3; *Health and Community Services Complaints Regulations 2005* (SA) Sch 2; *Health Complaints Act 2016* (Vic) Sch 2. In Queensland, the National Code of Conduct of Conduct for Health Care Workers (National Code) has been adopted, see *Health Ombudsman Regulation 2014* (Qld) s 5, *Health Ombudsman Act 2013* (Qld) s 288. The terms of the Code were endorsed by COAG, with a view to strengthening the regulation of unregistered health practitioners in Australian states and territories, For an overview, see Queensland Department of Health <www.health.qld.gov.au/system-governance/policies-standards/national-code-ofconduct/default.asp>.

45   Marie Bismark et al., 'Prevalence and Characteristics of Complaint-Prone Doctors in Private Practice in Victoria' (2011) 195(1) *Medical Journal of Australia* 25.

46   Marie Bismark et al., 'Identification of Doctors At Risk of Recurrent Complaints: A National Study of Healthcare Complaints in Australia' (2013) 22 *BMJ Quality and Safety in Healthcare* 532.

47   Ibid.

Civil legal proceedings

Patients who have suffered harm through preventable (negligent) adverse events in health-care provision may also elect to investigate and, where appropriate, pursue civil claims in the courts for financial compensation against their treating health professionals and/or health service organisations. The circumstances in which claims in medical negligence can be brought by injured patients are examined in more detail in Chapter 11. Patients who have suffered harm as a result of the use of products in the provision of healthcare, such as medicines or medical devices,[48] may also be able to bring claims under the Australian Consumer Law (ACL). The ACL creates a strict liability regime for products which are considered to have 'safety defects', and imposes statutory guarantees on manufacturers regarding their products. Note that fair trading legislation provides for the application of the ACL in all Australian states/territories.[49]

The coronial system

In general terms, Australian coroners have the power to investigate a range of 'reportable deaths' that are unexpected, unnatural or violent.[50] A range of approaches have been taken by Australian states and territories in relation to 'reportable deaths' that occur in healthcare settings.[51] They can be divided into three categories: (1) where such deaths occur as a result of an unexpected outcome of a health-related operation or procedure;[52] (2) where the death occurred as a result of an anaesthetic;[53] and (3) where the death was caused by or temporally associated with an operation or procedure.[54] There are also differences in relation to the elements of the offences relating to a failure to report such death, as well as in the penalties for breaching reporting obligations set out in the relevant legislation.[55]

Coroners investigate these types of 'reportable deaths' and in certain circumstances proceed to an inquest to determine the cause of death, as well as how and why the death occurred. Relatives of deceased patients can attend and be legally represented at such

---

48   Note that where patients suffer adverse events through taking medication or following the administration of a vaccine, a report may be submitted to the Therapeutic Goods Administration (TGA) by patients or treating health professional. For an overview of the role and powers of the TGA in this area, see Department of Health, *Therapeutic Goods Administration, Reporting Medicine and Vaccine Adverse Events* <www.tga.gov.au/reporting-medicine-and-vaccine-adverse-events#who>.

49   The ACL is contained in Schedule 2 of the *Competition and Consumer Act 2010* (Cth). 'Safety defects' are defined in ACL, Chapter 1, s 9; for a full list of statutory guarantees, see ACL, Chapter 3, Part 3.2, Div 1; a broad definition is given to 'manufacturer', see ACL, Chapter 1, s 7. For a more detailed overview of the ACL, see Commonwealth of Australia, *Australian Consumer Law* <www.consumerlaw.gov.au>.

50   For a general overview, see David Ranson and Ian Freckleton, *Death Investigation and the Coroner's Inquest* (OUP, 2006).

51   This draws on the three categories identified by Sarah Middleton and Michael Buist, 'The Coronial Reporting of Medical-Setting Deaths: A Legal Analysis of the Variation in Australian Jurisdictions' (2014) 37 *Melbourne University Law Review* 699.

52   *Coroners Act 2009* (NSW) s 6(1)(e) and (3); *Coroners Act 2003* (Qld) ss 8(3)(d) and 10AA; *Coroners Act 2008* (Vic) ss 3(1) and 4(2)(b).

53   *Coroners Act* (NT) s 12(1)(a)(v) and (vi); *Coroners Act 1995* (Tas) s 3(a)(v); *Coroners Act 1996* (WA) s 3(b), (c).

54   *Coroners Act 1997* (ACT) s 13(1)(c), (d) and (4); *Coroners Act 2003* (SA) s 3(1)(d)(i), (ii).

55   Middleton and Buist, above n 51, 724–32.

inquests.[56] The findings from inquests may lead to recommendations by coroners aimed at reducing preventable 'reportable deaths', so as to promote public health and safety and the administration of justice. For example, in Victoria such recommendations can be directed towards any public authority or entity, with a three-month time limit for responses, which are then published on the coronial website.[57] In NSW, Ministers and agencies also publish their responses to coronial recommendations online. [58]

The criminal law

There are diverse ways in which the criminal law may intersect with episodes of unsafe and poor quality healthcare practice.[59] One example involves the criminalisation of (grossly) negligent healthcare practice by health professionals resulting in the death of their patients, often referred to as 'medical manslaughter'. A relatively recent high-profile case involved Dr Jayant Patel, the Head of Surgery at Bundaberg Hospital between 2003 and 2005. Although initially convicted of manslaughter in relation to the deaths of three of his patients, and grievous bodily harm in relation to another patient, Patel successfully appealed his conviction and it was subsequently announced that there would be no retrial.[60] For families who lost loved ones as a result of being under the care of Dr Patel, the use of the criminal law in this instance failed to address their desire for justice and accountability.[61]

As has been noted in other jurisdictions, this case only served to highlight the difficulties that persist in the prosecution of and the obtaining of convictions against health professionals for medical manslaughter.[62] Various reasons have been put forward for this state of affairs. They include difficulties in separating recklessness from (gross) negligence in order to ground criminal liability;[63] whether there should be a subjective or objective assessment of the knowledge and/or conduct of the accused;[64] and how best to define the circumstances in which the standard of gross negligence will be satisfied in order to obtain a conviction.[65] It begs the question of whether the criminal jurisdiction is an appropriate forum in which to deal with sub-standard performance on the part of health professionals. Although it may have

---

56   Reference should be made to individual state and territory coroners' websites for the processes to be followed in relation to the conduct and outcomes of inquests.

57   Coroners Court of Victoria, *The Coroners Process: Information for Family and Friends* <www.mck .org.au/resources/Coroner's%20Process> 45–6.

58   NSW Government, Department of Justice <www.justice.nsw.gov.au/lsb/Pages/coronial-recommendations.aspx>.

59   See Danielle Griffiths and Andrew Sanders (eds), *Medicine Crime and Society, Bioethics, Medicine and the Criminal Law, Vol. II* (CUP, 2013).

60   David Carter, 'Correcting the Record: Australian Prosecutions for Manslaughter in the Medical Context' (2015) 22(3) *Journal of Law and Medicine* 588, 589.

61   Ibid.

62   Oliver Quick, 'Prosecuting "Gross" Medical Negligence: Manslaughter Discretion and the Crown Prosecution Service' (2006) 33 *Journal of Law and Society* 421.

63   Ian Dobinson, 'Medical Manslaughter' (2009) 28(1) *University of Queensland Law Journal* 101.

64   Quick, above n 62.

65   Margaret Brazier and Neil Allen, 'Criminalising Medical Malpractice' in Charles Erin and Suzanne Ost (eds), *The Criminal Justice System and Health Care* (OUP, 2007) 17.

symbolic effect,[66] it is not clear on the available evidence that invoking the criminal law either operates as a deterrent to health professionals or contributes to safer healthcare practice.[67]

Options for reform

In the third part of this chapter, we briefly consider various options that have been put forward regarding the reform of patient redress arising out of harm suffered in healthcare provision. One that has attracted enduring interest has been the proposal that state-sponsored administrative schemes for medical injury be established to process claims for financial compensation whether on their own, or as part of a wider redress package. Those in favour of such schemes have argued that their advantages include widened eligibility, lower costs, greater efficiency and the enhancement of systems learning for patient safety. This is in stark contrast to the current tort-based system for medical negligence.[68] In contrast, other commentators have challenged whether such schemes are sufficiently responsive to what patients say they want when harm is suffered in healthcare provision (see earlier). Additional concerns include whether the schemes operate in a fair and just manner in terms of access, eligibility and claims adjudication; whether pre-existing legal entitlements to bring civil claims should be removed or preserved; and what evidence is available to show that they actually promote professional and systems learning to enhance patient safety, rather than just having the potential to do so.[69]

Various approaches to the design of such schemes have been proposed. These include patient redress schemes for low value claims;[70] 'health courts' which adopt a broader standard for eligibility than negligence and more explicitly contribute to embedding a patient safety culture;[71] and the much-discussed option of a 'no-fault' scheme for medical injury which provides financial compensation for harm caused to patients. It has been suggested that the key principles that should guide the design of such schemes include accessibility, fairness, appropriateness of compensation, timeliness of adjudication and cost effectiveness.[72] Examples of schemes that have been established include the New Zealand Accident Compensation Scheme, which covers accidental personal injury;[73] no-fault administrative schemes for medical injury in the Nordic countries; and birth-related neurological injury schemes in Virginia and Florida in the US.[74]

---

66   Karen Yeung and Jeremy Horder, 'How Can the Criminal Law Support the Provision of Quality in Healthcare?' (2014) 23 *BMJ Quality and Safety* 519.

67   Alan Merry and Alexander McCall Smith, *Errors, Medicine and the Law* (CUP, 2001) 78.

68   David Weisbrot and Kerry Breen, 'A No-Fault Compensation System for Medical Injury is Long Overdue' (2012) 197(5) *Medical Journal of Australia* 296.

69   Anne-Maree Farrell, 'No-Fault Compensation for Medical Injury: Principles, Practice and Prospects for Reform' in Pamela Ferguson and Graeme Laurie (eds), *Inspiring a Medico-Legal Revolution: Essays in Honour of Sheila McLean* (Ashgate, 2015) 155–70.

70   Such a scheme was proposed but never implemented in England, but did happen in Wales. See National Health Service (Concerns, Complaints and Redress Arrangements) (Wales) Regulations 2011. For a review of the Wales redress scheme, see Mari Rosser, 'The Welsh NHS Redress Arrangements – Are They Putting Things Right for Welsh Patients?' (2015) 20(6) *Clinical Risk* 144.

71   See Michelle Mello et al., '"Health Courts" and Accountability for Patient Safety' (2006) 84(3) *Milbank Quarterly* 459.

72   No Fault Compensation Review Group, *Report and Recommendations, Vol. 1* (Scottish Government, 2011) para. 5.2 <www.gov.scot/Topics/Health/Policy/No-Fault-Compensation>.

73   See NZ Accident Compensation Scheme <www.acc.co.nz>.

74   For an overview of such schemes, see Farrell et al., above n 12.

Since the 1970s, the creation of no-fault schemes has been periodically on the political agenda in Australia, leading to reforms in the case of injuries caused in the workplace and as a result of motor vehicle accidents.[75] Greater awareness of the extent of harm suffered by patients in healthcare provision, as well as the medical indemnity insurance 'crisis' that emerged in Australia in the early 2000s,[76] led to renewed interest in the creation of no-fault schemes for medical injury.[77] In 2011, the Productivity Commission recommended that a National Injury Insurance Scheme (NIIS) be developed, in conjunction with the National Disability Insurance Scheme (NDIS), which would include 'catastrophic injuries caused by four types of accidents: motor vehicle accidents, workplace accidents, medical accidents and general accidents (occurring in the home or community)'.[78] The Commonwealth and state/territory governments are currently working towards developing the NIIS as a feder-ated model of separate, state-based no-fault schemes to provide lifetime care and support for those who have suffered a catastrophic injury. The current focus is on establishing such schemes in the case of motor vehicle accidents, with a view to extending them to include 'medical treatment injuries' over time.[79]

Conclusion

This chapter has explored patient safety and redress in Australia. The first part examined key aspects of the national safety and quality in healthcare agenda, including initiatives such as open disclosure, patient rights and patient safety education. While there is clearly a political commitment to promoting a national approach to the governance of safety and quality in healthcare, the lack of national patient safety legislation and the diverse approaches adopted at state/territory level makes this difficult to achieve in practice. The second part examined options for patient redress, which included making formal complaints and taking civil legal action, in addition to exploring the role of the coronial jurisdiction and the criminal law where patient deaths occur in healthcare settings. In the final part, select reforms in the area of patient redress were reviewed. Based on what injured patients have said they want in terms of redress, there is a need for a comprehensive approach to be taken. This should be underpinned by a commitment to access to justice, appropriate compensation and the provi-sion of explanations and apologies, combined with professional and institutional account-ability and lesson learning.

---

75   For a historical overview, see Mark Robinson, *Accident Compensation in Australia: No-Fault Schemes* (Legal Books, 1987).

76   See Talina Drabsch, *Medical Negligence: An Update*, Briefing Paper 0/04 (NSW Parliament Library Research Service, 2004).

77   Angus Corbett, 'Regulating Compensation for Injuries Associated with Medical Error' (2006) 28 *Sydney Law Review* 259.

78   Productivity Commission Inquiry Report, *Disability Care and Support*, No. 54, 31 July 2011 (Commonwealth of Australia, 2011) chs 17–19.

79   Australian Government, The Treasury, NIIS, *Supporting People with Catastrophic Injury* <www .treasury.gov.au/Policy-Topics/PeopleAndSociety/National-Injury-Insurance-Scheme>. For an overview of discussions between Australian governments on the NIIS, see <www.treasury.gov.au/ Access-to-Information/DisclosureLog2013/1318>. For an opposing view which questions whether the NIIS will work in practice to deliver appropriate redress, see the Australian Lawyers Alliance, NIIS <www.lawyersalliance.com.au/ourwork/the-national-injury-insurance-scheme>.

PART III

CONTEXT

PATIENTS, DOCTORS AND HEALTHCARE

9

CONSENT TO MEDICAL TREATMENT

John Devereux

Introduction

It is essential that, before a doctor performs any treatment on a patient, the doctor first obtains a valid consent to do so. Treatment performed in the absence of consent gives rise to actions in various areas of the law. Australian common law has traditionally narrowed the remit of contractual and intentional tort actions. This has meant that, on the whole, a patient on whom treatment was performed without consent was more likely to sue in negligence than in contract or intentional torts. Recent legislative enactments restricting the legal action in negligence have led to renewed interest in the applicability of contract and intentional tort actions.[1] While actions in medical negligence are examined in more detail in Chapter 11, this chapter aims to provide an overview and understanding of the role and operation of consent in contract and intentional torts.

The first part of this chapter outlines some general principles of consent and how this operates in contract law. The second part provides an overview of relevant intentional torts, analysing how consent operates in circumstances that would otherwise be a battery. This is done through examining the elements of a valid consent, focusing in particular on the troubling area of competency involving children. Competency involving those with mental illness and/or intellectual disability is examined in more detail in Chapter 10.

Consent: general principles

The concept of consent lies at the heart of the lawful provision of medical treatment. It is axiomatic that a competent patient may refuse consent to any treatment, even if doing so will result in adverse effects, even death. This is notwithstanding the very strong state interest in preserving life.[2] In terms of doctor-patient interactions, Alderson and Goodey have pointed out that consent is understood differently by various disciplines and professions, and also in various theoretical models, including the following:

- real consent (a positivist focus on the factual exchange of medico-legal information);
- social constructionism (consent is a complex, ambiguous process; not a single event);
- functionalism (consent is a formality);
- critical theories (emphasising the vital importance of consent); and
- postmodern theories (outlining the confusion which arises when the choice is assumed to matter more than any of the options chosen).[3]

How then does the law approach consent? It is clear that the law views consent as an ongoing process which lies at the heart of the doctor-patient interactions. To the law, consent is more than a formality. As is common with the law's view of consent in other contexts, consent authorises a person (in this case a doctor) to do what s/he would not otherwise be lawfully permitted to do. A failure to obtain a valid consent from a patient may lead to actions in breach of contract, in battery or in negligence.

---

1   See, for example, Tina Cockburn and Bill Madden, 'Intentional Torts Claims in Medical Cases' (2006) 13(3) *Journal of Law and Medicine* 311.

2   *Re T (adult: refusal of medical treatment)* [1993] Fam 95.

3   Priscilla Alderson and Christopher Goodey, 'Theories of Consent' (1998) 317 *British Medical Journal* 1313.

To put it another way, Teff refers to three models of doctor-patient interactions: medicine as trade; medicine as an intrusion into personal autonomy; and medicine as a therapeutic alliance.[4] If medicine amounts to the provision of a trade, then a patient unhappy with the way that trade is provided may, in some circumstances, have an action in contract against the person who provided that trade. The second focuses on the concept of battery, which will be the subject of later discussion in this chapter. The third is most relevant when we examine the law of negligence as applied to medical practice, which is examined in more detail in Chapter 11.

Contractual consent and medical practice[5]

The doctor-patient relationship is contractual in origin, with the doctor providing services in consideration for fees payable by the patient.[6] However, there are a number of caveats which should be noted. First, although this accurately describes the position between patient and private specialist or general practitioner, this is not the case where there is a relationship between a patient and a doctor employed by the state. So, in *Melchior v Cattanach*,[7] the plaintiff brought actions in contract and tort for damages arising out of a failed sterilisation procedure conducted by the defendant doctor. The action in contract was correctly abandoned as there was no privity between the patient and the doctor, since the procedure was carried out at a public hospital in Queensland.

Second, recall that the essential elements of contract are offer and acceptance (commonly called agreement), consideration and the intention to be legally bound (otherwise referred to as intention to create legal relations). It is not clear whether it is the doctor who makes the offer to provide treatment, or the patient who offers to pay a fee, if the doctor provides services. Picard suggests that it is the patient's request for treatment which is the offer, accepted by a doctor who provides treatment.[8] This analysis is consistent with those cases analysing the invitation to treat in respect of services and then provision of services.[9]

Finally, as consideration is essential for contract formation, there is an assumption that a patient will pay, or offer to pay for services. A patient who is unable to pay may have recourse through the Medicare system to 'bulk billing' by a doctor. In this event, the contract remains between doctor and patient. The Commonwealth does not pay the doctor. Were it otherwise, the contract would be between the Commonwealth and the doctor. Instead, the patient assigns their right to seek payment of a Medicare rebate to the doctor.[10] There is common law authority suggesting that, even if a patient cannot pay, consideration is

4   Harvey Teff, *Reasonable Care: Legal Perspectives on the Doctor-Patient Relationship* (Clarendon Press, 1994) xxviii.

5   The sections of this chapter on contract and battery draw heavily on material in John Devereux, *Australian Medical Law*, 3rd edn (Routledge, 2007) 147–303.

6   *Sidaway v Board of Governors of Bethlem Royal Hospital* [1985] AC 871, 874 per Lord Templeman. The position is also noted in *Breen v Williams* (1996) 186 CLR 71.

7   *Melchior v Cattanach* (2001) 217 ALR 640. The matter was ultimately heard by the High Court of Australia as *Cattanach v Melchior* (2003) 215 CLR 1.

8   Ellen Picard, *Legal Liabilities of Doctors and Patients in Canada*, 2nd edn (Carswell, 1984) 20.

9   *Pharmaceutical Society of Great Britain v Boots Cash Chemists (Southern) Ltd* [1953] 1 QB 401.

10   See Chapter 6 for further details on the Medicare system that operates in Australia.

provided by the patient's submission to treatment.[11] This is, of course, on the basis that consideration does not need to involve money. The giving up of a valid legal right can amount to consideration.

Action in breach of contract

A contract is where two or more parties have consented to entering into binding obligations. Identifying whether a breach has occurred requires in the first instance that the terms of the contract be identified. What is it, then, that a doctor and patient have given consent to? Unlike many commercial transactions, there are rarely express terms of the contract, to which the parties have provided consent.

Parties may agree such matters as payment, or who is to carry out the medical treatment or procedure. A consent form is an example of a contract containing express terms. A person may not agree to any terms which are contrary to public policy (eg. selling an organ).[12] Any such express terms as are agreed are enforceable in an action for breach of contract, or for breach of warranty. A breach of a term of a contract permits the injured party to terminate the contract and seek damages. A breach of the warranty only gives rise to an action in damages, with the contract remaining on foot.

Patients suing doctors for breach of contract have asserted that the law should imply a term into a contract between doctor and patient that the doctor promises to effect a cure.[13] If this term were to be implied, a patient who was not made better by a doctor would be able to sue for breach of contract. Implying such a term (or warranty) has been rejected by the courts on the grounds that medicine is an inexact science. Courts have said that, objectively speaking, it is most unlikely that a medical practitioner would promise a cure.[14] Courts have also noted that the engagement of a professional does not usually involve an undertaking to achieve a desired result. So, for example, a solicitor does not undertake to win a case.[15]

However, the courts are willing to imply a term that a doctor will use reasonable skill and care.[16] It has been noted that implying a term promising a cure would be inconsistent with implying a term to simply use reasonable skill and care.[17] It is also inconsistent with the fact that medicine is an inexact science.[18] So in *Eyre v Measday*,[19] a woman who consulted a gynaecologist/obstetrician seeking a sterilisation procedure was informed that the operation should be considered as 'irreversible'. However, she was not told of the risk of the procedure being unsuccessful. Upon resuming sexual relations with her husband, she became pregnant and subsequently gave birth to a healthy child. She brought legal actions in various torts.

---

11   *Coggs v Bernard* (1703) 92 ER 107; *Banbury v Bank of Montreal* [1918] AC 626; see also *Breen v Williams* (1996) 186 CLR 71.

12   See, generally, Ian Kennedy and Andrew Grubb, *Medical Law: Cases and Materials*, 3rd edn (Butterworths, 2000).

13   *Eyre v Measday* [1986] 1 All ER 488; *Thake v Maurice* [1986] 1 All ER 497.

14   *Thake v Maurice* [1986] 1 All ER 497.

15   *Thake v Maurice* [1986] 1 All ER 497; *Greaves & Co (Constructions) Ltd v Baynham Meikle & Partners* [1975] 1 WLR 1095 at 1100 per Denning LJ.

16   *Thake v Maurice* [1986] 1 All ER 497.

17   Ibid.

18   Ibid.

19   *Eyre v Measday* [1986] 1 All ER 488.

Her action in contract alleging that the doctor had promised to render her infertile did not succeed as the court was unwilling to imply such a term into the contract with her doctor.

Battery

Battery is a direct intentional application of force. Although there are many defences to what would otherwise be a battery, the most often applied is consent. Of course there is a threshold question: to what extent can the provision of medical treatment be regarded as the application of force? Surely force implies a hostile intent, but medical treatment is benign? Early cases suggested that an element of hostility was included in the term 'application of force'.[20] More recently, however, courts have made clear that hostility need not be proved.[21] Any medical treatment involving the slightest touching could give rise to an action in battery.[22] Not only would surgical intervention come within the realms of battery, but so too would carrying out a physical examination of a patient (eg. palpating, applying a blood pressure cuff, using instruments to examine a patient's ears or throat).

Defences other than consent

Before proceeding to the elements of a valid consent, it needs to be appreciated that in a small number of situations, treatment may lawfully proceed in the absence of consent. This is because another defence might be in play. For example, in the case of necessity, a doctor may proceed in the absence of consent, although caution is needed to ensure that what is happening is actually a matter of necessity.[23] Similarly, in some states there is statutory protection for a doctor or nurse acting in good faith at the scene of an emergency.[24]

Elements of consent

Consent must be freely and voluntarily given

It is clear that consent must be freely and voluntarily given. Consent given by force, or where the patient's will is overborne while under the influence of sedation, is not consent. In *Beausoleil v The Sisters of Charity*,[25] the patient had clearly indicated that she did not want a spinal anaesthetic. On the day of the surgery, however, and while under the influence of sedation, she was 'browbeaten' into agreeing to a spinal anaesthetic, the administration of which subsequently rendered her a paraplegic. An action brought by the patient for battery was successful. It was held that consent given by the patient while under sedation was no consent. It is insufficient that a person be in an inferior position to the doctor where their will might be overborne.[26] To invalidate consent, their will must actually be overborne.

---

20   See *Cole v Turner* (1704) 87 ER 907 where it is noted that 'the slightest touching in anger, if not consented to, can lead to an action in battery'.
21   *Re F (Mental Patient: Sterilisation)* [1990] 2 AC 1.
22   *Cole v Turner* (1704) 87 ER 907.
23   *Murray v McMurchy* [1949] 2 DLR 442.
24   *Law Reform Act 1995* (Qld) s 16; *Consent to Medical Treatment and Palliative Care Act 1995* (SA) s 13.
25   *Beausoleil v The Sisters of Charity* (1964) 53 DLR (2d) 65.
26   *Freeman v Home Office (No 2)* [1984] QB 524.

Consent must relate to the act to be performed

The consent provided may not be exceeded. For example, a patient who gives consent to a caesarean section does not give consent to a sterilisation procedure being performed as well. This is so even if undertaking the latter procedure is conveniently performed at the same time as the caesarean section.[27] The exception to this rule is a case of genuine emergency. So, when a patient was operated upon for the purpose of a hernia repair, and it was discovered that he had a diseased testicle, it was held that it was permissible for the surgeon to proceed to remove the testicle. This was because postponing the removal may have resulted in the patient dying of septicaemia.[28] Consent provided is generally only for that procedure. For example, doctors have been held to be liable in battery where a patient had consented to a toe operation, but woke up having had a spinal fusion performed;[29] and where a boy was admitted to hospital for a tonsillectomy, but was instead circumcised.[30]

Where an adult competent patient has expressed, in advance, that a treatment should be performed, or should not, then that consent or refusal of treatment must be respected. This was highlighted in the Canadian case of *Malette v Shulman*,[31] where a woman was admitted to hospital following a motor vehicle accident. A blood transfusion was clinically indicated and the treating doctor ordered a blood transfusion to treat her injuries. The doctor was found liable in battery as he had ignored a card the woman had which clearly indicated that she was a Jehovah's Witness and that she refused all blood transfusions, even if it led to her death. In the Australian context, regard must be had to state/territory substituted decision-making laws (including guardianship laws) on the broader issues raised by this case: these are discussed in further detail in Chapter 10.[32]

Sufficient information must be provided

There must be sufficient information provided so that the patient can decide whether or not to consent to treatment. In the event that a patient is provided with incorrect information, and makes a decision on that basis, the decision may later be invalidated on the basis that the patient did not truly turn his or her mind to the procedure to which consent was given. In the case of *Re T*,[33] T was a 20-year-old who was brought up by her mother, who was a Jehovah's Witness. Though not a member of that religion, she was sympathetic to its beliefs. She refused a blood transfusion having been told (incorrectly) that alternatives to a blood transfusion were available, and that a blood transfusion was not always necessary with a caesarean section. T gave birth to a stillborn child. T was sedated and placed on a ventilator. A blood transfusion was clinically indicated. T's boyfriend sought a declaration that it would not be unlawful for a hospital to administer a blood transfusion. The English Court of Appeal was persuaded that T had not validly refused consent since she had not turned her mind to the situation she was facing, having been given erroneous information.

27   *Murray v McMurchy* [1949] 2 DLR 442.
28   *Marshall v Curry* (1933) 3 DLR 260.
29   *Schweizer v Central Hospital* (1974) 53 DLR (3d) 494.
30   *Chatterton v Gerson* [1981] QB 432 per Bristow J.
31   *Malette v Shulman* (1990) 67 DLR (4th) 321.
32   See, generally, *Qumsieh v Guardianship and Administration Board* [1998] VSCA 45.
33   *Re T (adult: refusal of medical treatment)* [1993] Fam 95.

It is clear that once a patient has been informed in broad terms of the nature of a procedure, and gives consent, that consent is real. No action in battery will lie for a failure to advise of the risks of a procedure.[34] There is some dispute as to what amounts to 'the nature of a procedure'. A patient 'need not understand the precise physiological processes involved in medical treatment'.[35] It is consistent with the general nature of a battery action that consent 'is to the plaintiff's conduct, rather than its consequences'.[36]

Other circumstances where consent is not valid[37]

On rare occasions, the principles underpinning consent to medical treatment have been departed from, presumably on the grounds of public policy. So, in *Potts v North West Regional Health Authority*,[38] the plaintiff consented to being immunised against rubella. Unbeknownst to her, the syringe with which she was injected contained not only the rubella vaccine but Depo-Provera, which is a long acting contraceptive. An action in battery was successful.

Uncertainties in this area relate back to criminal cases concerning the impact of fraud on the validity of consent. Fraud as to the nature of an act (eg. pretending something is not sexual intercourse, when it is) vitiates consent.[39] Fraud, not as to the nature of the act, but as to the status of the person to whom consent to intercourse has been given (eg. pretending that following the signing of a document, the person having sex with you is your husband) does not vitiate consent.[40] The law draws a distinction between fraud as to the essential nature and quality of an act, which vitiates consent, and fraud 'in the inducement' (ie. to a collateral circumstance) in which case the consent is not vitiated.

It is clear that, at a minimum, the nature of a treatment includes the physical interventions which are proposed as part of that treatment. Unnecessary treatments can give rise to a battery action.[41] Medical treatment performed by a person whose registration to practise has been suspended probably does not give rise to a battery action.[42] Treatment carried out by lay people does, however, give rise to actions in battery, possibly because they are not being performed by doctors, so they lose their nature as medical treatment.[43] There is also some authority which suggests that the more serious the risks of a treatment are, the more likely they are to be regarded not merely as risks of the procedure, but as actually altering the nature of that treatment. This could arise, for example, where a patient is not

---

34 *Chatterton v Gerson*, above n 30, followed in *Rogers v Whitaker* (1992) 175 CLR 479.
35 *R v Mental Health Act Commission; Ex parte X* (1991) 9 BMLR 77 at 87 per Stuart-Smith LJ.
36 *R v Raabe* [1985] 1 Qd R 115 at 124 per Derrington J; followed in *Lergesner v Carroll* [1991] 1 Qd R 206 at 219 per Cooper J and at 206 per Kneipp J.
37 This part of the chapter draws heavily on John Devereux, 'When Practising Fails to Make Perfect: Medical Treatment and Battery' (2013) 21 *Tort Law Review* 120–6 and John Devereux, 'Continuing Conundrums in Consent' in Sheila McLean, *First Do No Harm: Law, Ethics and Health Care* (Ashgate, 2006) 235.
38 *Potts v North West Regional Health Authority*, (unreported, *The Guardian*, 23 July 1983).
39 *R v Williams* [1923] 1 KB 430.
40 *Papadimitropolous v The Queen* (1957) 98 CLR 249.
41 *Dean v Phung* [2012] NSWCA 223.
42 *R v Richardson* (1998) 2 Cr App R 200.
43 *R v Maurantonia* [1967] 65 DLR (2d) 674, *R v Naveed Tabassum* [2000] 2 Cr App R 328.

made aware that a treatment is experimental,[44] or that the risks of a treatment are very serious indeed.[45] However, these cases should be regarded as anomalous and confined to their particular facts.

Competence

Consent can only be given by a person competent to give consent. Every human being of adult years and sound mind has a right to determine what shall be done with his/her own body, and surgeons who perform operations without their patients' consent commit a battery, for which they are liable in damages.[46] Every adult of sound mind is presumed to be competent. That presumption may, however, be rebutted. Competency is a functional capacity referable to an ability to receive information about a proposed treatment, weigh that information in the balance, be able to apply it to one's own situation, to make a decision, and to communicate that decision.[47]

It has been noted that courts 'tend to use the words "inform" and "understand" interchangeably, reflecting a simplistic assumption that understanding is the natural and expected consequence of adequately informing an individual'.[48] It is important to note that competency is situation-specific, and treatment-specific. A person may be competent one day, in respect of one treatment option, but not so on another day, in respect of another treatment.

Competency can be affected by temporary factors, or permanent factors. Temporary factors include unconsciousness, confusion, the effect of fatigue, shock, pain or drugs,[49] and panic induced by fear;[50] however, this is only to the extent that those matters impair a person's capacity to make a decision.[51] Courts have warned that the fact that a patient makes a decision which others would not does not, of itself, indicate a lack of competency. A competent patient can make a decision for good reasons, bad reasons, or even no reason at all.[52]

Children

The traditional view was that children could not, themselves, consent to medical treatment.[53] Instead, that responsibility vested with parents or courts. Lord Denning noted 'that an older child's views should be sought, but even an older child's views were never decisive'.[54]

---

44   *Coughlan v Kuntz* [1990] 2 WWR 737, *R v Mental Health Act Commission; Ex parte X* (1991) 9 BMLR 77.

45   *Kelly v Hazlett* (1976) 15 OR (2d) 290; *D v S* (1981) 93 LS (SA) JS 405.

46   *Schloendorff v Society of New York Hospital*, 105 NE 92 (1914).

47   See, generally, *Re C (adult: refusal of medical treatment)* [1994] 1 All ER 819.

48   Harold I Schwartz and Loren H Roth, 'Informed Consent and Competency in Psychiatric Practice' in Allan Tasman, Robert E Hales and Allen J Frances (eds), *Review of Psychiatry*, Vol 8, (American Psychiatric Press, 1989) 409, 417.

49   *Re T (adult: refusal of medical treatment)* [1993] Fam 95.

50   *Re MB* [1997] EWCA Civ 1361.

51   Ibid.

52   *Re T (adult: refusal of medical treatment)* [1993] Fam 95; *Hunter and New England Area Health Service v A* (2009) 74 NSWLR 88; *H Ltd v J* (2010) 107 SASR 352.

53   See, generally, A Samuels, 'Can A Minor Under Sixteen Consent to a Medical Operation?' (1983) 13 *Family Law* 30; John Devereux, 'The Capacity of a Child in Australia to Consent to Medical Treatment – Gillick Revisited?' (1991) 11(2) *Oxford Journal of Legal Studies* 283.

54   *B(RB) v B(J)* [1968] P 466, 468.

That position has now been abandoned. In the House of Lords judgment in the leading case of Gillick, it was held that a child with sufficient maturity and understanding to understand fully what is proposed can consent to medical treatment.[55] This has become known as Gillick competence and is usually applied in the case of what have been called 'mature minors' (ie. children between 12 and 16 years of age). The principle, at least in England, applies not only to a child's right to make a decision as to medical treatment, but a child's right to information being provided to them as to medical treatment, being confidential as between the doctor and that child patient.[56]

Subsequent case law in England tended to the view that the right to consent vested in a mature minor but that this did not necessarily include the right to refuse treatment.[57] The Court of Appeal in *In re R*[58] and *Re W*[59] opined that while a child was under the age of Gillick competence, there were two groups of people who could give consent – either the child's parents or a court. Once the child had Gillick competence, however, there were three such groups – the child, the parents or the courts. If any one of them gave consent, this would provide a key to unlock the lock leading to lawful medical treatment.

In Marion's case, the leading Australian judgment on consent, the High Court endorsed the Gillick competence test. It also stated that two principles operate in respect of the parental power to provide consent: first, the subjective consent of a parent, in the sense of the parent speaking for the child, is ordinarily indispensable; and second, the overriding criterion to be applied in the exercise of parental authority on behalf of the child is the welfare of the child, objectively assessed. These two principles have become one for all practical purpose. This is a recognition that ordinarily a parent of a child who is not capable of giving consent is in the best position to act in the best interests of the child. Implicit in parental consent is the determination of what is best for the welfare of the child.[60] However, a parent's right to consent on behalf of their child is not an unfettered discretion. The High Court has clearly stated that a parent does not have the power to consent to do harm to a child.[61]

There are some forms of medical treatment to which no child or parent can consent, and court authorisation is required. These 'special medical procedures' including the following: first, invasive, irreversible and major surgery; second, where 'there is a significant risk of making the wrong decision, either as to a child's present or future capacity to consent, or about what is the best interests of the child'; and third, where the consequences of a wrong decision are particularly grave. Examples of such procedures include the sterilisation of a

55   *Gillick v West Norfolk and Wisbech Area Health Authority* [1986] AC 112; *Secretary, Department of Health and Community Services v JWB and SMB* (Marion's Case) (1992) 175 CLR 218.

56   *R (Axon) v Secretary of State for Health* [2006] EWCA 37.

57   One may query whether the approach of the English Court of Appeal in *Re R* and *Re W* – that capacity to consent does not include capacity to refuse – will be followed in Australia.

58   *Re R (a minor) (wardship: consent to treatment)* [1992] Fam 11.

59   *Re W (a minor) (medical treatment: courts jurisdiction)* [1993] Fam 64.

60   *Secretary, Department of Health and Community Services v JWB and SMB* (1992) 175 CLR 218 at 239–40 per Mason CJ.

61   See, for example, the discussion in *Secretary, Department of Health and Community Services v JWB and SMB* (1992) 175 CLR 218. The example provided by the High Court notes that no parent in Australia could consent to the amputation of a child's arm for the purpose of making the child a better beggar.

profoundly intellectually impaired young woman;[62] sex reassignment surgery;[63] and removal of an endotracheal tube of a severely brain-damaged infant.[64]

In terms of determining what is in the child's best interests, the Family Court has suggested the following factors as relevant:

- the medical condition involved
- the nature of the proposed treatment
- the reasons for the proposed treatment
- any alternative courses of action available
- the desirability and effect of authorising the proposed treatment, rather than the alternatives
- the physical, social and psychological effects on the child of authorising versus not authorising the proposed procedure
- the nature and degree of risk to the child of authorising versus not authorising the proposed treatment
- the views as the treatment and alternatives expressed by the guardians of the child – the person who has custody of the child, the person who is responsible for the daily care and control of the child – and the child.[65]

Statutory provision

In NSW and SA, legislation has altered common law rules relating to child consent to medical treatment.[66] In SA, a person who is 16 years of age or older is treated as an adult. For persons under 16 years of age, treatment may be administered if a parent consents or, in the absence of parental consent, where the doctor is of the opinion that the child understands the nature, consequences and risks of the treatment, and the treatment is in the best interests of the child and one other doctor (who has personally examined the child), is of the same view.[67] In NSW, treatment may be given to a child who is 16 years of age without parental consent or, where the child consents, where the patient is 14 years of age or older.[68]

Mental illness, intellectual disability and competency

There is no automatic denial of competency to people with intellectual disability or mental illness: competency is a question of each person's abilities. State/territory mental health legislation impacts upon the ability of some people who lack capacity due to mental illness or

---

62   *Secretary, Department of Health and Community Services v JWB and SMB* (1992) 175 CLR 218.
63   *Re Alex* (2009) 248 FLR 312.
64   *Re Baby D (No 2)* (2011) 258 FLR 290.
65   *Re Alex (hormonal treatment for gender dysphoria)* (2004) 31 Fam LR 503.
66   *Minors (Property and Contracts) Act 1970* (NSW); *Consent to Medical Treatment and Palliative Care Act 1995* (SA).
67   *Consent to Medical Treatment and Palliative Care Act 1995* (SA) s 12.
68   *Minors (Property and Contracts) Act 1970* (NSW) s 49.

intellectual disability to withhold consent to certain medical treatments. This is discussed in much more detail in Chapter 11.

Conclusion

This chapter has examined the role and operation of consent in contract and intentional torts such as battery. It is important to note that an action bought in contract alleging a failure to cure a patient is likely to be unsuccessful, as courts are slow to imply a term that the doctor has promised to cure. However, the courts will imply a term that the doctor will act using reasonable care and skill. A battery action alleging a failure to advise of risks will also likely fail. However, such an action is likely to succeed where the patient lacked competency to consent (save where an authorised decision-maker has provided consent) and where the procedure performed was different from that to which consent was provided by the patient (save in the case of necessity). The key elements of a valid consent under law were also examined. What constitutes competency to give consent was also explored in the case of adults, and was contrasted with what is required in the case of children, in particular 'mature minors' who have Gillick competence. It is clear that while the courts have been prepared to allow Gillick-competent children to consent to medical treatment, this has not been the case with respect to refusal of medical treatment.

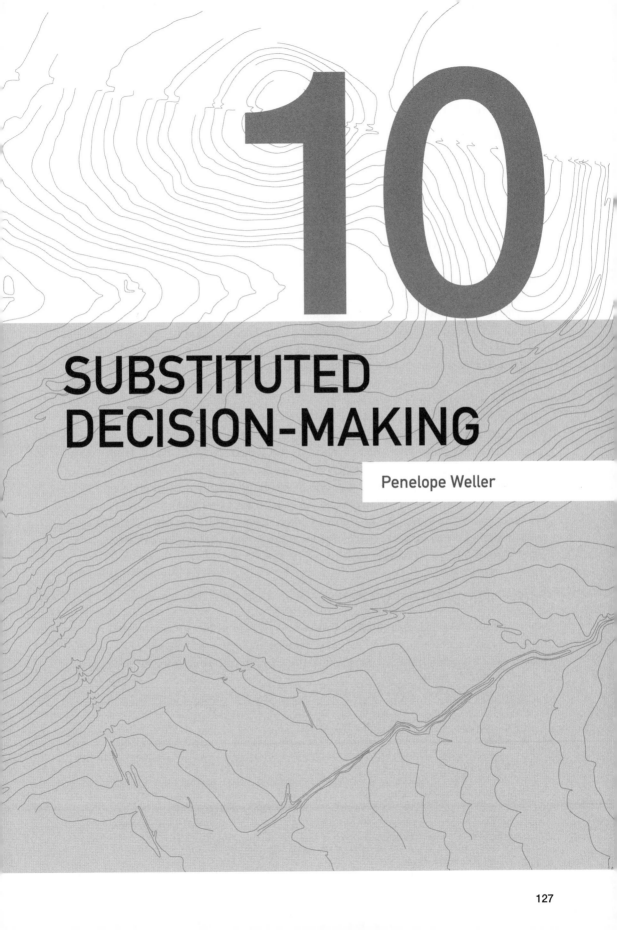

10

SUBSTITUTED DECISION-MAKING

Penelope Weller

Introduction

The term 'substituted decision-making' refers to a range of processes that create decision-making mechanisms for people who are unable to make decisions for themselves. Traditionally, substituted decision-making involves the appointment of a person to make decisions on behalf of another, usually on a 'best interests' basis. Such arrangements are thought necessary whenever an individual lacks the mental capacity to make decisions for themselves.[1] The concept of substituted decision-making has expanded to include self-appointed substitutes, advance directives and new forms of collaborative or supported decision-making.

Substituted decision-making mechanisms are used for a range of personal decisions, including medical, financial or lifestyle matters. Understanding who is authorised to make a particular decision, and on what basis, can be a complex area for healthcare professionals. This chapter focuses on substituted decision-making for general healthcare decisions. The first part of the chapter discusses the historical development of substituted decision-making and its place in the common law. The second part discusses substituted decision-making arrangements initiated by individuals with capacity, such as advance directives and enduring powers of attorney. The third part discusses guardianship law and provides a brief outline of such laws in Australian jurisdictions.[2]

It is very likely that current laws on substituted decision-making will change in the near future. Because of this, the fourth part of the chapter focuses on current critiques of substituted decision-making. The modern trend in substituted decision-making is for partial, time-limited arrangements that are linked to the wishes of the person who is the subject of the decision.[3] However, the Convention on the Rights of Persons with Disabilities (CRPD) calls for the replacement of all substituted decision-making arrangements with supported decision-making.[4] Moreover, the obligation to afford people with disabilities 'equal recognition before the law' in article 12 of the CRPD requires positive protection of the legal capacity of people who are cognitively impaired.[5]

Historical overview

Substituted decision-making existed in Roman law as early as the 5th century BC and has been invoked since that time as a method of protecting the interests of vulnerable citizens.[6] Recognition of substituted decision-making in the common law stems from the development

---

1 'Mental capacity' refers to the ability of an individual to understand information relevant to a decision, weigh the information in order to arrive at a decision and communicate the decision. See *Mental Capacity Act 2005* (England and Wales) s 4; *Powers of Attorney Act 2014* (Vic) s 4.

2 Substituted decision-making arrangements are also established by the compulsory treatment powers contained in mental health legislation. Discussion of mental health legislation is beyond the scope of this chapter.

3 Shih-Ning Then, 'Evolution and Innovation in Guardianship Laws: Assisted Decision-making' (2013) 33(1) *Sydney Law Review* 133.

4 Convention on the Rights of Persons with Disabilities (CRPD), adopted 13 December 2006, GA Res 61/106, UN Doc A/Res/61/106 (entered into force 3 May 2008). Australia ratified the CRPD on 17 July 2008.

5 Barbara Carter, 'Adult guardianship: Human Rights or Social Justice' (2010) 18(1) *Journal of Law and Medicine* 143, 154.

6 Denzil Lush, 'Roman Origins of Modern Guardianship Law' in Kimberly Dayton (ed.), *Comparative Perspectives on Adult Guardianship* (Carolina Academic Press, 2014).

of the English doctrine of *parens patriae* in the 16th century.[7] The doctrine of *parens patriae* recognises that the state (formerly the sovereign) has a duty to protect individuals who are unable to care for themselves.[8] With the rise of medical professional power, the *parens patriae* jurisdiction expanded to apply to all those in need of medical care, including children, the elderly, the sick, the disabled and the mentally ill.[9] In the 17th century, guardians were appointed court 'committees', giving rise to the concept of 'best interests'.[10] The best interests principle refers to the idea that decisions made on behalf of those in need of protection should reflect considerations of what is 'best'.[11]

In modern legal systems, the broad common law recognition of substituted decision-making frameworks has been gradually replaced by new common law standards and legislation, allowing individuals to make decisions for themselves. *Parens patriae* remains as a residual protective jurisdiction, exercised by the courts for the protection of children and adults who lack mental capacity.[12]

The 'best interests' standard

Until the late 20th century, the courts accepted that medical practitioners needed to make decisions on behalf of their patients in a range of circumstances.[13] The 'best interests' standard applied, but was largely left to medical discretion. The evolving common law principle of informed consent gradually limited the authority of medical professionals.[14] Over time, the English courts developed a broader approach to best interests. For example, in *Re A (Medical Treatment: Male Sterilisation)*, Dame Butler Sloss states that 'best interests encompasses medical, emotional and all other welfare issues'.[15] In the same case, Justice Thorpe used a 'checklist' approach that set out the relative advantages and disadvantages of proposed options, based on the Law Commission's *Report on Mental Incapacity* (1995).[16] The standard of best interests expressed in English case law has not been recognised in case law in Australia. However, in Victoria and the ACT, where human rights legislation applies, the determination of 'best interests' is limited by the principle of proportionality.[17]

---

7   Terry Carney and David Tate, *The Adult Guardianship Experiment: Tribunals and Popular Justice* (Federation Press, 1997) 10.

8   Erica Wood, 'The Paradox of Adult Guardianship: A Solution to and a Source for Elder Abuse' (2012) 36(3) *Generations* 79–82, 79.

9   Then, above n 3, 136; see also the section on children's capacity to consent and refuse medical treatment in Chapter 9.

10 Carney and Tate, above n 7, 10.

11 *Airedale NHS Trust v Bland* [1993] AC 789 (House of Lords).

12 Mental capacity is a common law concept describing the ability of a person to understand and weigh relevant information in order to make a decision. See *Mental Capacity Act 2005* (England and Wales) s 4.

13 Mary Donnelly, *Healthcare Decision-making and the Law: Autonomy, Capacity and Limits of Liberalism* (CUP, 2010) 180.

14 Ruth Faden and Tom Beauchamp, *A History and Theory of Informed Consent* (OUP, 1986).

15 [2000] 1 FCR 193, 200.

16 [2000] 1 FCR 193, 206; See Donnelly, above n 13, 181. 'Best interests' is defined in *Mental Capacity Act 2005* (England and Wales) s 4.

17 *PJB v Melbourne Health* (2011) 39 VR 373, [358]–[364]; *Charter of Human Rights and Responsibilities Act 2006* (Vic).

Substituted mechanisms instigated by individuals with capacity

The common law recognises that individuals with mental capacity 'are entitled to make their own decisions about health care'.[18] Provided a person has mental capacity, the law recognises that he or she may accept or reject healthcare that is offered to them.[19] In general, people with capacity may not be compelled to undergo medical treatment 'for their own good' or because it is 'best'.[20] Respect for individual autonomy and self-determination extends to the right to appoint one's own substituted decision-maker.[21] The key legal mechanisms enabling individuals with capacity to do this are common law advance directives, statutory advance directives and Enduring Powers of Attorney.[22]

Common law advance directives

Oral or written statements intended to apply to future health decisions, made by a person with mental capacity, are recognised by the common law and generally referred to as advance directives.[23] Common law advance directives are legally valid, provided it can be established that the person possessed capacity at the time the direction was given, that the directions are clear and applicable to the situation and that there are no other factors that might raise uncertainty about the person's wishes or intent.[24] Common law advance directives are recognised in NSW and Tasmania.

Advance health directives

Different types of statutory advance directives are available in the other Australian jurisdictions, where they are recognised alongside common law advance directives. Advance health directives are formal documents made in accordance with relevant statutory requirements by an adult with mental capacity. Advance directives allow a person to set out decisions or directives with respect to future healthcare. They are designed to come into operation once the person has lost capacity, although the document itself may vary the latter presumption. Some advance directive schemes provide for the appointment of a substituted decision-maker.[25]

---

18 *Re C (adult: refusal of medical treatment)* [1994] 1 All ER 819; *Rogers v Whitaker* (1992) 175 CLR 479; *Secretary, Department of Health and Community Services v JWB and SMB* (Marion's case) (1992) 175 CLR 218; *Re T (adult: refusal of medical treatment)* [1992] EWCA Civ 18.

19 *Secretary, Department of Health and Community Services v JWB and SMB* (1992) 175 CLR 218 at 258–60. Penelope Weller, *Mental Health Advance Directives: The Convention on the Rights of Persons with Disabilities and the Right to Choose* (Routledge, 2013) 4–8.

20 See Chris Ryan, 'Playing the Ferryman: Psychiatry's Role in End-of-life Decision-making' (2012) 46(10) *Australian and New Zealand Journal of Psychiatry* 932.

21 Weller, above n 19, 4–8.

22 A Power of Attorney authorises another person to exercise the first person's legal powers, but ceases to have effect if the person loses capacity; see, for example, *Powers of Attorney Act 2006* (ACT) s 13; *Powers of Attorney Act 1998* (Qld).

23 *Hunter and New England Area Health Service v A* (2009) 74 NSWLR 88; *Brightwater Care Group v Rossiter* (2009) 40 WAR 84.

24 Weller, above n 19.

25 For example, the *Medical Treatment and Decisions Act 2016* (Vic).

As discussed in Chapters 15 and 23, recent debate and law reform about advance directives has been principally concerned with end-of-life care.[26] In the ACT, a health direction may refuse treatment or require the withdrawal of medical treatment.[27] An ACT Enduring Power of Attorney (EPA) overrides a health directive.[28] In the NT, people can make an 'advance personal care plan' in which they may consent to future care, set out their views, wishes and beliefs with respect to future care, or appoint a person to make decisions on their behalf.[29] The NT decision-maker is required to make decisions on the basis of 'substituted judgment', which means the 'way the decision maker reasonably believes the represented adult would have done' except in circumstances where the decision-maker is excused from exercising substituted judgment: that is, with respect to excluded matters and restricted health matters.[30] An appointed guardian must give effect to a health directive.[31]

In Queensland, adults may make an advance health directive and/or appoint an eligible attorney.[32] The directive may consent to future healthcare, require the withholding or withdrawing of life-sustaining measures in specified circumstances, or authorise physical restraint.[33] In SA, a competent adult may make an advance care direction and appoint a substituted decision-maker.[34] Guardians in SA are required to give effect to an advance care directive.[35] They are required to give effect to the person's directions and wishes, but may not refuse the provision of pain relief or food and liquid by mouth.[36] In Victoria, medical treatment, but not palliative care, may be refused by instruction or by a person appointed under the Act.[37] The *Medical Treatment and Decisions Act 2016* (Vic), which comes into force in 2018, provides for medical treatment planning. The Act introduces binding advance directives and the appointment of supporters and medical treatment decision makers. In WA, the law simply states that adults may make an advance health directive. [38]

Enduring Power of Attorney

An EPA offers a relatively inexpensive and accessible mechanism for the appointment of one or more, single or joint substituted decision-makers who are authorised to make healthcare decisions for an adult person (the donor) in the event of incapacity.[39] Typically, individuals appoint family members or carers as substituted decision-makers. The powers contained in EPAs are broad, although some legislative schemes limit the range of decisions that a substituted decision-maker is entitled to make with respect to highly intrusive

26   Stephania Negri, *Self-Determination, Dignity and End of Life Care: Regulating Advance Directives in International and Comparative Perspective* (Martinus Nijhoff Publishers, 2012).
27   *Medical Treatment (Health Directions) Act 2006* (ACT) s 19.
28   Ibid s 139.
29   *Advance Personal Planning Act 2013* (NT) s 8.
30   Ibid ss 23–25.
31   *Adult Guardianship Act* (NT) s 20.
32   *Guardianship and Administration Act 2000* (Qld) s 35.
33   Ibid ss 35–36.
34   *Consent to Medical Treatment and Palliative Care Act 1995* (SA) ss 14, 21.
35   *Guardianship and Administration Act 1993* (SA) s 31A.
36   *Advance Care Directives Act 2013* (SA) ss 11–13, 34, 35.
37   *Medical Treatment Act 1988* (Vic) ss 5, 5A, 5B.
38   *Guardianship and Administration Act 1990* (WA) s 110P.
39   *Powers of Attorney Act 2006* (ACT) ss 6, 12–14, 37; *Guardianship and Administration Act 1990* (WA); *Powers of Attorney Act 2014* (Vic) ss 21–27.

medical procedures or personal matters.[40] In such instances, additional authorisation may be required.[41]

Statutorily appointed treatment decision-makers

Some jurisdictions make provision for the appointment of treatment decision-makers if other decision-making mechanisms are not in place. For example, with respect to health decisions in Victoria, a 'person responsible' is authorised to make decisions for a person who is unable to give consent.[42] The decision must be made on 'best interests' grounds:

> taking into account the wishes of the patient, the wishes of a nearest relative or any other family member, the consequence to the patient if the treatment is not carried out, any alternative treatment available, the nature and degree of any significant risks associated with the treatment or any alternative treatment, and whether the treatment to be carried out is only to promote and maintain the health and well-being of the patient.[43]

In NSW, individuals vested with power of attorney are not empowered to make decisions relating to healthcare, but an Enduring Guardian is so empowered.

Emergencies

In effect, advance directives and EPAs provide a mechanism of 'consent' when the person is no longer able to make decisions for themselves. The common law recognises that consent is not required in an 'emergency'.[44] An emergency is described in law as necessary medical interventions 'carried out in order either to save (their) lives or to ensure improvement or prevent deterioration in physical or mental health' in the absence of informed consent.[45] In general, the relevant standard for emergency decisions is the best interests standard. However, those who attend emergencies are obliged to check for clear applicable advance instructions, such as a card that may indicate the person's refusal of blood transfusions.[46]

Guardianship

Individuals who lack mental capacity (and have not had the opportunity to appoint a decision-maker or make an advance directive) may have a guardian appointed as a substituted decision-maker for health decisions. Guardianship legislation is rooted in 19th century laws devised as part of the great confinement.[47] For example, the powers of the *Lunacy Act 1890* (England) were transferred to superior courts in Australia in the 19th century.[48] The legal

---

40   *Powers of Attorney Act 2006* (ACT) s 37 (eg. tissue donation, sterilisation, termination of pregnancy, experimental research, treatment for mental illness including electro-convulsive therapy (ECT) and psychosurgery).
41   For example, see 'special health care' matters under *Powers of Attorney Act 2006* (ACT) s 37.
42   *Guardianship and Administration Act 1986* (Vic) s 37.
43   Ibid s 38.
44   Michael Eburn, *Emergency Law*, 4th edn (Federation Press, 2013).
45   *Re F (Mental Patient: Sterilisation)* [1990] 2 AC 1, 550 per Lord Brandon.
46   *Malette v Shulman* (1990) 67 DLR (4th) 321.
47   Michel Foucault, *Discipline and Punish* (Penguin, 1977).
48   Carney and Tate, above n 7, 11.

framework permitted people with mental illness and intellectual disabilities to be confined in institutions.[49] Individuals in 'care' were relieved of personal, day-to-day decision-making responsibilities, while their financial and property matters were managed by state agencies such as the public trustee or the courts.[50]

In the mid 20th century, the civil rights movement in the US and elsewhere demanded the dismantling of large stand-alone institutions, as too many had become places of entrenched abuse and neglect.[51] Plenary guardianship powers, which provided the legal basis for such confinements, were also widely criticised. In the 1980s, new types of guardianship arrangements were created to facilitate the release of individuals from institutions, promote integration into the community and provide the opportunity to 'live normally'.[52] Instead of plenary guardianship, limited forms of guardianship were made available for personal, financial or medical decisions.[53] Family members, rather than state proxies, were appointed as guardians and their decisions were guided by principles of 'substituted judgment'.[54] In Australia, 'substituted judgment' refers to the requirement that decisions are made in accordance with the wishes of the person.[55] In 2014, the Australian Law Reform Commission (ALRC) published its final report on disability-related laws, entitled *Equality, Capacity and Disability in Commonwealth Laws*.[56] The report includes consideration of the substituted decision-making arrangements under Commonwealth law (ie. federal law), recommending a uniform shift to substituted judgment.

At state level, several law reform reports have been completed. In Victoria the final report of a comprehensive review of guardianship laws was published in 2012.[57] The Queensland Law Reform Commission undertook a full review of the state's guardianship laws in 2010.[58] The NSW Standing Committee on Social Issues also undertook an inquiry into substituted decision-making for people lacking capacity in NSW, in 2010.[59] Many of the key recommendations of these reviews are yet to be translated into law; the exception is the introduction of supportive attorneys in Victoria.[60]

At present, guardianship legislation in most jurisdictions in Australia defines the standard of substituted decision-making as a combination of traditional 'best interests' and 'substituted judgment' considerations. In NSW, for example, guardianship decisions are guided

---

49   Michael Foucault, *Madness and Civilisation* (Tavistock, 1961).

50   Carney and Tate, above n 7, 12–13.

51   Lawrence Gostin and Lance Gable, 'The Human Rights of Persons with Mental Disabilities' (2004) 63 *Maryland Law Review* 20.

52   Carney and Tate, above n 7.

53   Usually financial, medical and/or personal guardians are appointed.

54   Carney and Tate, above n 7, 17–18.

55   Victorian Law Reform Commission, *Guardianship: Final Report* (2012) 387. In international jurisdictions the terms 'proxy' or 'surrogate' decision-makers refer to decision-makers who are obliged to follow a substituted judgment principle.

56   Australian Law Reform Commission, *Equality, Capacity and Disability in Commonwealth Laws*, Report No. 124 (2014).

57   Victorian Law Reform Commission, *Guardianship: Final Report* (2012).

58   Queensland Law Reform Commission, *A Review of the Queensland's Guardianship Law*, Vols 1–4 (2010).

59   New South Wales Standing Committee on Social Issues, *Substituted Decision-making for People Lacking Capacity* (2010); See also House of Representatives Standing Committee on Legal and Constitutional Affairs *Older People and the Law* (2007).

60   *Powers of Attorney Act 2014* (Vic) ss 86–92.

by consideration of the person's welfare and interests, their freedom to make decisions and the views of the person.[61] The guardian may not consent if they are aware that the person objects to the treatment, although exceptions apply.[62] In Queensland guardians must apply the general principles, which are set out in a Schedule to the Act. With respect to healthcare decisions they must consider what is 'in all the circumstances in the adult's best interests'.[63] In SA, consideration must be given to what would be 'the wishes of the person in the matter if he or she were not mentally incapacitated', the person's current wishes and the adequacy of existing informal arrangements, and the decision must be the least restrictive option.[64] In NT, the decision or action should be the least restrictive, promote best interests and give effect to the wishes of the person wherever possible.[65]

Substituted decision-making in context

The number of people subject to guardianship in Australia is rising.[66] The trend reflects the growing population, the ageing population, the proportion of individuals in the population living with cognitive impairment and the increased availability of substituted decision-making arrangements.[67] Most jurisdictions provide for the appointment of public guardians or 'guardians of last resort'.[68] There also appears to be an increased tendency for families, supporters and service providers to formalise substituted decision-making arrangements, in preference to informal arrangements.[69]

Research into substituted decision-making reveals a high degree of variation in practice,[70] poor understanding of the law and confusion about decision-making responsibilities.[71] Wilmott reports that substituted decision-making in healthcare is understood and applied in different ways throughout Australia.[72] Carney has also noted the willingness of substituted decision-makers to exploit those in their care.[73] The research also suggests that many substituted decision-makers appear to mistakenly assume that traditional 'best interests' considerations apply, rather than the applicable statutory standards. Such misunderstandings underpin the observation that substituted decision-makers tend to adopt

61   *Guardianship Act 1987* (NSW) s 4.
62   Ibid s 46.
63   *Guardianship and Administration Act 2000* (Qld) s 34; Sch 1 Part 2 12.
64   *Guardianship and Administration Act 1993* (SA) s 5.
65   *Adult Guardianship Act* (NT) s 4.
66   Carter, above n 5, 147.
67   Liz Dearn, *Too Much Guardianship? Reflections on Guardianship in Victoria: 1988 to 2008* (2010) Office of the Public Advocate Discussion Paper <www.publicadvocate.vic.gov.au>.
68   *Adult Guardianship Act* (NT) s 5.
69   John Chesterman, 'The Future of Adult Guardianship in Federal Australia: A Strategy for Social Work' (2013) 66(1) *Australian Social Work* 26, 32.
70   Terry Carney and Fleur Beaupert, 'Public and Private Bricolage – Challenges Balancing Law, Services and Civil Society in Advancing CRPD Supported Decision-Making' (2013) 36(1) *University of New South Wales Law Journal* 175.
71   See also Terry Carney, 'Participation and Service Access Rights for People with Intellectual Disability: Role of the Law?' (2012) 38(1) *Journal of Intellectual and Development Disability* 59.
72   Lindy Willmott, 'Advance Directives and the Promotion of Autonomy: A Comparative Study Statutory Analysis' (2010) 17 *Journal of Law and Medicine* 556, 558.
73   Carney and Beaupert, above n 69, 175; Nina A Kohn, Jeremy A Blumenthal and Amy T Campbell, 'Supported Decision-Making: A Viable Alternative to Guardianship?' (2013) 117(4) *Penn State Law Review* 1111.

a paternalistic stance, either ignoring the wishes of the person or overlooking their ability to participate in decision-making. Disability activists argue that the routine exclusion of people with disability from decision-making processes reinforces assumptions about their lack of decision-making skills, while at the same time preventing the development of such skills.

On the other hand, scholars have argued for a reconceptualisation of guardianship relationships as interactions that are capable of making meaningful contributions to a person's life.[74] They argue that guardianship, viewed holistically, is capable of seeking a range of outcomes for a person with cognitive impairment, including tangibles, such as access to appropriate accommodation support and services; and intangibles, such as social inclusion.[75] Finally, confusion may arise whenever the authority and interaction of the different mechanisms is unclear, or information about what substituted decision-making arrangements are in place is difficult to obtain or is not communicated to health practitioners, family members and others.

The human rights challenge to substituted decision-making

Capacity and 'best interests' are flexible standards that have been criticised for being narrow, indeterminate, discriminatory and paternalistic. The human rights challenge to substituted decision-making is based on the argument that the decisions of people with disabilities are entitled to the same level of respect as is accorded those who are not disabled. The CRPD aims to promote, protect and fulfil the human rights of people with disabilities. Its core ethos is the recognition of people with disabilities as holders of rights, rather than 'imperfect humans in need of medical correction and charitable intervention, and as active participants in all decision-making arrangements'.[76] The Convention's goal is the full and effective participation of people with disabilities in society.

With respect to substituted decision-making, the overarching requirement of the CRPD is that all decision-making measures 'respect(s) the person's autonomy, will and preferences'.[77] This phrase is interpreted as including the principle that in instances where an individual is unable to make decisions, the appropriate standard should be a 'best interpretation of the person's wishes'.[78]

Article 12 outlines the principle of equality before the law and the right to legal capacity, and its full meaning is explored in CRPD General Comment 1.[79] General Comment 1 explains that legal capacity is an 'inherent human right accorded to all people', consisting of the ability to hold legal rights and duties (legal standing) and to exercise those rights and

---

74   Carter, above n 5, 155.

75   Chesterman, above n 68, 34.

76   Carter, above n 5, 147.

77   CRPD, General Comment 1 [26]. UN Doc. No. CRPD/C/GC/1, adopted at the 11th Session (April 2014).

78   Eilionoir Flynn and Anna Arstein-Kerslake, 'The Support Model of Legal Capacity: Fact, Fiction, or Fantasy?' (2014) 32(1) *Berkeley Journal of International Law* 124.

79   CRPD, above n 76.

duties (legal agency).[80] The General Comment envisages a range of positive mechanisms to give effect to the substantive obligation contained in article 12. For example, General Comment 1 explains that the CRPD requires the replacement of all 'substituted decision-making' with 'supported decision-making' regimes.[81] Substituted decision-making is defined as instances where:

(i) legal capacity is removed from a person (even if this is just in respect of a single decision);

(ii) a substituted decision-maker is appointed by someone other than the person concerned (and this can be done against her will); and

(iii) any decision made by a substituted decision-maker is based on what is believed to be the objective 'best interests' of the person.[82]

The definition in General Comment 1 excludes forms of substituted decision-making that permit the person to choose the decision-maker, and substituted decision-making that requires the substituted decision-maker to make a substituted judgment. On this basis, most Australian substituted decision-making arrangements are at least minimally compatible with the CRPD. However, it is apparent that more is required with respect to, for example, the obligation to promote supported decision-making.[83]

'Supported decision-making' means arrangements that enable individuals to exercise legal capacity, as well as arrangements or strategies that support people with disabilities to exercise their decision-making abilities.[84] The latter meaning refers to a range of formal or informal measures that will assist a person to make decisions. It is best understood as a subset of the broader category of support for legal capacity.[85] With respect to legal recognition of supported decision-making in the former sense, several Canadian provinces have introduced supported decision-making and co-decision-making laws.[86]

In Victoria, the concept of 'supportive attorneys' was recently introduced via the *Powers of Attorney Act 2014* (Vic).[87] The new provisions respond to the experience of individuals with disabilities for whom the appointment of a guardian is not considered appropriate but who find they are recognised as legal actors in the community.[88] The supportive attorney's role is to give legal effect to the decisions of the person, described in the legislation as the

---

80 CRPD, General Comment 1 – Article 12: Equal Recognition Before the Law, Paragraph 15, General Comment 1, [13] and [14]. See Bernadette McSherry, 'Legal Capacity under the Convention on the Rights of Persons with Disabilities' (2012) 20 *Journal of Law and Medicine* 22.

81 CRPD, General Comment 1 [26].

82 Ibid [23].

83 Chesterman, above n 68, 31.

84 Eilionoir Flynn and Anna Arstein-Kerslake, 'Legislating Personhood: Realising the Right to Support in Exercising Legal Capacity' (2014) 10(1) *International Journal of Law in Context* 81, 83.

85 Piers Gooding, 'Navigating the "Flashing Amber Lights" of the Right to Legal Capacity in the United Nations Convention on the Rights of Persons with Disabilities: Responding to Major Concerns' (2015) 15 *Human Rights Law Review* 45, 48.

86 *Decision Making, Support and Protection to Adults Act 2003* (Yukon) c 21; *Adult Guardianship and Co-decision-making Act 2000* (Saskatchewan) c A-5.3), *Adult Guardianship and Trusteeship Act 2008* (Alberta) c A-4.2; *Representation Agreement Act 1996* (British Columbia) c 405; *Vulnerable Persons Living with a Mental Disability Act 1993* (Manitoba) c V90, s 6.

87 See *Powers of Attorney Act 2014* (Vic) Part 7. The provisions came into effect on 1 September 2015.

88 Second Reading Speech, Hansard, 2524.

'principal'. The legislation specifies that a supportive attorney does not make decisions for the principal but is authorised to give effect to their decisions. The principal may revoke the appointment when they have the capacity to do so.[89] The supportive attorney is authorised to access, collect, disclose and communicate relevant information,[90] as well as to undertake transactions, except 'significant financial transactions'.[91] More than one supportive attorney, or alternative supportive attorneys, may be appointed.[92]

Conclusion

Substituted decision-making is undergoing a transformation. From the plenary guardianship models of the 19th century, there was a shift in more developed jurisdictions to self-appointed substituted decision-making arrangements and limited, family-based guardianship. In the 21st century, jurisdictions are creating new legal mechanisms, such as supportive attorneys and co-decision-makers, that recognise the legal capacity of people with disabilities. Whether and how substituted decision-making laws should be modified remains a matter of debate in Australia. The full replacement of substituted decision-making with supported decision-making, as required by CRPD, is likely to be an ongoing process.

89   *Powers of Attorney Act 2014* (Vic) s 86.
90   Ibid ss 87–88.
91   Ibid s 89.
92   Ibid ss 92–93.

11

MEDICAL NEGLIGENCE

John Devereux

Introduction

Various legal options, grounded in contract, intentional torts, property and equity, are open to aggrieved patients who have suffered harm.[1] Nevertheless, there are restrictions implicit in those causes of action. So, for example, a patient could sue for breach of contract, although such an action is limited to the express terms of the doctor-patient contract (of which there are few), or breach of an implied term. Though a patient might claim there was an implied term that the doctor pledged to cure the patient, courts have been reluctant to imply such a term.

Similarly, save in the situation where a doctor carries out a physical intervention to which no consent was given by a patient (eg. the doctor operates on an arm instead of a leg), the action in battery is of limited use. Courts will not grant relief in battery where what is complained of by the patient is that no real consent was given because the patient was not informed of the risks of a treatment. However, there is another legal cause of action that may be considered in these circumstances – an action in negligence. The purpose of this chapter is to explain the use of such a cause of action in a healthcare setting. In the first part of the chapter, we consider the basis and first principles of claims made in negligence. In the second part, we consider the key elements of a claim in negligence – duty of care, breach, causation and remoteness – and how they apply in context of claims made against medical practitioners and in healthcase settings more generally.

The basis of negligence

Unlike contract, where the focus is upon what the parties agreed (or might reasonably have been presumed to have agreed), obligations in negligence (such as that in battery) arise by operation of law, irrespective of the intent of the parties. In its broadest sense, negligence refers to acting (or failing to act) in a way that falls below the standard of 'the reasonable person'. In the popular press, such a person is said to have 'breached his (or her) duty of care'. While this definition provides a useful start, it obscures more than it makes clear. If a person does act negligently, does this mean anyone who is harmed can claim? What, exactly is 'a reasonable person'? Is it the same as the ordinary person? If so, is this the standard by which we judge the conduct of medical practitioners?

First principles

Negligence is actionable where a duty of care exists, that duty has been breached, and that breach has caused damage which is not too remote. Some caution needs to be exercised here. Butler et al. point out that there is inevitably some overlap between the three elements,[2] noting that in *Gett v Tabet*[3] the NSW Court of Appeal suggested that:

---

1   For further details, see Chapter 9. The parts of this chapter covering pre-civil liability common law draw heavily upon John Devereux, *Australian Medical Law*, 3rd edn (Routledge, 2007) 313–559.

2   Desmond A Butler, Tina Cockburn and Jennifer M Yule, 'Negligence' in Benjamin P White, Fiona McDonald and Lindy Willmott (eds), *Health Law in Australia*, 2nd edn (Thomson Reuters, 2014) 255–370.

3   *Gett v Tabet* [2009] NSWCA 76.

The various elements (of negligence) are not to be treated as independent of one another and hence to be addressed entirely separately. The manner of defining a duty will frequently answer the question as to whether it has been breached in particular circumstances, [and] the means of identifying the harm will frequently determine whether the relevant causative connection exists. Accordingly, the intellectual discipline of separating the various elements must be exercised with an eye to the overall direction.[4]

Duty of care

A duty of care is not owed by a person to the world at large. In *Donoghue v Stevenson*[5] Lord Atkin suggested that:

> one must take reasonable care to avoid acts or omissions that could reasonably be foreseen as likely to injure one's neighbour. Who then in law is my neighbour? A neighbour is someone who is so closely and directly affected by the act that one ought to have them in contemplation as being so affected when directing one's mind to the acts or omissions in question.[6]

In terms of reasonable foreseeability, it is clear that a doctor's patient is reasonably foreseeable as being within a class of people who could suffer damage. A doctor owes a duty of care to her/his patients. In the seminal case of *Rogers v Whitaker*[7] the High Court described this duty as a single, comprehensive duty encompassing diagnosis, advice and treatment. The duty is not an absolute one. Rather, it is a duty to exercise reasonable care and skill.

When does the duty commence?

Generally, the law does not recognise a duty to rescue another. It has been said that Anglo-Australian law does not recognise a Good Samaritan principle:

> The dictates of charity and of compassion do not constitute a duty of care. The law casts no duty upon a man to go to the aid of another who is in peril or in distress, not caused by him. The call of common humanity may lead him to rescue. This the law recognizes, for it gives the rescuer its protection when he answer the call. But it does not require that he do so. There is no general duty to help a neighbour whose house is on fire.[8]

The NT recognises a statutory exception on this point in its Criminal Code, which provides that:

> Any person who, being able to provide rescue, resuscitation, medical treatment, first aid, or succour of any kind to a person urgently in need of it and whose life may be endangered if it is not provided, callously fails to do so is guilty of a crime and is liable to imprisonment for 7 years.[9]

---

4   Ibid at 321.
5   *Donoghue v Stevenson* [1932] AC 562.
6   Ibid at 580, per Lord Atkin.
7   *Rogers v Whitaker* (1992) 175 CLR 479.
8   *Hargrave v Goldman* (1963) 110 CLR 40 per Windeyer J.
9   *Criminal Code Act* (NT) s 155.

In exceptional circumstances, it has been held that even at common law a duty of care exists to those people who, though not currently patients of a doctor, are in such a position that, if the doctor is to act in a way that does not involve reasonable skill and care, might suffer damage. So, in *Lowns v Woods*[10] a teenage boy suffered a series of epileptic fits. His sister was despatched to a nearby doctor's surgery to seek help. Though the doctor subsequently denied being approached by the boy's sister, the court accepted that he had, in fact, been so approached. The doctor declined to attend. The boy suffered brain damage, an outcome which the court accepted would not have happened had the doctor promptly attended and treated the boy. The doctor was found liable in negligence for failing to attend and provide treatment.

Similarly, in *Hoffman v Medical Board of Australia*[11] a doctor was cautioned by the WA State Administrative Tribunal (WASAT). A woman with a sick child attended a medical centre before there was any doctor available to see her child. She approached the appellant (who was standing in the doorway of the medical centre) and asked if he was a doctor. He denied that he was. There was no previous relationship between the parties, but the Tribunal determined that what the doctor had done was 'acting improperly in the course of medical practice'.[12]

In contrast, the WA Court of Appeal quashed such a finding in the case of *Dekker v Medical Board of Australia*.[13] In that case, the doctor was returning from an outing when she swerved to avoid a car. The latter car ended up in a ditch, having crossed an embankment. The crash occurred at night. The doctor drove immediately to a police station (a one-minute drive away) to summon help. The Tribunal held:

> It is improper conduct in a professional respect for a medical practitioner who is aware that a motor vehicle accident has or may have occurred in their vicinity and that anyone involved has or may have suffered injury not to make an assessment of the situation, including the nature of any injuries and needs of persons involved, and render assistance, by way of first aid, when the practitioner is physically able to do so, notwithstanding that the practitioner immediately reports the matter to police or other emergency services. It matters not that there is no existing professional relationship between a medical practitioner and the persons involved in the accident. Because saving human life and healing sick and injured people is a core purpose and ethic of the medical profession, and because members of the profession have the knowledge and skills to do so, the failure by a medical practitioner to make an assessment and render assistance when he or she is aware that a motor vehicle accident has or may have occurred in their vicinity and that people have or may have been injured, when the practitioner is physically able to do so, would, notwithstanding that the practitioner reports the matter immediately to police or other emergency services, reasonably be regarded as improper by medical practitioners of good repute and competency, and there is a sufficiently close link or nexus with the profession of medicine.[14]

10   *Lowns v Woods* (1996) Aust Torts Reports 81–376.
11   *Hoffman v Medical Board of Australia* [2012] WASAT 110 at 35.
12   Ibid at 35 in 'Catchwords'.
13   *Dekker v Medical Board of Australia* [2014] WASCA 216.
14   Ibid at 26.

However, the WA Court of Appeal held that the Tribunal had insufficient evidence upon which to base its findings and set aside the decision. The Court was equally critical of the fact that the medical practitioner's obligations as outlined above failed to take into account the practitioner's particular circumstances. In this case, the practitioner neither owned, nor had with her, a mobile phone. She was distressed at having narrowly avoided physical injury, she had no medical equipment with her and the police station was only a very short drive away.[15]

Similar duties have been held to be owed to other third parties. When a doctor conducts an examination at the request of an employer, the doctor owes a duty not only to the potential employer, but also to the patient.[16] This may include a duty to advise a patient of the results of pathology tests, as well as to advise if further investigation and treatment is warranted.[17] Similarly, a doctor working at a factory was held liable for failing to order six-monthly medical reviews of workers, given his knowledge of their cancer risk.[18] Jones notes that there is English authority suggesting that a doctor will be held liable in circumstances where he has negligently discharged an infectious patient, who then infects others,[19] and where a doctor admits a person to a maternity home without first warning of the recent outbreak of disease there.[20]

The principle is clear: a doctor owes a duty of care not only to her/his individual patients, but also to a person who could foreseeably be harmed through the failure of the doctor to take reasonable care of the patient. So, in *BT v Oei*,[21] AT was a patient of Dr Oei, and attended for consultations with the doctor on a number of occasions, complaining of symptoms which, with the benefit of hindsight, were consistent with his having been infected with HIV. Subsequently, AT transmitted HIV to his partner, BT. Despite the fact that Dr Oei had no doctor-patient relationship with BT, and that Dr Oei was not aware of BT's existence, he was held to have breached a duty of care owed to BT. This was because he had failed to advise AT to undergo an HIV test, in circumstances where the Court was satisfied that, having been so advised he would have done so, and would have practised safe sex.

Though it is clear from the general law that a duty of care can be owed to a child *in utero* (ie. before the child is born and has legal status), it has been held that a duty of care may be owed to a person even prior to conception. Thus, in *Kosky v Trustees of the Sisters of Charity*,[22] where a woman was negligently transfused with the wrong type of blood, which affected a child conceived seven years later, that child was permitted to sue for breach of a duty of care owed to her.

The question of duties owed to other parties is particularly problematic where a doctor owes duties to two patients, in circumstances where the duty owed to one party might conflict with the duty owed to another. So, in *Harvey v PD*,[23] two people who intended to

---

15   Ibid at 3.
16   Michael Jones, *Medical Negligence* (Sweet & Maxwell, 1991) 27. The discussion in this chapter on duties owed to third parties draws heavily upon Devereux, above n 1, 324–98.
17   *Thomson v Davison* [1975] Qd R 93.
18   *Stokes v Guest, Keen and Nettlefold (Bolts and Nuts) Ltd* [1968] 1 WLR 1776.
19   *Evans v Mayor of Liverpool* [1906] 1 KB 160.
20   *Lindsey County Council v Marshall* [1937] AC 97.
21   *BT v Oei* [1999] NSWSC 1082.
22   *Kosky v Trustees of the Sisters of Charity* [1982] VR 961.
23   *Harvey v PD* (2004) 59 NSWLR 639.

marry sought to be tested for sexually transmitted infections. They attended together. The female partner tested negative. The male partner tested positive, for both HIV and Hepatitis B. The doctor was held liable for failing to identify the conflict of interest should either the male or female patient test positive, as well as for failing to obtain instructions as to how the information should be communicated, if this proved to be the case.

An interesting recent case is that of *McCann v Buck*,[24] where a doctor advised a patient, in the presence of her parents, that there was no more he could do for her. The doctor advised the patient that an experimental treatment was available in the US. On the strength of this representation, the patient's parents obtained a bank loan to fund the treatment, to be taken abroad. In fact, the experimental treatment was on offer at a local hospital which was conducting studies on such treatment. The WA District Court held the doctor liable for the economic loss suffered by the patient's parents. It was clear in this case that the interests of the patient and the parents did not conflict.

Compare this with the position adopted by the High Court in *Sullivan v Moody*.[25] In this case, the Court held that a doctor owed no duty to the father of a child who had been examined in respect of suspected child sexual abuse and where the father had subsequently suffered psychiatric harm and consequential financial loss. It was held that to hold that the doctor owed a duty to the father would place the doctor in a situation of potentially owing conflicting duties to the child and the father.

Breach

Breach is determined by reference to the relevant standard of care (a matter of law), then examining whether the defendant has fallen below that standard of care (a matter of fact). The traditional formula for breach was that found in *Bolam v Friern Barnett Hospital Management Committee*.[26] The test was not that of the reasonable person, but rather that which could reasonably be expected of a person holding out or professing a special skill. Inexperience was no excuse;[27] nor was being a rural, rather than an urban, medical practitioner.[28] Noting that medical technology and skills advance over time, the courts have made it clear that the relevant time for assessing breach is the date of the incident, not the date of trial.[29] There is now a bifurcated approach to breach, which is dependent upon whether the breach alleged is an error of diagnosis or treatment, or a failure to advise of material risks.

Diagnosis or treatment

The standard here is that established by the High Court in *Rogers v Whitaker*.[30] This area has been affected by the *Civil Liability Acts* (or equivalent) which have been adopted in Australian states/territories as a result of tort law reform recommended in the Ipp Report

---

24   *McCann v Buck* [2000] WADC 81.
25   *Sullivan v Moody* (2001) 207 CLR 562.
26   *Bolam v Friern Barnet Hospital Management Committee* [1957] 1 WLR 582.
27   *Wilsher v Essex Area Health Authority* [1988] AC 1074.
28   *Geissman v O'Keefe* (unreported, Supreme Court of New South Wales, Simpson J, 25 November 1994).
29   *Roe v Minister of Health* [1954] 2 QB 66.
30   See above n 7.

in the early 2000s.[31] The Act in each jurisdiction makes it a defence for the doctor to prove that 'he has acted in accordance with a practice that was widely accepted in Australia by peer professional opinion as professional practice'.[32] This defence will operate, subject to the courts determining that the practice is irrational. It will be appreciated that this is a 'modified' *Bolam* test. It was noted in the case of *Dobler v Halverson* that the relevant provisions of the Acts operate as a defence and not as a matter of plaintiff proof.[33]

The consequence is that a plaintiff will be required to prove the three steps of breach in the relevant Act.[34] That is, that a risk of harm was reasonably foreseeable, that it was not insubstantial, and that a reasonable person would have taken precautions to avoid the risk. Having done so, the onus then falls on the defendant to show that what was done was in accordance with reasonable medical practice. In terms of reasonable foreseeability, the High Court has stressed it is important to avoid 'hindsight bias'.[35] The fact that a risk is not insignificant is, according to the Ipp report, a higher standard than the common law test which formerly applied (ie. not 'far-fetched or fanciful'), but is not as high as 'a substantial risk'. In *Shaw v Thomas*[36] it was held that the test was to be determined by reference to what reasonable people would have been aware of in the circumstances of the appellants.

Examples of errors in diagnosis and treatment

Elsewhere a number of cases describing errors in diagnosis and treatment have been discussed.[37] The cases include *Chin Keow v Government of Malaysia*,[38] where liability was established when a doctor failed to take a medical history, which would have revealed a penicillin allergy. The patient died when the doctor injected penicillin into her as treatment for a leg ulcer. The duty to take a medical history is an ongoing one, such that a doctor who fails to revise a diagnosis when new information comes to light is liable if damage results to the patient.[39] A failure to prescribe the correct antibiotic for a patient who has an infection is negligence.[40] If a patient has an underlying medical condition, the duty of care owed by the doctor to that patient is higher.[41] This principle is reflective of the general law of negligence, as established in *Paris v Stepney Borough Council*.[42]

---

31   Such reform took place in the wake of the recommendations of what is known as the Ipp Report, see The Honourable David Ipp et al., *Review of the Law of Negligence: Final Report* (Commonwealth of Australia, 2002).

32   See, for example, *Civil Liability Act 2002* (NSW) s 50; *Civil Liability Act 2002* (Tas) s 22; *Civil Liability Act 1936* (SA) s 41; *Civil Liability Act 2003* (Qld) s 22(1); *Wrongs Act 1958* (Vic) s 59; *Civil Liability Act 2002* (WA) s 5PB. NT and ACT have not enacted mirror legislation to include the peer professional practice defence and, in this context, rely on *Rogers v Whitaker*.

33   *Dobler v Halverson* (2007) 70 NSWLR 151.

34   See, for example, *Civil Liability Act 2003* (Qld) s 9; *Civil Liability Act 2002* (WA) s 5PB; *Civil Liability Act 2002* (Tas) s 14; *Civil Liability Act 1936* (SA) s 35; *Wrongs Act 1958* (Vic) ss 52 and 56; *Civil Liability Act 2002* (NSW) s 5E.

35   *Rosenberg v Percival* (2001) 205 CLR 434.

36   *Shaw v Thomas* [2010] NSWCA 169.

37   See Devereux, above n 1, 399–559. This section of the chapter draws heavily on the cases discussed in that text. Reference should be made to that text for further details on the cases.

38   *Chin Keow v Government of Malaysia* [1967] 1 WLR 813.

39   *Giurelli v Girgis* (1980) 24 SASR 264.

40   *Geissman v O'Keefe* (unreported, Supreme Court of New South Wales, Simpson J, 25 November 1994).

41   *Markaboui v Western Sydney Area Health Service* [2005] NSWSC 649.

42   *Paris v Stepney Borough Council* [1951] AC 367.

Courts have made it clear that the fact that damage has happened does not mean, *ipso facto*, that a medical practitioner has been negligent. The fact that a child was born following a sterilisation procedure does not mean that the doctor who performed the operation must have done so negligently.[43] Proof that the doctor has fallen below the standard of care is required. So, leaving foreign matter inside a patient following surgery is not automatically negligent: where the surgeon went to a great deal of trouble to count in and count out swabs, the swabs were marked with flags, and a surgeon's assistant checked as well; but nonetheless a patient died when a swab was left inside him, the surgeon was found to be not negligent.[44] However, in cases where it can be demonstrated that there has been a clear lack of care in terms of accounting for foreign matter and making appropriate checks, negligence will often be found.[45] A failure to accurately diagnose a malignancy which results in a lost opportunity to have efficacious treatment will also amount to negligence,[46] as will a misdiagnosis of multiple sclerosis, where the correct diagnosis (tumour of the spine) was made too late to arrange efficacious treatment.[47]

If an operation is performed without negligence, but additional damage is caused to the patient, a doctor should advise the patient of that damage. A failure to do so in a timely fashion, which deprives the patient of the chance to seek remedial treatment, is negligence.[48] A failure by a doctor to follow up a patient when the doctor is aware, or should be aware, of medical results which indicate that treatment is required is negligence, with no set-off permitted for contributory negligence for the patient's failure to make further enquiries of the doctor.[49] Similarly, a specialist who refers a patient to a nearby hospital but fails to follow up when she does not appear on his surgical list, will be liable.[50] A patient who is suspected of being seriously ill, and is frustrated at the length of time he had to wait in casualty, should be counselled against leaving the hospital if there is a risk he might suffer damage as a result of failing to obtain efficacious diagnosis and treatment.[51] A doctor also has a duty to properly train staff to detect and prioritise serious illnesses.[52]

Failure to advise of material risks

A medical practitioner has a proactive and reactive duty to advise of material risks.[53] That duty is to provide information that a reasonable person in the patient's position would, in the circumstances, require to enable the person to make a reasonably informed decision about whether or not to undergo the treatment or follow the advice. It is information that

---

43 *Hancock v Queensland* [2002] QSC 27.
44 *Mahon v Osborne* [1939] 2 KB 14.
45 *Chasney v Anderson* (1950) 4 DLR 223; *Hocking v Bell* (1947) 75 CLR 125.
46 *Wood v Queensland Medical Laboratories* (unreported, Supreme Court of Queensland, Cullinane J, 16 December 1994); *O'Shea v Sullivan and Macquarie Pathological Services* (1994) Aust Torts Report 81–273.
47 *Flinders Medical Centre v Waller* (2005) 91 SASR 378.
48 *Wighton v Arnot* [2005] NSWSC 637.
49 *Kite v Malycha* (1988) 71 SASR 321.
50 *Tai v Hatzistavrou* [1999] NSWCA 306.
51 *Wang v Central Sydney Area Health Service* (2000) Aust Tort Reports 81-574.
52 *Alexander v Heise* [2001] NSWSC 69.
53 See, for example, *Civil Liability Act 2003* (Qld) s 21; *Civil Liability Act 2002* (WA) ss 5PB(2)(a)–(b); *Civil Liability Act 2002* (Tas) s 21; *Civil Liability Act 1936* (SA) s 41(5); *Wrongs Act 1958* (Vic) s 60; *Civil Liability Act 2002* (NSW) s 5P.

the doctor knows, or ought reasonably to know, the patient wants to be given before making the decision about whether or not to undergo the treatment or follow the advice. This duty was first established in *Rogers v Whitaker*. In that case a woman was successful in a negligence action when a surgeon failed to warn her of the one in 14,000 risk of developing sympathetic opthalmia: she became blind in both eyes. The patient was anxious prior to the procedure, asked questions about the procedure and, at one point, suggested covering her 'good eye', lest the doctor accidentally operate on the 'wrong eye'.[54]

Causation

It is not enough that a doctor owes a duty of care, and that s/he breached that duty by falling below the relevant standard. The plaintiff must additionally prove that that failure caused damage to the plaintiff. So in *Barnett v Chelsea and Kensington Hospital Management Committee*,[55] a group of night watchmen became ill after consuming tea and they attended their local hospital. A doctor on duty failed to attend and treat, and one of the men subsequently died. The doctor and the hospital avoided being held liable in negligence since it could not be shown that, even if the doctor had promptly attended and treated, the night-watchman would have survived. The evidence was that his poisoning was too far advanced. The test outlined in *Barnett v Chelsea* has become known as the 'but for test': but for the defendant's negligence, would the harm have occurred to the plaintiff?

Such a test has an important role to play, not only in failure of diagnosis or treatment cases, but also in failure to warn cases. The plaintiff needs to prove not only that the doctor owed a duty of care to advise of a material risk, but that the failure to do so caused damage to him or her. In other words, that had the patient been informed of the risk, he or she would not have gone ahead with the procedure. In assessing this last matter, courts have examined not only statements made by the plaintiff, but the surrounding circumstances. In *Bustos v Hair Transplant Pty Ltd and Peter Wearne*[56] the plaintiff claimed a failure to warn him of the side effects of a juri flap procedure (a hair transplant procedure). The court noted that, having seen the procedure successfully performed on his brother, the plaintiff was 'keen to the point of desperation' to have the procedure done. Similarly, in *Berger v Mutton*[57] the plaintiff alleged that there had been a failure to advise of the risk of a perforated bowel while undertaking a diagnostic laparoscopy. She claimed that had she been told of the risk, she would not have undergone the procedure. The court noted that the plaintiff was a nurse with extensive experience of surgery, trauma and oncology. She had a genuine fear that she might be suffering from cancer. In all the circumstances, the court did not accept that the information about the risk of bowel perforation was determinative for her.

Of course, the difficulty with the 'but for test' is that there may be multiple causes of damage. In *March v Stramere*,[58] the High Court formulated an alternative test of causation

---

54   *Rogers v Whitaker*, above n 7; note also the recent UK Supreme Court judgment in *Montgomery v Lanarkshire Health Board* [2015] UKSC 11.
55   *Barnett v Chelsea and Kensington Hospital Management Committee* [1968] 2 WLR 422.
56   *Bustos v Hair Transplant Pty Ltd and Peter Wearne* (unreported, NSW District Court, 20 December 1994).
57   *Berger v Mutton* (unreported, NSW District Court, Twigg DCJ, 22 November 1994).
58   *March v E & MH Stramere Pty Ltd* (1991) 171 CLR 506.

known as 'the common sense test'. If, as a matter of common sense, the defendant generated the very risk of harm which materialised, then the defendant could be said to have caused the plaintiff's harm. In *Chappel v Hart*,[59] for example, where the plaintiff (a teacher) was not warned of the risk of mediastinitis, which affected her voice, she sued in negligence for a failure to advise of a material risk. Under cross-examination, the plaintiff admitted that, even if she had have been warned of the risk of the procedure, she would have had the operation, but at a later stage, and with a more experienced surgeon. The fact that she would have had the procedure anyway precluded proof of the 'but for test'. The majority of the High Court found that, as a matter of common sense, the fact that a more experienced surgeon would have done the operation had the plaintiff been warned meant that the risk of the side effect occurring was less. This was notwithstanding expert evidence that mediastinitis could occur by random chance.

Since the adoption of the *Civil Liability Acts* (or equivalents), the 'but for test' has been re-established as the primary test of causation,[60] but the court may still, in exceptional cases, 'apply principles in accordance with established cases' (ie. common sense).[61] A plaintiff is now precluded from having admitted a statement s/he makes as to what s/he would have done, had things been different, except where such a statement is against her/his own interest.[62] This means, for example, that the statement made by the plaintiff in *Chappel v Hart* would no longer be admissible.

It needs to be emphasised that not all damage is recoverable at law. So, for example, while an action is maintainable for wrongful birth – where a doctor's negligence is responsible for the birth of a child, causing costs to the parents which are recoverable[63] – an action brought by a severely disabled child born as a result of a doctor's negligence, who claims s/he would rather not have been born, is not maintainable. This is because awarding damages would involve a court comparing existence while severely disabled with non-existence.[64]

Remoteness

The principle of remoteness governs the extent to which a defendant should be liable. For example, if a person's negligence causes a physical injury, which causes a loss of employment, which causes depression, which causes a breakdown of a relationship, which of these damages is recoverable? At common law, the operative principle is to be found in the *Wagon Mound* case.[65] Damage of a type or kind of harm which was reasonably foreseeable

---

59   *Chappel v Hart* (1998) 195 CLR 232.
60   See, for example, *Civil Liability Act 2003* (Qld) s 11(1)(a); *Civil Liability Act 2002* (WA) s 5C(1)(a); *Civil Liability Act 2002* (Tas) s 13(1)(a); *Civil Liability Act 1936* (SA) s 34(1)(a); *Wrongs Act 1958* (Vic) s 51(1)(a); *Civil Liability Act 2002* (NSW) s 5D(1)(a).
61   See, for example, *Civil Liability Act 2003* (Qld) s 11(2); *Civil Liability Act 2002* (WA) s 5C(2); *Civil Liability Act 2002* (Tas) s 13(2); *Wrongs Act 1958* (Vic) s 51(2); *Civil Liability Act 2002* (NSW) s 5D(2). There does not seem to be an equivalent provision in the SA legislation.
62   See, for example, *Civil Liability Act 2003* (Qld) s 11(3); *Civil Liability Act 2002* (WA) s 5C(3); *Civil Liability Act 2002* (Tas) s 13(3); *Wrongs Act 1958* (Vic) s 51(3); *Civil Liability Act 2002* (NSW) s 5D(3). There does not seem to be an equivalent provision in the SA legislation.
63   *Cattanach v Melchior* (2003) 215 CLR 1.
64   *Harriton v Stephens* (2006) 226 CLR 52.
65   *Overseas Tankship (UK) Ltd v Morts Dock & Engineering Co Ltd* (The Wagon Mound (No 1)) [1961] AC 388.

is recoverable. The precise sequence of events need not, however, be foreseen.[66] The same rule operates under the *Civil Liability Acts* (or equivalent),[67] but the courts may also consider policy factors.[68] Since the adoption of these Acts, remoteness has been called 'scope of liability'.

In *Wallace v Kam*[69] the High Court confronted the situation where there were two material risks of an operation to be performed on a patient's lumbar spine, neither of which was divulged to a patient. One of the risks materialised. The patient did not dispute that had he been told of this risk he would nevertheless have proceeded to have the treatment. The Court accepted that had he been told of the other risk, he would not have proceeded with the treatment. The High Court decided that while factual causation had been established, allowing recovery in such circumstances was not within the scope of liability.

Conclusion

This chapter has examined how and why the law of negligence may be invoked as a cause of action due to harm or injury suffered by a patient as a result of medical treatment. It is important to note that negligence consists of a number of elements: duty of care, breach of that duty, and that such breach causes damage. A doctor owes a duty of care to a patient to exercise reasonable skill and care. The duty extends to diagnosis, treatment and advice as to material risks. Diagnosis and treatment are judged by a modified *Bolam* standard. The duty to advise of material risks is governed by principles first outlined by the High Court case of *Rogers v Whitaker*. For a doctor to be liable, their breach of duty must have caused damage which is of a type or kind of harm which is reasonably foreseeable.

---

66   *Chapman v Hearse* (1961) 106 CLR 112.
67   See, for example, *Civil Liability Act 2003* (Qld) s 11(1)(b); *Civil Liability Act 2002* (WA) s 5C(1)(b); *Civil Liability Act 2002* (Tas) s 13(1)(b); *Civil Liability Act 1936* (SA) s 34(1)(b); *Wrongs Act 1958* (Vic) s 51(1)(b); *Civil Liability Act 2002* (NSW) s 5D(1)(b).
68   See, for example, *Civil Liability Act 2003* (Qld) s 11(4); *Civil Liability Act 2002* (WA) s 5C(4); *Civil Liability Act 2002* (Tas) s 13(4); *Civil Liability Act 1936* (SA) s 34(3); *Wrongs Act 1958* (Vic) s 51(4); *Civil Liability Act 2002* (NSW) s 5D(4).
69   *Wallace v Kam* (2013) 250 CLR 375.

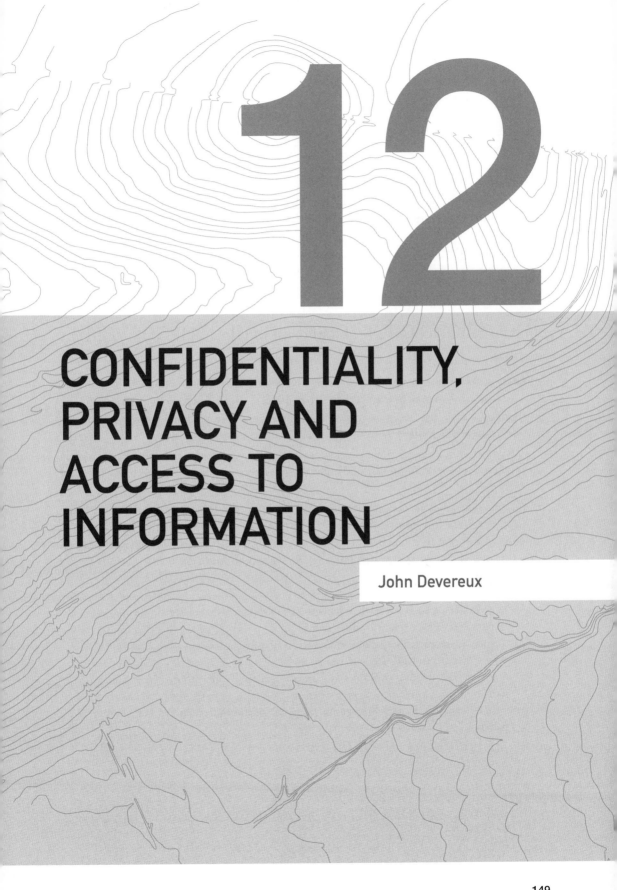

12

CONFIDENTIALITY, PRIVACY AND ACCESS TO INFORMATION

John Devereux

Introduction

Health information is among the most sensitive information. Details of illness, disease and treatment are highly personal. Historically, codes of ethics have carefully regulated the use to which such information can be put. While ethics continues to enjoin healthcare professionals from misusing private information, more modern formulations attempt to balance the confidentiality of health information with a lawful right of access by patients, and to ensure the legitimate use of information by doctors, institutions and researchers. This chapter first explores the ethical and legal obligation of confidence and the exceptions to it. In the second part, it examines 'the flip side': access to information. In the final part of the chapter, the limitations on a doctor's right to collect and disseminate information are explored.

The rationale for maintaining confidentiality

Skene has identified three rationales for maintaining confidentiality:

* *Medical*: from a medical point of view, maintaining a patient's confidentiality benefits a patient's treatment. Knowing that a patient can speak freely, unworried about the thought of what use might be made of the information means that a patient can divulge information which might be useful to making an accurate diagnosis.
* *Ethical*: from an ethical point of view, maintaining a patient's confidential information respects a patient's autonomy and right to self-determination, as well as the dignity of each person.
* *Public policy*: it is in the public interest that all people in society be given optimum treatment. This can best be achieved by ensuring accurate diagnosis, which, in turn, is dependent upon free and frank disclosure of information. This is most likely to happen when the patient is assured that information 'will go no further'.[1]

As Raanan Gillon notes:

> In order to do a good job for their patients, doctors often need to have information of a sort that people generally regard as private, even secret ... Some of the information is embarrassing to discuss, and some may be positively harmful to the patient or others if it is divulged. Doctors routinely ask a series of questions about bodily functions that people would not dream of discussing with anyone else ... Such intrusive medical inquiries are not based on prurience or mere inquisitiveness but on the pursuit of information that may assist the doctor in treating and helping the patient.[2]

---

1   Loane Skene, *Law and Medical Practice: Rights, Duties, Claims and Defences*, 2nd edn (LexisNexis, 2004) 256–7.
2   Raanan Gillon, 'Confidentiality' in Helga Kuhse and Peter Singer (eds), *A Companion to Bioethics* (Blackwell, 1998) 426–7, quoted in Sonia Allan and Meredith Blake, *The Patient and The Practitioner: Health Law and Ethics in Australia* (LexisNexis, 2014) 298–9.

Sources of confidentiality[3]

There are three main sources of confidentiality: ethics, contract or tort, and equity. We now consider each in turn.

Ethics

The traditional conception of confidentiality in medical ethics can be traced to the Code of Hippocrates:

> What I see or hear in the course of the treatment or even outside of the treatment in regard to the life of men, which on no account one must spread abroad, I will keep to myself holding such things shameful to be spoken about.[4]

A more modern formulation is to be found in The World Medical Association's Declaration of Geneva, which states:

> I will respect the secrets which are confided in me, even after the patient has died.[5]

The Australian Medical Association's (AMA's) Code of Ethics is less absolute. It notes:

> Maintain your patient's confidentiality. Exceptions to this must be taken very seriously. They may include where there is a serious risk to the patient or another person, where required by law, where part of approved research, or where there are overwhelming societal interests.[6]

Contract

As discussed in Chapter 9, there is usually a contractual relationship between a doctor and a private patient. An implied term of that contract is that the doctor will maintain confidentiality. It is clear that if a doctor breaches that implied term, then the doctor will be liable in damages. An alternative basis of liability is that grounded in the law of negligence. In *Furniss v Fitchett*,[7] a couple were both patients of the same doctor. Without the wife's knowledge or consent, the doctor supplied a note to the husband where he indicated that he thought the wife was mentally unsound and this note was subsequently produced in family law proceedings. When the wife suffered nervous shock as a result, she successfully sued the doctor in negligence.

---

3   The sections of this chapter on confidentiality and exceptions to it draw heavily on John Devereux, *Australian Medical Law*, 3rd edn (Routledge, 2007) 947–72.

4   Ludwig Edelstein, *The Hippocratic Oath: Test, Translation and Interpretation* (Johns Hopkins Press, 1943) quoted in Allan and Blake, above n 2, 298.

5   World Medical Association, *Declaration of Geneva, Editorial Revision 2006* (173rd Council Session of the World Medical Association, Divonne-Les-Bains, May 2006).

6   Australian Medical Association, *Code of Ethics* (2006) 1.1l, quoted in Allan and Blake, above n 2, 298; cf Medical Board of Australia, *Good Medical Practice: A Code of Conduct for Doctors in Australia*, para 3.4.

7   *Furniss v Fitchett* [1958] NZLR 396.

Equity

An equitable action for breach of confidence arises provided three pre-conditions are met:

- the information must have the necessary quality of confidence about it;
- the information must have been imparted in circumstances importing an obligation of confidence; and
- there has been an unauthorised use of that information.[8]

Courts have made it clear that the second element is to be judged according to an objective standard.[9] Objectively speaking, there seems little doubt that a doctor-patient consultation would be caught by the second element noted above. According to Allan and Blake, the first element means that certain comments or discussions in the context of a doctor-patient consultation would not be accorded the protection of the law of confidence, such as those about the weather or what either party did on the weekend.[10] It has been suggested that the protection extends not only to information gained directly from a patient, but also to information gleaned from other persons in the doctor's capacity as a health professional.[11]

Exceptions to the duty of confidence

The duty of confidence is not absolute. A number of exceptions have already been noted:

- *Consent:* Since the duty is for the benefit of the patient, the patient may waive the duty (ie. consent to disclosure of information). Consent may be express or implied. So, for example, a patient who is offered a referral to see a specialist, impliedly agrees to the general practitioner releasing medical information about the patient to the specialist.
- *Public interest:* There will be instances where the disclosure of confidential information could save lives. So, for example, a psychiatrist who is told of violent fantasies a patient has may by informing the subject of the violent fantasy, or the police, enable the subject to seek safety.[12]

The duty of confidence is often described as protecting a private interest – that of the patient. However, it also protects a public interest – public health is promoted indirectly because more people are encouraged to seek treatment when they know information imparted to a doctor is kept confidential. Viewed as a conflict of one public interest (confidentiality) against another (public safety), it is then easier for a court to determine whether one should take precedence over another.

In *W v Egdell*,[13] a patient was detained at Her Majesty's pleasure in the UK following a 'killing spree'. He commissioned a report from a private psychiatrist. This was part of a process by which the patient was seeking to be transferred to a less secure facility, which was

---

8   *Coco v AN Clark (Engineers) Ltd* [1969] RPC 41.
9   *Mense and Ampere Electrical Manufacturing Co Pty Ltd v Milenkovic* [1973] VR 784.
10   *Coco v AN Clarke*, above n 8.
11   Francis Gurry, *Breach of Confidence* (Clarendon Press, 1984).
12   See, for example, *Tarasoff v Regents of the University of California*, 17 Cal 3d 425 (1976). US courts have taken the view that doctors who do not breach the duty of confidentiality in such circumstances expose themselves to liability to a person who suffers injury, or their family.
13   *W v Egdell* [1990] Ch 359.

the first step towards eventual release into the community. The psychiatrist formed the view that the patient was not safe to move to a less secure facility. He expressed this view in a report. The patient, having been apprised of the report, tried to restrain the psychiatrist from releasing it. The psychiatrist sent it to the Home Office. The English Court of Appeal held that in circumstances where there was an identified threat of harm, disclosure was justified on the basis of preventing a greater harm.

However, the disclosure must be no greater than that which is necessary to avoid the risk of harm, and to a person or body who is empowered to remove the risk of harm. In *Duncan v Medical Practitioners Disciplinary Committee*[14] a disclosure about the health status of a bus driver made to bus passengers and the media was held to exceed these requirements as it was a disclosure to the general public. In that case, the Court made clear that before disclosure could be permitted, another person's life must be immediately endangered and urgent action must be required. This sense of a need for urgent intervention was re-emphasised in *X Health Authority v Y*.[15] In that case, the health authority's employees leaked information to a newspaper about two doctors who were practising medicine while they had AIDS. The Court's view was that there was no urgent need to protect the public through such publication.

Compulsion by law

A doctor may be compelled by law to disclose medical information. For example, public health statutes in each jurisdiction compel the reporting of certain communicable diseases.[16] Similarly, the National Law compels doctors, employers or educational facilities to report certain concerns about doctors or trainee doctors.[17] A clear direction to disclose information cannot be resisted on the basis that such disclosure would breach a patient's (or, in the case of mandatory reporting about doctors or trainee doctors, those doctors') confidence. In *Hunter v Mann*[18] an English High Court considered the interpretation of section 168 of the *Road Traffic Act 1972* (Imp), which provided, in part, that where the driver of a vehicle was alleged to have committed an offence, 'any person shall, if required, give any information which it is in his power to give and may lead to the identification of the driver'. A doctor had information which would have identified the driver of a stolen car. When asked by a policeman to divulge that information, he refused on the basis that he owed a duty of confidentiality to his patient. The Court held that the words of the statute were clear and unequivocal. The doctor was obliged to provide the information.

It is a normal part of litigation for disclosure to be ordered. This provides each party, subject to exemptions based on grounds of privilege, to have full access to relevant documents to prepare for trial. At trial, a court may additionally order a party to answer a question, even if doing so might breach confidentiality. In *BC (by her litigation guardian) v Australian Red Cross Society* the Supreme Court of Victoria ordered the Australian Red Cross Society to

---

14   *Duncan v Medical Practitioners Disciplinary Committee* [1986] 1 NZLR 513.

15   *X Health Authority v Y* [1988] RPC 379.

16   For further details, see Chapter 25, which examines public health law.

17   See *Health Practitioner Regulation National Law Act 2009* (Qld) ss 140–3; Medical Board of Australia, above n 6, para 8.3. See, generally, Chapter 7 for further details.

18   *Hunter v Mann* [1974] QB 767.

divulge the name and address of a person thought to have donated HIV-infected blood, which it was alleged had been transmitted to the recipient, 'BC'.[19] This order was upheld on appeal.[20] Legislation throughout Australia mandates disclosure of particular medical information:[21]

(a) Legislation on the registration of deaths requires details relating to the medical condition of a deceased person to be disclosed;[22]

(b) Coroners legislation contains a requirement on health professionals to inform the coroner of a death in certain circumstances;[23]

(c) Road traffic legislation requires doctors to take blood samples of people involved in road accidents and to report the results of those samples;[24]

(d) The *Health Acts* in the various Australian jurisdictions impose obligations to disclose information where the patient is suffering from certain types of communicable diseases, including HIV and other sexually transmissible diseases;

(e) Child welfare legislation imposes obligations to inform police and welfare authorities where the health professional has formed a reasonable suspicion that a child has been subjected to sexual or physical abuse;[25]

(f) The notification of cancer diagnosis.[26]

Privacy and medical information[27]

The concept of privacy encompasses what use may be made of private information. Since *Breen v Williams*[28] it has been clear that a patient has no common law right to access health information. In that case, the plaintiff, who had had a breast implant, became aware of a

---

19   *BC v Australian Red Cross Society* [1991] Vic SC 85 (25 February 1991).
20   *Australian Red Cross Society v BC* [1991] VicSC 87 (7 March 1991).
21   Drawing on Allan and Blake, above n 2, 309–10.
22   *Births, Deaths and Marriages Registration Act 1995* (NSW) s 39; *Births, Deaths and Marriages Registration Act 1998* (WA) s 44; *Births, Deaths and Marriages Registration Act 1997* (ACT) ss 33–5; *Births, Deaths and Marriages Registration Act 1996* (Vic) ss 34–7; *Births, Deaths and Marriages Registration Act 1996* (NT) ss 32–4; *Births, Deaths and Marriages Registration Act 2003* (Qld) ss 26–8; *Births, Deaths and Marriages Registration Act 1999* (Tas) ss 38–9. See Allan and Blake, above n 2, 309–10.
23   *Coroners Act 1997* (ACT) s77; *Coroners Act 2009* (NSW) s 53; *Coroners Act* (NT) s 12; *Coroners Act 2003* (Qld) s 7; *Coroners Act 2003* (SA) s 28; *Coroners Act 1995* (Tas) s 19; *Coroners Act 2008* (Vic) s 10; *Coroners Act 1996* (WA) s 17. See Allan and Blake, above n 2, 309–10.
24   *Road Transport (Alcohol and Drugs) Act 1977* (ACT) Divs 2.2, 2.5 and 2.7; *Road Transport (Safety and Traffic Management) Act 1999* (NSW) s 20; *Traffic Act* (NT) Div 5; *Road Traffic Act 1961* (SA) ss 47E and 47I; *Road Safety (Alcohol and Drugs) Act 1970* (Tas) Div 2; *Road Safety Act 1986* (Vic) ss 55, 55A, 55B and 55E; *Road Traffic Act 1974* (WA) ss 66B, 66F. See Allan and Blake, above n 2, 309–10.
25   *Children and Young People Act 2008* (ACT) s 356; *Care and Protection of Children Act 2007* (NT) s 26; *Child Protection Act 1999* (Qld) s 148; *Children's Protection Act 1993* (SA) s 11; *Children, Young Persons and their Families Act 1999* (Tas) s 14; *Children, Youth and Families Act 2005* (Vic) s 184; *Children and Community Services Act 2004* (WA) s 124B. See Allan and Blake, above n 2, 309–10.
26   *Public Health Act 1997* (ACT) Part 6; *Public Health Act 2010* (NSW) s 55, Sch 1; *Cancer (Registrations) Act 1988* (NT); *Public Health Act 2005* (Qld) Div 3; *Health Care Regulations 2008* (SA) Pt 6; *Public Health Act 1997* (Tas) Part 3; *Cancer Act 1958* (Vic) Part 3; *Health (Notification of Cancer) Regulations 2011* (WA). See Allan and Blake, above n 2, 309–10.
27   This section of the chapter is based heavily on a series of lectures given by Dr Donal Buchanan at the Australasian College of Legal Medicine.
28   *Breen v Williams* (1996) 186 CLR 71.

pending class action litigation in respect of breast implants in the US. A condition of her 'opting in' to the litigation was that she was required to provide copies of her medical records. She wrote to Dr Williams, the surgeon who had performed her breast implant surgery. On advice from his medical insurers, the surgeon replied saying that he was happy to provide the medical records for her, provided that she indemnified him against any liability arising out of the surgery. She commenced legal action for access to the records.

Eventually, the matter came before the High Court. The plaintiff's Counsel argued that there were five potential grounds to her action. The first was that Mrs Breen had a proprietorial right of interest in the medical records. The High Court rejected that argument. Although documents prepared by an agent are normally the property of the principal, the relationship between patient and doctor is not that of principal and agent. The doctor's notes in his records were prepared to assist him to fulfil his professional duties. The Court acknowledged that property rights in an item could be detached and divided among a number of persons. Unless otherwise provided by contract or statute, however, medical records prepared by the doctor are the property of the doctor.[29] While Counsel for Mrs Breen conceded that she did not own the medical records, it was nevertheless argued on her behalf that she had a proprietorial interest in them on the grounds that the records were not owned by anybody. The Court also found that 'the idea that an item of property that has not been abandoned has no owner is ill founded'.[30]

The Court also rejected the argument advanced by Mrs Breen that a right of access to medical records was an implied contractual term of the relationship between her and Dr Williams. In particular, the Court held there was no implied term to act in the best interests of the patient, which would form the greater part of an obligation to allow access. Such a term would be inconsistent with the tortious and contractual obligation to provide reasonable skill and care to a patient. A term to 'act in the best interests' would also fail as an implied term as it lacks sufficient certainty.[31]

The High Court found that there was no 'innominate' (ie. general or unfettered) common law right of access to medical records. It was equally dismissive of there being a fiduciary duty on a doctor to provide access to patient records. To decide otherwise would be to impose fiduciary obligations which would significantly alter the already existing complexity of legal obligations governing the doctor-patient relationship. The statement of Justice Sopinka in *Norberg v Wynrib* was quoted with approval: 'fiduciary duties should not be superimposed on … common law duties simply to improve the nature or extent of the remedy'.[32]

Counsel for Mrs Breen also argued that the move towards recognising patient autonomy in the landmark case of *Rogers v Whitaker*, which required that a doctor disclose all material risks,[33] was evidence of a broader trend in the common law which included 'a right to know'. While the High Court agreed that *Rogers v Whitaker* was part of a rejection of a paternalistic model of doctor-patient interactions, it noted that it would take 'a quantum leap' to justify this as the basis for the relief which Mrs Breen sought.[34] In conclusion, the High Court said that any change in the law was a matter for the legislature, not the Courts.[35]

29   Ibid; see Gaudron and McHugh JJ at [7].
30   Ibid at [8].
31   Ibid at [11]–[16].
32   *Norberg v Wynrib* (1992) 92 DLR (4th) 449, per Sopinka J at 481, quoted in *Breen v Williams* (1996) 186 CLR 71, per Gaudron and McHugh JJ at [33].
33   *Rogers v Whitaker* (1992) 175 CLR 479.
34   *Breen v Williams* (1996) 186 CLR 71, per Gaudron and McHugh JJ at [43]–[44]; see also Dawson and Toohey JJ at [29]–[32].
35   Ibid, see Gaudron and McHugh JJ at [45]–[48]; see also Dawson and Toohey JJ at [33].

Privacy Act 1988 (Cth) and Australian Privacy Principles

The Commonwealth government has taken up the challenge posed by the High Court in *Breen v Williams*. Through amendments to the *Privacy Act 1988* (Cth), it has extended the reach of those provisions so that they apply to doctor-patient interactions. The Privacy Act applies to Commonwealth government bodies, as well as to private bodies. It does not, therefore, apply to state or territory hospitals. It should be noted, however, that legislative provisions similar to the Privacy Act exist in most states and territories.[36] The Privacy Act, amongst other things, establishes 13 Australian Privacy Principles (APPs), as well as an Office of the Information Commissioner. It also mandates a patient's right of access to their medical records.

Definitions

Key definitions are outlined in section 6(1) of the Privacy Act, which provides:

> Health information (which is a subset of 'sensitive information') includes information or opinion about health or disability of a person; express wishes about future health care; health service provided; organ donation or genetic information.

Enforcement-related activity includes the prevention, detection, investigation and prosecution of a criminal offence or breach of a law that imposes a penalty; surveillance activities; and custodial activities or preparation for court proceedings.

Disclosure of health-related information

Section 16B of the Privacy Act permits health-related information to be disclosed to a person other than the patient in three specific circumstances, referred to in the Act as 'permitted health situations':

- conducting research, or compilation of statistics, relevant to public health and safety;
- where disclosure is necessary to prevent a serious threat to life, health or safety of a genetic relative; and
- where disclosure is made to a responsible person (eg. carer) for the person.

Collection of health information

Collection of health information is governed by APP 3, which provides that an entity must not collect sensitive information about an individual unless an individual consents or information is reasonably necessary for one or more of entity's functions or activities. What is 'reasonably necessary' is an objective test and is based on whether a reasonable person properly informed would agree that the collection is necessary in the circumstances.

36　*Health Records (Privacy and Access) Act 1997* (ACT); *Health Records and Information Privacy Act 2002* (NSW); *Information Act 2002* (NT); *Information Privacy Act 2009* (Qld); *Personal Information Protection Act 2004* (Tas); *Health Records Act 2001* (Vic).

Use of health information

The use of health information is governed by APP 6. This principle notes that an entity may collect sensitive personal information for a particular purpose (primary purpose). The entity must not use or disclose the information for another purpose (a secondary purpose) unless:

- the individual has consented to use or disclosure; or
- the individual would reasonably expect the entity to use or disclose sensitive personal information if the secondary purpose is directly related to the primary purpose; or
- use/disclosure is required by law or a court order; or
- the entity is an organisation and a 'permitted health situation' exists in relation to the use or disclosure; or
- the entity reasonably believes that the use or disclosure is reasonably necessary for one or more enforcement-related activities conducted by, or on behalf of, an enforcement body (written note is required, including the basis for the reasonable belief).

In terms of a reasonable belief, the entity must have a reasonable basis for the belief, and not merely a subjective, if genuine, belief. 'Reasonable belief' is an objective test which precludes arbitrary action. The entity bears the onus of justifying that its belief was a reasonable one.

In terms of a secondary purpose, a directly related secondary purpose is one which is closely associated with the primary purpose. An example is a doctor who decides she cannot treat a patient for ethical and therapeutic reasons, discloses the patient's need for treatment to another doctor and why she cannot treat the patient. The disclosure must be directly related to the primary purpose for which the information was collected.

Accuracy obligations

APP 10 imposes obligations on an entity to ensure that information it retains is accurate. The APP states than an entity must take reasonable steps to ensure that the personal information it collects and discloses is accurate, up to date and complete. Reasonable steps include: implementing internal practices and procedures; ensuring that updates are promptly added; and if personal information is to be used or disclosed for a secondary purpose, assessing the quality of that personal information.

Security obligations

APP 11 covers the need to ensure the security of personal information. It requires an entity that holds personal information to take reasonable steps to protect the information from misuse, interference or loss, as well as from unauthorised access, modification or disclosure.

Unauthorised disclosure

APP 6 covers unauthorised disclosure and states that this occurs when an entity makes personal information accessible or visible to others outside the entity; or releases the information from its effective control in a way that is not permitted by the Privacy Act. Reasonable steps to avoid such disclosure may include: governance, culture, training in privacy obligations; internal practices, procedures and systems (eg. what is required when personal information is requested for a secondary purpose); and external professional standards and guidelines, access and physical security.

Access to medical records[37]

The Privacy Act refers to health records. A health record is defined as recorded health information. 'Health information' is, in turn, defined as information or an opinion about the following: history, physical examination, investigations, diagnosis, treatment, review; and referrals, medications, advance health directives, organ donation or genetic status. Two key concepts are then used in the Act: access and privacy. Access refers to a patient's right to view his or her own records; and privacy refers to the right to prevent or limit access to those records by others.

Access

APP 12 requires that an entity that holds information about an individual should give that individual access to their information. Reasons for a valid refusal include where that access would pose a serious threat to life; to the health and safety of any individual; or to public health. An agency can refuse access if it is authorised to do so under the *Freedom of Information Act* or another relevant Commonwealth Act.

Correction of health records

APP 13 requires an entity to take reasonable steps to correct personal information. This is to be done independently of any request, or may be done at the request of the individual. Refusal of individual's request must be in writing, and must state reasons, such as the information being already 'accurate, up to date, complete, relevant, not misleading'; or that the request is unreasonable in the circumstances.

Breaches of the Privacy Act

The Privacy Act established the Office of the Information Commissioner (OIC). The Information Commissioner has powers to assess and investigate alleged breaches of privacy. An individual may complain to the Commissioner about an act or practice that may interfere with the individual's privacy.[38] The Commissioner is obliged to investigate the complaint, may also investigate matters on her/his own initiative, and must make a reasonable attempt to conciliate a complaint, if s/he considers that conciliation might work.[39] The Commissioner also has the power to obtain information,[40] and may compel a respondent to attend a conference.[41] There is $2000 fine for failing to appear before the Commissioner if required to do so.[42]

37   Access to records maintained in a state/territory facility is governed by the *Freedom of Information Act 1989* (ACT) and *Health Records (Privacy and Access) Act 1997* (ACT); *Government Information (Public Access) Act 2009* (NSW), *Health Records and Information Privacy Act 2002* (NSW) and *Information Act 2002* (NSW); *Information Act 2002* (NT); *Right to Information Act 2009* (Qld) and *Information Privacy Act 2009* (Qld); *Freedom of Information Act 2009* (SA); *Right to Information Act 2009* (Tas) and *Personal Information Protection Act 2004* (Tas); *Freedom of Information Act 1982* (Vic) and *Health Records Act 2001* (Vic); and *Freedom of Information Act 1992* (WA).

38   *Privacy Act 1988* (Cth) s 36.

39   Ibid ss 40, 40A.

40   Ibid s 44.

41   Ibid s 46.

42   Ibid s 65.

In terms of determinations which may be made, the Commissioner may dismiss a complaint or find that a complaint is substantiated. In the latter case, the Commissioner may declare that:

- the entity must take steps within a timeframe to ensure that the impugned conduct is not repeated; and/or
- the entity must redress any loss or damage suffered; and/or
- the complainant is entitled to a specified amount of compensation for loss or damage suffered; and/or
- it would be inappropriate to take further action.

Enforcement of orders

For constitutional reasons, the Information Commissioner cannot enforce its own orders and needs to apply to the Federal Court to enforce a determination, such as the payment of compensation.[43] In the case of serious or repeated interferences with privacy, an order can be made for payment of a civil penalty.[44]

eHealth records scheme

The Commonwealth has introduced an electronic health records scheme (eHealth record). Participation in the scheme is voluntary. The *Personally Controlled Electronic Health Records Act 2012* (Cth) (PCEHR Act) and the *Healthcare Identifiers Act 2010* (Cth) have established the overarching regulatory framework for the scheme. It is now possible for multiple health records to be joined via the scheme in order to provide a better overall picture of someone's health. eHealth records are forwarded by health providers to a national repository (Medicare), which is accessible to the patient (consumer) and others. Under the PCEHR Act, an electronic health record that is uploaded is considered to be a summary, and not the doctor's record.

A 'system operator' is authorised to collect the following information from the 'consumer':[45]

- current medications, allergies, adverse reactions;
- details about a consumer's health entered by consumer;
- information regarding an Advance Health Directive;
- information concerning an adult consumer's capacity.

Consumers can control their eHealth record by:[46]

- setting controls on the healthcare provider organisations and nominated representatives who may access the PCEHR; and
- imposing limits on the kind of health information to be collected, used or disclosed by such healthcare provider organisations and nominated representatives.

---

43   Ibid s 55A.
44   Ibid s 13G.
45   *Personally Controlled Electronic Health Records Act 2012* (Cth) s 13A and Part 2.
46   Ibid Part 2.

Conclusion

This chapter has provided an overview of the ethical and legal obligation of confidence and examined the nature and scope of the duty of confidentiality between doctor and patient. It was noted that the duty is not absolute and can be overridden in circumstances where there is patient consent; where there is a requirement for the doctor to disclose patient information which is imposed by law; and where disclosure of information would be in the public interest. Commonwealth privacy legislation imposes strict controls on the collection and dissemination of sensitive health-related information. Patients are able to access their medical records where the legislation applies, in the absence of a common law right to do so. Such legislation should be read in conjunction with relevant state/territory legislation regarding access to such records.

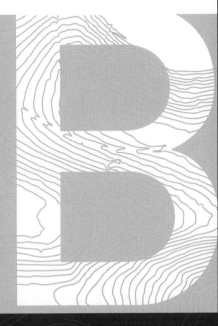

LAW AT THE BEGINNING AND THE END OF LIFE

13

REGULATING REPRODUCTION

Isabel Karpin

Introduction

Over the last decade, the use of assisted reproductive technologies (ART) across the globe has been steadily on the rise. In some parts of Europe, the uptake has been as much as three per cent of babies born.[1] In Australia, the numbers have dropped slightly, possibly due to changes in Medicare funding, but they are still significant. It is estimated that 3.6 per cent of all women who gave birth in Australia in 2009 received some form of ART treatment.[2] It is not surprising then that some Australian states and the Commonwealth government have sought to regulate its use. The regulation of human reproduction does, however, raise significant ethical issues.

The first part of this chapter focuses on ART regulation prior to pregnancy and the implications for women's reproductive freedom. This includes an examination of laws prohibiting the reproduction of cloned and hybrid human embryos; the freezing, storage, donation, testing, selection and disposal of 'sperm and egg' human embryos; access to ART; gamete donation, and posthumous reproduction. The second part examines the regulation of the next stage of the reproductive cycle (namely pregnancy), with a focus on the way in which the regulation of prenatal screening, abortion and surrogacy impact on women's reproductive choices and capacity for autonomous decision-making.

Overview of ART regulation and embryo research

Reproduction in Australia is regulated by a matrix of complicated and disharmonious Commonwealth, state and territory laws. At the Commonwealth level, there are two main Acts that have national coverage: The *Prohibition of Human Cloning for Reproduction Act 2002* (Cth) and the *Research Involving Human Embryos Act 2002* (Cth). While the constitutional status of the Commonwealth legislation has not yet been tested in the High Court, and health is not a constitutional head of power,[3] each of the states and the ACT has passed legislation that mirrors the Commonwealth legislation and works in tandem with other state and territory-based legislative regimes around reproductive technology.[4] This is an imperfect system as, over time, small changes have been made to the mirror legislation so

---

1   European Society of Human Reproduction and Embryology, *ART Fact Sheet* (April 2004) <www.eshre.eu/Guidelines-and-Legal/ART-fact-sheet.aspx>.

2   Alan Macaldowie et al., *Assisted Reproductive Technology in Australia and New Zealand 2010*, Assisted Reproduction Series Number 16 (Australian Institute of Health and Welfare Canberra, 2012) 1 <www.aihw.gov.au/WorkArea/DownloadAsset.aspx?id=10737423255>.

3   There are other possible heads of Commonwealth constitutional power that may support the legislation, including the external affairs power (s 51(xxix)); the trade and commerce power (s 51(i)); and the corporations power (s 51(xx)). See Chapter 6 for an overview of the constitutional position with respect to health powers.

4   *Human Cloning and Embryo Research Act 2004* (ACT); *Human Cloning for Reproduction and Other Prohibited Practices Act 2003* (NSW); *Research Involving Human Embryos and Prohibition of Human Cloning for Reproduction Act 2003* (Qld); *Prohibition of Human Cloning for Reproduction Act 2003* (SA); *Human Cloning for Reproduction and Other Prohibited Practices Act 2003* (Tas); *Prohibition of Human Cloning for Reproduction Act 2008* (Vic); *Human Reproductive Technology Act 1991* (WA). Legislation is currently being drafted in NT.

that there is no longer a uniform nationwide approach. In addition at the state and territory level, Victoria, NSW, WA and SA have laws specifically regulating some aspects of ART and In Vitro Fertilisation (IVF);[5] and the ACT, Victoria, SA, Queensland, NSW, Tasmania and WA all have laws regulating surrogacy.[6]

Alongside all of these state, territory and Commonwealth laws, sits the National Health and Medical Research Council Ethical Guidelines on the use of ART in Clinical Practice and Research (NHMRC ART Guidelines)[7] and the Reproductive Technology Accreditation Committee (RTAC) Code of Practice. The NHMRC ART Guidelines are currently undergoing a major review and draft guidelines were presented for public comment in 2015.[8] The NHMRC has indicated that the new guidelines are likely to be finalised in early 2017. Below is a graphical representation of this matrix of laws. As can be seen at a glance, no state has the same two sets of laws, some only regulate surrogacy and cloning, others only regulate ART, and some regulate ART, surrogacy and cloning. Once a child is born, the matrix grows ever more complex with state-based parentage laws, birth registration laws and the federal family law jurisdiction all having a regulatory impact. While it is not possible to provide a detailed account of all of the legislative regimes here, this chapter focuses on key issues that have generated significant ethical debate.

Figure 13.1   ART regulation in Australia

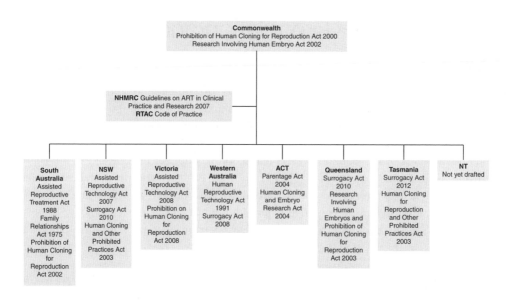

5   *Assisted Reproductive Treatment Act 2008* (Vic); *Assisted Reproductive Technology Act 2007* (NSW); *Assisted Reproductive Treatment Act 1988* (SA); *Human Reproductive Technology Act 1991* (WA).

6   *Parentage Act 2004* (ACT); *Assisted Reproductive Treatment Act 2008* (Vic); *Surrogacy Act 2008* (WA); *Family Relationships Act 1975* (SA); *Surrogacy Act 2010* (Qld); *Surrogacy Act 2010* (NSW); *Surrogacy Act 2012* (Tas).

7   NHMRC, *Ethical Guidelines on the Use of ART in Clinical Practice and Research* (2007) <www .nhmrc.gov.au/guidelines-publications/e78>.

8   NHMRC, *Draft Ethical Guidelines on the Use of Assisted Reproductive Technology in Clinical Practice and Research* (2015) (Draft NHMRC ART Guidelines) <http://consultations.nhmrc.gov.au/public_ consultations/assisted-reproductive-tech>.

Commonwealth regulation

Perhaps the newest genre of laws in this area is what we might call biotechnology laws: namely, laws governing how scientists may deal with new biotechnologies. A major focus of this genre of law, apart from genetically-modified foods, are laws regulating access to and use of reproductive materials including embryos, gametes, embryonic stem cells and other human tissue.

Prohibition on human cloning

In the last 20 years, science has made significant leaps forward in the field of mammalian cloning and this has sparked fears about the potential for human reproductive cloning, the creation of animal/human hybrids and chimeras and inheritable genetic modifications. Dolly the sheep was the first mammal successfully cloned from an adult cell in 1997 and shortly thereafter, the then US President, Bill Clinton, banned human cloning for reproductive purposes. It took five years for Australia to pass its own set of national laws dealing with cloning and, when it did, the laws prohibited human cloning for reproduction but also instituted a complex system of facilitated embryo research via a licensing regime that allowed cloning for research purposes. The legislation consisted of two Acts: the *Prohibition of Human Cloning Act 2002* (Cth) and the *Research Involving Human Embryos Act 2002* (Cth) (RIHE Act), both subsequently amended and the former renamed the *Prohibition of Human Cloning for Reproduction Act 2002* (Cth) (PHCR) in 2007.

The PHCR Act prohibits reproductive cloning,[9] the creation of hybrids and chimeras,[10] with specific exceptions, and deliberately and knowingly undertaking genetic modification that will be inheritable.[11] At the same time, the RIHE Act establishes a licensing system for the use of embryos in research. While it is still a speculative technology, it is possible to imagine that in the future women (men too, with the assistance of a woman to gestate the embryo) may wish to utilise human reproductive cloning technology to reproduce. Whether you accept the ethical limits placed on human reproductive cloning as appropriate or not, it is nevertheless uncontroversial that a ban on the use of the technology does constitute a limit on reproductive freedom. Yet this has received very little coverage in the bioethical literature.[12]

Requirement for ART clinic accreditation

The PHCR Act was intended to deal with, and comprehensively prohibit, certain reproductive possibilities while the RIHE Act was intended primarily to regulate and control the use of embryos for research. However, it is the latter Act that has ended up entrenching a national accreditation system for assisted reproduction. Sections 10 and 11 of the RIHE Act state that no embryo, including excess embryos (defined as an embryo created for ART

---

9   PHCR Act, s 9.

10   Ibid ss 17 and 18.

11   Ibid s 15.

12   For further discussion of this issue, see Isabel Karpin and David Ellison, 'Reproduction Without Women: Frankenstein and the Legal Prohibition of Human Cloning' in Catherine Kevin (ed.), *Feminism and the Body, Interdisciplinary Perspectives* (Cambridge Scholars Publishing, 2009) 29–48.

treatment of a woman but excess to her needs),[13] can be used for ART treatment unless the use is by an accredited ART centre. ART centres can gain accreditation from the RTAC of the Fertility Society of Australia or other bodies prescribed by the legislation.

This tiny provision in the Commonwealth legislation has had enormous consequences for the provision of ART services across Australia. Prior to the introduction of this section, there was no Commonwealth requirement for accreditation of ART clinics and legislation regulating ART had only been passed in three states: namely, Victoria, SA and WA. Queensland, NSW and Tasmania were unregulated but generally voluntarily complied with the NHMRC ART Guidelines. In 2004, the RTAC made accreditation of an ART clinic contingent on full compliance with the NHMRC ART Guidelines. By making the Guidelines a requirement for accreditation, itself a legislative requirement under the RIHE Act, the Guidelines have taken on the status of soft law and are what might be described as quasi-regulatory. The Guidelines are mostly written in advisory language but there are significant provisions that are more declaratory and most clinics view these as compulsory.

NHMRC ART Guidelines and the ban on non-medical sex selection

An example of the regulatory significance of the NHMRC ART Guidelines can be found in their impact on the practice of sex selection. Up until 2004, some ART clinics were conducting sex selection for non-medical purposes. However, the 2004 version of the NHMRC ART Guidelines specifically prohibited sex selection for non-medical reasons 'pending further community discussion', as does the current version.[14] Clinics, such as Sydney IVF (now known as Genea), took the view that it was no longer possible for them to continue sex selection for non-medical reasons since in order to retain their accreditation they needed to comply with the NHMRC ART Guidelines. Without accreditation, they would not be allowed to use in vitro embryos without breaching the RIHE Act. In this instance, even though no law was (or had ever been) in existence in NSW (where Genea is based) that prohibits sex selection for non-medical purposes, it has effectively been banned. [15]

Sex selection is specifically prohibited in legislation in some jurisdictions, such as Victoria and WA. In Victoria, the issue has been judicially considered in *JS and LS v Patient Review Panel*.[16] In this case, a couple were not allowed to use preimplantation genetic diagnosis (PGD) to select the sex of their child pursuant to section 28(2)(b) of the *Assisted Reproductive Treatment Act 2008* (Vic), which allowed non-medical sex selection at the discretion of the Patient Review Panel (PRP). In denying the couple's request, the court discussed the 'welfare of the child' principle in section 5 of the Act, which closely follows

---

13   RIHE Act s 9.
14   NHMRC, above n 7, para 11.1.
15   See <www.genea.com.au/my-fertility/im-a-patient/pgd-genetic-testing>: 'Using PGD to select the sex of your embryo is only allowed in Australia if the testing is being used to avoid passing on a specific sex-linked genetic disorder to a child. The NHMRC ART Guidelines restrict the use of PGD for sex selection in Australia, see ss 11 and 12.' It should be noted that at the time of writing, the 2015 Draft Revised NHMRC ART Guidelines do not advance a position on non-medical sex selection but rather invite further public consultation: see NHMRC, above n 8. The response to these submissions is not yet available.
16   [2011] VCAT 856.

the NHMRC ART Guidelines: (a) the welfare and interests of persons born or to be born as a result of treatment procedures are paramount.

The couple argued that they suffered from post-traumatic stress disorder brought on by the loss of a pregnancy at the point of birth. The pregnancy would have given them the child of the desired sex, a child that was the opposite sex to their existing three children. Furthermore, there was some suggestion that the pregnancy had been lost due to medical negligence and this compounded the harm. The couple, therefore, argued that being allowed to have a child of the desired sex would help them move on from this trauma. Having been refused PGD to select the sex of their next child, the woman chose to become pregnant without sex selection testing in order to try for a child of the desired sex. After four further attempts, including a spontaneous miscarriage, a twin pregnancy that was terminated due to medical complications and a twin pregnancy through IVF that the couple chose to terminate because they were of the undesired sex, the couple persisted with an appeal to the Victorian Civil and Administrative Tribunal. At the hearing, the couple indicated that they would continue to try to achieve a pregnancy of the desired sex in the same way as previously if they did not obtain approval for PGD for sex selection. The Victorian Civil and Administrative Tribunal (VCAT) denied the request, stating:

> In our view, arguments based on completion of family, replacement of a child, or family balance do not advance the welfare interests of a child born to fulfil that end. Expert witnesses, Professor Thomson and Associate Professor Tonti Filippini said, it is ethically undesirable, and contrary to the welfare of the child, to make acceptance of a child conditional on its sex.[17]

This is in stark contrast, however, to the practice of allowing sex selection for medical reasons. There is almost universal acceptance of the use of PGD for sex selection to avoid transmission of a sex-linked disability.

Some controversial issues in the regulation of ART treatment

The presumption against treatment and criminal record checks in Victoria

In Victoria, unlike any other jurisdiction in Australia, section 14 of the *Assisted Reproductive Treatment Act 2008* (Vic) includes a presumption against treatment where the person seeking treatment has a criminal history of sexual or violence offences or has had a child removed as a result of a child protection order. This is based on the overarching principle enunciated in section 5(a) of that Act which states that: '[t]he welfare and interests of the person born or to be born as a result of treatment procedures are paramount.'

Section 14 has already been adjudicated all the way to the Victorian Supreme Court of Appeal. The case involved a clinic's decision to refuse a couple access to ART on the basis that the husband had been convicted of having unlawful sex with a girl of 16 while he was

---

17   *JS and LS v Patient Review Panel* [2011] VCAT 856 [82].

a teacher's aide and the girl was in his care. The Victorian Patient Review Panel upheld the clinic's decision but the VCAT overturned that decision. The VCAT opted instead to impose conditions on the husband requiring him to complete 12 counselling sessions for sex offenders before his wife could access treatment.[18] The PRP appealed and the Court of Appeal of the Supreme Court of Victoria overturned the decision of the VCAT.[19] The Court of Appeal held that the *Assisted Reproductive Treatment Act 2008* (Vic) is 'clearly structured in such a way that in no situation can the best interests and the welfare of a child be ignored'.[20] In considering the meaning of 'best interests', the Court of Appeal stated: 'the best interests of a child could include the physical, sexual, emotional and developmental well-being of a child'.[21]

The difficulty here is that there is no existing child and therefore the clinic, the PRP and the Courts must all engage in speculation about what is in the best interests of someone who does not yet exist and may never come to exist. In light of this, it is interesting that the Court of Appeal in its judgment talks about 'the child' and not 'the person to be born'– the legislative language. Emily Jackson has criticised this approach in relation to a similar requirement that exists under s 13(5) of the *Human Fertilisation and Embryology Act 1990* (UK). She argues that the law missteps when it 'purports to make a child's best interests relevant to a judgement made prior to that child's conception'.[22]

Regulating access to PGD

The NHMRC ART Guidelines prohibit the use of PGD,[23] except to avoid a serious disability or in certain circumstances to identify an embryo that is a tissue match for an existing ill child, (commonly known as 'saviour sibling' embryos). This provision is carried forward in the Draft Revised NHMRC ART Guidelines,[24] however, more detail is provided as to when 'seriousness' may be present, as well as the different types of preimplantation testing including PGD and preimplantation genetic screening (PGS).[25] Unlike in the prenatal context, PGS and diagnosis are not routine. They are considered specialised procedures reserved for patients who have identified a history of a particular disorder in the family or who have a high rate of early miscarriage. Medicare does not currently cover PGD. WA is the only jurisdiction that goes beyond these Guidelines and adds additional levels of scrutiny. In section 14(2) of the *Human Reproductive Technology Act 1991* (WA) (as amended in 2004), the diagnostic testing of embryos, including via PGD, is allowed subject to the approval of the Reproductive Technology Council (RTC). The RTC is prohibited from approving such a procedure unless 'there is a significant risk of a serious genetic abnormality or disease being

---

18   *ABY, ABZ v Patient Review Panel* [2011] VCAT 905.

19   *Patient Review Panel v ABY and ABZ* [2012] 37 VR 634.

20   Ibid at 648.

21   Ibid at 639.

22   Emily Jackson, 'Conception and the Irrelevance of the Welfare Principle' (2002) 65(2) *Modern Law Review* 176, 181.

23   NHMRC, above n 7, para 12.1. Preimplantation Genetic Diagnosis (PGD) is a procedure where cells are removed from an embryo created using IVF, prior to implantation in a woman, to check for the presence of a genetic anomaly. It can also be used for sex selection (see above). It is also sometimes called Preimplantation Genetic Testing (PGT).

24   See NHMRC, above n 8.

25   Ibid paras 8.13–8.15.

present in the embryo.'[26] However, there is no definition in the legislation of either the word 'significant' or the word 'serious'.

The WA RTC Policy on Approval of Diagnostic Procedures Involving Embryos[27] governs the granting of permission to undertake PGD and provides some elaboration on the question of what constitutes a significant risk of a serious genetic abnormality or disease. In relation to a 'significant risk',[28] the policy states:

5. It is not appropriate to specify a statistical probability as the sole criterion for the risk of a genetic abnormality or disease being present in the embryo to be 'significant'.

6. The level of risk should be measured against the risk of the disease or disability occurring in the general population. The Council should be satisfied that there is a higher risk of the embryo in question being affected by the abnormality or disease being tested for than for embryos in the general population.

7. The significance of the risk for the persons seeking the testing may also be relevant, in that the persons seeking treatment may have varying perceptions of the significance of risk that need to be taken into account.

In relation to the concept of a 'serious genetic abnormality or disease', the policy states:

8. In assessing whether a genetic abnormality or disease is serious it is appropriate to look at environmental and personal factors as well as the impairment to body functions and structures that may arise from the condition. The assessment should consider the limits that these factors impose on the extent to which a person can engage in activities or participate in life situations.

9. The International Classification of Functioning Disability and Health (ICF) developed by the World Health Organisation provides a broad overview for assessment of seriousness, which covers many different aspects of disease, however, does not consider an individual's perspective of seriousness. The infrastructure of the ICF may be adapted to the assessment of the seriousness of a genetic abnormality or disease.

The adoption of the ICF is a very interesting development and is discussed in more detail in Chapter 22 which examines the relationship between health law and people with disability. However, what is particularly interesting about the policy is that the question of 'seriousness' includes a consideration of the 'environment' and 'personal factors.' Although these terms are vague, the policy provides a sample application form for approval of testing. It can be seen from that form that the RTC will take account of the capacity of a family to manage the disability when determining its seriousness. Questions such as: 'What experience with, and attitude to, the abnormality or disease does the family requesting the testing have?' and 'What is the capacity of the family who are requesting the testing to provide the level of support required by a child with the abnormality or disease?' are listed on the form.[29]

---

26   *Human Reproductive Technology Act 1991* (WA) (as amended) s 14(2b).

27   Reproductive Technology Council, *Policy on Approval of Diagnostic Procedures Involving Embryos* (March 2008) <www.rtc.org.au/clinics/docs/PGD_Policy_on_approval_of_diagnostic_procedures_ involving_embryos.pdf>.

28   Ibid section 2.1 paras 5–9.

29   Ibid section 2.2.3 para 20.

In the Draft Revised NHMRC ART Guidelines, similar kinds of considerations are fore-grounded. For instance, the new proposed paragraph 8.13.2 states:[30]

> It is not possible to definitively assign genetic conditions as 'serious' or 'non-serious' as context is important. Clinicians should consider the following criteria when assessing the ethical acceptability of the use of PGT:
>
> - current evidence and expert opinion on the impact of the condition of the life of the person who would be born, including the anticipated symptoms, age-of-onset and the degree/spectrum or severity of the condition
> - the concerns of the intended parent/s about their ability to financially and emotionally care for a person born with the condition
> - the available therapies or interventions to reduce the severity, delay onset or minimise the impact of the condition
> - the likelihood of false positive and false negative results
> - the distinction between the genotypic and phenotypic expression of the condition
> - the variable range of effects of the condition, including the likely rate of degeneration in the case of progressive disorders
> - the experiences of families living with the condition
> - the likely availability of effective therapy or management of the condition now and in the future
> - the extent of social support available to the intended parent/s and to the person who would be born.

The recognition that the significance of a disability is contextually driven is important and this is discussed in more detail in Chapter 22. A disability studies critique is vital to understanding the way in which disability is socially constructed. The answer to the question of when it is appropriate to use PGD to avoid a 'serious' disability, must be contingent on many more factors than the mere presence of a gene or chromosomal abnormality. Indeed, recent developments in genetic knowledge have further complicated the legal response because they have asserted that the gene is vulnerable to the environment and, as such, can be turned on or off by stress stimuli. This makes the determinative nature of genetic identity highly contingent. The field of epigenetics has begun to explore the myriad ways that genes interact with the environment, including for example, the social environment and social disparities such as discrimination on the grounds of race, or lower socio-economic status.[31]

Section 12.3 of the 2007 NHMRC ART Guidelines deals with the use of PGD to select an embryo with compatible tissue to an existing child. Usually, stem cells are harvested from the umbilical cord blood and transfused into the existing sick child, so no intervention with respect to the body of the newborn sibling is required. When this procedure was first publicised, concerns were raised that children would be conceived for the purpose of saving the lives of other relatives and that they would be viewed as potential

---

30   NHMRC, above n 8.
31   M Thayer Zaneta and Christopher W Kuzawa, 'Biological Memories of Past Environments: Epigenetic Pathways to Health Disparities' (2011) 6(7) *Epigenetics* 798; see Chapter 4 for a more detailed examination of the social determinants of health.

organ donors for living relatives. Therefore, the guidelines require that the procedure only be used to assist a sick sibling and not other members of a family group. A similar limit exists in the UK where the Human Fertilisation and Embryology Authority oversees preimplantation tissue typing to match with a sick sibling, approving it on a case-by-case basis.[32] The phenomenon of 'saviour siblings' is relatively new but as we see with many of the technological options in the area of ART, the medical community and the government tend to take a precautionary approach to regulating their use.

Identifying gamete and embryo donors

In recent years, we have seen an increase in privacy laws around genetic testing and genetic information.[33] However, in the context of reproduction, there is an opposite trend. Recent state laws in Victoria, NSW, SA and WA require gamete donors to be prepared to have their identity released to genetic offspring, where requested, after they turn 16 in WA and SA; and 18 in Victoria and NSW.[34] Changes to donor identification regimes can be very challenging for people who originally donated under the assumption they would remain anonymous and it has been suggested that the number of people willing to donate has declined as donor anonymity has become increasingly difficult. However, there is a very strong lobby of donor-conceived children who are slowly reforming the law to enable access to identifying records.

NSW is one of the newest jurisdictions in Australia to develop legislation on ART. Sections 32A–41M of the *Assisted Reproductive Technology Act 2007* (NSW) have created a Central Register to record information about gamete and embryo donors and participants in IVF and surrogacy. Although the Act was passed in 2007, it did not come into force until 2010. For all gamete donations that occurred after 1 January 2010, identifying information is kept on the Register and is released to a donor-conceived person upon request after they turn 18.[35] This has meant that people conceived from donor gametes and embryos prior to 2010 in NSW do not have the same access to information as those conceived after 2010.

This is an area of ongoing controversy, particularly given recent developments in Victoria. In 2016, the *Assisted Reproductive Treatment Amendment Act 2016* was passed, which amended the *Assisted Reproductive Treatment Act 2008* (Vic). This now permits individuals who were gamete donors prior to 1 January 1998, to be identified to persons conceived using their gametes, without need to obtain their consent to being identified. The changes also require donor-conceived children and donors to abide by pre-notified contact preferences, subject to heavy penalties where breached. Prior to this legislative amendment in Victoria, identifying information of gamete and embryo donors had only been required

---

32   Sch 2 s 1ZA(1)(d) of the *Human Fertilisation and Embryology Act 1990* (UK) permits the use of embryo testing to establish tissue compatibility only where the would-be sibling of that embryo suffers from a serious medical condition which could be treated by umbilical cord blood stem cells, bone marrow or other tissue.

33   See Chapter 12 for a more detailed discussion of health privacy laws; see Chapter 20 for the regulation of genetic testing.

34   *Assisted Reproductive Treatment Act 2008* (Vic) ss 56, 59: *Assisted Reproductive Technology Act 2007* (NSW) s 37; *Assisted Reproductive Treatment Regulations 2010* (SA) reg 8(4); *Human Reproductive Technology Act 1991* (WA).

35   *Assisted Reproductive Technology Act 2007* (NSW) s 37.

since January 1998. The information has been kept on the Central Register and released to a donor-conceived person upon request once they reach the age of 18.[36] The amendment now makes it possible for people who were conceived prior to 1998 as a result of gamete donation, to identify their donors. In SA, there is no Central Register, however, since September 2010 donors must be willing to be identified once a child conceived as a result of the donation reaches the age of 16.[37] In WA, people conceived using gametes donated after 2004 may access identifying information about the donor when they turn 16.[38]

Storage of embryos

Some IVF clinical practice has involved stimulating a woman's egg production so that as many eggs as possible can be harvested. The harvested eggs are fertilised outside the body to create in vitro embryos. Best clinical practice will not allow implantation of more than two embryos at a time and some Australian clinics recommend that only one is implanted. The remaining embryos will then be frozen and stored for later use or until family formation is complete. At that stage, the woman and her partner can choose to continue storing the embryos, to donate them for others to use for reproductive purposes, to donate them for research or to dispose of them.

If they choose to continue storage, there are limits on how long they may be stored in all regulated jurisdictions, except SA. In WA, an embryo may be kept in storage for a maximum of ten years, while in Victoria it is five years with the possibility of a further five years upon application. In NSW, the limit applies to donated embryos and embryos created using donor gametes and is also ten years. For all the unregulated jurisdictions (Tasmania, Queensland, NT and ACT) and SA, the NHMRC ART Guidelines apply which recommend that the maximum storage time is five years with the possibility of an extension for a further five years.[39] In a recent study, these storage limits were found to be highly problematic, with some women indicating that they felt coerced into disposing of their embryos before they were ready.[40]

Embryo disposal

As mentioned previously, sometimes ART clinics create more embryos during IVF than can be used by the woman for whom they are created. If not disposed of immediately or donated, these embryos are frozen and stored and an ongoing storage fee is charged until such time as the storage period expires. Where the embryos are disposed of either immediately or once the storage period expires, the NHMRC ART Guidelines specify that clinics must have 'protocols in place for the respectful disposal of embryos' and that the 'wishes of the persons for whom the embryos are stored, as to the method of disposal, should be

---

36   *Assisted Reproductive Treatment Act 2008* (Vic) ss 56, 59.

37   *Assisted Reproductive Treatment Regulations 2010* (SA) reg 8(4).

38   *Human Reproductive Technology Act 1991* (WA) s 43; see also <www.rtc.org.au/donor/docs/7-Access-to-information.pdf>.

39   NHMRC, above n 7, guideline 8.8. If accepted, the Draft Revised ART Guidelines, above n 8, will not include a limitation on the storage period; however, this will not alter state/territory ART legislation that does include a limit.

40   Isabel Karpin et al., 'Analysing IVF Participant Understanding of, Involvement in, and Control over Embryo Storage and Destruction in Australia' (2013) 20(4) *Journal of Law and Medicine* 811.

respected.' [41] However, Victoria is the only jurisdiction in Australia to have legislated about the manner of destruction: 'an embryo must be disposed of by allowing the embryo to stand in its container, at room temperature, in a secure area for a period of not less than 24 hours'.[42]

Although Victoria has laid down these requirements, disposal can take a number of forms in most Australian state and territorial jurisdictions. Sometimes, a request is made for a disposal ceremony to be held inside or outside the clinic. At other times, women choose to remove their frozen embryos from the clinic to dispose of them at home. 'Compassionate' or 'unviable' transfer is another method, primarily offered in the US. This involves placing the thawed embryos in the woman's vagina or cervix where it is understood by all parties that they cannot implant. It may also be at a non-viable time in the woman's cycle. As noted by Ellison and Karpin: 'The object here is to discontinue storage and discard the embryos in a way that enrols the woman's body in a ritualised practice that confers additional (ethical, ceremonial) meaning to the act of disposal.'[43]

A recently published study found that just under one third (*n*=110) of the survey respondents would have liked to participate 'in some way in the disposal of their embryos'. Of those who indicated they would like to be involved in the disposal, over half of them (59%; *n*=65) would have 'liked the option of removing the embryos from the clinic to then dispose of them in another environment'. Twenty per cent of those surveyed opted for being at the clinic to watch as the embryos were disposed of and 16 per cent expressed an interest in some kind of ceremony. The researchers did not specifically ask about non-viable transfer, however 5 per cent (*n*=6) of the participants indicated they would have liked that option.[44]

Posthumous conception and implantation

There are two main kinds of posthumous reproduction. The first kind is where a gamete provider has died and the surviving family or partner wishes to use the gametes to create an embryo with the remaining partner's gametes or a donor gamete. The second kind is where one or both of the gamete's providers for an existing embryo have died and a family member or donor recipient wishes to use the embryo.

Under the NHMRC ART Guidelines, there are specific rules relating to the use of embryos after the death of a gamete provider. They may only be used where the deceased person has made a clearly expressed directive that the embryo may be used after their death.[45] A similar requirement exists in those state jurisdictions where ART legislation has been enacted with small variations.[46] In Victoria, for instance, there are several requirements that need to be met for posthumous use of stored embryos, including PRP approval and counselling of

---

41   NHMRC, above n 7, guideline 8.9.
42   *Assisted Reproductive Treatment Regulations 2009* (Vic) reg 12.
43   David Ellison and Isabel Karpin, 'Death without Life: Grievability and IVF' (2011) 110(4) *South Atlantic Quarterly* 795, 797.
44   Karpin et al., above n 40.
45   NHRMC, above n 7, guideline 6.16. The Draft Revised NHMRC ART Guidelines, above n 8, make minor changes to these provisions but the substantive requirements are the same: that is to say, there needs to be a clear directive from the deceased person.
46   See *Assisted Reproductive Technology Act 2007* (NSW) s 23; *Assisted Reproductive Treatment Act 1988* (SA) s 9(1)(c)(iv)(C); *Assisted Reproductive Treatment Act 2008* (Vic) s 46(b).

the survivor.[47] In NSW, there must be consent by the deceased and written consent by the recipient to use the gametes. In SA, the person seeking to use the gametes or embryos must have the deceased's consent and have been living with the deceased person on a domestic basis prior to their death.[48]

Although there appear to be legislated avenues for posthumous use, posthumous reproduction is, nevertheless very rare. Not many people turn their mind to the possibility of death when they engage in ART and so consent to posthumous use is very hard to prove. In a recent study, a majority of participants said that they would want to be able to posthumously use the embryos or gametes of their partner.[49] In the circumstances, it seems incumbent on those engaged in ART – clinicians, counsellors and advising lawyers – to make sure people do examine this question before commencing ART treatment. Ironically, a woman undergoing IVF, whose partner dies without leaving consent to use his sperm posthumously will be unable to access his gametes, however, she will be able to obtain donor sperm from someone with whom she has no relationship, past or present.

Prenatal testing

Over the last several decades, there has been increasing emphasis placed on screening and testing before and during pregnancy to avoid a disability in a future child. Over the same period, screening and testing technologies have become simpler to administer and have expanded to capture a greater range of abnormalities. For instance, it is now possible to identify whether an individual is a carrier for nearly 500 recessive disorders.[50] Apart from expanded preconception testing, there is an emerging set of new technologies that make prenatal testing for some conditions very simple.

Non-invasive prenatal testing (NIPT) is a technology that makes it possible to test a pregnant woman's blood to identify whether the fetus she is carrying has Down syndrome, Edward syndrome and Patau syndrome (Trisomy 21, 18 and 13 respectively). These tests are only being rolled out slowly in Australia and the cost of such testing currently remains high at around $500–1,400.[51] As a result, most women still undergo the standard recommended prenatal testing. This involves an ultrasound at 11–13 weeks to identify anomalies and blood tests for placental protein and free human chorionic gonadotropin. These may be followed up with more invasive tests such as chorionic villus sampling (CVS) or amniocentesis. In each case a needle is inserted into the abdomen of the pregnant woman to extract cells from either the chorionic villi or the amniotic sac. Additional ultrasounds and blood tests may also be recommended.

---

47   *Assisted Reproductive Treatment Act 2008* (Vic) ss 46–8.

48   There has been recent Australian case law on requests for access to stored gametes for the purposes of posthumous reproduction; these are discussed in more detail in Chapter 18.

49   Anita Stuhmcke et al., 'Use of Stored Embryos in IVF Following Separation or Death of a Partner' (2013) 20(4) *Journal of Law and Medicine* 773–88.

50   Callum J Bell et al., 'Carrier Testing for Severe Childhood Recessive Diseases by Next-Generation Sequencing' (2011) 3 *Science Translational Medicine* 65ra4; Janice Edwards et al., 'Expanded Carrier Screening in Reproductive Medicine–Points to Consider: A Joint Statement of the American College of Medical Genetics and Genomics, American College of Obstetricians and Gynecologists, National Society of Genetic Counselors, Perinatal Quality Foundation, and Society for Maternal-Fetal Medicine' (2015) 125(3) *Obstetrics & Gynecology* 653. In addition, see Chapter 21 for further discussion on genetic testing.

51   Jane Woolcock and Rosalie Grivell, 'Noninvasive Prenatal Testing' (2014) 43(7) *Genetics* 432.

While there are some regulatory restrictions around the testing of embryos prior to implantation using PGD, there is no regulation of prenatal testing and screening, apart from the requirements around standards in medical devices,[52] pathology clinics and medical treatment. Instead, decisions about access to and availability of prenatal testing is left to best practice professional guidelines issued by peak representation bodies, such as the Royal Australian and New Zealand College of Obstetricians and Gynaecologists (RANZCOG). RANZCOG has issued guidelines for prenatal testing which require that all women are made aware of the availability of first trimester screening tests for Trisomy 21, 18 and 13, as well as carrier screening.[53] Although not currently the case in Australia, it is not unthinkable that carrier screening could be legally regulated and there are examples where this is the case, including in Cyprus where one in seven adults carries a mutation that causes ß-thalassaemia. Individuals who wish to marry must present documentation of thalassaemia screening to obtain a marriage licence.[54]

Further, although it is not compulsory for anyone to obtain genetic testing whether for preconception purposes or prenatally, once the information has been obtained the person may be required to disclose it in other circumstances such as, for instance, when applying for life insurance.[55] In addition, there are some special provisions involving genetic testing that arise in different areas of the law. For example, section 15 of the *Assisted Reproductive Technology Act 2007* (NSW) states that where it is necessary to make the disclosure to save a person's life or to warn the person to whom the information is disclosed about the existence of a medical condition that may be harmful to that person or to that person's offspring (including any future offspring of the person), an ART provider may disclose medical information about a donor to their adult offspring, or to the parent of their offspring if they are still a child. They can also choose to disclose it to the woman while she is pregnant. Interestingly, the permission is reciprocal in that an ART provider can also disclose medical information about the offspring to the donor. However, they do not require donors to be tested.

Furthermore, under Regulation 12 of the Assisted Reproductive Technology Regulations 2014 (NSW) an ART provider who obtains donated gametes must obtain the following information from the donor amongst other requirements:

(e) any medical history or genetic test results of the donor or the donor's family that are relevant to the future health of:

   (i) a person undergoing ART treatment involving the use of the donated gamete, or

---

52 See Chapter 21 for further details on the regulation of genetic testing (classified as medical devices).

53 RANZCOG, *Prenatal Screening and Diagnosis of Chromosomal and Genetic Abnormalities in the Foetus in Pregnancy* (Statement C-Obs 59, March 2015) 1.

54 Nicole E Cousens et al., 'Carrier Screening for Beta-thalassaemia: A Review of International Practice' (2010) 18(1) *European Journal of Human Genetics* 1077.

55 It is interesting to note that the UK Human Genetics Commission has recommended whole population preconception genetic screening and that children and young people should learn about antenatal and preconception screening in the final years of compulsory schooling. There is no suggestion, however, that the tests be mandatory. Rather, there is a recognition that key ethical principles are reproductive autonomy, the protection of the interests of children who will be born, genetic solidarity and the moral duty of individuals to share relevant results with family members: see Human Genetics Commission, Advisory Committee on Genetic Testing, *Increasing Options, Informing Choice: A Report on Preconception Genetic Testing and Screening* (April 2011) <https://f.hypotheses.org/wp-content/blogs.dir/257/files/2011/04/2011.HGC_.-Increasing-options-informing-choice-final1.pdf>.

(ii) any offspring born as a result of that treatment, or

(iii) any descendent of any such offspring

Abortion

Together with laws governing access to ART and regulating the behaviour of pregnant women, laws that seek to regulate abortion are key to discussion of laws that regulate reproduction. Abortion is often assumed to be the next step, once a diagnosis of disability is identified prenatally. Given that testing undertaken prenatally is primarily aimed at identifying genetic or other anomalies, it is interesting to compare the sparse regulatory response to genetic testing with the complex and highly regulated approach to abortion. One argument for this intense regulatory scrutiny is the notion that the fetus has a special status as a potential person worthy of protection.[56] Yet it is also clear that the key moment when a fetus is said to be a distinct rights bearing individual in law is when it is born alive and exists independently of the gestating woman.[57] Karpin has argued that:

> [t]his seeming contradiction illustrates the ongoing struggle within law to find a way to account for fetal value. The debate often polarizes between those who wish to attribute individuality to the foetus at varying stages of development and those who wish to deny it any value until it is born. Neither of these positions, however, adequately deals with, nor attempts to document, the way in which women themselves value their pregnancies.[58]

As with ART regulation, there is a complex matrix of laws that exist in the Australian states and territories in relation to abortion. However, before turning to the regulatory regime around abortion two points need to be made. First, although it may be an assumption tied to a positive test result for a disabling condition, that termination of a pregnancy will follow, there is a significant body of scholarship that challenges this assumption and critiques the way in which testing followed by abortion may be a form of soft eugenics or discrimination against people with disability.[59] Secondly, many women obtaining abortions do so for reasons unconnected with the presence of a disability, which may include reasons which relate to their own personal wellbeing and health.

While a number of Australian jurisdictions have decriminalised abortion, only the ACT has removed it entirely from its criminal code. In the ACT, a woman can access abortion services where she makes an informed request in accordance with the *Health Act 1993* (ACT) and it is performed by a doctor in an approved medical facility as defined in the

---

56   Sonia Harris-Short, 'Regulating Reproduction: Frozen Embryos, Consent, Welfare and the Equality Myth' in Stephen W Smith and Rohan Deazley (eds), *Legal Medical and Cultural Regulation of the Body* (Ashgate, 2009) 47.

57   Kristin Savell, 'Is the "Born Alive" Rule Outdated and Indefensible?' (2006) 28 *Sydney Law Review* 625.

58   Isabel Karpin, 'Regulating Reproduction: A Bioethical Approach' in John D Arras, Elizabeth Fenton and Rebecca Kukla (eds), *The Routledge Companion to Bioethics* (Routledge, 2014) 370–80.

59   The critical literature in this area is vast. See, for example, Erik Parens and Adrienne Asche, 'Special Supplement: The Disability Rights Critique of Prenatal Genetic Testing: Reflections and Recommendations' (1991) 29(5) *Hastings Centre Report* S1-S22; Loane Skene and Janna Thompson (eds), *The Sorting Society: The Ethics of Genetic Screening and Therapy* (CUP, 2008); Rosamund Scott, *Choosing Between Possible Lives: Law and Ethics of Prenatal and Preimplantation Genetic Diagnosis* (Hart, 2007).

legislation.[60] In Victoria, a woman may obtain an abortion upon request at any time up until 24 weeks gestation.[61] After 24 weeks, a doctor must consider the abortion 'appropriate in all the circumstances' and a second doctor must support that view. The doctor must have regard to: (a) all relevant medical circumstances; and (b) the woman's current and future physical, psychological and social circumstances.[62]

In the remaining Australian jurisdictions, we find a mixture of criminal law and statutory exceptions, as well as defences of necessity. In SA, for example abortion is legal if two doctors agree that a woman's physical and/or mental health is endangered by the pregnancy, or for serious fetal abnormality.[63] Similarly in the NT, abortion is legal up until 14 weeks of pregnancy (and this is extended to 23 weeks to prevent serious harm to the woman), provided that two doctors agree that a woman's physical and/or mental health is endangered by the pregnancy, or for serious fetal abnormality.[64] In NSW and Queensland, abortion is a criminal offence, however, the courts have recognised a defence of necessity where the pregnancy poses a serious danger to the physical and mental health of the woman. This has been interpreted broadly to encompass social and economic circumstances, as well as medical harm.[65] In WA, the law limits the availability of abortion to 20 weeks after which time, a woman must obtain the approval of two or more members of a ministerially appointed panel in order to obtain an abortion.[66]

Surrogacy and parentage

ART and IVF have been utilised by many women and men to overcome infertility but there are still persons in the community who are unable to form a family without the assistance of a woman who can gestate their fetus. Surrogacy, as this is known, can involve a woman carrying a fetus to which she has also donated her own genetic material to create or carrying a fetus that contains the genetic material of one, both or indeed neither of the intending parents or herself. In Australia, all the states and territories (except the NT) have laws prohibiting commercial surrogacy. Commercial surrogacy is defined in many different ways in the various Australian jurisdictions but a general definition involves payments to a woman amounting to more than reasonable expenses to carry a child to term. On the other hand, so-called altruistic surrogacy is permitted in most jurisdictions, or at least is not prohibited.

Concerns over the commercialisation of reproductive material and the sale of services such as surrogacy can be seen in the proliferation of state and territory-based laws aimed at prohibiting these practices.[67] At the same time, more flexible laws around parentage

---

60   *Health Act 1993* (ACT) ss 10, 80–3.

61   *Abortion Law Reform Act 2008* (Vic).

62   Ibid s 5.

63   *Criminal Law Consolidation Act 1935* (SA) s 82A; *Criminal Law Consolidation (Medical Termination of Pregnancy) Regulations 2011* (SA) Reg 4; Sch 1.

64   *Medical Services Act 1982* (NT) s 11.

65   *Crimes Act 1900* (NSW) ss 82–4; *R v Wald* (1971) 3 DCR (NSW) 25; *CES v Superclinics v Superclinics (Australia) Pty Ltd* (1995) 38 NSWLR 47; *Criminal Code Act 1899* (Qld) ss 224–6; *R v Bayliss & Cullen* (1986) 9 Qld Lawyer Reps 8.

66   *Health Act 1911* (WA) ss 334, 335.

67   *Parentage Act 2004* (ACT) s 41; *Assisted Reproductive Treatment Act 2008* (Vic) s 44; *Surrogacy Act 2008* (WA) s 8; *Family Relationships Act 1975* (SA) ss 10G, 10H; *Surrogacy Act 2010* (Qld) s 56; *Surrogacy Act 2010* (NSW) s 8; *Surrogacy Act 2012* (Tas) s 40.

orders,[68] and more complex laws around passport acquisition and the nationality of children born through international surrogacy arrangements, are also being introduced.[69] There is substantial disagreement amongst feminist scholars and others about whether there should be commercially compensated surrogacy and egg donation, however, it is clear that many people are bypassing Australian law by travelling overseas to jurisdictions where it is legally available because they are unable to form a family inside the law.[70] Given this is the case, it must be asked whether regulated commercial surrogacy and egg donation ought to be available in Australia to ensure harm minimisation to individuals and their future children.

Conclusion

The regulation of human reproduction is complex and multifaceted, with developments in reproductive technology being unevenly regulated both within and beyond Australia. This means that not only is there an imperative to simplify the complex array of jurisdictional variations in ART regulation, surrogacy and abortion but there is also increasingly a need to ensure harmonisation with jurisdictions beyond our shores, such as the UK and Europe. It is worth asking whether limits on cloning, and forms of embryo selection through PGD, enhance or limit women's reproductive choices and whether the regulatory system ought to take account of women's rights to make autonomous reproductive decisions not just about their fetuses, but also about the storage and destruction of embryos

---

68   In NSW, Queensland, Victoria, WA, SA and Tasmania, the birth mother and father (if known) are registered on the child's birth certificate until the surrogate parents get an order from the court to transfer the child's parentage: *Surrogacy Act 2010* (NSW) s 39; *Surrogacy Act 2010* (Qld) s 17; *Status of Children Act 1974* (Vic) s 19; *Artificial Conception Act 1985* (WA) ss 5–7 and *Surrogacy Act 2008* (WA) s 21; *Family Relationships Act 1975* (SA) ss 10C and 10HB; *Surrogacy Act 2012* (Tas) ss 12–18, 22. In the ACT, an order of the Supreme Court is required, which is similar to the requirement for an adopted child under s 28 of *Parentage Act 2004* (ACT). In Queensland, Victoria, WA, SA, ACT and Tasmania, same-sex female parents can record the names of both the birth mother and the female de facto mother on the child's birth certificate: *Status of Children Act 1978* (Qld) s 19C; *Status of Children Act 1974* (Vic) s 13; *Artificial Conception Act 1985* (WA) s 6A; *Family Relationships Act 1975* (SA) s 10C; *Parentage Act 2004* (ACT) s 8; *Status of Children Act 1974* (Tas) s 10C.

69   A person born overseas to an Australian citizen, such as a surrogate child, does not obtain Australian citizenship automatically under law. However, the person may apply for Australian citizenship by descent. Citizenship by descent requires that one of the parents is an Australian citizen. This means that there will need to be legal parentage under Australian state and territory laws or an order from the Family Court of Australia. Being named on a foreign birth certificate as the parent will not be sufficient on its own to prove legal parentage in Australia. The surrogate mother would retain parental responsibility under Australian law, even if there is a foreign court order that expressly extinguishes her parental responsibility. Applications for Australian citizenship by descent are assessed according to requirements set out in the *Australian Citizenship Act 2007* (Cth): the policy guidelines can be accessed at Australian Government, Department of Immigration and Border Protection, *Fact sheet – International surrogacy arrangements* <www.border.gov.au/about/corporate/information/fact-sheets/36a-surrogacy#offshore>.

70   Jenni Millbank, 'Rethinking "Commercial" Surrogacy in Australia' (2015) 12(2) *Journal of Bioethical Inquiry*, 477–90; Emily Jackson et al., 'Learning from Cross Border Reproduction' (forthcoming).

that are maintained outside the woman's body.[71] Thus it might be argued that, even if they involve new technologies that challenge our core understandings of reproductive processes, people who wish to use such technologies are best placed to assess the risks and ethics of their use. Suffice to say, IVF was once viewed as a suspect and unnatural technology and today it is a Commonwealth funded, mainstream technology that falls into the category of medical treatment.

---

71   Isabel Karpin, 'The Legal and Relational Identity of the "Not-Yet" Generation' (2012) 4(2) *Law, Innovation and Technology* 122–43; Anita Stuhmcke, 'Tick Tock Goes the Clock: Rethinking Policy and Embryo Storage Limits' (2014) 22(3) *Feminist Legal Studies* 285–306; Karpin, above n 58.

14

REGULATING EMERGING REPRODUCTIVE TECHNOLOGIES

Isabel Karpin

Introduction

In this chapter, the future of reproductive technology and its regulation is examined. When dealing with emerging technologies, regulators have to determine whether it is appropriate to regulate prospectively or reactively, taking account of a range of ethical, social and legal issues that may be raised by such developments.[1] While there have been some significant legislative changes in Australia to address speculative technologies, there is generally a legal lag when it comes to technologies that are no longer speculative but are nevertheless very new. In addition, it may be the case that such technologies are approved for use in other jurisdictions, but not in Australia.

This chapter will examine a range of emerging technologies which are proposed to be or are currently being used as part of Assisted Reproductive Technology (ART) treatment. There is much more that could be included within the remit of this topic, but for reasons of space there is a need to narrow the focus to some of the more high-profile and contested emerging technologies in the area. Specifically, the technologies that are examined in this chapter are: non-invasive prenatal tests, otherwise known as NIPT; technologies being employed to address mitochrondrial disease; new vitrification techniques to preserve oocytes; the creation of in vitro-derived artificial gametes and induced pluripotent stem cells (iPS) for reproduction.

Non Invasive Prenatal Testing (NIPT)

NIPT is already available in Australia, but it is not yet routinely used and is not covered by Medicare. It involves a simple blood test that can be performed on a pregnant woman from nine weeks, and analyses cell-free fetal nucleic acids found in low levels in maternal blood. While scientists claim to have successfully scanned the entire DNA of a fetus from the mother's blood, the test is not currently used for that purpose in Australia.[2] Instead, it is used to detect fetal chromosomal abnormalities, such as Trisomy 13 (Patau syndrome), Trisomy 18 (Edward syndrome), Trisomy 21 (Down syndrome), and sex chromosome abnormalities.[3] NIPT is not currently viewed as a diagnostic test, although many would argue that the accuracy rate brings it close to that standard.[4] In Australia, when NIPT testing produces a positive result, follow-up diagnostic tests such as Chorionic Villus Sampling (CVS) and Amniocentesis may be recommended to confirm a diagnosis. In the future NIPT could be classified as diagnostic, and may then replace these invasive tests, which carry a risk of miscarriage.

---

1   For an overview, see Roger Brownsword and Morag Goodwin, *Law and the Technologies of the Twenty-First Century* (CUP, 2012); Mark Flear et al., 'A European Law of New Health Technologies?' in Mark Flear et al. (eds), *European Law and New Health Technologies* (OUP, 2013) 389–414.

2   YM Dennis Lo et al., 'Maternal Plasma DNA Sequencing Reveals the Genome-Wide Genetic and Mutational Profile of the Fetus' (2010) 2(61) *Science Translational Medicine* 61ra91, doi: 10.1126/scitranslmed.3001720.

3   Jane Woolcock and Rosalie Grivell, 'Noninvasive Prenatal Testing' (2014) 43(7) *Australian Family Physician* 432.

4   This may account for the fact that there is still some confusion in the literature about whether it should be called NIPT or NIPD (where the D stands for diagnosis). For Down syndrome, the false positive rate is only 0.2% while it is a bit higher for Trisomies 13 and 18. These rates are considered significant enough to warrant invasive testing to confirm diagnosis: see above n 3.

The potential future routine use of NIPT has raised a number of ethical concerns, particularly with regard to whether it is used for screening or diagnostic purposes. De Jong et al. argue that the test is likely to replace the initial screening test, thus capturing women who would usually only undergo more invasive diagnostic tests if they were found to be at high risk in the initial screen, or were of advanced maternal age.[5] If NIPT is used for routine diagnostic testing, it could present problems in terms of obtaining informed consent. This is because different approaches are currently taken to obtaining consent and offering counselling when conducting diagnostic, as opposed to screening, tests. In addition, whole genome scanning from fetal cells in maternal blood is on the horizon. As outlined in Chapter 20, genetic testing generally raises a range of concerns about consent, privacy and protection from stigmatisation, and in the case of this new technology the impact will fall on those not yet born. The simplicity of NIPT may also result in pressure on women to utilise it. This may in turn create greater pressure to respond to the results of any test in line with what are purported to be socially desirable outcomes: in other words, to terminate a pregnancy where there is the possibility of an abnormality.[6]

Mitochondrial donation and inheritable genetic modification

In March 2015, the House of Lords in the UK voted in favour of allowing technology that facilitates the creation of embryos with the use of donor mitochondria to cure mitochondrial disease. This is a disease in which the cell's batteries (the mitochondria) malfunction, disabling energy production.[7] The law allowing Assisted Reproduction Technology (ART) clinics in the UK to apply to the national regulator, known as the Human Fertilisation and Embryology Authority (HFEA), for a licence to undertake the technique, came into force in late 2015.[8] This was a watershed moment, making legal what will effectively be inheritable genetic modification, and eventually leading to the creation of an embryo, and (hopefully) ultimately a child, with genetic material from three people.

How does the technique work? There are a number of methods, but the one most likely to be used involves the mitochondria from a donor cell being merged with the nuclear DNA of an egg of a woman who has mitochondrial disease. This process, known as ooplasmic transfer, involves taking the nucleus containing the genetic material from one cell and inserting it into a donor egg from which all the genetic material, except the mitochondrial DNA, has been removed. This produces what is called a cybrid or cytoplasmic hybrid embryo, which is then transferred to the woman's uterus, where it develops and hopefully results in a full-term pregnancy and the birth of a child. The child will have three genetic contributors – the genetic mother and father, and the female mitochondria donor.

---

5   Antina de Jong et al., 'Non-invasive Prenatal Testing: Ethical Issues Explore' (2010) 18(3) *European Journal of Human Genetics* 272.
6   Isabel Karpin, 'Protecting the Future Well: Access to Preconception Genetic Screening and Testing and the Right Not to Use It' (2016) 25 *Griffith Law Review* doi:10.1080/10383441.2016.1203274.
7   For further details about mitochondrial disease, <www.amdf.org.au/mito-info>.
8   *Human Fertilisation and Embryology (Mitochondrial Donation) Regulations 2015* (UK).

Currently, the use of this new technology is not allowed in Australia, as the creation of these types of cybrid or cytoplasmic hybrid embryos would most likely contravene sections 9 and 13 of the *Prohibition of Human Cloning for Reproduction Act 2002* (Cth) (PHCR Act). Section 13 of the Act specifically prohibits the development of an embryo with genetic material from more than two persons. The rationale behind the provision that was offered during law reform debates over its adoption was that it would avoid 'confusion of genetic identity for the person born'.[9] This is a significant limitation given that mitochondrial disease affects 1 in 5000 births and probably a higher proportion of fetuses (which may be non-viable and may spontaneously abort).[10]

Nevertheless, there are many commentators who argue that techniques that lead to inheritable genetic modification should not be permitted because they alter the human gene pool in perpetuity. For instance, Scully notes that members of the deaf community, who consider deafness to be a cultural attribute, would view the intergenerational eradication of this trait as highly undesirable.[11] Survey evidence of public attitudes to the use of inheritable genetic modification technologies reveals a nuanced approach. For example, one UK study on public attitudes to gene therapy found that people were more accepting of gene therapy that was not inheritable, but that the key determinant was the trait for which the therapy was being undertaken. For instance, the public broadly supported gene therapy for heart disease, but while 82 per cent supported non-inheritable gene therapy, a lesser number (63 per cent) supported germ line or inheritable genetic modification for the same condition.[12] In both cases, it was notable that the support for therapy of one kind or another was well over 50 per cent. Given that inheritable genetic modification (including for mitochondrial disease) is still an untested proposition and will have an impact on future generations, it is worth asking whether there are means to address the same concerns without impacting future populations.

Vitrification of human oocytes and the rise of 'social' egg freezing

While sperm and embryo freezing are techniques that have been common in ART for many years now, the availability of reliable egg or oocyte freezing technology has only been developed over the last ten years. Because oocytes have a high proportion of liquid, initial attempts at egg cryopreservation that involved a slow cooling process were for the most part unsuccessful. However, this has now changed with the development of a new 'freezing' technology known as vitrification. The US Society for Reproductive Medicine has noted that

---

9   Lockhart Committee, *Legislation Review: Prohibition of Human Cloning Act 2002 and Research Involving Human Embryos Act 2002, Issues Paper: Outline of Existing Legislation and Issues for Public Consultation* (2005) 14.

10   Human Fertilisation and Embryology Authority (HFEA), 'Scientific Review of the Safety and Efficacy of Methods to Avoid Mitochondrial Disease through Assisted Conception' (April 2011) para 4.1.3 <www.hfea.gov.uk/docs/2011-04-18_Mitochondria_review_-_final_report.PDF>.

11   Jackie Leach Scully, 'IGM and Disability: Normality and Identity' in John EJ Rasko, Gabrielle M O'Sullivan and Rachel A Ankeny (eds), *The Ethics of Inheritable Genetic Modification: A Dividing Line?* (CUP, 2006) 175–92, 179.

12   Wellcome Trust, *What do People Think about Gene Therapy? A Report Published by the Wellcome Trust* (2005) <https://wellcome.ac.uk/sites/default/files/wtx026421_0.pdf>

because success rates in achieving clinical pregnancies were similar whether using frozen or fresh eggs, it is now no longer appropriate to categorise the use of the technology as experimental.[13] This was despite also noting that 'there are not yet sufficient data to recommend oocyte cryopreservation for the sole purpose of circumventing reproductive ageing in healthy women'.[14] Similarly, in the UK, the British Fertility Society and the Association of Clinical Embryologists support egg freezing on medical grounds, but do not recommend it for women who wish to put childbearing on hold for non-medical reasons.[15]

Nevertheless, the term 'social egg freezing' has taken hold and is now being used to describe egg freezing for fertility preservation where there is no medical cause of future infertility, such as might be found where a person is undergoing cancer treatment, for example.[16] Some commentators have described this as egg freezing for 'lifestyle reasons',[17] suggesting that it offers women 'more time to find an appropriate partner with whom to have a child and it permits women to delay childbearing until they are psychologically, financially and occupationally ready for parenthood'.[18] This view has been buoyed by the recent decision of multinational corporations, such as Facebook and Apple, to offer insurance coverage for the cost of egg freezing for women as part of their employment benefits package.[19] Conversely, there are those who argue that the process of egg freezing is physically onerous for women and extremely costly,[20] especially if you include ongoing storage expenses. Furthermore, it has been suggested that it would be better if companies such as Facebook and Apple worked harder to provide more family-friendly workplaces and flexible job options as a means to assist their female employees to manage both a career and a family.[21]

Although the success rate with fresh and frozen eggs is comparable, the evidence to date suggests that women deciding to freeze their eggs for social reasons are doing so in their mid 30s, when their eggs are already on the mature side. The older the eggs, the less likely it is that a successful pregnancy will result. Given that egg freezing is still a relatively new technology and there is not a lot of evidence-based research on its efficacy for women who have delayed childbearing, there is concern that companies offering the technology stand to make a considerable amount of money on the promise of not very much. In the circumstances, it

---

13   Society for Reproductive Medicine and Society for Assisted Reproductive Technology, 'Mature Oocyte Cryopreservation: A Guideline' (2013) 99(1) *Fertility and Sterility* 41.

14   Ibid 42.

15   British Fertility Society, *New Clinical Guidelines for Egg Freezing in the UK* (2009) <www.fertility .org.uk/news/pressrelease/09_11-EggFreezinGuidelines.html>.

16   Helen Mertes and Guido Pennings, 'Social Egg Freezing For Better Not For Worse' (2011) 23(7) *Reproductive Biomedicine Online* 824; Kylie Baldwin et al., 'Reproductive Technology and the Life Course: Current Debates and Research in Social Egg Freezing' (2014) 17(3) *Human Fertility* 170.

17   Julian Savulescu and Imogen Goold, 'Freezing Eggs for Lifestyle Reasons' (2008) 6 *American Journal of Bioethics* 32.

18   Baldwin et al., above n 16, 171.

19   Mark Tran, 'Apple and Facebook to Offer to Freeze Eggs for Female Employees', *The Guardian*, 15 October 2014.

20   See the newspaper article by Wendy Tuohy, 'Freezing Your Eggs: How 30-Something Single Women are Challenging Infertility', *Herald Sun*, 22 November 2014. In this article, Professor of Gynaecology and Monash IVF doctor Gab Kovacs was quoted as saying 'if you want a family of three kids, that means you'd need 60 eggs, it's not feasible at $10,000 to $15,000 a pop (a cycle of egg collection)'. He noted that an average of 22 eggs is necessary to be collected for freezing for one likely pregnancy.

21   Helen Mertes, 'Does Company-Sponsored Egg Freezing Promote or Confine Women's Reproductive Autonomy?' (2015) 32 *Journal of Assisted Reproduction and Genetics* 1205.

has been argued that ART clinics should be required by law to provide detailed information to women seeking to use the technology about their relative chances of success, based on age and other factors. Further, it is argued that, in essence, it is a medical response to a social problem.[22]

Stem cells for research and reproduction

The aim of both the PHCR Act and the *Research Involving Human Embryos Act 2002* (Cth) (RIHE Act) has been primarily to manage the use of human embryos in research and to prohibit certain practices that are seen as breaking the boundaries of appropriate scientific exploration. It is important to note that those engaged in ART research proved to be an influential interest group in the design of the first iteration of the legislation, as well as of amendments that were adopted in 2007. On behalf of the group, it was strongly argued that being able to use embryonic stem cells for research offered the best chance of finding cures for many debilitating diseases and disabilities. Adult stem cells, it was argued, were not adequate because they were not easily reprogrammed, as they lacked totipotency, as well as pluripotency.[23] In contrast, embryonic stem cells are totipotent in the first cell divisions and pluripotent thereafter.

Prior to perfecting human cloning techniques, scientists were limited to harvesting embryonic stem cells from embryos created through ART that were excess to needs. It was, and indeed still is, illegal under Australian law to create a traditional sperm and egg embryo using IVF merely for research purposes. Such embryos may only be created for the purpose of reproduction and during the course of IVF treatment. Once human cloning was achieved, however, a new source of embryonic stem cells became available through the creation of embryos by somatic cell nuclear transfer (SCNT). Commonwealth legislation (see above) makes a clear distinction between SCNT embryos and traditional sperm and egg embryos. Only the former can be deliberately created for the purposes of research, whereas the latter may only be used where they are excess to needs and were created originally for the purposes of ART treatment.

Section 14 of the PHCR Act prohibits the development of an embryo beyond 14 days and it is a criminal offence to implant an SCNT embryo in a woman and bring it to term. An egg with its nucleus removed is needed for the creation of an SCNT embryo. As a consequence of a last-minute amendment to the RIHE Act, it is not possible to use animal eggs as the denucleated package for human SCNT – this would be a prohibited hybrid embryo under section 19(3) of the same Act. Therefore, scientists wishing to create human SCNT embryos for research need to have a supply of human ova. In order to ensure that unethical or illegal scientific behaviour does not occur, section 22 of the PHCR Act requires anyone who wishes to create and develop a human embryo, other than through the fertilisation of a human egg by a human sperm, to obtain a licence under the RIHE Act to do so.

---

22   Angel Petropanagas et al., 'Social Egg Freezing: Risk, Benefits and Other Considerations' (2015) 187(9) *Canadian Medical Association Journal* 666.

23   Totipotency means cells that can be programmed to develop into any cell in the body, whereas pluripotency means cells that are capable of developing into any type of cell, except those that form a placenta or embryo.

At the time of writing, there are 10 active licences that have been issued by the NHMRC Licensing Committee.[24] Four of those licences are held by Genea, a Sydney-based ART clinic, for the use of eggs and the creation of SCNT embryos.[25] In relation to such licences, the Committee has authorised the use of up to 2400 eggs in three of those licences and 1000 in the fourth licence.[26] In fact, Genea has only used about 759 across the four licences, out of a potential 8200, and none in the 2014/15 reporting period. In addition, they have only created 41 embryos, although they were authorised to create 1080. Out of those 41 embryos, only one has developed to the compacted morula stage in the development of an embryo.

Artificial gametes

Research using embryonic stem cells has led to an interesting development – the creation of artificial gametes. The research is currently in its early stages and there has been controversy about the extent of its success so far. In 2014, Cambridge-based researchers reported that they had made primitive forms of artificial sperm and eggs by culturing embryonic stem cells.[27] While they were not the first researchers to make this claim, they have continued to develop the technology by showing that the same process can be done using adult skin tissue.[28]

If it becomes possible to create sperm and even ova from embryonic stem cells, or from induced pluripotent adult stem cells (iPS – see below), the question arises whether ART clinics would be allowed to use these artificially derived gametes to fertilise and create an embryo. Artificial gametes would allow an adult who is infertile – due to cancer treatment, for example – to create a gamete containing their own DNA. It is not difficult to imagine that if and/or when this technology is more fully developed, it would become desirable for a range of people with fertility issues.

The question to be addressed, however, is whether it would be legal to use an in vitro-derived artificial sperm under current Australian laws to fertilise an egg for the purposes of reproduction. While it is illegal to create an embryo for research by fertilising an egg with a sperm, it is unclear whether it would be illegal under Australian legislation to create an embryo for implantation and reproduction using an artificial sperm and/or egg. Such an embryo would probably be caught by section 20(4)(f) of the PHCR Act, which prohibits the creation of a human embryo that contains a human cell (within the meaning of section 15) whose genome has been altered in such a way that the alteration is inheritable by human descendants of the human whose cell was altered. While there is some ambiguity in Australian law, the UK Parliament has been sufficiently concerned about this new

24   National Health and Medical Research Council (NHMRC), *Stem Cells, Cloning and Related Issues* (20 February 2014) <www.nhmrc.gov.au/about/nhmrc-committees/embryo-research-licensing-committee/human-embryos-and-cloning/stem-cells-clon>.

25   NHMRC Embryo Research Licensing Committee, *Report to the Parliament of Australia for the Period 1 September 2014 to 28 February 2015* (June 2015) <www.nhmrc.gov.au/_files_nhmrc/publications/attachments/hc46_nhmrc_licensing_committee_25th_biannual_report_to_parliament.pdf>. For further details about Genea, see <www.genea.com.au>.

26   Ibid.

27   Ian Sample, 'Scientists Use Skin Cells to Create Artificial Sperm and Eggs', *The Guardian*, 25 December 2014.

28   Naoko Irei et al., 'SOX17 Is a Critical Specifier of Human Primordial Cell Fate' (2015) 160(1–2) *Cell* 253.

technology to explicitly prohibit the use of artificial gametes in assisted reproduction at the current time.[29]

If it becomes safe to use artificial gametes, one of the most significant applications will be the capacity of two men (and possibly two women) to have a child that is genetically related to both of them. Or indeed, as Jackson points out: 'a child might have only one genetic parent whose natural gametes could be used to fertilise their artificially derived gametes'.[30] This would not produce a clone, because the genes would be reshuffled through the process of fertilisation. However, even if such technology were proved safe, its (potential) use gives rise to a range of other issues. For example, what of those people who have donated their cells for the production of stem cell lines without the knowledge that those stem cell lines could be turned into gametes? Because those stem cell lines are immortal, gametes and embryos could be created several generations into the future, notwithstanding that the original genetic progenitors are long dead.[31]

Induced pluripotent stem cells

The development of a cell reprogramming method resulting in induced pluripotent stem cells (iPS) from skin cells avoids some of the concerns previously raised by SCNT, given that the process by which embryonic stem cells are harvested results in the destruction of the embryo. iPS derived from skin cells avoids the necessity for embryo creation and destruction and allows the debate regarding the development of this technology to avoid concerns about the moral status of the embryo. However, from a regulatory perspective, the potential uses of iPS cells needs further interrogation. While the technology around iPS cells is still in its infancy and their clinical use on human beings is still some time off, successes in reprogramming these cells indicate that their pluripotency may well be as potent as 'gold standard' human embryonic stem cells (hESC). In China, for example, iPS cells and related technology have been used to generate entire mice.[32]

Given that advances in stem cell technology in the UK have already shown the capacity to produce what appears to be a mature human sperm from hESC, it seems likely that iPS cells could also be used to achieve this end. In this way both iPS and hESC might be used in the future to create artificial gametes. This raises significant implications for ART regulatory regimes which so far have not contemplated this kind of reproductive possibility. If pluripotency means that, theoretically, the stem cell has the capacity to generate any cell type in

---

29   Note that Clause 3ZA of the *Human Fertilisation and Embryology Act 2008* (UK) (HFE Act) defines the terms, 'permitted embryo', 'permitted sperm' and 'permitted eggs'. Paragraph 29 of the *Explanatory Notes* to the HFE Act states that: 'permitted eggs' are defined as eggs produced by or extracted from the ovaries of a woman and 'permitted sperm' is 'sperm produced by or extracted from the testes of a man.' There is no such clear definition in Australian legislation.

30   Emily Jackson, 'Degendering Reproduction?' (2008) 16 *Medical Law Review* 346.

31   Note the concerns of John Moore, the plaintiff in the well-known case of *Moore v Regents of the University of California*, 51 Cal. 3d 120 (1990); 271 Cal. Rptr. 146; 793 P.2d 479, about the fact that tissue from his excised spleen was used by his treating doctor (and colleagues) to create a lucrative and immortal cell line, known as the Mo cell line. This was done without his knowledge or consent. For further details, see Chapters 18 and 20.

32   Monya Baker, 'iPS Cells Make Mice That Make Mice' (2009) *Nature Reports Stem Cells*, published online 6 August 2009, doi:10.1038/stemcells.2009.106.

the body, then what are – or should be – the limits to how such cells should be used in the future, and who gets to decide? Is it the tissue donor or the law that determines whether or not, for instance, an individual can use their own skin cell to develop a new organ or body part or potentially an entire human embryo? While it is unlikely that scientific researchers will have an interest in using iPS cells to create entire human beings, there is nevertheless arguably a role for law in creating a regime where if the community is opposed to such a use (or not) that is reflected in the law.

Under Australian law, it appears that it would be illegal to place a human embryo created by iPS into the body of a woman. Section 20(3) of the PHCR Act makes it an offence for a person to intentionally place an embryo in the body of a woman, knowing that it is a prohibited embryo. In addition, section 20(4) describes all the kinds of prohibited embryos that there might be. An iPS-created embryo would contravene the very first category: (a) a human embryo created by a process other than the fertilisation of a human egg by a human sperm. Of course this assumes that that embryo could be considered to be a human embryo within the definition set down in the PHCR Act. Either way, it might also fall under section 20(4)(f), which refers to a prohibited human embryo as one which contains a human cell with an altered genome that is inheritable. It seems then that the reproduction of a human being in this manner would be as illegal as the reproduction of a human using SCNT, whether or not the iPS-derived human being could be considered a clone in the same way as one derived via SCNT.

It is possible to imagine a situation in which it might be useful for scientific researchers to create a human embryo via iPS, but they may have no intention of developing it beyond a certain number of cell divisions or days. They might want to do this in order to test the embryo's reprogramming mechanisms and to identify whether or not they were (like their mouse counterparts) fully pluripotent. iPS researchers could then no longer side-step the debate about research involving human embryos and would need to comply with existing regulatory mechanisms under Australian law in order to lawfully conduct such research. For example, section 22 of the PHCR Act, and sections 8 and 20 of the RIHE Act, place limits on who may create an embryo, as well as on what kind of embryo may be created.

If it were possible to avoid the use of human eggs, iPS would offer significant advantages. Mice iPS cells can functionally differentiate into all cell lineages, including germ cells that can ultimately give rise to offspring. In addition, if iPS cells can be used to create a plentiful supply of ova, this would remove a significant and, some would argue, controversial burden placed on women to provide eggs for the creation of embryos via SCNT. Finally, if iPS cells can be used for reproductive purposes, then it is possible that stem cell lines currently stored in stem cell banks could at some point in the future be used for the production of gametes and future children. This would constitute a new kind of posthumous reproduction, and raises a range of ethical and legal issues around donors' consent for future use of stem cells.[33] If we are to ensure that today's stem cell donors comprehend the possibilities of the future, then we may have to countenance the possibility that things that are repugnant today, such as human cloning, may not always be so.

---

33   For further discussion on obtaining consent for future use of human tissue in the context of biobanking, see Chapter 19.

In terms of the impact of reproductive technologies, the development of iPS technology that can make any cell in the body pluripotent is highly significant. Together with embryonic stem cell technology, iPS technology moves us closer to the possible development of whole organs, including artificial wombs. [34]

Conclusion

The development of a reliable and non-invasive form of prenatal testing to detect possible fetal abnormalities, together with inheritable genetic modification techniques to deal with mitochondrial disease, are examples of the current scientific focus on what might be described as 'disability avoidance' technologies. In light of the contested understanding of disability which is outlined in Chapter 22, it is suggested that more attention needs to be paid to the appropriate use of such technologies. At the same time, the capacity to create in vitro-derived artificial gametes is on the horizon, and combined with growing corporate and social acceptance of deferred parenthood and egg freezing, this suggests that there is also a social and scientific commitment to genetic reproduction and fertility preservation.

It is thus necessary to consider how these new technologies will impact on ART and related regulation in Australia and to critically reflect on how such technological developments are likely to impact on the rights and freedoms of women and men to reproduce and form families. In particular, given the more onerous role women play in ART and IVF, it is worth considering whether regulation is necessary to enhance or limit women's reproductive choices. A key question that needs to be addressed is whether, or to what extent, the law should take account of women's right to make autonomous reproductive decisions, even if they involve new technologies that challenge our core understandings of reproductive processes.

---

[34]   Notably, in 2015, the UK regulator approved a clinical trial of womb transplants involving ten women. This followed a similar program in Sweden which resulted in the birth of a child in 2014, from a woman who had received a donor womb, see Chris Johnston, 'Womb Transplants: First 10 British Women Given Go-Ahead', *The Guardian*, 30 September 2015. If a womb could be developed from stem cells the necessity for a transplant may be removed.

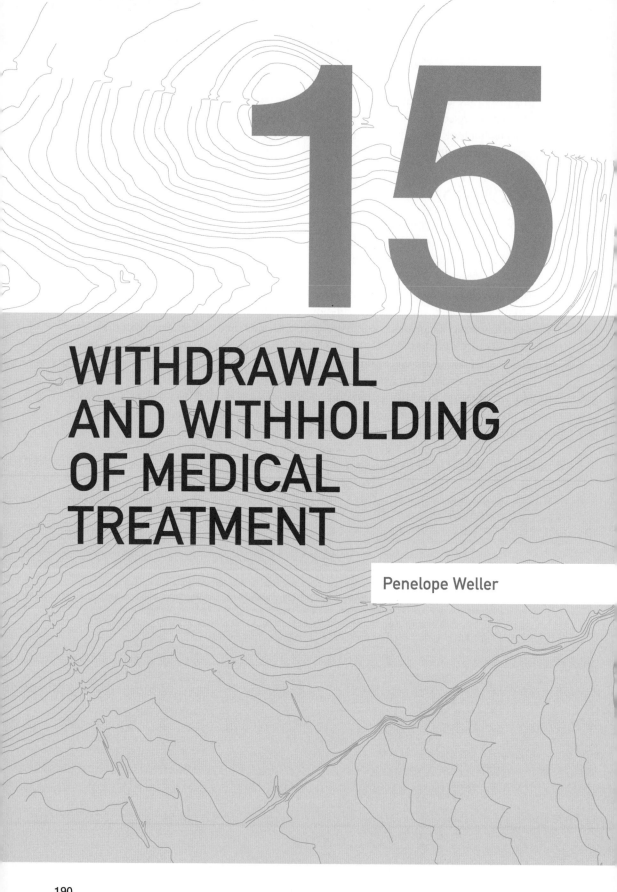

15

WITHDRAWAL AND WITHHOLDING OF MEDICAL TREATMENT

Penelope Weller

Introduction

Approximately 440,000 deaths occur annually in Australia as a result of decisions to withdraw or withhold life-sustaining treatment from both competent and incompetent adults.[1] The consequences for doctors who misapprehend the law or misinterpret their legal responsibilities may be criminal charges for murder or manslaughter if treatment is withheld inappropriately,[2] or assault charges,[3] or civil actions, or disciplinary and coronial proceedings, if treatment is provided without appropriate consent or authorisation. The issue is not purely a legal one. Conflict among family, friends, supporters, doctors and other health professionals during end-of-life decision-making is associated with adverse consequences for everyone involved.

Whether, and how, to regulate the provision of end-of-life healthcare has emerged as a prominent theme in law and policy debates in recent decades.[4] There is an ongoing discussion about the ethical, philosophical, theological and practical dimensions of dying.[5] In the midst of this debate, the courts are required to resolve the particular disputes that come before them.[6] The disputes reveal changing social attitudes towards end-of-life

---

1   Ben White et al., 'The Legal Role of Medical Professionals in Decisions to Withhold or Withdraw Life-Sustaining Treatment: Part One (New South Wales)' (2011) 18(3) *Journal of Law and Medicine* 498, 502.

2   Lindy Wilmott, Ben White and Shih-Ning Then, 'Withholding or Withdrawing Life-Sustaining Medical Treatment' in Ben White, Fiona McDonald and Lindy Wilmott (eds), *Health Law in Australia* (Thomson Reuters, 2010) [13.20].

3   *Secretary, Department of Health and Community Services (NT) v JWB and SMB* (Marion's case) (1992) 175 CLR 218, 232 per Mason CJ, Dawson Toohey and Gaudron JJ; *Hunter and New England Area Health Service v A* (2009) 74 NSWLR 88, [40].

4   Margaret Otlowski, *Voluntary Euthanasia and the Common Law*, 2nd edn (OUP, 2000). The Voluntary Euthanasia Society in the UK was established in 1935.

5   In Australia the following inquiries have been undertaken: Parliament of Victoria, *Enquiry Into Options For Dying With Dignity* (1987); South Australia Parliament, *Final Report of the Select Committee of the House of Assembly on the Law and Practice Relating to Death and Dying* (1992); Legislative Assembly of the Australian Capital Territory, Select Committee on Euthanasia, *Report: Voluntary and Natural Death Bill* (1994); Parliament of Tasmania, Community Development Committee, *Report on the Need for Legislation of Voluntary Euthanasia* (1998); Parliament of South Australia Social Development Committee, *Enquiry into the Voluntary Euthanasia Bill 1996* (1999); NSW Parliamentary Research Service, *Euthanasia: An Update* (2001); Attorney General/Minister for Health for Western Australia, *Medical Treatment for the Dying: Discussion Paper* (2005); Parliament of Victoria, *Medical Treatment (Physician Assisted Dying) Bill 2008*, Current Issues Brief Number One (2008); Parliament of Tasmania, Joint Standing Committee on Community Development, *Report on the Dying with Dignity Bill 2009*; Australian Government Productivity Commission, *Caring for Older Australians*, Productivity Commission Inquiry Report Overview, No. 53 (2011); Health and Community Services Committee, *Inquiry into Palliative Care Services and Home and Community Care Services in Queensland* (2012); Australian Senate Standing Committee on Community Affairs, *Inquiry into Palliative Care in Australia* (2012); Australian Commission on Safety and Quality in Health Care, *Safety and Quality of End-of-Life Care in Acute Hospitals – A Background Paper* (2013); Australia21, *The Right to Choose an Assisted Death: Time for Legislation*, Report following a Roundtable in Brisbane (2013); Lindy Wilmott and Benjamin P White, Australia21, *How Should Australia Regulate Voluntary Euthanasia and Assisted Suicide?* (2012) <http://eprints.qut.edu.au/54757/>; Australian Centre of Health Research, *Leadership and Quality in End of Life Care Australia: Round Table Recommendations* (2013); Senate Community Affairs Committee, *Inquiry into the Living Longer Living Better Aged Care Bills 2013* (2013); NSW Parliament Issues Backgrounder, *Euthanasia* (2013); Senate Legal and Constitutional Affairs Legislation Committee Inquiry, Exposure Draft of the Medical Services (Dying with Dignity) Bill 2014.

6   Landmark cases are *Airedale NHS Trust v Bland* [1993] AC 789, *Re Quinlan*, 70 NJ 10, 355 A 2d 647 (1976) and *Bush v Schiavo*, 885 So 2d 321 (2004) in the US.

decision-making and care, and the struggle to come to terms with sophisticated medical technology and the consequent relocation of death from the home to the hospital. They also reveal a changing regulatory landscape and the impact of international human rights principles on this area of law.[7]

End-of-life care raises questions about how the law should engage with concepts such as the quality of life,[8] medically futile treatment,[9] the distribution of scarce medical resources,[10] who should be entitled to make end-of-life decisions and, if so, on what basis.[11] The current position in law is that a distinction is drawn between: (1) withdrawing and withholding life-sustaining treatment at the end of life; and (2) actions that are intended to cause death, such as (active) euthanasia and assisted suicide.[12] Within these two categories, the rules that apply with respect to individuals who have the capacity to make their own decisions are different from those that apply to those who do not. In either situation, the legal responsibilities of all parties warrant scrutiny, both because the determination of capacity or competence is uncertain and because the law in many jurisdictions arises at the interface of common law, statutory provisions and practice guidelines, where the legal landscape is often complex, opaque and in flux.

This chapter examines legal, ethical and social issues relating to the withdrawing and withholding of medical treatment near the end of life, including management of post-coma unresponsive or minimally responsive patients. The first part of the chapter provides an overview of the prohibition against murder and assisted suicide. The second explores end-of-life decision-making in relation to those with legal competence, before going on to examine how such decision-making is approached in the case of those who lack such competence, including children. The final part of the chapter examines whether there is a right to demand treatment in end-of-life care, by reference to recent case law on this issue. The law relating to euthanasia and assisted suicide is examined in Chapter 16. It is important to note that both Chapter 15 and Chapter 16 should be read in conjunction with Chapter 10 on substituted decision-making.

The prohibition against murder and assisted suicide

The law governing end-of-life decisions has developed against the backdrop of the prohibition against murder and assisted suicide. While the prohibition against murder remains absolute,[13] in many jurisdictions suicide is no longer a criminal offence. However, the offence

---

7   Dale Gardner, 'Diagnosing Death in the 21st Century' (Keynote address at the International Conference on End of Life Care: Law, Ethics, Policy and Practice, Brisbane, 13–15 August 2014).

8   Martha C Nussbaum and Amartya Sen, *The Quality of Life* (OUP, 1993).

9   Robert Truog, Allan Brett and Joel Frader, 'The Problem with Futility' in Francoise Baylis et al. (eds), *Health Care Ethics in Canada*, 3rd edn (Cengage Learning, 2011) 408.

10   Robert H Blank, *Rationing Medicine* (Columbia University Press, 2013).

11   Nancy Berlinger, Bruce Jennings and Susan M Wolf, *The Hastings Center Guidelines for Decisions on Life-Sustaining Treatment and Care Near the End of Life*, revised and expanded 2nd edn (OUP, 2013).

12   See *Airedale NHS Trust v Bland* [1993] AC 789.

13   See Chapter 16.

of assisting a person to commit suicide is often retained.[14] Doctors and other health professionals caring for people at the end of life are inevitably implicated in the latter offence. Some Australian jurisdictions have responded by providing legislative protection to doctors who act in good faith when providing medical treatment to their patients who are at the end of life.[15]

The law's first response is to distinguish between lawful withdrawing and withholding of medical treatment at the end of life, and the withholding and withdrawing of treatment that may invoke criminal law sanctions. For example, in the US, the courts have recognised that the decision to refuse life-sustaining treatment is not equivalent to attempting suicide because there is no intent to die;[16] that refusing medical treatment merely allows the disease or injury to take its natural course, death being the result of the primary or underlying disease or injury;[17] and that the decision to refuse life-sustaining procedures made before an accident does not amount to suicide because the injury is not self-inflicted.[18] Similarly in Australia, it is established that refusal of nutrition by a quadriplegic patient is not analogous to euthanasia or lethal treatment; does not engage with concepts such as the right to life or death; and should not be considered in terms of the best interests of a medical patient.[19] The determining question in end-of-life decision-making for legally competent patients is: what are the wishes of the patient?

End-of-life decisions for those with legal competence

In general, the emphasis in the law is on individual self-determination and the value of one's own life in relation to individuals who are recognised as being able to make their own decisions. The common law recognises that competent individuals have a right to autonomy and self-determination,[20] including the right to control what is done to their bodies now, and in the foreseeable future.[21] The first consideration is whether or not the person has capacity to make decisions with respect to their medical treatment.[22] The starting point of the law is the rebuttable presumption that an adult person has decision-making capacity.[23] The common

---

14   *Crimes Act 1900* (ACT) s 17; *Crimes Act 1900* (NSW) s 31C; *Criminal Code Act* (NT) s 162; *Criminal Code* (Qld) s 311; *Criminal Law Consolidation Act 1935* (SA) ss 13A(5)–(7), 13(6)(b); *Criminal Code* (Tas) s 163; *Crimes Act 1958* (Vic) s 6B(2); *Criminal Code* (WA) s 288.

15   *Criminal Code* (WA) s 259; *Criminal Code* (Qld) s 282A(1); *Criminal Code (Palliative Care) Amendment Act 2003* (Qld); *Consent to Medical Treatment and Palliative Care Act 1995* (SA) s 17(1).

16   *Guardianship of Doe*, 411 Mass 512, 583 NE 2d 1263 (1992); *McKay v Bergstedt*, 106 Nev 808, 801 P 2d 617 (1990).

17   *McConnell v Beverly Enterprises-Connecticut*, 209 Conn 692, 533 A 2d 596 (1989); *McKay v Bergstedt*, 106 Nev 808, 801 P 2d 617 (1990); *Matter of Conroy*, 98 NJ 321, 486 A 2d 1209, 48 ALR 4th 1 (1985).

18   *H Ltd v J* (2010) 107 SASR 352.

19   *Brightwater Care Group v Rossiter* (2009) 40 WAR 84; *Re F (Mental Patient: Sterilisation)* [1990] 2 AC 1.

20   *Airedale NHS Trust v Bland* [1993] AC 789, 826; *Rogers v Whitaker* (1992) 175 CLR 479, 487; *Brightwater Care Group v Rossiter* (2009) 40 WAR 84, [24].

21   *Schloendorff v Society of New York Hospital*, 211 NY 125, 105 NE 92 (1914), 129.

22   *Hunter and New England Area Health Service v A* (2009) 74 NSWLR 88, [23].

23   *Brightwater Care Group v Rossiter* (2009) 40 WAR 84, [23] per Martins CJ; *Hunter and New England Area Health Service v A* (2009) 74 NSWLR 88, [23] per McDougall J; *Re MB* [1997] 2 FCR 541 per Lady Justice Butler-Sloss; *Ms B v An NHS Hospital Trust* (2002) 2 FCR 1, [10].

law test for capacity is functional. A person demonstrates capacity if s/he is able to comprehend material information, use or weigh the information to arrive at a decision and communicate the decision.[24] It is recoguised in law that capacity is decision and context-specific.[25]

Once capacity is established, the second consideration is whether the competent
adult person wishes to receive the proposed treatment. The right to autonomy and self-
determination is underpinned by the legal requirement of informed consent, which encompasses the right to refuse medical treatment.[26] The law requires informed consent to be given
voluntarily, by a competent person, and without undue influence.[27] The person must be
informed of the material risks associated with the proposed treatment, including those risks
that are of special importance to the person.[28] Although refusal of medical treatment may
be based on assessment of the information provided, there is no requirement for the refusal
of treatment to be 'informed'.[29] This is because a valid refusal of treatment may be based on
religious, social or moral grounds; may have no apparent rational basis;[30] or may be 'for any
reason or no reason at all'.[31] Neither is a competent adult 'obliged to give consent to medical
treatment':[32] 'They are always free to decline. On the other hand, health professionals are
not entitled to provide treatment without consent, even if the failure to treat will result in
loss of the patient's life.'[33]

It is clear that the general right to refuse medical treatment includes the right to refuse
life-sustaining medical treatment.[34] A competent adult may also instruct health professionals
to withdraw hydration and nutrition in order to bring about death,[35] unless the refusal is
precluded by statute. For example, in the SA case of *H Ltd v J*, H wished to cease food hydration and insulin because of a deep-seated sense of medical despair about her deteriorating
medical condition and the need for full-time care.[36] The SA Supreme Court ruled that the
health facility had no duty to feed or hydrate her and it had no right to do so against her
wishes, even if such action would result in her death. Kourakis J stated: 'I would accept the

---

24   *Re MB* [1997] 2 FCR 541, [30].
25   *Secretary, Department of Health and Community Services v JWB and SMB* (1992) 175 CLR 218.
26   *Secretary, Department of Health and Community Services v JWB and SMB* (1992) 175 CLR 218, 233;
        Rogers v Whitaker (1992) 175 CLR 479, 489; *Airedale NHS Trust v Bland* [1993] AC 789, 857; *Hunter
        and New England Area Health Service v A* (2009) 74 NSWLR 88, [23].
27   *Re C* [1994] 1 WLR 290.
28   *Rogers v Whitaker* (1992) 175 CLR 479.
29   *Hunter and New England Area Health Serivce v A* (2009) 74 NSWLR 88.
30   *Malette v Shulman* (1990) 72 OR (2d) 417 (Ontario Court of Appeal); *Re C* [1994] 1 WLR 290.
31   *Re T (adult: refusal of medical treatment)* [1993] Fam 95.
32   *Re JS* [2014] NSWSC 302; *Brightwater Care Group v Rossiter* (2009) 40 WAR 84, [26] per Martin
        CJ; *Hunter and New England Area Health Service v A* (2009) 74 NSWLR 88, [9]–[15]; *Bouvia v
        Superior Court of Los Angeles County*, 179 Cal App 3d 1127 (1986), 1137, 1139–41; *Nancy B v Hotel
        de Québec* (1992) 86 DLR (4th) 385 (Quebec Superior Court); *Airedale NHS Trust v Bland* [1993]
        AC 789, 857, 864; *Auckland Area Health Board v Attorney-General* [1993] 1 NZLR 235, 245.
33   *Brightwater Care Group v Rossiter* (2009) 40 WAR 84, [26] per Martin CJ; *Hunter and New England
        Area Health Service v A* (2009) 74 NSWLR 88, [9]–[15]; *Bouvia v Superior Court of Los Angeles
        County*, 179 Cal App 3d 1127 (1986), 1137, 1139–41; *Nancy B v Hotel de Québec* (1992) 86 DLR
        (4th) 385 (Quebec Superior Court); *Airedale NHS Trust v Bland* [1993] AC 789, 857, 864; *Auckland
        Area Health Board v Attorney-General* [1993] 1 NZLR 235, 245.
34   *Reibl v Hughes* [1980] 2 SCR 880; *Malette v Shulman* (1990) 72 OR (2d) 417 (Ontario Court of
        Appeal); *Fleming v Reid* (1991) 4 OR (3d) 74 (Ontario Court of Appeal); *B v NHS Trust* [2002]
        EWHC 429.
35   *H Ltd v J* (2010) 107 SASR 352, 373; cf *R (Nicklinson) v A Primary Care Trust* [2013] EWCA Civ 961.
36   *H Ltd v J* (2010) 107 SASR 352.

distinction … between suicide and an individual merely speeding "the natural and inevitable part of life known as death" by refusing food and water.'[37]

A practical consequence of the law accepting a person's wishes as determinative in relation to end-of-life treatment decision-making is an increased emphasis on advance care planning, Advance Health Directives and the appointment of medical and/or Enduring Powers of Attorney.[38] These mechanisms give legal weight to the wishes of the competent person at a time in the future when the person is no longer able to make decisions.[39] The courts have made it clear that objective best interests considerations do not arise if a person has capacity and is competent to make legally binding decisions, or has done so in an advance directive. With respect to advance directives, the common law recognises written refusals of treatment when the person's wishes are clear, apply to the situation at hand, and are made voluntarily when the person is competent. Where there is doubt, the law favours the preservation of life.[40]

End-of-life decisions for those who lack legal competence

A key feature of the debate about appropriate end-of-life care is a concern that vulnerable people will be disadvantaged if the law moves away from the preservation of life principle.[41] The law requires a person or authority to provide consent for the provision of medical treatment to those who lack capacity, including treatment that might be needed at the end of life.[42] In instances where an individual is unable to formulate or communicate their views, a substituted decision-maker is appointed, usually pursuant to state or territory guardianship legislation. Substituted decision-makers are generally required to make decisions on a best interests basis, or in accordance with the views of the person, depending on the form of the statutory provision.[43]

---

37   Ibid [56].

38   *Guardianship Act 1987* (NSW); *Guardianship and Administration Act 1993* (SA); *Guardianship and Administration Act 1995* (Tas); *Guardianship and Administration Act 1986* (Vic); *Guardianship and Administration Act 1990* (WA); *Powers of Attorney Act 1998* (Qld); *Powers of Attorney Act 2006* (ACT). See also *Medical Treatment (Health Directions) Act 2006* (ACT); *Advance Care Directives Act 2013* (SA); *Advance Personal Planning Act 2013* (NT); *Medical Treatment and Decisions Act 2016* (Vic).

39   *Hunter and New England Area Health Service v A* (2009) 74 NSWLR 88; *Cruzan v Director, Missouri Department of Health*, 497 US 261 (1990); *Malette v Shulman* (1990) 72 OR (2d) 417 (Ontario Court of Appeal); see Stephania Negri, *Self-Determination, Dignity and End of Life Care: Regulating Advance Directives in International and Comparative Perspective* (Martinus Nijhoff Publishers, 2012).

40   *HE v A Hospital NHS Trust* [2003] EWHC 1017 (Fam), [46] per Munby J.

41   House of Lords, *Report of the Select Committee on Medical Ethics* (HL paper 21–1, 1994), [239]; Parliamentary Assembly of the Council of Europe, *Recommendation 1418 (1999) 1: Protection of the Human Rights and Dignity of the Terminally Ill and the Dying* (Text adopted by the Assembly on 25 June 1999, 24th sitting), [9].

42   *Guardianship and Management of Property Act 1991* (ACT); *Medical Treatment (Health Directions) Act 2006* (ACT) Parts 2 and 3; *Adult Guardianship Act* (NT); *Advance Personal Planning Act 2013* (NT); *Guardianship and Administration Act 2000* (Qld); *Powers of Attorney Act 1998* (Qld) Ch 3, Part 3; *Advance Care Directives Act 2013* (SA); *Guardianship and Administration Act 1993* (SA); *Guardianship and Administration Act 1995* (Tas); *Guardianship and Administration Act 1986* (Vic); *Medical Treatment and Decisions Act 2016* (Vic); *Guardianship and Administration Act 1990* (WA) Part 9B; see also Chapters 8 and 10.

43   For a more detailed examination of substitute decision making, see Chapter 10.

Doctors are also required to consider the best interests of their patients.[44] Objective best interests standards have been criticised as a vehicle of paternalism. Commentary surrounding the Convention on the Rights of Persons with Disabilities (CRPD) has argued that as the principle of self-determination is the relevant standard for non-disabled people, it should also apply to individuals with disabilities, including those with cognitive disabilities.[45] The consequences of this argument are yet to be resolved. Legal disputes between substituted decision-makers and doctors about whether or not treatment should be discontinued have arisen when doctors have determined that continuing treatment is futile, and therefore not in the person's best interests.[46]

State and territory laws

Some Australian states and territories have specific legislative provisions relating to end-of-life care.

SA

The *Consent to Medical Treatment and Palliative Care Act 1995* (SA) must be read in conjunction with the *Advance Care Directives Act 2013* (SA). Section 17 of the *Consent to Medical Treatment and Palliative Care Act 1995* (SA) provides that a 'medical practitioner' is not under a duty to prolong life, and must withdraw life-sustaining measures at the request of the patient or the patient's representative.[47]

NT

The *Advance Personal Planning Act 2013* (NT) provides a comprehensive scheme for healthcare decisions that encompasses end-of-life decisions by both competent and incompetent individuals.

Victoria

At present, the relevant law is the *Medical Treatment Act 1988* (Vic). It allows a proxy decision-maker to be appointed by the person, or otherwise provides for the appointment of a medical guardian. The Act permits the decision-maker to refuse medical treatment, but not palliative care, for a current medical condition. Artificial nutrition with Percutaneous Endoscopic Gastronomy (PEG) (which involves the placement of a tube through the abdominal wall and into the stomach), is defined as medical treatment.[48] In the case of Maria Korp, the Victorian Public Guardian authorised the removal of PEG feeding for a woman in a persistent vegetative state.[49] In *Slaveski v Austin Health*, the Victorian Supreme Court authorised the withdrawal of treatment for a man who was considered to have a negligible chance of neurological recovery. Applying a best

---

44   *Re MB* [1997] 2 FCR 541, [543] (Dame Butler-Sloss CJ).
45   Eilionoir Flynn and Anna Arstein-Kerslake, 'This Support Model of Legal Capacity: Fact or Fiction or Fantasy?' (2014) 32(1) *Berkeley Journal of International Law* 1; see also Chapters 22 and 23.
46   *Cuthbertson v Rasouli* [2013] 3 SCR 341 (CanLII).
47   *Consent to Medical Treatment and Palliative Care Act 1995* (SA) s 17(2).
48   *Re BWV; Ex parte Gardner* (2003) 7 VR 487.
49   Ibid; *Public Advocate v RCS (Guardianship)* [2004] VCAT 1880; *Korp v Deputy State Coroner* [2006] VSC 282.

interests test, Dixon J held that the *parens patriae* jurisdiction of the Court protected the right of an unconscious person to receive ordinary, reasonable and appropriate care, but not 'extraordinary, excessively burdensome, intrusive or futile medical treatment and support'.[50]

The *Medical Treatment and Decisions Act 2016* (Vic) comes into operation on 12 March 2018 (unless it is proclaimed earlier). The Act replaces the *Medical Treatment Act 1988* (Vic) and amends the *Mental Health Act 2014* (Vic) with respect to the approval of electroconvulsive therapy for those who lack decision-making capacity. The Act establishes a scheme of medical treatment planning. It provides for binding advance directives, the appointment of support persons who will represent the interests of the person, and the appointment of medical decision makers who will make decisions about medical treatment and participation in medical research when the person lacks capacity.

NSW

Decisions for those who lack competence are made pursuant to the *Guardianship Act 1987* (NSW). With respect to end-of-life care decisions, the NSW Department of Health issued guidelines for end-of-life care and decision-making in 2005.[51] The guidelines set out a collaborative process for decision-making. If there is disagreement about end-of-life decisions, the NSW guidelines advise interested parties to seek recourse to the NSW Supreme Court or the NSW Administrative Decision Tribunal (ADT).

In *Northridge v Central Sydney Area Health Service* O'Keefe J ordered the reinstatement of active treatment for a 37-year-old patient who was unconscious following a drug overdose.[52] The Area Health Service had withdrawn treatment following a premature and inaccurate diagnosis of a persistent vegetative state. In *Messiha v South East Health* the Supreme Court held that a 70-year-old patient in a deep coma should not continue to receive treatment because there was no realistic prospect of him regaining consciousness.[53] In *FI v Public Guardian* the ADT determined that the Public Guardian was authorised to participate in and authorise an advance care planning process for a patient in a persistent vegetative state.[54] In *Application of Justice Health; re a Patient* the NSW Supreme Court held that section 702A of the *Crimes (Administration of Sentences) Act 1999* (NSW) did not preclude withdrawing and withholding medical treatment in circumstances where further active treatment would be futile.[55]

Queensland

The *Guardianship and Administration Act 2000* (Qld) provides that a guardian may be appointed where a decision is to be made that involves an 'unreasonable risk' to the health of a person who has impaired capacity.[56] The Act defines a life-sustaining measure as 'health care intended to sustain or prolong life and that supplants or maintains the operation of

50   *Slaveski v Austin Health* (2010) 32 VR 129, [35].
51   NSW Health, *Guidelines For End-of-Life Care and Decision-Making* (March 2005) <www.health.nsw
      .gov.au/policies/gl/2005/GL2005_057.html>.
52   (2000) 50 NSWLR 549.
53   [2004] NSWSC 1061.
54   [2008] NSWADT 263 cf *WK v Public Guardian* (No 2) [2006] NSWADT 121 holding that the
      Guardianship Act 1987 (NSW) did not authorise the Public Guardian to consent to withholding
      treatment that would prolong life.
55   (2011) 80 NSWLR 354.
56   *Guardianship and Administration Act 2000* (Qld) s 12.

vital bodily functions that are temporarily or permanently incapable of independent operation'.[57] Decisions with respect to life-sustaining measures may be dealt with according to the
person's advance directive, the directions of a guardian, or the directions of an appointed
attorney or statutory health attorney.[58]

A consent to the withholding or withdrawal of a life-sustaining measure will only operate
if the adult's health provider considers that the commencement or continuation of the measure
would be inconsistent with good medical practice.[59] The decision to withhold and withdraw
life-sustaining treatment may be challenged by an interested person on application to the
Queensland Civil and Administration Tribunal.[60] For example, in the case of *Re HG* the carers
of HG challenged the Adult Guardian's decision to withdraw artificial hydration and nutrition.
In that case, the Tribunal upheld the decision to withdraw treatment, applying the common
law test of best interests, as articulated in the English House of Lords judgment in *Bland*.[61]

End-of-life decision-making and children

The debate about the law at the end of life is predominantly concerned with adults, but it
also encompasses end-of life decision-making involving children. In such cases, the *parens
patriae* jurisdiction of the court may be invoked. As outlined in Chapter 9, the general principle at law is that parents are authorised to make healthcare decisions for their children,
including decisions about withholding or withdrawing life-sustaining treatment, provided
that such decisions are in the best interests of the child. There are two exceptions: first, where
a 'mature minor' is able to make decisions for themselves;[62] and second, where the proposed
medical treatment falls into the category of a 'special case' requiring court authorisation.[63]

The case of *Re Baby D (No 2)* provides a relevant example.[64] Baby D was a severely
brain-injured child. The hospital sought authorisation to respond to Baby D's anticipated
respiratory distress – when the endotracheal tube was removed – with medication to sup-
press her breathing, rather than through the use of a tracheotomy. The Court held that the
decision to withdraw and withhold life-prolonging treatment for a child in circumstances
where the treatment would provide no benefit, remained within the scope of parental
authority.[65] The case illustrates the limitations of a legal formula that sanctions the withdrawing and withholding of treatment at the end of life, but not the provision of treatment that
will actively bring about death.

---

57   Sch 2, s 5A(1). The definition includes cardiopulmonary resuscitation, assisted ventilation; and
      artificial nutrition and hydration s 5A(2); but not blood transfusions s 5A(3).
58   *Guardianship and Administration Act 2000* (Qld) s 66.
59   Ibid s 66A.
60   Ibid s 41. See also *Airedale NHS Trust v Bland*, above n 12.
61   *Re HG* [2006] QGAAT 26. See Lindy Willmott and Ben White, 'Charting a Course Through Difficult
      Legislative Waters: Tribunal Decisions of Life-Sustaining Measures' (2005) 12(4) *Journal of Law and
      Medicine* 441.
62   *Secretary, Department of Health and Community Services v JWB and SMB* (1992) 175 CLR 218.
63   Ibid; *Re Alex* (2009) 248 FLR 312; *Re Baby D (No 2)* (2011) 258 FLR 290; *Family Law Act 1975* (Cth)
      ss 67ZC, 60CA, 64B(2)(i). See *X v Sydney Children's Hospitals Network* [2013] NSWCA 320, where
      an application to the High Court was dismissed as the applicant reached the age of majority: *X v
      Sydney Children's Hospitals Network* [2014] HCASL 97 (13 May 2014).
64   (2011) 258 FLR 290.
65   Ibid per Young J [198], [234].

The right to demand treatment in end-of-life care

The common law has shied away from recognising a right to demand treatment for adults. In *R (Burke) v General Medical Council* Mr Burke challenged a guidance, issued by the General Medical Council in the UK, that permitted doctors to withdraw artificial nutrition or hydration if they were of the opinion that such provision would cause suffering or would be likely to be too burdensome.[66] Mr Burke, who suffered from a degenerative condition, was concerned that medical treatment or artificial feeding might be withdrawn while he was still competent, but unable to communicate his wishes. He sought an order that he would be provided with nutrition and hydration until he died, on the grounds, inter alia, that to do otherwise would breach his rights under the *Human Rights Act 1998*, specifically Article 2 (the right to life); Article 3 (the prohibition against … inhuman or degrading treatment); and Article 8 (the right to respect for private and family life).[67]

At first instance, before Munby J, Mr Burke was successful in his legal challenge. However, this judgment was subsequently overturned when the matter came before the English Court of Appeal. In the leading judgment, Lord Phillips MR rejected Munby J's rights-based approach, holding that patients could not insist on treatment above and beyond the doctor's general duty to care for the patient to keep them alive, if they are competent (and have not refused treatment); or if they are incompetent, then in their best interests.[68] Subsequent jurisprudence in the European Court of Human Rights (ECHR) has established that Article 8 does entitle individuals to participate in treatment decisions and to actively choose between available treatment options.[69] Overall, these developments highlight the shift towards incorporating rights-based arguments and reasoning in healthcare treatment and decision-making in the UK and continental Europe, particularly at the end of life. This will be discussed in more detail in Chapter 16.

Conclusion

It is lawful in Australia to withdraw or withhold life-sustaining treatment near the end of life in certain circumstances.[70] Nevertheless, it is difficult to identify a 'bright' line between legally permissible and legally impermissible treatment. Determining the legality of end-of-life decisions should entail consideration of applicable legislation, the doctor's intention, the

---

66   [2004] EWHC 1879 (Admin).
67   See *Human Rights Act 1998* (UK) Sch 1, Part I. This Act incorporates key Articles of the European Convention on Human Rights (ECHR) into UK law.
68   *R (Burke) v General Medical Council* [2005] EWCA Civ 1003, [32]; see David Gurnham (2006) (14(2) *Medical Law Review* 253.
69   *Tysiac v Poland* (2007) 45 EHRR 42, [113]; see Penelope Weller, *New Law and Ethics in Mental Health Advance Directives: the Convention on the Rights of Persons with Disabilities and the Right to Choose* (Routledge, 2013) 123–5.
70   Ben White, Lindy Willmott and John Allen, 'Withholding and Withdrawing Life-Sustaining Treatment: Criminal Responsibility for Established Medical Practice?' (2010) 17(5) *Journal of Law and Medicine* 849; Cameron Stewart, 'Euthanasia and Assisted Suicide' in Ben White, Fiona McDonald and Lindy Donnelly (eds), *Health Law in Australia* (Thomson Reuters, 2010) 416–49.

standard of healthcare provided, the patient's condition, whether or not there is consent or there is valid refusal, and whether or not the power to make decisions has been lawfully devolved to another person. The complexity of law, coupled with the sensitivity of the issues involved, continues to prompt calls for law reform. In the interim, advance care planning strategies and programs are being developed to address the gaps in both the common law and legislation. This chapter has shown that law and practice surrounding withholding and withdrawing of medical treatment increasingly privilege the principle of individual self-determination. Such developments underpin the argument that competent individuals should be permitted to make a full range of informed choices near or at the end of life, including the ability to choose treatments that may lead to their death.

16

EUTHANASIA AND ASSISTED SUICIDE

Penelope Weller

Introduction

While the prohibition against murder is absolute, the law in most common law jurisdictions has decriminalised suicide and recognised the right of competent individuals to refuse life-prolonging healthcare and treatment.[1] The focus of current legal debates is on whether the right to self-determination should encompass a positive right to choose the manner and circumstances of one's own death, including the right to seek and receive assistance to end one's life.[2] This chapter considers the current law, as well as law reform debates, about euthanasia and assisted suicide in Australia; the prosecution of those who have assisted others to suicide; the regulation of assisted suicide in other national jurisdictions; and examines recent legal challenges in the courts in these areas.[3]

The right to end one's own life in certain circumstances is referred to as euthanasia and assisted suicide.[4] The key ethical argument put forward by supporters of euthanasia and assisted suicide laws is that individuals suffering from terminal or chronic conditions lead painful and undignified lives and wish to die, but are prevented from obtaining the assistance they need by the current state of the law. Those who are opposed to a change in the law invoke the sanctity of life principle, or voice concerns that relaxing the law will weaken the social commitment to protecting the lives of people who are unwell or otherwise vulnerable. Beyond Australia, legislative schemes that permit euthanasia and assisted suicide have been introduced in the Benelux countries – Belgium[5], the Netherlands[6] and Luxembourg;[7] three state jurisdictions in the US;[8]

---

1   See *Crimes Act 1900* (ACT) s 16; *Crimes Act 1900* (NSW) s 31A; *Criminal Law Consolidation Act 1935* (SA) s 13A(1); *Crimes Act 1958* (Vic) s 6A; see also Chapter 15.

2   Ottawa Senate, Canada, *Still Not There: Quality End-of-Life Care: A Progress Report* (2005); Ottawa Senate, Canada, *Raising the Bar: A Roadmap for the Future of Palliative Care in Canada* (2010); National Assembly of Quebec, Canada, Select Committee on Dying With Dignity, *Dying with Dignity Report* (2012); Daniel Hillyard and John Dombick, *Dying Right: the Death with Dignity Movement* (Psychology Press, 2001); Howard Ball, *At Liberty to Die: the Battle with the Death With Dignity in America* (New York University Press, 2012).

3   See Australian Commission on Safety and Quality in Health Care, *Safety and Quality of End-of-Life Care in Acute Hospitals – A Background Paper* (2013); Australia21, *The Right to Choose an Assisted Death: Time for Legislation*, Report following a Roundtable in Brisbane (January 2013); Lindy Willmott and Benjamin P White, Australia21, *How Should Australia Regulate Voluntary Euthanasia and Assisted Suicide?* (2012) <http://eprints.qut.edu.au/54757/>; Australian Centre of Health Research, *Leadership and Quality in End of Life Care Australia: Round Table Recommendations* (2013); Senate Community Affairs Committee, *Inquiry into the Living Longer Living Better Aged Care Bills 2013* (2013); NSW Parliament Issues Backgrounder, *Euthanasia* (2013); Senate Legal and Constitutional Affairs Legislation Committee Inquiry, Exposure Draft of the Medical Services (Dying with Dignity) Bill 2014.

4   For a discussion of various terminology in this area see Benjamin P White and Lindy Willmott, 'How Should Australia Regulate Voluntary Euthanasia and Assisted Suicide?' (2012) 20 *Journal of Law and Medicine*, 410–38.

5   *Act on Euthanasia 2002* (Belgium). In 2014, the Belgian courts sparked controversy by accepting a request to die from a convicted prisoner on the grounds of unbearable mental suffering (4 January 2015) <www.telegraph.co.uk/news/worldnews/europe/belgium/11324579/Belgian-rapist-and-murderer-to-be-put-to-death-by-lethal-injection.html>.

6   *Termination of Life on Request and Assisted Suicide (Review Procedures) Act 2000* (Netherlands) See also *Dutch Criminal Code* (Netherlands) article 294.

7   *Law of 16 March 2009 on Euthanasia and Assisted Suicide* (Luxembourg).

8   *Death with Dignity Law*, O.R.S. §§ 127.800–127.995 (Oregon, US); *Death with Dignity Act*, RCW. 70.245 (Washington, US); *Patient Choice and Control at End of Life Act*, 18 VSA. chapter 113 §§ 5281–5292 (Vermont, US);

and in the province of Quebec.[9] The Canadian Parliament introduced legislation in June 2016.[10] Euthanasia and assisted suicide programs are also available in Switzerland.[11] See Table 16.1 for information relating to legislative schemes in international jurisdictions.

The usual form of such schemes is that a person who qualifies under the law is provided with a prescription for lethal medication after a specified waiting period. Generally, the person must be competent, fully informed, must have made the decision voluntarily and is suffering from a terminal or untreatable illness or experiencing unbearable suffering. The courts in Australia, the UK and Canada have considered the legal issues surrounding euthanasia and assisted suicide. In each of these jurisdictions, new laws are being considered that will permit individuals to access euthanasia and assisted suicide programs.

Australia

Murder is defined in Australian law as the deliberate act of causing the death of another person.[12] All states and territories prohibit intentional acts or omissions that are designed to cause the death of another person, including when the person requests those actions.[13] The NT Criminal Code specifically provides that 'a person cannot authorise or permit another person to kill him'.[14] There is an express prohibition against actions that aid, assist or encourage suicide in all states and territories.[15] The Criminal Codes in WA and Queensland also prohibit acts that 'deliberately accelerate' death.[16] In WA, section 262 of the *Criminal Code* imposes a positive duty to 'provide the necessaries' of life to a person 'under one's charge'.[17]

As discussed in Chapter 15, the complex legal issues raised by end-of-life care have prompted some jurisdictions to introduce statutory protections from criminal liability for those who provide end-of-life care in good faith.[18] These provisions include specific prohibitions against euthanasia and assisted suicide. Section 282A(3) of the *Criminal Code* (Qld) states that: 'Nothing in this section justifies, authorises or excuses an act that is made with the intent to kill a person or aid

---

9   *An Act Respecting End of Life Care*, RSQ 2014, c S-32.001 (Quebec, Canada).
10   C-14 An Act to amend the Criminal Code and to make related amendments to other Acts (medical assistance in dying) <www.justice.gc.ca/eng/17_06_2016>.
11   *Swiss Criminal Code of 21 December 1937* (S.R. 311.0) arts 114–115 (Switzerland).
12   *Crimes Act 1900* (ACT) ss 12(1)(a)–(b); *Crimes Act 1900* (NSW) s 80(1)(a); *Criminal Code Act* (NT) ss 161–2; *Criminal Code* (Qld) ss 291, 293, 300 302(1)(a); *Criminal Law Consolidation Act 1935* (SA) s 12A; *Criminal Code* (Tas) ss 156, 159; *Crimes Act 1958* (Vic) s 3A; *Criminal Code* (WA) s 279(1).
13   *Crimes Act 1900* (ACT) s 17; *Crimes Act 1900* (NSW) ss 31B–31C; *Criminal Code Act* (NT) s 162; *Criminal Code* (Qld) s 311; *Criminal Law Consolidation Act 1935* (SA) s 13A(5); *Criminal Code* (Tas) s 163; *Crimes Act 1958* (Vic) ss 6B(1)–(2); *Criminal Code* (WA) s 288.
14   *Criminal Code Act* (NT) s 26(3).
15   *Crimes Act 1900* (ACT) s 17 (suicide – aiding or abetting suicide or attempted suicide); *Crimes Act 1900* (NSW) ss 31B (survivor of suicide pact), 31C (aiding suicide); *Criminal Code Act* (NT) s 162 (assisting and encouraging suicide); *Criminal Code* (Qld) s 311 (aiding suicide); *Criminal Law Consolidation Act 1935* (SA) s 13A(5) (criminal liability in relation to suicide); *Criminal Code* (Tas) s 163 (aiding suicide); *Crimes Act 1958* (Vic) s 6B(1) (survivor of suicide pact who kills deceased party is guilty of manslaughter), s 6B(2); *Criminal Code* (WA) s 288 (aiding suicide).
16   *Criminal Code* (Qld) s 296; *Criminal Code* (WA) s 273.
17   See Chapter 15 for a discussion of withholding and withdrawing medical treatment under Australian law.
18   *Criminal Code* (WA) s 259; *Criminal Code* (Qld) s 282A(1); *Criminal Code (Palliative Care) Amendment Act 2003* (Qld); *Consent to Medical Treatment and Palliative Care Act 1995* (SA) s 17(1).

Table 16.1: International Legislation Permitting Active Voluntary Euthanasia[19]

Jurisdiction	Law	Commencement	Effect	Summary
Switzerland	Swiss Criminal Code of 21 December 1937 (S.R. 311.0) arts 114–15 (Switzerland)	1 January 1942	Assisted suicide legal	• Implicit that assisting a person to commit suicide (where the assistance does not directly cause the death) is legal unless there is a selfish motive • No requirement that the person providing assistance be a physician • No requirement for terminal illness • No residency requirement

Belgium	Act on Euthanasia 2002 (Belgium)	Law passed on 28 May 28 2002, commenced operation on 3 September 2002, and amended on 13 February 2014	Euthanasia legal including for minors	• Physician must ensure:
				  o legal competency
				  o the request is voluntary, well considered and repeated
				  o that the adult or emancipated minor patient is 'in a medically futile condition of constant and unbearable physical or mental suffering that cannot be alleviated, resulting from a serious and incurable disorder caused by illness or accident' or
				  o that the minor patient is 'in a medically futile condition of constant and unbearable physical or mental suffering that cannot be alleviated and that will result in death in the short term, resulting from a serious and incurable disorder caused by illness or accident'
				• Physician and person must both consider there is no reasonable alternative
				• No minimum age, however consent of the minor's parents and a mental health specialist is required
				• Second opinion requirement (and third opinion if person not expected to die in the near future)
				• Request must be written (and for a minor must include the agreement of the minor's legal representatives)
				• Advance statement may be made
				• Oversight by committee
				• Residency requirement

19   Based on unofficial translations of relevant legislation.

| Netherlands | Termination of Life on Request and Assisted Suicide (Review Procedures) Act 2000 (Netherlands) | Entered into force 1 April 2002 (codification of common law) | Euthanasia and assisted suicide legal | • Requires physician to exercise due care, including:
  o being satisfied that the person's request is voluntary and well considered and that the person's suffering be 'lasting and unbearable'
  o informed request
  o through discussions, coming to the joint conclusion that there is no other reasonable solution
  o consult an independent physician
• Euthanasia or assisted suicide may be requested by a person aged 16 and above. For children aged 12 to 16 parental consent is required.
• Advance statement may be made
• No residency requirement
• Oversight by review committee |
| Luxembourg | Law of 16 March 2009 on Euthanasia and Assisted Suicide (Luxembourg) | Law commenced 1 April 2009 | Euthanasia and assisted suicide legal | • Person must be capable and conscious, request must be voluntary
• Person must be in a severe and incurable terminal medical situation and have constant and unbearable physical or mental suffering without prospect of improvement
• Request must be written and registered
• Doctor must hold several interviews with the person to: confirm that request is informed and voluntary; ensure the person's suffering is persistent; consult a second doctor; consult with the person's care team and any person of trust; and check the advance statement register before performing euthanasia
• Second opinion requirement
• No child or incapable person may validly request assisted suicide or euthanasia
• Advance statement may be made by capable adult
• Person of trust may be appointed to communicate wishes to doctors in the event the person is no longer able to communicate
• Oversight by committee
• No residency requirement |

Table 16.1: (cont.)

Jurisdiction	Law	Commencement	Effect	Summary
Montana, US	*Baxter v Montana*, 2009 MT 449	Ruling 31 December 2009	Pursuant to Montana Supreme Court ruling, the *Rights of the Terminally Ill Act*, Mont Code Ann §§ 50.9.101 – 50.9.206 (1991), permits physician-assisted suicide	• The Montana Supreme Court held that physicians can use a patient's request in writing as a defence to the charge of homicide • No regulatory framework
Oregon, US	Oregon *Death with Dignity Act* enacted by Ballot Measure 16 (1994), Or. Rev. Stat. §§ 127.800–127.995	Passed 27 October 1997 and came into effect in November 1997	Physician-assisted suicide legal	• Two physicians must determine that the person is capable and suffers from a terminal disease • Informed request required • Request must be in writing and witnessed • If the physician believes the person may be suffering from a psychiatric or psychological disorder the person must be referred to counselling and the counsellor must determine that the person does not have impaired judgment • Residency requirement • Physician may dispense the medication directly or request that a pharmacist dispense the medication • Waiting periods apply, of 15 days between an oral request and writing of prescription, and 48 hours between the written request and writing of prescription • Oversight by government health department

Jurisdiction	Legislation	Date	Status	Requirements
Vermont, US	*Patient Choice and Control at the End of Life Act* (Act 39) 18 V.S.A. Chapter 113 (Bill s77 'End of Life Choices' (2013))	Came into effect 20 May 2013	Physician-assisted suicide legal	• A physician must determine that the person is suffering from a terminal condition, capable, making an informed decision, and suffers from a terminal disease • Second opinion required • Request must be in writing and witnessed • The physician must verify that the person does not have impaired judgment or refer the person for an evaluation by a psychiatrist, psychologist or clinical social worker for confirmation that the person is capable and does not have impaired judgment • Residency requirement • Physician may dispense the medication directly or request that a pharmacist dispense the medication • Waiting period applies, of 48 hours between the last of the following: the written request/second oral request/the physician offering an opportunity to rescind the request, and writing of prescription • No oversight established by law
Washington, US	Washington *Death with Dignity Act*, Initiative 1000 (2008), R.C.W. 70.245.	Passed 4 November 2008 and came into effect 5 March 2009	Physician-assisted suicide legal	• Two physicians must determine that the person is competent and suffers from a terminal disease • Informed request required • Request must be in writing and witnessed • If the physician believes the person may be suffering from a psychiatric or psychological disorder the person must be referred to counselling and the counsellor must determine that the person does not have impaired judgment • Residency requirement • Physician may dispense the medication directly or request that a pharmacist dispense the medication • Waiting periods apply, of 15 days between an oral request and writing of prescription, and 48 hours between the written request and the writing of the prescription • Oversight by government health department
Canada	*C-14 An Act to amend the Criminal Code and to make related amendments to other Acts (medical assistance in dying)*	Passed June 2016	Permits 'medically assisted dying'	• Over 18 years • Suffering from 'grievous and irremediable medical condition' • Formal, signed, application • Two witnesses who are not beneficiaries • 15-day wait

another person to kill him or herself.' Under section 18 of the *Consent to Medical Treatment and Palliative Care Act 1995* (SA), protection from liability 'does not authorise' the administration of medical treatment for the purpose of causing the death of the person to whom the treatment is administered, or of assisting the suicide of another. Although SA and the NT have introduced advance care planning legislation, euthanasia and assisted suicide are not permitted.[20]

There have been several prosecutions in Australia of individuals who have assisted others to die.[21] Two physicians in Australia have been, or are the subject of, police investigation; however, none has been charged with criminal offences to date. In 2004, Dr Andrew Hollo, the former director of the NSW Voluntary Euthanasia Society, was charged with administering a potentially lethal dose of insulin to an elderly woman during a visit to her Sydney home, but the case was dismissed in the Magistrates' Court.[22] In 2014, police interviewed Dr Rodney Syme after he made a public admission that he had given a man Nembutal. Nembutal (or pentobarbital) is promoted by euthanasia campaigners as a peaceful way to die, and is known to be illegally imported into Australia for that purpose.[23] A test case on the question of physician-assisted suicide in Victoria is expected in the near future.[24] A third physician, Dr Philip Nitschke, who is a well-known advocate for euthanasia and assisted suicide, is currently suspended pending an investigation into whether actions he took relating to euthanasia and assisted suicide constitute professional misconduct.[25]

In several Australian states and territories there have been attempts to introduce legislation that permits euthanasia and assisted suicide.[26] In the NT, the *Rights of the Terminally Ill*

---

20   *Advance Care Directives Act 2013* (SA) s 12; *Advance Personal Planning Act 2013* (NT) s 51.

21   Murder: *DPP v Rolfe* (2008) 191 A Crim R 213; *R v Justins* [2008] NSWSC 1194 and *Justins v The Queen* (2010) 79 NSWLR 544; Attempted murder: *DPP v Riordan* (unreported, Victorian Supreme Court, Cummins J, 20 November 1998); *R v Marden* [2000] VSC 558; *R v Nicol* [2005] NSWSC 547; *R v Catherine Anne Pryor* (unreported, Tasmanian Supreme Court, Hill AJ, 19 January 2005); Manslaughter: *R v Mathers* [2011] NSWSC 339; Aiding suicide: *R v Hood* (2002) 130 A Crim R 473; *R v Maxwell* [2003] VSC 278; *John Stuart Godfrey* (unreported, Tasmanian Supreme Court, Underwood J, 26 May 2004); *R v Fred Thompson* (unreported, NSW Magistrates Court, Railton J, 25 January 2005); *R v Ann Leith* (unreported, Melbourne Magistrates Court, Lesser J, 15 April 2010); *R v Justins* [2011] NSWSC 568; *R v Victor Rijn* (unreported, Melbourne Magistrates Court, Letherbridge J, 23 May 2011); *R v Nielsen* [2012] QSC 29.

22   Natasha Wallace, 'Doctor Cleared of Trying to Kill Patient', *Sydney Morning Herald* (online), 5 November 2004 <www.smh.com.au/news/National/Doctor-cleared-of-trying-to-kill-pati ent/2004/11/04/1099547322756.html>; Leonie Lamont, 'Widow, 93, Almost Died, But Kept Faith in Her Doctor', *Sydney Morning Herald* (online), 28 July 2004 <www.smh.com.au/ articles/2004/07/27/1090693965268.html>.

23   *My Right to Die* <www.myrighttodie.com>.

24   Julia Medew, 'Euthanasia Advocate Rodney Syme Interviewed by Police Over Death Drug Confession', *The Age* (Victoria, online), 22 October 2014, <www.theage.com.au/victoria/euthanasia-advocate-rodney-syme-interviewed-by-police-over-death-drug-confession-20141022-119t9b.html>.

25   Caitlyn Gribbin and Norman Hermant, 'Medical Board of Australia Proposes to Suspend Euthanasia Advocate Philip Nitschke's Medical Licence', *ABC News* (Western Australia, online), 17 July 2014 <www.abc.net.au/news/2014-07-17/medical-board-proposes-suspension-of-nitschkes-licence/5604958>; see Philip Nitschke and Fiona Stewart, 'What's It Got To Do With You? Challenging the Medical Profession's Future in the Assisted Suicide Debate' (2011) 45 *Australian and New Zealand Journal of Psychiatry* 1017–19.

26   See Lorana Bartels and Margaret Otlowski, 'A Right to Die? Euthanasia and the Law in Australia' (2010) 17 *Journal of Law and Medicine* 532.

Act 1995 (NT) legalised euthanasia in limited circumstances. This piece of legislation was only in force for a period of nine months. It was effectively nullified by the *Euthanasia Laws Act 1997* (Cth), which removed the power of Australian territories to legislate with respect to euthanasia.[27] More recently, a number of private members' Bills on the issue have been introduced, in WA,[28] SA,[29] NSW[30] and Tasmania.[31] It is expected that the Victorian (Andrews) government will introduce a euthanasia bill into parliament in 2017. All were defeated by narrow margins. The final report of the Victorian Legal and Social Issues Parliamentary Committee inquiry into end-of-life choices, released in June 2016, has recommended the introduction of legislation to legalise assisted dying in limited circumstances.[32] At the federal level, an exposure draft of the Medical Services (Dying with Dignity) Bill 2014 (Cth) was referred to the Senate Standing Committee on Legal and Constitutional Affairs in 2014. The Senate Committee conducted an inquiry with 'particular reference to the rights of terminally ill people to seek assistance in ending their lives, and an appropriate framework and safeguards with which to do so'.[33] The Senate Committee released its final report on November 2014, recommending that the proponents of the Bill address the 'technical and other issues raised in evidence to the Committee before the Bill is taken further'.[34] In particular, the Committee noted conflicting evidence with respect to the constitutionality of the Bill.

White and Willmott have argued that the introduction of such legislation in Australia is justified on the grounds of compassion, non-discrimination, transparency and the rule of law. They identify the overarching ethical considerations as follows:

- the inherent value of human life
- the need to respect a person's autonomy
- the need to protect vulnerable members of society
- the need to alleviate pain and suffering of individuals who are unwell
- the need for the law to be coherent and transparent
- the need for the law to be followed.

They have also formulated a range of legal options that would modify the position of the criminal law, including sentencing reform, context-specific offences, and prosecutorial guidelines.[35] At the time of writing, the debate in Australia is in abeyance, but it is far from resolved.

27   *Wake v Northern Territory* (1996) 109 NTR 1 the Supreme Court of Northern Territory held that the *Rights of the Terminally Ill Act 1995* (NT) was valid.
28   Voluntary Euthanasia Bill 2010 (WA).
29   Criminal Law Consolidation (Medical Defences – End of Life Arrangements) Amendment Bill 2011 (SA); Voluntary Euthanasia Bill 2012 (SA) defeated 22–20, 14 June 2012 <www.parliament.sa.gov.au>.
30   Rights of the Terminally Ill Bill 2011 (NSW) defeated on division, 23 May 2013 <www.parliament.nsw.gov.au>.
31   Voluntary Assisted Dying Bill 2013 (Tas) defeated 13–12 <www.parliament.tas.gov.au>.
32   <www.parliament.vic.gov.au/lsic/article/2611>.
33   Parliament of Australia, Exposure Draft of the Medical Services (Dying with Dignity) Bill 2014 <www.aph.gov.au/Parliamentary_Business/Committees/Senate/Legal_and_Constitutional_Affairs/Dying_with_Dignity>.
34   Ibid Recommendation 5.5.
35   Benjamin P White and Lindy Willmott, 'How Should Australia Regulate Voluntary Euthanasia and Assisted Suicide?' (2012) 20 *Journal of Law and Medicine* 410–38.

England

English law has decriminalised suicide, but prohibits murder and assisted suicide.[36] As is the case elsewhere, there is an active right-to-die movement in England.[37] Following the incorporation of the European Convention on Human Rights (ECHR)[38] into English law by the *Human Rights Act 1998*,[39] there have been three significant legal challenges in this area. In each case, individuals have sought legal recognition of a right to assistance to end their lives. In the first case, in 2001, Diane Pretty suffered from a progressive degenerative disorder and wished to end her life, but required assistance to do so. She sought an undertaking from the Director of Public Prosecutions (DPP) that her husband would not be prosecuted under section 2(1) of the *Suicide Act 1961* (1961 Act) for aiding and abetting her suicide.[40]

At first instance, the court held that the DPP did not have the power to give the undertaking sought by Pretty.[41] Her appeal to the House of Lords was also unsuccessful. Although Pretty alleged that there had been a breach of a number of Articles under the ECHR, we focus here on the main finding in the judgment regarding the alleged breach of Pretty's Article 8(1) rights with regard to respect for private and family life. For ease of reference, Article 8 is set out here in full:

1. Everyone has the right to respect for his private and family life, his home and his correspondence.

2. There shall be no interference by a public authority with the exercise of this right except such as is in accordance with the law and is necessary in a democratic society in the interests of national security, public safety or the economic well-being of the country, for the prevention of disorder or crime, for the protection of health or morals, or for the protection of the rights and freedoms of others.

It was held, inter alia, that Pretty could not rely on Article 8 as it was directed to the protection of personal autonomy and did not confer a right to decide when or how to die.[42] Pretty subsequently appealed to the European Court of Human Rights (ECtHR). The ECtHR found that section 2(1) of the 1961 Act constituted an interference with her Article 8(1) rights, but that such interference was justified under Article 8(2):

> It does not appear to be arbitrary to the Court for the law to reflect the importance of the right to life, by prohibiting assisted suicide while providing for a system of enforcement and adjudication which allows due regard to be given in each particular case to the public interest in bringing a prosecution, as well as to the fair and proper requirements of retribution and deterrence.[43]

---

36   See *Suicide Act 1961*.
37   *Campaign for Dignity in Dying* <www.dignityindying.org.uk>.
38   Council of Europe, *European Convention for the Protection of Human Rights and Fundamental Freedoms, as amended by Protocols Nos. 11 and 14*, 4 November 1950, ETS 5.
39   See *Human Rights Act 1998* (UK) Sch 1, Part I.
40   *Suicide Act 1961* (UK) s 2(1) states: 'A person who aids, abets, counsels or procures the suicide of another, or an attempt by another to commit suicide, shall be liable on conviction on indictment to imprisonment for a term not exceeding fourteen years.'
41   *R (Pretty) v Director of Public Prosecutions* [2001] EWHC Admin 788.
42   *R (Pretty) v Director of Public Prosecutions* (2001) 1 AC 800, per Lord Bingham at [18].
43   *Pretty v United Kingdom* (2002) 35 EHRR 1 [67], [76].

The second case was brought by Debbie Purdy, who sought a declaration that her husband would not be prosecuted under section 2(1) of the 1961 Act if he assisted her to travel to Switzerland to end her life there. Purdy argued that the 1961 Act contravened her rights under Article 8(1) (see above), and that the absence of an offence-specific policy by the DPP meant that such contravention was not 'in accordance with the law', as required by Article 8(2). The English Court of Appeal followed the decision in *Pretty v DPP* and denied relief to Purdy.[44] On appeal, the House of Lords found that the requirements of Article 8(2) entitled Purdy to know what factors would influence the decision to prosecute her husband. The Lords directed the DPP to publish specific guidance on the issue.[45]

The third case was brought by Tony Nicklinson, who was left profoundly disabled following a stroke. He wanted to be able to legally access assistance to end his 'demeaning' and 'intolerable' life.[46] Arguing that the prohibition against assisted suicide under the 1961 Act gave him no option but to kill himself by an uncomfortable process of self-starvation, he sought a declaration that it would be lawful for someone to inject him with a lethal drug, such as a barbiturate, or to otherwise assist him to die with the use of a machine invented by Philip Nitschke, an Australian doctor (see earlier). Alternatively, Nicklinson sought a declaration that the current law as set out in the 1961 Act was incompatible with his rights under Article 8. At first instance, he was denied relief:[47]

> It is not for the court to decide whether the law about assisted dying should be changed and, if so, what safeguards should be put in place. Under our system of government these are matters for Parliament to decide, representing society as a whole, after Parliamentary scrutiny, and not for the court on the facts of an individual case or cases.[48]

In 2012, Mr Nicklinson passed away as a result of self-starvation. His widow continued with an appeal to the UK Supreme Court (formerly the House of Lords), but this was ultimately unsuccessful.[49] The Nicklinson appeal was heard with two others which had similar fact circumstances, with the appellants also wishing to end their lives. With respect to the question of whether it was lawful for a doctor to assist Nicklinson to die, the Supreme Court found that section 2(1) of the 1961 Act fell within the 'margin of appreciation' afforded to Member States under the ECHR, because it did not constitute an impermissible 'blanket ban' on assisted suicide.[50] With respect to the question of compatibility of the 1961 Act with the ECHR, the majority of the Supreme Court held that it was compatible, with two dissenting.

Of the two dissenting, Lady Hale held that the prohibition on assisted suicide in the 1961 Act 'does not provide for any exception for people who have made a capacitous, free and

---

44   *R (Purdy) v Director of Public Prosecutions* [2008] EWHC 2565 (Admin).

45   *R (Purdy) v Department of Public Prosecutions* [2010] 1 AC 345, 378 [1] (Lord Phillips), 396 [56] (Lord Hope), 400 [69] (Baroness Hale), 405 [86]–[87] (Lord Brown), 409 [106] (Lord Neuberger).

46   *R (Nicklinson) v Ministry of Justice* [2012] EWHC 2381 (Admin).

47   Ibid per Toulson LJ, Royce and Macur JJ agreeing.

48   Ibid per Lord Toulson at [150].

49   *R (Nicklinson) v Ministry of Justice* [2014] UKSC 38.

50   Ibid per Lord Neuberger at [148], with Lords Mance, Wilson, Sumption, Hughes, Clarke, Reed, Kerr and Lady Hale agreeing. For a further discussion on what is meant by the 'margin of appreciation' under the ECHR and in ECtHR jurisprudence, see, for example, Dean Spielmann, President of the European Court of Human Rights, *Whither the Margin of Appreciation?*, UCL – Current Legal Problems Lecture (at 20 March 2014) <www.echr.coe.int/Documents/Speech_20140320_London_ENG.pdf>.

fully informed decision to commit suicide but require help to do so'.[51] Lord Kerr argued that the starting point for analysis for individuals in the position of Nicklinson should be that they have a right to end their lives pursuant to Article 8(1). This should extend to being able to access willing and informed assistance to bring about their wish to end their life. He stated that to 'insist that these unfortunate individuals should continue to endure the misery that is their lot is not to champion the sanctity of life; it is to coerce them to endure unspeakable suffering'.[52]

The result of the Supreme Court's judgment in *Nicklinson* is that the law remains unchanged in England, except for the modifications to the DPP guidance on prosecutorial policy which arose in the wake of the *Purdy* case.[53] In 2015 Nicklinson's widow made an application to the ECtHR that was held to be inadmissible.[54] It is interesting to note that since the *Pretty* judgment in 2002, the ECtHR has consolidated its position with regard to the interpretation of Article 8.[55] The ECrtHR recognises that an individual's Article 8(1) rights encompass the right to decide how and when to die in some instances.[56] In particular, it has emphasised that this includes a right to be free from a distressing and undignified end to life, provided the decision to end one's life is made freely.[57] It will be interesting to see how the English common law develops in response to the influence of rights-based jurisprudence under the ECHR.[58]

In England, there have also been several attempts at legislative reform in the area. Lord Joffe introduced Bills into the House of Lords in 2003, 2004 and 2005. A Commission on Assisted Dying, chaired by Lord Falconer, was established in 2010 to inquire into the question of assisted dying.[59] The Commission published its final report in 2012. An Assisted Dying Bill was also introduced to the House of Lords in 2014, with the stated aim of enabling 'competent adults who are terminally ill to be provided at their request with specified assistance to end their own life'. The Bill was scrutinised at a committee hearing in January 2015, but failed because of the general election in May 2015. A subsequent Bill was also defeated.

---

51   *R (Nicklinson) v Minsistry of Justice* [2014] UKSC 38 per Lady Hale at [351].

52   Ibid per Lord Kerr at [358].

53   Crown Prosecution Service (CPS), Policy for Prosecutors in Respect of Cases of Encouraging or Assisting Suicide (updated October 2014) <www.cps.gov.uk/publications/prosecution/assisted_suicide_policy.html>.

54   *Nicklinson and Lamb v United Kingdom* Apps 2478/15 and 1787/15, Decision of 23 June 2015; see Elizabeth Wicks, '*Nicklinson and Lamb v United Kingdom*: Strasbourg Fails to Assist on Assisted Dying in the UK' (2016) *Medical Law Review* doi:10.1093/medlaw/fwv045.

55   Ibid.

56   *Haas v Switzerland* (2011) 53 EHRR 33 (ECHR); *Koch v Germany* (2013) 56 EHRR 6 (ECHR); *Gross v Switzerland* (2014) 58 EHRR 7 (ECHR).

57   *Haas v Switzerland* (2011) 53 EHRR 33 (ECHR) [51]; *Koch v Germany* (2013) 56 EHRR 6 (ECHR) [46], [51]; *Gross v Switzerland* (2014) 58 EHRR 7 (ECHR) [60].

58   See *R (Nicklinson) v Ministry of Justice* [2012] EWHC 2381 (Admin) [45]–[49]. Robert Orfali, *Death with Dignity: The Case for Legalising Physician-Assisted Dying and Euthanasia*, (Hillcrest Publishing Group, 2011).

59   The Commission on Assisted Dying, *The Aim of the Commission* (7 August 2010) <www.commissiononassisteddying.co.uk/the-aim-of-the-commission>.

Canada

The first 'right to die' case in Canada was considered in the Supreme Court of Canada in 1993.[60] The case involved Mrs Rodriguez, who suffered from a degenerative neurological condition. She sought an order that would allow a medical practitioner to establish through technological means a mechanism by which she could end her life. A majority of the British Columbia Court of Appeal had held that the right to life, liberty and security of the person under Article 7 of the Canadian Charter of Rights and Freedoms (Charter) had been infringed by the prohibition against assisted suicide, but that the latter proposition was in accordance with the principles of fundamental justice as required by Article 7.[61]

On appeal, a majority of the Supreme Court of Canada held that section 7 (the right to security of the person) was engaged but could not encompass 'a right to take action that [would] end one's life as the security of the person is intrinsically concerned with the well-being of the living person'.[62] A clear concern of the majority was a fear that 'the relaxation of a clear standard set by the law, [would] undermine the protection of life and lead to abuse of the exception'.[63] Of those who dissented, McLachlin J invoked the ground of discrimination in Article 15 to find a violation of section 7 of the Charter. Her Honour stated:

> Parliament has put into force a legislative scheme which does not bar suicide but criminalizes the act of assisting suicide. The effect of this is to deny to some people the choice of ending their lives solely because they are physically unable to do so. This deprives Sue Rodriguez of her security of the person (the right to make decisions concerning her own body, which affect only her own body) in a way that offends the principles of fundamental justice, thereby violating section 7 of the Charter.[64]

In a more recent case, in 2012, *Carter v Canada*, the Supreme Court of British Columbia held that criminal law provisions against assisted suicide[65] violate the rights of the seriously ill and are thus unconstitutional, infringing Articles 7 and 15 of the Charter.[66] The key argument in the case was that such laws restrict the liberty of physicians to deliver compassionate end-of-life care to incurably ill patients. The Supreme Court gave the government of British Columbia 12 months to introduce legislation that would legalise assisted suicide. However, the judgment was appealed by the Canadian federal government and was subsequently overturned by the Court of Appeal for British Columbia, in 2013.[67] On appeal to the Supreme

---

60   *Rodriguez v British Columbia (Attorney-General)* [1993] 3 SCR 519 (Canada).
61   *Canada Act 1982* (UK) cl 11, Sch B, Part I (Canadian Charter of Rights and Freedoms).
62   *Rodriguez v British Columbia (Attorney-General)* [1993] 3 SCR 519 (Canada), 585 (Sopinka J).
63   Ibid Sopinka J at [613].
64   Ibid McLachlin J at [617].
65   Section 241(b) and s 14 of the *Criminal Code*, R.S.C. 1985, c C-46.
66   *Carter v Canada (Attorney-General)* (2012) 287 CCC (3d) 1; cf *R (Nicklinson) v Ministry of Justice* [2012] EWHC 2381 (Admin) (UK).
67   *Carter v Canada (Attorney-General)* [2013] BCCA 435 (Canada).

Court of Canada, in a judgment handed down in February 2015, it was held that the relevant criminal law provisions against assisted suicide infringed section 7 of the Charter:

> [They] are of no force or effect to the extent that they prohibit physician-assisted death for a competent adult person who (1) clearly consents to the termination of life and (2) has a grievous and irremediable medical condition (including an illness, disease or disability) that causes enduring suffering that is intolerable to the individual in the circumstances of his or her condition.[68]

The court suspended the ruling for one year to give the federal government the opportunity to bring forward appropriate legislative amendments. In June 2016, the Canadian Parliament passed legislation, C-14 *An Act to amend the Criminal Code and to make related amendments to other Acts (medical assistance in dying)*, in response to *Carter v Canada*.

Conclusion

The European and Canadian courts have made it clear that criminal law prohibitions preventing competent adults from choosing the manner of their own death are contrary to human rights principles in certain circumstances. The challenge for law reform is how to develop a framework that strikes a reasonable balance between allowing some individuals to receive assistance to end their lives, while protecting those who are thought to be vulnerable. In Australia, there has been consistent public support for law reform in this area.[69] Individuals are interested in seeking assistance to die, and many would consider assisting another person. Some Australians also travel abroad to access assisted suicide services or source lethal medication to end their lives.[70]

One of the more persuasive arguments for regulating euthanasia and assisted suicide is the need to stem illegal conduct and protect those who are correctly seeking assistance to die outside the law. Anecdotal evidence that physicians accede to their patients' requests for treatment that will end their lives lends weight to the related argument that such decisions should be made in a transparent manner and in accordance with established criteria.[71] Although Australia is a signatory to a number of international human rights conventions, it lacks its own national human rights legislation. While the absence of such legislation is not an absolute barrier to successful law reform, it seems unlikely that a right to die will be recognised by Australian courts any time soon. Moreover, if right to die legislation is adopted in Australia, it is likely to face a strong constitutional challenge.

---

68   *Carter v Canada (Attorney-General)* [2015] 1 SCR 331. The declaration of invalidity was suspended for 12 months.

69   Brendan Hills, 'Poll Backs Euthanasia', *Herald Sun* (online) 25 September 2010 <www.heraldsun .com.au/archive/news/poll-backs-euthanasia/story-e6frf7l6-1225929316349>, reported 78% support. A Newspoll published in *The Australian* in 2009 reported 85% support: AAP, '85 Per Cent Support Voluntary Euthanasia – Poll', *The Australian* (online) 28 October 2009 <www.theaustralian.com.au/ news/latest-news/per-cent-support-voluntary-euthanasia-poll/story-fn3dxiwe-1225791455181>.

70   Sarah Steele and David Worswick, 'Destination Death: Review of Australian Legal Regulation Around International Travel to End of Life' (2013) 21 *Journal of Law and Medicine* 415–28.

71   Helga Khuse et al., 'End-of-Life Decisions in Australian Medical Practice' (1997) 166(4) *Medical Journal of Australia* 191–6, reporting that 1.8% of deaths in Australia occurred due to voluntary euthanasia and 0.1% were due to physician-assisted suicide, although the study reported 3.5% of deaths being assisted without the patient's explicit request.

LAW AND THE
HUMAN BODY

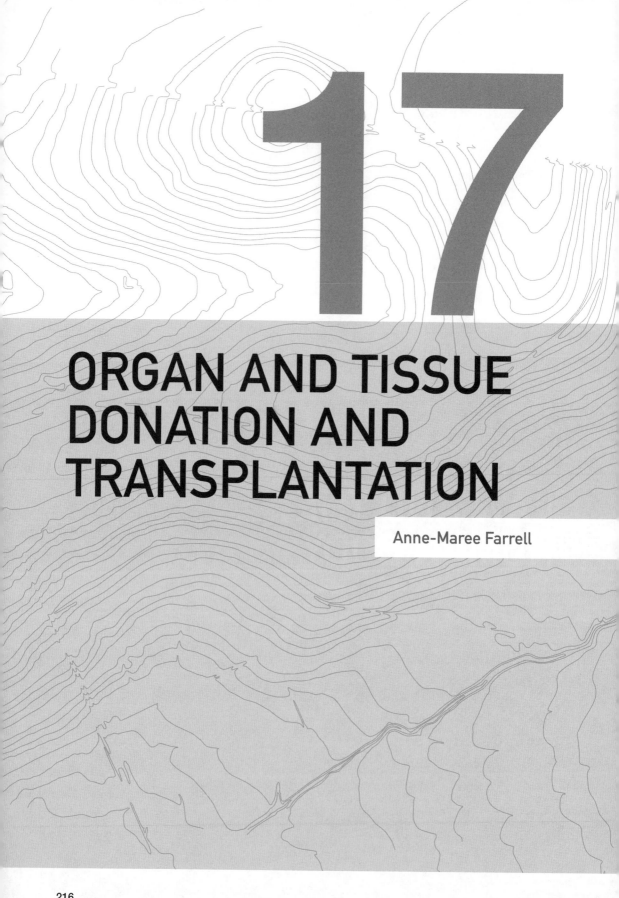

17

ORGAN AND TISSUE DONATION AND TRANSPLANTATION

Anne-Maree Farrell

Introduction

In the 21st century, advances in scientific research, biotechnology and clinical care have greatly expanded the potential for organ and tissue donation and transplantation. Although the promise of xenotransplantation has not yet been realised,[1] there have been recent successes with womb and face transplant surgery.[2] Tissue which can be used for transplantation purposes is already being created through the use of 3D bioprinting.[3] There is also hope that advances in both stem cell and 3D printing technologies will lead, in the not too distant future, to the creation of (solid) organs which are suitable for transplantation.[4]

Developments in machine (or ex-vivo) perfusion of organs also offer the potential for repair and regeneration of organs, enabling more organs to be available for transplant.[5] Notwithstanding the promise of such technologies, the current reality in Australia is that demand for human organs and tissue greatly exceeds supply.

Currently, there are around 1500 individuals on national organ transplant waiting lists.[6] New medical treatments and technological advances, as well as the rise in the number of Australians with chronic medical conditions which require organ transplants, means that the gap between supply and demand looks set to increase in the future. Whether or not demand for tissue and organs can ever be met remains a contested issue.[7] If demand cannot be met, it is argued that the key question in policy terms should be the design of just and fair allocation criteria in order to ensure 'appropriate use of a scarce resource'.[8] Nevertheless, much of the academic and policy literature in the field is focused on how best to increase rates of both deceased and living organ donation in circumstances which are ethically justified, legally permissible and politically acceptable.

This chapter examines key aspects of the organ and tissue donation and transplantation system in Australia. The types of human tissue considered are those donated and supplied for the purposes of transplantation, such as hearts, lungs, kidneys, livers, intestines and pancreases. Tissues that can be used include eyes, bones, tendons, ligaments, skin and heart valves. In addition, there are also 'vascularised composite tissue allografts', which involve transplantation of multiple tissues such as muscle, bone, nerve and skin, as a functional unit (for example, face or hand).[9] A detailed examination of the donation and supply of blood

---

1   Burcin Ekser et al., 'Clinical Xenotransplantation: The Next Medical Revolution?' (2012) 379 *The Lancet* 672.

2   Maggie Fazeli Fard, 'Face Transplant for Virginia Man is Lauded as Most Extensive in History', *The Washington Post*, 27 March 2012; Chris Johnston, 'Womb Transplants: First 10 British Women Given Go-Ahead', *The Guardian*, 30 September 2015.

3   3D bioprinting has been used to create tissue, such as skin, bone, vascular grafts, tracheal splints, heart tissue and cartilaginous structures. See Sean Murphy and Anthony Atala, '3D Bioprinting of Tissues and Organs' (2014) 32 *Nature Biotechnology* 773.

4   Jonathan Pearlman, 'Kidney Grown from Stem Cells by Australian Scientists', *The Telegraph*, 16 December 2013; Melissa Davey, '3D Printed Organs Come a Step Closer', *The Guardian*, 4 July 2014.

5   National Health and Medical Research Council (NHMRC), *Ethical Guidelines for Organ Transplantation from Deceased Donors* (2016) para 3.3.

6   Australian Government, Organ and Tissue Authority (OTA), *Facts and Statistics* <www.donatelife .gov.au/discover/facts-and-statistics>.

7   Anne-Maree Farrell, 'Addressing Organ Shortage: Are Nudges the Way Forward?' (2015) 7(2) *Law Innovation and Technology* 253, 256–8.

8   NHMRC, above n 5, para 3.2.2.

9   Ibid Explanation of Key Terms, iv.

and plasma products is outside the scope of this chapter, but brief reference is made to key provisions dealing with blood in the relevant human tissue legislation.

The first part provides an overview of institutional arrangements, before moving in the second part to examine ethical and legal issues impacting organ and tissue donation from deceased persons, as well as an analysis of strategies to increase rates of such donation. Thereafter, the ethical and legal issues involved in the diagnosis of death are considered, as well as those involved in allocating organs and tissues from deceased donors. In the third part, ethical and legal issues associated with living organ and tissue donation and transplantation are examined. The final part of the chapter considers key aspects of donor tissue banking in Australia.

National policy and institutional arrangements

In 2008, the Council of Australian Governments (COAG) endorsed the Australian Government's national reform agenda to implement a world's best practice approach to organ and tissue donation for transplantation. The twin objectives were to increase the capability and capacity within the health system so as to maximise donation rates and to raise community awareness and stakeholder engagement to promote organ and tissue donation.[10] To date, the Australian government has committed approximately $250 million towards the implementation of the reform program.[11] In conjunction with such developments, a number of reviews have been undertaken by state Parliaments to examine the operation and reform of their organ and tissue donation systems.[12]

In the years since the reform program began, Australia's deceased organ donation rate has increased from 11.4 donor per million population (dpmp) to 18.3 dpmp – this is a 61 per cent increase over the period 2009–15.[13] While there has been some variation in the growth in the rate of deceased organ donation (with a 3 per cent decrease in 2014), the overall trend is positive. While this has been welcomed, it still lags behind other developed countries, such as Spain (35.7 dpmp), France (25.3 dpmp), the US (26.6 dpmp) and the UK (20.6 dpmp).[14] In the Australian context, it is also worth noting that there are some significant differences between the states and territories, with SA having achieved a rate of 24.7 dpmp in contrast to Queensland's rate of 15.1 dpmp.[15]

---

10   OTA, National Reform Programme <www.donatelife.gov.au/about-us/national-reform-programme>.

11   Georgina Connery, 'The Painful Wait for Australia's Organ Donation Rates to Rise', *Sydney Morning Herald*, 8 August 2015.

12   For an overview, see Parliament of Victoria, Legislative Council, Legal and Social Issues References Committee, *Inquiry into Organ Donation in Victoria Report No. 1*, March 2012, (No. 119, Session 2010–12), paras 2.7.1–2.7.4.

13   OTA, *Australian Donation and Transplantation Activity Report 2015*, 1 <www.donatelife.gov.au/sites/default/files/Australian%20Donation%20and%20Transplantation%20Activity%20Report%202015.pdf>.

14   Council of Europe, TRANSPLANT Newsletter 2015. *International Figures on Organ Donation and Transplantation Activity*. Year 2014, 4, 15.

15   OTA, above n 13, 6.

In 2009, the Australian Organ and Tissue Donation and Transplantation Authority (Organ and Tissue Authority (OTA)) was established as an independent statutory authority, in order to further the national reform agenda.[16] The OTA works with state and territory governments, as well as with a range of organ and tissue organisations and stakeholders, to develop a nationally coordinated approach to organ and tissue donation for transplantation. It is responsible for administering funds to non-government organisations to provide essential associated services aligned to its purpose. In its current Strategic Plan (2015–19), the OTA has stated that it plans to bring about an overall national increase in the rate of deceased organ donation, from 15.1 dpmp to 25 dpmp, by 2018.[17]

A nationally coordinated approach and system for organ and tissue donation, known as the DonateLife Network, has also been established. The DonateLife Network comprises Organ and Tissue Donation Agencies (OTDAs), as well as hospital-based staff across Australia who work specifically on organ and tissue donation. Such staff include Medical Directors who are responsible for the delivery of the reform program in their respective states and territories. They manage hospital-based staff who are clinical specialists in organ and tissue donation, as well as OTA employees who specialise in organ donor coordination, donor family support, education and communication coordination and data and audit.[18]

There are also a number of professional and stakeholder groups involved in national organ and tissue donation and transplantation policy. These include the Australasian Transplant Coordinators Association (ATCA), which represents organ and tissue donor and transplant coordinators. ATCA publishes guidance on protocols and procedures for health professionals in relation to organ and tissue donation, transplantation and allocation.[19] ATCA does this in conjunction with the Transplantation Society of Australia and New Zealand (TSANZ), which is the Australasian peak body representing clinicians and scientists in the field of organ transplantation.[20] Another key professional representative body is the Australian and New Zealand Intensive Care Society (ANZICS), which represents, inter alia, intensive care physicians who have a critical role in the organ donation process, being involved with potential donor patients and their families, as well as in the care of donor recipients immediately following organ donation. ANZICS also publishes regularly updated guidance on the diagnosis of death (see later in this chapter).[21] There are also a number of lay stakeholder groups that engage in advocacy and support to organ donors, their families

---

16   The OTA was created pursuant to the *Australian Organ and Tissue Donation and Transplantation Authority Act 2008* (Cth).

17   OTA, *Strategic Plan (2015–19)* <www.donatelife.gov.au/strategic-plan>. Note that the OTA's current strategic plan reflects in part the findings of successive reviews of its performance in recent years: see, for example, Auditor General, *Organ and Tissue Donation: Community Awareness, Professional Education and Family Support*, ANAO Report No. 33 2014–15 (Australian National Audit Office, 2015); Parliament of Australia, Senate Select Committee on Health, *First Interim Report*, December 2014 (Commonwealth of Australia, 2014).

18   OTA, *About Us* <www.donatelife.gov.au/about-us>; Australian Government, Department of Health, *Review of the Implementation of the National Reform Agenda on Organ and Tissue Donation and Transplantation* (2015) [Ernst & Young Report] <www.health.gov.au/internet/main/publishing.nsf/Content/review-implementation-of-national-reformagenda-organ-tissue-donation-transplantation>.

19   ACTA, *National Guidelines for Organ and Tissue Donation*, 4th edn (2008). For a detailed list of guidance and procedures published by ACTA, see <www.atca.org.au>.

20   TSANZ <www.tsanz.com.au>.

21   ANZICS <www.anzics.com.au>.

and organ recipients.[22] In addition, various registries have been established to gather and publish data on organ and tissue transplantation in Australia and New Zealand.[23]

Regulation of organ and tissue donation and transplantation

In this section we will consider a range of ethical, legal and social issues that influence the way in which organ and tissue donation and transplantation take place in Australia. The relevant legislation for organ and tissue donation is what are commonly known as the state/territory *Human Tissue Acts* (HT Acts). The HT Acts were adopted as a result of recommendations contained in the Australian Law Reform Commission report, *Human Tissue Transplants*, which was published in 1977.[24] They deal with the donation of blood, tissue and organs for transplantation, as well as for scientific, therapeutic or medical purposes. The HT Acts do not contain provisions dealing with storage of and access to tissue samples, nor with access or transfer to other researchers, or the future use of samples.[25] For further examination of such issues, see Chapters 19 and 20.

Key definitions

It is important to be clear about what sort of human tissue is covered by the HT Acts:

- **Tissue**: an organ, or part, of a human body or a substance extracted from, or from a part of, the human body.[26]
- **Regenerative tissue:** tissue which, after injury or removal, is replaced in the body of a living person by natural processes of growth or repair (Victoria and SA omit the phrase 'of growth or repair').[27]

---

22   See, for example, Transplant Australia <http://transplant.org.au>; Kidney Health Australia <www .kidney.org.au>; Gift of Life Inc. <www.giftoflife.asn.au>; Share Life <www.sharelife.org.au>.

23   See Australia and New Zealand Organ Donation (ANZOD) Registry, the Australia and New Zealand Dialysis and Transplant Registry (ANZDATA); the Australia and New Zealand Cardiothoracic Organ Transplant Registry (ANZCOTR); the Australia and New Zealand Liver Transplant Registry (ANZLTR) and the National Pancreas Transplant Registry (NPTR).

24   Australian Law Reform Commission (ALRC), *Human Tissue Transplants*, Report No. 7 (AGPS, 1977).

25   This created a gap in the legislative coverage relating to the use of human tissue in research settings, including the collection, storage and use of such samples by biobanks. Instead, such research activity is now covered by a combination of national ethical guidance and privacy legislation, see Chapters 12, 19 and 20 for further details.

26   *Transplantation and Anatomy Act 1978* (ACT) Dictionary, s 6; *Human Tissue Act 1983* (NSW) s 4; *Transplantation and Anatomy Act 1979* (NT) s 4; *Transplantation and Anatomy Act 1983* (SA) s 5; *Human Tissue Act 1985* (Tas) s 3; *Human Tissue Act 1982* (Vic) s 3; *Human Tissue and Transplant Act 1982* (WA) s 3. Under s 4 of the *Transplantation and Anatomy Act 1979* (Qld), the expanded definition of 'tissue' includes 'organs, blood or part of (and substances extracted therefrom), a human fetus and which excludes immunoglobulins and laboratory reagents, or reference and control materials derived wholly or in part from pooled human plasma'.

27   *Transplantation and Anatomy Act 1978* (ACT) Dictionary; *Human Tissue Act 1983* (NSW) s 4; *Transplantation and Anatomy Act 1979* (NT) s 4; *Transplantation and Anatomy Act 1979* (Qld) s 4; *Transplantation and Anatomy Act 1983* (SA) s 5; *Human Tissue Act 1985* (Tas) s 3; *Human Tissue Act 1982* (Vic) s 3; *Human Tissue and Transplant Act 1982* (WA) s 3.

- **Non-regenerative tissue**: tissue other than regenerative tissue.[28]

Other relevant issues include the fact that reproductive tissue, such as fetal tissue and gametes, are excluded from coverage under the HT Acts with respect to donation of such tissue by living persons.[29] A detailed examination of Australian law regarding reproductive tissue is to be found in Chapter 13. In addition, blood is considered to be tissue for the purposes of the HT Acts. Although a detailed examination of blood donation and supply is outside the scope of this chapter, we note that the Acts set out the circumstances in which consent may be given to blood donation. This may occur for the purposes of blood transfusion to another or for the purpose of using the blood or any of its constituents for other therapeutic purposes or for medical or scientific purposes. Reference is also made to the age of consent to the removal of blood being 16 years, and the circumstances in which blood can be removed from children who have not attained the age of 16 years.[30]

Trade and commerce

In Australia, there is a longstanding ethical and policy commitment to the gift relationship as the central ethical principle underpinning national organ and tissue donation. It is predicated on the altruistic motivation of individuals who donate their organs and tissue (usually on an anonymous basis) without expectation of financial reward.[31] Altruism in this context is seen as an important part of the community's social capital. This commitment also underpins the legal prohibition on trading in human tissue used for transplantation purposes: this is set out in the HT Acts, and is supported in relevant professional guidance.[32] Two approaches

---

28   *Transplantation and Anatomy Act 1978* (ACT) Dictionary; *Human Tissue Act 1983* (NSW) s 4; *Transplantation and Anatomy Act 1979* (NT) s 4; *Transplantation and Anatomy Act 1979* (Qld) s 4; *Transplantation and Anatomy Act 1983* (SA) s 5; *Human Tissue Act 1985* (Tas) s 3; *Human Tissue Act 1982* (Vic) s 3; *Human Tissue and Transplant Act 1982* (WA) s 3.

29   *Transplantation and Anatomy Act 1978* (ACT) Dictionary; *Human Tissue Act 1983* (NSW) s 6; *Transplantation and Anatomy Act 1979* (NT) s 4; *Transplantation and Anatomy Act 1979* (Qld) s 8; *Transplantation and Anatomy Act 1983* (SA) s 7; *Human Tissue Act 1985* (Tas) s 5; *Human Tissue Act 1982* (Vic) s 5; *Human Tissue and Transplant Act 1982* (WA) s 6.

30   *Transplantation and Anatomy Act 1978* (ACT) Div 2.5, ss 20–3; *Human Tissue Act 1983* (NSW) Part 3, ss 18–20H (note also Part 3A, which deals with the regulation of businesses supplying blood and blood products); *Transplantation and Anatomy Act 1979* (NT) Part 2, Div 4, ss 14–15; *Transplantation and Anatomy Act 1979* (Qld) Part 2, Div 4, ss 16–20; *Transplantation and Anatomy Act 1983* (SA) Part 2, Div 5, ss 17A–20; *Human Tissue Act 1985* (Tas) Part II, Div 5, ss 17A–20; Div 5A, ss 21–2; *Human Tissue Act 1982* (Vic) Part III, ss 20–4; *Human Tissue and Transplant Act 1982* (WA) Part II, Div 5, ss 18–21.

31   The origins of the gift relationship as a key ethical principle underpinning tissue donation is to be found in the work of Richard Titmuss on blood donation: see *The Gift Relationship: From Human Blood to Social Policy* (George Allen & Unwin, 1970).

32   Note, for example, the Australian and New Zealand Intensive Care Society (ANZICS). The ANZICS Statement on Death and Organ Donation Edition 3.2 2013, para 1.2 [ANZICS Statement] states that: 'ANZICS believes that no person, organisation or company should profit financially from organ or tissue donation; and neither the estate of an organ or tissue donor nor his or her family should incur any cost from the processes that occur to facilitate organ and tissue donation.'

can be identified in the HT Acts. The first is to be found in the ACT, NSW, NT and Tasmania, where the scope of the general prohibition is as follows:

> A person must not enter into or offer to enter into a contract or arrangement under which any person agrees for valuable consideration … to the sale or supply of tissue from any such person's body or the body of any other person, whether before or after that person's death or the death of that other person; or to the post-mortem examination of any person's body after their death.[33]

The second approach is to be found in the HT Acts in Queensland, SA and Victoria, where reference is made to a number of specific prohibitions focused on unauthorised selling and buying of tissue (including one's own tissue) and the right to remove tissue. In addition, there is a prohibition on disseminating through various media any advertisements relating to the donation, selling or buying of tissue, or the right to take tissue from bodies of persons, unless it has been approved by the relevant Minister and there is a statement to that effect accompanying the advertisement.[34] The WA HT Act appears to be a mixture of these two approaches.[35]

There are a number of exceptions to the general prohibition on trade and commerce in human tissue, which include the following. First, there is a sale or supply of tissue (except blood) that has been subject to processing or treatment and this was done (by a medical practitioner/doctor) for the purpose of enabling it to be used for therapeutic, medical or scientific purposes.[36] Second, there is a contract or arrangement which only provides for reimbursement of expenses necessarily incurred by a person in relation to the removal of tissue in accordance with the relevant HT Act.[37] Third, there is Ministerial (or governmental) authorisation to permit a contract or arrangement for the sale and/or supply of tissue.[38] As noted previously, the HT Acts do not cover reproductive tissue or human embryos. There

---

33   *Transplantation and Anatomy Act 1978* (ACT) s 44(1); *Human Tissue Act 1983* (NSW) s 32(1); *Transplantation and Anatomy Act 1979* (NT) s 22E [must also intentionally engage in such conduct]; *Human Tissue Act 1985* (Tas) s 27(1).

34   *Transplantation and Anatomy Act 1979* (Qld) ss 40, 42(1); *Transplantation and Anatomy Act 1983* (SA) s 35(1)–(7); *Human Tissue Act 1982* (Vic) ss 38, 39, 40(1).

35   *Human Tissue and Transplant Act 1982* (WA) ss 29, 30.

36   *Transplantation and Anatomy Act 1978* (ACT) s 44(2); *Human Tissue Act 1983* (NSW) s 32(2); *Transplantation and Anatomy Act 1979* (NT) s 22E(2); *Transplantation and Anatomy Act 1979* (Qld) s 42AA(1); *Transplantation and Anatomy Act 1983* (SA) s 35(3); *Human Tissue Act 1985* (Tas) s 27(2); *Human Tissue and Transplant Act 1982* (WA) s 29(4).

37   *Transplantation and Anatomy Act 1978* (ACT) s 44(3); *Human Tissue Act 1983* (NSW) s 32(3); *Transplantation and Anatomy Act 1979* (NT) s 22E(3); *Transplantation and Anatomy Act 1983* (SA) s 35(4); *Human Tissue Act 1985* (Tas) s 27(3); *Human Tissue and Transplant Act 1982* (WA) s 29(3). Note that in Queensland, a person who owns a prescribed tissue bank may charge an amount (cost-recovery amount) to cover reasonable costs associated with removing, evaluating, processing, storing or distributing donated tissue (see *Transplantation and Anatomy Act 1979* (Qld) s 42A. This is also echoed in the *Human Tissue Act 1982* (Vic) s 39A(1).

38   *Transplantation and Anatomy Act 1978* (ACT) s 44(4); *Human Tissue Act 1983* (NSW) s 32(4); *Transplantation and Anatomy Act 1979* (NT) s 22F; *Transplantation and Anatomy Act 1979* (Qld) ss 40(2), (3); *Transplantation and Anatomy Act 1983* (SA) s 35(6); *Human Tissue Act 1985* (Tas) s 27(4); *Human Tissue Act 1982* (Vic) ss 39(1A), (2), (3) [Note: donor tissue banks can recover 'reasonable costs' involved in the removal, evaluation, storage, processing and distribution of donated tissue provided it is in accordance with the Act, s 39A]; *Human Tissue and Transplant Act 1982* (WA) s 29(4).

are specific legislative provisions dealing with trade and commerce in such tissue, and the circumstances in which payment of reasonable expenses is permitted, details of which are set out in Chapter 13.

Notwithstanding the prohibitory approach taken in Australia to trade and commerce in human tissue (save for the exceptions noted above), there are ongoing international academic and policy debates about whether trade, incentives and markets in organs and tissue can be ethically justified and should be legally permitted in certain circumstances. Proposals have included whether one (state-sponsored) provider or regulatory agency should be responsible for administering what has been described as a 'monopsonistic market';[39] whether a model of collaboration between the state and not-for-profit organisations would instead work better;[40] or whether a futures market in organs is the way forward.[41]

For those who object to markets for organs, it has been argued that the use of direct financial payment is ethically problematic for a number of reasons: its potential negative impact upon the altruistic motivation to donate;[42] the increased commodification of the body; and the potential for donor harm and exploitation.[43] Financial incentives may also serve to entrench power, wealth and race disparities, with poor or lower income donors servicing a more wealthy recipient population.[44] Incentivising organ donation can also be non-financial, and can take different forms. It may involve recognition in some shape or form valued by donors; it may also involve benefits-in-kind or benefit sharing. An approach based on benefits-in-kind sets priorities in organ allocation, and is used in countries such as Israel.[45]

Given that direct financial payment for organs as an incentivisation strategy has not attracted widespread political or public support, there is now an increased government focus on removing financial disincentives in order to encourage organ donation.[46] In the case of deceased organ donation, this has included proposals for payment of a specified amount for funeral expenses to families who consent to donate organs after the death of a family member. This proposal has not been taken up in Australia, but it is offered in other countries, such as Spain.[47] We will consider how the question of financial payments and the removal of financial disincentives have been approached in the case of living organ donation in a later section of the chapter.

---

39   Charles Erin and John Harris, 'An Ethical Market in Human Organs' (2003) 29(3) *Journal of Medical Ethics* 137.

40   Ahad Ghods and Shekoufeh Savaj, 'Iranian Model of Paid and Regulated Living-Unrelated Kidney Donation' (2006) 1(6) *Clinical Journal of the American Society of Nephrology* 1136.

41   Lloyd Cohen, 'Increasing the Supply of Transplant Organs: The Virtues of a Futures Market' (1989) 58(1) *George Washington Law Review* 1.

42   See Titmuss, above n 31; cf. Scott Halpern et al., 'Regulated Payments for Living Kidney Donation: An Empirical Assessment of the Ethical Concerns (2010) 152 *Annals of Internal Medicine* 358.

43   Nuffield Council on Bioethics, *Human Bodies: Donation for Medicine and Research* (Nuffield Council on Bioethics, 2011) para 22.

44   Francis Delmonico et al., 'Ethical Incentives – Not Payment – For Organ Donation' (2002) 346(25) *New England Journal of Medicine* 2002.

45   Nuffield Council on Bioethics, above n 43, paras 3.68–3.74.

46   Alexander C Wiseman, 'Removing Financial Disincentives to Organ Donation: An Acceptable Next Step?' (2012) 7(12) *Clinical Journal of the American Society of Nephrology* 1917.

47   David Rodriguez-Arias et al., 'Success Factors and Ethical Challenges of the Spanish Model of Organ Donation' (2010) 376 *The Lancet* 1109.

Consent to deceased organ donation

Consent has been described as the 'central ethical and legal justification for the removal and use of organs' and tissue.[48] Various models of consent have been proposed in an attempt to increase rates of deceased organ donation. We consider here the opt-in, opt-out (presumed consent) and required choice models, before going on to consider the specific legislative requirements that must be fulfilled in order for deceased organ and tissue donation to take place in Australia.

Opt-in model

The opt-in model requires an individual to expressly state that they wish to become an organ donor. Australia operates an opt-in model of consent. Individuals can decide to become organ donors in the event of their death by registering their intention to do so on the Australian Organ Donation Register (AODR) or otherwise discussing their wishes with their families. Recently published data has shown that over 32 per cent of Australians 16 years and older (six million people) have registered their decision regarding organ and tissue donation. This includes people who do not wish to donate, which amounts to less than 0.5 per cent of all registrations.[49] Notwithstanding the fact that an individual may have signed up to the AODR, it is considered ethically appropriate for families to be asked to confirm the donation decision of their deceased family member. These donors are referred to as 'consented organ and tissue donors'.[50] In the event that families do not consent, it is accepted that organs and tissue of their deceased family member will not be removed.[51]

Opt-out model (presumed consent)

An opt-out model presumes that individuals are willing to donate after their death, unless they have expressed or formally registered the fact that they do not wish this to take place. There are 'hard' and 'soft' versions of the model. The 'hard' model does not take account of families' views before donation takes place. The 'soft' model involves consulting with families about their views: if they object, the donation does not proceed.

There has been considerable debate over whether or not the presumed consent model is likely to make more organs available for transplant. On the basis of cross-country analysis and systematic reviews, it has been argued that presumed consent models increase rates of deceased organ donation.[52] However, this view has been challenged on the

---

48   David Price, *Human Tissue in Transplantation and Research: A Model Legal and Ethical Donation Framework* (CUP, 2010) 99.

49   Ibid 9.

50   OTA, above n 6, 2.

51   NHMRC, *Organ and Tissue Donation After Death, for Transplantation – Guidelines for Ethical Practice for Health Professionals* (2007) <www.nhmrc.gov.au/guidelines-publications/e75>.

52   Alberto Abadie and Sebastien Gay, 'The Impact of Presumed Consent Legislation on Cadaveric Organ Donation: A Cross-Country Study' (2006) 25(4) *Journal of Health Economics* 599; Amber Rithalia et al., 'Impact of Presumed Consent for Organ Donation on Donation Rates: A Systematic Review' (2009) 338 *British Medical Journal* a3162. Note that Wales recently adopted a 'soft' version of the opt-out model, known as a 'deemed consent' model, which states that 'if you do not register a clear decision either to be an organ donor (opt in) or not to be a donor (opt out), you will be treated as having no objection to being a donor'. This model was introduced pursuant to the *Human Transplantation (Wales) Act 2013*, which came into force on 1 December 2015 <http://organdonationwales.org/FAQs/Organ-donation-from-december-2015/?lang=en>. Since it was introduced, there has been a noticeable increase in deceased organ donation in Wales. See Steven Morris, 'Welsh "Deemed Consent" Organ Donation System Shows Promising Results', *The Guardian*, 4 September 2016.

grounds that such reviews are not sufficiently nuanced to capture the range of factors contributing to such increase.[53] Specifically, it fails to take account of the fact that in several countries with presumed consent models, such as Spain, families are consulted by doctors and their consent is still sought for organ and tissue donation following the death of a family member. It has also been suggested that the presumed consent model does not result in a sustained increase in organ donation in the absence of institutional reform and incentivisation strategies.[54]

Required choice

Another strategy has been to employ different forms of forced or required choice in order to elicit a decision from individuals as to whether or not they wish to become organ and tissue donors in the event of their death. One such approach is referred to as mandated choice, which involves individuals being required to state whether or not they wish to register as an organ and tissue donor. The format in which such choice is registered can vary, ranging from 'yes/no' to a 'yes/no/I would prefer to leave the decision to my family'. Although it has been argued that using mandated choice as a 'default' strategy will lead to more individuals signing up to become organ donors in the event of their death, it has met with mixed success in the US.[55] In the UK, a 'prompted choice' approach has been implemented, when individuals apply online for (or to renew) their driving licences. During the online process, they are prompted to answer a question about whether they would like to join the national organ donor register. They are presented with three options: '(1) yes, I would like to register; (2) I am already registered; and (3) I do not want to answer this question now. Almost half of all registrations for organ donation in the UK take place via this route.'[56]

Family consent

Given that it is considered ethically appropriate to seek the consent of families before organ and tissue donation takes place under the Australian opt-in model, national guidance has been developed which sets out an ethical framework by which health professionals should seek consent from families following the death of a family member. It is emphasised that organ and tissue donation should only be raised with the family once a decision has been made to discontinue treatment of the family member and there should be no financial burden for families where they do consent to donation.[57]

Notwithstanding significant public support for becoming an organ and tissue donor after death, family refusal to consent currently sits at around 40 per cent.[58] This is a relatively high rate of refusal when compared to other developed countries, such as Spain

---

53   Brian Willis and Muireann Quigley, 'Opt-Out Organ Donation: On Evidence and Public Policy' (2014) 107(2) *Journal of the Royal Society of Medicine* 56.

54   Muireann Quigley et al., 'The Organs Crisis and the Spanish Model: Theoretical versus Pragmatic Considerations' (2007) 34 *Journal of Medical Ethics* 223; John Fabre et al., 'Presumed Consent: A Distraction in the Quest For Increasing Rates of Organ Donation' (2010) 341 *British Medical Journal* 922; Parliament of Victoria, above n 12, paras 4.2–4.3.

55   Richard Thaler and Cass Sunstein, *Nudge: Improving Decisions about Health, Wealth and Happiness* (Penguin, 2009) 189–92.

56   Farrell, above n 7, 264.

57   NHMRC, above n 51, paras 3.1–3.2.

58   OTA, above n 6.

(17.9 per cent) and the US (21.9 per cent), although it is on a par with countries such as the UK (42 per cent).[59] Data published by the OTA for the year 2015 showed that requests were made to families for donation in around 940 cases, with consent subsequently being provided by 564 families. As noted by the OTA, key reasons offered by families as to why they did not wish to proceed with donation include: 'they believed their loved one did not want to donate, they did not like the idea of organ donation and for cultural or religious reasons'.[60]

Research commissioned by the OTA has revealed that prior family discussions about willingness of family members to donate organs plays a central role in families' consenting to such donation after the death of a family member.[61] Other international research has also shown that many families struggle to come to terms with their family member being subjected to further medical intervention and being 'cut up' as part of the retrieval of organs and tissue and this has led to their refusal to consent to donation.[62] The OTA recognises that more work needs to be done to reduce rates of family refusal, as well as to assist health professionals in communicating with and supporting families in relation to decision-making around organ and tissue donation after death.[63]

Key legislative provisions

Under the HT Acts, there are a number of important issues that must be taken into account in relation to obtaining consent for organ donation from deceased adults. While there are some differences between the various Australian state/territory jurisdictions, key provisions are summarised below:

- **A designated officer** may authorise removal of tissue from the body of a deceased person where the body is at a hospital and the purpose is for transplantation to a living person or other therapeutical, medical of scientific purposes.[64]

- **Where the deceased's views are known and death has occurred/body located in a hospital**: the designated officer may, after making reasonable inquiries, authorise removal of organs and tissue if the deceased donor had expressed a wish or given consent to the donation of organs and tissue which had not been revoked and where the donor had not expressed an objection to donation. Note that there is some variation

---

59   Council of Europe, above n 14, 48.

60   OTA, above n 13, 12.

61   OTA, *National Study of Family Experiences in Organ and Tissue Donation Wave 1 2010 and 2011* <www.donatelife.gov.au/national-wave-1-donor-family-study-0>. Note that the OTA plans to undertake successive studies on this issue at two-year intervals.

62   Magi Sque and Dariusz Galasinski, '"Keeping Her Whole": Bereaved Families' Accounts of Declining a Request for Organ Donation' (2013) 22(1) *Cambridge Quarterly of Healthcare Ethics* 53.

63   See OTA, *Professional Education Package* (PEP) <www.donatelife.gov.au/professional-education-package>.

64   *Transplantation and Anatomy Act 1978* (ACT) s 27(1); *Human Tissue Act 1983* (NSW) ss 23, 36(3); *Transplantation and Anatomy Act 1979* (NT) ss 18, 19; *Transplantation and Anatomy Act 1979* (Qld) s 22; *Transplantation and Anatomy Act 1983* (SA) s 21(1); *Human Tissue Act 1985* (Tas) s 23(1); *Human Tissue Act 1982* (Vic) s 26(1); *Human Tissue and Transplant Act 1982* (WA) s 22(1).

between jurisdictions as to how donors may make their views known regarding consent to organ and tissue donation prior to their death.[65]

- **Where the deceased's views are unknown and death has occurred/body located in a hospital**: where the deceased had not explicitly indicated their wishes regarding organ donation prior to death, but had not expressed an objection to donation during their lifetime, and the senior available next of kin cannot provide consent, then the designated officer may, after making reasonable inquiries, authorise the removal of tissue.[66]

- **Where the deceased's views are known and death has occurred/body located outside of hospital**: where the deceased, during their lifetime, gave consent to tissue removal and this had not been withdrawn or revoked, then tissue removal is authorised.[67]

- **Where the deceased's views are unknown and death has occurred/body located outside of hospital**: senior available next of kin may authorise tissue removal unless, after making reasonable inquiries, it appears that the deceased had expressed an objection to such removal which had not been withdrawn or revoked. If there is an objection by one (same or higher order) senior available next of kin, then the removal will not take place.[68]

- **Senior available next of kin**: are set out in order of priority with regard to who may provide consent to the removal of organs and tissue for transplantation. Note that where

---

65   *Transplantation and Anatomy Act 1978* (ACT) s 27(1); *Human Tissue Act 1983* (NSW) s 23(1) [consent to be in writing]; *Transplantation and Anatomy Act 1979* (NT) s 19B [consent to be in writing]; *Transplantation and Anatomy Act 1979* (Qld) s 22(5) [consent to be in writing]; *Transplantation and Anatomy Act 1983* (SA) s 21(2); *Human Tissue Act 1985* (Tas) s 23(1); *Human Tissue Act 1982* (Vic) s 26 [consent to be in writing or, during last illness, orally in the presence of two witnesses]; *Human Tissue and Transplant Act 1982* (WA) s 22.

66   *Transplantation and Anatomy Act 1978* (ACT) s 27(2) [senior available next of kin may make objections to removal of tissue known to designated officer (s 27(4)]; *Human Tissue Act 1983* (NSW) s 22(3) [senior next available kin may consent verbally if audio or audiovisual recording is made of deceased's consent prior to death and senior available next of kin consented to such recording – see *Human Tissue Regulations 2015* (NSW) reg 8]; *Transplantation and Anatomy Act 1979* (NT) s 18; *Transplantation and Anatomy Act 1979* (Qld) s 22; *Transplantation and Anatomy Act 1983* (SA) s 21(3); *Human Tissue Act 1985* (Tas) s 23(2); *Human Tissue Act 1982* (Vic) ss 26, 26A; *Human Tissue and Transplant Act 1982* (WA) ss 22, 33(2).

67   *Transplantation and Anatomy Act 1978* (ACT) s 28(3); *Human Tissue Act 1983* (NSW) s 24(1) [consent to be in writing]; *Transplantation and Anatomy Act 1979* (NT) s 19B [consent to be in writing]; *Transplantation and Anatomy Act 1979* (Qld) s 23(3) [consent to be in writing]; *Transplantation and Anatomy Act 1983* (SA) s 22(3); *Human Tissue Act 1985* (Tas) s 24(3); *Human Tissue Act 1982* (Vic) s 26(2) and (3) [consent to be in writing or during last illness, orally in the presence of two witnesses]. There are no express provisions in the *Human Tissue and Transplant Act 1982* (WA) for removal of tissue from deceased persons outside of a hospital, save for some exceptions if the death comes under the coronial jurisdiction (*Coroners Act 1996* (WA) ss 24, 34).

68   *Transplantation and Anatomy Act 1978* (ACT) s 28; *Human Tissue Act 1983* (NSW) s 24(3), (4) [senior next available kin may consent verbally if audio or audiovisual recording is made of deceased's consent prior to death and senior available next of kin consented to such recording – see *Human Tissue Regulations 2015* (NSW) reg 8]; *Transplantation and Anatomy Act 1979* (NT) s 19A; *Transplantation and Anatomy Act 1979* (Qld) s 23(1), (2); *Transplantation and Anatomy Act 1983* (SA) s 22(1) and (2); *Human Tissue Act 1985* (Tas) s 24(1), (2); *Human Tissue Act 1982* (Vic) s 26(2)(d) [note: registered medical practitioner or authorised person may remove tissue from deceased if, after having reasonable inquiries, they are unable to ascertain existence or whereabouts of next of kin and has no reason to believe that deceased objected to such removal (s 26(2)]; there are no express provisions in the *Human Tissue and Transplant Act 1982* (WA), but see also *Coroners Act 1996* (WA).

the coronial jurisdiction is invoked as a result of the death of the family member being a 'reportable death' (see below), then there is a need to obtain consent to organ and tissue donation from the coroner, rather than senior available next of kin, to organ and tissue donation.[69]

Diagnosis of death

Death is a biological process, rather than an event: this can make it difficult to define when death occurs. Nevertheless, it is important to have a legal definition of death for various reasons. It can be important for property purposes, as well as in relation to organising estate and probate matters. Clearly, defining death is also vitally important for those involved in organ transplantation from deceased donors, as organs cannot be lawfully removed until the donor has been declared dead. This is underpinned by what is colloquially known as the 'dead donor rule', which holds that 'patients must be declared dead before the removal of any vital organs for transplantation'.[70] Historically, it was relatively easy to determine death – a person's heart ceased to beat, and they stopped breathing. With advances in medicine and (bio)technology, however, the cessation of the heartbeat or of breathing does not necessarily mean a person is dead. Cardiac arrest has been followed by successful resuscitation and artificial ventilation has also improved techniques in resuscitation and provided life support for those who are severely ill or have been seriously injured.

Brain death

The advent of organ transplantation provided a catalyst to rethink the definition of death, mainly because of the need to move quickly once such a diagnosis was made in order to preserve organs for transplant.[71] With the exception of WA, all Australian states/territories have adopted a legislative definition of death. Brain death is defined in such legislation as:

- irreversible cessation of all function of the brain of the person; or
- irreversible cessation of circulation of blood in the body of the person.[72]

This definition provides the basis for the majority of organ and tissue donation by deceased donors in Australia.[73]

---

69   *Transplantation and Anatomy Act 1978* (ACT) Dictionary; *Human Tissue Act 1983* (NSW) s 4; *Transplantation and Anatomy Act 1979* (NT) s 4; *Transplantation and Anatomy Act 1979* (Qld) s 4; *Transplantation and Anatomy Act 1983* (SA) s 5; *Human Tissue Act 1985* (Tas) s 3; *Human Tissue Act 1982* (Vic) s 3; *Human Tissue and Transplant Act 1982* (WA) s 3.

70   Robert D Truog and Franklin G Miller, 'The Dead Donor Rule and Organ Transplantation' (2008) 359 *New England Journal of Medicine* 674.

71   Ibid.

72   *Transplantation and Anatomy Act 1978* (ACT) s 45; *Human Tissue Act 1983* (NSW) s 33; *Transplantation and Anatomy Act 1979* (NT) s 23; *Transplantation and Anatomy Act 1979* (Qld) s 45(2); *Death (Definition) Act 1983* (SA) s 2; *Human Tissue Act 1985* (Tas) s 27A; *Human Tissue Act 1982* (Vic) s 41. In the case of WA, s 24(2) of the *Human Tissue and Transplant Act 1982* (WA) states that tissue must not be removed from a body unless certain specified conditions are met, including a declaration that irreversible cessation of all function of the brain of the person has occurred. No independent definitions of either brain death or cardiac death are provided in the Act.

73   In the latest published data, 72 per cent of deceased organ donors in 2015 were from the Donation after Brain Death (DBD) pathway: see OTA, above n 13, 7.

Detailed criteria for determining the diagnosis of death is set out in professional guidance. This is published (and regularly updated) in the Australian and New Zealand Intensive Care Society Statement on Death and Organ Donation (ANZICS Statement).[74] The ANZICS Statement aims to provide a framework for best practice with respect to the determination of death, to deal with aspects of end-of-life care in the intensive care unit, and to facilitate the provision of the best possible care when patients or their families support organ and tissue donation after death.[75]

A number of ethical concerns have been raised about defining death as brain death. First, the variations in state and territory legislation regarding the circumstances in which brain death can be diagnosed, and who can make such a diagnosis, make for a lack of consistency in both interpretation and clinical practice across Australia.[76] Second, concerns have been raised about whether a definition of death, such as brain death, does in practice offend the dead donor rule. Accepting that a family member has died as a result of brain death may be particularly difficult for families given that they may still see their family member breathing (albeit with artificial ventilation) and with their heart continuing to beat. Although brain-dead patients will not recover, withdrawal of treatment may nevertheless be required in order to bring about the cessation of heartbeat.[77]

In the circumstances, it has been suggested that death should instead be defined by reference to cardiorespiratory criteria, as this would be well understood by the public. Patients with brain death could then be accepted as dying, rather than dead. Withdrawal of treatment would be initiated on the basis that they have no hope for recovery due to brain stem death, and thereafter they could be considered as potential organ and tissue donors. Although this would involve a change in the current Australian legal position, it has been argued that it might offer a way forward that would be acceptable to the public and would still allow organ and tissue donation to proceed in the case of deceased donors.[78]

Finally, concerns have been raised about the ethical framework that should operate in relation to managing perceived or real conflicts of interest for those health professionals involved in end-of-life care and those involved in organ donation and transplantation. In order to clarify this matter, both the ANZICS Statement and relevant NHMRC Guidance on organ and tissue donation after death make clear that it is ethically and professionally necessary to draw a clear distinction between the two. In the first instance, consideration

---

74   ANZICS, above n 32. Note that the 'sunset date' for the Statement is 2016, so a revised Statement will be published in the near future.

75   Ibid.

76   Ibid, para 4.1. Note, for example, the judgment in *Kryommydas v Sydney West Area Health Service* [2006] NSWSC 901, where it was held that a diagnosis of death based on brain stem death criteria was acceptable. This is contrary to the definition of death as being brain death, as set out in the *Human Tissue Act 1983* (NSW). For a critique, see James Tibballs, 'The Non-Compliance of Clinical Guidelines for Organ Donation with Australian Statute Law' (2008) 16 *Journal of Law and Medicine* 335. Note that in the UK, the definition is based on brain stem death, rather than whole brain death, and this is supported by English common law authority. See Academy of Medical Royal Colleges, *A Code of Practice for the Diagnosis and Confirmation of Death* (AMRC, 2008). Relevant English common law authority includes the joined cases of *R v Malcherek; R v Steel* [1981] 2 All ER 422; *Re A* [1992] 3 Med LR 303; *Airedale NHS Trust v Bland* [1993] AC 789.

77   Truog and Miller, above n 70.

78   Ian Kerridge et al., *Ethics and Law for the Health Professions*, 4th edn (Federation Press, 2013) 760–1.

should be given to end-of-life care and whether there should be withdrawal of treatment (see Chapter 15 for further details). It is only after a decision has been taken in this regard by the patient or the patient's family/guardians that any discussion should take place regarding organ and tissue donation.[79]

Donation after circulatory death

Where deceased organ donation takes place, it is usually because it has been determined that the donor has suffered brain death. However, the growing gap between supply and demand has led to organs and tissue now being transplanted from individuals via what is known as donation after circulatory death (DCD).[80] In the 2014–15 period there was a 22 per cent increase in organ and tissue donation via the DCD pathway in Australia, with an overall 41 per cent increase in the 2009–15 period.[81] The use of DCD as a pathway for organ and tissue donation usually takes place where the decision has been taken by families to withdraw treatment in intensive care for their severely brain injured, but not yet brain dead, family member.[82] The complex ethical, legal and medical issues raised by DCD led the OTA to develop the National Protocol for DCD. It also has responsibility for the implementation and application of DCD practices across Australia.[83] The NSW government has also recently published its own DCD guidelines.[84]

The internationally accepted protocol for the DCD pathway is known as the Maastricht criteria. Although there are a number of different criteria, Australia only currently accepts the following as suitable for DCD:[85]

- Category 3: withdrawal of treatment in ICU – known and limited warm ischaemic time (WIT)[86] – 'controlled';
- Category 4: cardiac arrest following formal determination of brain death but before planned organ procurement – known and potentially limited WIT – 'uncontrolled'.

In determining death for the purposes of DCD, the ANZICS Statement recommends that organ and tissue procurement only take place when all of the following features are present: immobility, apnoea, absent skin perfusion and absence of heart activity for a minimum of two minutes.[87] The National DCD Protocol adopts the ANZICS recommendation and

---

79   ANZICS, above n 32, para 3.9.5; NHRMC, above n 51, para 3.2; NHRMC, above n 5, para 2.2.6.
80   Note that the term 'donation after circulatory death' is used here rather than 'donation after cardiac death', as it is consistent with international standards, is more clinically accurate and is in line with the legislative language used in Australia regarding the definition of death:, see NSW Government, Ministry of Health, *Organ Donation After Circulatory Death: NSW Guidelines* (11 June 2014) Doc No: GL2014_008, 1.
81   OTA, above n 13.
82   ANZICS, above n 32, para 5.6.1.
83   OTA, *National Protocol for Donation After Cardiac Death* <www.donatelife.gov.au/national-protocol-donation-and-cardiac-death> [OTA, National Protocol for DCD].
84   Ministry of Health, above n 80.
85   ANZICS, above n 32, para 5.5.
86   Warm Ischaemic Time (WIT) refers to the time an organ or tissue remains at body temperature after its blood supply has been reduced or cut off but before it is cooled or reconnected to a blood supply.
87   ANZICS, above n 32, para 5.5. For an overview of how DCD is approached in different jurisdictions, see Anne Laure Dalle Ave et al., 'An Analysis of Heart Donation After Circulatory Determination of Death' (2016) 42(5) *Journal of Medical Ethics* 312–7.

adds that the period of observation of absent heart activity should be for a minimum of two minutes and not more than five minutes.[88] Recently published NHMRC Guidelines state that 'clinical interventions that support and maintain organ viability before death are ethically supportable, providing there is no legal impediment and they comply with Clinical Guidelines developed by TSANZ'.[89]

Notwithstanding national and international DCD guidance, and its increasing use for the purposes of facilitating organ and tissue transplantation in Australia, concerns continue to be raised about its ethical and legal probity. For example, the recent procurement of hearts for transplantation through DCD in NSW led some commentators to argue that the circumstances in which such procurement had taken place were not in accordance with current Australian law.[90] Others have argued to the contrary, particularly in light of specific NSW guidelines which deal with the issue.[91] Concerns in this regard have mainly revolved around whether the concept of irreversibility of cessation of circulation has been established in accordance with requirements under the relevant state and territory legislation for the diagnosis of death (see above).[92]

Coronial jurisdiction

There are certain circumstances in which deaths must be reported to the Coroner for further investigation. There is some variation across state/territory jurisdictions as to what constitutes a 'reportable death',[93] but in all such circumstances, it is necessary to obtain the Coroner's consent before organ and tissue donation from deceased donors for transplantation purposes

---

88   OTA, above n 83, para 3.8.
89   NHMRC, above n 5, para 1.2.
90   James Tibballs and Neera Bhatia, 'Transplantation of the Heart After Circulatory Death of the Donor: Time for a Change in the Law?' (2015) 203(6) *Medical Journal of Australia* 268; cf Craig Butt, 'Surgeons Hit Back at Claims Heart Transplants are Against the Law', *Sydney Morning Herald*, 22 September 2015.
91   See Butt, above n 90. See also Ministry of Health, above n 80, para 2.3.8, which deals specifically with the use of DCD hearts for transplantation. It states that circulation is considered to have irreversibly stopped when there is 'terminal pathology within the patient's body that causes the heart and circulation to cease ... Although it may be technically possible to restore the arrested circulation, it should not and therefore must not be restored in this context' ... [Where circulation has been absent for two minutes, then it is considered to have] 'irreversibly stopped and death is then certified ... There are no legal barriers to using hearts removed from DCD donors for transplantation provided death of the patient is declared consistent with the law in NSW.' This is also supported by ANZICS, Circulatory Death Determination, 23 October 2015 <www.anzics.com.au/Pages/DaOD.aspx>.
92   The OTA's National Protocol for DCD, above n 83, para 3.8, states that 'irreversible' means that 'sufficient time has elapsed to eliminate the possibility of auto-resuscitation so that, in the absence of resuscitative attempts, cessation is irreversible; and resuscitative attempts are either contraindicated on medical grounds, given that it has been determined that meaningful recovery of the patient is unlikely, or the patient ... has decided that resuscitative measures would be unduly burdensome'.
93   These 'reportable deaths' are described in all jurisdictions, and typically include deaths that are unexpected, unnatural or violent or have resulted from an accident, fire or injury; where cause of death is unknown; where death has occurred during or after a medical procedure; while the person was in custody; or where cause of death is unknown. See *Coroners Act 1997* (ACT) s 77; *Coroners Act* (NT) s 12(3); *Coroners Act 2003* (Qld) s 7; *Coroners Act 2003* (SA) s 28; *Coroners Act 1995* (Tas) s 19; *Coroners Act 2008* (Vic) ss 10–13; *Coroners Act 1996* (WA) s 17.

can proceed. Organ donation via the DCD pathway is very time-sensitive, given the need to keep cold ischaemic time to a minimum. In the NSW DCD guidelines, it is recognised that timely referral and liaison with the Coroner is vital where a death is likely to be a 'reportable death'.[94] This will assist in determining whether the Coroner's consent will be forthcoming and therefore whether organ and tissue donation is likely to proceed. [95]

Allocation of organs for transplantation from deceased donors

Australia has enjoyed considerable success with its organ and tissue transplantation program. It has one of the highest organ transplantation success rates in the world, with a five-year survival rate of 80 per cent for most organs.[96] In 2015, 1483 individuals received an organ transplant from deceased donors, which represents a 58 per cent increase in the 2009–15 period.[97] Given that approximately 1500 people are on waiting lists for organs at any given time, a key policy question is how best to determine the criteria for eligibility and allocation of organs for transplantation. Determining such criteria must necessarily balance the needs of individuals who need organs and would benefit most from them with 'responsible stewardship' of what is a valuable but scarce resource on behalf of the community as a whole.[98] There is a need to ensure that there is a principled approach to applying such criteria that is consistent with ethical and rights-based norms and in line with best international scientific and clinical practice.

For many years, the TSANZ was responsible for publishing guidelines (Consensus Statements) that provided nationally uniform eligibility criteria to ensure that the process of listing potential recipients for organ transplantation was equitable and transparent. The TSANZ also previously provided nationally uniform allocation protocols to ensure consistency in organ allocation. Following a request from the OTA and the TSANZ, the NHMRC has now adopted Ethical Guidelines for Organ Transplantation from Deceased Donors (Guidelines). These Guidelines have now replaced the TSANZ Consensus Statement and are accompanied by Clinical Guidelines developed by TSANZ.[99] Together, they now comprise the overarching ethical and clinical framework for allocation criteria for the transplantation of organs from deceased donors in Australia.[100]

Organ suitability criteria

The Guidelines note that various terms have been used to describe different types and levels of quality of organs which may be assessed as suitable for transplantation. Such terms include 'standard criteria organs', 'extended criteria (or high-risk) organs', 'marginal

---

94   For further details on 'reportable deaths', see Chapter 8.
95   Ministry of Health, above n 80, paras 2.3.2 and 2.3.4.
96   NHMRC, above n 5, v.
97   OTA, above n 13, 8.
98   NHMRC, above n 5, v.
99   TSANZ, *Clinical Guidelines for Organ Transplantation from Deceased Donors* <www.tsanz.com.au/organallocationguidelines>.
100   NHMRC, above n 5, v.

donors' and 'alternative listing'. The decision was taken not to use such terminology in the Guidelines on the grounds that their use implies that there are 'distinct categories', rather than acknowledging that there is a 'spectrum' of considerations that need to be taken into account in determining organ suitability for a particular recipient. The Guidelines note that such terminology can 'be misleading and do[es] not reflect the careful consideration of balance between benefit and risk when organs are considered for allocation and transplantation'.[101] Instead, the Guidelines underline the importance of considering organ suitability on a 'case-by-case basis', taking account of the 'benefits and risks associated with the quality of the organ and the circumstances of the individual'.[102] Emphasis is also placed on conducting discussions with potential recipients about likely organ suitability well ahead of the time when an offer of an organ may be made.[103]

Human rights, ethical principles and values

The Guidelines identify key ethical principles and values underpinning the allocation of organs for transplantation from deceased donors in Australia, which include respect, justice, equity, solidarity, reciprocity, altruism, care and wellbeing, welfare and security, transparency, effectiveness and efficiency. In addition, they also emphasise the importance of taking account of relevant human rights norms, such as the right of individuals to access adequate and affordable healthcare. How and why such principles, values and rights should be taken account of in determining eligibility and allocation criteria for transplantation are elaborated upon in some detail in the Guidelines.[104]

Eligibility and allocation criteria

Eligibility and allocation criteria for organs for transplantation from deceased donors should take account of the ethical principles, values and rights outlined above. Decisions regarding eligibility must exclude unreasonable and unlawful discrimination against potential recipients on 'medically irrelevant grounds'. Such grounds include race, cultural and religious belief, gender, relationship status, sexual preference, social or other status, disability or age, past lifestyle, capacity to pay for treatment, location of residence, previous refusal of an offer of an organ for transplantation, and refusal to participate in research.[105] However, there are some factors which will need to be taken into account, including the relative severity of illness and disability of potential recipients; urgency of medical need (subject to clinical peer review and oversight); length of time waiting for a transplant; risks of transplantation weighed against the potential benefits to the recipient; closeness of tissue-matching and organ quality; and whether such recipients are likely to adhere to the post-transplant treatment regime.[106]

At times, where the donor and recipient are located may also be relevant in determining allocation. This is because there is a need to limit cold ischaemic time between organ donation and transplant. As a result, it is often the case that organs are donated and transplanted

---

101   Ibid para 1.3.
102   Ibid.
103   Ibid.
104   Ibid paras 2.1, 2.2.1–2.2.6.
105   Ibid para 3.2.1; see also para 2.2.2.
106   Ibid paras 3.2.1, 3.2.2.

in the same state or territory. If there is no suitable match, however, the organ may be offered to transplant units in other states/territories and NZ on the basis of a rotation system designed to promote equity. It is also made clear that the allocation criteria should be transparent and that potential recipients have the right to know whether or not they are considered suitable candidates for transplant and, if not, what the basis for determining ineligibility was.[107]

In terms of the practicalities of organ allocation, it is important to note that the kidney allocation process differs from the one used for other organs. The Australian Red Cross Blood Service (ARCBS) is currently responsible for allocating kidneys via the National Organ Matching Service (NOMS).[108] Information about all other organs that become available is sent directly to transplant units through the Electronic Donor Record (EDR).[109] The OTA is now developing the Australian Organ Matching Service (AOMS), which will employ best practice algorithms to allow for optimal matching of organ recipients on a national basis.[110]

Living organ donation

Until the late 1980s, living donor organ donation and transplantation was essentially confined to kidneys, but this situation has now changed. Since the 1990s, successful segmental liver and partial lobe transplants from living donors have been performed in a range of countries.[111] As a result of medical and scientific advances, organ donation by living donors has now become the preferred clinical option for transplantation, particularly in the case of kidneys. Currently, a range of both regenerative and non-regenerative tissue – such as kidneys, liver lobe/portion, lung lobe, intestinal portions, pancreas islets, and bone marrow – may be donated by living donors.[112] In Australia, kidney donors comprise the vast majority of living organ donors. Recently published data showed that there were 267 living donor kidney transplants performed in 2014, which represented 29 per cent of all transplants performed. The proportion of genetically unrelated donors was 49 per cent, with 41 per cent of living unrelated donors being spouses or partners. Overall, living donor transplants have been falling as a result as a proportion of all transplants since 2009.[113]

---

107   Ibid para 3.2.1.
108   NOMS is a computer program which determines the allocation of kidneys from a deceased donor
         to patients on the waiting list and is administered by the ARCBS. Further details regarding allocation
         criteria for kidneys are provided in NHMRC, above n 5, para 1.4.
109   The Electronic Donor Record (EDR) was established in 2014. The EDR is a clinical information
         system used by donation specialists, providing real-time access to essential information about organ
         donors and organ retrieval processes:, see Senator the Honourable Fiona Nash, 'Electronic Donor
         Record Enhances Australian Organ and Tissue Donation Processes', 11 July 2014 <www.health.gov
         .au/internet/ministers/publishing.nsf/Content/health-mediarel-yr2014-nash038.htm>.
110   OTA, above n 17, 27. The Framework provides a system of assessment and controls that must be
         completed before products can be marketed.
111   Mark L Barr et al., 'Living Donor Lobar Lung Transplantation: Current Status and Future Directions'
         (2005) 37(9) *Transplant Proceedings* 3983; Alice Tung Wan Song et al., 'Liver Transplantation: Fifty
         Years of Experience' (2014) 20(18) *World Journal of Gastroenterology* 5363.
112   Bone marrow donation and transplantation are well established in Australia, involving donation by
         both related and unrelated living donors. The Australian Bone Marrow Donor Registry (ABMDR),
         which works in close collaboration with the ARCBS, maintains a national register of potential bone
         marrow donors: see ABDMR Purpose <www.abmdr.org.au/abmdr2/page/abmdr-purpose>.
113   ANZDATA Registry, *38th Annual Report 2016, Kidney Donors*, Ch 9, <www.anzdata.org.au/v1/
         report_2015.html>.

The available evidence shows that recipients who receive organs, such as kidneys, from living donors are usually healthier post-transplant surgery than would be the case if the organ was received as a result of deceased organ donation. In addition, tissue compatibility is usually closer. As a result, there tends to be a reduction in the need for immunosuppression therapy to prevent rejection of the organ by the recipient. Better results in terms of longer life expectancy and lower mortality rates have been achieved over time for recipients of organs from living donors.[114] Medical follow-up of recipients has also shown that the pattern of long-term complications for recipients is changing. Although overall rates of rejection, infection and organ loss are decreasing, cardiovascular disease and cancer have now emerged as some of the more significant problems facing recipients. In the case of Indigenous Australians, worse long-term outcomes have also been reported, which has been attributed to higher rates of co-morbidity with other diseases. This is combined with the fact that many reside in remote locations, which makes medical follow-up and monitoring more difficult.[115]

For living organ donors, there may be some significant short-term risks from the surgery to remove a kidney. However, a large body of retrospective evidence has suggested that adverse health consequences for kidney donors are minimal.[116] It is nevertheless important to take account of more recently published data that has questioned whether such donors do in fact face a higher risk of end-stage renal disease. Clearly, a strengthening of the evidence base on this issue, involving carefully designed prospective studies which engage in long-term follow-up of living organ donors, would be welcomed.[117]

Ethical issues

Living organ donation raises a number of ethical concerns. Developing an ethically acceptable framework which facilitates this form of donation has presented a significant challenge in policy terms. There may also be different ethical concerns depending on whether the donation is directed to a relative or friend (most common); or is a non-directed donation to a recipient who is unknown to the donor.[118] Clearly, there is also a need to consider the respective interests of the donor and recipient in circumstances where the donor is undergoing a medical procedure which has no therapeutic benefit for them.[119]

As discussed in Chapter 2, various bioethical perspectives can be employed to consider the ethical conundrums raised by these issues. Within the principlist ethical framework this would involve respecting the autonomy of the individual to consent to such a procedure on the one hand, but it could be said to infringe upon the 'do no harm' principle on the other hand. A consequentialist perspective would tend to favour living organ donation,

---

114   OTA, above n 13, 2.
115   NHMRC, *Organ and Tissue Donation by Living Donors: Guidelines for Ethical Practice for Health Professionals* (2007) para 1.3, 12. For an overview of the Indigenous health issues, see Chapters 4 and 23.
116   Ibid paras 1.3, 10.
117   Geir Mjoen et al., 'Long-term Risks for Kidney Donors' (2014) 86(1) *Kidney International* 162; cf Hassan N Ibrahim et al., 'Long-Term Consequences of Kidney Donation' (2009) 360 *New England Journal of Medicine* 459.
118   NHMRC, above n 115, 1.
119   Ibid.

especially in the case of kidneys, where outcomes are extremely good. This could be said to outweigh the minor risks faced by living donors. In contrast, a deontological perspective would identify concerns about the individual human body and its parts being used as a means to an end.[120]

Added to this would be concerns about whether the dignity of the individual had been infringed, particularly in circumstances where there is trade, commerce or trafficking involved in living organ donation.[121] This would contravene the ethical principle against the commodification of the body, which is embedded in a number of prominent international ethical and legal instruments. Although these instruments have not specifically been incorporated into Australian domestic law, they are considered important in terms of establishing norms or principles in the area. Key instruments include the WHO Guiding Principles on Organ Donation and Transplantation (WHO Guiding Principles);[122] the Council of Europe's Convention on Human Rights and Biomedicine,[123] together with the Additional Protocol on the Transplantation of Organs and Tissue of Human Origin (Additional Protocol).[124] Important instruments dealing with organ trafficking include the Istanbul Declaration on Organ Trafficking and Transplant Tourism[125] and the Council of Europe's Convention Against Trafficking in Human Organs.[126]

Australian position

The current NHMRC ethical guidance on living organ donation and transplantation mirrors much of the international position. The key principles that underpin the guidelines include the following. First, organ and tissue donation by living donors is an act of altruism and human solidarity. Second, there is a need to show respect for all those involved in living organ donation, which involves ensuring that fully informed consent is obtained in circumstances that are free from coercion, undue emotional pressure or the use of material incentives. Third, there should be only minimal risks to donors in terms of both short- and long-term harm, in addition to there being a high likelihood of a successful transplant outcome for the recipient. Fourth, the risks must be minimal for those who lack capacity. There should be no alternative donors available, and the recipient must be a close relative of the donor. An independent judgment needs to be made that the donation is in the overall best interests of the potential donor. Finally, conflicts of interest should be minimised through the use of independent and separate assessment and advocacy for potential donors.[127]

---

120   See Chapter 2 for an overview of these differing ethical perspectives.
121   For an examination of the concept of human dignity in bioethics and law, see Derek Beyleveld and Roger Brownsword, *Human Dignity in Bioethics and Biolaw* (OUP, 2001).
122   <www.who.int/transplantation/en>.
123   *Convention for the Protection of Human Rights and Dignity of the Human Being with regard to the Application of Biology and Medicine: Convention on Human Rights and Biomedicine*, ETS No. 164 – Oviedo, 4.IV.1997.
124   *Additional Protocol to the Convention on Human Rights and Biomedicine concerning concerning Transplantation of Organs and Tissue of Human Origin*, CETS No. 186 – Strasbourg 24.I.2002.
125   <www.declarationofistanbul.org>. For an overview of issues raised by organ trafficking, see Nancy Scheper-Hughes, 'Human Trafficking in "Fresh Organs" for Illicit Transplants: A Protected Crime' in Molly Dragiewicz (ed.), *Global Human Trafficking: Critical Issues and Context* (Routledge, 2015) 76–90.
126   <www.coe.int/en/web/conventions/full-list/-/conventions/treaty/216>.
127   NHMRC, above n 115, 6.

Strategies to increase living organ donation

Financial payment and removal of financial disincentives

As mentioned previously in this chapter, whether or not there should be direct financial payment and/or (in)direct financial incentives for donating organs has been the subject of ongoing debate in the academic and policy literature. In the case of living organ donation, those in favour of financial payments have focused on individual donor autonomy and the right to decide to donate in circumstances where no harm is caused to another, provided that informed consent is given. It has also been argued that many individuals are happy to become living organ donors and it should therefore be a matter for them how they want to use the monies received from the donation. In such circumstances, it is not clear that financial payments for organs are against the interests of donors. It has also been suggested that objections to payment for organs from living donors are Western-centric; such payments may not be objectionable in other cultures. At a broader level, it has been argued that there are significant benefits to using financial payments to encourage higher rates of living organ donation and transplantation, as they are likely to result in significant cost savings for national health systems in the long term.[128]

The arguments against the use of financial payments or incentives in the case of deceased organ donation have been discussed earlier in this chapter. Many also apply in the case of living organ donation. The main concerns centre on the need to avoid commodification of the body, and the problem of donor exploitation, particularly where donors reside in less developed countries and are supplying organs (for example, kidneys) to more wealthy recipients in developed countries. Such exploitation is said to be exacerbated by the lack of any medical follow-up post-transplant and any monitoring of donors' long-term health. The lack of donor protection has been raised as a matter of particular concern in the case of Iran, which is 'one of the few countries in the world which operates a compensated and regulated living unrelated donor renal transplant program'.[129] In addition, establishing a market for living organ donation through direct financial payments to donors would mean that governments would be less likely to provide proper funding and infrastructure for programs to encourage deceased organ donation, or dialysis programs for patients with kidney disease.[130]

Notwithstanding such debates, direct financial payment to living organ donors has not attracted public or political support in Australia. In terms of ethical acceptability, it has been suggested that the focus should be on reimbursement for financial costs associated with becoming a living donor, although it is recognised that there may be a fine line between reimbursement and direct financial payment for organs, particularly where a potential donor

---

128   See Janet Radcliffe Richards et al., 'The Case for Allowing Kidney Sales' (1998) 351 *The Lancet* 1950; Erin and Harris, above n 39; James S Taylor, 'Autonomy and Organ Sales, Revisited' (2009) 34 *Journal of Medicine and Philosophy* 632.

129   Ghods and Savaj, above n 40, 1137; Dianne Tober, 'Kidneys and Controversies in the Islamic Republic of Iran: The Case of Organ Sale' (2007) 13(3) *Body & Society* 151, 165–6.

130   See Samuel J Kerstein, 'Kantian Condemnation of Commerce in Organs' (2009) 19 *Kennedy Institute of Ethics Journal* 147; Kate Greasley, 'A Legal Market in Organs: The Problem of Exploitation' (2014) 40 *Journal of Medical Ethics* 51; Julian Koplin, 'Assessing the Likely Harms to Kidney Vendors in Regulated Organ Markets' (2014) 14(10) *American Journal of Bioethics* 7.

is unemployed.[131] Nevertheless, it has been recognised that there is a need to remove financial disincentives to becoming a living organ donor, in particular a kidney donor. Donors may face particular financial hardship or difficulties as a result of their decision to donate. It may involve significant time off work in preparation for the donation, as well as post-operative recovery and medical follow-up.[132] In recognition of such difficulties, the Australian government has established the Supporting Leave for Living Organ Donors Programme (SLLODP). At the present time, it is funded until 2017 and is administered by the Department of Health. SLLODP provides reimbursement to employers for payments made or credits given in relation to employees who wish to take leave for kidney or partial liver lobe donation, which includes a convalescence period for recovery from surgery. The amount that is reimbursed is up to 'a maximum of nine weeks at the national minimum wage rate, based on a 38 hour week'.[133]

Paired kidney exchange programs

The chronic shortage of kidneys available to treat end-stage kidney disease (ESKD) has led to some living donors agreeing to participate in what is known as paired or pooled living kidney donor exchange programs. This involves exchanging donor kidneys, enabling two incompatible recipients to receive a kidney which is more compatible with their blood or tissue type.[134] Although ethical concerns have been raised about whether the decision to donate has been made under coercion or as a result of manipulation, and whether donors and recipients have been fully informed about and understand the risks and benefits associated with this type of organ donation,[135] the persisting gap between supply and demand for kidneys has led to such programs being established in several countries. In Australia, the Australian Paired Kidney Exchange (AKX) program facilitates these types of transplants. In 2015, 45 Australians received a live kidney transplant through AKX; a total of 154 KPD transplants have been performed since 2010.[136]

Legal position

In general terms, the common law position is that no living person is capable of giving consent to being killed under the common law. Therefore, the donation of a heart from a living person is precluded.[137] In addition, it has been held that there are limits to what living persons can do with their bodies without attracting criminal sanction.[138] In the early days of transplantation medicine, it was perhaps conceivable that the courts would have hesitated

---

131   NHMRC, above n 115, 54.
132   OTA, *Living Donation* <www.donatelife.gov.au/donor-family-support/living-donors>.
133   Australian Government, Department of Health, *Leave for Living Organ Donors* <www.health.gov.au/internet/main/publishing.nsf/content/leave-for-living-organ-donors>.
134   Sommer Gentry et al., 'Kidney Paired Donation: Fundamentals, Limitations and Expansions' (2011) 57(1) *American Journal of Kidney Diseases* 144.
135   Linda Wright et al., 'Ethical Guidelines for the Evaluation of Living Organ Donors' (2004) 47(6) *Canadian Journal of Surgery* 408, 410–412.
136   OTA, above n 13, 2.
137   *R v Coney* (1882) 8 QBD 534.
138   See, for example, *R v Brown* [1993] 2 All ER 75.

to approve the removal of a healthy organ or tissue from a living donor. Such concerns have now been removed as a result of Australia's HT Acts, which set out the nature and scope of consent that is required and what procedural safeguards must be in place. While current Australian legislation permits adults with capacity to become living organ donors provided consent conditions in the prescribed terms have been met, it has adopted a restrictive approach in the case of children or adults lacking capacity. As we shall see, such an approach may sit uneasily at times with case law on the matter.

Adults with capacity

The legislative requirements for adults with capacity consenting to living organ and tissue donation are set out in the HT Acts. Note that the same definitions of regenerative and non-regenerative tissue apply as would be the case in relation to deceased organ and tissue donation (see above). There is a need to satisfy a number of consent requirements regarding the donation of regenerative and specified non-regenerative tissue by adults with capacity. Although there is some variation among the HT Acts, in general terms the following requirements must be met:

- **Consent to donation of regenerative tissue**: an adult person may give their consent in writing to the removal from their body of specified regenerative tissue (other than blood) for the purpose of the transplantation of the tissue to the body of another living person; or for use for other therapeutic, medical or scientific purposes.[139]

- **Consent to donation of non-regenerative tissue**: an adult person may give their consent in writing to the removal from their body, at any time after the expiration of 24 hours from the time at which the consent is given, of specified non-regenerative tissue for the purpose of the transplantation of the tissue to the body of another living person. The time at which such consent is given should be specified in writing.[140]

- **Certificate of consent**: a doctor or (registered) medical practitioner may certify in writing that the consent of the adult person to donate specified regenerative and/or non-regenerative tissue was given in their presence and that an explanation was provided to the person before the consent was given as to the nature and effect of the removal from the body of the person of the tissue specified in the consent. In addition, they must be satisfied that at the time consent was given the person was 18 years of age or was 'not a child', had capacity, and gave the consent freely.[141]

---

139   *Transplantation and Anatomy Act 1978* (ACT) s 8; *Human Tissue Act 1983* (NSW) s 7; *Transplantation and Anatomy Act 1979* (NT) ss 4, 8; *Transplantation and Anatomy Act 1979* (Qld) s 10; *Transplantation and Anatomy Act 1983* (SA) s 9(1); *Human Tissue Act 1985* (Tas) s 7; *Human Tissue Act 1982* (Vic) s 7; *Human Tissue and Transplant Act 1982* (WA) s 8(1).

140   *Transplantation and Anatomy Act 1978* (ACT) s 9; *Human Tissue Act 1983* (NSW) s 8; *Transplantation and Anatomy Act 1979* (NT) s 8; *Transplantation and Anatomy Act 1979* (Qld) s 11; *Transplantation and Anatomy Act 1983* (SA) s 10(1); *Human Tissue Act 1985* (Tas) s 8(1); *Human Tissue Act 1982* (Vic) s 8; *Human Tissue and Transplant Act 1982* (WA) s 9(1).

141   *Transplantation and Anatomy Act 1978* (ACT) s 10; *Human Tissue Act 1983* (NSW) s 9; *Transplantation and Anatomy Act 1979* (NT) s 10(2); *Transplantation and Anatomy Act 1979* (Qld) s 12 [designated officer is used rather than doctor or (registered) medical practitioner]; *Human Tissue Act 1985* (Tas) s 9; *Human Tissue Act 1982* (Vic) s 9. Note that there are no certificate of consent requirements in relation to adults with capacity who donate regenerative and non-regenerative tissue set out in the *Transplantation and Anatomy Act 1983* (SA) or the *Human Tissue and Transplant Act 1982* (WA).

Adults who lack capacity

The legal position as to whether regenerative and/or non-regenerative tissue can be removed from adults who lack capacity is complex and inconsistent across Australia's states and territories. In particular, there is a need to take account of state and territory guardianship legislation, as well as other miscellaneous laws, in order to determine whether it is permissible for such removal to take place and, if so, in what circumstances.[142] See Chapter 10 for a detailed overview of the legal approach taken to adults who lack capacity in relation to authorisation being provided for medical treatment or procedures to take place.

Children

The HT Acts are highly restrictive with regard to children becoming living organ and tissue donors. In relation to the extent of the legal prohibition, a distinction needs to be drawn between non-regenerative and regenerative tissue. Has there is some variation in the HT Acts. Key aspects are highlighted in summary form below:

- **Non-regenerative tissue**: there is a prohibition on children becoming living organ and tissue donors in the case of non-regenerative tissue (with the exception of the ACT in specified circumstances).[143]

- **Regenerative tissue**: a parent of a child may give consent in writing to the removal from the body of the child of specified regenerative tissue for the purpose of transplantation of

---

142   *Guardianship and Management of Property Act 1991* (ACT) ss 69, 70 and *Transplantation and Anatomy Act 1978* (ACT) s 16A; *Guardianship Act 1987* (NSW) Part 5; *Advance Personal Planning Act 2013* (NT) Part 4; *Guardianship and Administration Act 2000* (Qld) s 69; *Consent to Medical Treatment and Palliative Care Act 1995* (SA) s 14A, Part 3A and *Guardianship and Administration Act 1993* (SA) s 3; *Guardianship and Administration Act 1995* (Tas) s 3, Part 6; *Guardianship and Administration Act 1986* (Vic) ss 3, 39; *Guardianship and Administration Act 1990* (WA) ss 3, 110ZD.

143   The removal of non-regenerative tissue from children for the purpose of transplantation is prohibited: see *Transplantation and Anatomy Act 1983* (SA) s 12(a); *Human Tissue Act 1982* (Vic) s 14(2); *Human Tissue and Transplant Act 1982* (WA) s 12(2). There are no legislative provisions dealing with the removal of non-regenerative tissue from children: see *Human Tissue Act 1983* (NSW); *Transplantation and Anatomy Act 1979* (NT); *Transplantation and Anatomy Act 1979* (Qld); *Human Tissue Act 1985* (Tas). In the ACT, a person who is a parent of a child may give their written consent to the removal from the body of the child, at any time after the end of 24 hours from the time when the consent is given, of specified non-regenerative tissue for the purpose of transplantation of the tissue into the body of another member of the family (*Transplantation and Anatomy Act 1978* (ACT) s 14(1)). A doctor needs to certify that they have discussed the removal and its consequences with the parents, as well as with the child, and that their consent was given in the doctor's presence; that the family member recipient was in danger of dying unless the tissue was provided; and the doctor should be satisfied that at the time the consent was given the child understood the nature and effect of the removal and of the transplantation and was in agreement (s 14(3)). Thereafter, the doctor must refer the matter to a specially convened committee for review (ss 9(5), 14(4)). There are also special provisions where only one parent is available to provide consent (s 14(6)).

the tissue to the body of family members (there is some variation as to what constitutes 'family').[144]

- **Medical certificate required**: where donation of specified regenerative tissue by a child is permitted, this can only take place where there is a certificate from a registered medical practitioner that the child was (a) a mature minor and was 'Gillick competent';[145] and (b) consent was obtained from both the parents and the child. The only exception to this may be where the specified regenerative tissue will save the life of a sibling. In that case, it may be possible for both a 'Gillick competent' mature minor and a much younger child or infant to donate such tissue in particular circumstances.[146]

- **Revocation of consent:** a child may revoke any consent given, either orally or in writing.[147]

Case law

The *parens patriae* jurisdiction of states' Supreme Courts has been invoked in order to seek approval for the donation of both regenerative and non-regenerative tissue by an adult who lacks capacity.[148] In the case of *Northern Sydney and Central Coast Area Health Service v CT*,[149] the NSW Supreme Court approved a bone marrow donation by an intellectually disabled adult (CT) to his brother (NT), who was suffering from non-Hodgkin's lymphoma. It was necessary to invoke the *parens patriae* jurisdiction in this case because of the restrictive nature of the guardian's consent powers under the *Guardianship Act 1987* (NSW). As mentioned previously, the position may be different under other guardianship laws in other Australian states and territories.[150]

---

144   *Transplantation and Anatomy Act 1978* (ACT) s 13(1) ['member of the family' and 'relative' are not defined]; *Human Tissue Act 1983* (NSW) s 10 [can transplant regenerative tissue from child into body of sibling or biological, step or adoptive parent]; *Transplantation and Anatomy Act 1979* (Qld) s 12B [can transplant regenerative tissue from child into body of a sibling or parent, where parent is defined quite widely (s 4)]; *Transplantation and Anatomy Act 1983* (SA) s 13(1) [only in prescribed circumstances (s 13(2)], [parent of child includes a guardian of the child (s 5)]; *Human Tissue Act 1985* (Tas) s 12 [parent of child does not include guardian or person standing in loco parentis for child (s 11)]; *Human Tissue Act 1982* (Vic) s 15(1) [parent of child does not include guardian or person standing in loco parentis for child (s 14)]; *Human Tissue and Transplant Act 1982* (WA) s 13 [in specified circumstances]. There are no specific provisions in relation to the donation of regenerative tissue by children in the *Transplantation and Anatomy Act 1979* (NT).

145   See Chapter 9 for further details about what constitutes *Gillick* competence.

146   *Transplantation and Anatomy Act 1978* (ACT) s 13(2); *Human Tissue Act 1983* (NSW) ss 11, 11A; *Transplantation and Anatomy Act 1979* (Qld) ss 12C, 12D, 12E; *Human Tissue Act 1985* (Tas) s 13; *Human Tissue Act 1982* (Vic) ss 15, 16. There are no specific provisions concerning the need for a medical certificate for the donation of regenerative tissue by children under the *Transplantation and Anatomy Act 1979* (NT); *Transplantation and Anatomy Act 1983* (SA); and *Human Tissue and Transplant Act 1982* (WA).

147   *Transplantation and Anatomy Act 1978* (ACT) ss 24, 25(1); *Human Tissue Act 1983* (NSW) ss 16(2), 17 [does not specify whether consent has to be revoked orally or in writing]; *Transplantation and Anatomy Act 1979* (Qld) s 21(1); *Transplantation and Anatomy Act 1983* (SA) s 14; *Human Tissue Act 1985* (Tas) s 22; *Human Tissue Act 1982* (Vic) ss 18(2), 19; *Human Tissue and Transplant Act 1982* (WA) s 14. There are no specific provisions in this regard in the *Transplantation and Anatomy Act 1979* (NT).

148   See Chapter 9 for an overview of the *parens patriae* jurisdiction; see Chapters 9, 10 and 24 for a more detailed discussion about capacity issues in the context of medical treatment.

149   *Northern Sydney and Central Coast Area Health Service v CT* [2005] NSWSC 551.

150   See Chapter 10 for further details regarding Australian state and territory guardianship laws.

Because of the restrictive nature of the HT Acts, applications to approve living donation by children have also been made to the Family Court pursuant to its welfare jurisdiction.[151] An example is the case of *Re GWW and CMW*,[152] which involved an application by parents of a 10-year-old boy to the Family Court to authorise a bone marrow donation by the child to his aunt. Based on evidence submitted to the Court, the child understood the nature of the medical procedure but was not competent to give consent. After reviewing the evidence, the Court held that the bone marrow donation would be in the best interests of the child. This was on the grounds of psychological benefit to the child in providing the donation to his aunt. This outweighed the minimal risks and potential adverse consequences of the procedure.

A further example is the case of *Re Inaya (Special Medical Procedure)*,[153] where an application was made to the Family Court to authorise a bone marrow donation from a 13-month-old child to a 7-month-old cousin who suffered from infantile osteoporosis. The condition was fatal and the bone marrow transplant was the only potential cure. The relevant legislation was section 15(1) of the *Human Tissue Act 1982* (Vic) (Victorian HTA), which prohibits the removal of tissue from a child for donation to anyone bar a sibling or a parent of the child. The Court held that donation by a living child of regenerative tissue was within parental consent powers, as the Act already recognised the parents' right to consent to donations to siblings or parents. Given that the regenerative tissue in question was bone marrow, its removal was also considered to pose minimal risk, and was not serious or irreversible. In short, the legislative prohibition in the Victorian HTA regarding donation of regenerative tissue beyond immediate family members by living children was struck down by the Family Court as being inconsistent with the *Family Law Act 1975* (Cth) (FLA). In effect, the judgment rendered this prohibition void. In the circumstances, it has been argued that this legal prohibition should be either removed or amended to ensure that there is consistency with the FLA. To date, there has been no move on the part of Australian state and territory governments to do so.[154]

Tissue banks

In Australia there are a number of tissue banks that collect and store various types of tissue received from both living and deceased donors for transplantation purposes. Although the Donor Tissue Bank of Victoria (DBTV) operates a major multi-tissue facility, most are single-tissue banks – they only store and process a single tissue, such as eyes, heart valves or bone.[155] Living donors can also donate bone, such as the femoral head, through hip

---

151   Note that the Family Court's powers are derived from Commonwealth legislation. Under *Commonwealth Constitution* s 109, Commonwealth laws can override state laws.

152   (1997) FLC 92-478.

153   (2007) 38 Fam LR 546. Note that when the case came before the Family Court, it was recognised that there was a potential conflict between the relevant provisions of the *Human Tissue Act 1982* (Vic) and the *Commonwealth Constitution* s 109. All state/territory Attorneys-General were notified but none sought to intervene in the case.

154   For an overview of the legal issues, see Shih-Ning Then and Gabrielle Appleby, 'Tissue Transplantation from Children: Difficulties in Navigating the State and Federal Systems' (2010) 33(2) *UNSW Law Journal* 305.

155   For an overview of single tissue banks, see OTA, *Eye and Tissue Banks* <www.donatelife.gov.au/eye-and-tissue-banks>.

replacement surgery.[156] The types of tissue that can be collected from deceased donors include eyes; musculo-skeletal tissue (bone, tendons, cartilage, ligaments); skin (outermost layers only); and cardiac tissue (pulmonary and aortic valves and pericardium).

There is more flexibility in tissue donation from deceased donors than in organ donation, as it is possible to arrange for the removal of tissue up to 24 hours after the donor's death. For example, bone, skin, heart valves and corneas can be donated 12–24 hours following the death of the donor.[157] In addition, tissue can be stored for longer periods of time before transplantation: examples include corneas from donated eyes (up to 30 days) and heart tissue, bone and skin tissue (up to five years).[158]

There is a growing demand for all these types of tissue, as they are supplied to treat patients with a diverse range of medical conditions. Indeed, multi-tissue donation from one deceased donor can benefit between 20 and 30 recipients. The latest published data shows that there has been a 74 per cent increase in tissue donation over the 2012–15 period. In the case of eye donation, for example, there has been a 37 per cent increase in donation by deceased donors in the 2009–15 period and this has facilitated a 45 per cent increase in corneal transplants. In 2015, Australian eye banks were able to meet all requests for eye tissue for transplantation.[159]

It is important to note that the actual process of tissue donation is different from that of organ donation. Where tissue donation from a deceased donor is identified, donor coordinators from either DonateLife or the relevant tissue bank will contact the family of the deceased person by phone to discuss potential tissue donation. If family consent is obtained, details need to be solicited about the deceased donor's medical and social history. Retrieval of relevant tissue from a deceased donor usually takes place in an operating theatre or in a dedicated area set aside in a state/territory mortuary. In the case of a living tissue donor, such as donation of femoral heads as a result of hip replacement surgery, retrieval also takes place in operating theatres. It is currently the case that tissue retrieval from deceased donors only takes place in Australia's major cities, as regional hospitals/mortuaries are not properly equipped to undertake the retrieval procedures.

Legal requirements regarding consent and retrieval of tissue from both living and deceased donors are set out in the HT Acts (see above). Where tissue banks manufacture donated tissue into transplantable grafts, they are required to be licensed under the *Therapeutic Goods Act 1989* (Cth). Under the Act, tissue banks must also satisfy requirements set out under the Australian Regulatory Guidelines for Biologicals (ARGB), which regulate human cell and tissue-based products as distinct therapeutic goods known as 'biologicals'. The ARGB establishes a system of assessment and controls that must be complied with before products, including biologicals, can be included on the Australian Register of Therapeutic Goods (ARTG). It is only once they are on the ARTG that they can then be marketed and supplied in Australia.[160]

---

156   OTA, above n 13, 11.
157   NHMRC, above n 51.
158   OTA, *Tissue Donation Process* <www.donatelife.gov.au/tissue-donation-process>.
159   OTA, above n 13, 10–11.
160   Australian Government, Department of Health and Ageing, Therapeutic Goods Administration, *Australian Regulatory Guidelines for Biologicals* (ARGB) <www.tga.gov.au/publication/australian-regulatory-guidelines-biologicals-argb>.

It is recognised that there is a need for reform of the donor tissue bank sector in Australia.[161] There is currently no uniform national approach in the sector, which has resulted in a range of processes and models which cover funding, administration, donor selection, consent, data management, and retrieval and distribution systems being adopted. Variation in state and territory legislative requirements for tissue donation and the lack of information sharing between tissue banks have also adversely impacted upon equity of access and the development of a uniform national approach.[162] How best to reform the sector is currently being considered by the OTA, with a view to bringing the matter before the Council of Australian Governments' Health Council (CHC). It is hoped that a decision can then be made at a national level on the future structure and sustainability of the sector.[163]

Conclusion

This chapter has examined the key institutional, ethical and legal issues that arise in the context of both deceased and living organ and tissue donation and transplantation. There are a range of agencies, organisations, professional and lay stakeholder groups which contribute to policy-making in the area at state/territory and Commonwealth levels, which in turn has contributed to the development of detailed ethical and professional guidance on key aspects of organ and tissue donation and transplantation. Such guidance must be read in conjunction with an established legal framework which sets out requirements that deal with obtaining consent, undertaking retrieval, the diagnosis of death, the scope of coronial jurisdiction and procedural safeguards. While there is a good degree of commonality regarding such requirements across Australian state/territory jurisdictions, there are also important differences.

While the national reform agenda has clearly resulted in an increase in the rate of deceased organ and tissue donation, and has facilitated better state-federal co-ordination, there is still much that needs to be done with regard to institutional and legal reform, as well as in providing appropriate support for health professionals, families, donors and recipients. Maintaining an ethically principled approach to the design and implementation of such reform will be vital to ensuring the success of the reform program in addressing the persisting gap between supply and demand for organs and tissue in Australia.

---

161   See Parliament of Victoria, above n 12, Ch 5; OTA, above n 155.
162   OTA, *Report on the Options for More Effective Eye and Tissue Retrieval, Processing and Storage* (July 2011) <www.donatelife.gov.au/sites/default/files/etwgreport.pdf>; Ernst & Young Report, above n 18, para 5.11.1.
163   OTA, above n 17, Objectives 3.6, 24.

18

PROPERTY AND HUMAN TISSUE

Anne-Maree Farrell

Introduction

As a result of advances in scientific research and biotechnology, there is increasing demand for human tissue for therapeutic and research purposes. The changing dynamics of supply and demand have contributed to lively academic and policy debates about the relationship between property and human tissue, which engage with broader issues around value, (self-) ownership and control over our bodies.[1] Key questions that have arisen in such debates include: should individuals have property rights in their own tissue? Conversely, should such rights only be enjoyed by third parties, such as researchers, clinicians or companies, where they make use of such tissue for the purposes of research and/or commercialisation activities? What are the advantages and disadvantages of a property-based approach to human tissue?

The aim of this chapter is to examine important legal developments that have taken place in relation to recognising (some) property rights in human tissue, as well as to consider what this might mean in terms of addressing these key questions. The chapter begins with a brief overview of key terms and principles before going on to explore how these have been applied in case law in Australia, England and the US. The advantages and disadvantages of a property-based approach to human tissue are also examined and the legislative position in Australia is briefly reviewed.

Key terms

There are a number of key terms in property law which are relevant in terms of understanding the relationship between property and human tissue. The idea of property is multifaceted. In law, it is used to describe types of rights, as well as rights in relation to things. As a result, property has been described as a 'bundle of rights' involving legal, equitable or even beneficial rights. Examples include the right to use or enjoy property, the right to exclude others and the right to sell or give away things.[2] Such rights may also take on different forms depending on what type of property is involved, and legislative frameworks may affect different types of property. It is also important to be aware that property rights are not frozen and may change over time, a case in point being property rights involving human tissue.

There are different categories of property. Personal property refers to items which are subject to the control of a person, whereas real property covers land and anything attached to the land under common law annexation rules. Intellectual property deals with the right to reproduce the expression of an idea, or an invention or process that comes from the mind or intellect of the person who produced it. Possession and ownership are different, and it is important to distinguish between the two. Possession involves an intent to control an item, plus physical control,[3] whereas ownership, as noted, should be viewed as a bundle of rights, rather than just a single right.[4] For present purposes, there is also a need to be familiar with the term 'bailment', as it arises in recent case law involving posthumous reproduction,

---

1   Muireann Quigley, 'Property and the Body: Applying Honoré' (2007) 33(11) *Journal of Medical Ethics* 631.

2   For an overview of 'bundle of rights' theory, see Anthony Honoré, 'Ownership' in *Making Law Bind: Essays Legal and Philosophical* (Clarendon Press, 1987), originally published in Anthony G Guest (ed.), *Oxford Essays in Jurisprudence* (OUP, 1961).

3   See generally *Powell v McFarlane* (1979) 38 P & CR 452.

4   See Honoré, above n 2.

which is examined later in this chapter. Bailment recognises that an owner can divest themselves of possession of goods, but still retain ownership of them. Where this occurs, the owner is the bailor and the person who currently possesses the goods is the bailee.

Other key terms include 'alienability' and 'abandonment'. Property rights can be alienable in the sense that they can be the subject of transfer to others:

> if a hospital had property rights in a [tissue] sample, it could transfer them to a pharmaceutical company for a fee. That company would then have the right to use the samples to produce a product and would be entitled to any income that was generated by this activity.[5]

In contrast, the principle of abandonment under common law holds that a person who owns personal property can relinquish all rights to its control and a person who finds abandoned property may claim it. Where the principle applies, it extinguishes any property interest that would otherwise operate. Examples of human tissue that could be said to have been abandoned include cut hair, amputated limbs and tissue excised during surgery. Where scientific researchers use such tissue to later develop a new diagnostic test or cell line, for example, they could argue that they now have a proprietary interest in such tissue, given that it has been abandoned by the source or originator of the tissue.[6]

Where property rights have been infringed, three causes of action may arise under the law of torts: trespass, conversion and detinue. Trespass to goods protects against any unauthorised interference with the possession of goods, provided that the person had actual possession at the time of the interference.[7] Conversion involves a serious interference with a person's goods or assuming the rights of an owner of goods, provided there is a right to immediate possession on the part of the person alleging such interference.[8] A person may sue in detinue where there has been wrongful detention of goods.[9]

Having identified key terms which are relevant for understanding the relationship between property and human tissue, we now turn to examining a number of key legal principles that have developed over time in the area, drawing on examples from Australian, English and US case law.

No property in the human body

Traditionally, it was considered that there could be no property interest in the human body, whether living or dead.[10] There were a number of historical factors that led to the development of this principle. Christian religious traditions involving the human body played an

---

5   Australian Law Reform Commission (ALRC), *Essentially Yours: The Protection of Human Genetic Information in Australia*, Report 96, (2003) para 20.18.

6   For a critique which challenges the idea that human tissue taken from the body can be 'abandoned', see Imogen Goold, 'Abandonment and Human Tissue' in Imogen Goold et al. (eds), *Persons Parts and Property: How Should We Regulate Tissue in the 21st Century* (Hart, 2014) 125–55.

7   See *Bailiffs of Dunwich v Sterry* (1831) 109 ER 995; *Tharpe v Stallwood* (1843) 5 Man and G 760; *Barker v Furlong* (1891) 2 Ch 172.

8   See *Penfolds Wines Pty Ltd v Elliott* (1946) 74 CLR 204; *Healing (Sales) Pty Ltd v Inglis Electrix* (1968) 121 CLR 584.

9   See *Lloyd v Osborne* (1899) 15 WN (NSW) 267.

10   Shawn Harmon and Graeme Laurie, '*Yearworth v North Bristol NHS Trust*: Property, Principles, Precedents and Paradigms' (2010) 69(3) *Cambridge Law Journal* 476, 480.

important role and common law courts considered that they had no jurisdiction over a dead body; instead, it was considered a matter for the ecclesiastical courts.[11] The poor treatment and use of human corpses, as well as the nefarious activities of the 'body snatchers' who secretly removed corpses from burial sites to supply the burgeoning demand for bodies for medical dissection in the UK,[12] were also influential factors.

In relation to the living body, it is clear that a person cannot own another person and is prohibited from buying or selling another: this would amount to slavery, which is illegal.[13] It has also been argued that unauthorised interference with a living body infringes a personal, rather than a proprietary, right.[14] Over time, this legal prohibition has been extended to cover separated human body parts and tissue, although the justification for this extension has been the subject of lively academic debate.[15] Nevertheless, the position in Australia and other common law jurisdictions is that there is no property in a whole human body, nor in separated human body parts or tissue, except in specified circumstances such as what is known as the 'work/skill exception', which is discussed in the next section.[16]

Work/skill exception

One of the key issues that courts have had to confront in this area is what kind of property rights, if any, can be acquired in the human body, its parts and tissue. One of the earlier cases in which this was considered was *Doodeward v Spence*, which was heard before the High Court.[17] The facts of this case involved a doctor who had preserved and kept a two-headed child in a bottle, following its stillbirth. Subsequent to the doctor's death, the bottle and its contents came into Doodeward's possession, who then made it a public exhibit. It was seen by Spence, a policeman, who subsequently seized the exhibit. Doodeward demanded its return, but all that was returned to him was the bottle in which the child had been preserved. Doodeward then successfully sued in detinue for the return of the child. The leading judgment was delivered by Chief Justice Griffith, who stated that:

> when a person has by the lawful exercise of work or skill so dealt with a human body or part of a human body in his lawful possession that it has acquired some attributes differentiating it from a mere corpse awaiting burial, he acquires a right to retain possession of it, at least as against any person not entitled to have it delivered to him for the purpose of burial …

This statement has since come to be known as the work/skill exception (or *Doodeward* exception). It identifies the circumstances in which a person may acquire property rights in human tissue in the form of a right to possession through the application of lawful work or skill on such tissue. It is important to note that the person who uses such tissue must have

---

11	*Hayne's case* (1614) 12 Co Rep 113; *Exelby v Handyside* (1749) 2 East PC 652.
12	Harmon and Laurie, above n 10, 480–1.
13	See, for example, *Criminal Code Act 1995* (Cth) Div 270.
14	Paul Matthews, 'Whose Body? People as Property' (1983) 36(1) *Current Legal Problems* 193.
15	For an overview, see Muireann Quigley, 'Property in Human Biomaterials – Separating Persons and Things?' (2012) 32(4) *Oxford Journal of Legal Studies* 659.
16	*Doodeward v Spence* (1908) 6 CLR 406 per Griffiths CJ.
17	Ibid.

the lawful authority to do so and they must apply some work or skill to its preservation. It is only where both such requirements are satisfied that they will have acquired property rights in the tissue.

This exception has subsequently been considered in a number of English and Australian cases. In the English case of *Dobson v North Tyneside Health Authority*,[18] for example, a woman had died of a brain tumour and her brain had been preserved in paraffin following a post-mortem. It was subsequently disposed of by the second defendant. Her mother, as administratrix for the estate, sued in negligence, alleging that there would have been a different medical outcome if her daughter's brain tumour had been diagnosed at an earlier stage. She also sued in conversion in relation to the disposal of the brain, as this had been needed to prove the claim. The court found, inter alia, that although the *Doodeward* exception applied to the case, simply preserving the brain in paraffin was insufficient to convert it into property.

In the later case of *R v Kelly and Lindsay*,[19] Lindsay (a technician) removed a range of body parts from the Royal College of Surgeons at the behest of Kelly (a sculptor). The body parts were subsequently found at various locations, including Kelly's attic, a nearby field and a friend's flat. The key question before the English Court of Appeal was whether the men could be prosecuted for theft (of property) under the *Theft Act 1968* (Act). It was argued, on their behalf, that such a prosecution was not possible given the 'no property' in the human body rule. The Court rejected this argument, holding that the body parts in question were capable of being property for the purposes of prosecution for theft under the Act if they had 'acquired different attributes by virtue of the application of skill, such as dissection or preservation techniques, for exhibition or teaching purposes'.[20]

There have also been a number of Australian cases where the courts have found that preserved human tissue samples are property. In the case of *Roche v Douglas*,[21] for example, an application was made under the rules of the WA Supreme Court to allow DNA testing on the preserved tissue samples of a deceased person in order to determine whether or not the applicant was the daughter of the deceased. In the absence of direct legislation on point, and in view of the substantial savings in court time and costs that would result, it was held that the samples in question were property for the purposes of conducting such testing.

The way in which the work/skill exception has been interpreted and applied by English and Australian courts means that it could be said to cover activities undertaken by scientists/clinicians such as dissection; the use of preservation techniques on human tissue for teaching purposes or for exhibit at a trial; and DNA extraction and analysis. Nevertheless, the nature and scope of the exception remains unclear. Although the *Doodeward* exception remains good law in Australia,[22] its continuing relevance has been brought into question in recent judicial pronouncements in England.[23]

---

18   *Dobson v North Tyneside Health Authority* [1996] 4 All ER 474.
19   *R v Kelly and Lindsay* [1999] QB 621.
20   Ibid 623.
21   *Roche v Douglas* (2000) 22 WAR 331.
22   Loane Skene, 'Proprietary Interests in Human Bodily Material: *Yearworth*, Recent Australian Cases on Stored Semen and Their Implications' (2012) 20(2) *Medical Law Review* 227, 236.
23   *Yearworth v North Bristol NHS Trust* [2010] QB 1.

Case law

England and Australia

In recent years, the question of property rights in human tissue has arisen in a number of English and Australian cases involving stored human semen samples. In the leading English judgment of *Yearworth v North Bristol NHS Trust*,[24] six men who had been diagnosed with cancer had provided samples of their semen prior to undergoing chemotherapy. The samples had been kept in frozen storage at a hospital for which the defendant was responsible. The requisite storage temperature was not maintained and the samples perished. Proceedings were commenced alleging negligence by the defendant, with the men claiming damages for psychological injury and for damage to property.

By the time the case reached the English Court of Appeal, a key issue for determination was whether the semen samples could be considered the men's property. While the court conceded that the *Doodeward* exception could apply, it was viewed as problematic and 'not entirely logical'. It was stated that developments in medical science 'now require a re-analysis of the common law's treatment of and approach to the ownership of parts or products of a living human body'.[25] The Court found that the men had ownership of their sperm for the purposes of their claims in negligence. The sole object of the production of such sperm had been that it might later be used for their benefit. No person other than each man had any rights in relation to the sperm which he produced.[26]

The Court held that there had been a gratuitous bailment of the sperm by the men to the hospital where the storage unit was kept. Liability as a gratuitous bailee was therefore established in principle. Bailment entitled the bailor (in this case, the men) or their representatives to call for the property's return, subject to the terms of the contract that existed between bailer and bailee. Factors held to be relevant in establishing a bailment in these circumstances included the men's right of control over the stored semen; their intention to use the semen at some later stage; and the nature of the agreement between the parties. This involved the men expressing their intention with regard to the purpose of the storage of the semen and its use and this being accepted by the defendant who agreed to such storage. In agreeing to take possession in such circumstances, the defendant had accepted responsibility for the safekeeping of the semen samples, even in the absence of any consideration. It was a gratuitous bailment that the Court considered to be 'closely akin to contracts'.[27]

Following *Yearworth*, there have been a number of Australian cases involving the use of stored semen samples.[28] The first of these cases was *Bazley v Wesley Monash IVF Pty Ltd*,[29] which involved an application by a widow who wished the respondent (fertility clinic) to continue to store her deceased husband's sperm samples, which had been collected prior

---

24   Ibid.
25   Ibid.
26   Ibid [47].
27   Ibid [57].
28   For an overview, see Skene, above n 22. Note that account should also be taken of the relevance of the state/territory Human Tissue Acts in this line of cases. For further details, see Chapter 17.
29   *Bazley v Wesley Monash IVF Pty Ltd* [2011] 2 Qd R 207.

to his death. Following his death, the respondent informed the applicant in her capacity as personal representative of her deceased husband's estate, that it could no longer store the samples. The applicant issued legal proceedings to restrain the respondent from destroying them. In the Queensland Supreme Court, Justice White found that the stored semen samples were the property of the deceased prior to his death and therefore became the property of his personal representative after his death. Drawing on *Yearworth*, it was held that the relationship between the applicant and respondent was one of bailor and bailee for reward, provided that storage fees were paid and the contract was maintained. This was so notwithstanding the deceased having not left a written directive as to what should happen with his stored sperm in the event of his death.[30]

There was a similar fact scenario in the case of *Edwards*,[31] save for the fact that the sperm samples had been collected after the death of the husband. The widow had previously brought a successful application for sperm samples to be collected from her deceased husband and stored for later use. A subsequent application was made to determine whether the widow had the right to possession of the samples for the purposes of fertility treatment. The matter came before Justice Hulme in the NSW Supreme Court. He found that as the sperm samples had been extracted post death, they were not the deceased's property at that time. Therefore, they did not pass under his estate. He was nevertheless persuaded by the reasoning in *Yearworth* and *Bazley* that the law should recognise that sperm could be considered property in certain circumstances. He went on to hold that the widow was the 'only person in whom an entitlement to property in the deceased's sperm would lie'.[32]

The subsequent case of *Re H, AE*[33] involved a number of applications which were brought before Justice Gray in the SA Supreme Court by a widow who sought possession of her deceased husband's sperm samples for the purposes of fertility treatment. As in *Edwards*, the samples had been collected and stored posthumously. Following the judgment in *Edwards*, the Court found that the applicant was entitled to possession of the sperm samples. Given the application of the NHMRC ART Guidelines in SA,[34] however, the Court was advised by the relevant state Minister that the applicant was unable to make use of the samples for the purposes of fertility treatment in the state. The applicant subsequently applied for permission to remove the sperm samples to the ACT, where it was permissible to make use of sperm which had been collected posthumously. The order for removal was granted by the Court.

It is interesting to note that Australian courts' reasoning regarding the recognition of human sperm samples as property has differed depending on whether they had been collected pre or post death. Where they were collected prior to death, as in *Bazley*, for example, it was found that the samples were the property of the deceased before his death. No further steps needed to be taken for the samples to be recognised as property. Where the samples were collected after death, however, the courts in *Edwards* and *Re H, AE* considered that the work/skill exception (per *Doodeward*) applied with regard to the storage and preservation

---

30   Ibid [33]. Note also the more recent case of *Roblin v Public Trustee for the Australian Capital Territory* (2015) 10 ACTLR 300, where the applicant was successful on fact circumstances similar to *Bazley*.

31   *Re Edwards* (2011) 81 NSWLR 198.

32   Ibid [91].

33   *Re H, AE (No 2)* [2012] SASC 177; *Re H, AE (No 3)* (2013) 118 SASR 259.

34   NHMRC, *Ethical Guidelines on the Use of Assisted Reproductive Technology in Clinical Practice and Research* (2007); see Chapter 13.

process, thus transforming the samples into property, and a further step was needed in the reasoning process to give the applicants' possession of the samples. This involved finding that the staff who undertook such work did so as 'agents' (for the applicants) and 'so did not acquire any proprietary rights for their own sake'.[35]

It has been suggested that *Yearworth*, as well as the recent Australian cases dealing with stored semen samples, represent an innovative turn in the judicial approach to recognising property rights in human tissue. There is clearly a greater judicial willingness to assign property rights in human tissue to the source and the source's personal representatives. What is not clear, however, is whether this approach will be confined to particular types of human tissue or whether a more expansive judicial approach will prevail. As evidenced in *Yearworth*, there was a recognition that the common law had moved on from recognising property rights as being grounded only in the *Doodeward* exception. Nevertheless, it could be argued that the use of a property model by the courts in the cases examined in this section was designed to achieve a particular outcome, rather than being grounded in a principled and coherent approach to dealing with property rights in human tissue.[36]

United States

There have also been a number of important US cases that have highlighted the extent to which third party property rights in relation to human tissue have priority over those of individuals who were the source of such tissue.[37] In the well-known case of *Moore v Regents of the University of California*,[38] John Moore was treated by Dr Golde at UCLA Medical Center in Los Angeles for hairy cell leukaemia between 1976 and 1983. Blood, bone marrow and other tissue, including his spleen, were removed from Moore as part of the treatment. Unbeknownst to Moore, Dr Golde and his colleagues had used his tissue to develop and subsequently patent a financially lucrative cell line (known as the Mo cell line). Moore subsequently became aware that his tissue had been used in this way and brought legal proceedings for damages for, inter alia, breach of fiduciary duty, lack of informed consent and conversion.

The case eventually came before the Californian Supreme Court, where a majority found in favour of Moore on the grounds that there had been a lack of informed consent and a breach of fiduciary duty. However, the court rejected his claim in conversion on the basis that, as a patient, he retained no proprietary interest in his excised tissue under the relevant laws. Therefore, he was not able to control or direct its future use. On policy grounds, the majority was also clearly concerned that a finding of conversion, which would involve recognising that Moore had ownership of his tissue, would significantly hinder scientific research and restrict access to necessary raw materials.

---

35   See *Edwards*, above n 31, [88].
36   Muireann Quigley, 'Property: The Future of Human Tissue' (2009) 17(3) *Medical Law Review* 457, 464; Harmon and Laurie, above n 10; Muireann Quigley and Loane Skene, 'Property Interests in Human Tissue: Is the Law Still an Ass?' in Catherine Stanton et al. (eds), *Pioneering Healthcare Law: Essays in Honour of Margaret Brazier* (Routledge, 2016) 165–7.
37   It is an approach that has been the subject of academic criticism: see, for example, Harmon and Laurie, above n 10, 481; Ian Kerridge et al., *Ethics and Law for the Health Professions*, 4th edn (Federation Press, 2013) 742–44; Dianne Nicol et al., 'Impressions on the Body, Property and Research' in Goold et al., above n 6, 15–17.
38   (1990) 793 P 2d 479.

In *Greenberg v Miami Children's Hospital Research Institute Inc.*[39] the plaintiffs had donated tissue samples to a researcher so that he could conduct research into Canavan disease. However, a conflict arose between the parties about making the results of the research publicly available and ensuring that any tests developed from the research would be affordable and accessible. Legal proceedings were issued alleging, inter alia, conversion and lack of informed consent. Relying on *Moore*, the court rejected both claims, with concerns being expressed about the problems that would arise if too much control was ceded to research participants, including the chilling effect this might have on scientific research.[40]

In *Washington University v Catalona*[41] an internationally renowned researcher had established a tissue bank at Washington University (WU) which held thousands of tissue samples. The samples had been collected for the purposes of conducting a study into prostate cancer. When the researcher subsequently took up a position at another university, he sought to take the tissue samples with him, with the support of the majority of research participants. WU was successful in legal action to retain ownership of the tissue bank and to prevent the removal of the tissue bank by the researcher. At first instance, the court found that WU was the owner of the samples; that neither the researcher nor the research participants had any ownership or proprietary interests in the samples; and that none of the informed consent forms signed by the participants were effective to transfer ownership or proprietary interests of the samples to the researcher. The first instance judgment was affirmed on appeal.

A property-based approach to human tissue

In this section of the chapter, we briefly consider a number of key arguments that have been put forward in the academic literature regarding the advantages and disadvantages of a property-based approach to human tissue.[42]

Advantages

It has been suggested that there are a number of advantages to recognising a property-based approach to human tissue. In general terms, it would clarify the legal rights of both donors and recipients. It would also overcome one of the major problems with the current consent-based approach to the donation of tissue samples, namely the lack of control by the individual

---

39   *Greenberg v Miami Children's Hospital Research Institute Inc.* 264 F Supp 2d 1064 (Fla 2003).

40   Ibid 1071.

41   *Washington University v Catalona* 437 F Supp 2d 985 (Miss 2006).

42   This section draws on a voluminous literature on this topic, of which select reference is made for the purposes of outlining the advantages and disadvantages of a property-based approach to human tissue. For example, see Stephen R Munzer, *A Theory of Property* (CUP, 1990); James E Penner, *The Idea of Property Law* (OUP, 1997); John W Harris, *Property and Justice* (OUP, 2001); J Kenyon Mason and Graeme Laurie, 'Consent or Property? Dealing with the Body and its Parts in the Shadow of Bristol and Alder Hey' (2001) 64(5) *Modern Law Review* 710; Loane Skene, 'Proprietary Rights in Human Bodies, Body Parts and Tissue: Regulatory Contexts and Proposals for New Laws' (2002) 22(1) *Legal Studies* 102; ALRC, above n 5, Ch 20; Barbro Bjorkman and Sven Ove Hansson, 'Bodily Rights and Property Rights' (2006) 32(4) *Journal of Medical Ethics* 209; Margaret Otlowski, 'Donor Perspectives on Issues Associated With Donation of Genetic Samples and Information: An Australian Viewpoint' (2007) 4 *Journal of Bioethical Inquiry* 135; Quigley, above n 1, 15 and 36; Goold et al., above n 6.

who donated the material over its future use. It would also clarify the nature of the gift made by such individuals, in particular the terms under which transfer to recipients took place.

It would also ensure greater equity and fairness between donors and recipients, rather than the current lopsided approach under law whereby most of the power to make use of the donor's tissue is vested with the recipient and other third parties, rather than with the donor as the source. Property rights could be asserted by donors against the recipient and other third parties who wish to make use of their tissue, in circumstances where it has not been alienated or abandoned. As a result, legal remedies would be available to individuals where it could be established that there was unlawful interference with their rights by such parties. They would also have a legal entitlement to share in the financial rewards resulting from commercialisation activities by such parties.

Disadvantages

It has been suggested that the principles underpinning property law do not sit comfortably with the recognition of property rights in human tissue. The rights that currently exist are grounded in the common law. Inevitably, law in the area has developed in response to judicial findings in individual cases. This has made for a piecemeal approach to date, rendering any reliance on the common law to offer a comprehensive approach to dealing with such rights problematic. The preferred approach would be to recognise any rights the source might have in their tissue as grounded in a justice-based approach, which recognises the importance of equality, autonomous choice and bodily integrity.

The provision of human tissue for both therapeutic and research purposes is currently predicated on altruistic participation. This is an important aspect of Australia's social capital. It would be detrimental to such social capital, as well as to the public interest more broadly, if there was a public perception that human tissue had become commodified. This is against a background where a range of international legal instruments view commodification of the human body as an affront to human dignity that should not be permitted.

A property-based approach would also potentially undermine the current system of ethical approval for health and medical research in Australia, as set out in the National Statement on Ethical Conduct in Human Research.[43] Pursuant to the National Statement, consent to use of human tissue samples can be waived in some situations by human research ethics committees (HRECs). It is questionable whether it would be lawful to waive consent where an individual holds property rights over their tissue. If human tissue samples were to be regarded as property, de-identification would not extinguish the rights of the person from whom the tissue sample was taken. De-identification is one of the main mechanisms currently used by researchers to provide a degree of privacy protection for research participants, whilst at the same time permitting scientific research to be carried out.

Rather than relying on property law, there are other areas of law that would provide most, if not all, of the legal protections required by individuals as the source of human tissue used in research. Privacy laws, which include penalties for non-compliance, address concerns regarding third party or public disclosure of identifying genetic information and data derived from human tissue. Where issues of control and future use of human tissue are relevant for

---

43   NHMRC, *National Statement on Ethical Conduct in Human Research* (2007/2015) (*National Statement*) <www.nhmrc.gov.au/guidelines-publications/e72>.

individuals, this could be better addressed through showing due respect for their autonomy as expressed in the law of consent. In the case of human tissue samples held by biobanks, a range of consent models have been proposed to address these concerns about future use.[44]

Even if it is accepted that a property-based approach is to be preferred, it is not clear that individuals would in fact have control over commercialisation activities by third parties arising out of the use of their tissue. Recognition of property rights of sources of human tissue would not on its own, and without further elaboration, set out the extent of legal obligations imposed upon third parties engaged in such activities. If such an approach were to be employed, it would be likely to substantially increase the costs of research, with the risk that such costs would be passed on to consumers.

Legislative position

At present, Australian legislation does not specifically address the issue of property rights in human tissue. In order to understand the ethical and legal issues associated with the donation, use, control and (future) use of such tissue, reference must be had to case law, the Human Tissue Acts which operate in various states/territories, privacy legislation and relevant NHMRC ethical guidelines, including those dealing with human research and various types of human tissue (for example, organs and gametes).[45]

In the early 2000s there was considerable debate, in the context of law reform around the use of genetic material and related data, about whether property rights in human tissue should be recognised. In the end, such an approach was not supported, on the grounds that the common law was not sufficiently well developed in the area and would therefore not be able to offer a comprehensive solution to the issues at stake. In particular, concerns were expressed that if such an approach were adopted, it would contribute to uncertainty about (the extent of) legal obligations by third parties towards sources of human tissue. This would have potentially adverse implications for scientific research and innovation in Australia. Instead, it was recommended that privacy legislation be used to protect the rights of individuals regarding their genetic material and related data.[46]

Conclusion

This chapter has explored the relationship between property and human tissue, examining important recent legal developments. Key terms and principles in property law, including the no property rule and the work/skill exception, were also examined. This was done with a view to better understanding the evolution in judicial thinking about legal recognition of property rights in human tissue, against a background of rapid scientific and technological advances involving the use of such tissue. In light of such advances, there is a need to carefully consider whether or not a property-based approach may offer a more equitable way forward in providing the sources of human tissue – be they patients and/or research participants – with a greater degree of control over the future use of their tissue under the law.

---

44   See Chapters 19 and 20 for further details regarding consent for future use of tissue samples and related genetic data arising out of biobanking.
45   For further details, see Chapters 12, 13 and 17.
46   ALRC, above n 5, Ch 8, Recs 20–2. See Chapters 12, 19 and 20 for further details.

19

BIOBANKS

Anne-Maree Farrell

Introduction

In recent decades there has been an upsurge in interest in the formation and development of biobanks. This has been for two main reasons: first, to promote research that will better understand the risk factors underlying disease;[1] and second, to facilitate the translation of scientific research into healthcare practice, particularly in the areas of pharmacogenomics and personalised medicine.[2] Traditionally, collections of human tissue samples and related information were created for the purposes of treatment and diagnosis, and they continue to exist. However, what is new is the creation of large-scale entities involving systematic (and automatised) approaches to the collection of human tissue and related data. This has opened up new opportunities for data linkage and data mining, both nationally and internationally.[3] This chapter explores key definitions, institutions and concepts in biobanking. A number of ethical, legal and social concerns that have arisen in this context are also examined, with a particular focus on the topics of consent, privacy and confidentiality, property rights and commercialisation.

Key definitions

The term 'biobanks' is commonly used to describe a range of entities that store human tissue (or what are referred to as 'human biospecimens' in this context),[4] as well as genetic information and other health-related information collected from participants.[5] For present purposes, we shall refer to human biospecimens and related information collected by biobanks

---

1   This includes genetic, genomic and molecular epidemiological research. *Genetic* research involves the study of heredity and hereditability, whereas *genomic* research involves the study of genes and their functions, and related techniques. The main difference between the two is that genetics scrutinises the functioning and composition of a single gene whereas genomics addresses all genes and their inter-relationships in order to identify their combined influence on the growth and development of organisms: see <www.who.int/genomics/geneticsVSgenomics/en>. *Genomics molecular epidemiology* combines research in molecular biology and epidemiology in order to better understand biomarkers (genes and other molecules) for disease, in particular interactions between external environmental exposure and genetic and other susceptibility factors. This will assist in identifying likely at-risk populations and individuals.

2   *Pharmacogenomics* involves the study of how a person's genes respond to the use of medication. Not everyone responds to medication in the same way, so the aim is to develop safe and effective medications that are better tailored to a person's genetic makeup. *Personalised medicine* is defined as 'the capacity to predict disease development and influence decisions about lifestyle choices or to tailor medical practice to an individual': see NHMRC, *Clinical Utility of Personalised Medicine* (2011) 1 <www.nhmrc.gov.au/_files_nhmrc/publications/attachments/ps0001_clinical_utility_personalised_medicine_feb_2011.pdf>; see also Don Chalmers et al., 'Personalised Medicine in the Genome Era' (2013) 20(3) *Journal of Law and Medicine* 577.

3   Barbara Prainsack and Alena Buyx, 'A Solidarity-Based Approach to the Governance of Research Biobanks' (2013) 21(1) *Medical Law Review* 71, 73.

4   *Human biospecimens* refers to 'any biological material obtained from a person including tissue, blood, urine, sputum and any derivative from these including cell lines … Sources of human biospecimens include voluntary donation, material taken for clinical purposes, and material collected post-mortem (after death)': see NHMRC, *National Statement on Ethical Conduct in Human Research* (2007/2015) (National Statement) Chapter 3.4, Introduction <www.nhmrc.gov.au/guidelines-publications/e72>.

5   NHMRC, *Biobanks Information Paper* (2010) 6 <www.nhmrc.gov.au/_files_nhmrc/file/your_health/egenetics/practitioners/biobanks_information_paper.pdf>. See also Chapter 20 for a more detailed examination of the relationship between law, genetics and biobanks.

as 'material'. In using the term 'biobanks', however, we note that there are also other terms in use which reflect the origin, type and reasons for the material being stored. They include 'repositories', 'tissue banks', 'databanks' and 'human genetic research databases'. It is also important to note that biobanks have also been established for purposes other than health and medical research, such as for forensic purposes (for example, DNA databases).[6]

Key institutions

A diverse range of biobanks operate in Australia.[7] They operate largely autonomously, with each biobank having independent processes to manage its operations and deal with any requests for material from researchers or other third parties. Currently, a lack of national coordination in the field has resulted in a duplication of effort. It has led to different processes being applied to the same diseases using a range of protocols, as well as inadequate linkage between data collected from clinical trials and that resulting from laboratory-based research. It is recognised that facilitating such linkage would be particularly beneficial for advancing research in the areas of pharmacogenomics and personalised medicine.[8] Biobanks can be established through public or private funding sources or a mixture of both. Not-for-profit biobanks may acquire funding through being associated with universities or hospitals, and/or through a range of grants or subsidies by government and research funding bodies. For Australian biobanks that receive predominantly public funding, ensuring long-term financial sustainability remains an ongoing problem.[9]

Principles

It has been argued that the principles underpinning the establishment of a national approach to biobanking should include the following:

- national focus and vision
- participation by a range of health and research organisations
- scalability (ie. a single national biobanking strategy should facilitate growth in the number and type, or in the scale, of biobanks)
- a streamlined national approach to ethics and approvals
- a plan for financial sustainability
- operational efficiency
- promotion of maximum benefits to patients and the health sector
- a national IT and informatics system to facilitate linkage of data and research outcomes

---

6   See, for example, *The National Criminal Investigation DNA Database* (NCIDD) <www.crimtrac.gov
      .au/dna>.
7   Examples include The Australasian Biospecimen Network – Oncology (ABN-Oncology) <http://
      abrn.net>; Victorian Cancer Biobank <www.viccancerbiobank.org.au>; The Australian Bone Marrow
      Donor Registry <www.abmdr.org.au>.
8   NHMRC, *National Biobanking Strategy* (November 2012) <www.nhmrc.gov.au/_files_nhmrc/file/
      research/nhmrc_national_biobanking_strategy_130628.pdf>.
9   Tim Caulfield et al., 'A Review of the Key Issues Associated with the Commercialization of
      Biobanks' (2014) 1(1) *Journal of Law and the Biosciences* 94.

- minimal bureaucracy
- involvement of consumers (patients, research participants) and advocacy groups
- transparent and independent governance.[10]

Governance

Ensuring that there is appropriate governance of biobanks is recognised as an important issue in terms of attracting participants and researchers, ensuring the conduct of high-quality research, and enhancing public trust in biobanks and their activities. In Australia, the National Statement on Ethical Conduct in Human Research[11] (National Statement) requires that biobanks develop a model of governance to deal with the 'collection, storage, use and disposal of human tissue in research'. Considerations to be taken into account in designing such a model include deciding what sort of information needs to be collected and recorded; what the consent requirements should be; how participants' confidentiality and privacy should be managed; and what policies should be in place regarding access and disposal of material. Biobanks are also required to take socio-cultural considerations that may relate to their activities into account.[12]

Biobanks are encouraged to establish independent (ethical) oversight mechanisms in relation to their activities. Given the potential for national and international transfer of material, as well as data linkage, it is also important that systems are developed for monitoring third parties who seek to access such material/data. As part of developing such policies, biobanks should consider what sanctions and dispute resolution mechanisms should apply in the event that third parties do not deal with material/data appropriately.[13] In the case of not-for-profit biobanks in particular, it is difficult to see what resources would be available to them to actively engage in such enforcement activities, which in any case may be limited by restrictions imposed by law.[14]

Australia has no specific legislation dealing with biobanks. Given that the state/territory Human Tissue Acts (or their equivalent) do not deal with health and medical research involving human tissue,[15] where should biobanks turn to for guidance in designing their governance models? As previously noted, the National Statement does provide guidance and is highly influential, but it does not address all aspects of biobanking activity. Other sources include the draft Policy Directive that has recently been published by the NSW government, which sets out a standardised approach for biobanks to use when obtaining consent.[16] The Genetic Register Guidelines may be useful with respect to some aspects of biobanking

---

10   Ibid Appendix 1.
11   NHMRC, above n 4.
12   Ibid para 3.4.1.
13   Yann Joly et al., 'Genomic Databases Access Agreements: Legal Validity and Possible Sanctions' (2011) 130(3) *Human Genetics* 441; Carole Grady et al., 'Broad Consent for Research with Biological Samples: Workshop Conclusions' (2015) 15(9) *The American Journal of Bioethics* 34, 39.
14   For further discussion on this point, see Lorena Aparicio et al., 'Biobanking of Blood and Bone Marrow: Emerging Challenges for Custodians of Public Resources' (2013) 21(2) *Journal of Law and Medicine* 343, 349.
15   For a more detailed examination of the Human Tissue Acts (or their equivalent), see Chapter 17.
16   NSW Government, Office of Health and Medical Research (OHMR), *Consultation – Statewide Biobanking Consent* <www.health.nsw.gov.au/ohmr/biobankregistry/Pages/biobanking-consent.aspx>.

activity, as may other NHMRC guidance. Aspects of anti-discrimination and intellectual property law may also be relevant.[17]

Biobanks may also take account of principles set out in a number of international instruments, including the following:

- UNESCO International Declaration on Human Genetic Data (16 October 2003)[18]
- OECD Guidelines on Human Biobanks and Genetic Research Databases (2009)[19]
- OECD Privacy Framework (2013)[20]
- Human Genome Organisation (HUGO) statements covering ethical and legal issues impacting upon the human genome and genetic databases[21]
- WHO *Statement on Genetic Databases: Assessing the Benefits and Impact on Human and Patient Rights.*[22]

There is also a range of state, national and international standards that apply in relation to the collection, annotation, storage and access of material held by biobanks. Meeting international standards may be particularly advantageous because it has the potential to create a clear and consistent approach across biobanks that can in turn better facilitate international research collaborations. This could prove to be particularly cost-effective, especially in the case of research on rare human tissue samples.[23] Key international standards include those published by the International Society for Biological and Environmental Repositories (ISBER)[24] and laboratory standards developed by the International Standards Organization (ISO) in relation to quality, risk management, and the use of in-vitro diagnostic devices.[25]

Ethical, social and legal issues

A number of ethical, social and legal concerns have been raised in response to the growth of biobanks both nationally and internationally. A key overarching concern has been how best to balance the individual against the collective: that is to say, between promoting the individual participant's autonomy and rights as a result of providing their material to biobanks on the one hand and the desire of researchers to draw on such material for health and medical research for the greater common good on the other hand. Within this context, it has been argued that biobanks should be viewed as 'custodians' of the material they collect and store on behalf of participants.[26] The concept of custodianship speaks to each biobank's ethical duty to 'ensure its data and/or samples are used responsibly and carefully

---

17   NHMRC, above n 5, 20.
18   <http://portal.unesco.org/en/ev.php-URL_ID=17720&URL_DO=DO_TOPIC&URL_SECTION=201 .html>.
19   <www.oecd.org/sti/biotech/44054609.pdf>.
20   <www.oecd.org/sti/ieconomy/oecd_privacy_framework.pdf>.
21   For an overview, see Bartha Knoppers et al., 'The Human Genome Organisation: Towards Next-Generation Ethics' (2013) 5 *Genome Medicine* 38.
22   <www.codex.vr.se/texts/whofinalreport.rtf>.
23   NHMRC, *Biobanking Roundtable: Summary of Discussion* (29 June 2012) 3, <www.nhmrc.gov .au/_files_nhmrc/file/research/biobanking_roundtable_outcome_june_2012.pdf>.
24   ISBER, *Best Practice Guidelines for Repositories: Collection, Storage, Retrieval and Distribution of Biological Materials for Research* <www.isber.org/?page=BPR>.
25   International Organization for Standardization (ISO) <www.iso.org/iso/home.html>.
26   NHMRC, above n 4, paras 3.2.5–3.2.8.

in accordance with its purpose for the public good, and to ensure that research participants' interests are taken into account'.[27] This is considered to be particularly important where biobanks receive public funds and where they have therapeutic objectives, in addition to those related to research.

Questions of trust, solidarity and community may also loom large, particularly where the material collected by biobanks has implications for family, identity and kinship.[28] In the circumstances, independent ethical oversight of biobanks is considered vital if there is to be public trust in their operations.[29] Such oversight – through a panel or a board of appointees from different professional and lay backgrounds, for example – is also considered useful in providing guidance in key areas of biobanking activity that give rise to ethical, social and legal concerns, including consent; confidentiality and privacy; property rights; and commercialisation. We will now deal briefly with each of these issues in turn.

Consent

The nature and type of consent obtained from participants in biobanks have been much examined and debated within the academic and policy literature. Indeed, it has been noted that 'the issue of consent has proven to be one of the most divisive topics in the context of biobanking research'.[30] One key concern has been the type of consent that should be obtained in relation to the future use of participants' material. In Australia, the National Statement draws a distinction between specific consent for a particular project and extended or unspecified consent where consent is needed for the future use of material.[31] In practice, however, biobanks have used a range of processes and practices in this regard. This has included obtaining initial consent at the time of collection for a specified use now and in the future; re-consent for any subsequent future use; and having participants identify what sort of research they would consent to in the future.[32]

It has been argued that there is a strong ethical obligation for participants to remain fully informed about all direct and indirect dealings by biobanks regarding health and medical research conducted on their material. In such circumstances, there is a need to ensure the confidentiality and privacy of participants and their material. In turn, this influences the nature and type of consent obtained by biobanks.[33] There have been a number of studies which have surveyed the views of participants about the issue of future use of their material. Some studies have found that while most participants wanted to be asked about the use of their material for biomedical research as part of the initial consent process, they were willing

---

27   Aparicio et al., above n 14, 345.

28   Klaus Hoeyer and Niels Lynöe, 'Motivating Donors to Genetic Research? Anthropological Reasons to Rethink the Role of Informed Consent' (2006) 9(1) *Medicine, Health Care and Philosophy* 13; Prainsack and Buyx, above n 3, 74.

29   Alistair V Campbell, 'The Ethical Challenges of Genetic Databases: Safeguarding Altruism and Trust' (2007) 18(2) *King's Law Journal* 227, 245.

30   Caulfield et al., above n 9, 102.

31   NHMRC, above n 4, paras 2.2.14 – 2.2.18.

32   Teresa Edwards et al., 'Biobanks Containing Clinical Specimens: Defining Characteristics, Policies, and Practices' (2014) 47(4–5) *Clinical Biochemistry* 245.

33   Jane Kaye et al., 'Dynamic Consent: A Patient Interface for Twenty-First Century Research Networks' (2015) 23 *European Journal of Human Genetics* 141.

to give a fairly open-ended consent about what was done with the material after that.[34] In contrast, other studies have shown that there is a sizeable number of participants who do want to be kept informed and/or asked for specific consent about the future use of their material. Key areas of concern for such participants include research involving human cloning and indigenous peoples, as well as the commercialisation of research.[35]

Various proposals have been put forward to address the issue of consent for future use of material. One option that has been proposed is the use of a model of broad consent. This is seen as offering an ethically acceptable way forward, and it is finding increasing support in the Australian context.[36] This model has three components: (1) obtaining initial broad consent; (2) establishing a process of oversight and approval of future research activities; and (3) implementing an ongoing process of providing information to or communicating with donors (where feasible).[37] Obtaining broad consent from participants is said to involve the following:

> Briefly [describing] that the samples will be stored, that samples may be shared with a wide range of researchers and institutions and the conditions under which sharing would be allowed, that general health information accompanies the material, the possibility of commercial or therapeutic applications, the oversight process that will review proposed research, the potential for re-contact or ongoing communication, and the possibility of donors opting out of further research on their stored material in the future.[38]

For some academic commentators, however, broad consent is not considered appropriate in ethical or legal terms. Kaye et al. have argued that participants are being asked to consent to involvement in ongoing or future research where there may be multiple and changing research questions and methods. In such circumstances there are risks that their privacy may be infringed, particularly with regard to the use of identifying health information.[39] Where such risks exist, be they direct or indirect, there may be a need to obtain specific consent under national data protection and privacy laws and this is not possible in the context of a broad consent model. In the circumstances, they propose the adoption of a dynamic consent process as a way of addressing the issue. It involves the following:

> The creation of a personalised communication interface to enable greater participant engagement in clinical and research activities. It is a participant-centred initiative that places patients and research participants at the centre of decision-making, providing an interactive IT interface to engage with participants. This approach is 'dynamic' because it allows interactions over time; it enables participants to consent to new projects or to alter their consent choices in real time as their circumstances change and to have confidence that these changed choices will take effect.[40]

---

34   Wendy Lipworth, Rowena Forsyth and Ian Kerridge, 'Tissue Donation to Biobanks: A Review of Sociological Studies' (2011) 33(5) *Sociology of Health and Illness* 792.

35   For an overview of the studies, see Grady et al., above n 13, 36–7.

36   Don Chalmers, 'Biobanking and Privacy Laws in Australia' (2015) 43(4) *Journal of Law, Medicine & Ethics* 703.

37   Grady et al., above n 13, 37.

38   Ibid 37–8.

39   Kaye et al., above n 33, 142.

40   Grady et al., above n 13, 142–3.

Ploug and Holm have also expressed concerns about broad consent. They argue that for all intents and purposes, it is likely to operate as a blanket consent. In practice, it is likely to operate to minimise the administrative burden to biobanks so that they can offer 'a uniform, one-off request to the individual that does not introduce any limits to [health and medical] research and so cannot subsequently give rise to problems in reinterpreting the original consent'.[41] Instead, they propose that a meta-consent model be adopted which 'does not involve asking individuals for consent but rather asking them when and how they would like to be asked for consent'.[42] Participants could choose what sort of model of consent and type of research they prefer, whilst still acting in line with their altruistic support for future research.[43]

For commentators who oppose these types of models, the preference is for re-consenting processes once the identity of specific researchers and details of their research projects are known. This includes ensuring that participants have the opportunity to opt in or opt out of future projects.[44] The UK Biobank, a large-scale population biobank, has adopted the position that it will provide regular updates on research to participants as a whole, rather than providing individual feedback. In this way, participants are kept informed, but without the need for a formal re-consenting process for future research.[45] Whether and how such an approach is likely to fit with the increasingly networked approach to international exchange of biobank material, and whether or not there is likely to be ongoing compliance with data protection and privacy laws, remain contested.[46]

Return of individual or incidental research findings

There is considerable variability among biobanks regarding how they obtain consent from, and provide feedback to, participants. This has given rise to a range of concerns about how best to deal with the return of individual or incidental findings from research conducted on participants' material. Such concerns have grown in the context of an increase in the use of genomic technologies. This means that there may be incidental findings which may be relevant for participants, though they may not have been the target of specific research projects.[47] Concerns that have been raised in relation to the return of such findings include how best to manage participants' confidentiality and privacy; the risk of potential legal liability; and the financial and other resources that will be involved in returning such results.[48]

---

41   Thomas Ploug and Soren Holm, 'Going Beyond the False Dichotomy of Broad or Specific Consent: A Meta-Perspective on Participant Choice in Research Using Human Tissue' (2015) 15(9) *The American Journal of Bioethics* 44, 45.

42   Ibid 46.

43   Thomas Ploug and Soren Holm, 'Meta Consent: A Flexible and Autonomous Way of Obtaining Informed Consent for Secondary Research' (2015) 350 *British Medical Journal* h2146.

44   Angela Ballantyne, 'In Favor of a No-Consent/Opt-Out Model of Research with Clinical Samples' (2015) 15(9) *The American Journal of Bioethics* 65; see also NHMRC, above n 4, paras 2.3.5–2.3.8.

45   See, for example, UK Biobank Participant Events, <www.ukbiobank.ac.uk/participant-events>.

46   Wendy Lipworth and Ian Kerridge, 'Consent to Biobank Research: Facing Up to the Challenge of Globalization' (2015) 15(9) *The American Journal of Bioethics* 58.

47   Marianna J Bledsoe et al., 'Practical Implementation Issues and Challenges for Biobanks in the Return of Individual Research Results' (2012) 14(4) *Genetics in Medicine* 478.

48   Ibid.

Although guidelines have been published, there is currently no clear consensus on how best to address this issue.[49] On the one hand, it has been suggested that on ethical grounds it is important that ways are found to return such findings to participants in biobanks, in the interests of promoting respect, beneficence, reciprocity and justice. On the other hand, it has been argued that the return of such findings should not be required, on the grounds that individuals originally agreed to participate on altruistic grounds in order to further the broader aims of health and medical research for the greater common good. For yet other commentators, context – in terms of how and why the material was gathered, as well as some participants' desire 'not to know' – matters, as this may influence whether or not there should be a return of individual findings.[50]

In Australia, the National Statement recommends that biobanks submit an ethically defensible plan for the return of individual research results to their oversight research ethics committees. It is also emphasised that returning such findings should be considered on a case-by-case basis, underpinned by an evaluation of the risks and benefits to individuals and costs to society.[51] Published findings from a recent Australia-wide survey showed that a strong majority of the sample ($n = 800$) were interested in receiving such findings if they had consented to their material being used in biobank research. This was particularly so where it involved specific information which was important to their health or medical treatment and/or involved any potential genetic risks associated with inherited disease.[52]

Confidentiality and privacy

Ensuring the confidentiality and privacy of material provided by participants to biobanks is vital. In ethical terms, it is underpinned by human dignity, respect, autonomy and the welfare of participants. Information privacy is also recognised as a (qualified) fundamental human right.[53] In relation to protecting the personal health information of participants from third parties, it is important to distinguish between privacy and confidentiality. In the former, the concern is with the collection of information; in the latter, the issue is disclosure of such information to third parties.[54] The general principles that apply to the confidentiality and privacy of health information under Australian law are set out in more detail in Chapter 12.[55] How these issues are dealt with in the case of genetic information in particular is covered in Chapter 20.

For biobanks, there are a number of important issues that need to be taken into account where genetic, health and family history information need to remain linked for research

---

49   Susan M Wolf et al., 'Managing Incidental Findings and Research Results in Genomic Research Involving Biobanks and Archived Data Sets' (2012) 14 *Genetics in Medicine* 361.

50   Bartha M Knoppers, 'Introduction: From the Right to Know and the Right Not to Know' (2014) 42(1) *Journal of Law Medicine & Ethics* 6.

51   NHMRC, above n 4, see Chapters 3.4 and 3.5.

52   Jennifer Fleming et al., 'Attitudes of the General Public Towards the Disclosure of Individual Research Results and Incidental findings from Biobank Genomic Research in Australia' (2015) 45 (12) *Internal Medicine Journal* 1274.

53   See, for example, the International Covenant on Civil and Political Rights (ICCPR), Art 17.1. Australia has signed and ratified the ICCPR.

54   NHMRC, above n 5, 44.

55   See also Dianne Nicol et al., 'Time To Get Serious about Privacy Policies: The Special Case of Genetic Privacy' (2014) 42 *Federal Law Review* 149.

purposes.[56] Although it has been suggested that it is possible to de-identify material through anonymisation, the National Statement states that 'human tissue samples should always be regarded as, in principle, re-identifiable'.[57] Where such samples may be linked to genetic material stored by biobanks, identifiers should not be removed without the consent of participants, particularly if removal would make it difficult to communicate individual results to them.[58] It is important, therefore, that participants are informed by biobanks, as part of the process of obtaining consent, about what steps are being taken to address confidentiality and privacy concerns, as well as how biobanks propose to deal with any (incidental) findings derived from the material provided by participants.

At an operational level, biobanks also need to consider how participant confidentiality and privacy will be managed in policies established with respect to data identifiability, linkage and storage,[59] and in how they facilitate the transfer of material to third parties. The latter would ordinarily take place subject to material transfer agreements (MTAs), which aim to ensure that third parties comply with all relevant laws in relation to the use of such material, as well as with any conditions specified by human research ethics committees and the National Statement. The objective is to ensure that third parties do not use material other than for the specific research set out in the relevant MTA.[60] Although it has been suggested that research ethics committees need to take a more active role in policing such agreements,[61] it is not clear how compliance would be enforced in the event of breach of privacy, particularly if it takes place beyond jurisdictional boundaries.[62]

Property rights

Property rights, ownership and control of human tissue are examined in detail in Chapter 18. Such issues are also relevant in relation to material held by biobanks. As a result of collecting, storing and working on participants' material, biobanks would be in a strong position to argue that they now possessed (some) property rights in such material as a result of the 'work/skill exception'.[63] It has been suggested that as part of the consent process, participants should be informed that they do not 'own' their material held by biobanks. However, this should not preclude participants from either negotiating a right to access their personal information or withdraw from research projects undertaken or facilitated by biobanks.[64] There may also be intellectual property rights associated with the biobank itself, as well as arising out of the use of biobank resources. In the case of not-for-profit biobanks, for example, it has been suggested that they would be likely to view

---

56   Don Chalmers and Dianne Nicol, 'Human Genetic Research Databases and Biobanks: Towards Uniform Terminology and Australian Best Practice' (2008) 15 *Journal of Law and Medicine* 538, 539.

57   NHMRC, above n 4, Ch 3.2, Introduction.

58   Ibid para 3.5.5.

59   Data linkage involves linking data from different data sets in and across biobanks nationally and internationally. See ibid paras 3.2.4–3.2.5. For further information on managing the data linkage and on the question of storage, see ibid paras 3.2.2 and 3.4.1.

60   NHMRC, above n 5, 22.

61   Don Chalmers et al., 'A Role for Research Ethics Committees in Exchanges of Biospecimens through Material Transfer Agreements' (2014) 11 *Journal of Bioethical Inquiry* 301.

62   For further discussion, see Aparicio et al., above n 14; Caulfield et al., above n 9, 109.

63   Aparicio et al., above n 14, 347–48.

64   NHMRC, above n 5, 72.

the material they hold as a 'common resource for research', with ownership of intellectual property arising out of the use of such material vesting in the researchers who created it or in their employer institution.[65]

Commercialisation

The question of commercialisation of biobank resources, and related activities, has been the subject of considerable debate. This is particularly so where it involves the use of resources from not-for-profit, publicly funded biobanks. Such biobanks may struggle with ensuring financial sustainability or with participation in large-scale collaborative research, due to limited financial means.[66] For present purposes, commercialisation is defined as involving trade or commerce where monies are charged or exchanged, or (intellectual property) rights or entitlements are acquired for the purposes of making a profit. Commercialisation in relation to such biobanks can be direct or indirect. While the more direct forms are noted above, indirect forms may involve the commercial use of the results of research drawn from material held by not-for-profit biobanks;[67] or such biobanks operating in partnership with, or otherwise receiving some degree of funding from, the private sector (eg. biotech companies, or the pharmaceutical or medical device industries).[68]

With these scenarios in mind, key policy questions to consider include how partnerships with the for-profit sector can be reconciled with the institutional settings in which not-for-profit biobanks operate; and whether and, if so how, any (commercial) benefit-sharing from such partnerships should be managed. Important factors to be taken into account when addressing such questions include:

- the potential for public trust in biobanks to be adversely impacted[69]
- how questions of consent are to be addressed, including the potential need to re-consent participants
- exacerbation of privacy issues, which may require additional oversight or protection mechanisms
- the design and implementation of mechanisms to ensure appropriate ethical and regulatory oversight and monitoring of research
- how to address possible tensions regarding the ownership and sharing of material and related data
- how to manage the use and control of the resource if biobanks become bankrupt or lose financial support.[70]

---

65   Ibid 72–3.
66   Ibid 95.
67   Chalmers and Nicol, above n 56, 539.
68   Caulfield et al., above n 9, 96.
69   On the question of public trust, commercialisation and biobanking in Australia, see Christine Critchley et al., 'The Impact of Commercialisation and Genetic Data Sharing Arrangements on Public Trust and Intention to Participate in Biobank Research' (2015) 18(3) *Public Health Genomics* 160.
70   Caulfield et al., above n 9, 110.

It has been suggested that deep-seated public and political unease about the commodification of human material, particularly where it may have genomic significance, lies at the heart of such concerns. This may have implications not only for individual participants, but also for particular ethnic or racial groups and communities as a whole, an issue which is examined in more detail in Chapter 20. It may also conflict with broader public health issues.[71] A general prohibition on commercialisation remains a policy option which can be ethically justified on the grounds of the need to avoid commodification and the need to uphold the dignity of the human body, its parts and tissue. However, it is also recognised that a range of scientific and community benefits may flow from providing commercial incentives, such as desired therapeutic applications in the medium to long term.

In seeking a principled way forward, it has been argued that how biobanks' resources are publicly framed, as well as managed, is vital.[72] Classifying material held by biobanks by the extent to which it has become 'attenuated' has also been suggested as another way forward in identifying whether and, if so under what circumstances, commercialisation should be considered. Attenuation involves taking account of the significance that participants are likely to attach to material donated to biobanks. For example, material which contains genetic or cellular information that individuals and their families are likely to attach significance to may mean that either no commercialisation is permitted, or that specific research protocols, agreement to ongoing ethical oversight and identification of individual and community benefit is needed before it can proceed. Commercialisation of material that does not have such significance may not be seen as ethically problematic,[73] although some degree of regulatory oversight may be required for quality and safety purposes.

More broadly, it has been argued that we need to consider what rights are being established, and for whose benefit, when the issue of commercialisation of biobanks' resources is under consideration. For example, while the prospect of acquiring intellectual property rights may offer a clear commercial incentive for third parties, this should not be, on its own, a reason to exclude the use of biobanks' resources in this way. In addition, further consideration may be required as to the extent to which property rights vested in the source of the material held by biobanks should be recognised in the context of commercialisation activities (see Chapter 18 for further discussion on this point). The more important question to consider may be how such rights are to be controlled and used, and what oversight mechanisms need to be in place in order to ensure that community benefit gained from a not-for-profit resource is taken into account.[74]

---

71   Klaus Hoeyer, 'Trading in Cold Blood? Trustworthiness in Face of Commercialized Biobank Infrastructures' in Peter Dabrock, Jocken Taupitz and Jens Ried (eds), *Trust in Biobanking: Dealing with Ethical, Legal and Social Issues in an Emerging Field of Biotechnology* (Springer, 2012).

72   See, for example, Prainsack and Buyx, above n 3.

73   See NHMRC, *Ethics and the Exchange and Commercialisation of Products Derived from Human Tissue: Background and Issues* (2011) paras 2.1.4, 3.3 <www.nhmrc.gov.au/guidelines-publications/e103>.

74   Klaus Hoeyer, 'The Role of Ethics in Commercial Genetic Research: Notes on the Notion of Commodification' (2005) 24 *Medical Anthropology* 45, 64; for specific decision-making criteria that could be taken into account in this regard, see NHMRC, above n 73, Ch 4.

Conclusion

This chapter has examined key definitions, institutions and concepts in biobanking. New opportunities for the conduct of scientific research and international collaborations are emerging as a result of the development of systematic approaches to data linkage and data mining of biobanks' resources. While this is to be welcomed, it has also given rise to a number of ethical, social and legal challenges, particularly for not-for-profit, publicly funded biobanks. A number of such challenges were examined in this chapter, including consent, confidentiality and privacy, property rights and commercialisation. If public trust in biobanks is to be maintained, it is vital that such challenges are adequately addressed in both ethical and legal terms so that the best use can be made of the range of opportunities now available in the increasingly globalised research environment.

20

HUMAN GENETICS AND THE LAW

Isabel Karpin and Karen O'Connell

Introduction

The law as it applies to genetic technologies and their therapeutic applications is complex and constantly evolving. The complexity stems in part from the way that genetic health issues span so many and such disparate areas of legal regulation: from therapeutic goods to discrimination; from privacy laws to consent over future use of information; from Indigenous rights to private ownership and cloning. However, recent developments in genetic knowledge have further complicated the legal response to genetics, as the contextual and constructed nature of the gene is brought to the fore. In particular, epigenetics has begun to explore the myriad ways in which genes interact with the environment, including, for example, the social environment in the form of health.[1]

From a legal perspective, many questions arise, such as where do we draw the line between what is considered a medical problem and what is considered a social or legal problem? How will law determine the responsibility of those 'diagnosed' with genetic conditions that undermine their capacity to make decisions? How will the law respond to the claim that someone has committed a crime because they have a particular genetic profile? Indeed, some geneticists have – controversially – claimed that they have identified a gene for criminality.[2] How will society perceive its responsibility to respond if the problems being addressed are viewed as genetically determined? Conversely, what protections will law offer to avoid discriminatory outcomes for individuals identified with undesirable genetic traits? Genetics has significantly expanded the ambit of health law, requiring law to respond to the biological attributes of legal actors in novel ways. In order to explore these questions, the first part of the chapter provides a brief overview of recent historical developments in relation to genetic knowledge, before moving on in the second part to examine the relationship between genetics, race and indigeneity. The final part examines a number of current and contested areas of genetics-related regulation, including testing, discrimination, privacy, biobanks and property, as well as genetic modification and gene therapy.

Historical overview

Over the last 30 years there has been a growing reliance on genes and gene sciences as the key to understanding why we are the way we are. Genes have been called on to explain not just medical conditions or 'genetic illnesses', but also social problems and challenging behaviours. Not surprisingly, therefore, there has been an unprecedented growth in gene testing technologies[3] and a push by some health organisations and governments to encourage universal 'preconception' genetic testing of adults to ascertain their carrier status prior to

---

1   For further discussion on the social determinants of health, see Chapter 4.
2   Melissa Hogenboom, 'Two Genes Linked with Violent Crime', *BBC News* (online), 28 October 2014 <www.bbc.com/news/science-environment-29760212>. Note that Monoamine Oxidase A (MAOA) has been referred to as a 'crime gene', see ABC Radio National, 'The Crime Gene', *The Law Report* (online) 23 February 2010 <www.abc.net.au/radionational/programs/lawreport/the-crime-gene/3120754>.
3   Callum Bell et al., 'Carrier Testing for Severe Childhood Recessive Diseases by Next-Generation Sequencing' (2011) 3(65) *Science Translation Medicine* 65.

having children.[4] At the same time, however, there has been mounting unease about the way in which genes have been used to expand the category of disease and disability to include the not-yet-sick.[5] Indeed, our health status often now includes an assessment of our genetic risk of future ill-health. Thus, how we define a genetic disease or disability has become an important matter for ethical debate.

The gene acquired 'cult status'[6] with the launch of the Human Genome Project (HGP) in 1990.[7] This was a major US government-sponsored initiative to study the entirety of human genetic inheritance, with a budget of US$3 billion.[8] The aim of the HGP was to analyse the structure of human chromosomes, to sequence the genes in that structure, to locate and map the structure, and to find the location of 'defective' genes that cause or contribute to human genetic disease. Initially, it was claimed that the HGP would provide the definitive story of human identity and would allow scientists to locate genes for all sorts of hitherto elusive medical and social problems. There were predictions of genes for alcoholism, unemployment, domestic and social violence, as well as addiction and homelessness.[9] The push to provide a genetic explanation for conditions or characteristics that were previously socially defined, and a move to medicalise that which was previously only understood as social, has raised troubling questions for bioethics and health law.

However, 25 years on from the mapping of the human genome the scientific community now accepts that genes are not a simple determinant of biological states. Instead, there is a flourishing of scientific work on the interplay among genes and their environment. Scientific research has shifted to a focus on epigenetics: the study of cellular and physiological trait variations that result from chemical reactions that activate and deactivate parts of the genome. Scientists are discovering that intergenerational and environmental influences can affect whether or not a gene is 'turned on' and thus whether a person's phenotype, or expressed genetic traits, matches their genotype, their genetic material. It is relatively rare to be able to isolate a single gene as being responsible for a disease or disability, and in the many cases where there is more than one cause, epigenetics highlights that 'biological difference – not reduced to genomics – can be an effect of social relations'.[10]

4   UK Human Genetics Commission, *Increasing Options, Informing Choice: A Report on Preconception Genetic Testing and Screening* (April 2011) <www.hypotheses.org/wp-content/blogs.dir/257/files/2011/04/2011.HGC.-Increasing-options-informing-choice-final2.pdf>.

5   Abby Lippman, 'The Inclusion of Women in Clinical Trials: Are We Asking the Right Questions?' (March 2006) <www.whp-apsf.ca/pdf/clinicalTrialsEN.pdf>.

6   David Le Breton, 'Genetic Fundamentalism or the Cult of the Gene' (2004) 10(4) *Body and Society* 1.

7   The project was undertaken cooperatively by the National Institutes of Health and the US Department of Energy; for more information, see the Human Genome Project Information Archive 1990–2003, *Human Genome Project* (21 March 2014) <www.ornl.gov/sci/techresources/Human_Genome/home.shtml>; Le Breton, above n 6.

8   The US government has reported the total cost of the HGP (excluding construction costs) at US$437 million: see the Human Genome Project Information Archive 1990–2003, *Human Genome Project Budget* (23 July 2013) <www.ornl.gov/sci/techresources/Human_Genome/project/budget.shtml>.

9   Daniel Koshland, 'Sequences and Consequences of the Human Genome' (1989) 246 *Science* 189; Steven Rose, 'The Genetics of Blame' (1998) 300 *New Internationalist* 20.

10   Julie Guthman and Becky Mansfield, 'The Implications of Environmental Epigenetics: A New Direction for Geographic Inquiry on Health, Space, and Nature-Society Relations' (2013) 37(4) *Progress in Human Geography* 486, 496.

Genetics and race

The social and scientific interaction of genetics and race is complex and fraught, given the complicated history of racial stigmatisation using the language of genetics and eugenics.[11] Genetics, along with other scientific disciplines, has revealed that 'race' is not a purely biological category at all and that while a study of genetics can reveal certain knowledge around, for example, population level movements or common genetic markers shared by kinship groups, 'race' itself is a social construction.[12]

Some of the early suggestions of the uses to which genetic knowledge could be put clearly demonstrated the coupling of racist stereotypes with scientific developments. The Violence Initiative, for example, was a US government program which sought to identify the genetic underpinnings of violence in American cities by focusing on the supposed genetic propensity to aggression of individuals in areas of high crime, specifically African-American inner-city youth. The initiative, which was marked by controversy from the start, failed to garner adequate support for continued funding and has been mostly discontinued.[13]

The Human Genome Diversity Project (HGDP), another ambitious scientific initiative, aimed to collect genetic information from indigenous populations around the world.[14] Indigenous communities expressed concern that genetic material was being collected in order to develop improved medicine and health outcomes for non-indigenous populations in developed countries.[15] The project was met with clear hostility from many indigenous groups, who termed it the 'Vampire' project, and they rallied to oppose it.[16] These concerns were also shared by some Indigenous Australians.[17] Instead, the difficult history of genetics and indigeneity meant that there has been little genetic health research involving Indigenous Australians,[18] and specific legislation to address these concerns is minimal. As with many other areas of health regulation in Australia, genetic health research involving Aboriginal and Torres Strait Islander (ATSI) peoples is regulated by NHMRC guidelines.[19] In this case the relevant document is the National Statement in Ethical Conduct in Human Research. These guidelines are not directly enforceable, but compliance with them will assist research organisations in meeting their obligations at common law, including contractual obligations to conduct research without harm to participants.

---

11   Jon Beckwith, 'A Historical View of Social Responsibility in Genetics' (1993) 43(5) *BioScience* 327.
12   Audrey Smedley and Brian Smedley, 'Race as Biology Is Fiction, Racism as a Social Problem Is Real' (2005) 60(1) *American Psychologist* 16.
13   Robert Wright, 'The Biology of Violence', *New Yorker*, 13 March 1995, 68.
14   Meika Foster, 'Human Genome Diversity Project and the Patenting of Life: Indigenous Peoples Cry Out' (1999) 7(2) *Canterbury Law Review* 343; Leota Lone Dog, 'Whose Genes Are They?' 10(4) *Journal of Health and Social Policy* 51, 58.
15   Bette-Jane Crigger, 'The "Vampire Project" (Human Genome Diversity Project)' (1995) 25(1) *The Hastings Center Report* 2.
16   The Indigenous Peoples' Council on Biocolonialism, formed in 1999.
17   Michael Dodson and Robert Williamson, 'Indigenous Peoples and the Morality of the Human Genome Diversity Project' (1999) 25 *Journal of Medical Ethics* 204.
18   Emma Kowal, 'Genetic Research in Indigenous Health: Significant Progress, Substantial Challenges' (2012) 197(1) *Medical Journal of Australia* 19.
19   See NHMRC, *National Statement on Ethical Conduct in Human Research* (2007/2015) (*National Statement*); NHMRC, *Values and Ethics: Guidelines for Ethical Conduct in Aboriginal and Torres Strait Islander Health Research* (ATSI Guidelines); NHMRC, *Medical Genetic Testing: Information for Health Professionals* (April 2010) <www.nhmrc.gov.au/_files_nhmrc/publications/attachments/e99.pdf>.

Genetics and regulation

In this part of the chapter, we examine six specific areas of genetics-related regulation. As outlined in the Introduction, they have been chosen for their topicality and because they have been the subject of considerable debate within the relevant academic and policy literature.

Genetic testing

Genetic testing has become a common part of healthcare in Australia and has a long history here. For example, the routine use of the newborn 'heel prick test' to check for genetic conditions such as phenylketonuria and cystic fibrosis has been in place for many decades.[20] In recent years, however, the availability of increasingly sophisticated technology that can identify multiple genetic mutations in one test has led to a growth in pre-symptomatic and predictive testing for genetic disorders and more routine use of genetic testing at prenatal and preconception stages. Legislation has not kept pace with technological developments in genetic testing; it tends, instead, to be governed by government health department policy directives,[21] and by ethical guidelines produced by peak bodies representing health professionals in the relevant fields.[22] These documents set out the requirements for informed consent and pre- and post-test counselling.

The Royal Australian and New Zealand College of Obstetricians and Gynaecologists (RANZCOG) has produced a number of ethical guidelines for doctors on the use of genetic tests.[23] The NHMRC Ethical Guidelines on the Use of Assisted Reproductive Technology in Clinical Practice and Research (NHMRC ART Guidelines) limit the use of pre-implantation genetic diagnosis of embryos by ART clinics to the detection of serious genetic conditions, sex selection for medical reasons and, on rare occasions, selection of an embryo with compatible tissue for a sibling.[24] Furthermore, the *Research Involving Human Embryos Act 2002* (Cth) makes compliance with these guidelines a condition of accreditation for all ART clinics, giving them quasi-legislative force.[25] For a more detailed discussion of the regulation of reproduction, see Chapter 13.

One aspect of genetic testing for 'therapeutic' purposes which is statutorily regulated is genetic testing devices. This occurs through the *Therapeutic Goods Act*

20   Bridget Wilcken, 'Newborn Screening Methods for Cystic Fibrosis' (2003) 4(4) *Paediatric Respiratory Reviews* 272.

21   The NSW Ministry of Health has produced a policy directive on genetic testing: see NSW Health, *Policy Directive: Genetic Testing* (8 August 2007) <www0.health.nsw.gov.au/policies/pd/2007/pdf/ PD2007_066.pdf>.

22   Human Genetics Society of Australasia, *Guideline Pre-symptomatic and Predictive Testing for Genetic Disorders* (March 2014) <www.hgsa.org.au/documents/item/1574>.

23   The Royal Australian and New Zealand College of Obstetricians and Gynaecologists, *Joint HGSA/ RANZCOG Prenatal Diagnosis Policy* (November 2006) <www.ranzcog.edu.au>. Australian state health departments also provide guidelines: see, for example, NSW Health, *Policy Directive; Prenatal Testing/Screening for Down Syndrome and Other Chromosomal Abnormalities* (8 August 2007) <www0.health.nsw.gov.au/policies/pd/2007/pdf/PD2007_067.pdf>.

24   NHMRC, *Ethical Guidelines on the Use of Assisted Reproductive Technology in Clinical Practice and Research 2004* (revised 2007) <www.nhmrc.gov.au/_files_nhmrc/publications/attachments/ e78.pdf.>.

25   *Research Involving Human Embryos Act 2002* (Cth) ss 10, 11.

1989 (Cth) (TGA 1989) and the regulations dealing with in-vitro diagnostic medical devices, defined as 'in general, pathology tests and related instrumentation used to carry out testing on human samples, where the results are intended to assist in clinic diagnosis or in making decisions concerning clinical management'.[26] From 2010, with a transitional period that was intended to finish in 2014 but was extended further, genetic tests for therapeutic purposes have been brought within the purview of the TGA 1989. They are described as in-vitro diagnostic medical devices (IVDs), class three.[27] The Therapeutic Goods Administration (TGA) notes that these types of medical devices present 'a moderate public health risk, or high individual risk, and often provide the critical or sole basis for correct diagnosis'.[28]

Human genetic testing, prenatal screening of women and screening of fetal congenital disorders are all captured by this classification.[29] The classification system determines what the TGA requires in terms of compliance with quality and safety standards, as well as performance characteristics of genetic tests. However, the TGA 1989 only regulates those tests that are used for therapeutic purposes. Non-therapeutic tests, such as those used for parentage and kinship, are not subject to the TGA 1989.[30] The new framework applies to all IVDs that are imported, supplied in, or exported from Australia. [31]

Given that the subjects of genetic testing may include some of the most vulnerable members of the community, such as children, concerns must be raised about appropriate rules regarding consent, capacity and privacy and protection from potential stigmatisation. With the development of inexpensive, non-invasive and easily accessible gene-testing kits, more people are starting to access genetic testing as a risk assessment device, rather than for diagnosis of an existing condition.[32] Following genetic testing, an otherwise non-symptomatic individual can find themselves with a list of pre-symptomatic conditions that are certain to manifest (such as Huntington's disease) and/or a list of predicted conditions that may never eventuate. This spectrum of genetic information may include results that impact an individual's life, both by altering their perception of themselves and their future life course, and in other material ways, such as their ability to access insurance.

As with healthcare practice more generally, the usual laws with respect to informed consent and best practice will apply to the provision of genetic testing services.[33] Notably, the kind of information that can be disclosed to third parties as a consequence of genetic testing is already subject to privacy legislation.[34] However, decisions about who may access genetic tests and for

---

26   See Australian Government, Department of Health, Therapeutic Goods Administration (TGA), *Overview of the Regulatory Framework for In-Vitro Diagnostic Medical Devices* (6 July 2011) <www.tga.gov.au/overview-regulatory-framework-vitro-diagnostic-medical-devices>.

27   TGA, *Classification of IVD Medical Devices* (Version 2.0, December 2015) 17 <http://www.tga.gov.au/sites/default/files/classification-ivd-medical-devices.pdf>.

28   Ibid 10.

29   *Therapeutic Goods (Medical Devices) Regulations 2002* (Cth) Sch 2A.

30   See TGA, above n 26. Tests used in Family Court cases and other legal contexts must be conducted by accredited testing facilities: see, for example, reg 21D of the *Family Law Act Regulations 1984* (Cth).

31   Ibid.

32   Darrol Baker et al., 'Genetic Tests Obtainable through Pharmacies: The Good, the Bad, and the Ugly' (2013) 7 *Human Genomics* 17.

33   For further details on the issue of the consent and the law, see Chapter 9.

34   For further details on privacy in the health context, see Chapter 12.

what reason are really a matter for health professionals. Reliance on their judgment in areas where the technology is developing rapidly makes sense because legislation can be rigid, and has a limited capacity for amendment and renewal. Nevertheless, there are special situations that may not be adequately covered by healthcare decision-making and existing laws.

As previously discussed, genetic testing of indigenous people raises specific cultural issues and demands special attention because of the need to maintain cultural self-determination. These issues may mean a requirement for different modes of consent and information-giving.[35] Genetic testing also raises other concerns – such as, for example, the need for pre- and post-test counselling – that are addressed in the relevant policy and ethical guidance documents. It may be that these should be legally binding requirements. This would have a flow-on effect to allied health services and their accreditation practices, which are currently inadequately codified.

The decision to offer genetic testing relies on shared assumptions about what constitutes a serious disease or disability. These assumptions are often unexpressed and therefore inadequately tested or nuanced; this is explored in more detail in Chapter 22. The conditions for which tests are offered may sometimes be viewed as stigmatising of people living with them. While most organisations have ruled out producing a list of conditions for which testing ought to be offered, it is certainly possible – and indeed desirable – to mandate structures that implement complex decision-making processes that take account of these concerns when offering testing, and to develop strategies to minimise the potential for any harm.[36]

Genetic discrimination

'Genetic discrimination' is a term that is generally used to describe discrimination against people based on their genetic predisposition to a characteristic or disease. Genetic information, with its capacity to reveal the health status of individuals and their kin, and to be predictive of potential future health developments, makes people vulnerable to discrimination in a range of areas, but particularly in employment and insurance. Genetic discrimination is indirectly covered by Australia's federal and state systems of anti-discrimination laws. Federal anti-discrimination legislation covers disability, sex, race and age discrimination, with genetic discrimination covered primarily by the *Disability Discrimination Act 1992* (Cth) (DDA). The DDA was amended in 2009 in order to clarify that the legislation applies to a 'disability' that 'may exist in the future (including because of a genetic predisposition to that disability)'.[37]

35   NHRMC, *Medical Genetic Testing: Information for Health Professionals* (2010) [4.3.5] <www.nhmrc .gov.au/_files_nhmrc/publications/attachments/e99.pdf>.

36   Ibid [1.5]: 'There are 1,787 genetic tests available, [and] of these approximately 400 types of tests were provided in Australia in 2006. Approximately 1% of these types of test were funded by Medicare; the remainder were funded by the patients themselves or through State and Territory governments.' But they go on to say: 'In 2007, the volume of Medicare-funded medical testing (of all types) was 7% higher than during 2006. However, the volume of Medicare-funded genetic testing increased by 90% during this period. In other words, genetic testing is expanding at a much faster rate than other forms of medical testing', drawing on findings from the Royal College of Pathologists of Australasia (RCPA), *Report of the Australian Genetic Testing Survey 2006*, prepared for the Commonwealth Department of Health and Ageing in consultation with the Human Genetics Society of Australasia (2008). Notably, Preimplantation Genetic Diagnosis (PGD) is not eligible for a Medicare rebate. For further details about PGD, see Chapter 13.

37   *Disability Discrimination Act 1992* (Cth) (DDA) s 4(1).

It would be possible for complaints of discrimination to fall within the scope of other anti-discrimination laws. For example, in the case of race, if a person is discriminated against because of being Jewish and therefore more likely to be a carrier of Tay Sachs disease; or in the case of sex, if a woman is fired from her employment because she has tested positive to the 'breast cancer' gene. An example of a genetic discrimination complaint that has been made public is the case of a man who was denied life insurance because he carried a mutation in the MSH6 gene, which made him more susceptible to cancer.[38] Another complaint involved a man who was denied parole following genetic testing for Huntington's disease.[39] There are no reported court decisions on genetic discrimination in Australia to date.[40]

Significant problems remain with using current anti-discrimination laws in relation to genetic status. First, the area of public life where genetic discrimination seems most prevalent is in the provision of insurance. Yet the DDA contains a broad exemption for insurance providers, who are permitted to discriminate if their actions are based upon actuarial or statistical data on which it is reasonable to rely;[41] or, in the absence of such data, where the discrimination is reasonable having regard to any other relevant factors.[42] This very broad industry exemption is justified on the basis that 'some discrimination is part of the nature of most types of insurance in Australia';[43] however, it makes genetic discrimination in insurance much more difficult to counter. Second, the inclusion of asymptomatic individuals in the definition of 'disability' in disability discrimination laws does theoretically mean that these individuals are protected. However, there is a conceptual problem that undermines the practical impact of the existing legal protections. Asymptomatic individuals are unlikely to conceptualise themselves as 'disabled' and thus discriminated against on the grounds of their disability, whereas they may well recognise that they are being discriminated against on the basis of their genes. This is an additional hurdle in accessing protection.

Genetic privacy

The idea that genetic information about an individual is uniquely powerful has been the rationale for proposed privacy law reform measures that regulate genetic information differently from other health information.[44] A counterargument to this rationale, however, is that genetic information is just one aspect of an individual's life, along with, for example, lifestyle choices and family history, and that all these aspects are, or can be, predictive of health status. Despite these opposing positions, there are aspects of genetic information that invest it with particular significance: first, the capacity of genetic information, particularly from genetic testing, to reveal health information about an individual's family members; and

---

38   Louise Keogh and Margaret Otlowski, 'Life Insurance and Genetic Test Results: A Mutation Carrier's Fight to Achieve Full Cover' (2013) 199(5) *The Medical Journal of Australia* 363.

39   Karen O'Connell, 'The Clean and Proper Body: Genetics, Stigma and Disability Discrimination Laws' (2009) 14(2) *Australian Journal of Human Rights* 139, 154.

40   In the US, see *Burlington Northern and Santa Fe Railway Co v Sheila White*, 126 S Ct 2405 (2006).

41   DDA s 46(1)(f).

42   DDA s 46(1)(g).

43   Australian Human Rights Commission, *Guidelines for Providers of Insurance and Superannuation* (2005) <www.humanrights.gov.au/guidelines-providers-insurance-and-superannuation>.

44   Australian Law Reform Commission (ALRC), *Essentially Yours: The Protection of Human Genetic Information in Australia*, Report 96 (2003) vol 1, 137–44.

second, the predictive nature of genetic information, which gives a stronger sense of an individual's future health risks than other health information.

In Australia, the privacy of genetic information is protected, along with other health information, under the *Privacy Act 1988* (Cth) (Privacy Act) and Australian Privacy Principles (APPs).[45] The Privacy Act also acknowledges the significance of genetic information for an individual's relatives by permitting the disclosure of genetic information about an individual to family members without consent in limited circumstances. Under the APPs, an organisation must not collect sensitive information, and must not use or disclose personal information for a purpose other than the primary purpose of collection without consent, unless an exception applies (APP 6). An exception applies to genetic information where 'the organisation reasonably believes that the use or disclosure is necessary to lessen or prevent a serious threat to the life, health or safety of another individual who is a genetic relative of the first individual'.[46] However, it is difficult to demonstrate a 'serious threat' where many genetic diseases or disorders manifest with varying and unknown degrees of severity or the genetic information indicates a 'risk' rather than a known outcome.

Genetic testing and the storage of genetic information also raises the question of whether a person should have a 'right not to know', since genetic testing can inform an individual of genetic risks and latent disorders they may not wish to know about. In addition, this information can also affect an individual's family members in terms of their own genetic risk. Privacy legislation builds in some minimal protection through requiring consent for testing and disclosure to others, but apart from the relatives' exception to consent outlined above, there is no specific 'right not to know' protected in law.

Biobanks

Biobanks have become crucial to genetic research programs. As outlined in Chapter 19, biobanks containing genetic information (any human tissue or blood sample is also genetic information) pose particular ethical challenges around privacy and consent. Privacy issues, for instance, are amplified, as genetic information can reveal the health status and other traits of familial and other kin groups. Further, it is difficult, if not impossible, for consent to be given to all future uses of human tissue samples and related genetic information. Given the pace of biotechnological development, it is likely that currently unimaginable uses of such information will emerge in the not-so-distant future.

So what would an ethical form of consent look like, in relation to genetic specimens held at biobanks? It has been proposed that the way forward is to operate a 'broad' consent, being a form of consent in which participants agree to categories or types of use, rather than the specific use(s) of their genetic material.[47] The relevant guideline, the NHMRC National Statement on Ethical Conduct in Human Research (NHMRC National Statement), allows for consent for future use of tissue or data to be 'specific', 'extended' or 'unspecific', thus providing a spectrum of valid consent, from narrow to broad.[48] Another way of adapting consent

---

45   For further details on privacy law as it applies in the health context, see Chapter 12.
46   *Privacy Act 1988* (Cth) s 16B(4).
47   NHMRC, *Biobanks Information Paper* (2010) <www.nhmrc.gov.au/_files_nhmrc/file/your_health/
      egenetics/practioners/biobanks_information_paper.pdf>; NHMRC, *National Statement*, above n 19,
      [2.2.14] <www.nhmrc.gov.au/book/chapter-2-2-general-requirements-consent>.
48   NHMRC, *National Statement*, above n 19, [2.2.14].

to genetic information is to allow it to be withdrawn or renegotiated.[49] The NHMRC National Statement also allows for these possibilities. A third debate concerning consent in biobanking arises in the case of group rights. Where the genetic information held for research impacts familial or kinship groups, communities, or racial or ethnic groups, should there be a form of group consent required? Given the difficult history of race and genetics, there is a strong argument to be made for group consent. However, the question then becomes who is authorised to give that consent?[50] How best to address the issue of consent in the context of biobanking is examined in detail in Chapter 19.

Property rights in genes

In Australia, the UK, Canada and the US, the courts and the legislatures have been reluctant to allow property claims by individuals over their own discarded human tissue samples. Instead, the more usual path has been to frame the rights we have as rights of control and consent to use. Nevertheless, third parties that have managed to obtain a commercial advantage using human tissue samples to isolate genes or create cell lines that have a medical benefit have been granted property rights in those products. Perhaps the most famous case is the US case of *Moore v Regents of the University of California*, in which the Supreme Court ruled that Moore's spleen, which had been used to create the 'Mo' cell line, was not his property but rather was the property of the researchers who had been granted a patent upon it.[51] The Court reasoned that a person's discarded cells cannot be their property. However, it did permit Moore's claims for breach of fiduciary duty and lack of informed consent.

In a similar case, *Greenberg v Miami Children's Hospital*, the US District Court for the state of Florida held that the bodily material provided by the plaintiffs were not their property, and that the gene responsible for their disease was the property of the scientists who had isolated it and the hospital that had patented it.[52] This is despite the fact that, unlike *Moore*, where there was a significantly different product created using Mr Moore's spleen, the scientists in *Greenberg* did not make a cell line but arguably merely discovered (or isolated) what is known as the Canavan gene. In the further case of *Washington University v Catalona* it was held that both the intellectual property in the body and the tangible physical parts of the body (ie. blood, DNA and tissue samples) were owned by the University, which had stored the parts in its biorepository.[53] The issues raised by this line of US cases in relation to how we (should) conceptualise property rights in human tissue is discussed in detail in Chapter 18.

---

49   For example, the National Centre for Indigenous Genomics, which holds thousands of samples of indigenous DNA from past collections, is developing a model of 'dynamic consent' that 'pursue[s] processes of ongoing consent, which allow a participant to change his/her consent at any time using a secure electronic interface' <http://ncig.anu.edu.au/ncig-collection/engagement-consent>.

50   David Winickoff, 'Governing Population Genomics: Law, Bioethics, and Biopolitics in Three Case Studies' (2003) 43 *Jurimetrics* 187, 197–8.

51   *Moore v Regents of the University of California*, 793 P 2d 479 (Supreme Court of California, 1990).

52   *Greenberg v Miami Children's Hospital Research Institute Inc*, 264 F Supp 2d 1064 (US District Court for the Southern District of Florida, 2003).

53   *Washington University v Catalona*, 490 F 3d 667 (8th Circuit 2007).

In Australia, the most significant case on this question was heard by the High Court in 2015. That case concerns the patent owned by the company Myriad Genetics over the BRCA1 and 2 breast cancer genes. While section 18(2) of the *Patents Act 1990* (Cth) states that: 'Human beings and the biological processes for their generation, are not patentable inventions', this does not preclude the patenting of genes that satisfy the criteria of a patentable invention under sections 18(1) and (1A) of the Act. Such criteria include the manner of manufacture as per the statute of monopolies, as well as the fact that it is novel and useful. If the isolated gene is an 'artificially created state of affairs', then it can be patented even if it also exists in nature. This is how the Federal Court viewed the process of isolating the BRCA1 and 2 genes by Myriad Genetics. The Court upheld the patent on the two breast cancer genes held by the company.[54] This was in direct contrast to an earlier US Supreme Court judgment that had struck the very same patents down, in the case of *Association for Molecular Pathology v Myriad Genetics*.[55] So it is perhaps not surprising that when the case eventually came before the Australian High Court, it overturned the Federal Court decision unanimously, holding that the isolated nucleic acid in question was not a patentable invention within the meaning of the Patents Act.[56]

The granting of property rights over genetic material has generated concerns that access to healthcare and pharmaceutical treatments for genetic diseases will be restricted because of economic interests. Activists have countered the move towards a 'corporatised' model of genetic ownership with a call to protect genes in a collective form, known as a 'genetic commons'. In an attempt to halt the patenting of genes, as well as micro-organisms, plants, animals and human bodily material, a number of non-government organisations (NGOs) have attracted significant support for their proposal for the adoption of a Treaty to Share the Genetic Commons.[57]

Genetic modification and gene therapy

Germ line gene therapy involves modifying a person's egg/sperm cells and thus results in an inheritable gene change, whereas somatic gene therapy involves the modification of non-reproductive cells, so theoretically, changes will not be passed on to future generations. In Australia, gene therapy is for the most part regulated as an IVD under the TGA 1989. However, it is the Office of the Gene Technology Regulator (OGTR) that oversees the approval of such therapy. Genetically modified cells are regulated as biologicals under the TGA 1989 and are generally classified as a class four IVD. This means that to be included on the Australian Register of Therapeutic Goods (ARTG) they must, similarly to class three IVDs, be evaluated by the TGA for safety, efficacy and quality.

In the case of class four IVDs, however, more onerous standards of analysis of supporting data are applied. Furthermore, the TGA must notify the OGTR whenever an application

---

54   *D'Arcy v Myriad Genetics Inc* (2014) 224 FCR 479.

55   *Association for Molecular Pathology v Myriad Genetics Inc*, 569 US (2013) (US Supreme Court, No 12–398, 13 June 2013).

56   *D'Arcy v Myriad Genetics Inc* (2015) 325 ALR 100.

57   'Activists Call for a Treaty to Share the Genetic Commons', *Biores* (online) 7 February 2002 <www .ictsd.org/bridges-news/biores/news/activists-call-for-a-treaty-to-share-the-genetic-commons>.

is made to place a genetically modified product on the ARTG. The OGTR will then provide written advice to the TGA which will take that advice on board when determining the application.[58] However, regulation of this kind does not stop people seeking out unproven stem cell 'treatments'. Indeed, a significant number of Australians travel overseas every year for these treatments, to countries such as China, India, Germany, the US and Panama.[59]

New and emerging genetic modification techniques demonstrate that there will continue to be regulatory challenges in the field of human genetics and health. The gene editing technique known as CRISPR, for example, shows promise in addressing genetic disorders more effectively. Its relative simplicity and accessibility as a technology, however, has also raised concerns about its use by 'biohackers' or 'DIY biologists' – people who conduct biological experiments in places that are outside of formal laboratory settings and so can be more difficult to monitor.[60]

Conclusion

While the 'cult of the gene' may seem to have subsided, this is in part because genetic explanations of human characteristics and health status have become embedded in our expectations of medical treatment, and our understandings of what it means to be 'well'. This chapter has shown that law primarily regulates genetic technologies in Australia 'behind the scenes', relying on a framework of guidelines and policies rather than direct legislative interventions. Moreover, the use of autologous cells or tissue is currently exempt from the Biologicals framework. This means that people intending to use their own cells or tissue can do so without the intervention of the TGA. However, given the complex and evolving nature of genetic knowledge, amendments to current legislation and new regulatory measures are inevitable, as the law continues to respond to the challenge of genetic knowledge.

---

58   TGA, *Australian Regulatory Guidelines for Biologicals* (June 2011) <www.tga.gov.au/sites/default/files/biologicals-argb-p1.pdf>.

59   Alan Petersen, Casimir MacGregor and Megan Munsie, 'Stem Cell Tourism Exploits People by Marketing Hope', *The Conversation* (online) 16 July 2014 <http://theconversation.com/stem-cell-tourism-exploits-people-by-marketing-hope-29146>.

60   Heidi Ledford, 'Biohackers Gear Up For Genome Editing' (2015) 524 *In Focus News, Nature* 398 <www.nwabr.org/sites/default/files/pagefiles/Ledford2015_Nature%7BBiohackersGearUpforCRISPR%7D.pdf>.

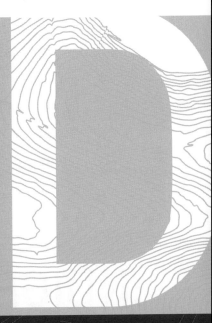

LAW AND
POPULATIONS

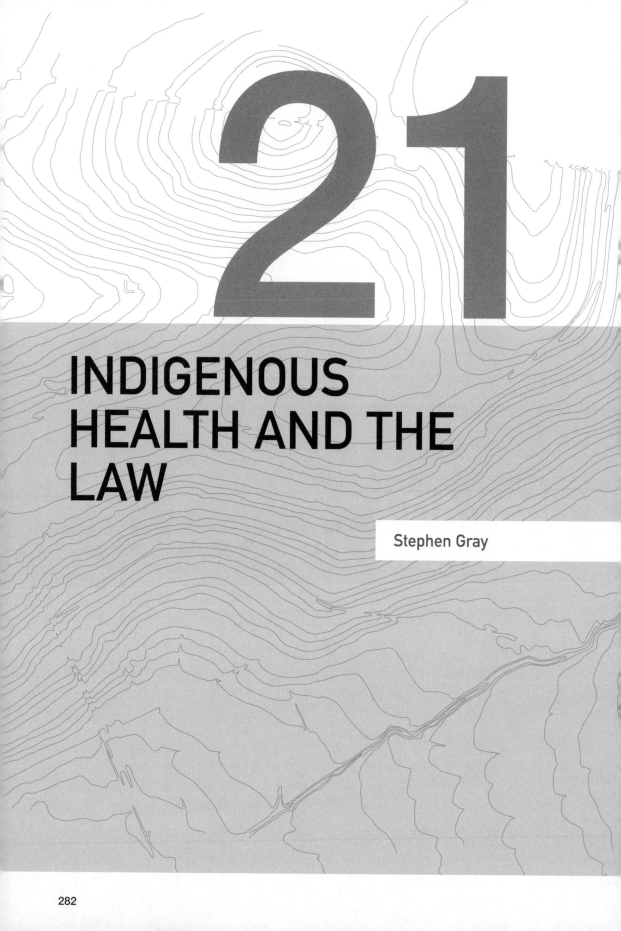

21

INDIGENOUS HEALTH AND THE LAW

Stephen Gray

Introduction

An examination of the way in which law interacts with Indigenous health in Australia must begin with an obvious question: why, after more than a century of apparently well-intentioned legal interventions, is Indigenous health still so dramatically worse than that of the non-Indigenous population? To begin to answer this question, it is necessary to understand that non-Indigenous law and Indigenous health have never existed in a neutral, interdependent relationship. Rather, non-Indigenous law is historically complicit in – and sometimes, directly responsible for – near-catastrophic damage to Indigenous bodies.

It is important to understand this history as far as possible in an 'Indigenous informed conceptual framework', a framework that respects the ways Indigenous people view health and the world.[1] This will help a non-Indigenous observer to both understand why Indigenous health has historically been so poor, and make some sense of the way the barriers to closing the gap between Indigenous and non-Indigenous health might be overcome. The first part of this chapter provides a brief snapshot of some key recent statistics on Indigenous health. The second part outlines some of the historical and policy issues that intersect with Indigenous health issues. The third part examines how law has interacted with and impacted upon Indigenous health for better and for worse.

Indigenous health: key indicators

Australian Indigenous peoples are 'probably one of the most researched and written about groups on earth'.[2] For example, a staggering 98 government and consultant reports into Indigenous people were produced between 2007 and October 2012. In just one month alone in 2011, these reports formed a stack of paper half a metre high.[3]

In 2016, the Prime Minister's 8th *Closing the Gap* report was published. The figures in this report build on an earlier and much more detailed report by a government steering committee, entitled *Overcoming Indigenous Disadvantage: Key Indicators 2014* (OID Report).[4]

These reports show some improvements in Indigenous health, as well as a number of significant problems:

- Life expectancy at birth for Aboriginal and Torres Strait Islander (ATSI) peoples increased from 67.5 years to 69.1 years for males and from 73.1 to 73.7 years for females between 2005 and 2012.[5] This represented a narrowing of the 'gap' between Indigenous and non-

---

1   Juanita Sherwood, 'Colonisation – It's Bad for Your Health: The Context of Aboriginal Health' (2013) 46(1) *Contemporary Nurse* 28; Juanita Sherwood and Sacha Kendall, 'Reframing Spaces by Building Relationships: Community Collaborative Participatory Action Research with Aboriginal Mothers in Prison' (2013) 46(1) *Contemporary Nurse*, 83, 86.

2   Ian Kerridge, Michael Lowe and Cameron Stewart, *Ethics and Law for the Health Professions*, 4th edn (Federation Press, 2013) 987.

3   As Altman and Russell argue, this 'evaluation fetishism' is a problem in itself: Jon Altman and Susie Russell, 'Too Much 'Dreaming': Evaluations of the Northern Territory National Emergency Response Intervention 2007–2012' (2012) 3 *Evidence Base* 1, 7–8.

4   Commonwealth of Australia, *Closing the Gap: Prime Minister's Report* (2016) (Closing the Gap Report) <http://closingthegap.dpmc.gov.au>; see also SCRGSP (Steering Committee for the Review of Government Service Provision), *Overcoming Indigenous Disadvantage: Key Indicators 2014* (2014) (Overcoming Indigenous Disadvantage or OID Report). The report comprised 13 chapters, multiple appendices and came to 3200 pages in total.

5   OID Report, above n 4, 16 (Overview 4.1).

Indigenous Australians from 11.4 years to 10.6 years for males and from 9.6 to 9.5 years for females. While this represented 'improved wellbeing' in the language of the OID Report, it does not represent much progress in 'closing the gap'.[6] On these statistics, it would take men 66.5 years and women 49.5 years to 'close the gap' – well short of the Commonwealth government's target of equality in life expectancy by 2031.

- Indigenous child mortality has declined by 33 per cent since 1998, and from 217 to 146 deaths per 100,000 population between 1998 and 2012.[7] Although this is arguably 'on track' to meet the 'closing the gap' target of halving the difference in mortality rates for Indigenous children within the decade to 2018, it is still significantly above the non-Indigenous child mortality rate.

In other areas, however, Indigenous health is actually getting worse:

- Rates of disability and chronic disease among Indigenous people rose from 21 per cent to 23 per cent between 2009 and 2013.
- Three-quarters of Indigenous deaths were classified as potentially avoidable during this period, compared to two-thirds of non-Indigenous deaths.
- Substantiated cases of child abuse and neglect of Indigenous children increased from 30 to 38 per 1000 children between 2009 and 2013: this rate is around 10 times higher than the rate for non-Indigenous children.[8]
- Hospitalisations for all chronic diseases except cancer are higher for Indigenous than for non-Indigenous Australians, with rates ranging from 9.9 times the rate for kidney failure to 1.6 times for circulatory disease.[9]
- Rates of reported psychological distress for Indigenous adults are increasing, with 30 per cent of Indigenous adults reporting high or very high levels of distress; this is about three times the rate for non-Indigenous adults.[10]
- Rates of suicide and intentional self-harm among Indigenous people are also increasing. The Indigenous suicide rate is almost twice the rate for non-Indigenous Australians, while hospitalisations for intentional self-harm increased by almost 50 per cent between 2004 and 2013.[11]

Statistics also suggest that violent crime rates are increasing, although this could possibly be an effect of increased attention being paid to this issue by police and other authorities. In 2013, the rate of imprisonment for Indigenous adults was 13 times the non-Indigenous imprisonment rate. Indigenous imprisonment rates increased by 77.4 per cent between 2000 and 2015, leading to a widening of the 'gap' between the rates for Indigenous and non-Indigenous people; however, significantly, equality in imprisonment rates is not actually a 'closing the gap' target.[12] Hospitalisation rates for family violence are extremely high: 34.2 times the rate for Indigenous as opposed to non-Indigenous women.[13]

6	Closing the Gap Report, above n 4, 42.
7	Ibid 9; OID Report, above n 4, 17.
8	OID Report, above n 4, 22–3 (figures 4.8 and 4.10), and 46 for figures on potentially avoidable deaths.
9	Ibid 979, table 4A, 8.18.
10	Ibid 48, figure 8.7.
11	Ibid 49, figure 8.8; see also Closing the Gap Report, above n 4, 47.
12	OID Report, above n 4, 252, box 4.12.1; Closing the Gap Report, above n 4, 51.
13	OID Report, above n 4, 1111, table 4A, 11.22.

Indigenous Australians remain over-represented as victims of violence. For example, recent data shows that Indigenous Australians were five times more likely to be victims of homicide than non-Indigenous Australians. The victim and offender were intimate partners in 47.4 per cent of Indigenous homicides, compared with just over 20 per cent of homicides among non-Indigenous people. Surprisingly, there were no Indigenous homicides where the victim and offender were strangers – this is a statistic which raises questions about the nature and causes of Indigenous crime, to which we will return later in the chapter.[14]

What do all these figures 'mean'? Unsurprisingly, they suggest that Indigenous health continues to be 'in crisis', even a 'national scandal'.[15] It is apparent that poor health outcomes are linked to other types of socio-economic disadvantage, such as inadequate schooling, low household income, overcrowding, unemployment and poor health choices (such as smoking).[16] To this can be added inadequate access to health services, a factor sometimes directly responsible for the death of Indigenous children from common childhood illnesses which would have been easily treatable had the child been within reach of a hospital.[17]

Equally unsurprisingly, Indigenous people identify broader factors as responsible. These include the destruction of culture, limited education, racism, alienation from their land, and the effects of grief and childhood violence:[18] a 'testament to the history of colonisation and its continuation'.[19] This clearly suggests that poor Indigenous health is not a 'lifestyle choice', in then Prime Minister Tony Abbott's now notorious use of the phrase;[20] instead, it is an effect of Australia's colonial and post-colonial history. This picture is complicated by evidence of Aboriginal resistance to white authority taking the form of 'non-compliance' with the well-intentioned plans of health professionals.[21]

Indigenous health and the law: a historical overview

In 1992, when the High Court first recognised Indigenous native title as part of the common law, Deane and Gaudron JJ described Australia's colonial history of dispossession and degradation of Aboriginal people as a 'national legacy of unutterable shame'.[22] Whether shame is an appropriate reaction to the history has been intensely debated ever since. Former Prime

---

14   Ibid 218 (para 4.93).

15   Sherwood, above n 1, 29.

16   As the OID Report notes, different aspects of disadvantage often occur together: see above n 4, 61 ('multiple disadvantage').

17   See, for example, the account of the death of Zena Stevens in Chris Howse, *Living Heart* (Charles Darwin University Press [CDU Press], 2007) 1–21.

18   Kerridge et al., above n 2, 989.

19   Sherwood, above n 1, 30.

20   In March 2015, the Prime Minister caused deep distress and offence in Indigenous communities by commenting that it was not the job of the taxpayer to subsidise the 'lifestyle choice' of Indigenous people to live in remote communities: see, for example, Michael Gordon, 'Tony Abbott's Lifestyle Choice Remark Leaves "Everyone Hurting Inside" in Remote Indigenous Communities', *Sydney Morning Herald*, 14 March 2015.

21   See further on this issue Kerridge et al., above n 2, 996–7.

22   *Mabo v Queensland (No 2)* (1992) 175 CLR 1 at 104 per Deane and Gaudron JJ.

Minister John Howard famously declared that he 'refuses to feel inter-generational guilt'[23] over past actions such as the Stolen Generations policies. Even during the purportedly bipartisan apology to the Stolen Generations of 2008, then Opposition Leader Brendan Nelson argued that 'good in many cases was sought to be done'.[24]

It is clear that since British colonisation, Aboriginal people have suffered conditions of great disadvantage and discrimination. Massacres were common during the early years, and persisted until at least the late 1920s in the less 'settled' areas in the north.[25] Sexual abuse by white men of Aboriginal women and children was widespread. The practice of 'running down' – or kidnapping – Aboriginal boys and girls on the frontier and keeping them for work and sexual companionship provided the major catalyst for 'protective' legislation governing Indigenous people, such as that passed in Queensland in 1897, and in the NT in 1910.[26] Nevertheless these and similar practices continued. As late as 1968, Stevens noted that Aboriginal women were 'fair game' for any white desirous of sexual adventure, and that 'the incidence of first sexual contact between Indigenous females and Caucasian males has risen only slightly above the seven-year-old females mentioned by Berndt [in 1946]'.[27] If sexual abuse is inter-generational, it is difficult not to see current problems of sexual abuse in Indigenous communities as having these historical roots.

The 'protective' era

Early 'protective' legislation was partly the product of some liberal white Australians' desire to shield Aboriginal people from the worst excesses of the colonial frontier. These 'good intentions' were mingled with other, less salubrious, impulses, such as a moral panic about interracial sex, or the desire to sweep the shame of 'comboism' – the practice of white men cohabiting with Indigenous women, and their mixed race progeny – under the carpet.[28] Consequently, the laws of the 'protection' era established strict controls over almost every aspect of Aboriginal peoples' lives, including place of residence, marriage, education and employment. Mixed-race children were frequently separated from their parents and communities. Justified at the time by the notion that such children were doomed to lives of squalor, sexual abuse and early death, these practices resulted in thousands of Aboriginal children being raised in harsh institutions where they were frequently

23   Desmond Manderson, 'Unutterable Shame/Unuttered Guilt: Semantics, Aporia and the Possibility of Mabo', (1998) 4 *Law, Text, Culture* 234.

24   Brendan Nelson, Leader of the Opposition, Parliament of Australia, House of Representatives, *Parliamentary Debates* (13 February 2008) 173–7. For the Apology to the Stolen Generations, Kevin Rudd, Prime Minster, Parliament of Australia, House of Representatives, *Parliamentary Debates* (13 February 2008) 167–73. This is the now-famous speech in which Prime Minister Rudd apologised to the members of the 'Stolen Generations', those Indigenous children removed from their families pursuant to previous government policies designed to assimilate them with the non-Indigenous population.

25   On the Northern Territory, see, for example, Stephen Gray, *Brass Discs, Dog Tags and Finger Scanners: the Apology and Aboriginal Protection in the Northern Territory 1863–1972* (CDU Press, 2011) 18ff. The Forrest River massacre occurred just west of the Territory's border in 1926; the equally famous, and officially sanctioned, Coniston massacre occurred in 1928.

26   See further discussion in ibid 29.

27   Frank Stevens, *Aborigines in the Northern Territory Cattle Industry* (ANU Press, 1974) 187. The reference to Berndt is to a report carried out by the anthropologists Ronald and Catherine Berndt between 1944 and 1946: see further discussion in Gray, above n 25, 99–102.

28   Gray, above n 25, 31–3.

physically or sexually abused. By the 1990s, this group had become widely known as the 'Stolen Generations'.[29] These strict controls also permitted unauthorised use of cultural heritage, including genetic material, an issue with ramifications for health and medical research even today.[30]

While in many respects the lives of Indigenous (and particularly part-Aboriginal) people were minutely managed, in other ways almost nothing was known about those lives. In 1912, for example, NT Chief Protector Baldwin Spencer airily estimated the number of Indigenous people in the NT as 'probably … more nearly 50,000 than 20,000'.[31] His successor during the 1930s, Dr Cecil Cook, proclaimed that 'in those days the Aboriginal person was like a gumtree – nobody cared, and nobody worried, he was just there – and nothing was done'. Aboriginal people were not counted as citizens. Nor, with rare exceptions, were they eligible for social security benefits such as widow's and old age pensions, and sickness or unemployment benefits, which were being created for other Australians at this time.[32]

The assimilation era

The assimilation era of the 1950s represented a small step forward in white Australians' understanding of these issues. In the NT, the list of Aboriginal people, known as the Register of Wards, allowed authorities to obtain statistics for the first time on endemic problems such as infant mortality, leprosy, tuberculosis, malaria and eye diseases: a 'rod for our own backs', as the NT's Director of Welfare, Harry Giese, observed. While those working in the field may have known more than their predecessors about the dire state of Aboriginal health, the broader community knew little, and cared less. For example, Giese claimed that he 'fought the department for a number of years to attach doctors to my staff. I wanted a doctor at Papunya in 1959.'[33]

Recognition of citizenship and rights

The civil rights era of the 1960s changed the political landscape, if not Aboriginal living conditions. These great upheavals are represented in popular memory today by the 'Wave Hill' walk-off of 1967, the 1967 referendum, the *Aboriginal Land Rights Act 1975* (Cth) and Prime Minister Gough Whitlam's announcement of the 'self-determination' era in 1972.[34] For the first time, some Aboriginal people had their own land. Outstations were created and

---

29	Human Rights and Equal Opportunity Commission, *Bringing Them Home – the Report* (1995).
30	For further details on the relationship between genetics and race, see Chapter 20.
31	Alan Powell, *A Far Country: A Short History of the Northern Territory* (CDU Press, 2009) 141–4.
32	For Cook's comments, see Gray, above n 25, 120, and for more detailed discussion of the situation regarding social security, see 139–42.
33	Oral history interview with Harry Giese, NTRS 226, TS 755, Northern Territory Archives Service, Darwin, tape 14 (4 October 1989) 6, quoted in Gray, above n 25, 152–3.
34	For further discussion of these events, see, for example, Gray, above n 25, 170–90. The Wave Hill walk-off was a strike of Aboriginal stock workers who were being paid at near slave rates. It led to a promise by Gough Whitlam to return Aboriginal land to its traditional owners, and ultimately therefore to the land rights legislation of the 1970s. The 1967 referendum led to Aboriginal people being counted in the Census as citizens and also to the removal of some (but by no means all) of the provisions in the Australian Constitution which discriminated against them.

Aboriginal people were legally free of discriminatory bureaucratic control, again for the first time since colonisation. Theoretically, they could aspire to determine or create their own lives as they wished.

Indigenous health, crime and the criminal process

Perhaps the first detailed and sympathetic scrutiny of Aboriginal living conditions came with the Royal Commission into Aboriginal Deaths in Custody, whose Final Report was released in 1991. Originally, the Royal Commission was established to investigate how and why 99 Aboriginal people had died in custody between 1980 and 1989. It began as a response to several particularly controversial deaths, and the firm belief of many in the Aboriginal community that Aborigines in custody were being murdered by the police. Following its establishment, however, the Commission's investigation of the issue broadened as it quickly became apparent that once in jail or police custody, an Aboriginal person was no more likely to die than a non-Aboriginal person. Rather, the significant number of Aboriginal people dying in custody was the product of the disproportionate number being arrested and put in custody in the first place. Nor were these figures the result of Aboriginal people committing more, and more serious, crimes. Aboriginal people were being arrested, put in jail and consequently dying as a result of minor crimes such as public drunkenness or failing to pay fines.[35]

However, the underlying issues went deeper. Of the 99 deaths in custody investigated by the Royal Commission, 30 were death by hanging, two deaths by other trauma, 23 by trauma other than hanging, 4 from substance abuse, and 37 by natural causes.[36] Somewhat counterintuitively, the proportion of Aboriginal people who died violent (trauma-related) deaths while in custody was actually less than the proportion of non-Aboriginal people who died such deaths. This in turn was the result of the poor general health of Aboriginal people in comparison to others. Thus, as the Royal Commission pointed out:

> [a] clear link exists between Aboriginal health and Aboriginal deaths in custody, or, more accurately, between Aboriginal sickness and Aboriginal deaths in custody ... Since so many Aboriginal people experience serious sickness and injury as part of their everyday lives, it should be *no* surprise to find that they bring this impaired health status with them into the custodial situation.[37]

Consequently, the Royal Commission made numerous recommendations relating to custodial health and safety. These included recommendations concerning police training to identify health issues, health screening of persons in custody, the introduction of a regular nursing or medical presence in principal watch-houses, and the development of protocols

---

35   'By far the most potentially significant area for [diverting Aboriginal people from police custody] ... is that of public drunkenness', see Elliott Johnston, *Royal Commission into Aboriginal Deaths in Custody, National Report* (AGPS, 1991) 21.1.1 (Decriminalisation of the Offence of Public Drunkenness and Other Offences).

36   Ibid 1.2.8 (Vol. 1).

37   Ibid 31.1.1 (Vol. 4) Chs 3 and 24.

for the care and management of Aboriginal prisoners at risk. There were also various recommendations made relating to Aboriginal health more generally.[38] These recommendations continue to be breached today.[39]

For some years after the Royal Commission, governments in all states and territories paid at least lip service to the idea that jail for Aboriginal people should be an option of last resort. This changed in 2006, when an Alice Springs public prosecutor, Dr Nanette Rogers, went public on the ABC's *Lateline* program about the alleged 'long silence' about child sexual abuse in Aboriginal communities in central Australia. While hardly new, the debate focused public attention on the supposed leniency of courts passing sentence in cases of serious crimes committed by Aboriginal men. In response, the NT government commissioned a report into the 'extent, nature and factors contributing to the sexual abuse of Aboriginal children'.[40] This report directly preceded the NT Intervention, discussed further below.

Indigenous health and the role of the coroner

Non-Indigenous law typically intervenes most immediately in issues of Indigenous health only when something has gone wrong. Most often and tragically, this is when an Indigenous person has died. Thus the law's intervention is likely to take the form of recommendations designed to ensure that similar situations do not occur again. This was the case with the 339 recommendations of the Royal Commission into Aboriginal Deaths in Custody (see earlier discussion). It is also true of coronial inquests, which are intended to reflect the fundamental principle of respect for and protection of human life. Whether such recommendations are implemented is traditionally viewed as a matter for government.

Coroners investigate unexpected deaths. Their traditional role is to identify the medical or medico-legal cause of death, and to make recommendations or comments in relation to that death; for example, whether any person should be prosecuted. More recently, the role of Coroners has broadened, and they are now empowered to make recommendations relating to public health and safety; about how to prevent avoidable deaths in future; and around identifying breaches of human rights.[41]

This expanded role has not escaped controversy. Some coroners have been resistant to a broader conception of their powers. An Aboriginal legal aid lawyer, Chris Howse, has

---

38   Ibid recommendations 122–67 (Custodial Health and Safety) and 246–71 (Towards Better Health).

39   For example, see Christine Clements, Acting State Corner, Office of the Queensland State Coroner, *Inquest into the death of Mulrunji* (27 September 2006) and further coronial investigations discussed below.

40   Northern Territory Government, *Little Children Are Sacred, Report of the Northern Territory Board of Inquiry into the Protection of Aboriginal Children from Sexual Abuse* (2007). For a more detailed discussion of this and the publicity surrounding the ABC's *Lateline* episode, see Stephen Gray and Jenny Blokland, *Criminal Laws Northern Territory*, 2nd edn (Federation Press, 2012) 40–2.

41   See Roy Watterson, Penny Brown and John McKenzie, 'Coronial Recommendations and the Prevention of Indigenous Death' (2008) 12(6) *Australian Indigenous Law Review* 4; Jonathon Hunyor, 'Disgrace: The Death of Mr Ward' [2009] *IndigLawB* 42; (2009) 7(15) *Indigenous Law Bulletin* 3.

written at length about his dispute with the Coroner during an inquiry into the death of a two-year old Aboriginal child in the NT's Barkly region. Howse asked the Coroner to recommend to the Attorney-General that a doctor be provided in the Barkly. The Coroner refused to make such a recommendation, arguing that his power to make recommendations on matters of public health and safety did not extend to such matters. The Coroner added that his 'recommendations have to be rooted in realism ... Otherwise people aren't really going to listen to me.'[42] The clear implication was that the provision of funding for a doctor was a matter for the executive, and that for a judicial officer to trespass into such matters would be tactically and politically unwise.

Coroners have not always taken such a narrow view. A state Coroner in WA, Alistair Hope, made wide-ranging recommendations in an inquiry into the death of Mr Ward, an Aboriginal elder from the Ngaanyatjarrra lands, who died in 2008 after spending several hours in extreme heat in the back of a prisoner transport van between Laverton and Kalgoorlie. The Coroner found that Mr Ward was subjected to degrading treatment and was not treated with humanity or respect for the inherent dignity of the human person, which was in breach of international law. He also reported on systemic issues with a view to formulating constructive recommendations to reduce the incidence of future avoidable deaths.[43]

Of course, recommendations 'can only save lives if they are responded to by the agencies and entities responsible'.[44] That this is the case is apparent in the history of the recommendations of the Royal Commission into Aboriginal Deaths in Custody, which led to a flood of government reports claiming successful implementation, but no actual reduction in Indigenous imprisonment rates. Evidence suggests that coronial recommendations were often not communicated to the agencies at whom they were directed; were lost within bureaucratic processes; or were ignored.[45] One suggested solution to such problems is to create a 'uniform national coronial public reporting and review scheme', making coronial recommendations easily publicly available, and hopefully ensuring that they are considered and responded to by relevant government agencies and others. [46]

The NT Intervention

In 2007, the Commonwealth government announced that it would make an 'immediate and urgent response' to the perceived problem of child sexual abuse in the NT. This soon became known as the NT Intervention, or the NT Emergency Response (NTER). The Commonwealth government's package of legislation was wrapped up in the language of urgency and disaster, with then Prime Minister Howard justifying action on the grounds that it represented 'Australia's Hurricane Katrina'.[47] It involved bypassing ordinary civil

---

42   Howse, above n 17, 16.
43   Hunyor, above n 41, 6.
44   See Australian Inquest Alliance, *Submission to the National Human Rights Action Plan Baseline Study Consultation* (2011) 9 <www.ag.gov.au/Consultations/Documents/Publicsubmissionsonthedraftbaselinestudy/AustralianInquestAlliance.pdf>.
45   Watterson et al., above n 41, 4, 5.
46   Australian Inquest Alliance, above n 44, 15.
47   Kerridge et al., above n 2, 1004.

rights and obligations, such as those involving non-discrimination on the basis of race. In its initial incarnation, aspects of the NTER legislation were excluded from the operation of the *Racial Discrimination Act 1975* (Cth). The legislation contained extensive restrictions on the possession, consumption and sale of liquor in Aboriginal communities; instituted a land acquisition scheme over Aboriginal townships and town camps; and introduced a controversial income management regime (IMR) under which a proportion of welfare recipients' payments would be quarantined, ostensibly so that it would not be spent on alcohol.[48]

In late 2007 there was a federal election and the then Liberal government under John Howard lost power and was replaced by a Labor government under Kevin Rudd. Once in power, Rudd apologised to members of the Stolen Generations in February 2008 and at the same time launched a campaign to 'close the gap' between Indigenous and non-Indigenous people. He also committed to 'reinstating' or restoring the operation of the *Racial Discrimination Act 1975* (Cth). In 2010, the Labor government passed legislation repealing those aspects of the original NTER legislation which explicitly contravened (or suspended the operation of) the Act. In 2012, the NTER legislation was repealed in its entirety and was replaced by a new package of legislation known as the *Stronger Futures in the Northern Territory Act 2012* (Cth).[49] However, the Stronger Futures legislation continues to receive criticism on the basis that it is inconsistent with Australia's human rights obligations, including the UN Declaration on the Rights of Indigenous People.[50]

So is the Intervention working? For some observers, it is a 'return to the ration days' of control by white authority.[51] For others, the increased funding and attention given to Aboriginal disadvantage as a result of Intervention policies provides 'some grounds for optimism'.[52] This is so even if much of the funding in practice appears to have gone to non-Indigenous bureaucrats and government consultants.[53] Some measures of health have improved, but in the process, human rights obligations have been contravened, or at the very least, only been paid lip service. Many Aboriginal people have been disempowered. Even where short-term improvements have occurred, it seems unlikely that the long-term aim of empowering Aboriginal people to determine their own healthy futures (improving health being a stated aim of the NTER) has been advanced.

---

48   *Northern Territory National Emergency Response Act 2007* (Cth) Parts 3, 4 and 7. For further discussion see Gray and Blokland, above n 40, 43–5, and Kerridge et al., above n 2, 1004.

49   For the 2010 changes, see the *Social Security and Other Legislation Amendment (Welfare Reform and Reinstatement of Racial Discrimination Act) Act 2010* (Cth).

50   See, for example, Parliamentary Joint Committee on Human Rights, Commonwealth of Australia, *Examination of Legislation in accordance with the Human Rights (Parliamentary Scrutiny) Act 2011: Stronger Futures in the Northern Territory Act 2012*, Eleventh Report, (2013).

51   Paddy Gibson, 'Return to the Ration Days: the NT Intervention: Grass-Roots Experience and Resistance', Jumbunna Indigenous House of Learning, (2012) 3 *Ngaya – Talk the Law*.

52   Kerridge et al., above n 2, 1004.

53   For further discussion of the cost of the NTER, including the excessive cost of evaluation reports and of the 'Government Business Manager', see Altman and Russell, above n 3, 14–15.

Analysing the relationship between Indigenous health and the law

This chapter has outlined the historically negative impact of Australia's legal system upon Indigenous health. It has also pointed out some of the potentially positive impacts of legal changes such as those recommended by the Royal Commission into Aboriginal Deaths in Custody, or in some coronial reports. However, these can only have practical impact to the extent that they are listened to and implemented by government, and to the extent that they are consistent with the needs and wishes of Indigenous people themselves (as the history of the NT Intervention suggests).

International law is increasingly relevant to issues of Indigenous health. Relevant international law rights include the right to self-determination; the right to equal protection and non-discrimination; the right to social security; the right to an adequate standard of living; and the right not to have one's privacy, home or family unlawfully or arbitrarily interfered with.[54] The UN Declaration on the Rights of Indigenous People provides further rights, such as the right to determine and develop priorities and strategies for exercising their right to develop. This includes 'the right to be actively involved in developing and determining health, housing and other economic and social programmes affecting them and, as far as possible, to administer such programs through their own institutions'.[55]

There is, however, a further source of law that is of arguably even greater relevance to issues of Indigenous health. As long ago as 1986, the Australian Law Reform Commission noted the clear desire of Aboriginal people for the recognition of their law.[56] As was noted above, Aboriginal people often locate the source of their own ill-health in the destruction of Aboriginal culture, or the effects of colonisation. Indigenous people have argued that the way forward is through a 'collaborative community' approach that affirms and respects Indigenous knowledge, including 'ways of sharing and collating data such as storytelling and yarning'.[57] Perhaps the law most relevant to issues of Indigenous health, therefore, is Indigenous custom and law itself.

Conclusion

This chapter has looked first at statistics on Indigenous health. It has demonstrated that Indigenous health is still significantly worse than non-Indigenous health in key areas. It has outlined some of the major historical and policy developments that have contributed to this situation. Finally, it has outlined some of the legal avenues that might be used to overcome Indigenous health problems, including international and Indigenous law. A better relationship between non-Indigenous law and Indigenous health would involve the law respecting an 'Indigenous informed conceptual framework', which at the very least involves listening to the concerns of Indigenous people, and ensuring that their views are taken into account.

---

54   See further detail and discussion of these rights in Parliamentary Joint Committee on Human Rights, above n 50, 17 ff.

55   UN Declaration on the Rights of Indigenous People, Art 23, discussed in ibid 18.

56   ALRC, *The Recognition of Aboriginal Customary Law*, Report No 31 (1986), discussed in Gray and Blokland, above n 40, 46.

57   Sherwood and Kendall, above n 1, 87–8.

22

HEALTH LAW AND PEOPLE WITH DISABILITY

Isabel Karpin

Introduction

The relationship between health law and disability is not straightforward. The traditional *medical model* of disability, that views disability as a physical problem, intrinsic to the individual, has been the subject of sustained criticism by disability scholars and others working in the field.[1] Instead, in recent regulatory and policy instruments, the *social model* of disability has replaced the medical model. The social model proposes that disability is the consequence of structural and systemic breakdowns that fail to create inclusive and responsive environments to non-normative bodies. This model arguably reached a highpoint when, together with a human rights model, it was used in the development of the Convention on the Rights of Persons with Disabilities (CRPD).[2]

In contexts where advocacy for the rights of people living with disability has been effective, the social model has demanded changes that promote broader accessibility and challenge assumptions about capabilities. Disability advocates have argued that rather than, or in addition to, offering a medical or health fix, what is needed is a reimagining of the social and a reconstruction of the environment. In recent disability studies debates, the key assertion is that people are both embodied and constituted within and by particular social, political and medical contexts.[3]

This chapter, then, explores the way disability is both constructed and managed through legal, as well as medical and social, discourses. The institution of law forms part of the social context that constitutes the embodied subject and contributes to the construction of notions of ability and disability. The law thus has an important role to play in addressing and redressing differential and discriminatory treatment, and in the administrative mechanisms for managing difference in our community. In order to explore these issues, the first part of the chapter examines some of the definitions of disability used in law and social policy and

---

1   For a small sample of this rapidly growing field, see: Gary L Albrecht, Katherine Delores Seelman and Michael Bury (eds), *Handbook of Disability Studies* (Sage Publications, 2001) 97; Lennard J Davis (ed.), *The Disability Studies Reader*, 4th edn (Routledge, 2013); Lennard J Davis, 'Constructing Normalcy' in Lennard J Davis (ed.), *The Disability Studies Reader*, 4th edn (Routledge, 2013) 3; Barbara M Altman, 'Disability Definitions, Models, Classification Schemes, and Applications' in Gary L Albrecht, Katherine Delores Seelman and Michael Bury (eds), *Handbook of Disability Studies* (Sage Publications, 2001) 97; Carol Thomas, 'How is Disability Understood? An Examination of Sociological Approaches' (2004) 19(6) *Disability and Society* 569; Tom Shakespeare, 'The Family of Social Approaches' in Tom Shakespeare, *Disability Rights and Wrongs* (Routledge, 2006) 9; Anita Silvers, 'On the Possibility and Desirability of Constructing a Neutral Conception of Disability' (2003) 24 *Theoretical Medicine* 471; Fiona Kumari Campbell, 'Refusing Able(ness): A Preliminary Conversation about Ableism' (2008) 11(3) *M/C Journal: A Journal of Media and Culture*; Mairian Corker and Tom Shakespeare, 'Mapping the Terrain' in Mairian Corker and Tom Shakespeare (eds), *Disability/Postmodernity: Embodying Disability Theory* (Continuum, 2002) 1; Rosemarie Garland-Thomson, 'The Case for Conserving Disability' (2012) 9(3) *Journal of Bioethical Inquiry* 339; Arlene S Kanter, 'The Law: What's Disability Studies Got to Do With It or An Introduction to Disability Legal Studies' (2010–11) 42 *Columbia Human Rights Law Review* 403.

2   *Convention on the Rights of Persons with Disabilities* (CRPD), opened for signature 30 March 2007, 2515 UNTS 3 (entered into force 3 May 2008) <www.un.org/disabilities/convention/conventionfull .shtml>. The CRPD was unprecedented in its involvement of people with disability when being drafted. It is also the international Convention with the most number of ratifications by Member States in UN history.

3   See above n 1; Gillian Einstein and Margrit Shildrick, 'The Postconventional Body: Retheorising Women's Health' (2009) 69(2) *Social Science and Medicine* 293.

the second part explores contemporary models of disability posed by legal theorists, sociologists and bioethicists. There are many important areas of concern that might have been considered in this chapter, but given the constraints of space, rather than attempt to cover all issues at a superficial level, the chapter instead provides the tools for interrogating laws dealing with people with disability in a health law context.

That said, it should be noted that some important and relevant areas for people with disability that have not been included in this chapter appear elsewhere in this book. For example, the regulation of consent, coercion and capacity in the context of disability are touched on in Chapters 9 and 10; and a discussion of this area as it relates to mental health is examined in Chapter 23. For a discussion of the regulation of end-of-life decision-making where a disability is diagnosed, see Chapters 15 and 16. A discussion of constraints on reproductive decision-making using assisted reproductive technology (ART) and abortion for disability is briefly covered in Chapter 13.

Defining disability in law

'Disability' is a broad term encompassing physical and intellectual impairments, mental illness, brain injuries and difficulties in communication and developing social relations among others. Each of these in itself is heterogeneous and applies to a complex and richly diverse community of people.

Convention on the Rights of Persons with Disabilities and the National Disability Insurance Scheme

A good place to begin a discussion of the meaning of 'disability' is in the international sphere. We find an agreed set of norms or standards in the CRPD.[4] The Convention aims to enable the full participation of persons with disabilities in society. It does so by acknowledging that bodily impairment is constructed as disability by the socio-economic and political contexts in which it is embedded. The Convention states:

> Persons with disabilities include those who have long-term physical, mental, intellectual or sensory impairments which in interaction with various barriers may hinder their full and effective participation in society on an equal basis with others.[5]

By incorporating the existence of barriers, this definition acknowledges the social component of the construction of disability. Whether a difference is one that is disabling will depend on how well the particular difference is accommodated or incorporated into what is viewed as normal in the relevant social context.

By contrast, it is instructive to look at the definition of disability that appears in the Australian National Disability Insurance Scheme (NDIS). The Scheme is being rolled out across Australia in order to provide a range of disability services. The legislation which establishes the Scheme is the *National Disability Insurance Scheme Act 2013* (Cth) (NDIS Act). Those who seek services under the terms of the NDIS Act must first make an access

4   CRPD, above n 2.
5   Ibid Art 1.

request.[6] There are a number of threshold measures needed to meet the access criteria, including age and residence requirements, as well as disability or early intervention requirements.[7] Taking a closer look at the 'disability requirements', it becomes clear that these are highly contextual. Section 24 of the NDIS Act reads as follows:

> (1) A person meets the disability requirements if:
>
> (a) the person has a disability that is attributable to one or more intellectual, cognitive, neurological, sensory or physical impairments or to one or more impairments attributable to a psychiatric condition; and
>
> (b) the impairment or impairments are, or are likely to be, permanent; and
>
> (c) the impairment or impairments result in substantially reduced functional capacity to undertake, or psychosocial functioning in undertaking, one or more of the following activities:
>
> (i) communication;
>
> (ii) social interaction;
>
> (iii) learning;
>
> (iv) mobility;
>
> (v) self-care;
>
> (vi) self-management; and
>
> (d) the impairment or impairments affect the person's capacity for social and economic participation; and
>
> (e) the person is likely to require support under the National Disability Insurance Scheme for the person's lifetime.
>
> (2) For the purposes of subsection (1), an impairment or impairments that vary in intensity may be permanent, and the person is likely to require support under the National Disability Insurance Scheme for the person's lifetime, despite the variation.

It can be seen from the list of activities set out in section 24(1)(c) above that impairment and functioning are as much determined by the limits of the existing social, communications and economic environment as by the person's physiological make-up.[8] This is further borne out by the way in which the NDIS Act has been translated into a user-friendly format with an online questionnaire on the NDIS website. Question 4 in the series of questions on the website asks:[9]

> 4. Do you usually need support from a person or equipment to do everyday things for yourself because of an impairment or condition that is likely to be permanent?

---

6   *National Disability Insurance Scheme Act 2013* (NDIS Act) ss 18–20.

7   Ibid ss 21–25.

8   Interestingly, the first NDIS case to come before the Federal Court, *Mulligan v National Disability Insurance Agency* (2015) 146 ALD 418, dealt with a question of context. The appellant argued that the Administrative Appeals Tribunal had erred when it found him ineligible for the scheme on the basis that his impairment did not result in 'substantially reduced functional capacity for mobility and self-care'. In overturning the decision, the Federal Court made it clear that the Tribunal must examine the individual circumstances of the applicant and may not apply a global standard.

9   NDIS, *NDIS Access Checklist* <https://myplace.ndis.gov.au/ndisstorefront/ndis-access-checklist.html>.

The question goes on:

> To meet the NDIS disability rules you need to have an impairment or condition that is likely to be permanent (lifelong) and that stops you from doing everyday things by yourself.
>
> The following questions may help you decide if your answer is 'yes'. Do you usually need support from a person or assistive equipment so you can:
>
> - understand and be understood by other people?
> - make and keep friends and cope with feelings and emotions?
> - understand, remember and learn new things?
> - get out of bed and move around the home and outside the home?
> - take a bath or shower, dress and eat?
> - do daily jobs, handle money and make decisions?[10]

As we can see, part of the eligibility criteria relies on a concept of 'everyday things'. But what is an 'everyday thing' is highly subjective and depends on the specific social infrastructure and culture that makes 'everyday things' commonplace and possible. In this sense, if one has a difference that is stigmatised or marginalised in the social context, social structures will not necessarily be created to accommodate that difference. Such a person will be less accommodated than a person whose body is socially and politically valued or considered normal or mainstream. This is compounded when bodily variation intersects with stigma attached to varying identities, such as those based on race and gender.[11]

Anti-discrimination laws and social welfare benefits

Disability has been described from a variety of standpoints, including medical, economic, socio-political and administrative. It has been argued that it is not possible to provide a global definition of disability and, as Altman has said, this is most dramatically demonstrated when a person is:

> defined as disabled in one context and not in another, such that he or she receives therapies for serious impairments but does not qualify for certain disability-related benefits provided by his or her employer or by the government.[12]

A similar issue arises when disability is defined broadly for anti-discrimination purposes, but still narrowly for social welfare benefits. In Australia, for example, the definition of disability contained in the *Disability Discrimination Act 1992* (Cth) (DDA) is broader than definitions of disability found in legislation that provides benefits to people living with disabilities. Note that in section 4 of the DDA, disability in relation to a person, means:

> (a) total or partial loss of the person's bodily or mental functions; or
>
> (b) total or partial loss of a part of the body; or
>
> (c) the presence in the body of organisms causing disease or illness; or

---

10   Ibid.

11   Einstein and Shildrick, above n 3; Subini Ancy Annamma, David Connor and Beth Ferri, 'Dis/ability Critical Race Studies (DisCrit): Theorizing at the Intersections of Race and Dis/ability' (2013) 16(1) *Race Ethnicity and Education* 1.

12   Altman, above n 1, 98.

(d) the presence in the body of organisms capable of causing disease or illness; or

(e) the malfunction, malformation or disfigurement of a part of the person's body; or

(f) a disorder or malfunction that results in the person learning differently from a person without the disorder or malfunction; or

(g) a disorder, illness or disease that affects a person's thought processes, perception of reality, emotions or judgment or that results in disturbed behaviour;

and includes a disability that:

(h) presently exists; or

(i) previously existed but no longer exists; or

(j) may exist in the future (including because of a genetic predisposition to that disability); or

(k) is imputed to a person.

To avoid doubt, a *disability* that is otherwise covered by this definition includes behaviour that is a symptom or manifestation of the disability.

This definition can be contrasted with that found in the NDIS (see above) and other state-based legislation that aims to provide disability services rather than protect those classified as disabled from discrimination. For example, the *Disability Act 2006* (Vic) aims to provide a framework for the provision of services and supports to people with a disability. The Act defines 'disability' in relation to a person as:

(a) a sensory, physical or neurological impairment or acquired brain injury or any combination thereof, which—

    (i) is, or is likely to be, permanent; and

    (ii) causes a substantially reduced capacity in at least one of the areas of self-care, self-management, mobility or communication; and

    (iii) requires significant ongoing or long term episodic support; and

    (iv) is not related to ageing; or

(b) an intellectual disability; or

(c) a developmental delay.[13]

While it is still a broad definition, the requirement that it is permanent and that it actively hinder the person's capacity for self-care and management, among other things, limits the coverage of the legislation to a narrower class than would be captured under the DDA. For instance, would it apply, as the DDA does, to people who have not yet become disabled though they have a genetic predisposition to a condition, such as breast cancer? Would it cover people who were once disabled but no longer are? Finally, would it include people who, for whatever reason, have had a disability imputed to them?

Similarly, the *Disability Inclusion Act 2014* (NSW), which aims to regulate disability supports and services until mid 2018, at which point the NDIS will be extended to the whole of NSW, also offers a narrower definition of disability than that found in the DDA. Drawing on the definition found in the CRPD, disability in relation to a person is defined as including:

a long-term physical, psychiatric, intellectual or sensory impairment that, in interaction with various barriers, may hinder the person's full and effective participation in the community on an equal basis with others.[14]

---

13   *Disability Act 2006* (Vic) s 3.

14   *Disability Inclusion Act 2014* (NSW) s 7.

Contrast this to the expansive definition provided in relation to disability in section e of the Preamble of the CRPD:

> e. ... disability is an evolving concept and ... results from the interaction between persons with impairments and attitudinal and environmental barriers that hinders [sic] their full and effective participation in society on an equal basis with others.

Disability can thus be defined according to varying criteria, and each has its own problematic component. If the definition is based on functional capacity or permanent limitation, then the availability of a prosthesis, the effectiveness of therapy or the provision of pharmaceuticals may mean that the person is no longer classified as disabled within the relevant definition. Ironically, a state or territory that provides these assistive devices as part of disability service provision may render the recipient definitionally no longer disabled.[15] For example, Altman refers to the US case of *Sutton v United Airlines Inc*,[16] where the US Supreme Court limited the applicability of employment discrimination protection where the individual had access to assistive technologies such as mobility aids and other kinds of prosthesis.[17] This is despite the fact, one has to assume, that the provision of a prosthesis may not eliminate stigma and the impulse towards discriminatory treatment.[18]

Defining 'disability' in social policy

Disability at the beginning of life

An expanded definition of disability operates in the context of discrimination and protection from stigmatisation. As we have already seen, a much narrower view of disability is used in the provision of social services. However, an expanded definition of disability, or a narrow conceptualisation of normalcy, do not just operate in the context of anti-discrimination laws; they also operate in the context of decisions made at the beginning and end of life. For example, the diagnosis of a genetic or morphological anomaly or deviation in the context of prenatal testing of fetuses may facilitate legal access to abortion in some jurisdictions.[19] Further, the intention to avoid the birth of a child with a serious disability will provide the

---

15   For another example of this definitional problem, the story of Amy Silverman and her daughter, broadcast on *This American Life* in 2008, is instructive: *This American Life*, 'Educated Guess', 358: *Social Engineering Act Three* (27 June 2008) <www.thisamericanlife.org/radio-archives/episode/358/social-engineering?act=3>.

16   *Sutton v United Airlines Inc*, 527 US 471 (1999).

17   Joan Biskupic, 'Supreme Court Limits Meaning of Disability', *Washington Post*, 23 June 1999, 1, cited in Altman, above n 1.

18   In a number of cases, including *Sutton v United Airlines Inc* (see above n 16), the US Supreme Court held that the *Americans with Disabilities Act* 42 USC § 12102 does not protect those individuals who can mitigate or correct their disability by medication, for example.

19   For example, abortion is legal in SA, if two doctors agree that a woman's physical and/or mental health is endangered by the pregnancy, or for serious fetal abnormality: see *Criminal Law Consolidation Act 1935* (SA) s 82A; *Criminal Law Consolidation (Medical Termination of Pregnancy) Regulations 2011* (SA) reg 4, Sch 1. Similarly, in the NT, abortion is legal up to 14 weeks of pregnancy; this is extended to 23 weeks if two doctors agree that a woman's physical and/or mental health is endangered by the pregnancy, or for serious fetal abnormality: see *Medical Services Act 1982* (NT) s 11. For further discussion of abortion in the law, see Isabel Karpin and Kristin Savell, *Perfecting Pregnancy: Law Disability and the Future of Reproduction* (CUP, 2012) 106; Kristin Savell, 'The Legal Significance of Birth' (2006) 29(2) *The University of New South Wales Law Journal* 200.

legal justification for the use of preimplantation genetic diagnosis to select embryos that are identified as 'unaffected' by a condition in the context of in-vitro fertilisation (IVF).[20]

Defining disability for statistical purposes

Furthermore, for statistical purposes, a broad definition of disability is preferred, as it increases the capacity to refine statistical analysis of the category based on specific criteria. According to the Australian Institute of Health and Welfare (AIHW), and as used in the Australian Bureau of Statistics (ABS) Survey of Disability, Ageing and Carers, 'disability' is defined as 'any limitation, restriction or impairment which restricts everyday activities and has lasted, or is likely to last, for at least six months'.[21] This is a much more inclusive definition than that found in the *Disability Inclusion Act 2014* (NSW), the *Disability Act 2006* (Vic) or the *National Disability Insurance Scheme Act 2013* (Cth), all of which require a long-term or permanent impairment. The resource implications of this broader definition, which again relies on a shared understanding of what constitutes the 'everyday', is demonstrated by the finding in the 2011 Census that based on this criteria, just under one in five Australians reported having a disability.[22]

As part of their classification and coding, the ABS also classifies disability by level of severity. There are four levels of severity: profound, severe, moderate and mild.[23] A profound disability would be one where an individual 'is unable to do, or always needs help with, a core activity task',[24] whereas a severe disability would be where an individual sometimes needs help or has difficulty communicating.[25] Core activities are self-care, mobility and communication, and include washing, toileting, dressing and eating.[26] On this definition, it appears that 'core' is something like the 'everyday' used in legal definitions discussed earlier.

In 2011, the Productivity Commission published a report, Disability Care and Support, which recommended that the NDIS be established.[27] In its report, the Commission found that:

> under the ABS's approach, many intellectual disabilities might not be categorised as severe or profound (reflecting the omission of learning as a 'core activity limitation').

---

20   See Chapter 13; Karpin and Savell, above n 19, 157; NHMRC ART Guidelines.

21   ABS, *4430.0 – Disability, Ageing and Carers, Australia: Summary of Findings, 2012* (18 September 2014) <www.abs.gov.au/ausstats/abs@.nsf/Lookup/A813E50F4C45A338CA257C21000E4F36?opendoc ument>.

22   Ibid.

23   ABS, *Rates of Disability in Australia* (6 August 2013) <www.abs.gov.au/ausstats/abs@.nsf/Lookup/ 4429.0main+features100232009>.

24   Ibid.

25   Ibid.

26   Ibid.

27   Australian Government, Productivity Commission, *Disability Care and Support*, Inquiry Report No 54, Productivity Commission (Commonwealth of Australia, 2011) <www.pc.gov.au/inquiries/ completed/disability-support/report>.

However, in the Commission's view, there were strong grounds for a disability scheme to provide funded supports to people with an intellectual disability.[28]

The DALY and the ICF

Another method used to define disability was developed by the World Health Organization (WHO), together with the World Bank, and provides a basis for comparison of the impact of disabilities across nations. This method uses a metric known as the daily adjusted life years (DALY) and it is calculated by the sum of years of life lost from premature mortality in the population (termed YLL), plus years of life lost due to a disability (termed YLD), adjusted for the severity of disability.[29] The calculation of the YLD for a particular disability includes a number of factors, such as the severity of the disease on a scale from zero (perfect health) to one (dead).[30]

The WHO also uses another method of classification, known as the International Classification of Functioning, Disability and Health (ICF). The ICF is used in conjunction with other accepted measures, such as (for mental and behavioural disorders) the American Psychiatric Association's Diagnostic and Statistical Manual of Mental Disorders, known as the DSM.[31] The WHO website describes the ICF as follows:

> Since 2001, ICF has been demonstrating a broader, more modern view of the concepts of 'health' and 'disability' through the acknowledgement that every human being may experience some degree of disability in their life through a change in health or in environment. Disability is a universal human experience, sometimes permanent, sometimes transient. It is not something restricted to a small part of the population.[32]

Clearly, there are a range of definitions of disability that serve different objectives and purposes and these definitions vary across legal and policy documents. It has not been possible to come up with a global definition of disability in law and social policy, although clearly a definition of some kind seems essential. Sociologists, philosophers, bioethicists, disability scholars and lawyers have therefore engaged in a complex and nuanced debate about how disability should be defined, if at all, and how it should be understood. The second part of this chapter considers models of disability that have been proposed and developed within the contemporary academic and policy literature.

---

28   Ibid 95.

29   Altman, above n 1, 99.

30   WHO, *Metrics: Disability-Adjusted Life Year* (DALY) <www.who.int/healthinfo/global_burden_disease/metrics_daly/en>.

31   See American Psychiatric Association, *Diagnostic and Statistical Manual of Mental Disorders* (DSM-5), 5th edn (2013) <www.psychiatry.org/psychiatrists/practice/dsm/dsm-5>.

32   WHO, *International Classification of Functioning, Disability and Health* (ICF) (16 December 2015) <www.who.int/classifications/icf/icf_more/en/>.

Defining 'disability': contemporary scholarship

The social model

As noted in the introduction to this chapter, there has been a clash between the social model of disability, which attributes the inability of people with impairments to undertake social activities to the barriers imposed by the non-disabled majority; and the medical model, which is commonly used to determine the distribution of resources. The social model of disability was originally developed by a group called the Union of the Physically Impaired Against Segregation (UPIAS), which defined disability as:

> The disadvantage or restriction of activity caused by a contemporary social organisation which takes no or little account of people who have physical impairments and thus excludes them from participation in the mainstream of social activities. [33]

In contrast, the medical model equates disability with impairment and demands the adjustment and adaptation of disabled individuals. The medical model's test for impairment, however, inevitably takes us back to the social model when it uses the calculus of capacity to undertake 'everyday activities'.

The contemporary understanding of disability as a social construct directly influences the modern view of disability and reflects a broader positional shift of major medical and policy organisations in the field both nationally and internationally. For instance, the American Institute of Medicine has described disability as 'the expression of the gap between a person's capabilities and the demands of the environment – the interaction of a person's limitations with social and physical environmental factors'.[34] This accords with the model proposed by disability scholars Verbrugge and Jette, who draw a distinction between what they call 'intrinsic disability (without personal or equipment assistance) and actual disability (with such assistance)',[35] and state that 'Disability is not a personal characteristic, but is instead a gap between personal capability and environmental demand.'[36]

Disability studies approaches

Postmodern theorists argue that individual limitations are constructed by the socio-cultural expectations themselves. One of the major advantages to understanding disability in this way is that it prompts us to question our assumptions about what is normal and what is not.

---

33   Michael J Oliver, 'Capitalism, Disability and Ideology: A Materialist Critique of the Normalization Principle' in Robert J Flynn and Raymond A Lemay (eds), *A Quarter-Century of Normalization and Social Role Valorization: Evolution and Impact* (University of Ottawa Press, 1999) 163, 168.

34   Edward N Brandt and Andrew M Pope (eds), *Enabling America Assessing the Role of Rehabilitation Science and Engineering* (National Academy Press, 1997) 26 <http://iom.nationalacademies .org/reports/2005/enabling-america-assessing-the-role-of-rehabilitation-science-and-engineering .aspx#sthash.EuqIzBb2.dpuf>.

35   Lois M Verbrugge and Alan M Jette, 'The Disablement Process' (1994) 38(1) *Social Science & Medicine* 1.

36   Ibid. See also Saad Nagi, 'Disability Concepts Revisited: Implications for Prevention' in Andrew M Pope and Alvin R Tarlov (eds), *Disability in America: Toward a National Agenda for Prevention* (National Academy Press, 1991) 309, 315.

If people who consider themselves to be without disability could understand all the ways in which society aids and assists them in their everyday tasks, it has been argued, it may be possible to change attitudes to these differences and to create a fuller understanding of normalcy.[37]

For example, Davis argues that the concept of normal did not really exist until the mid to late 1800s, and that it arose through the development of the discipline of statistics.[38] Davis views the development of an administrative structure based on statistical norms as instrumental in limiting the acceptance of people who do not fit within statistical norms.[39] Disability, then, is not just associated with injury, or debilitating physical conditions, but includes mere existence outside the range of normal – a statistical category that refers to a lack of significant variation from the average.[40] Where the difference is viewed as 'abnormal', it may also be viewed as presumptively bad and therefore undesirable. When the standard, or average, shifts so that normal expands or contracts, that which is undesirable, or viewed as limiting, also shifts. In his most recent work, Davis has suggested that normalcy now incorporates a concept of diversity derived from a neo-liberal emphasis on maximising personal liberty and eschewing government regulation. That neo-liberal concept of diversity, therefore, still excludes disability, because disability is not (usually) born out of personal choice. He goes on to state:

> Disability … is the resistant point in the diversity paradigm. In other words, you can't have a statement like 'we are all different, and we celebrate that diversity' without having some suppressed idea of a norm that defines difference in the first place.[41]

Einstein and Shildrick argue that the assumption endemic to current Western biomedicine, that 'the health care consumer is a free, rational, self-determining subject with unexamined and unchallenged agency through, and property rights over, her own body',[42] is, however, unrealistic. So whether disability sits inside or outside the 'norm', it seems clear that an approach that prioritises the self-actualising individual will necessarily exclude people who are dependent on others to survive. As discussed briefly below, there are a number of theorists who insist that dependency is actually the normal state of being for the majority of people and that we should organise law and social policy around the assumption that we *all* rely on others for our survival. Corker and Shakespeare, for example, argue that greater value should be attributed to 'uncertainty, instability, hybridity, contingency, embodiment and reflexivity'.[43]

37   Fiona Kumari Campbell, 'Refusing Able(ness): A Preliminary Conversation about Ableism' (2008) 11(3) *M/C Journal: A Journal of Media and Culture*.

38   Davis, 'Constructing Normalcy', above n 1, 4.

39   Ibid.

40   Isabel Karpin and Roxanne Mykitiuk, 'Going Out on a Limb: Prosthetics, Normalcy and Disputing the Therapy Enhancement Distinction' (2008) 16 *Medical Law Review* 413, 416; Kerry Taylor and Roxanne Mykitiuk, 'Genetics, Normalcy and Disability' (2001) *ISUMA* 65, 66.

41   Ibid. See also Roxanne Mykitiuk and Isabel Karpin, 'Fit or Fitting in: Deciding Against Normal When Reproducing the Future' (forthcoming, 2017) *Continuum Journal of Media and Cultural Studies*.

42   Einstein and Shildrick, above n 3, 294.

43   Corker and Shakespeare, above n 1, 3–4.

Fineman has put forward a vulnerability analysis which suggests that we replace the autonomous and independent subject asserted in the liberal legal tradition with the vulnerable embodied and embedded person of real life.[44] She goes on to say:

> The vulnerable subject approach does what the one-dimensional liberal subject approach cannot: it embodies the fact that human reality encompasses a wide range of differing and interdependent abilities over the span of a lifetime.[45]

In her most recent work, she has argued that 'vulnerability can form the foundation on which to build ideas about appropriate social and state responsibility for all'.[46]

Other contemporary models of disability have attempted to develop understandings that meld the medical and the social. For instance, Bickenbach synthesises the medical and social models into what he describes as a 'biopsychosocial model'.[47] In contrast, Campbell rejects a binary model altogether and instead critiques existing models as 'ableist'. According to Campbell, 'ableism' refers to:

> a network of beliefs, processes and practices that produces a particular kind of self and body (the corporeal standard) that is projected as the perfect species-typical and therefore essential and full human. Disability then, is cast as a diminished state of being human.[48]

Conclusion

In this chapter, ideas of disability, as constructed and managed through legal, as well as medical and social, discourses have been canvassed and the various theoretical models of disability have been explained. It has been demonstrated that legal definitions of disability contract and expand depending on context. For instance, the definition found in the CRPD is broad, as is the definition found in the DDA. On the other hand, regulatory regimes that provide social services, such as the NDIS Act, define disability according to a narrower set of criteria. Universal standards that depend on generalist application cannot, therefore, be relied on when dealing with important health law questions. All these legal definitions, however, draw on social as well as medical accounts of disability, suggesting that the approaches offered by the disability studies scholars discussed in the second half of the chapter may offer a way forward. These approaches should be regarded as providing tools that can be used by judges, lawyers and other legal actors to assist in the development of legal responses that recognise that all legal subjects, including those with disabilities, are heterogeneous and embedded in historical, cultural and political structures.

---

44   Martha Albertson Fineman, 'The Vulnerable Subject: Anchoring Equality in the Human Condition' (2008–09) 20 *Yale Journal of Law and Feminism* 1, 10.

45   Ibid 12.

46   Martha Albertson Fineman, 'Equality, Autonomy and the Vulnerable Subject in Law and Politics' in Martha Albertson Fineman and Anna Grear (eds), *Vulnerability: Reflections on a New Ethical Foundation of Law and Politics* (Ashgate, 2014) 20.

47   Jerome E Bickenbach, 'Disability Human Rights, Law, and Policy' in Albrecht, Seelman and Bury, above n 1, 565, 567.

48   Fiona Kumari Campbell, 'Inciting Legal Fictions: Disability's Date with Ontology and the Ableist Body of the Law' (2001) 10 *Griffith Law Review* 42, 44.

23

MENTAL HEALTH LAW

Penelope Weller

Introduction

Modern mental health laws provide a comprehensive regulatory framework for the operation of mental health systems.[1] In Australia, mental health legislation typically includes,
among other matters, provisions for compulsory mental health assessment, detention and
treatment, the regulation of special procedures such as Electroconvulsive Therapy (ECT),
psychosurgery, the use of the seclusion and restraint in mental health facilities, and the rights
of patients, the rights of carers and families. This is in addition to legislative provisions for
forensic psychiatric detention, including the interface between criminal justice and mental
health systems and the interstate transfer of detained patients, as well as provisions relating
to the establishment of oversight mechanisms including Mental Health Tribunals, the Office
of the Chief Psychiatrist and community visitors. Law reform debates about mental health
legislation are concerned with many of these features. Over the past few decades, the most
controversial and widely debated aspect of modern mental health legislation has been the
compulsory detention and treatment provisions. More recently, a new set of human rights
considerations arising from the Convention on the Rights of Persons with Disabilities (CRPD)
has influenced such debates.

As this book is primarily concerned with health matters, the main focus of this chapter
is on the laws that permit compulsory mental health treatment, and the debates related to it
that arise in response to the CRPD. Aspects of the law that relate to the criminal justice system and the management of forensic matters are not considered. The first part of the chapter
provides a brief history of mental health law in other common law jurisdictions followed by
a discussion of trends in the formulation of the involuntary treatment criteria and a summary
of current civil commitment requirements. The second half the chapter considers the human
rights critique of mental health legislation, drawing on current debates about the impact
of the CRPD. This chapter should be read in conjunction with Chapter 22, which critically
examines models of disability, as well as Chapters 9, 10 and 15, which deal, inter alia, with
issues of capacity in the context of decision-making about medical treatment.

Mental health law: from rights to risk

The development of mental health law during the course of the 20th century has been
described as a pendulum that has swung between laws that privileged either medical or legal
professional power;[2] and between institutional treatment settings or community facilities.[3] In
the 1960s and 1970s, civil rights perspectives informed the international critique of mental
health laws. In several jurisdictions, sociologists, psychiatrists, lawyers and patients highlighted
the detrimental effects of institutional care and the dangers of unregulated medical power.[4]

---

1   Clive Unsworth, *The Politics of Mental Health Legislation* (Clarendon Press, 1987).

2   Kathleen Jones, 'The Limitations of the Legal Approach to Mental Health' (1980) 3(1) *International
        Journal of Law and Psychiatry* 15; Gillian Lipton, 'Politics of Mental Health' (1983) 17(1) *Australian
        and New Zealand Journal of Psychiatry* 50.

3   Patricia Allderidge, 'Hospitals, Madhouses and Asylums: Cycles in the Care of the Insane' (1979) 134
        British Journal of Psychiatry 31.

4   Penelope Weller, *New Law and Ethics in Mental Health Advance Directives: The Convention on The
        Rights of Persons With Disabilities and the Right to Choose* (Routledge, 2013) 54–5.

These critiques prompted a new legislative approach, which has been described as 'rights-based mental health laws'.[5] The rights-based model, which was first expounded by Gostin, was taken up in the UK and then in other Western countries, including Australia, in the second half of the 20th century.[6]

Rights-based mental health laws in Australia seek to balance liberal principles of individual rights and freedoms with welfare-based principles and mechanisms designed to protect vulnerable individuals.[7] They do this by positioning medical professional discretion at the heart of mental health legislation, while limiting the scope of professional power and providing 'safeguard' mechanisms. The primary limiting mechanism is the involuntary commitment criteria.[8] In Australia, the key components of the civil commitment criteria are that the person has a mental illness (that requires treatment) and there is a 'risk of harm' to themselves or to others. Other statutory elements, including the principle of the 'least restrictive alternative' also limit the scope of mental health legislation.[9] The primary safeguard in rights-based mental health laws is legal oversight, which is provided by an administrative tribunal.

In Australia, such tribunals are typically composed of a lawyer, a psychiatrist and a community representative.[10] While the functions and powers of Mental Health Tribunals differ in each jurisdiction, tribunals usually take the form of 'inquisitorial' forums that are not bound by the rules of evidence. They are empowered to make a range of decisions concerning the care of people with mental illness, and are required to balance a number of competing statutory obligations and considerations.[11]

In the 1980s and 1990s, rights-based mental health laws highlighted the global trend towards de-institutionalisation.[12] The dismantling of large stand-alone institutions has since been associated with the dislocation of individuals with complex health and social problems and with a crisis of homelessness among individuals with mental health problems. For example, in the US, Isaac and Armat describe the phenomenon as 'madness in the streets'.[13] Concerns about the consequences of overly strict civil commitment criteria prompted many countries, including Australia, to expand such criteria on the basis of a risk of deterioration of the person's health or mental health.

In Australia, the latter measure was preceded by the introduction of 'community treatment orders', a novel form of community-based involuntary treatment that was thought to provide a 'safety net', enabling appropriate transitions from institutional care to the community. The use of involuntary treatment orders in the community has been criticised for

---

5   Penelope Weller, 'Lost in Translation: Human Rights and Mental Health Law' in Bernadette McSherry and Penelope Weller (eds), *Rethinking Rights-Based Mental Health Laws* (Hart, 2010) 51.

6   See Lawrence O Gostin, *The Human Condition (Vol. 1): The Mental Health Act from 1959 to 1975: Observations Analysis and Proposals for Reform* (MIND 1975) <www.mind.org.uk>.

7   Nikolas Rose, 'The Ethos of Welfare' (unpublished conference paper presented at Metamorphoses and Variations in Governmentality (University of Helsinki, 2000)).

8   Rights-based laws were the subject of strong criticism from the outset: see Darold Treffert, 'Dying With Their Rights On' (1974) 2(2) *Prism* 49.

9   See *S v South Eastern Sydney and Illawarra Area Health Service* [2010] NSWSC 178.

10   There is a range of patient-centred and institutional safeguard mechanisms that are also important, but they are beyond the scope of this chapter.

11   Terry Carney et al., 'Pushing the Boundaries: Realising Rights Through Mental Health Tribunal Processes?' (2008) 30 *Sydney Law Review* 329.

12   Lawrence O Gostin, '"Old" and "New" Institutions for Persons with Mental Illness: Treatment, Punishment or Preventive Confinement?' (2008) 122(9) *Public Health* 906.

13   Rael Jean Isaac and Virginia C Armat, *Madness in the Streets: How Psychiatry and the Law Abandoned the Mentally Ill* (Free Press, 1990).

continuing to expose individuals to unnecessary psychiatric intervention,[14] preventing timely access to acute care[15] and driving people away from mental healthcare and treatment.[16] Despite several large international studies, the supposed benefits of community treatment orders have not been demonstrated.

Mental health legislation in Australia

Mental health is the legislative responsibility of the Australian states and territories. As a consequence, there is separate legislation across the eight Australian jurisdictions, with significant differences among them.[17] Mental health law is an area of law in constant flux, with the current cycle of law reform being influenced by the debates surrounding the CRPD.[18] New mental health legislation was adopted in Tasmania in 2013, in Victoria and WA in 2014, in the ACT in 2015 and in Queensland in 2016.[19] In NSW, amendments to the current legislation were passed in 2014.[20] Amendments to the SA legislation are yet to commence.[21] The most important legal standard in mental health legislation in Australia is the overall scope of the involuntary detention and treatment provisions. The scope of mental health legislation is contributed to by the statutory definition of mental illness, the treatment criteria and the least restrictive principle.

Definition of mental illness

The starting point for the civil commitment criteria is the definition of mental illness. All jurisdictions include the requirement that the person has a mental illness.[22] Mental illness is defined differently in each Act. The definitions of mental illness are invariably accompanied by a list of characteristics or conduct that may not be regarded as constituting mental illness. The definitions, which are set out in Table 23.1, dovetail with the requirement that treatment is available and necessary.[23]

---

14   Bernadette McSherry and Kaye Wilson, 'Detention and Treatment Down Under: Human Rights and Mental Health Laws in Australia and New Zealand' (2011) 19(4) *Medical Law Review* 548.
15   Stuart Lee et al., 'What is Needed to Deliver Collaborative Care to Address Comorbidity More Effectively for Adults with a Severe Mental Illness?' (2013) 47 *Australian and New Zealand Journal of Psychiatry* 333.
16   Matthew M Large et al., 'The Danger of Dangerousness: Why We Must Remove the Dangerousness Criterion from our Mental Health Acts' (2008) 34 *Journal of Medical Ethics* 877.
17   *Mental Health Act 2015* (ACT); *Mental Health Act 2007* (NSW); *Mental Health and Related Services Act* (NT); *Mental Health Act 2016* (Qld); *Mental Health Act 2009* (SA); *Mental Health Act 2013* (Tas); *Mental Health Act 2014* (Vic); *Mental Health Act 2014* (WA).
18   Convention on the Rights of Persons with Disabilities (CRPD), adopted 13 December 2006, GA Res 61/106, UN Doc A/Res/61/106, entered into force 3 May 2008. Australia ratified the CRPD on 17 July 2008.
19   *Mental Health Act 2013* (Tas); *Mental Health Act 2014* (Vic); *Mental Health Act 2014* (WA); *Mental Health Act 2015* (ACT); *Mental Health Act 2016* (Qld).
20   *Mental Health Amendment (Statutory Review) Act 2014* (NSW).
21   *Mental Health (Review) Amendment Act 2016* (SA).
22   *Mental Health Act 2015* (ACT) s 58(2)(a); *Mental Health Act 2007* (NSW) s 9(1); *Mental Health and Related Services Act* (NT) s 14(a); *Mental Health Act 2016* (Qld) s 12(1)(a); *Mental Health Act 2009* (SA) s 21(a); *Mental Health Act 2013* (Tas) s 40(a); *Mental Health Act 2014* (Vic) s 5(a); *Mental Health Act 2014* (WA) s 25(1)(a).
23   *Mental Health Act 2009* (SA) s 21(b); *Mental Health Act 2013* (Tas) s 40(d); *Mental Health Act 2014* (Vic) s 5(c); *Mental Health Act 2014* (WA) s 26(1)(a). There are no equivalent provisions in ACT, NSW or Qld.

Table 23.1: Involuntary Treatment Criteria

AUSTRALIAN CAPITAL TERRITORY
Mental Health Act 2015 – ss 58(2) and 66(2)
	52 Psychiatric treatment order
	
	(2) The ACAT may make a psychiatric treatment order in relation to a person if—
	
	  (a) the person has a mental illness; and
	
	  (b) either
	
	    (i) the person does not have decision-making capacity to consent to the treatment, care or support and refuses to receive the treatment, care or support; or
	
	    (ii) the person has decision-making capacity to consent to the treatment, care or support, but refuses to consent; and
	
	  (c) the ACAT believes on reasonable grounds that, because of the mental illness, the person—
	
	    (i) is doing, or is likely to do, serious harm to themself or someone else; or
	
	    (ii) is suffering, or is likely to suffer, serious mental or physical deterioration; and
	
	  (d) in relation to a person mentioned in paragraph (b) (ii)—
	
	  (e) the ACAT is satisfied that psychiatric treatment, care or support is likely to—
	
	    (i) reduce the harm or deterioration, or the likelihood of the harm or deterioration, mentioned in paragraph (c); or
	
	    (ii) result in an improvement in the person's psychiatric condition; and
	
	  (f) if an application has been made for a forensic mental health order—the ACAT is satisfied that a psychiatric treatment order should be made instead; and
	
	  (g) the ACAT is satisfied that the treatment, care or support to be provided under the psychiatric treatment order cannot be adequately provided in another way that would involve less restriction of the freedom of choice and movement of the person.

NEW SOUTH WALES (NSW)
Mental Health Act 2007 – ss 14 and 15
	14 Mentally ill persons
	
	(cf 1990 Act, s 9)
	
	(1) A person is a <u>mentally ill person</u> if the person is suffering from <u>mental illness</u> and, owing to that illness, there are reasonable grounds for believing that care, treatment or control of the person is necessary:
	
	  (a) for the person's own protection from serious harm, or
	
	  (b) for the protection of others from serious harm.
	
	(2) In considering whether a person is a <u>mentally ill person</u>, the continuing condition of the person, including any likely deterioration in the person's condition and the likely effects of any such deterioration, are to be taken into account.

Table 23.1: (cont.)

NORTHERN TERRITORY (NT)
Mental Health and Related Services Act – ss **14, 15, 15A** and **7**

15 Mentally disordered persons

(cf 1990 Act, s 10)

A person (whether or not the person is suffering from mental illness) is a <u>mentally disordered person</u> if the person's behaviour for the time being is so irrational as to justify a conclusion on reasonable grounds that temporary care, treatment or control of the person is necessary:

(a) for the person's own protection from serious physical harm, or

(b) for the protection of others from serious physical harm.

14 Involuntary admission on grounds of mental illness

The criteria for the involuntary admission of a person on the grounds of mental illness are that:

(a) the person has a mental illness; and

(b) as a result of the mental illness:

   (i) the person requires treatment that is available at an approved treatment facility; and

   (ii) without the treatment, the person is likely to:

      (A) cause serious harm to himself or herself or to someone else; or

      (B) suffer serious mental or physical deterioration; and

   (iii) the person is not capable of giving informed consent to the treatment or has unreasonably refused to consent to the treatment; and

(c) there is **no less restrictive means** of ensuring that the person receives the treatment.

15 Involuntary admission on grounds of mental disturbance

The criteria for the involuntary admission of a person on the grounds of mental disturbance are that:

(a) the person does not fulfil the criteria for involuntary admission on the grounds of mental illness or complex cognitive impairment; and

(b) the person's behaviour is, or within the immediately preceding 48 hours has been, so irrational as to lead to the conclusion that:

   (i) the person is experiencing or exhibiting a severe impairment of or deviation from his or her customary or everyday ability to reason and function in a socially acceptable and culturally appropriate manner; and

   (ii) the person is behaving in an abnormally aggressive manner or is engaging in seriously irresponsible conduct that justify a determination that the person requires psychiatric assessment, treatment and care that is available at an approved treatment facility; and

(c) unless the person receives treatment and care at an approved treatment facility, he or she:

   (i) is likely to cause serious harm to himself or herself or to someone else; or

(ii) will represent a substantial danger to the general community; or

(iii) is likely to suffer serious mental or physical deterioration; and

(d) the person is not capable of giving informed consent to the treatment and care or has unreasonably refused to consent to the treatment and care; and

(e) there is *no less restrictive means* of ensuring that the person receives the treatment and care.

15A Involuntary admission on grounds of complex informed consent cognitive impairment

The criteria for the involuntary admission of a person on the grounds of complex cognitive impairment are:

(a) the person is an adult who does not fulfil the criteria for involuntary admission on the grounds of mental illness or mental disturbance; and

(b) the person has significant cognitive impairment; and

(c) unless the person receives treatment and care at an approved treatment facility, the person:

(i) is likely to cause serious harm to himself or herself or to someone else; or

(ii) will represent a substantial danger to the general community; or

(iii) is likely to suffer serious mental or physical deterioration; and

(d) the person is likely to benefit from the treatment and care; and

(e) the person is not capable of giving informed consent to the treatment and care; and

(f) there is no less restrictive way of ensuring the person receives the treatment and care.

7 Informed consent

(2) A person gives informed consent under this act:

(a) when the person's consent is freely and voluntarily given without any inducement being offered; and

(b) the person is capable of understanding the effects of giving consent; and

(c) the person communicates his or her consent on the approved form.

(Also see requirements in s7(3). 'Capable' is not defined.)

12 Meaning of treatment criteria

(1) The treatment criteria for a person are all of the following—

(a) the person has a mental illness;

(b) the person does not have capacity to consent to be treated for the illness;

QUEENSLAND (Qld)
Mental Health Act 2016 –
ss 12 and 14

Table 23.1: (cont.)

(c) because of the person's illness, the absence of involuntary treatment, or the absence of continued involuntary treatment, is likely to result in

    (i) imminent serious harm to the person or others; or

    (ii) the person suffering serious mental or physical deterioration.

(2) For subsection (1)(b), the person's own consent only is relevant.

(3) Subsection (2) applies despite the *Guardianship and Administration Act 2000*, the *Powers of Attorney Act 1998* or any other law.

14 Meaning of capacity to consent to be treated

(1) A person has capacity to consent to be treated if the person

  (a) is capable of understanding, in general terms

    (i) that the person has an illness, or symptoms of an illness, that affects the person's mental health and wellbeing; and

    (ii) the nature and purpose of the treatment for the illness; and

    (iii) the benefits and risks of the treatment, and alternatives to the treatment; and

    (iv) the consequences of not receiving the treatment; and

  (b) is capable of making a decision about the treatment and communicating the decision in some way.

(2) A person may have capacity to consent to be treated even though the person decides not to receive treatment.

(3) A person may be supported by another person in understanding the matters mentioned in subsection (1)(a) and making a decision about the treatment.

(4) This section does not affect the common law in relation to

  (a) the capacity of a minor to consent to be treated; or

  (b) a parent of a minor consenting to treatment of the minor.

21 Level 1 inpatient treatment orders

(1) A medical practitioner or authorised health professional may make an order that a person receive treatment as an inpatient in a treatment centre (a "level 1 inpatient treatment order) if it appears to the medical practitioner or authorised health professional, after examining the person, that—

  (a) the person has a mental illness; and

  (b) because of the mental illness, the person requires treatment for the person's own protection from harm (including harm involved in the continuation or deterioration of the person's condition) or for the protection of others from harm; and

  (c) there is no less restrictive means than an inpatient treatment order of ensuring appropriate treatment of the person's illness.

SOUTH AUSTRALIA (SA)
Mental Health Act 2009 –
s 21, see also ss 25, 29

TASMANIA (Tas)
Mental Health Act 2013
(No. 2 of 2013) – ss 40
and 7

40 Treatment criteria

The treatment criteria in relation to a person are –

(a) the person has a mental illness; and

(b) without treatment, the mental illness will, or is likely to, seriously harm –

   (i) the person's health or safety; or

   (ii) the safety of other persons; and

(c) the treatment will be appropriate and effective in terms of the outcomes referred to in section 6(1); and

(d) the treatment cannot be adequately given except under a treatment order; and

(e) the person does not have decision-making capacity.

7 Capacity of adults and children to make decisions about their assessment and treatment

(1) For the purposes of this Act, an adult is taken to have the capacity to make a decision about his or her own assessment or treatment (decision-making capacity) unless it is established, on the balance of probabilities, that –

(a) he or she is unable to make the decision because of an impairment of law disturbance in the functioning of the mind or brain; and

(b) he or she is unable to–

   (i) understand information relevant to the decision; or

   (ii) retain information relevant to the decision; or

   (iii) use or weigh information relevant to the decision: or

   (iv) communicate the decision (whether by speech gesture or other means).

VICTORIA (Vic)
Mental Health Act 2014
– s 5

5 What are the treatment criteria?

The treatment criteria for a person to be made subject to a Temporary Treatment Order or Treatment Order are—

(a) the person has mental illness; and

(b) because the person has mental illness, the person needs immediate treatment to prevent—

   (i) serious deterioration in the person's mental or physical health; or

   (ii) serious harm to the person or to another person; and

(c) the immediate treatment will be provided to the person if the person is subject to a Temporary Treatment Order or Treatment Order; and

(d) there is no less restrictive means reasonably available to enable the person to receive the immediate treatment.

Table 23.1: (cont.)

WESTERN AUSTRALIA (WA)
Mental Health Act 2014 –
s 25, 18

25 Criteria for involuntary treatment order

(1) A person is in need of an inpatient treatment order only if all of these criteria are satisfied –

(a) that the person has a mental illness for which the person is in need of treatment;

(b) that, because of the mental illness, there is –

    (i) a significant risk to the health or safety of the person or to the safety of another person; or

    (ii) a significant risk of serious harm to the person or to another person;

(c) that –

    (i) the person does not have the capacity required by section 18 to make a treatment decision about the provision of the treatment to himself or herself; or

    (ii) the person has unreasonably refused treatment;

(d) that treatment in the community cannot reasonably be provided to the person;

(e) that the person cannot be adequately provided with treatment in a way that would involve less restriction on the person's freedom of choice and movement than making an inpatient treatment order.

(3) A decision whether or not a person is in need of an inpatient treatment order or a community treatment order must be made having regard to the guidelines published under section 543(1)(a) for that purpose.

18 Determining capacity to make treatment decision

A person has the capacity to make a treatment decision about the provision of treatment to a patient if another person who is performing a function under this Act that requires that other person to determine that capacity is satisfied that the person has the capacity to—

(a) understand the things that are required under section 19 to be communicated to the person about the treatment; and

(b) understand the matters involved in making the treatment decision; and

(c) understand the effect of the treatment decision; and

(d) weigh up the factors referred to in paragraphs (a), (b) and (c) for the purpose of making the treatment decision; and

(e) communicate the treatment decision in some way.

Mental dysfunction or impairment

Two jurisdictions permit compulsory detention and treatment on the grounds of 'mental disturbance', 'complex cognitive impairment',[24] or 'mental disorder'.[25] The provisions expand the available grounds for civil commitment in these jurisdictions. In NSW, 'mental disorder' is defined as behaviour that 'for the time being is so irrational as to justify a conclusion on reasonable grounds that temporary care, treatment or control of the person is necessary: (a) for the person's own protection from serious physical harm, or (b) for the protection of others from serious physical harm' as an additional ground for psychiatric detention.[26] The NT legislation defines 'complex cognitive impairment' as 'intellectual impairment, neurological impairment or acquired brain injury (or any combination of these) that is, or is likely to be, permanent'. Additional grounds include substantially reduced capacity in self-care or management, decision-making, problem-solving, communication or social functioning.

Detention and treatment criteria

The core of the civil commitment criteria is the treatment criteria set out in Table 23.2. The general requirement is that treatment must be necessary to prevent harm to the person or to other people, or to prevent deterioration of the person's physical or mental health. The scope of the harm criteria differs across jurisdictions. Provisions in the ACT,[27] NSW,[28] the NT,[29] Tasmanian[30] and Victorian[31] Acts refer to the prevention of 'serious' harm. The Queensland legislation requires that there is a risk of 'imminent serious harm' to the person or to someone else or that the person is 'likely to suffer serious mental or physical deterioration'.[32] The reference to harm in SA is unqualified in this respect.[33] The current WA legislation refers to 'a significant risk to the health or safety of the person or the safety of another person' or 'a significant risk of serious harm to the person or to another person'.[34] Despite these differences in description, it seems that in practice the criteria operate similarly across Australian jurisdictions.[35]

---

24   *Mental Health and Related Services Act* (NT) ss 15, 15A.
25   *Mental Health Act 2007* (NSW) s 15.
26   Ibid s 15.
27   *Mental Health Act 2015* (ACT) s 58(2)(c).
28   *Mental Health Act 2007* (NSW) ss 14, 15.
29   *Mental Health and Related Services Act* (NT) ss 14, 15, 15A.
30   *Mental Health Act 2013* (Tas) s 40.
31   *Mental Health Act 2014* (Vic) s 5(b).
32   *Mental Health Act 2016* (Qld) s 12.
33   *Mental Health Act 2009* (SA) ss 21, 25, 29.
34   *Mental Health Act 2014* (WA) s 25.
35   Terry Carney et al., 'Mental Health Tribunals – Space of Rights, Protection, Treatment and Governance? (2012) 35(1) *International Journal of Law and Psychiatry* 1.

Table 23.2: Definitions of Mental Illness

AUSTRALIAN CAPITAL TERRITORY (ACT) *Mental Health Act 2015* – ss 10 and 11	**10 Meaning of mental illness**

In this Act:

'mental illness' means a condition that seriously impairs (either temporarily or permanently) the mental functioning of a person in 1 or more areas of thought, mood, volition, perception, orientation or memory, and is characterised by—

(a) the presence of at least 1 of the following symptoms:

    (i) delusions;

    (ii) hallucinations;

    (iii) serious disorders of streams of thought;

    (iv) serious disorders of thought form;

    (v) serious disturbance of mood; or

(b) sustained or repeated irrational behaviour that may be taken to indicate the presence of at least 1 of the symptoms mentioned in paragraph (a).

11 People not to be regarded as having mental disorder or mental illness

For this Act, a person is not to be regarded as having a mental disorder or mental illness only because of any of the following:

(a) the person expresses or refuses or fails to express, or has expressed or has refused or failed to express, a particular political opinion or belief;

(b) the person expresses or refuses or fails to express, or has expressed or has refused or failed to express, a particular religious opinion or belief;

(c) the person expresses or refuses or fails to express, or has expressed or has refused or failed to express, a particular philosophy;

(d) the person expresses or refuses or fails to express, or has expressed or has refused or failed to express, a particular sexual preference or sexual orientation;

(e) the person engages in or refuses or fails to engage in, or has engaged in or has refused or failed to engage in, a particular political activity;

(f) the person engages in or refuses or fails to engage in, or has engaged in or has refused or failed to engage in, a particular religious activity;

(g) the person engages in or has engaged in sexual promiscuity;

(h) the person engages in or has engaged in immoral conduct;

(i) the person engages in or has engaged in illegal conduct;

(j) the person takes or has taken alcohol or any other drug;

(k) the person engages in or has engaged in antisocial behaviour.

4 Definitions

'mental illness' means a condition that seriously impairs, either temporarily or permanently, the mental functioning of a person and is characterised by the presence in the person of any one or more of the following symptoms:

(a) delusions,

(b) hallucinations,

(c) serious disorder of thought form,

(d) a severe disturbance of mood,

(e) sustained or repeated irrational behaviour indicating the presence of any one or more of the symptoms referred to in paragraphs (a)–(d).

16 Certain words or conduct may not indicate mental illness or disorder

(cf 1990 Act, s 11)

(1) A person is not a mentally ill person or a mentally disordered person merely because of any one or more of the following:

(a) the person expresses or refuses or fails to express or refused or failed to express a particular political opinion or belief,

(b) the person expresses or refuses or fails to express or refused or failed to express a particular religious opinion or belief,

(c) the person expresses or refuses or fails to express or refused or failed to express a particular philosophy,

(d) the person expresses or refuses or fails to express or refused or failed to express a particular sexual preference or sexual orientation,

(e) the person engages in or refuses or fails to engage in, or refused or failed to engage in, a particular political activity,

(f) the person engages in or refuses or fails to engage in, or refused or failed to engage in, a particular religious activity,

(g) the person engages in or has engaged in a particular sexual activity or sexual promiscuity,

(h) the person engages in or has engaged in immoral conduct,

(i) the person engages in or has engaged in illegal conduct,

(j) the person has developmental disability of mind,

(k) the person takes or has taken alcohol or any other drug,

(l) the person engages in or has engaged in anti-social behaviour,

(m) the person has a particular economic or social status or is a member of a particular cultural or racial group.

(2) Nothing in this Part prevents, in relation to a person who takes or has taken alcohol or any other drug, the serious or permanent physiological, biochemical or psychological effects of drug taking from being regarded as an indication that a person is suffering from mental illness or other condition of disability of mind.

Table 23.2: (cont.)

NORTHERN TERRITORY (NT)
Mental Health and Related Services Act – ss 6 and 6A

6 Mental illness

(1) A mental illness is a condition that seriously impairs, either temporarily or permanently, the mental functioning of a person in one or more of the areas of thought, mood, volition, perception, orientation or memory and is characterised:

   (a) by the presence of at least one of the following symptoms:

      (i) delusions;

      (ii) hallucinations;

      (iii) serious disorders of the stream of thought;

      (iv) serious disorders of thought form;

      (v) serious disturbances of mood; or

   (b) by sustained or repeated irrational behaviour that may be taken to indicate the presence of at least one of the symptoms referred to in paragraph (a).

(2) A determination that a person has a mental illness is only to be made in accordance with internationally accepted clinical standards.

(3) A person is not to be considered to have a mental illness merely because he or she:

   (a) expresses or refuses or fails to express a particular political or religious opinion or belief, a particular philosophy or a particular sexual preference or sexual orientation; or

   (b) engages, or refuses or fails to engage, in a particular political, religious or cultural activity; or

   (c) engages, or has engaged, in sexual promiscuity, immoral or illegal conduct or anti-social behaviour; or

   (d) has a sexual disorder; or

   (e) is intellectually disabled; or

   (f) uses alcohol or other drugs; or

   (g) has a personality disorder or a habit or impulse disorder; or

   (h) has, or has not, a particular political, economic or social status; or

   (i) communicates, or refuses or fails to communicate, or behaves or refuses or fails to behave, in a manner consistent with his or her cultural beliefs, practices or mores; or

   (k) is, or is not, a member of a particular cultural, racial or religious group; or

   (m) is involved, or has been involved, in family or professional conflict; or

   (n) has been treated for mental illness or has been detained in a hospital that provides treatment of mental illness; or

   (p) has been admitted as an involuntary patient on the grounds of mental disturbance or complex cognitive impairment; or

   (q) has acquired brain damage.

6A Complex cognitive impairment and related terms

(1) A person has a **complex cognitive impairment** if the person has a cognitive impairment with a behavioural disturbance.

(2) A person has a **cognitive impairment** if the person has an intellectual impairment, neurological impairment or acquired brain injury (or any combination of these) that:

(a) is, or is likely to be, permanent; and

(b) results in substantially reduced capacity in at least one of the following:

    (i) self-care or management;

    (ii) decision making or problem solving;

    (iii) communication or social functioning.

(3) A person has a **behavioural disturbance** if the person's mental condition has deteriorated to the extent the person is behaving in an aggressive manner or is engaging in seriously irresponsible conduct.

12 What is mental illness

(1) Mental illness is a condition characterised by a clinically significant disturbance of thought, mood, perception or memory.

(2) However, a person must not be considered to have a mental illness merely because of any 1 or more of the following—

(a) the person holds or refuses to hold a particular religious, cultural, philosophical or political belief or opinion;

(b) the person is a member of a particular racial group;

(c) the person has a particular economic or social status;

(d) the person has a particular sexual preference or sexual orientation;

(e) the person engages in sexual promiscuity;

(f) the person engages in immoral or indecent conduct;

(g) the person takes drugs or alcohol;

(h) the person has an intellectual disability;

(i) the person engages in antisocial behaviour or illegal behaviour;

(j) the person is or has been involved in family conflict;

(k) the person has previously been treated for mental illness or been subject to involuntary assessment or treatment.

(3) Subsection (2) does not prevent a person mentioned in the subsection having a mental illness.

Examples for subsection (3)—

1 A person may have a mental illness caused by taking drugs or alcohol.

2 A person may have a mental illness as well as an intellectual disability.

QUEENSLAND (Qld)
Mental Health Act 2000 – s 12

Table 23.2: (cont.)

(4) On an assessment, a decision that a person has a mental illness must be made in accordance with internationally accepted medical standards.

Editor's note—

See United Nations Principles for the protection of persons with mental illness and for the improvement of mental health care, principle 4, paragraph 1.

SOUTH AUSTRALIA (SA)
***Mental Health Act 2009* – s 3 and Sch 1**

3 Interpretation

'mental illness' means any illness or disorder of the mind; see also Schedule 1 (Certain conduct may not indicate mental illness);

Schedule 1—Certain conduct may not indicate mental illness

A person does not have a mental illness merely because of any 1 or more of the following:

(a) the person expresses or refuses or fails to express, or has expressed or refused or failed to express, a particular political opinion or belief;

(b) the person expresses or refuses or fails to express, or has expressed or refused or failed to express, a particular religious opinion or belief;

(c) the person expresses or refuses or fails to express, or has expressed or refused or failed to express, a particular philosophy;

(d) the person expresses or refuses or fails to express, or has expressed or refused or failed to express, a particular sexual preference or sexual orientation;

(e) the person engages in or refuses or fails to engage in, or has engaged in or refused or failed to engage in, a particular political activity;

(f) the person engages in or refuses or fails to engage in, or has engaged in or refused or failed to engage in, a particular religious activity;

(g) the person engages in or has engaged in a particular sexual activity or sexual promiscuity;

(h) the person engages in or has engaged in immoral conduct;

(i) the person engages in or has engaged in illegal conduct;

(j) the person has developmental disability of mind;

(k) the person takes or has taken alcohol or any other drug;

(l) the person engages in or has engaged in anti-social behaviour;

(m) the person has a particular economic or social status or is a member of a particular cultural or racial group.

However, nothing prevents, in relation to a person who takes or has taken alcohol or any other drug, the serious or permanent physiological, biochemical or psychological effects of drug taking from being regarded as an indication that a person is suffering from mental illness.

4 Meaning of mental illness

(1) For the purposes of this Act –

  (a) a person is taken to have a mental illness if he or she experiences, temporarily, repeatedly or continually –

    (i) a serious impairment of thought (which may include delusions); or

    (ii) a serious impairment of mood, volition, perception or cognition; and

  (b) nothing prevents the serious or permanent physiological, biochemical or psychological effects of alcohol use or drug-taking from being regarded as an indication that a person has a mental illness.

(2) However, under this Act, a person is not to be taken to have a mental illness by reason only of the person's –

  (a) current or past expression of, or failure or refusal to express, a particular political opinion or belief; or

  (b) current or past expression of, or failure or refusal to express, a particular religious opinion or belief; or

  (c) current or past expression of, or failure or refusal to express, a particular philosophy; or

  (d) current or past expression of, or failure or refusal to express, a particular sexual preference or orientation; or

  (e) current or past engagement in, or failure or refusal to engage in, a particular political or religious activity; or

  (f) current or past engagement in a particular sexual activity or sexual promiscuity; or

  (g) current or past engagement in illegal conduct; or

  (h) current or past engagement in an antisocial activity; or

  (i) particular economic or social status; or

  (j) membership of a particular cultural or racial group; or

  (k) intoxication (however induced); or

  (l) intellectual or physical disability; or

  (m) acquired brain injury; or

  (n) dementia; or

  (o) temporary unconsciousness.

Table 23.2: (cont.)

VICTORIA (Vic)
Mental Health Act
2014 – s 4

4 What is mental illness?

(1) Subject to subsection (2), mental illness is a medical condition that is characterised by a significant disturbance of thought, mood, perception or memory.

(2) A person is not to be considered to have <u>mental illness</u> by reason only of any one or more of the following—

   (a) that the person expresses or refuses or fails to express a particular political opinion or icbelief;

   (b) that the person expresses or refuses or fails to express a particular religious opinion or belief;

   (c) that the person expresses or refuses or fails to express a particular philosophy;

   (d) that the person expresses or refuses or fails to express a particular sexual preference, gender identity or sexual orientation;

   (e) that the person engages in or refuses or fails to engage in a particular political activity;

   (f) that the person engages in or refuses or fails to engage in a particular religious activity;

   (g) that the person engages in sexual promiscuity;

   (h) that the person engages in immoral conduct;

   (i) that the person engages in illegal conduct;

   (j) that the person engages in antisocial behaviour;

   (k) that the person is intellectually disabled;

   (l) that the person uses drugs or consumes alcohol;

   (m) that the person has a particular economic or social status or is a member of a particular cultural or racial group;

   (n) that the person is or has previously been involved in family conflict;

   (o) that the person has previously been treated for <u>mental illness.</u>

(3) Subsection (2)(l) does not prevent the serious temporary or permanent physiological, biochemical or psychological effects of using drugs or consuming alcohol from being regarded as an indication that a person has <u>mental illness.</u>

6 When a person has a mental illness

(1) A person has a mental illness if the person has a condition that –

    (a) is characterised by a disturbance of thought, mood, volition, perception, orientation or memory; and

    (b) significantly impairs (temporarily or permanently) the person's judgment or behaviour.

(2) A person does not have a mental illness merely because one or more of these things apply –

    (a) the person holds, or refuses or fails to hold, a particular religious, cultural, political or philosophical belief or opinion;

    (b) the person engages in, or refuses or fails to engage in, a particular religious, cultural or political activity;

    (c) the person is, or is not, a member of a particular religious, cultural or racial group;

    (d) the person has, or does not have, a particular political, economic or social status;

    (e) the person has a particular sexual preference or orientation;

    (f) the person is sexually promiscuous;

    (g) the person engages in indecent, immoral or illegal conduct;

    (h) the person has an intellectual disability;

    (i) the person uses alcohol or other drugs;

    (j) the person is involved in, or has been involved in, personal or professional conflict;

    (k) the person engages in anti-social behaviour;

    (l) the person has at any time been –

        (i) provided with treatment; or

        (ii) admitted by or detained at a hospital for the purpose of providing the person with treatment.

(3) Subsection (2)(i) does not prevent the serious or permanent physiological, biochemical or psychological effects of the use of alcohol or other drugs from being regarded as an indication that a person has a mental illness.

(4) A decision whether or not a person has a mental illness must be made in accordance with internationally accepted standards prescribed by the regulations for this subsection.

The least restrictive requirement

The third requirement is that treatment be provided in the least restrictive manner possible. This requirement is phrased differently across the jurisdictions and is not statutorily defined.[36] In *S v South Eastern Sydney and Illawarra Area Health Service*[37] Brereton J overturned a community treatment order on the basis that the oral medication preferred by the person was a less restrictive option compared to fortnightly injections. His Honour explained that to uphold a treatment order he:

> must be satisfied that no other care of less restrictive kind consistent with safe and effective care is appropriate and reasonably available and that the patient would benefit from the least restrictive alternative consistent with safe and effective care.[38]

With respect to treatment decisions, the Victorian *Mental Health Act 2014* requires authorised psychiatrists and the Mental Health Review Tribunal to be satisfied that there is no less restrictive way for the patient to be treated. Decision-makers must 'have regard to' the patient's views and preferences; the views and preferences expressed in an advance statement; and the views of other relevant persons, such as nominated persons guardians or carers.[39]

Capacity

The civil commitment criteria in Queensland, Tasmania, the NT and WA are further limited by the requirement that the person must lack capacity to make a treatment decision.[40] In the NT, the incapacity criteria is satisfied if the person has 'unreasonably refused the proposed treatment'.[41] In Victoria, the civil commitment criteria do not contain a capacity requirement. While a person with capacity is entitled to consent to treatment, if they do not do so the authorised psychiatrist may make a treatment decision. [42]

Treatment

The statutory definitions of treatment also affect the scope of the legislative power by narrowing or expanding the ambit of the legislation. Table 23.3 sets out the statutory definitions in legislation across the Australian jurisdictions.

---

36   *Mental Health Act 2015* (ACT) s 5(c); *Mental Health Act 2007* (NSW) ss 12(1)(b), 31, 35, 38, 61, 62, 64, 68, 166; *Mental Health and Related Services Act* (NT) ss 8, 9, 11, 14(c), 15(e), 15A(f), 42, 56; *Mental Health Act 2016* (Qld) s 13; *Mental Health Act 2009* (SA) ss 7, 10(d), 16(d), 21(c), 25(1)(c), 29; *Mental Health Act 2013* (Tas) ss 12(d), 54(2); *Mental Health Act 2014* (Vic) ss 5(d), 10(b), 11(1)(a), 16(1)–(3), 93, 94, 96; *Mental Health Act 2014* (WA) s 25(2)(e).
37   [2010] NSWSC 178.
38   Ibid [40] per Brereton J.
39   For example, see s 71(4).
40   *Mental Health and Related Services Act* (NT) ss 14(b)(iii), 7; *Mental Health Act 2016* (Qld) s 12(1)(b); *Mental Health Act 2013* (Tas) ss 7, 40; *Mental Health Act 2014* (WA) ss 18, 25(1)(c), 25(2)(c).
41   *Mental Health and Related Services Act* (NT) s14(b)(iii).
42   *Mental Health Act 2014* (Vic) s 71(1)(a)(ii).

Table 23.3: Definitions of Treatment

Jurisdiction	Definition
AUSTRALIAN CAPITAL TERRITORY (ACT) *Mental Health Act 2015* – Notes, Dictionary	**"treatment**, care or support", for a mental disorder or mental illness— (a) means things done in the course of the exercise of professional skills to remedy the disorder or illness or lessen its ill effects or the pain or suffering it causes; and (b) includes the giving of medication and counselling, training, therapeutic and rehabilitation programs, care or support. **Examples—rehabilitation support** 1 support to improve social confidence and integration 2 assistance to improve work skills *Note* An example is part of the Act, is not exhaustive and may extend, but does not limit, the meaning of the provision in which it appears (see *Legislation Act 2001* (ACT), s 126 and s 132)
NEW SOUTH WALES (NSW) *Mental Health Act 2007*	**4 Definitions** 'treatment', in relation to mental illness, mental disturbance or complex cognitive impairment, means things done in the course of the exercise of professional skills: (a) to remedy the illness, disturbance or impairment; or (b) to lessen the effects or the pain and suffering caused by the illness, disturbance or impairment.
NORTHERN TERRITORY (NT) *Mental Health and Related Services Act* – s 4	No definition.
QUEENSLAND (Qld) *Mental Health Act 2016* – Schedule 3 – Dictionary	'treatment' of a person who has a mental illness, means anything done, or to be done, with the intention of having a therapeutic effect on the person's illness.
SOUTH AUSTRALIA (SA) *Mental Health Act 2009* – s 3	**3 Interpretation** 'treatment' or 'medical treatment' means treatment or procedures administered or carried out by a medical practitioner or other health professional in the course of professional practice, and includes the prescription or supply of drugs;

Table 23.3: (cont.)

TASMANIA (Tas)
Mental Health Act 2013 – s 6

6 Meaning of treatment

(1) For the purposes of this Act, treatment is the professional intervention necessary to –

    (a) prevent or remedy mental illness; or

    (b) manage and alleviate, where possible, the ill effects of mental illness; or

    (c) reduce the risks that persons with mental illness may, on that account, pose to themselves or others; or

    (d) monitor or evaluate a person's mental state.

(2) However, this professional intervention does not extend to –

    (a) special psychiatric treatment; or

    (b) a termination of pregnancy; or

    (c) a procedure that could render a person permanently infertile; or

    (d) the removal, for transplantation, of human tissue that cannot thereafter be replaced by natural processes of growth or repair; or

    (e) general health care.

VICTORIA (Vic)
Mental Health Act 2014 – ss 6 & 7

6 What is treatment?

For the purposes of this Act—

(a) a person receives treatment for mental illness if things are done to the person in the course of the exercise of professional skills—

    (i) to remedy the mental illness; or

    (ii) to alleviate the symptoms and reduce the ill effects of the mental illness; and

(b) "treatment" includes electroconvulsive treatment and neurosurgery for mental illness.

7 What is medical treatment?

In this Act, 'medical treatment' means—

(a) medical treatment (including any medical or surgical procedure, operation or examination and any prophylactic, palliative or rehabilitative care) normally carried out by, or under, the supervision of a registered medical practitioner; or

(b) dental treatment (including any dental procedure, operation or examination) normally carried out by or under the supervision of a registered dental practitioner; or

(c) the administration of a pharmaceutical drug for which a prescription is required; or

(d) any other treatment that is not referred to in paragraph (a), (b) or (c) and is prescribed by the regulations to be medical treatment for the purposes of this Act— but does not include—

(e) a special procedure or medical research procedure within the meaning of the Guardianship and Administration Act 1986; or

Note:

Part 4A of the *Guardianship and Administration Act 1986* applies to the carrying out of a special procedure or medical research procedure on persons who are incapable of giving consent to that procedure.

(f) any non-intrusive examination made for diagnostic purposes (including a visual examination of the mouth, throat, nasal cavity, eyes or ears); or

(g) first-aid treatment; or

(h) any treatment for mental illness or the effects of mental illness

4 Definitions and notes

treatment means the provision of a psychiatric, medical, psychological or psychosocial intervention intended (whether alone or in combination with one or more other therapeutic interventions) to alleviate or prevent the deterioration of a mental illness or a condition that is a consequence of a mental illness, and does not include bodily restraint, seclusion or sterilisation;

treatment decision, in relation to a person, means a decision to give consent, or to refuse to give consent, to treatment being provided to the person;

treatment in the community means treatment that can be provided to a patient without detaining the patient at a hospital under an inpatient treatment order;

Human rights, equality and mental health laws

The various elements of the civil commitment criteria are generally thought to provide a reasonable balance between respect for the rights of people with mental illness and community protection. However, human rights debates surrounding the CRPD are challenging the scope and content of mental health laws. The purpose of the Convention is to extend international human rights protections to individuals with disabilities. It does this by providing for the respect, protection and fulfilment of the human rights of people with disabilities, including individuals with mental health problems, without discrimination on the basis of disability.[43] In particular, it recognises the social, political and personal contexts in which individuals with disabilities live, work and seek access to services.[44] It also responds to the marginalisation of individuals with disability by insisting on equality, non-discrimination and participation in society.

The most important contribution of the CRPD with respect to legal developments in the area is the requirement that there be equal access to the law: access to justice,[45] equal protection of the law,[46] and equal recognition by the law.[47] Article 12 has the most significance for mental health law and it is therefore useful to set out the Article in full:

ARTICLE 12: EQUAL RECOGNITION BEFORE THE LAW

1. States Parties reaffirm that persons with disabilities have the right to recognition everywhere as persons before the law.

2. States Parties shall recognize that persons with disabilities enjoy legal capacity on an equal basis with others in all aspects of life.

3. States Parties shall take appropriate measures to provide access by persons with disabilities to the support they may require in exercising their legal capacity.

4. States Parties shall ensure that all measures that relate to the exercise of legal capacity provide for appropriate and effective safeguards to prevent abuse in accordance with international human rights law. Such safeguards shall ensure that measures relating to the exercise of legal capacity respect the rights, will and preferences of the person, are free of conflict of interest and undue influence, are proportional and tailored to the person's circumstances, apply for the shortest time possible and are subject to regular review by a competent, independent and impartial authority or judicial body. The safeguards shall be proportional to the degree to which such measures affect the person's rights and interests.

5. Subject to the provisions of this article, States Parties shall take all appropriate and effective measures to ensure the equal right of persons with disabilities to own or

---

43   CRPD, Art 1 (Purpose).
44   Penelope Weller, 'Supported Decision-Making and the Achievement of Non-Discrimination: The Promise and Paradox of the Disabilities Convention' in Bernadette McSherry (ed.), *International Trends in Mental Health Laws in Context Special Issue* (Federation Press, 2008).
45   CRPD, Art 13 (Access to Justice).
46   CRPD, Art 5 (Equality and Non-Discrimination).
47   CRPD, Art 12 (Equal Recognition before the Law).

inherit property, to control their own financial affairs and to have equal access to bank loans, mortgages and other forms of financial credit, and shall ensure that persons with disabilities are not arbitrarily deprived of their property.

Article 12 makes it clear that individuals with disabilities must be recognised as 'legal persons' who possess legal agency and are entitled to the rights and benefits of the law. Those entitlements are the two limbs of legal capacity. As a consequence, the Committee on Rights of Persons with Disabilities, the UN body that oversees the implementation of the CRPD, states that substituted decision-making arrangements are no longer permitted.[48] CPRD General Comment 1 is an authoritative explication of Article 12. It defines substituted decision-making as situations where:

(a) a person's legal capacity is removed;

(b) a substitute decision-maker is appointed by someone other than the person; and

(c) a decision is made on a best interests basis.[49]

In other words, it is a regime that has the effect of removing the person, their perspective and their wishes from the decision-making equation, which is contrary to human rights principles.

General Comment 1 notes that the intention of Article 12 is not to attribute mental capacity, or decision-making ability, to all individuals with disability. Rather, it asserts the requirement that individuals with mental illness are entitled to retain legal control of decision-making processes throughout their illness. The effect of the requirement is two-fold. First, people with mental disabilities are entitled to a presumption of capacity. That is, an individual's decision-making abilities must be recognised and respected, untainted by discriminatory assumptions.[50] Second, the person must be supported to exercise legal capacity.

With respect to the presumption of capacity, US research has demonstrated that individuals with mental illness may be able to give informed consent to treatment even during acute episodes of mental illness.[51] The MacArthur Studies provide an evidence base for changing ideas about the abilities of individuals with severe mental illness. If it can be demonstrated that people with mental illness retain decision-making capacity, the best interests test, which is the key ethical and legal requirement for the conduct of compulsory mental health treatment decisions, may be undermined.

With respect to the obligation to provide support, General Comment 1 indicates that while support for decision-making may take many forms, it must be provided in accordance with the abilities and needs of the individual. The obligation to recognise and respect the decision-making abilities of individuals with mental health problems is supported by

---

48   CRPD, General Comment No. 1 (2014) Art 12 (Equal Recognition before the Law), CRPD/C/GC/1, 11 April 2014.

49   Ibid 13.

50   Chris Ryan, 'One Flu Over the Cuckoo's Nest: Comparing Legislated Coercive Treatment of Mental Illness with the Other Illness' (2011) 8 *Bioethical Inquiry* 93.

51   Thomas Grisso and Paul S Appelbaum, *Assessing Competence to Consent to Treatment: A Guide for Physicians and Other Health Professionals* (OUP, 1998); Thomas Grisso et al., 'The MacArthur Treatment Competence Study II: Measures of Abilities Related to Competence to Consent to Treatment' (1995) 19(2) *Law and Human Behavior* 127; Thomas Grisso and Paul S Appelbaum, 'The MacArthur Treatment Competence Study III: Abilities of Patients to Consent to Psychiatric and Medical Treatments' (1995) 19(2) *Law and Human Behavior* 149.

the principle of 'reasonable accommodation' in the CRPD. 'Reasonable accommodation' is defined as:

> necessary and appropriate modification and adjustments not imposing disproportionate or undue burden, where needed in a particular case, to ensure to persons with disabilities the enjoyment or exercise on an equal basis with others of all human rights and fundamental freedoms.[52]

From a CRPD perspective, the combination of a presumption of capacity and the provision of support to exercise legal capacity should work to limit the 'default settings' for compulsory treatment.

Article 12(4) contemplates the need for additional 'measures to support capacity' in some circumstances. The principle that a person's legal capacity must always be recognised means that s/he is entitled to delegate decision-making responsibilities to another person or to benefit from the implementation of other forms of decision-making processes in appropriate circumstances and with appropriate protections. The critical components of Article 12(4) are that the decisions that are made: (a) 'respect the rights, will and preferences of the person'; (b) are 'free of conflict of interest and undue influence'; (c) are 'proportional and tailored to the person's circumstances'; (d) 'apply for the shortest time possible'; and (e) 'are subject to regular review by a competent, independent and impartial authority or judicial body'. The CRPD requires that measures conform to the CRPD definition and that substituted decision-making arrangements are adjusted to conform to these requirements.

The CRPD and mental health law reform

Mental health laws in Australia have been criticised for being infused with discriminatory practices, including substituted decision-making, and therefore contrary to the CRPD. For example, in its *Concluding Observations for Australia*, the Committee on Rights of Persons with Disabilities states:

> 35. The Committee recommends that Australia should repeal all legislation that authorises medical interventions without free and informed consent of the persons with disabilities concerned, and legal provisions that authorize commitment of individuals to detention in mental health services, or the imposition of compulsory treatment either in institutions or in the community via Community Treatment Orders (CTOs).[53]

The Committee's comments urge an extension of the legal standards that are enjoyed by people who do not have disabilities to those who do. Throughout the developed world,

---

52   CRPD, Art 2 (Definitions).
53   Committee on the Rights of Persons with Disabilities, *Consideration of Reports Submitted by States Parties under Article 35 of the Convention*: Concluding observations on the initial report of Australia, adopted by the Committee at its tenth session (2–13 September 2013) CRPD/C/AUS/CO/1, 4 October 2013.

individuals seek and receive general healthcare according to the laws of (informed) consent. Consent laws were developed in response to the civil rights critique of medical power in the second half of the 20th century.[54] They govern the relationship between doctors and their patients, providing a protective framework that ensures that prospective patients are fully informed of the consequences of accepting recommended medical treatment.[55]

As outlined in Chapter 9, the law of consent recognises the entitlement of competent adults to decline medical treatment on any basis whatsoever, even when doing so exposes the person to danger.[56] Many people with mental health problems seek and receive mental healthcare as voluntary patients. However, should a person with a mental health problem fall within the civil commitment criteria, the right to refuse medical treatment or choose a preferred treatment may be overridden by a compulsory psychiatric treatment order. The CRPD requires that the general standard be applied to people with mental illness except in circumstances where special measures constitute reasonable accommodation or positive discrimination.

As they stand, Australian mental health laws are contrary to the principles set out in Article 12 of CPRD, primarily because they continue to provide a framework for substituted decision-making that permits the responsible psychiatrist to make treatment decisions for the person. There are currently no statutory provisions in Australian mental health law that could be interpreted as fully recognising the principle of support articulated in the CPRD standard. In addition, there are no provisions that adequately capture the inter-relationship between mental health powers and other decision-making processes, such as guardianship laws or powers of attorney, or that impose requirements to ascertain and follow the will and preferences of the person, or otherwise implement the content of advanced care plans or statements.

Exceptions to the general trend are beginning to emerge. Victoria has introduced legislation that recognises the validity of mental health advance planning statements, Queensland has applied advance health directives to the mental health context, and the ACT has introduced advance agreements and advance consent directions.[57] Victoria, Queensland, WA and the ACT offer 'nominated person' schemes.[58] The Victorian and WA legislation requires decision-makers to 'have regard to' the wishes and preferences of the person.[59] The new WA Act also introduces 'mental health advocates'.[60] While these features are promising, the CRPD's vision of equality appears to demand a more exacting and consistent law reform response on an Australia-wide basis.

---

54   Penelope Weller, 'Towards a Genealogy of "Coercive Care"' in Bernadette McSherry and Ian Freckleton (eds), *Coercive Care: Rights Law and Policy* (Routledge, 2013) 21.

55   Alasdair Maclean, *Autonomy, Informed Consent and Medical Law: A Relational Challenge* (CUP, 2009).

56   *Re C (adult: refusal of medical treatment)* [1994] 1 All ER 819.

57   *Mental Health Act 2014* (Vic) ss 19–22.

58   Ibid ss 23–7; *Mental Health Act 2000* (Qld) ss 340–9 (allied persons); *Mental Health Act 2015* (ACT) ss 19–23.

59   *Mental Health Act 2014* (WA) s 7; *Mental Health Act 2014* (Vic) s 11(1)(c) and throughout.

60   *Mental Health Act 2014* (WA) ss 348–71.

Conclusion

This chapter has outlined the core content of mental health laws in Australia in light of its historical antecedents and continuing evolution under the influence of human rights debates and law reform. It highlights the fact that the content of mental health laws in Australia reflects the entrenched discrimination that continues to shape the law as it applies to people with disabilities. Discrimination in the law clearly hinders the realisation of human rights goals. The question that is yet to be settled is how to craft mental health laws that articulate the boundaries of legislative power in a way that is consistent with human rights standards.

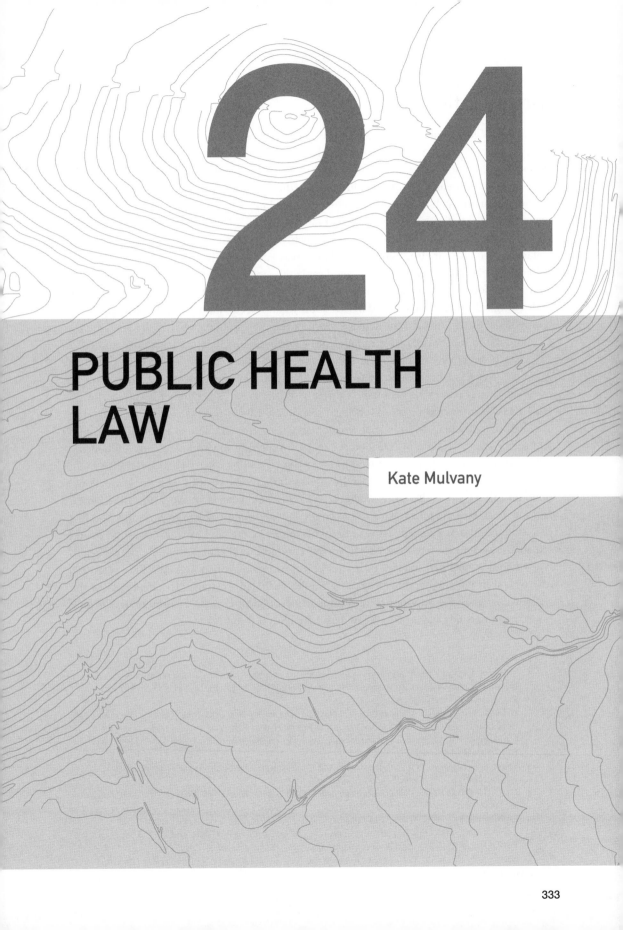

24

PUBLIC HEALTH
LAW

Kate Mulvany

Introduction

The ability of law to influence health at the population level has long been recognised.[1] In the 19th century, a range of policy and legislative initiatives were introduced in England and Wales. These proved to be highly influential in the subsequent development of the law in relation to public health in Australia. In England, the consequences of rapid industrialisation and urbanisation, such as overflowing cesspools leading to typhoid and cholera epidemics, were associated with life expectancies as low as 15 years.[2] This led the government of the UK to adopt the *Public Health Act 1848*, which promoted the improved management of water, sewage and rubbish.[3] Similar legislation was subsequently enacted in the Australian colonies.[4] Early public health laws targeted sanitation and noxious environments.[5] They created inspection and notification provisions, with the aim of controlling infectious disease and setting safety standards regarding food, drugs and occupational health.[6] This relatively narrow legal focus persisted throughout much of the 20th century.

Although in recent decades a number of health issues, including tobacco use and HIV/AIDS, have generated renewed interest in the intersection of law and public health in Australia,[7] there has been only limited policy and political engagement regarding the role of public health law more generally. Currently, Australia faces a number of public health challenges that demand multifaceted legal responses. Law is increasingly being looked to as a tool that can help address such challenges. Beyond its traditional focus on sanitation and safety standards, law is considered capable of altering environments and influencing behaviour to improve population health.

Examination of law's role in public health is a broad topic, worthy of a book in its own right, and this chapter therefore engages with only key aspects of the field. The chapter critically examines the relationship between the law and public health in Australia. The first part examines the problematic issue of defining 'public health law', as well as its sources and scope. The second part examines key principles and institutions underpinning public health law, while the third part focuses on a number of examples which highlight the (potential) role of law in influencing and promoting public health in Australia. The final part of the chapter examines the importance of a supportive political context in promoting a strong public health agenda within which law has a significant role to play.

This chapter draws upon an earlier paper by the author: Kate Mulvany, 'Prevention of Non-Communicable Diseases in Australia: What Role Should Public Health Law Play?' (2015) 23(1) *Journal of Law and Medicine* 83.

1   Helen L Walls, Kevin L Walls and Bebe Loff, 'The Regulatory Gap in Chronic Disease Prevention: A Historical Perspective' (2012) 33(1) *Journal of Public Health Policy* 89, 90.

2   Christopher Hamlin and Sally Sheard, 'Revolutions in Public Health: 1848, and 1998?' (1998) 317 *British Medical Journal* 587, 587.

3   Roger S Magnusson, 'Mapping the Scope and Opportunities for Public Health Law in Liberal Democracies' [2007] *Journal of Law Medicine & Ethics* 571, 572.

4   *Public Health Act 1854* (Vic); *Health Act 1884* (Qld); *Public Health Act 1896* (NSW); *Public Health Act 1885* (Tas); *Public Health Act 1886* (WA); *Public Health Act 1873* (SA).

5   Christopher Reynolds, *Public and Environmental Health Law* (Federation Press, 2011) 11.

6   Ian Bidmeade and Chris Reynolds, Commonwealth Department of Health and Family Services, *Public Health Law in Australia. Its Current State and Future Directions* (1997) 4.

7   Christopher Reynolds, 'Public Health Law in the New Century' (2003) 435 *Journal of Law and Medicine* 435, 436.

D

Public health law: sources, scope and principles

What exactly constitutes public health law is contentious. It is therefore necessary to make clear how the term is defined in this chapter, before exploring the sources and scope of such law. Broadly speaking, public health activities comprise 'collective interventions that aim to protect and promote the health of the public'.[8] Consequently, in contrast to health law, which traditionally focuses on the interaction between individuals and health professionals, public health law aims to act upon populations.[9] Furthermore, public health law emphasises preventive strategies rather than treatment.[10]

Definitions

Multiple definitions of public health law have been proposed, originating from a number of jurisdictions.[11] These range from those that take a narrow approach to the field, regarding both the sources and the scope of public health law, to those that adopt a more inclusive view.[12] For example, Hall suggests that 'public health law is about enforcing government efforts to promote health', and should be limited to the 'classic subjects of communicable diseases … sanitary water and sewer systems, safe food and injury prevention'.[13]

Gostin's widely cited definition similarly emphasises the role of government, yet also recognises the importance of other stakeholders:

> The legal powers and duties of the state, in collaboration with its partners (e.g. health care, business, the community, the media and academe) to assure the conditions for people to be healthy (e.g. to identify, prevent and ameliorate risks to health in a population) and the limitations on the power of the state to constrain the autonomy, privacy, liberty, proprietary or other legally protected interests of individuals for the common good.[14]

These US perspectives contrast with more holistic definitions from England and Australia.[15] In the Australian context, for example, Reynolds defines public health law as 'the body of law that provides for good public health powers, responses and programs, and that applies the legal process to securing public health outcomes'.[16] For the purposes of this chapter, Reynolds' broad definition of public health law will be used. As explored in the following

---

8   Angus Dawson and Marcel Verwij, 'Public Health Ethics: A Manifesto' (2008) 1(1) *Public Health Ethics* 1.

9   Keith Syrett and Oliver Quick, 'Pedagogical Promise and Problems: Teaching Public Health Law' (2009) 123 *Public Health* 222, 223.

10   Lawrence O Gostin, 'Legal Foundations of Public Health Law and Its Role in Meeting Future Challenges' (2006) 120 *Public Health* 8, 10.

11   Syrett and Quick, above n 9, 222.

12   Micha L Berman, 'Defining the Field of Public Health Law' (2013) 15(2) *DePaul Journal of Health Care Law* 45, 71.

13   Mark A Hall, 'The Scope and Limits of Public Health Law' (2003) 46(3 Suppl) *Perspectives in Biology and Medicine* S199.

14   Lawrence O Gostin, *Public Health Law: Power, Duty, Restraint*, 2nd edn (University of California Press, 2008).

15   Syrett and Quick, above n 9, 223.

16   Reynolds, above n 5, at 9.

sections, such a broad definition offers advantages regarding both the sources and scope of public health law.

Sources of law

When considering the sources, or types, of law that may be regarded as public health law, the role of the state and its ability to legislate is central. Gostin underscores this through his taxonomy of state powers, which include the power to tax and spend, to alter the informational environment, to alter the built environment, to alter the socioeconomic environment, to regulate persons, professionals and businesses, and to undertake deregulation.[17] The state may, for example, enact legislation to restrict the density of fast food outlets in particular geographic locations. Arguably, however, the state's role should not be over-emphasised. Public health law may also include the normative effects of civil and criminal litigation,[18] international sources of law, and 'soft law'.[19]

Civil litigation, although acting through individuals, can have substantial population-wide effects. According to Reynolds, 'without the threat of litigation, it is unlikely that smoking bans in public places would have developed in many countries to the extent that they did'.[20] Similarly, there is evidence that the threat of civil action in the US was able to influence the marketing practices of Kraft Foods and McDonalds.[21] International law, such as the right to health,[22] and the World Health Organization (WHO) Framework Convention on Tobacco Control,[23] places obligations on Member States to improve their population health. Its role and impact should not be overlooked,[24] particularly regarding the influence of multinational corporations over the consumption of products such as food and tobacco.

Finally, public health law should encompass forms of 'soft law', such as policies, guidelines and codes. These can promote and develop normative standards. An example of soft law is the Alcohol Beverages Advertising Code, which aims to ensure that alcohol is marketed responsibly and is administered by a management committee consisting of representatives from industry and government.[25]

---

17   Gostin, above n 10, 11.

18   Magnusson, above n 3, 577; see, for example, *Hawkins v Van Heerden* (2014) 240 A Crim R 364; *Cole v South Tweed Heads Rugby League Football Club Ltd* (2004) 217 CLR 469; *Pelman v McDonald's Corporation*, 237 F Supp 2d 512 (SDNY, 22 January 2003); *McCabe v British American Tobacco Australia Services Ltd* [2002] VSC 73.

19   See Roger S Magnusson, Lawrence Gostin and David Studdert, 'Can Law Improve Treatment and Prevention in Cancer?' (2011) 125 *Public Health* 813, 817.

20   Chris Reynolds, 'Legal Issues in Public Health', *International Encyclopedia of Public Health* (Springer, 2008) 45, 54.

21   Jane Mundy, 'Tobacco, No Time for Complacency' (2007) 5(3) *Of Substance* 19.

22   *International Covenant on Economic, Social and Cultural Rights*, opened for signature 16 December 1966, 993 UNTS 3 (entered into force 3 November 1976) Art 12. See Chapter 5 for a detailed examination of the right to health under international law.

23   *WHO Framework Convention on Tobacco Control*, opened for signature 21 May 2003, 2302 UNTS 166 (entered into force 27 February 2005). See Chapter 25 for more detail on this Convention.

24   Wendy K Mariner, 'Law and Public Health: Beyond Emergency Preparedness' (2005) 38(2) *Journal of Health Law* 247.

25   ABAC, *Responsible Marketing Code* <www.abac.org.au/wp-content/uploads/2014/06/ABAC-Responsible-Alcohol-Marketing-Code-30-4-14.pdf >; see Australian National Preventative Health Agency, *Alcohol Advertising: The effectiveness of current regulatory codes in addressing community concern, Draft Report* (2014).

The use of soft law as part of self-regulatory regimes within the tobacco, alcohol, food and advertising industries is contentious, due to the conflict between maximising profit and limiting the provision of harmful products.[26] Including soft law within the ambit of public health law is warranted, however, as it aligns with modern theories of regulation,[27] may foster innovative market solutions,[28] allows flexibility, and reduces oversight and enforcement costs borne by governments.[29] It also leaves open the possibility of positive self-regulatory outcomes. Marteau has recognised, for example, that self-regulation of the food industry in the UK led to a reduction in estimated per person salt intake.[30] Such outcomes may be particularly important where it is difficult to negotiate and achieve sufficient stakeholder or political support for the adoption of legislation.[31]

Scope of law

Public health law may include both laws specifically aiming to improve public health, and those that have an indirect or incidental impact. Notably, the field's core, laws intending to improve public health, overlaps with other areas of law such as environmental law, product safety law, and road safety law. Looking beyond this core, public health law extends to laws that do not primarily focus upon health, but have an impact on public health nonetheless.[32] These may include laws that influence social determinants of health,[33] such as employment and education, which affect health indirectly.[34]

To include laws that influence social determinants of health or incidentally impact upon health within the scope of public health law may be criticised as 'overreaching'.[35] As identified by Magnusson, however, 'to ignore law's role in shaping the social determinants of health is to ignore real, structural causes of population health outcomes'.[36] This does not necessarily mean that government health departments become responsible for education and employment portfolios.[37] Rather, it supports the concept of 'Health in all Policies',[38] which means considering the health impacts of policy decisions across all government activities.[39] This brief examination of the sources and the scope of public health law suggests

26   Stephen Sugarman, 'No More Business as Usual: Enticing Companies to Sharply Lower the Costs of the Products They Sell' (2009) 123 *Public Health* 275.

27   Julia Black, 'Constructing and Contesting Legitimacy and Accountability in Polycentric Regulatory Regimes' (2008) 2 *Regulation & Governance* 137.

28   Gail Pearson, 'Business Self-Regulation' (2012) 20 *Australian Journal of Administrative Law* 34.

29   Ibid.

30   Theresa Marteau, 'Judging Nudging: Can Nudging Improve Population Health?' (2011) 342 *British Medical Journal* 263, 264.

31   See Caroline White, 'Nudging, Fishing and Improving the Public's Health' (2011) 343 *British Medical Journal* d8046.

32   Scott Burris, 'From Health Care Law to the Social Determinants of Health: A Public Health Law Research Perspective' (2011) 59(6) *University of Pennsylvania Law Review* 1649, 1663.

33   Magnusson, above n 3, 573.

34   Andrew W Siegal, 'The Jurisprudence of Public Health: Reflections on Lawrence O. Gostin's *Public Health Law*' (2002) 18 *Journal of Contemporary Health Law & Policy* 359, 371.

35   Syrett and Quick, above n 9, 227.

36   Magnusson, above n 3, 583.

37   Ibid.

38   Ilona Kickbusch, 'Health in All Policies: Setting the Scene' (2008) 5(1) *Public Health Bulletin* 3.

39   See Chapter 4 for a detailed examination of the (potential) role of law in shaping the social determinants of health.

that there are many types of law capable of falling within its definition.[40] Though claims that public health law is 'uncoordinated'[41] and 'disparate' may be made,[42] the complexities of health issues demand a broad approach, and schemas of public health law based on core and peripheral elements can assist analysis.

Key principles

Analysis of the role of public health law often draws upon three key principles. First, the role of such law can be justified on multiple theoretical grounds. Adopting a market analysis viewpoint, state intervention in the form of public health law can be defended as protecting a 'public good', correcting information asymmetries or addressing negative externalities.[43] Alternatively, state action may be viewed as necessary as part of the state's 'stewardship' duties, to look after the needs of both individuals and the community.[44] While tensions may exist between the collective interest inherent in the approach taken in public health law and individual liberties,[45] the use of such law may in fact also be necessary to enhance autonomy or promote social justice overall.[46]

The second key principle of note is that there is evidence of the effectiveness of law in promoting public health in practice. While tobacco control measures provide a persuasive example in this regard,[47] evidence in support of public health law's effectiveness can also be identified in areas as diverse as advertising to children[48] and supervised injecting facilities.[49] Evidence of effectiveness can help justify the use of public health law.[50] Where detailed evidence is yet to be gathered, though, political leadership,[51] and a 'learning by doing' approach,[52] also provide ways to advocate for public health law in practice.

The third key principle is that law should be adopted as part of a comprehensive package of measures aimed at improving public health. Public health law is often presented as an isolated, top-down answer to a health problem. Even some public health advocates tend

40   Robyn Martin, 'Public Health Law' (2009) 129 *Perspectives in Public Health* 200.

41   Reynolds, above n 20, 46.

42   Ibid 45.

43   Reynolds, above n 5, 141.

44   Nuffield Council on Bioethics, *Public Health: Ethical Issues* (2007) 25.

45   Michael Keane, 'I Want to Consume This Product; Should Public Health Experts Stop Me?' (2011) 195(7) *Medical Journal of Australia* 379.

46   Kate Mulvany, 'Prevention of Non-Communicable Diseases in Australia: What Role Should Public Health Law Play?' (2015) 23 *Journal of Law and Medicine* 83, 96. See also Chapter 2 for a discussion of ethical concepts of autonomy and justice.

47   See Michelle Scollo, 'The Pricing and Taxation of Tobacco Products in Australia' in Michelle Scollo and Margaret Winstanley (eds), *Tobacco in Australia: Facts and Issues* (Cancer Council Victoria, 2015) <www.tobaccoinaustralia.org.au>.

48   Sarah MacKay, 'Food Advertising and Obesity in Australia: To What Extent Can Self-Regulation Protect the Interests of Children?' (2009) 35(1) *Monash University Law Review* 118, 126.

49   See Melissa de Vel-Palumbo et al., 'Supervised Injecting Facilities: What the Literature Tells Us' (2013) Series 1 *Drug Policy Modeling Program Bulletin*.

50   Scott Burris et al., 'Making the Case for Laws that Improve Health: A Framework for Public Health Law Research' (2010) 88(2) *Milbank Quarterly* 169, 172.

51   See Mulvany, above n 46, 102.

52   National Preventative Health Taskforce, *Australia: The Healthiest Country by 2020 A Discussion Paper* (2008) 14.

to assume that complex health issues can be solved directly by legislative intervention.[53] Care needs to be taken, however, to avoid oversimplification of the role of public health law. Rather than a stand-alone intervention, public health law should be viewed as complementing other measures aimed at improving population health. These measures may include social marketing campaigns, school education initiatives, and altering environmental cues to encourage healthier decision-making.[54] For example, images on cigarette packets depicting tobacco-related pathology act as environmental cues to discourage tobacco use, yet law is required to ensure that companies adopt such images on their packaging.

Ultimately, public health law may 'create significant shifts in culture, attitudes and behaviour',[55] and is a potent and cost-effective measure to help address contemporary public health issues.[56] In some areas of public health policy the use of law has made Australia a world leader.[57] This is especially evident regarding tobacco control and, more recently, in relation to the revised Public Health Acts.[58] Overall, however, the examination of key institutions and laws in the following section demonstrates that the body of public health law in Australia is perhaps best characterised as fragmented and inconsistent.

Key institutions

Numerous institutions are involved in the development and implementation of public health law in Australia. For present purposes, it is useful to classify these as government, private and not-for-profit. In practice, however, there is significant interaction between them. Although their role in creating and implementing public health law should not be overstated, governments remain central to any analysis of the field.[59] Parliaments are capable of enacting legislation, and the executive can adopt certain policy positions, as well as developing standards or guidelines via health departments or agencies.

In Australia, the Commonwealth, state and territory governments all play a significant role in the acceptance and adoption of public health law. When seeking to identify key institutions in the field, however, it becomes clear that their very existence and ongoing program of work has proven susceptible to the changing political hue of governments over the years. In 2011, for example, the Commonwealth Labor government established the Australian National Preventative Health Agency.[60] Although the agency set out a bold program, including advocating for the adoption of a more coherent approach to public health

---

53   See Roger Magnusson and Belinda Reeve, '"Steering" Private Regulation? A New Strategy for Reducing Population Salt Intake in Australia' (2014) 36 *Sydney Law Review* 255, 258.

54   See Mulvany, above n 46, 92.

55   Helen Walls et al., 'Public Health Campaigns and Obesity – a Critique' (2011) 11 *BMC Public Health* 136.

56   Bebe Loff and Helen Walls, 'Filling the Regulatory Gap in Chronic Disease Prevention', *The Conversation* (online) 29 June 2012 <http://theconversation.com/filling-the-regulatory-gap-in-chronic-disease-prevention-6127>.

57   Ben White, Fiona McDonald and Lindy Willmott, *Health Law in Australia*, 2nd edn (Thomson Reuters, 2014) 660.

58   Ibid.

59   Magnusson and Reeve, above n 53, 273.

60   See Australian National Preventative Health Agency website <www.anpha.gov.au/internet/anpha/publishing.nsf>.

law, it was abolished three years later by the incoming Liberal/National government in a streamlining and cost-cutting process.[61]

Private institutions also have substantial influence in the design and practice of public health law in Australia. They include corporate entities, as well as representative bodies of particular industries. The role of these institutions is extensive. They can lobby governments regarding the proposed adoption of government-sponsored public health law, and they can also generate their own body of soft law. Tobacco corporations, for example, challenged the Commonwealth government's enactment of the *Tobacco Plain Packaging Act 2011* (Cth),[62] and industry bodies such as the Australian Beverages Council, the Australian Food and Grocery Council and the Australian Association of National Advertisers have developed standards and codes that seek to regulate food labelling and advertising.

Numerous not-for-profit organisations are involved in the development of public health law. They range from local groups to internationally recognised organisations,[63] which may lobby state institutions, create publicity regarding specific issues, and generate research in support of such law. These groups also directly engage in public health law processes. For example, a complaint to the Australian Competition and Consumer Commission by a coalition of Australian public health groups led to changes in Coca Cola's advertising claims.[64] Notably, when the same complaint was made to the advertising industry's self-regulatory body, it was dismissed.[65]

Interaction between government, private and not-for-profit institutions may be both formal and informal. Often, Australian governments will facilitate a body that draws upon all three sectors. For example, the Commonwealth government established the Food and Health Dialogue, now known as the Healthy Foods Partnership, which aimed to encourage lower levels of salt, saturated fat and sugar in food. Members of the Dialogue included representatives of the Commonwealth Minister for Health, from the Public Health Association of Australia, the Australian Food and Grocery Council, Woolworths Ltd and McDonald's Australia (as a member of the Quick Service Restaurant Forum). The Healthy Food Partnership has a governance structure made up of an executive committee, five working groups and industry roundtables (where required).[66] Conversely, interaction between the three sectors may be less overt. The withdrawal of the Health Star Rating website, which was initiated by the states and territories, and which aimed to introduce

---

61   Explanatory Memorandum, Australian National Preventative Health Agency (Abolition) Bill 2014 (Cth).

62   *JT International SA v Commonwealth of Australia* (2012) 291 ALR 669.

63   For example, the Cancer Council, Diabetes Australia, the National Alliance for Action on Alcohol, the McCabe Centre for Law and Cancer and the Public Health Association of Australia.

64   Sandra Davoren and Nicole Antonopoulous, 'Alcohol and Food Regulation in Australia – Legal Issues in Cancer Prevention' (2012) 36(1) *Cancer Forum* 15.

65   Reynolds, above n 5, 422.

66   Australian Government, Department of Health, Healthy Food Partnership <www.health.gov.au/internet/main/publishing.nsf/Content/Healthy-Food-Partnership-Home>.

easy-to-understand front-of-pack food labelling, provides a stark example.[67] After two years in development, the website was temporarily withdrawn by the Commonwealth government amidst claims that members of the Commonwealth Department of Health had links to the food industry.[68]

Public health laws: some key examples

There is a wide range of both hard and soft law that could be said to influence public health in Australia. For present purposes, however, we focus on a number of key examples. As Reynolds has noted, the original state and territory Public Health Acts have generally stood the test of time.[69] They primarily aim to control unsanitary and unhealthy conditions through licensing, inspection and enforcement provisions,[70] and provide for emergency management powers regarding infectious diseases and disease registers. Almost all of the Public Health Acts have been updated in the last 20 years.[71] Updates have included, for example, broadening the regulatory approach to environmental nuisances[72] and introducing tobacco control provisions.[73]

Apart from the Public Health Acts, there is a range of laws that address specific health issues, including: strategies to control infectious, or communicable, diseases (at both levels of government); discrete biomedical interventions such as water fluoridation and food fortification; and strategies to impact upon behavioural risk factors for non-communicable diseases (NCDs), which are diseases that are chronic but cannot be passed from person to person.[74] Key examples of these laws are outlined in Table 24.1. Two attributes of this collection of laws can be noted: the broadening of public health law approaches over time, and inconsistencies in approach to health issues.

---

67   Amy Corderoy, 'Senator Fiona Nash Accused over Adviser's Junk Food Lobbying', *Sydney Morning Herald* (online), 22 February 2014 <www.smh.com.au/national/senator-fiona-nash-accused-over-advisers-junk-food-lobbying-20140221-337k1.html>.

68   Amy Corderoy, 'Healthy Food Star Ratings Website: Senior Bureaucrat Stripped of Responsibility', *Sydney Morning Herald* (online), 13 February 2014 <www.smh.com.au/federal-politics/healthy-food-star-ratings-website-senior-bureaucrat-stripped-of-responsibility-20140213-32jsq.html>.

69   Reynolds, above n 5, 179.

70   Ibid 192.

71   *Public Health Act 1997* (ACT); *Public Health Act 2010* (NSW); *Public and Environmental Health Act 2011* (NT); *Public Health Act 2005* (Qld); *South Australian Public Health Act 2011* (SA); *Public Health Act 1997* (Tas); *Public Health and Well Being Act 2008* (Vic); cf *Public Health Act 1886* (WA).

72   *South Australian Public Health Act 2011* (SA) s 56.

73   *Public Health Act 1997* (Tas) Part 4.

74   World Health Organization, *Noncommunicable Diseases Fact Sheet* (March 2013) <www.who.int/mediacentre/factsheets/fs355/en/>.

Table 24.1: Key Public Health Laws in Australia

Issue	Key Examples of Public Health Law	General Description
Sanitation, control of noxious environments	*Public Health Act 1997* (ACT); *Public Health Act 2010* (NSW); *Public and Environmental Health Act 2011* (NT); *Public Health Act 2005* (Qld); *South Australian Public Health Act 2011* (SA); *Public Health Act 1997* (Tas); *Public Health and Well Being Act 2008* (Vic); *Public Health Act 1886* (WA).	Control of public health nuisances, through licensing, inspection and enforcement; emergency management powers; disease registers; disclosure requirements regarding HIV/AIDS; regulation of childhood vaccination.
	Food Act 2001 (ACT); *Food Act 2003* (NSW); *Food Regulation 2010* (NSW); *Food Act 2004* (NT); *Food Act 2006* (Qld); *Food Act 2006* (Qld); *Food Act 2001* (SA); *Food Act 2003* (Tas); *Food Act 1984* (Vic); *Food Act 2008* (WA).	Criminalise unsafe food preparation and handling practices; food premises registration, inspection and audit powers; enforcement provisions for the Australian and New Zealand Food Standards Code.
Management of infectious diseases	*National Health Security Act 2007* (Cth); *Quarantine Act 1918* (Cth)	Commonwealth powers for surveillance, response and quarantine regarding public health events of national significance.
	Emergency Management Act 2006 (Tas); *HIV/AIDS Preventative Measures Act 1993* (Tas)	State emergency management powers. Prescribes testing, disclosure and needle exchange programs.
	Criminal Code (WA) s 1(1); *Crimes Act 1900* (NSW) s 4(1)(c); *Crimes Act 1958* (Vic) s 22; *Criminal Code 1899* (Qld) s 317(b).	Criminalise certain infectious disease transmission.
Childhood vaccination	*A New Tax System (Family Assistance) Act 1999* (Cth) Part 2 Div 2.	Pricing incentives to increase childhood vaccination rates.
	Public Health Regulations 2000 (ACT); *Public Health Act 2010* (NSW) Part 5 Div 4; *Public Health Act 1997* (Tas) Part 3 Div 2; *Public Health and Well Being Act 2008* (Vic) Part 8 Div 7; *School Education Act 1999* (WA) s 16.	Mandatory disclosure requirements when enrolling children in childcare facilities or schools.
Dental health	*Public Health Act 1997* (ACT) s 133; Public Health (Drinking Water) Code of Practice 2007 (ACT); *Fluoridation of Public Water Supplies Act 1957* (NSW); *Water Fluoridation Act 2008* (Qld); Safe Drinking Water Regulations 2012 (SA); *Fluoridation Act 1968* (Tas); *Health (Fluoridation) Act 1973* (Vic); *Fluoridation of Public Water Supplies Act 1966* (WA).	Prescribe levels of fluoride to be maintained in supplied drinking water.
Tobacco use	*Tobacco Plain Packaging Act 2011* (Cth); Tobacco Plain Packaging Regulations 2011 (Cth); Tobacco Plain Packaging Enforcement Policy; Competition and Consumer (Tobacco) Information Standard 2011; *Tobacco Advertising Prohibition Act 1992* (Cth); *Excise Tariff Act 1921* (Cth); *Customs Tariff Act 1995* (Cth); Air Navigation Regulations (Amendment) 1996 (Cth) reg 4; Interstate Road Transport Regulations 1986 (Cth) reg 51B.	Restrictions on the advertising and promotion of tobacco products; mandatory plain packaging, health warning labels and salient images; general pricing strategies; bans on cigarette smoking on planes and buses.

Category	Legislation	Description
	Tobacco Act 1927 (ACT); *Smoke-Free Public Places Act 2003* (ACT); *Public Health (Tobacco) Act 2008* (NSW); *Public Health (Tobacco) Regulation 2009* (NSW); *Smoke-free Environment Act 2000* (NSW); NSW Health Smoke-free Health Care Policy; *Tobacco Control Act 2002* (NT); *Tobacco Control Regulations 2002* (NT); *Tobacco and Other Smoking Products Act 1998* (Qld); *Tobacco and Other Smoking Products Regulations 2010* (Qld); *Tobacco Products Regulation Act 1997* (SA); *Tobacco Products Regulations 2004* (SA); *Public Health Act 1997* (Tas); *Tobacco Act 1987* (Vic); *Tobacco Regulations 2007* (Vic); *Tobacco Products Control Act 2006* (WA); *Tobacco Products Control Regulations 2006* (WA).	Prohibit smoking in enclosed workplaces, outdoor dining/drinking areas, enclosed restaurants, shopping centres, schools, playgrounds, sporting venues, skate parks, and cars occupied by children; prohibit certain advertising and sponsorship; certify specialist tobacconists; and provide inspection powers.
Alcohol	*Excise Tariff Validation Act 2009* (Cth); *Customs Tariff Validation Act 2009* (Cth); *Stronger Futures Northern Territory Act 2012* (Cth); Australian and New Zealand Food Standards Code, Standard 2.7.1	Isolated pricing strategy to reduce consumption of ready-to-drink spirit-based beverages; prohibits possession or supply of liquor in an alcohol-protected area; approval powers for alcohol management plans; prescribes labelling requirements for packaged alcohol including displaying basic identifying information, information about alcohol content and equivalent standard drinks; prohibits certain health claims.
	Alcohol Mandatory Treatment Act 2013 (NT)	Mandatory assessment, treatment and management powers regarding 'alcohol misusers' in the Northern Territory.
	Alcoholic Beverages Advertising Code (Scheme and Responsible Marketing Code)	Industry code with the aim of marketing alcohol in a responsible manner.
	Liquor Act 2010 (ACT); *Liquor Licensing Act 1997* (SA); *Public Intoxication Act 1984* (SA); *Liquor Control Reform Act 1998* (Vic); *Liquor Act 1992* (Qld); *Liquor Control Act 1988* (WA); *Liquor Licensing Act 1990* (Tas); *Liquor Act 2007* (NSW); *Northern Territory Liquor Act 1979* (NT); *Alcohol Mandatory Treatment Act 2013* (NT)	Licensing and investigatory strategies for premises that sell or supply alcohol; prohibitions on sale or supply to minors; powers to declare restricted alcohol areas; prescribed free drinking water.
	Australian and New Zealand Food Standards Code, Standard 1.2.7	Prescribes the nutritional claims and health claims that can be made on food labels or advertisements.
Unhealthy foods, inactivity and obesity	*Food Act 2003* (NSW) Part 8, Div 4; *Food Act 2001* (SA) s 112; *Food Act 2001* (ACT) s 110	Fast food outlets to display kilojoule content and average adult daily intake on menu boards.

Table 24.1: (cont.)

Issue	Key Examples of Public Health Law	General Description
	Health Star Rating	Voluntary front-of-packet labelling rating overall nutritional profile of food. Jointly developed by government, industry and public health groups.
	Responsible Children's Marketing Initiative	Voluntary advertising framework to help promote healthy dietary choices and lifestyles to Australian children. Developed by the Australian Food and Beverage Industry and Australian Association of National Advertisers.
	The Food Dialogue	Voluntary food reformulation program to decrease saturated fat, salt, added sugar in food, and increase the fibre, wholegrain, fruit and vegetable content. Developed by government, industry and public health representatives.
	Australian Beverages Council Commitment Addressing Obesity and Other Health and Wellness Issues 2009	Voluntary Commitment to provide additional beverage labelling, restrict advertising to children and beverage promotion in schools. Developed by the Australian Beverages Council.
Iodine deficiency disorders	Australian and New Zealand Food Standards Code, Standard 2.1.1	Mandatory fortification of salt used in bread making with iodine.
Birth defects and thiamine deficiencies	Australian and New Zealand Food Standards Code, Standard 2.1.1	Mandatory fortification of wheat flour for bread making with folic acid and thiamine.
Skin cancers	National Directory for Radiation Protection 2014 part 5.4.1; Radiation Protection Regulation 2007 (ACT) s 5; Radiation Control Regulation 2013 (NSW) cl 41; Radiation Protection Regulations (NT) reg 6(1); *Radiation Safety Act 1999* (Qld) s 47; Radiation Safety Regulation 2010 (Qld) s 64A; Radiation Protection and Control (Non-Ionising Radiation) Regulations 2013 (SA) reg 5; *Public Health Act 1997* (Tas) s 184; Guidelines for the Operation of Solaria in Tasmania 2014; *Radiation Act 2005* (Vic) s 23D. *Radiation Safety Act 1975* (WA) s 36; Radiation Safety (General) Regulations 1983 (WA).	Commercial solariums prohibited in all states.

Over the last 30 years, the use of law to improve public health has become more nuanced. Rather than relying on licensing, or prohibition and enforcement provisions alone, various other strategies have been adopted. These include pricing measures, restrictions on the informational environment and soft law schemes. While there may be a range of reasons for this more diverse approach, it is also perhaps indicative of increased Commonwealth government involvement. As outlined in Chapter 6, the only explicit constitutional power afforded to the Commonwealth government regarding health is quarantine,[75] so alternative powers, including the power to tax,[76] need to be engaged to support Commonwealth strategies in the field of public health.

In drawing on examples of the use of public health law, what is noticeable is that there are often glaring inconsistencies in approach. This is apparent in two respects. First, there are large discrepancies between the approaches of Australian governments to NCDs. Tobacco control strategies are extensive, nuanced, and primarily based on legislative responses. Measures to control skin cancers, although perhaps not as extensive, similarly involve key legislative measures which complement broader public health strategies.[77] In contrast, legal frameworks with a large emphasis on self-regulation and soft law are the favoured approach of governments concerning alcohol consumption and unhealthy food.[78]

Second, while legislative measures have been adopted prescribing the fortification of food with healthy elements, only voluntary schemes exist relating to the reduction in levels of unhealthy components such as salt.[79] These inconsistencies do not necessarily reflect the size and threat of particular health issues. Instead, they are the result of a complex interplay between varying degrees of public and political acceptance, industry resistance, and the evidence of effectiveness for the use of the particular measures. Overall, examination of the key institutions and laws in the field of Australian public health law has revealed significant differences in the extent and type of law adopted, and that key public health initiatives have not stood the test of time. We now turn to assess the current state of and future options for public health law in Australia.

Assessing the present and future of public health law

There are currently a number of critical public health challenges in Australia. One key challenge is the need to control NCDs. The increasing prevalence of risk factors for these diseases poses an enormous threat to a health system that is already under considerable strain. The magnitude of the problem is perhaps best demonstrated by current concerns

---

75 *Commonwealth Constitution* s 51(ix).

76 Ibid s 51(ii).

77 *Radiation Protection Regulation 2007* (ACT) reg 5; *Radiation Control Regulation 2013* (NSW) reg 41; *Radiation Protection Regulations* (NT) reg 6(1); *Radiation Safety Act 1999* (Qld) s 47; *Radiation Safety Regulation 2010* (Qld) reg 64A; *Radiation Protection and Control (Non-Ionising Radiation) Regulations 2013* (SA) reg 5; *Public Health Act 1997* (Tas) s 184; *Radiation Act 2005* (Vic) s 23D; *Radiation Safety (General) Regulations 1983* (WA) reg 57B.

78 Julie Henderson et al., 'Governing Childhood Obesity: Framing Regulation of Fast Food Advertising in the Australian Print Media' (2009) 69 *Social Science & Medicine* 1402.

79 Magnusson and Reeve, above n 53, 257.

regarding diabetes. Over the last 20 years in Australia, the prevalence of diabetes has more than doubled.[80] If not addressed, it is estimated that a third of today's young adults will go on to develop the disease, which has no cure, requires lifelong management and can lead to complications such as blindness and limb amputation.[81] Economic predictions suggest that Australian health spending on diabetes will rise by 400 per cent between 2003 and 2033.[82] Notably, comparisons have been drawn between current diabetes 'epidemics' and those of cholera and typhoid in the 19th century.[83] Although public health law has been advocated for as a strategy to tackle diabetes, it has only been used for this purpose in a very limited way to date.[84]

If Australia is to curb the threat posed by diabetes and other NCDs, those in political leadership need to address both inconsistencies in the current body of public health law and the vulnerability of key national institutions. However, the political will to make these changes is lacking. Unlike in the 19th century, where politicians were compelled into action by communicable diseases,[85] the slow-moving nature of NCDs affords opportunity for political lassitude. This is reflected in two areas: continued reliance on self-regulation and the dominance of the theme of personal responsibility.

The limits of self-regulation

While self-regulation has a justified role in public health law, this role should be situated within the context of a 'responsive' regulatory approach. Such an approach escalates the regulatory measure adopted if voluntary industry self-regulation is shown to be ineffective.[86] There are several examples of the ineffectiveness of self-regulatory codes, one being the Responsible Children's Marketing Initiative (RCMI). The RCMI aims to provide a 'framework for food and beverage companies to help promote healthy dietary choices and lifestyles to Australian children'.[87] However, there are deficiencies in the RCMI.[88] Difficulties arise in defining 'advertising to children', leading to outcomes where children may actually be exposed to increased advertising of unhealthy food by signatories to the RCMI.[89] Furthermore, the

---

80   Australian Institute of Health and Welfare, *Australia's Health 2012, Biennial Report* (2012) 299.
81   Baker Heart and Diabetes Institute, *Diabetes the Silent Pandemic* (2012) 27.
82   Victorian Department of Human Services, *Future Prevalence of Overweight and Obesity in Children and Adolescents 2005–2025 Report* (2008), referred to in Jenny C Kaldor, Roger S Magnusson and Stephen Colagiuri, 'Government Action on Diabetes Prevention: Time to Try Something New' (2015) 202(11) *Medical Journal of Australia* 578.
83   Cate Swannell, 'Diabetes Epidemic an "Emergency"' (2013) 31 *Medical Journal of Australia InSight* <www.mja.com.au/insight/2013/31/diabetes-epidemic-emergency>
84   Soft law schemes aiming to prevent obesity have been the preferred option: see Kaldor et al., above n 82.
85   Loff and Walls, above n 56.
86   Belinda Reeve, 'The Regulatory Pyramid Meets the Food Pyramid: Can Regulatory Theory Improve Controls on Television Food Advertising to Australian Children?' (2011) 19 *Journal of Law and Medicine* 128, 133.
87   Australian Food and Grocery Council (AFGC), *Responsible Children's Marketing Initiative* (2011) <www.afgc.org.au/industry-codes/advertising-to-children/rcmi.html>.
88   Lisa G Smithers, Tracy L Merlin and John W Lynch, 'The Impact of Industry Self-Regulation on Television Marketing of Unhealthy Food and Beverages to Australian Children. Could Recent Initiatives in Industry Self-Regulation be Missing the Mark?' (2013) 199(3) *Medical Journal of Australia* 148.
89   Ibid.

initiative neglects the cumulative effect of frequent advertising,[90] and suffers from enforcement limitations.[91] As such, the role and the effectiveness of the RCMI may be questioned. There is little indication, however, that the Commonwealth government plans to escalate the regulatory response through an enforceable legislative framework.[92]

The political context

The second area in which political leadership is lacking involves the entrenched mantra of 'personal responsibility'.[93] With respect to the growing obesity problem, Tony Abbott, the former Minister for Health and Prime Minster, once observed that:

> In the end, our weight is largely a product of the amount of exercise we do and the amount of food that we put in our mouths. And obviously we are in almost total control of both of those issues.[94]

The theme of personal responsibility inappropriately frames NCDs as solely caused by, and amenable to, individual behaviour. This narrow focus is inappropriate, as it not only fails to account for social and environmental influences upon health, but also shifts accountability for public health issues from both governments and industries to individuals.[95]

If the growing problem of NCDs is to be curbed, greater political leadership is required: to confront ineffective self-regulatory regimes and move on from the notion of personal responsibility. The issue of NCDs needs to be viewed as one of 'shared responsibility',[96] and regulation in the areas of alcohol consumption and unhealthy food should be escalated via legislation, addressing the current gaps and inconsistencies in Australian public health law. Such political action is likely to require 'constant active public pressure'.[97]

Previously, community acceptance of public health law, particularly in the form of legislation, may have been limited. In 2011, for example, on the topic of obesity, Reeve noted that personal responsibility appeared to be the dominant popular discourse.[98] In the last few years, however, surveys have demonstrated high levels of support for government intervention, including through public health law, to address obesity[99] and in areas such as alcohol

---

90   Henderson et al., above n 78.
91   Smithers et al., above n 88.
92   Henderson et al., above n 78, 1406.
93   Sarah MacKay, 'Legislative Solutions to Unhealthy Eating and Obesity in Australia' (2011) 125 *Public Health* 896.
94   The Hon Tony Abbott MHR, 'Pandemic Flu and Obesity Issues' (Media Release, 14 September 2005) <www.health.gov.au/internet/ministers/publishing.nsf/Content/health-mediarel-yr2005-taabbsp140905.htm> as quoted in Roger Magnusson, 'What's Law Got to Do With It? Part I: A Framework for Obesity Prevention' (2008) 5(10) *Australian and New Zealand Health Policy* 1, 3.
95   Mackay, above n 93, 898.
96   Benjamin Brooks, 'Personal Responsibility or Shared Responsibility: What is the Appropriate Role of Law in Obesity Prevention?' (2015) 23 *Journal of Law and Medicine* 106, 110.
97   Rob Moodie et al., 'Profits and Pandemics: Prevention of Harmful Effects of Tobacco, Alcohol, and Ultra-Processed Food and Drink Industries' (2013) 381 *Lancet* 670, 676.
98   Reeve, above n 86, 129.
99   B Morley et al., 'Public Opinion on Food-Related Obesity Prevention Policy Initiatives' (2012) 23 *Health Promotion Journal of Australia* 86; see also Christina M Pollard et al., 'Public Say Food Regulatory Policies to Improve Health in Western Australia are Important: Population Survey Results' (2013) 37(5) *Australian & New Zealand Journal of Public Health* 475.

warning labels,[100] and alcohol promotion at major sporting events.[101] Public support is higher for tools addressing the provision of information and restricting advertising, than for more intrusive strategies such as taxation. However, in relation to certain health issues, it seems the tide is perhaps turning towards greater community recognition of the role of public health law, as well as acceptance that legislative intervention may be necessary at times. If this kind of public sentiment gains momentum, the increased level of political leadership required to address the inconsistencies in the current body of Australian public health law may follow.

Conclusion

This chapter has explored the relationship between law and public health in Australia. It has identified that in certain areas, namely sanitation, infectious disease prevention and control, and tobacco use, the body of public health law is both extensive and progressive. This sits in contrast to responses regarding alcohol consumption, unhealthy foods and inactivity. In these areas, reliance is placed on narrow legislative measures and soft law of questionable effectiveness. These inconsistencies are likely to reflect a lack of political will rather than evidence of risk and effectiveness. There are encouraging signs, however, that public support for greater government legislative intervention is increasing. Such intervention is vital, if critical health challenges in Australia are to be addressed.

---

100   Paula O'Brien, 'The Contest Over 'Valuable Label Real Estate': Public Health Reforms to the Laws on Alcohol Beverage Labelling in Australia' (2014) 37(2) *UNSW Law Journal* 565, 586.

101   Rob Moodie and Caroline Mills, 'Beer and Chips Protected Species as Sports Ban Healthy Eating Ads', *The Conversation* (online) 10 May 2013 <http://theconversation.com/beer-and-chips-protected-species-as-sports-ban-healthy-eating-ads-14045>.

25

GLOBAL HEALTH AND THE LAW

Anne-Maree Farrell

We live in an era of globalisation, which has contributed to challenges and greater complexity in dealing with health issues. It has influenced patterns of health and disease worldwide, in addition to facilitating the rapid cross-border spread of pathogens and behavioural risk factors.[1] Against this background, there is currently a multi-level and often fragmented approach to the management of both communicable and non-communicable diseases (NCDs) at global level.[2] As a result, there have been calls for a clearer and more coherent approach to global health governance in order to address the problem of the disproportionate burden of disease and early death borne by the world's poorest people, as well as the health disparities across continents that produce such a result.

In order to understand the role of law in this context, there is a need to take account of national, regional and global health institutions, regulatory regimes, trade agreements and a range of other 'soft law' and consensus mechanisms. This chapter aims to explore how law intersects with global health governance. It begins with a brief historical overview of the emergence of the global health agenda, focusing in particular on the role and activities of the World Health Organization (WHO). In the second part, consideration is given to the way in which law intersects with global health, drawing on select examples such as infectious disease outbreaks, the management of NCDs and trade agreements that touch on health-related matters.

The emergence of the global health agenda

Historically, international cooperation between States in matters of health was focused on the management and regulation of infectious diseases. In the early part of the 20th century, a number of multilateral institutions were established across different continents to manage infectious disease. However, there was little in the way of harmonisation in terms of goals or practices. Following the end of World War II, this began to change. In 1948, with the founding of the UN, provision was also made for the creation of a new specialised health agency, known as the World Health Organization (WHO).[3]

World Health Organization

The WHO was established with a constitutional mandate of working towards the attainment by all peoples of the highest possible level of health. This was seen as 'one of the fundamental rights of every human being without distinction of race, religion, political belief, economic or social condition'.[4] Its mandate reflected the growing importance attached to human rights in the postwar era. The aim was for the WHO to be at the 'vanguard of [promoting] the right to health' at both global and local levels.[5] Over time, the WHO's global

---

1   Colin McInnes et al., 'Framing Global Health: The Governance Challenge' (2012) 7(S2) *Global Health Law* S83.
2   Communicable diseases are infectious diseases that are contagious and can be transmitted from one source to another by infectious bacteria or viral organisms. Non-communicable diseases (NCDs) are not passed from person to person, progress slowly and can be of long duration. They are also referred to as chronic diseases.
3   Lawrence O Gostin, *Global Health Law* (Harvard University Press, 2014) 179.
4   WHO, *Constitution of the World Health Organization* (1984), in force 7 April 1948.
5   John Hall and Richard Taylor, 'Health for All Beyond 2000: The Demise of the Alma-Ata Declaration and Primary Health Care in Developing Countries' (2003) 178(1) *Medical Journal of Australia* 17.

health agenda has oscillated between a focus on technical disease-specific strategies and the strengthening of the universal provision of healthcare and social services more generally.[6] In the mid to late 20th century, much of its work program focused on malaria control, the eradication of smallpox and the development of rural health programs. The WHO was also significantly influenced during this period by the emergence of African nationalism in the wake of decolonisation and the spread of nationalist and socialist movements, as well as by new theories of development that emphasised long-term socio-economic growth rather than short-term technological intervention.[7] In the 1970s, this led to an increased focus on the provision of primary healthcare and related services. This was underpinned by the Alma Ata Declaration, which called for 'health for all by 2000' and underscored issues of inequalities, rights and duties.[8]

In the 1980s, the WHO began to face a challenge from the World Bank (WB) in terms of global health leadership. Although the WB had initially been founded to assist in the reconstruction of Europe after World War II, it subsequently expanded its mandate to cover the provision of loans, grants and technical assistance to developing countries. By the 1970s, it was investing in population control, as well as health and education programs. Support for such programs was provided on the grounds that improving health and nutrition would accelerate economic growth. The WB called for a more efficient use of available resources, and explored the roles of both private and public sectors in financing healthcare. This was against a background of supporting free markets and a diminished role for national governments.[9]

The rise of the WB in terms of its influence in global health initiatives corresponded with a decline in influence of the WHO, which was exacerbated by budgetary problems.[10] From the mid 1990s onwards, the WHO embarked upon a reform process aimed at restoring its international standing. It was also around this time that the WHO began to use terminology such as 'global health' rather than 'international health' in its policy agenda. In the 2000s, the WHO again emerged as an influential player in global health, although as we shall see later in this chapter it has had difficulties in maintaining its leadership role.[11]

Apart from problems with institutional leadership and organisational capacity, the WHO has also faced significant financial constraints over time. Its core budget has effectively been frozen for decades. Indeed, the majority of its 2014–15 budget came from voluntary donations,[12] many of which were earmarked for specific projects. One private donor, the Bill and Melinda Gates Foundation, has become the second largest funder of the WHO after the US. Over time, this state of affairs has led to excessive donor dependence on the part of the

6   Theodore Brown et al., 'The World Health Organization and the Transition from "International" to "Global" Public Health' (2006) 96(10) *American Journal of Public Health* 62.
7   Hall and Taylor, above n 5.
8   Alma Ata Declaration, International Conference of Primary Health Care, Alma Ata, USSR, 6–12 September 1978.
9   Hall and Taylor, above n 5.
10   Brown et al., above n 6.
11   Lawrence O Gostin, 'Reforming the World Health Organization After Ebola' (2015) 313(14) *Journal of the American Medical Association* 1407.
12   Kelley Lee and Tikki Pang, 'WHO: Retirement and Reinvention' (2014) 128 *Public Health* 119; Gostin, above n 11.

WHO and the establishment of a range of stand-alone health programs at the expense of strengthening health systems.[13]

Recent global initiatives

In 2000, the UN General Assembly adopted the Millennium Development Goals (MDGs), which set out a global agenda and targets for development.[14] The MDGs identified targets to be achieved by 2015 in key health areas, such as malaria and HIV/AIDS, as well as child and maternal health. One of the consequences of the MDG agenda was an upsurge in the number of actors, organisations and resources involved in promoting global health. One of the downsides was that it in practice it restricted a broader range of health initiatives. This was because the focus was on select disease groups and sub-populations, rather than on strengthening population health and related services more generally.[15] As a result, the WHO has sought to re-emphasise the need for 'universal health coverage' as part of the post-2015 global health agenda.[16]

In 2015, the UN adopted the 2030 Agenda for Sustainable Development, which sets out a number of Sustainable Development Goals (SDGs).[17] Specifically, SDG3 refers to the need to 'ensure healthy lives and promoting well-being for all at all ages'. Targets associated with SDG3 include the reduction of global maternal mortality, the end of preventable deaths of newborns, the end of the epidemics of AIDS, tuberculosis and malaria, and the reduction by one-third of premature mortality from non-communicable diseases.[18] It has been suggested that this approach may provide an opportunity to better integrate human rights, as well as the role of law more generally, in global health governance.[19]

Global health and the role of law

Traditionally, law has been described as inadequate in dealing with the phenomenon of globalisation and its consequences, and in dealing with increasing global health inequalities. International law is said to offer only vague standards, weak enforcement and an approach that favours States' views over collective public health. It has often proven difficult to adopt legally binding instruments at global level, given political tensions and ongoing problems with resource constraints.[20] It has been suggested that the use of non-binding mechanisms

---

13 Remco van de Pas and Louise van Schaik, 'Democratizing the World Health Organization' (2014) 128 *Public Health* 195.

14 UN General Assembly, Resolution 55/2, Millennium Declaration, 18 September 2000.

15 Claire Brolan et al., 'Global Governance for Universal Health Coverage: Could a Framework Convention on Global Health Hold It Together? (2013) VI(2) *Global Health Governance* 1.

16 UN, *Transforming Our World: the 2030 Agenda for Sustainable Development*, Sustainable Development Goal 3, Target 3.8: 'Achieve universal health coverage, including financial risk protection, access to quality essential health-care services and access to safe, effective, quality and affordable essential medicines and vaccines for all' <https://sustainabledevelopment.un.org/sdg3>.

17 UN General Assembly, *Transforming Our World: the 2030 Agenda for Sustainable Development*, A/Res/70/1, 25 September 2015 <www.un.org/ga/search/view_doc.asp?symbol=A/RES/70/1&Lang=E>.

18 UN, above n 16.

19 Benjamin Meier and William Onzivu, 'The Evolution of Human Rights in World Health Organization Policy and the Future of Human Rights through Global Health Governance' (2014) 128 *Public Health* 179.

20 Lawrence O Gostin and Devi Sridhar, 'Global Health and the Law' (2014) 370(18) *New England Journal of Medicine* 1732.

could prove more effective in bringing about positive change in the long term. Such an approach might be likely to attract political support, in addition to offering greater flexibility in interpretation and implementation.[21]

Gostin and Sridhar have argued that law (broadly defined) has the potential to play an important role in dealing with many global health challenges.[22] Gostin himself has defined 'global health law' as:

> [The] study and practice of international law [both hard law in the form of binding treaties and soft law in terms of codes of practice and guidelines] that shapes norms, processes, and institutions to attain the highest attainable standard of physical and mental health for the world's population.[23]

In advocating for a greater role to be played by law in promoting global health, Gostin has also called for a Framework Convention on Global Health to be adopted, on the grounds that it would both promote leadership and coordination and ensure sustainable funding in the field.[24] This would require participating States to initially agree to a framework instrument that would establish broad principles for global health governance. Subsequently, specific protocols would be developed on an incremental basis, with a view to achieving objectives set out in the framework and fostering global health leadership over time.[25] Over time, these protocols would lead to the development of legal norms, structures and processes in key areas impacting global health governance.[26]

The role of human rights law

It has been argued that human rights law offers a clear and coherent framework in which to articulate the aspirations for global public health governance. However, some commentators have been sceptical about the promise of human rights in global health governance. They have argued that while there is much promise, there is a lack of precision in how it might work in practice. In particular, it is unclear how one determines when a right is violated or what the enforcement mechanisms are or should be when there is a breach.[27] In addition, there is a lack of evidence of the impact of the use of a human rights legal framework on health outcomes.[28] Notwithstanding such criticisms, the right to health is now viewed as an integral part of global health governance. The relationship between health and human rights law is discussed in more detail in Chapter 5.

---

21   Allyn L Taylor et al., 'Leveraging Non-Binding Instruments for Global Health Governance: Reflections From the Global AIDS Reporting Mechanism for WHO Reform' (2014) 128 *Global Health* 151.

22   Gostin and Sridhar, above n 20.

23   Gostin, above n 3, 60.

24   Ibid 435.

25   Gostin and Sridhar, above n 20.

26   Lawrence O Gostin, 'A Framework Convention on Global Health' (2012) 207(19) *Journal of the American Medical Association* 2087. For a critique, see Brolan et al., above n 15.

27   Lawrence O Gostin and James G Hodge, 'Global Health Law, Ethics, and Policy' (2007) 35(4) *Journal of Law Medicine and Ethics* 519, 522.

28   Lance Gable, 'The Proliferation of Human Rights in Global Health Governance' (2007) 35(4) *Journal of Law Medicine and Ethics* 534–44, 542.

Infectious diseases

The historical impetus for global regulation of infectious diseases was provided by the cholera epidemics in Europe in the 19th century. These led to the adoption of two international Conventions, one dealing with cholera and the other dealing with plague. In 1903 they were replaced by the International Sanitary Convention, which was also amended over time. However, there was still a lack of harmonisation in terms of the management of infectious diseases, given differing institutional and States' approaches, goals and practices. With the founding of the WHO, however, this began to change.[29] In line with its constitutional powers,[30] the WHO adopted the International Sanitary Regulations (ISR), replacing the earlier International Sanitary Convention, in 1951. The ISR were renamed the International Health Regulations (IHR) in 1969, but they applied to only a limited range of diseases, including cholera, plague and yellow fever.

In the late 20th century, the WHO experienced considerable difficulties with enforcement of the then IHR, as they had not been significantly updated since 1951. Times had changed and they were not considered sufficiently responsive to the challenges posed by the global spread of infectious diseases.[31] It was also recognised that taking effective action at national level was becomingly increasingly problematic for more vulnerable developing countries. All this led to the adoption of the revised IHR by the World Health Assembly in 2005. The Regulations entered into force as a binding instrument of international law in 2007. They are binding on 194 countries, including all WHO Member States.[32]

Australia has implemented the IHR through the adoption of the *National Health Security Act 2007* (Cth). The Act establishes a national system of public health surveillance to enhance the capacity of the Commonwealth, states and territories to identify and respond to public health events of national significance, and provides for the sharing of information with the WHO and other countries affected by such events. The Act also created a National Security Agreement, which establishes a framework for a coordinated national response to public health emergencies,[33] and a National Notifiable Disease List.[34] Currently, the Commonwealth Office of Health Protection coordinates responses to public health emergencies and disease outbreaks, and provides technical and policy advice on best practice in relation to managing such events.[35]

The International Health Regulations: key aspects

The IHR are the only global regulations for the control of infectious diseases. The purpose and scope of the IHR are stated to be:

> to prevent, protect against, control and provide a public health response to the international spread of disease and ... to avoid unnecessary interference with international traffic and trade.[36]

29   Gostin, above n 3, 179.
30   WHO Constitution, Art 21.
31   Gostin, above n 3, 182.
32   WHO, International Health Regulations (2005), 2nd edn <www.who.int/ihr/ publications/9789241596664/en>.
33   *National Health Security Act 2007* (Cth) Part 2, Div 2, s 7.
34   Ibid Part 2, Div 5, s 11.
35   See Australian Government, Department of Health, Communicable Diseases Information <www .health.gov.au/internet/main/publishing.nsf/Content/ohp-communic-1>.
36   IHR, Art 2.

The IHR are no longer limited to specific diseases; instead, they are concerned with infectious disease risk, whatever its origin or source.[37] Trade calculations determined the scope of the previous IHR, but the scope of the current IHR is determined by risks to human health. States are required to notify the WHO of events that may constitute a 'public health emergency of international concern' (PHEIC). A PHEIC is defined as follows:

> an extraordinary public health event which is considered to constitute a public health risk to other States through the international spread of disease and to potentially require a coordinated international response.[38]

In relation to notification obligations, States are required to notify the WHO of all events within their territories that may constitute a PHEIC,[39] to be determined by reference to whether or not: the public health impact of the event is serious; the event is unusual or unexpected; there is a significant risk of international spread; and there is a significant risk of international travel or trade restrictions.[40] A real-time event management system works alongside routine IHR environmental and epidemiological provisions, relying upon a variety of sources to identify a PHEIC.[41] States must also establish national Focal Points and responsible authorities for the implementation of health measures under the IHR,[42] and develop core surveillance and response capacities.[43]

A dispute settlement mechanism was also established under the IHR to resolve conflict arising between States and the WHO in relation to the application and/or interpretation of the IHR. Options open under this mechanism include negotiation, mediation and conciliation. Disputes can be referred to the WHO Director-General or to arbitration, if agreed to by all parties to such disputes.[44] However, States are not bound to follow the WHO's recommendations and there are limits to what it can do in the event of their non-compliance. This represents a real weakness of the current Regulations, given that non-compliance by States was a major problem in the previous version of the IHR.[45]

The IHR incorporate human rights principles and recognise the potential effect of public health interventions on civil and political rights.[46] They require States to: identify a public health risk that justifies imposing health measures against persons; apply an appropriate health response to such risk; and implement measures that are no more intrusive of persons than reasonably available alternatives that would achieve the level of health protection needed. It has been argued that implementing the IHR at national level has provided a welcome opportunity to better incorporate human rights principles into the operation of

---

37   Ibid Art 1.
38   Ibid.
39   Ibid Art 6.
40   Ibid Art 6, Annex 2.
41   Ibid Art 9.
42   Ibid Art 4.
43   Ibid Arts 5, 13, Annex 1.
44   Ibid Art 56.
45   See Steven J Hoffman, 'Making the International Health Regulations Matter: Promoting Compliance through Effective Dispute Resolution' in Simon Rushton and Jeremy Youde (eds), *Routledge Handbook on Global Health Security* (Routledge, 2015) 239–51.
46   See IHR, Art 3.1; see Chapter 5 for further discussion of the relationship between health and civil and political rights.

States' public health systems, and to take more account of the relationship between health security and human rights.[47]

Health security

It has been suggested that the adoption of the current IHR occurred at a 'moment when public health security and democracy have become intertwined, addressed at the highest levels of government'.[48] Their adoption marked a significant departure from the framework that informed the design of the previous IHR, and they have transformed the global legal context in which States now exercise their public health sovereignty. The normative frame of reference is now the promotion of 'health security', which the WHO has defined as:

> The activities required, both proactive and reactive, to minimize vulnerability to acute public health events that endanger the collective health of populations living across geographical regions and international boundaries.[49]

While the notion of protection of collective public health has traditionally been central to understanding this concept, the fallout from the recent West African Ebola epidemic highlighted the importance of also taking account of individual health security, in terms of ensuring access to safe and effective health services, products and technologies. In short, one of the key lessons learned from the epidemic was the importance of taking a broader view of the concept of health security, a view that encompasses both individual and collective aspects.[50]

The IHR and WHO's leadership role

The IHR envision a global leadership role for the WHO in managing the spread of infectious diseases, particularly as it now has the authority to determine whether a disease event constitutes a PHEIC.[51] If such a determination is made, it is able to issue guidance to States in the form of non-binding 'appropriate temporary recommendations'.[52] Notwithstanding the WHO's enhanced powers under the IHR, however, the problems of capacity-building and insufficient institutional and financial resources, as well as broader political tensions, have made it difficult for the WHO to take on an effective global leadership role in this area. This has been highlighted by its response to a number of infectious disease outbreaks in recent years.

In 2009, the development of the H1N1 influenza pandemic led to the WHO invoking the IHR. A review of the WHO's role in responding to the pandemic found that while it had responded well overall, there were also a number of significant problems. In particular,

---

47   Joseph J Amon, 'Health Security and/or Human Rights?' in Rushton and Youde, above n 45, 293–303.

48   David P Fidler and Lawrence O Gostin, 'The New International Health Regulations: An Historic Development for International Law and Public Health' (2006) 34(1) *Journal of Law Medicine and Ethics* 85.

49   WHO, *The World Health Report 2007: A Safer Future – Global Public Health Security in the 21st Century* (2007) ix.

50   David Heymann et al., 'Global Health Security: The Wider Lessons from the West African Ebola Disease Epidemic' (2015) 385 *Lancet* 1884; see, generally, Adam Kamradt-Scott, *Managing Global Health Security: The World Health Organization and Disease Outbreak Control* (Palgrave, 2015).

51   IHR, Art 12.

52   Ibid Art 12.2.

it was found that there were insufficient personnel and financial resources available to respond to such global health emergencies, and this needed to be addressed.[53] The WHO failed to act on the report's recommendations, instead opting to decrease funding and staffing for both surveillance and response to public health emergencies. This led to it being ill-prepared to response to the West African Ebola epidemic, which first emerged in 2013.[54]

The WHO's response to the Ebola epidemic has been described as a 'debacle', with weak surveillance and response capacities in West Africa, incompetent staff, limited funding and difficulties with regional offices. It avoided taking on a global leadership role as the epidemic progressed and did not declare it to be a PHEIC under the IHR until it was quite advanced. The affected low-income West African States also clearly did not have the core capacities to deal with the epidemic.[55] Overall, the epidemic revealed a lack of political will, as well as an institutional failure on the part of the WHO and other agencies, to mount an effective public health emergency response.[56] The WHO Secretary-General has since set out a range of reforms designed to address the perceived failures in dealing with the Ebola epidemic, which include strengthening its global health security and emergency response capacities. As a result, the WHO has now established a new Health Emergencies Programme, which is underpinned by substantial renewable funding and the development of a global health emergency workforce.[57]

Given a range of persisting institutional and political tensions, however, it remains to be seen whether this will substantially alter the WHO's response to global health crises in the future.[58] This has recently been tested in relation to the WHO's response to the spread of the Zika virus,[59] which was declared to be a PHEIC in February 2016.[60] The WHO has since published a strategic response plan to assist in building States' capacities and preparedness to respond to the virus's spread.[61] However, political tensions and concerns about conflicts of interest on the part of the WHO persist. These were alluded to in the call by prominent international health experts for the 2016 Rio Olympics to be postponed in the wake of the Zika virus outbreak in Brazil.[62]

53   WHO, *Report of the Review Committee on the Functioning of the International Health Regulations (2005) in Relation to the Pandemic H1N1 2009* (2011) <www.who.int/ihr/review_committee/en>.

54   David P Fidler, 'The Ebola Outbreak and the Future of Global Health Security' in Heymann et al., above n 50, 1888.

55   Ibid.

56   WHO, *Report of the Ebola Interim Assessment Panel – July 2015* <www.who.int/csr/resources/publications/ebola/ebola-panel-report/en>; Adam Kamradt-Scott, WHO's To Blame? The World Health Organization and the 2014 Ebola Outbreak in West Africa' (2016) 37(3) *Third World Quarterly* 401, 407–10.

57   WHO, *Health Emergencies Programme* <www.who.int/about/who_reform/emergency-capacities/en>.

58   Laurie Garrett, 'The Ebola Review, Part 1' *Foreign Policy*, 6 June 2015 <http://foreignpolicy.com/2015/06/06/ebola-review-world-health-organization-g-7-merkel>; Kamradt-Scott, above n 56, 410.

59   Zika virus is transmitted primarily by *Aedes* mosquitoes, but cases of sexual transmission have also been reported. Most people who contract Zika virus disease experience mild symptoms but there is now a scientific consensus that it is also a cause of a range of much more serious complications, such as microcephaly in newborns and Guillain-Barré syndrome, see WHO, *Zika Virus* <www.who.int/mediacentre/factsheets/zika/en>.

60   WHO, *WHO Director-General Summarizes the Outcome of the Emergency Committee Regarding Clusters of Microcephaly and Guillain-Barré Syndrome* <www.who.int/mediacentre/news/statements/2016/emergency-committee-zika-microcephaly/en>.

61   WHO, *Zika Virus Outbreak Global Response* <www.who.int/emergencies/zika-virus/response/en>.

62   For an overview, see <https://rioolympicslater.org>.

Non-communicable diseases (NCDs)

NCDs are those diseases that are chronic and cannot be transmitted from person to person. The four major NCDs that have been identified as impacting on global health are cardio-vascular diseases, diabetes, chronic respiratory diseases and cancers. NCDs share several risk factors including tobacco use, unhealthy diets, inactivity and harmful levels of alcohol intake. The rapid spread of NCDs has been attributable to globalisation, underpinned by international trade, rapid urbanisation and ageing populations.[63] Given the global upsurge in NCDs, there is now a looming health crisis which threatens to undermine progress made in global health and living standards over the past century.[64] The impact of NCDs traverses almost all States and income groups, although the burden is particularly felt by middle and low-income countries.[65] In recent years, it is estimated that NCDs have been responsible for over two-thirds of all deaths globally.[66]

A series of instruments have been adopted by the WHO in recognition of the challenges posed to global health by NCDs. These have included a series of global action plans for the prevention and control of NCDs (2000, 2008–13, 2013–20), as well as global strategy plans for diet, physical activity and health, and reduction in harmful alcohol use.[67] The Framework Convention on Tobacco Control (FCTC) was adopted in 2003, entering into force in 2005. The FCTC was the first instrument negotiated by the WHO using its treaty-making powers and 'it has since become one of the more rapidly and widely embraced treaties in the UN's history'.[68] A 2012 review showed that 79 per cent of State parties had adopted or strengthened tobacco control legislation after ratifying the FCTC. A key issue which remains unresolved in the FCTC, however, is the extent to which tobacco control measures should take priority over trade agreements.[69] This remains problematic, as was highlighted in Big Tobacco's ultimately unsuccessful challenge, brought under a regional trade agreement, to Australia's *Plain Packaging Legislation Act 2011* (Cth).[70]

---

63 WHO, *Global Status Report on Noncommunicable Diseases 2014* <www.who.int/nmh/publications/ncd-status-report-2014/en>.

64 Robert Beaglehole et al., 'Priority Actions for the Non-Communicable Disease Crisis' (2011) 377 *Lancet* 1438.

65 Karl-Heinz Wagner and Helmut Brath, 'A Global View on the Development of Non Communicable Diseases' (2012) 54 *Preventative Medicine* S38.

66 WHO, above n 63.

67 For an overview, see WHO, *Noncommunicable Diseases and Mental Health* <www.who.int/nmh/en>.

68 WHO, *Framework Convention on Tobacco Control* <www.who.int/fctc/about/en>; Kate Lannan, 'The WHO Framework on Tobacco Control: The International Context for Plain Packaging' in Tania Voon et al. (eds), *Public Health and Plain Packaging of Cigarettes: Legal Issues* (Edward Elgar, 2012) 11–29.

69 Hadii Madmudu et al., 'International Trade versus Public Health during the FCTC Negotiations, 1999–2003' (2011) 20 *Tobacco Control* e3.

70 Daniel Hurst, 'Australia Wins International Legal Battle with Philip Morris over Plain Packaging' *The Guardian*, 18 December 2015. Note that Ukraine brought a challenge to Australia's plain packaging legislation under the WTO dispute settlement mechanism. This was subsequently suspended at the request of Ukraine and the dispute panel's jurisdiction has now lapsed: see World Trade Organization (WTO), *Australia – Certain Measures Concerning Trademarks and Other Plain Packaging Requirements Applicable to Tobacco Products and Packaging (DS434)* <www.wto.org/english/tratop_e/dispu_e/cases_e/ds434_e.htm>.

In 2011, the UN General Assembly adopted a Political Declaration on the Prevention and Control of NCDs. The Declaration called for greater multi-sectoral, population-wide interventions; the promotion of research and development; and the strengthening of national policies, monitoring and evaluation.[71] In the wake of the Declaration, the WHO set nine measurable voluntary targets, which include a 25 per cent relative reduction in premature mortality from NCDs by 2025 (known as the '25 x 25' target).[72] In reviewing the work undertaken since the Declaration, the WHO recently reported that progress on the prevention and monitoring of NCDs had been 'insufficient and uneven', particularly in developing countries. This has led to the adoption of a series of State-based implementation targets for the period 2014 to 2016.[73] A further review of progress towards meeting targets will be undertaken by the third UN High Level Meeting on NCDs, which will be held in 2018.

Global health and trade agreements

The inter-relationship between global health and trade has long been recognised.[74] It has been argued that liberalisation of trade can bring positive changes in terms of enabling the transfer of much-needed health services and technologies. At the same time, it has also been seen as bringing negative changes, which include increased poverty and inequality.[75] It is important to note that there are key differences between the systems of governance for global health and those for global trade. The former involve a range of disparate actors and often soft, non-binding legal instruments. The latter involve a 'highly structured, formalised and demanding system of governance' that draws on legally binding frameworks and dispute resolution mechanisms.[76] In addition, businesses tend to have easier access to key policy-makers than those involved in the health policy arena. While there have been calls for the development of (binding) mechanisms to ensure that there is a balanced representation of views, it is unclear whether and how this would work in practice.[77]

There are a number of international and regional trade agreements which touch on health-related matters and/or treat such matters as an exception to certain international trade obligations. Suffice it to say that any such exceptions tend to be interpreted rather narrowly. They have been subject to challenge on the grounds that they are in fact an attempt by States to circumvent obligations relating to trade liberalisation, rather than genuine exceptions that are justified on the ground of public health protection.[78] Of increasing concern within the global health arena is the expansion of what are known as 'free trade agreements'

---

71   *Political Declaration of the High-level Meeting of the General Assembly on the Prevention and Control of Non-Communicable Diseases* (Document A/66/L.1).

72   Vasilis Kontis et al., 'Contribution of Six Risk Factors to Achieving the 25 x 25 Non-Communicable Disease Mortality Reduction Target: A Modeling Study' (2014) 384 *Lancet* 427.

73   UN, High-level Meeting on the Comprehensive Review and Assessment of the Progress Achieved in the Prevention and Control of Non-Communicable Diseases, 10–11 July 2014.

74   Brown et al., above n 6.

75   Jonathan Liberman and Andrew Mitchell, 'In Search of Coherence between Trade and Health: Inter-Institutional Opportunities' (2010) *University of Melbourne Law School Research Series* 7.

76   Ibid. A detailed examination of this system of governance is outside the scope of this chapter. At global level, the WTO plays a prominent role in such governance: see <www.wto.org>.

77   Ibid.

78   Tania Voon, 'Flexibilities in WTO Law to Support Tobacco Control Regulation' (2013) 39 *American Journal of Law and Medicine* 199.

or 'regional trade agreements'. In the wake of a perceived failure to promote greater world trade liberalisation measures, the focus has now shifted to the adoption of such agreements between States and/or 'economic coalitions of the willing'.[79] Critics of the reach of such agreements, particularly in health-related matters, have argued that they should more accurately be described as 'investor treaties'.[80] This is because such agreements contain clauses that offer protections and/or opportunities for legal challenges to be made by investors against signatory States where investors suffer losses due to the imposition of measures such as those that relate to health.

One example of such an agreement is the Trans Pacific Partnership (TPP). Following seven years of negotiations, the TPP was signed in February 2016. The 12 countries who are signatories to the TPP represent 40 per cent of the world's total Gross Domestic Product (GDP).[81] They have welcomed the agreement on the grounds that it will: promote economic growth; enhance innovation, productivity and competitiveness; raise living standards; reduce poverty; and promote transparency, good governance and enhanced labour and environmental protections. More generally, it is seen as promoting the ultimate goal of open trade and regional integration.[82] To date, only New Zealand and Japan have ratified the TPP, with Australia maintaining that it also wishes to proceed with ratification.[83] However, newly elected US President Donald Trump has indicated that he does not support ratification of the TPP and so it is unlikely to proceed in its current form, if at all.[84]

Whatever the fate of the TPP, it appears likely that signatory countries will want to push ahead with regional trade agreements in the future, whether they be bilateral or multilateral. What this means is that key provisions in the TPP may be imported in part or in whole into such agreements. It is therefore worth briefly considering some of the concerns that have been expressed by commentators about TPP provisions with regard to their potential adverse impact upon public health. Of concern are intellectual property provisions, in particular those relating to access to medicines and the use of 'evergreening' provisions, which may operate to prolong patent protection on pharmaceuticals. This may prove particularly costly for national pharmaceutical schemes.[85] In addition, the extent to which States will be able to adopt measures in the interests of public health may be subject to challenge under the investor-state dispute settlement (ISDS) mechanism.

---

79   Heather Stewart, 'Doha is Dead. Hopes for Fairer Global Trade Shouldn't Die Too', *The Guardian*, 20 December 2015.

80   Sharon Friel et al., 'A New Generation of Trade Policy: Potential Risks to Diet-Related Health from the Trans Pacific Partnership Agreement' (2013) 9 *Globalization and Health* 46.

81   The signatories to the TPP are the following Pacific Rim countries: Australia, Brunei, Canada, Chile, Japan, Malaysia, Mexico, New Zealand, Peru, Singapore, the US and Vietnam.

82   Office of the US Trade Representative, *Summary of the Trans Pacific Partnership Agreement* <https://ustr.gov/about-us/policy-offices/press-office/press-releases/2015/october/summary-trans-pacificpartnership>.

83   Australian Government, Department of Foreign Affairs and Trade, Trans Pacific Partnership Agreement <http://dfat.gov.au/trade/agreements/tpp/pages/trans-pacific-partnership-agreement-tpp.aspx>.

84   Michael C. Bender and Damian Paletta, 'Donald Trump Calls for List of Day-One Executive Actions, Outlines First 100 Days', *Wall Street Journal*, 22 November 2016.

85   For an overview, see Amy Kapczynski, 'The Trans-Pacific Partnership – Is It Bad for Your Health? (2015) 373 *New England Journal of Medicine* 201.

The ISDS mechanism provides that investor companies may obtain compensation from signatory States for the implementation of health laws that lead to investor losses. It has been argued that the inclusion of such a mechanism in trade agreements was originally designed to encourage foreign investment by providing a form of investor protection. Where appropriate, ISDS provisions can – and indeed have been – excluded from such agreements in order to protect health. An example of this is the China–Australia preferential trade agreement.[86] However, such exclusion was not provided for in the TPP, and where this happens in trade agreements, the concern is that it may narrow the scope of States to adopt health measures in the public interest. There are also concerns about the compatibility of trade agreements with the UN SDGs, as noted above. In the absence of substantive engagement with such Goals, the danger is that such agreements may in fact contribute to the exacerbation of poverty and inequality both within sigatory States and beyond.[87]

Conclusion

This chapter has examined the role of law in global health governance. Understanding law's role in this context means taking account of a multi-level and often fragmented governance environment, involving a diverse range of institutional arrangements and programs, differing normative legal frameworks, hard and soft law instruments, and other consensus mechanisms. The way in which law intersects with global health was explored through the examples of health security as exemplified by the IHR, the management of NCDs and the increasing use of trade agreements which touch upon matters of health. Global health is a complex decision-making environment with competing political and economic priorities, under-resourced global institutions, and enduring power asymmetries between the North and the South. Recent global health emergencies have highlighted the need for, and indeed the importance of, proactive leadership in managing global health challenges. In this context, there is much potential for law to support such leadership and make it more effective. Whether or not this is realised in practice remains to be seen.

---

86   Craig Applegate, 'We've Agreed to Investor-State Dispute Clauses Before – It's All in the Wording' *The Conversation* (online), 3 July 2015 <http://theconversation.com/weve-agreed-to-investor-state-dispute-clauses-before-its-all-in-the-wording-43851>.

87   Joseph Stiglitz, 'The Secret Corporate Takeover' *Project Syndicate*, 13 May 2015, <www.project-syndicate.org/commentary/us-secret-corporate-takeover-by-joseph-e-stiglitz-2015-05>.

INDEX